World Soccer Atlas – First Edition

Compiled and created by Kemari, Inc.: Marc Asmode, Rebecca Gilsdorf, Daniel Lopez
www.soccerexplorers.com
info@soccerexplorers.com

Published in the United States by Kemari, Inc.

ISBN: 0-9770451-090000

Printed and bound in Hong Kong by A.F. Printing.

Please visit us at www.soccerexplorers.com. Also see our sister site www.goaltv.com.

Acknowledgements

This book has come to life because of very good friends who were there every step of the way over the past six years. Thank you Rebecca and Dan! I would like to thank my dad Roland for the inspiration he gave me for this sport, and the love and support of my mother Monick, stepdad Bob Jr., my sister Christine, including family and friends. Inline Graphics, thank you so much for your kindness and dedication. Thanks a million, Louise Yoder, Mike Barton and John Coelho. The pictures in this book would never have been put together without the support and time given by Emmanuel Previnaire, David Storey, Philippe Piron, Timberlake Lewis, Jason Krause, Jaime Baquero, Louis Prezelin, Sarah Krinz and the rest of the Flying-Cam team. Tami Larsen, for your incredible dedication and help on the maps and friendship, thank you. Other people I would like to thank for their support are Annie Sundberg, Jenny Burton, Gene and Betty Gilsdorf, Susan Newton, Ashley Borg, Joel Malmen, Offer Touboul, James Cross, Kirsten Heckes, Rick Hofmann, Christian Miles, Scott Bucolla, Bill Hodson of LiveWire, Dawn Cochran for a great logo, Joel Rome for your creativity and patience for our website, Wivern for keeping us on track from Hong Kong with A. F. Printing Company, Eric and Deborah Valli for your inspiration, and of course the "Ballbusters" Tuesday and Sunday teams for keeping my sanity.

- Marc

Like most major undertakings, this book would not have been realized without the help of some wonderful people. Susan – your expertise and generosity helped us get the ball rolling. Tami – without your hard work and willingness, those maps still would not be finished. Louise – your kindness, persistence and skill are appreciated more than you can imagine and more than words can say. Joel – thank you a million for your work and know-how. I would also like to acknowledge the support and generosity of Kirsten, Ashley, Dawn, Mike and John of Inline Graphics, Monick, Anne, and of course Mom and Dad. Huge thanks to Dan for sticking with it and paying for it these six years and to my dear friends and family for asking how it's going on a regular basis. But most of all, Marc – I don't think I have fully appreciated how much your passion for this has impacted me and how it will affect the rest of my life. I count myself blessed to work with someone so inspirational, motivated and positive.

- Rebecca

Table of Contents

WORLD SOCCER ATLAS

Explore and Learn
6000 Clubs / 4000 Cities
in more than
270 countries & dependencies Worldwide

From the Top of the Himalayas
to the most remote island nations.

Futebol-Fussball-Soccer-Football-Futbol-Voetbal

1st Edition

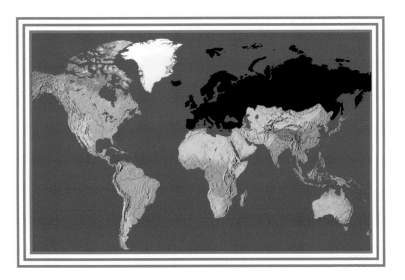

EUROPE

ALBANIA

THE FOOTBALL ASSOC. OF ALBANIA
Rruga Dervish Hima #31, Tirana
TEL 355-42/50 275 FAX /27 877
WEB www.fshf.org

REFERENCE
Official name
   Republic of Albania
Date of formation   1913
Capital   Tirana
Population   3.3 million
Total area   11 sq MI (28,750 sq KM)
Time zone   GMT +1
Density   312 per sq MI (117 per sq KM)
Languages   Albanina,Greek
Literacy rate   85%
Currency   Lek
Economy   Agriculture 55%
Religions   Muslim 70%
Ethnic Mix   Albanian 96%

GEOGRAPHY
Elevation
lowest point: Adriatic Sea 0 m
highest point: Maja e Korabit
             (Golem Korab) 2,753 m
Geography Note
strategic location along Strait of Otranto
(links Adriatic Sea to Ionian Sea and
Mediterranean Sea)
Natural Resources
petroleum, natural gas, coal, chromium,
copper, timber, nickel, hydropower
Climate
mild temperate; cool, cloudy, wet winters;
hot, clear, dry summers; interior is cooler
and wetter
Albanian Food
tave kosi/qofte te ferguara/tasqebap

WORLD CUP		COUNTRY LEAGUE CHAMPIONS	
1930	Did not qualify		
1934	Did not qualify		
1938	Did not qualify	2004	SK Tirana
1950	Did not qualify	2003	SK Tirana
1954	Did not qualify	2002	Dinamo tirane
1958	Did not qualify	2001	Vllaznia Shkoder
1962	Did not qualify	2000	Sk Tirana
1966	Did not qualify	1999	Sk Tirana
1970	Did not qualify	1998	Vllaznia Shkoder
1974	Did not qualify	1997	Sk Tirana
1978	Did not qualify	1996	Sk Tirana
1982	Did not qualify	**WOMEN'S LEAGUE CHAMPIONS**	
1986	Did not qualify	2004	Not Known
1990	Did not qualify	2003	Not Known
1998	Did not qualify	2002	Not Known
2002	Did not qualify	2001	Not Known
		2000	Not Known

NATIONAL TEAM COLORS

WORLD PICTURES OF SOCCER

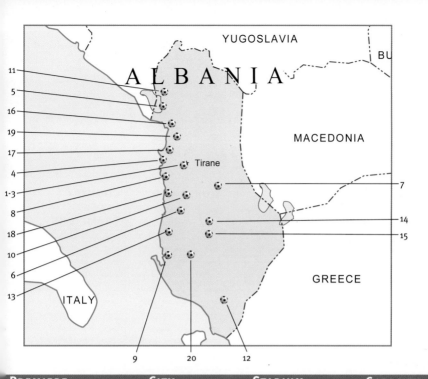

PREMIERE LEAGUE CLUBS	CITY	STADIUM	CAPACITY
1-SK Tirana	Tirana	Selman Stermasi	12 500
2-Partizan Tirana	Tirana	Selman Stermasi	12 500
3-Dinamo Tirana	Tirana	Selman Stermasi	12 500
4-Teuta Durres	Durres	Niko Dovana	12 000
5-Vllaznia Skhoder	Skhoder	Loro Borici	16 000
6-KS Lushnja	Lushnja	Roza Haxhiu	12 000
7-SK Elbasani	Elbasani	Ruzhdi Bizhuta	13 000
8-Besa Kavaje	Kavaje	Besa	8 000
9-Flamurtari Vlore	Vlore	Flamurtari	8 500
10-Shkumbini Peqin	Peqin	Peqin	6 000
11-Veleciku Koplik	Koplik		
12-Luftetari Gjirokaster	Gjirokaster	Subi Bakiri	8 400
13-Apolonia Fier	Fier	Loni Papucu	6 000
14-Naftetari Kucove	Kucove		
15-Tomori Berat	Berat	Tomori	14 500
16-Beselidhja Lezhe	Lezhe	Beseldhja	5 000
17-Erzeni Shijak	Shijak	Teufik Jashari	4 000
18-Egnatia Rrogozhine	Rrogozhine		
19-Laci Lac	Laci	Laci	5 000

ANDORRA

FED. ANDORRANA DE FUTBOL
c/ Verge del Pilar #52-5,Ed. Galerias Plza
BP 65,Andorra La Vella
TEL 376/862 003   FAX /862 006
WEB www.fedanfut.com

REFERENCE
Official name
Principality of Andorra

Date of formation	1278
Capital	Andorra La Vella
Population	58,000
Total area	181 sq MI (468 sq KM)
Time zone	GMT +1
Density	357 per sq MI (146 per sq KM
Languages	French,Spanish
Literacy rate	99%
Currency	Euro
Economy	Tourism
Religions	Catholic
Ethnic Mix	Spanish 60%,Andorran 30%

GEOGRAPHY
Elevation
lowest point: Riu Runer 840 m
highest point: Coma Pedrosa 2,946 m
Geography Note
landlocked; straddles a number of important crossroads in the Pyrenees
Natural Resources
hydropower, mineral water, timber, iron ore, lead.
Climate
temperate; snowy, cold winters and warm, dry summers.
Andorran Food
onion salad with honey

WORLD CUP		COUNTRY LEAGUE CHAMPIONS	
1930	Did not qualify		
1934	Did not qualify		
1938	Did not qualify	2004	FC Santa Coloma
1950	Did not qualify	2003	FC Santa Coloma
1954	Did not qualify	2002	Encamp Dicoansa
1958	Did not qualify	2001	FC Santa Coloma
1962	Did not qualify	2000	Constel-Lacio Esp
1966	Did not qualify	1999	CE Principat
1970	Did not qualify	1998	CE Principat
1974	Did not qualify	1997	CE Principat
1978	Did not qualify	1996	Encamp Dicoansa
1982	Did not qualify	**WOMEN'S LEAGUE CHAMPIONS**	
1986	Did not qualify	2004	Not Known
1990	Did not qualify	2003	Not Known
1998	Did not qualify	2002	Not Known
2002	Did not qualify	2001	Not Known
		2000	Not Known

NATIONAL TEAM COLORS

WORLD PICTURES OF SOCCER

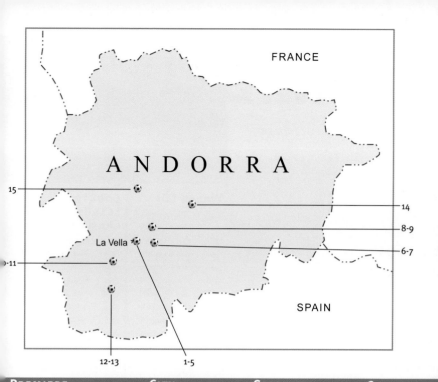

PREMIERE LEAGUE CLUBS	CITY	STADIUM	CAPACITY
1-CE Principat	Andorra La Vella	Aixovall	5 000
2-FC Rangers	Andorra La vella	Aixovall	5 000
3-Don Denis Principat	Andorra La Vella	Aixovall	5 000
4-FC Lusitanos	Andorra La Vella	Aixovall	5 000
5-FC Cerni	Andorra La Vella	Aixovall	5 000
6-Inter Club D'Escaldes	Les Escaldes		
7-SC D'Escaldes	Les Escaldes		
8-Construccions Modernes	Engordany		
9-UE Engordany	Engordany		
10-FC Santa Coloma	Santa Coloma		
11-Don Pernil	Santa Coloma		
12-Matecosa UE	Sant Julia de Loria		
13-UE Sant Juila	Sant Julia de Loria		
14-FC Encamp Docoansa	Encamp		
15-Deportivo La Massana	La Massana		

ARMENIA

FOOTBALL FEDERATION OF ARMENIA
Saryan 38,375 010 Yerevan
TEL 374-1/535 084 FAX /539 517
WEB www.armenia.fifa.com

REFERENCE
Official name
   Republic of Armenia

Date of formation	1991
Capital	Yerevan
Population	3.6 Million
Total area	11,505 sq MI (29,000 sq KM)
Time zone	GMT +4
Density	296 per sq MI (114 per sq KM)
Languages	Armenian,Russian
Literacy rate	99%
Currency	Dram
Economy	Industry26%,Agriculture27%, services 26%
Religions	Armenian Orthodox 94%
Ethnic Mix	Armenian 93%,European,Asian

GEOGRAPHY
Elevation
lowest point: Debed River 400 m
highest point: Aragats Lerrnagagat 4,090 m
Geography Note
landlocked in the Lesser Caucasus Mountains;
Sevana Lich (Lake Sevan) is the largest lake in
this mountain range
Natural Resources
small deposits of gold, copper, molybdenum, zinc, alumina
Climate
highland continental, hot summers, cold winters
Armenian Food
achot/gatnabour/tahnabour/topig

WORLD CUP		COUNTRY LEAGUE CHAMPIONS	
1930	Did not qualify		
1934	Did not qualify		
1938	Did not qualify	2004	Pyunik Yerevan
1950	Did not qualify	2003	Pyunik Yerevan
1954	Did not qualify	2002	Pyunik Yerevan
1958	Did not qualify	2001	Pyunik Yerevan
1962	Did not qualify	2000	Araks Ararat
1966	Did not qualify	1999	Shirak Gyumri
1970	Did not qualify	1998	Tsement Ararat
1974	Did not qualify	1997	Fk Yerevan
1978	Did not qualify	1996	Pyunik Yerevan
1982	Did not qualify	**WOMEN'S LEAGUE CHAMPIONS**	
1986	Did not qualify	2004	Not Known
1990	Did not qualify	2003	Not Known
1994	Did not qualify	2002	Not Known
1998	Did not qualify	2001	Not Known
2002	Did not qualify	2000	Not Known

NATIONAL TEAM COLORS

WORLD PICTURES OF SOCCER

PREMIERE LEAGUE CLUBS	CITY	STADIUM	CAPACITY
1-Pyunik Yerevan	Yerevan	Hanrapetakan	16 000
2-Banants Yerevan	Yerevan	Kotayk Stadium	3 000
3-Dinamo2000	Yerevan	Kasakh	3 000
4-Ararat Yerevan	Yerevan	Kotayk Stadium	3 000
5-Lernayin Artsakh	Yerevan	Lernargorts	3 000
6-Kilikia Yerevan	Yerevan	Hrazdan	69 000
7-Pyunik2	Yerevan	Hanrapetakan	16 000
8-Lokomotiv Yerevan	Yerevan		
9-Spartak Yerevan	Yerevan	Hanrapetakan	16 000
10-Dinamo FA	Yerevan		
11-Norq-Marash	Yerevan		
12-Yerazank	Yerevan		
13-Zvartnots Yerevan	Yerevan		
14-Mika Ashtarak	Ashtarak	Vardanank-451,Voskehat	3 000
15-Mika2 Ashtarak	Ashtarak	Vardanank-451,Voskehat	3 000
16-Shirak Gyumri	Gyumri	Gyumri City Stadium	3 000
17-Shirak2 Gyumri	Gyumri	Gyumri City Stadium	3 000
18-Kotaik Abovyan	Abovyan	Kotayk Stadium	3 000
19-Kotaik2003	Abovyan	Kotayk Stadium	3 000
20-Lernagorts Kapan	Kapan	Kotayk Stadium	3 000
21-Araks Ararat	Ararat		
22-FC Tsement	Ararat	Tsement Stadium	3 000
23-Vagharshapat Ejmiatsin	Ejimiatsin		
24-Lori Vanadzor	Vanadzor	Lori Stadium	3 000

AUSTRIA

OSTERRREICHER FUSSBALL BUND
Ernst -Happel Stadion sektor A/F
Postfach 340,meiereistrasse 7,1021 Wien
TEL 43-1/727 180 FAX /728 1632
WEB www.oefb.at

REFERENCE
Official name
Republic of Austria

Date of formation	1918/1945
Population	7.8 million
Capital	Vienna
Total area	32 sq MI (83,850 sq KM)
Time zone	GMT +1
Density	251 per sq MI (97 per sq KM)
Languages	German
Literacy rate	99%
Currency	Schilling
Economy	Services 66%
Religions	Catholic 85%
Ethnic Mix	Germans 98%

GEOGRAPHY
Elevation
lowest point: Neusiedler See 115 m
highest point: Grossglockner 3,798 m
Geography Note
landlocked; strategic location at the cross-roads of Central Europe with many easily traversable Alpine passes and valleys; major river is the Danube.
Natural Resources
iron ore, oil, timber, magnesite, lead, coal, lignite, copper, hydropower
Climate
temperate; continental, cloudy; cold winters with frequent rain in lowlands and snow in mountains; cool summers with occasional showers
Austrian Food
wiener schnitzel/speckknoedel

WORLD CUP

1930	Did not qualify
1934	Finish 4th
1938	Did not qualify
1950	Did not qualify
1954	Finish 3rd
1958	First round exit
1962	Did not qualify
1966	Did not qualify
1970	Did not qualify
1974	Did not qualify
1978	First round exit
1982	First round exit
1986	Did not qualify
1990	First round exit
1998	First round exit
2002	Did not qualify

COUNTRY LEAGUE CHAMPIONS

2004	GAK
2003	Austria Wien
2002	FC Tirol Innsbruck
2001	FC Tirol Innsbruck
2000	FC Tirol Innsbruck
1999	Sturm Graz
1998	Sturm Graz
1997	Austria Salzburg
1996	Rapid

WOMENS' LEAGUE CHAMPIONS

2004	SV Neulengbach
2003	SV Neulengbach
2002	Innsbrucker AC
2001	USC Landhaus
2000	USC Landhaus

NATIONAL TEAM COLORS

WORLD PICTURES OF SOCCER

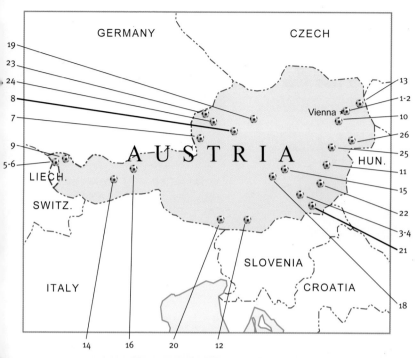

PREMIERE LEAGUE CLUBS	CITY	STADIUM	CAPACITY
1-FK Austria Wien	Wien	Franz Horr	11 800
2-SK Rapid	Wien	Gerhard-Hanappi	19 600
3-Grazer AK	Graz	Arnold Schwarzenegger	15 400
4-SK Sturm Graz	Graz	Arnold Schwarzenegger	15 400
5-SC Austria	Lustenau	Reichshofstadion	11 750
6-FC Lustenau 1907	Lustenau	An Der Hotzstrasse	5 500
7-SV Austria Salzburg	Salzburg	Stadion Salzburg	18 200
8-SV Pasching	Pasching	Waldstadion	7 000
9-Casino Schwarz-Weib	Bregenz	Casino	14 000
10-VFB Admira/Wacker	Modling	Sudstadt	12 000
11-SV Mattersburg	Mattersburg	Pappelstadion	10 000
12-FC Karntern	Klagenfurt	Wortherseestadion	10 500
13-SC	Untersiebenbrunn	Marchfeldstadion	5 000
14-FC Wacker	Tirol		
15-Kapfenberger SV	Kapfenberger	Alpenstadion	12 000
16-SV Worgl	Worgl	Sportzentrum Worgl	4 000
17-SV Ried im	Innkreis		
18-DSV Leoben	Leoben	Stadion Donawitz	6 000
19-LASK Linz	Linz	Stadion Der Stadt Linz	25 138
20-BSV Juniors	Villach	Stadthalle Villach	4 500
21-SEZ Bad Bielberg	Bad Bielberg	InfornStadion	6 500
23-SV Branau	Branau	Grenzlandstadion	7 500
24-SV Ried	Ried	Stadion Der Stadt Ried	9 500
25-Wiener Neustadt SC	Wiener Neust.	Wiener Neustadter Stad.	10 000
26-SC Eisenstadt	Eisenstadt	Lindenstadion	12 000

AZERBAIJAN

ASSOC. OF AZERBAIJAN FOOTBALL FEDERATION

Husu Haciyev Kuc,st 42,370 009,Bakau
TEL 994-12/944 916   FAX /989 393
WEB www.affa-az.com

REFERENCE

Official name
Republic of Azerbaijan

Date of formation   1991
Capital   Baku
Population   7.3 Million
Total area   33,436 sq MI(86,600 sq KM)
Time zone   GMT +4
Density   236 per sq MI (91 per sq KM)
Languages   Azerbaijani,Russian,Armenian
Literacy rate   97%
Currency   Manat
Economy   Services 42%
Religions   Muslim 94%
Ethnic Mix   Azervaijani,Russian

GEOGRAPHY

Elevation
lowest point: Caspian Sea -28 m
highest point: Bazarduzu Dagi 4,485 m
Geography Note
both the main area of the country and the
Naxcivan exclave are landlocked
Natural Resources
petroleum, natural gas, iron ore,
nonferrous metals, alumina
Climate
dry, semiarid steppe
Azerbaijan Food
green gutab/dill pilaf

WORLD CUP		COUNTRY LEAGUE CHAMPIONS	
1930	Did not qualify		
1934	Did not qualify		
1938	Did not qualify	2004	Neftchi Baku
1950	Did not qualify	2003	No League
1954	Did not qualify	2002	FK Samkir
1958	Did not qualify	2001	FK Samkir
1962	Did not qualify	2000	FK Samkir
1966	Did not qualify	1999	Kepez Ganca
1970	Did not qualify	1998	Kepez Ganca
1974	Did not qualify	1997	Neftchi Baku
1978	Did not qualify	1996	Neftchi Baku
1982	Did not qualify	**WOMEN'S LEAGUE CHAMPIONS**	
1986	Did not qualify	2004	Not Known
1990	Did not qualify	2003	Not Known
1998	Did not qualify	2002	Not Known
2002	Did not qualify	2001	Not Known
		2000	Not Known

NATIONAL TEAM COLORS

WORLD PICTURES OF SOCCER

PREMIERE LEAGUE CLUBS	CITY	STADIUM	CAPACITY
1-Neftchi Baku	Baku	Tofig Bakhramov	37 000
2-Shafa Baku	Baku	Shafa Stadium	17 000
3-Bakili Baku	Baku	Tofig Bakhramov	37 000
4-Dinamo Baku	Baku		
5-MOIK Baku	Baku		
6-Adliyya Baku	Baku		
7-Karat Baku	Baku		
8-SAF Baku	Baku		
9-Xazar Universiteti	Baku		
10-Azrebaijan-U17	Baku		
11-Baku Fehlesi	Baku	Ismet Gayibov	10 000
12-Xazar Sumqayit	Sumqayit	Mehdi Huseyn-Zade	14 000
13-Ganclarbirliyi	Sumqayit		
14-Lider Qarabag	Agdam		
15-Qarabag Azarsun	Agdam	Karabakh	15 000
16-FK Samkir	Samkir	Samkir Shehar	11 000
17-Turan Tovuz	Tovuz	Shehar	10 000
18-Sadag-Samur	Qusar		
19-Kapaz Gyanja	Gyanja	Shehar	25 000
20-Lokomotiv Imisli	Ismisli		
21-Goyazan Qazax	Qazax		
22-Energetik Mingacevir	Mingacevir		
23-Kur-Nur Mingacevir	Mingacevir	Shehar	16 000
24-Khazri Buzovna	Buzovna	Genclik	5 000
25-Karabakh Barda	Barda	Municipal	10 000

BELARUS

BELARUS FOOTBALL FEDERATION
8-2 Kyrov Street, 220 600 Minsk
TEL 375-17/227 2990 FAX /227 2920
WEB www.feesmg.minsk.by/bbf.htm

REFERENCE
Official name
Republic of Belarus

Date of formation	1991
Population	10.3 Million
Capital	Minsk
Total area	80,154 sq MI (207,600 sq KM)
Time zone	GMT +3
Density	80,154 sq MI (207,600 sq KM)
Languages	Bearussian, Russian
Literacy rate	98%
Currency	Belarussian Rouble
Economy	Industry 40%
Religions	Eastern Orthodox
Ethnic Mix	Belarussian79%, European, Asian

GEOGRAPHY
Elevation
lowest point: Nyoman River 90 m
highest point: Dzyarzhynskaya Hara 346 m
Geography Note
landlocked; glacial scouring accounts for the
flatness of Belarusian terrain and for its
11,000 lakes; the country is geologically well
endowed with extensive deposits of granite,
limestone, marl, chalk, sand, gravel, and clay
Natural Resources
forests, peat deposits, small quantities of
oil and natural gas, granite, dolomitic,
limestone, marl, chalk, sand, clay.
Climate
cold winters, cool and moist summers; transitional between continental and maritime
Belarusian Food
honey apples tart

WORLD CUP		COUNTRY LEAGUE CHAMPIONS	
1930	Did not qualify		
1934	Did not qualify		
1938	Did not qualify	2004	Dynamo Minsk
1950	Did not qualify	2003	FK Homel
1954	Did not qualify	2002	Bate Barysau
1958	Did not qualify	2001	Belshyna Babruisk
1962	Did not qualify	2000	Slavia Mazyr
1966	Did not qualify	1999	Bate Barysau
1970	Did not qualify	1998	Dnepr - Transmash
1974	Did not qualify	1997	Dynamo Minsk
1978	Did not qualify	1996	Dynamo Minsk
1982	Did not qualify	**WOMEN'S LEAGUE CHAMPIONS**	
1986	Did not qualify	2004	Babruichanka Babruisk
1990	Did not qualify	2003	Babruichanka Babruisk
1994	Did not qualify	2002	Babruichanka Babruisk
1998	Did not qualify	2001	Babruichanka Babruisk
2002	Did not qualify	2000	Babruichanka Babruisk

NATIONAL TEAM COLORS

WORLD PICTURES OF SOCCER

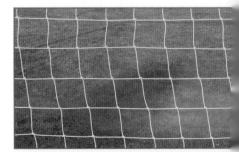

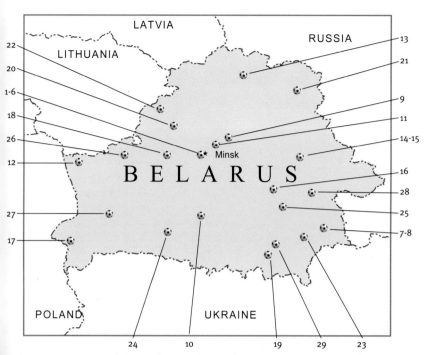

Premiere League Clubs	City	Stadium	Capacity
1-Dynama Minsk	Minsk	Dinamo Stadium	42 375
2-Torpedo-SKA	Minsk	Torpedo Stadium	7 000
3-Zvyazda VABDU	Minsk		
4-Lakamatyu Minsk	Minsk		
5-MTZ-RIPA Minsk	Minsk		
6-Dynama Juni	Minsk		
7-FK Homel	Homel	Homel Stadiom	10 000
8-ZLIN Homel	Homel		
9-BATE Barisau	Barisau	City Stadium	4 000
10-Shakhtsyor Salihorsk	Salihorsk	Shakhtsyor	5 000
11-Tarpeda Zhodzina	Zhodzina		
12-Neman Hrodna	Hrodna	Neman	15 000
13-Naftan Navapolatsk	Navapolatsk	Atlant	6 500
14-Dnepr-Transmash	Mahilyou	Spartak	11 200
15-Tarpeda-Kadzina	Mahilyou		
16-Belshyna Babruisk	Babruisk	Spartak	4 800
17-Dynama Brest	Brest	Dinamo	15 000
18-Daryda	Kuntsevchina		
19-Slavia Mazy	rMazyr	Yunost	6 500
20-FK Maladzechna2000	Maladzechna	Metallurg	5 500
21-Lakamatyu Vitsebsk	Vitsebsk	Dinamo	5 500
22-FK Smarhon	Smarhon		
23-Vedrych-97 Rechytsa	Rechytsa		
24-Hranit Mikashevichy	Mikashevichy		
25-Khimik Svetlahorsk	Svetlahorsk		
26-FK Lida	Lida	Yunost	5 000
27-Kamunalnik Slonim	Slonim	Yunost	5 000
28-Dnepr-DYUSSH-1	Dneprvosk		
29-Vertykal Kalinkavichy	Kalinkavichy		

BELGIUM

UNION ROYALE BELGE DES SOCIETES DE FOOTBALL ASSOC.
145 Av.Houba de Strooper,1020 Bruxelles
TEL 32-2/477 12121   FAX /478 2391
WEB www.footbel.com

REFERENCE
Official name
  Kingdom of Belgium
Date of formation   1830
Capital   Brussels
Population   10 Million
Total area   12,780 sq Mi (37,330 sq KM)
Time zone   GMT +1
Density   864 per sq MI (334 per sq KM)
Languages   French,Dutch
Literacy rate   99%
Currency   Euro
Economy   Services 77%
Religions   Catholic77%
Ethnic Mix   Fleming 55%,Walloon 35%

GEOGRAPHY
Elevation
lowest point: North Sea o m
highest point: Signal de Botrange 694 m
Geography Note
crossroads of Western Europe; majority of
West European capitals within 1,000 km of
Brussels, the seat of both the European
Union and NATO
Natural Resources
coal, natural gas
Climate
temperate; mild winters, cool summers;
rainy, humid, cloudy
Belgium Food
moule frites/gauffres

WORLD CUP

1930	First round exit
1934	First round exit
1938	First round exit
1950	Did not qualify
1954	First round exit
1958	Did not qualify
1962	Did not qualify
1966	Did not qualify
1970	First round exit
1974	Did not qualify
1978	Did not qualify
1982	First round exit
1986	Finish 4th
1990	First round exit
1994	First round finish
1998	First round exit
2002	Second round

COUNTRY LEAGUE CHAMPIONS

2004	Anderlecht
2003	Club Brugge
2002	Racing Genk
2001	Anderlecht
2000	Anderlecht
1999	Racing Genk
1998	Club Brugge
1997	Lierse SK
1996	Club Brugge

WOMEN'S LEAGUE CHAMPIONS

2004	K.F.C Rapid Wezemaal
2003	SK Lebeke-Aalst
2002	K.S.C Eendracht Aalst
2001	K.S.C Eendracht Aalst
2000	K.S.C Eendracht Aalst

NATIONAL TEAM COLORS

WORLD PICTURES OF SOCCER

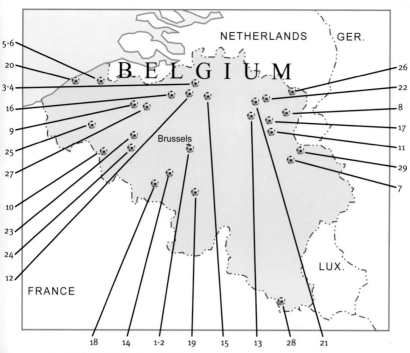

PREMIERE LEAGUE CLUBS	CITY	STADIUM	CAPACITY
1-RSC Anderlecht	Brussels	Constant Vanden Stock	26 261
2-FC Brussels	Brussels	Edmond Machtens	12 430
3-Royal Antwerp FC	Antwerp	Bosuil	16 649
4-Germinal Beerschot	Antwerp	Olympisch Stadion	12 148
5-Club Brugge KV	Brugge	Jan breydel	29 975
6-Cercle de Brugge KSV	Brugge	Jan Breydel	29 975
7-Standard de Liege	Liege	Sclessin	29 173
8-KRC Genk	Genk	Fenix Stadion	24 604
9-RAA Gent	Gent	Jules Otten	12 919
10-Excelsior Mouscron	Mouscron	Le Cannonier	11 300
11-Sint Truidense VV	Sint Truiden	Staaienveld	11 250
12-SK Beveren Waas	Beveren	Freethiel	12 930
13-VC Westerlo	Westerlo	T Kuipje	10 278
14-AA Louviereroise	La Louviere	Tivoli	13 500
15-Lierse SK	Lier	Herman Vanderpoorten	14 538
16-Sporting Lokeren SNW	Lokeren	Darknam	12 000
17-K Heusden-Zolder	Zolder	Belfortstadion	2 561
18-RAEC Mons	Mons	Charles Trondeau	12 000
19-Royal Charleroi SC	Charleroi	Stade Du Pays Charleroi	25 149
20-KV Oostende	Oostende	Albertparkstadion	10 800
21-KFC Verbroedering Geel	Geel	De Leunen	10 022
22-KFC Dessel Sport	Dessel	Lorzestraat	5 000
23-SV Zulte-Waregem	Waregem	Regenboogstadion	15 000
24-KRC Zuid-West	Harelbeke	Forestierstadion	9 937
25-KSV Roeselare	Roeselare	Schiervelde	8 836
26-K.Patro	Maasmechelen	Patrostadion	9 600
27-KFC Vigor Wuitens	Hamme	Vigor Wuitenstadion	6 000
28-R.Excelsior Virton	Virton	Yvan Georges	4 000
29-KAS Eupen	Eupen	Stadion Am Kehrweg	7 500

BOSNIA & HERZEGOVINA

FOOTBALL FEDERATION OF BOSNIA HERZEGOVINA

Ferhadija 30,71000 Sarajevo
TEL 387-33/276 660   FAX /444 332
WEB www.nsbih.ba

REFERENCE
Official name
Republic of Bosnia

Date of formation	1992
Capital	Sarajevo
Population	3.5 Million
Total area	19,741 sq MI (51,130 sq KM)
Time zone	GMT +1
Density	176 per sq MI (68 per sq KM)
Languages	Serbian,Croatian
Literacy rate	82%
Currency	Dinar
Economy	Services 41%
Religions	Muslim 49% Orthodox 31%
Ethnic Mix	Bosnian 44%,Serb 31%, Croat 17%

GEOGRAPHY
Elevation
lowest point: Adriatic Sea o m
highest point: Maglic 2,386 m
Geography Note
within Bosnia and Herzegovina's recognized borders, the country is divided into a joint Bosniak/Croat Federation and the Bosnian Serb-led Republika Srpska or RS; the region called Herzegovina is contiguous to Croatia and Serbia and Montenegro (Montenegro)
Natural Resources
coal, iron, bauxite, manganese, forests, copper, chromium, lead, zinc, hydropower
Climate
the country has hot summers and cold winters; mild, rainy winters along coast
Bosnia & Herzegovina Food
chorba burek/apple pie

WORLD CUP

1930	Did not qualify
1934	Did not qualify
1938	Did not qualify
1950	Did not qualify
1954	Did not qualify
1958	Did not qualify
1962	Did not qualify
1966	Did not qualify
1970	Did not qualify
1974	Did not qualify
1978	Did not qualify
1982	Did not qualify
1986	Did not qualify
1990	Did not qualify
1994	Did not qualify
1998	Finish 3rd
2002	First round exit

COUNTRY LEAGUE CHAMPIONS

2003	Leotar
2002	Zeljeznicar
2001	Zeljeznicar
2000	Brotnjo
MUSLIM CHAMPIONSHIP	
2004	Jedinstvo Bihac
2003	FK Sarajevo
2002	Bosna
2001	Celik Zenica
2000	Celik Zenica
SERBIAN CHAMPIONSHIP	
2003	Discontinued
2002	Leotar Borac
2001	Borac Banja Luka
2000	Boksit Mili

NATIONAL TEAM COLORS

WORLD PICTURES OF SOCCER

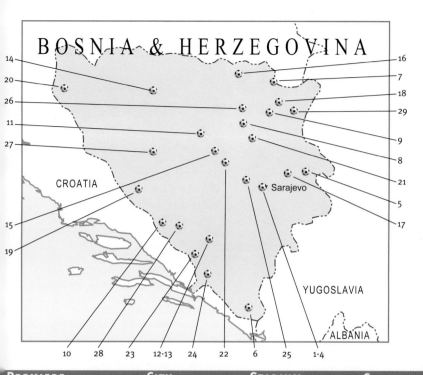

BOSNIA & HERZEGOVINA

CROATIA

Sarajevo

YUGOSLAVIA

ALBANIA

Premiere League Clubs	City	Stadium	Capacity
1-Sarajevo FC	Sarajevo	Olimpisjski Kosevo	37 500
2-Zeljeznicar	Sarajevo	Grbavica	24 500
3-Olimpik	Sarajevo		
4-SASK Napredak	Sarajevo		
5-Siroki Brijeg	Ljuti Brijeg		
6-Leotar	Trebinje		
7-Orasje	Orasje		
8-Zepce Limorad	Zepce		
9-Sloboda	Tuzla	Tusanj	15 000
10-Posusje	Posusje	Mokri Dolac	12 000
11-Travnik	Travnik		
12-Zrinjski	Mostar	Bijeli Brijeg	20 000
13-Velez	Mostar	Vrapcici	7 000
14-Borac	Banja Luka		
15-Celik	Zenica		
16-Modrica Maksima	Modrica		
17-Glasinac	Sokolac		
18-Rudar	Ugljevik		
19-Brotnjo	Citluk	Bare	8 000
20-Jedinstvo	Bihac	Gradski	16 000
21-Buducnost	Banovici		
22-Rudar	Kakanj		
23-Ljubuski	Ljubuski		
24-GOSK	Gabela		
25-NC Bosna	Visoko	Luke	10 000
26-Radnicki	Lukavac		
27-Iskra	Bugojno		
28-Grude	Grude		
29-Kiseljak	Kiseljak		

BULGARIA

BULGARIAN FOOTBALL UNION
19 Karnigradska Street, 1000 Sofia
TEL 359-2/987 7490 FAX /986 2538
WEB www.bfunion.bg

REFERENCE
Official name
    Republic of Bulgaria
Date of formation   1908/1923
Capital   Sofia
Population   9 Million
Total area   42,822 sq MI (110,910 sq KM)
Time zone   GMT +1
Density   191 per sq MI (74 per sq KM)
Languages   Bulgarian,Turkish
Literacy rate   93%
Currency   Lev
Economy   Services 45%
Religions   Bulgarian Orthodox 86%
Ethnic Mix   Bulgarian 86%,Turkidh 9 %

GEOGRAPHY
Elevation
lowest point: Black Sea 0 m
highest point: Musala 2,925 m
Geography Note
strategic location near Turkish Straits; controls key land routes from Europe to Middle East and Asia
Natural Resources
bauxite, copper, lead, zinc, coal, timber, arable land
Climate
temperate; cold, damp winters; hot, dry summers
Bulgarian Food
rice with olives/spinach zagora

WORLD CUP

1930	Did not qualify
1934	Did not qualify
1938	Did not qualify
1950	Did not qualify
1954	Did not qualify
1958	Did not qualify
1962	First round exit
1966	First round exit
1970	First round exit
1974	First round exit
1978	Did not qualify
1982	Did not qualify
1986	Scd round exit
1990	Did not qualify
1994	Finish Fourth
1998	First round exit
2002	Did not qualify

COUNTRY LEAGUE CHAMPIONS

2004	Lokomotiv Plovdiv
2003	CSKA
2002	Levski Sofia
2001	Levski Sofia
2000	Levski Sofia
1999	Litex
1998	Litex
1997	CSKA Sofia
1996	Slavia

WOMEN'S LEAGUE CHAMPIONS

2004	Not Known
2003	Not Known
2002	Not Known
2001	Grand Hotel
2000	Grand Hotel

NATIONAL TEAM COLORS

WORLD PICTURES OF SOCCER

PREMIERE LEAGUE CLUBS	CITY	STADIUM	CAPACITY
1-CSKA Sofia	Sofia	Balgarska Armiya	22 150
2-Levski Sofia	Sofia	Georgi Asparoukhov	29 980
3-Slavia sofia	Sofia	Slavia Stadion	32 000
4-Lokomotiv Sofia	Sofia	Lokomotiv Stadion	25 000
5-Koneliano Sofia	Sofia		
6-Septemvri	Sofia	Septemvri	20 000
7-Lokomotiv Plovdiv	Plovdiv	Lokomotiv Plovdiv	20 000
8-Botev	Plovdiv	Hristo Botev	21 000
9-Spartak Varna	Varna	Spartak Stadion	12 000
10-Cherno More	Varna	Ticha Stadion	12 000
11-Vihar-Vladislav	Varna		
12-Naftex	Burgas	Neftokhimik Stadion	18 689
13-Chernomorets	Burgas	Stadion 9 Septembri	14 000
14-Litex	Lovech	Gradski Stadion	6 488
15-Marek	Dupnitsa		
16-Vidima-Rakovski	Sevlievo		
17-Rodopa	Smolyan		
18-Belasitsa	Petrich	Tsar Samuil	12 000
19-Makedonska Slava	Simitli		
20-Beroe	Stara Zagora	Beroe Stadion	24 000
21-Pirin	Blagoevgrad	Hristo Botev	32 000
22-Nesebar	Pleven		
23-Belite Orli	Pleven		
24-Spartak Pleven	Pleven	Slavi Aleksiev	25 000
25-Svetkavitsa	Turgovishte		
26-Shumen 2001	Shumen	Panaiot Volov	30 000
27-Rilski Sportist	Samokov		
28-Vihren	Sandanski		
29-Akademik	Svishtov		

CROATIA

CROATIAN FOOTBALL FEDERATION
Rusanova 13, 10.000 Zagreb
TEL 385-1/236 1555   FAX /244 1500
WEB www.hns-cff.hr

REFERENCE
Official name
 Republic of Croatia

Date of formation	1991
Capital	Zagreb
Population	4.9 Million
Total area	21,830 sq MI (56,540 sq KM)
Time zone	GMT +1
Density	214 per sq MI (83 per sq KM)
Languages	Croatian,Serbian
Literacy rate	97%
Currency	Kuna
Economy	Services 56%
Religions	Catholic 77%,Orthodox 11%
Ethnic Mix	Croat 78%,Serb 12%

GEOGRAPHY
Elevation
lowest point: Adriatic Sea 0 m
highest point: Dinara 1,830 m
Geography Note
controls most land routes from Western
Europe to Aegean Sea and Turkish Straits
Natural Resources
oil, some coal, bauxite, low-grade iron
ore, calcium, natural asphalt, silica, mica,
clays, salt, hydropower
Climate
mediterranean and continental; continental
climate predominant with hot summers and
cold winters; mild winters, dry summers
along coast
Croatian Food
janjecu/croatian bow knots

WORLD CUP		COUNTRY LEAGUE CHAMPIONS	
1930	Did not qualify		
1934	Did not qualify		
1938	Did not qualify	2004	Hajduk Split
1950	Did not qualify	2003	Dinamo Zagreb
1954	Did not qualify	2002	NK Zagreb
1958	Did not qualify	2001	Hajduk Split
1962	Did not qualify	2000	Dinamo Zagreb
1966	Did not qualify	1999	Croatia Zagreb
1970	Did not qualify	1998	Croatia Zagreb
1974	Did not qualify	1997	Croatia Zagreb
1978	Did not qualify	1996	Croatia Zagreb
1982	Did not qualify	**WOMEN'S LEAGUE CHAMPIONS**	
1986	Did not qualify	2004	Maksimir Zagreb
1990	Did not qualify	2003	ZNK Osijek
1994	Did not qualify	2002	ZNK Osijek
1998	Finish 3rd	2001	ZNK Osijek
2002	First round exit	2000	ZNK Osijek

NATIONAL TEAM COLORS

WORLD PICTURES OF SOCCER

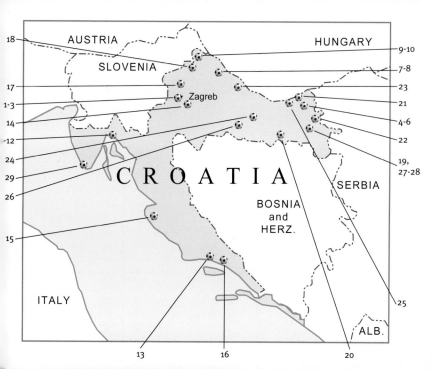

PREMIERE LEAGUE CLUBS	CITY	STADIUM	CAPACITY
1-Dinamo Zagreb	Zagreb	Stadion Maksimir	38 923
2-NK Zagreb	Zagreb	Stadion Kranjceviceva	15 000
3-Hrvatski Dragovoljac	Zagreb	Stadion Sigetu U	5 000
4-NK Osijek	Osijek	Stadion Gradski Vrt	19 500
5-Metalac Osijek	Osijek		
6-Graficar Vodovod	Osijek		
7-Slaven Belupo	Koprivnica	Stadion Gradski	5 054
8-NK Koprivnica	Koprivnica	Stadion gradski	5 054
9-Medimurje Cakovec	Cakovec		
10-NK Cakovec	Cakovec	Stadion Mladost	7 000
11-HNK Rijeka FC	Rijeka	Stadion Kantrida	12 124
12-Orijent Rijeka	Rijeka	Stadion Krimeja	7 000
13-Hajduk Split	Split	Stadion Poljud	39 941
14-NK Kamen Ingrad	Velika	Stadion Gradski	1 500
15-NK Zadar	Zadar	Stadion Stanovi	10 000
16-Mosor Zmovnica	Zmovnica	Stadion Pricvice	3 000
17-INKER Zapresic	Zapresic		
18-Varteks	Varazdin	Stadion Varteksa	9 300
19-Cibalia	Vinkovici		
20-Marsonia	Slavonski Brod		
21-NK Belisce	Belisce	Stadion Gradski	5 000
22-HNK Vukovar 91	Vukovar	Stadion Gradski	6 000
23-NK Virovitica	Virovitica		
24-Slavonija	Slavonska Pozega		
25-Valpovka Valpovo	Valpovo		
26-Sloga Nova Gradiska	Gradiska		
27-Dilj Vinkovci	Vinkovci		
28-HNK Cibala Vinkovci	Vinkovci	Stadion Cibalije	12 000
29-Pula 1856	Pula		

CYPRUS

CYPRUS FOOTBALL ASSOC.

1, Stasinos Street, Engomi
pb 25071, 2404 Nicosia
TEL 357-2/259 0960   FAX /259 0544
WEB www.uefa.com

REFERENCE

Official name
Republic of Cyprus

Date of formation	1960/1983
Capital	Nicosia
Population	700,000
Total area	3,572 sq MI (9,251 sq KM)
Time zone	GMT +2
Density	215 per sq MI (83 per sq KM)
Languages	Greek, Turkish
Literacy rate	77%
Currency	Cypryot Pound, Turkish Lira
Economy	Services 67%
Religions	GreekOrthodox
Ethnic Mix	Greek 78%,Turkish 18%

GEOGRAPHY

Elevation
lowest point: Mediterranean Sea 0 m
highest point: Olympus 1,951 m
Geography Note
the third largest island in the Mediterranean
Sea (after Sicily and Sardinia)
Natural Resources
copper, pyrites, asbestos, gypsum, timber, salt, marble, clay earth pigment
Climate
temperate; Mediterranean with hot, dry
summers and cool winters
Cyprus Food
saltsa domata/marinated olives

WORLD CUP		COUNTRY LEAGUE CHAMPIONS	
1930	Did not qualify		
1934	Did not qualify		
1938	Did not qualify	2004	Apoel Nicosia
1950	Did not qualify	2003	Omonia Nicosia
1954	Did not qualify	2002	Apoel Nicosia
1958	Did not qualify	2001	Omonia Nicosia
1962	Did not qualify	2000	Anorthosis Famagus
1966	Did not qualify	1999	Anorthosis Famagus
1970	Did not qualify	1998	Anorthosis Famagus
1974	Did not qualify	1997	Anorthosis Famagus
1978	Did not qualify	1996	Apoel Nicosia
1982	Did not qualify	**WOMEN'S LEAGUE CHAMPIONS**	
1986	Did not qualify	2004	Not Known
1990	Did not qualify	2003	Not Known
1994	Did not qualify	2002	Not Known
1998	Did not qualify	2001	Lefkothea Nicosia
2002	Did not qualify	2000	Not Known

NATIONAL TEAM COLORS

WORLD PICTURES OF SOCCER

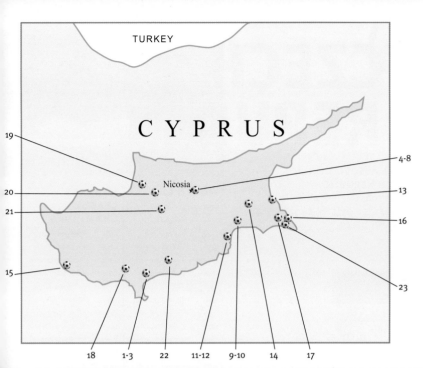

PREMIERE LEAGUE CLUBS	CITY	STADIUM	CAPACITY
1-Apollon	Limassol	Tsirion Stadium	13 152
2-A.E.L	Limassol	Tsirion Stadium	13 152
3-Aris Lemesos	Limassol	Tsirion Stadium	13 152
4-A.P.O.E.L	Nicosia	Neo GSP Stadium	23 400
5-Omonia	Nicosia	Neo GSP Stadium	23 400
6-Olympiakos	Nicosia	Neo GSP Stadium	23 400
7-Ethnikos Assias	Nicosia	Makario Stadium	16 000
8-Dighenis Morphou	Nicosia	Kykkos Stadium	2 000
9-Ermis Aradippou	Aradipou	Aradippou Stadium	1 000
10-Omonia Aradippou	Aradipou		
11-Anorthosis	Larnaca	Antonis Papadopoulos	9 139
12-A.E.K	Larnaca	Zenon Stadium	13 032
13-Nea Salamina	Famagusta	Ammohostos Stadium	4 000
14-AS Ethnicos	Athna	Dasaki Achnas Stadium	4 000
15-A.E.Paphos	Paphos	Paphiakos Stadium	7 650
16-Enosis Neon	Paralimni	Paralimni Stadium	5 800
17-Anagennisi	Dherinia	Anagennisi Stadium	4 500
18-Onisilos	Sotira		
19-Digenis	Morphou		
20-Doxa	Katokopia		
21-Doxa Katokopias	Peristerona	Peristerona Stadium	4 000
22-S.E.K.A.Y	Athanasios		
23-Aya Napa	Aya Napa		
Northern Cyprus			
1-Cetinkaya Turk SK			
2-Duzkaya SK			
3-Magusa Turk Gucu SK			
4-Yenicami Agdelen SK			
5-Gonyeli SK			

CZECH REPUBLIC

FOOTBALL ASSOCIATION OF THE CZECH REPUBLIC
Diskarska 100, 16017 Praha 6
TEL 420-2/3320 9111 FAX /3335 3107
WEB www.fotbal.cz

REFERENCE
Official name
  Czec Republic

Date of formation	1933
Capital	Prague
Population	10 Million
Total area	30,260 sq MI (78370 sq KM)
Time zone	GMT +1
Density	338 per sq MI (130 per sq KM)
Languages	Czech,Slovak
Literacy rate	99%
Currency	Koruna
Economy	Industry 47%
Religions	Catholic 40%
Ethnic Mix	Czech 95%,Slovak 3%

GEOGRAPHY
Elevation
lowest point: Elbe River 115 m
highest point: Snezka 1,602 m
Geography Note
landlocked; strategically located astride some of oldest and most significant land routes in Europe.
Natural Resources
hard coal, soft coal, kaolin, clay, graphite, timber
Climate
temperate; cool summers; cold, cloudy, humid winters
Czech Republic Food
poppy seed kolaches

WORLD CUP

1930	Did not qualify
1934	Finish Fourth
1938	1/4 final exit
1950	Did not qualify
1954	First round exit
1958	First round exit
1962	Finish Second
1966	Did not qualify
1970	First round exit
1974	Did not qualify
1978	Did not qualify
1982	First round exit
1986	Did not qualify
1990	1/4 final exit
1994	Did not qualify
1998	Did not qualify
2002	Did not qualify

COUNTRY LEAGUE CHAMPIONS

2004	FC Banik Ostrava
2003	AC Sparta Praha
2002	FC Slovan Liberec
2001	AC Sparta Praha
2000	AC Sparta Praha
1999	AC Sparta Praha
1998	AC Sparta Praha
1997	AC Sparta Praha
1996	SK Slavia Praha

WOMEN'S LEAGUE CHAMPIONS

2004	AC Sparta Praha
2003	AC Sparta Praha
2002	AC Sparta Praha
2001	AC Sparta Praha
2000	AC Sparta Praha

NATIONAL TEAM COLORS

WORLD PICTURES OF SOCCER

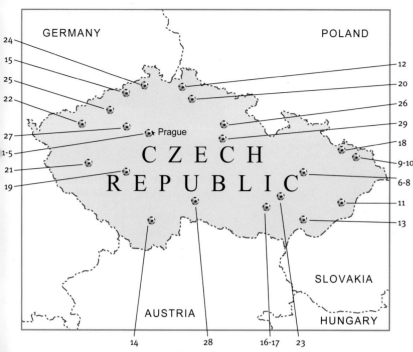

PREMIERE LEAGUE CLUBS	CITY	STADIUM	CAPACITY
1-AC Sparta Praha	Praha	Toyota Arena	20 565
2-SK Slavia Praha	Praha	Evzena Rosickeho	19 336
3-FC Bohemians Praha	Praha	V.Dolicku	10 500
4-AC Sparta Praha B	Praha	Toyota Arena	20 565
5-Viktoria Zizkov	Praha	FK Viktoria	8 000
6-SK Sigma Olomouc	Olomouc	Andruv	12 119
7-SK Sigma Olomouc B	Olomouc	Andruv	12 119
8-FK Helice Olomouc	Olomouc/Helice	Staskova	3 030
9-FC Banik Ostrava	Ostrava	Bazaly	18 020
10-FC Nova Hu	Ostrava	Nova Hut	20 000
11-FC Tescoma Zlin	Zlin	Letna	7 500
12-FC Slovan Liberec	Liberec	U.Nisy	9 090
13-FC Synot	Stare Masto	Siruch	4 700
14-SK Ceske Budejovice	Budejovice	Na Strelecky Ostrov	12 000
15-FK Teplice	Teplice	Na Stinadlech	18 428
16-FC Brno	Brno	Na Srbske	12 500
17-FC Brno B	Brno	Na Srbske	12 500
18-SFC Opava	Opava	Mastskych Sadech	14 800
19-FK Marila Pribram	Pribram	Na Litavcè	9 000
20-FK Jablonec 97	Jablonec	Strelnice	14 577
21-FC Viktoria Plzen	Plzen	Struncovy Sady	18 500
22-FK Chmel Blsany	Blsany	FK Chmel	3 300
23-Petra Drnovice	Drnovice	Sportovni Areal	7 000
24-FK Mlada Boleslav	Boleslav	Mestsky	13 000
25-FC MUS Most	Most	Letni	20 000
26-SK Hradec Kralove	Kralove	Vsesportovni Areal	25 000
27-Kladno	Kladno		
28-FC Vysocina Jihlava	Jihlava		
29-FK AS Pardubice	Pardubice	Letni	6 000

DENMARK

DANISH FOOTBALL ASSOC.
Idraettens Hus, Brondby Stadion 20,
2605 Brondby
TEL 45-43/262 222 FAX /262 245
WEB www.dbu.dk

REFERENCE
Official name
  Kingdom of Denmark
Date of
formation   AD 960/1953
Capital   Copenhagen
Population   5.2 million
Total area   16,629 sq MI (43,069 sq KM)
Time zone   GMT +1
Density   322 per sq Mi (124 per sq KM)
Languages   Danish,Faroese,Greenlandic
Literacy rate   99%
Currency   Euro
Economy   Services 75%
Religions   Lutheran 92%
Ethnic Mix   Scanidavian,Eskimos,Faroese

GEOGRAPHY
Elevation
lowest point: Lammefjord -7 m
highest point: Yding Skovhoej 173 m
Geography Note
controls Danish Straits (Skagerrak and
Kattegat) linking Baltic and North Seas;
about one-quarter of the population lives in
greater Copenhagen
Natural Resources
petroleum, natural gas, fish, salt, limestone, stone, gravel and sand
Climate
temperate; humid and overcast; mild, windy
winters and cool summers
Danish Food
cucumbers in sour cream/potato dumplings

WORLD CUP

1930	Did not qualify
1934	Did not qualify
1938	Did not qualify
1950	Did not qualify
1954	Did not qualify
1958	Did not qualify
1962	Did not qualify
1966	Did not qualify
1970	Did not qualify
1974	Did not qualify
1978	Did not qualify
1982	Did not qualify
1986	Scd round exit
1990	Did not qualify
1994	Did not qualify
1998	1/4 finals exit
2002	Scd round exit

COUNTRY LEAGUE CHAMPIONS

2004	FC Kobenhavn
2003	FC Kobenhavn
2002	Brondby IF
2001	FC Kobenhavn
2000	Herfolge BK
1999	Aab
1998	Brondby IF
1997	Brondby IF
1996	Brondby IF
WOMEN'S LEAGUE CHAMPIONS	
2004	Brondby IF
2003	Brondby IF
2002	Fortuna Hjoring
2001	OB
2000	OB

NATIONAL TEAM COLORS

WORLD PICTURES OF SOCCER

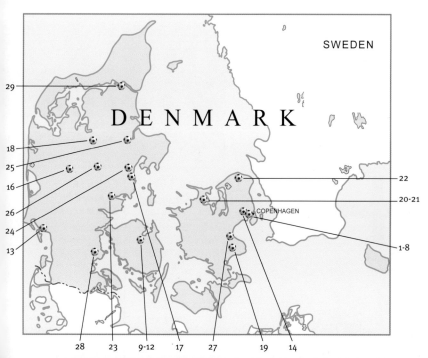

PREMIERE LEAGUE CLUBS	CITY	STADIUM	CAPACITY
1-FC Kobenhavn	Copenhagen	Parken	41 781
2-BK Frem	Copenhagen	Valby Idraetspark	12 000
3-Brondby IF	Copenhagen	Brondby Stadion	32 700
4-Lyngby FC	Copenhagen	Lyngby Stadion	9 680
5-Fremad Amager	Copenhagen	Sundby Idraetspark	7 200
6-B 1893	Copenhagen	Osterbro Stadion	6 000
7-Akademisk IF	Copenhagen	Gladsaxe Idraetspark	13 800
8-Hvidovre IF	Copenhagen	Hvidovre stadion	15 000
9-Odense BK	Odense	Odense Stadion	15 633
10-Dalum	Odense	Dalum Stadion	4 000
11-B 1909	Odense	B1909 Opvsningsbane	6 000
12-B 1913	Odense	Campus Road	5 000
13-Esbjerg FB	Esbjerg	Esbjerg Idraetspark	15 000
14-Glostrup	Glostrup	Glostrup Stadion	4 000
15-AAB Aalborg	Aalborg	Aalborg Stadion	16 000
16-FC Midtjylland	Herning		
17-AGF Arhus	Viby		
18-Viborg FF	Viborg	Viborg stadion	9 796
19-Herfolge BK	Herfolge	Herfolge Stadion	7 500
20-FC Nordsjaelland	Farum		
21-Farum BK	Farum	Farum Park	9 551
22-AB	Soborg		
23-AC Horsens	Horsens	Horsens Idraetspark	12 000
24-Randers FC	Randers	Randers Stadion	18 000
25-Vorup	Randers	Ulvehoj Idraetscenter	3 000
26-Silkeborg IF	Silkeborg	Silkeborg stadion	9 800
27-Koge	Koge	Koge Stadion	9 777
28-HFK Sonderjylland	Haderslev	Haderslev Stadion	8 500
29-FC Nordjylland	Aalborg		

ENGLAND

THE FOOTBALL ASSOCIATION
25 Soho Square, London W1 4 FA
TEL 44 20/7745 4545 FAX /77454546
WEB www.the-fa.org

REFERENCE
Official name
England
Date of formation 1536/1707
Capital London
Total area 93.218 sq Mi, 241,600 sq Km
Time zone GMT 0
Density 625 per sq Mi
Languages English
Literacy rate 99%
Currency British Pound
Economy Engineering, Energy, Services
Religions 55% Protestant
Ethnic Mix English 80%, Scottish 10%

GEOGRAPHY
Elevation
lowest point: Fenland -4 m
highest point: Ben Nevis 1,343 m
Geography Note
lies near vital North Atlantic sea lanes; only 35 km from France and now linked by tunnel under the English Channel
Natural Resources
coal, petroleum, natural gas, tin, limestone, iron ore, salt, clay, chalk, gypsum, lead, silica, arable land
Climate
temperate; moderated by prevailing south-west winds over the North Atlantic Current; more than one-half of the days are overcast
English Food
fish & chips

WORLD CUP

1930	Did not qualify
1934	Did not qualify
1938	Did not qualify
1950	First round exit
1954	1/4 final exit
1958	First round exit
1962	1/4 final exit
1966	World cup champ
1970	1/4 final exit
1974	Did not qualify
1978	Did not qualify
1982	Scd round exit
1986	1/4 final exit
1990	Finish Fourth
1994	Did not qualify
1998	Scd round exit
2002	Scd round exit

COUNTRY LEAGUE CHAMPIONS

2004	Arsenal
2003	Manchester United
2002	Arsenal
2001	Manchester United
2000	Manchester United
1999	Manchester United
1998	Arsenal
1997	Manchester United
1996	Manchester United

WOMEN'S LEAGUE CHAMPIONS

2004	Arsenal
2003	Fulham
2002	Arsenal
2001	Arsenal
2000	Croydon

NATIONAL TEAM COLORS

WORLD PICTURES OF SOCCER

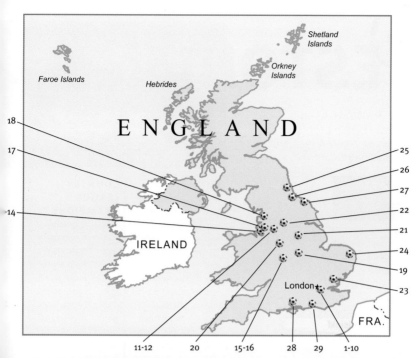

Premiere League Clubs	City	Stadium	Capacity
1-Arsenal FC	London	Highbury	38 500
2-Charlton Athletic FC	London	The Valley	26 500
3-Chelsea FC	London	Stamford Bridge	42 449
4-Fulham FC	London	Loftus Road	19 148
5-Tottenham Hotspurs	London	White Hart Lane	36 214
6-West Ham United	London	Boleyn Ground	35 056
7-Millwall Crusaders	London	The Den	20 146
8-Queenspark Rangers	London	Loftus Road	19 148
9-Crystal Palace	London	Selhurst Park	26 309
10-Leyton Orient FC	London	Matchroom Stadium	13 842
11-Manchester United	Manchester	Old Trafford	68 174
12-Manchester City	Manchester	City of Manchester Stad.	48 000
13-Liverpool FC	Liverpool	Anfield	45 000
14-Everton	Liverpool	Goodison Park	40 200
15-Aston Villa	Birmingham	Villa Park	43 275
16-Birmingham City	Birmingham	St.Andrew's	30 200
17-Blackburn Rovers	Blackburn	Ewood Park	31 367
18-Bolton Wanderers	Bolton	Reebok Stadium	28 000
19-Leicester City	Leicester	Walkers Stadium	32 000
20-Derby County	Derby	Pride Park	34 000
21-Nottingam Forrest	Nottingham	City Ground	30 602
22-Burnley FC	Burnley	Turf Moore	22 619
23-Ipswich Town	Ipswich	Portman Road	30 000
24-Norwich City FC	Norwich	Carrow Road	21 468
25-Newcastle United	Newcastle	St.James Park	52 143
26-Sunderland FC	Sunderland	Stadium of Light	48 300
27-Middlesbrough	Middlesbrough	Riverside Stadium	35 000
28-Southampton	Southampton	St. Mary's Stadium	32 000
29-Portsmouth FC	Portsmouth	Fratton Park	16 789

ESTONIA

ESTONIA FOOTBALL ASSOC.
Voidu 16,11213 Tallinn
TEL 372-6/542 715 FAX /542-719
WEB www.estfootball.ee

REFERENCE
Official name
Republic of Estonia

Date of formation	1917/1920
Capital	**Tallinn**
Population	1.4 Million
Total area	130,522 sq MI (338,130 sq KM)
Time zone	GMT +3
Density	84 per sq MI (32 per sq KM)
Languages	Estonian,Latvian, Lithuanian
Literacy rate	99%
Currency	Kroon
Economy	Industry 42%
Religions	Lutheran
Ethnic Mix	Estonian 62%,Russian, Ukrainian

GEOGRAPHY
Elevation
lowest point: Baltic Sea o m
highest point: Suur Munamagi 318 m
Geography Note
the mainland terrain is flat, boggy, and partly wooded; offshore lie more than 1,500 islands
Natural Resources
oil shale, peat, phosphorite, clay, limestone, sand, dolomite, arable land, sea mud.
Climate
maritime, wet, moderate winters, cool summers
Estonian Food
butter cookies/fish stew

WORLD CUP

1930	Did not qualify
1934	Did not qualify
1938	Did not qualify
1950	Did not qualify
1954	Did not qualify
1958	Did not qualify
1962	Did not qualify
1966	Did not qualify
1970	Did not qualify
1974	Did not qualify
1978	Did not qualify
1982	Did not qualify
1986	Did not qualify
1990	Did not qualify
1994	Did not qualify
1998	Did not qualify
2002	Did not qualify

COUNTRY LEAGUE CHAMPIONS

2004	FC Levadia
2003	FC Flora Talinn
2002	FC Flora Tallinn
2001	FC Flora Tallinn
2000	Levadia Maardu
1999	Levadia Maardu
1998	FC Flora Tallinn
1997	FC Lantana Tallinn
1996	FC Lantana Tallinn
WOMEN'S LEAGUE CHAMPIONS	
2004	Parnu JK
2003	Parnu JK
2002	TKSK Visa
2001	TKSK Visa
2000	KSK Visa

NATIONAL TEAM COLORS

WORLD PICTURES OF SOCCER

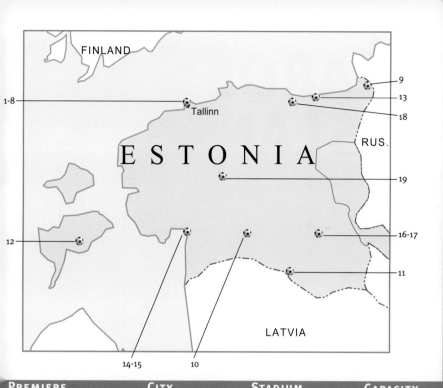

Premiere League Clubs	City	Stadium	Capacity
1-FC Flora	Tallinn	Lillekula Staadion	15 000
2-FC Tallinna VMK	Tallinn	Kalev Staadion	12 000
3-FC Levadia	Tallinn	Viimsi	2 000
4-JK Val	Tallinn	Kalev Staadion	12 000
5-M.C Tallinn	Tallinn		
6-F.C.A Estel	Tallinn		
7-Tallinna Jalgpalli Klubi	Tallinn		
8-FC Levadia	Maardu	Kadriorg	4 700
9-JK Trans	Narva	Kreenholm	3 000
10-JK Tulevik	Viljandi	Linnastaadion	1 000
11-FC Valga	Valga		
12-FC Kuressaare	Saaremaa		
13-FC Lootus	Kothla-Jarve		
14-JK Tervis	Parnu		
15-JK Vaprus	Parnu		
16-JK Merkuur	Tartu		
17-JK Tammeta	Tartu		
18-EP Johvi	Johvi	Kaevur	2 000
19-Lelle SK	Lelle	Kehtna Football School	1 500

FAROE ISLANDS

THE FAROE ISLANDS FOOTBALL ASSOCIATION
Gundadalur, PB 3028, 110 Torshavn
TEL 298/316 707 FAX/319 079
WEB www.football.fo

REFERENCE
Official name
Faroe Islands,
Self Governing (Denmark)

Date of formation	1948
Population	41,059
Capital	Torshavn
Total area	541 sq MI (1,400 sq KM)
Time zone	GMT 0
Density	30 per sq Km
Languages	Faroese, Danish
Literacy rate	99%
Currency	Danish Krone
Economy	Mainly Fishing
Religions	Lutheran
Ethnic Mix	Faroese

GEOGRAPHY
Elevation
lowest point: Atlantic Ocean 0 m
highest point: Slaettaratindur 882 m

Geography Note
archipelago of 17 inhabited islands and one uninhabited island, and a few uninhabited islets; strategically located along important sea lanes in northeastern Atlantic; precipitous terrain limits habitation to small coastal lowlands

Natural Resources
fish, whales, hydropower

Climate
mild winters, cool summers; usually overcast; foggy, windy

Faroe Islands Food
fried eels with creamed potatoes/stewed cod fish

WORLD CUP		COUNTRY LEAGUE CHAMPIONS	
1930	Did not qualify		
1934	Did not qualify		
1938	Did not qualify	2004	HB 04
1950	Did not qualify	2003	HB 04
1954	Did not qualify	2002	HB 04
1958	Did not qualify	2001	B 36
1962	Did not qualify	2000	VB
1966	Did not qualify	1999	KI
1970	Did not qualify	1998	HB 04
1974	Did not qualify	1997	B 36
1978	Did not qualify	1996	GI
1982	Did not qualify	**WOMEN'S LEAGUE CHAMPIONS**	
1986	Did not qualify	2004	KI Klaksvik
1990	Did not qualify	2003	KI Klaksvik
1994	Did not qualify	2002	KI Klaksvik
1998	Did not qualify	2001	KI Klaksvik
2002	Did not qualify	2000	KI Klaksvik

NATIONAL TEAM COLORS

WORLD PICTURES OF SOCCER

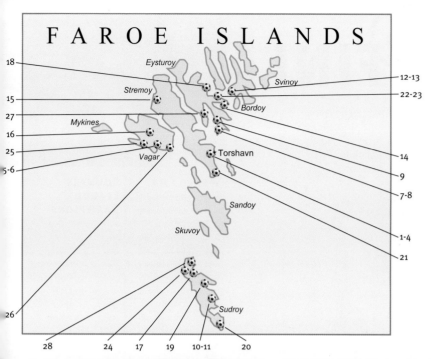

PREMIERE LEAGUE CLUBS	CITY	STADIUM	CAPACITY
1-HB	Torshavn	Gundalur	8 020
2-B36Torshavn	Gundalur	8 020	
3-B36-2	Torshavn	Gundalur	8 020
4-FRAM	Torshavn	Gundalur	8 020
5-FS Vorgar	Sandavagur	Sandavagur	2 000
6-SIF	Sandavagur	Sandavagur	2 000
7-B68	Toftir	Svangaskar	7 000
8-B68-2	Toftir	Svangaskar	7 000
9-NSI	Runavik	Runavik	2 000
10-VB	Vagur	Vesturi A Eiminum	3 000
11-VB-2	Vagur	Vesturi A Eiminum	3 000
12-KI	Klaksvik	Klaksvik	4 000
13-KI-2	Klaksvik	Klaksvik	4 000
14-GI	Gota	Serpurgergui	3 000
15-EB/Streymur	Streymoy		
16-FS Vagar	Vagar		
17-Skalar	Skalar	Skala	2 000
18-IF	Fuglafjoronur	Fuglafjoronur	3 000
19-TB	Tvoroyri	Sevmyra	3 000
20-Sumba IF	Sumba	A Krossinum	1 000
21-AB	Argir	Argir	1 000
22-B71	Leirvik	Sandur	2 000
23-LIF	Leirvik	Leirvik	2 000
24-Royn	Hvalba	Hvalba	2 000
25-SI	Sorvagur	Sorvagur	2 000
26-MB	Midvagur	Midvagur	1 000
27-Skali	Skali		
28-Sandvik	Sandvik		

FINLAND

SUOMEN PALLOLIITTO
Urheilukatu 1,ppb 191,00251
TEL 358-9/7421 51 FAX /7421 5200
WEB www.palloliitto.fi

REFERENCE

Official name
  Republic of Finland

Date of formation	1917/1920
Capital	Helsinki
Population	5 Million
Total area	130,552 sq Mi (338,130 sq KM)
Time zone	GMT +1
Density	42 per sq MI
Languages	Finnish,Swedish
Literacy rate	99%
Currency	Markka
Economy	Services 76%
Religions	Lutheran 89%, Finnish 94%,
Ethnic Mix	Swedish

GEOGRAPHY

Elevation
lowest point: Baltic Sea 0 m
highest point: Halti 1,328 m

Geography Note
long boundary with Russia; Helsinki is
northernmost national capital on European
continent; population concentrated on small
southwestern coastal plain

Natural Resources
timber, copper, zinc, iron ore, silver

Climate
cold temperate; potentially subarctic, but
comparatively mild because of moderating
influence of the North Atlantic Current,
Baltic Sea, and more than 60,000 lakes.

Finnish Food
kukkakaalialaatikko/finish coffee bread

WORLD CUP		COUNTRY LEAGUE CHAMPIONS	
1930	Did not qualify		
1934	Did not qualify		
1938	Did not qualify	2004	Haka Valkeakoski
1950	Did not qualify	2003	HJK Helsinki
1954	Did not qualify	2002	HJK Helsinki
1958	Did not qualify	2001	United Tempere
1962	Did not qualify	2000	Haka Valkeakoski
1966	Did not qualify	1999	Haka Valkeakoski
1970	Did not qualify	1998	Haka Valkeakoski
1974	Did not qualify	1997	HJK Helsinki
1978	Did not qualify	1996	Jazz Pori
1982	Did not qualify	**WOMEN'S LEAGUE CHAMPIONS**	
1986	Did not qualify	2004	United Pietarsaari
1990	Did not qualify	2003	MPS Helsinki
1994	Did not qualify	2002	United Pietarsaari
1998	Did not qualify	2001	HJK Helsinki
2002	Did not qualify	2000	HJK Helsinki

NATIONAL TEAM COLORS

WORLD PICTURES OF SOCCER

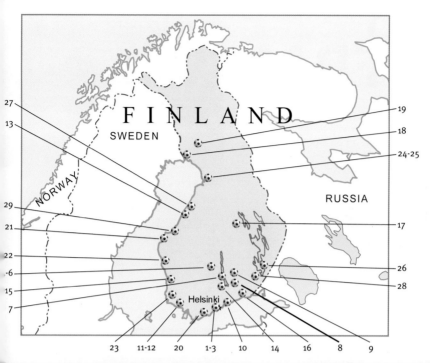

Premiere League Clubs	City	Stadium	Capacity
1-HJK Helsinki	Helsinki	Finnair	10 770
2-Jokerit Helsinki	Helsinki	Finnair	10 770
3-Viikingit Helsinki	Helsinki		
4-Tampere United	Tampere	Tammela	5 040
5-PP-70 Tampere	Tampere	Tammela	5 040
6-Tamper PV	Tampere	Tammela	5 040
7-FC Haka	Valkeakoski	Tehtaankentla	6 400
8-MYPA FC	Anjalan	Anjakosken Jalkapallo	4 067
9-FC Lahti	Lahti	Lahden Stadion	14 000
10-Allianssi Vantaa	Vantaa	Pohjola	4 600
11-Inter Turku	Turku	Veritas	9 000
12-Turun PS Turku	Turku	Veritas	9 000
13-FF Jaro Pietarsaari	Pietarsaari	Keskuskentla	5 000
14-FC Hameenlinna	Hameenlinna	Kaurialan Kentla	3 100
15-FC Jazz Pori	Pori	Porin Stadion	11 000
16-Kooteepee Kotka	Kotka	Arto Tolsa Areena	4 780
17-KUPS Kuopio	Kuopio	Vainolanniemi	9 000
18-TPP-47	Tornio		
19-ROPS Rovaniemi	Rovaniemi	Keskuskentla	4 000
20-FC Honka Espoo	Espoo		
21-VPS Vaasa	Vaasa	Hietalahti	4 300
22-Kraft Naarpio	Naarpio		
23-VG-62	Naantali		
24-AC Oulu	Oulu		
25-OLS Oulu	Oulu		
26-FC Rakuunat	Lappeenranta		
27-GBK Kokkola	Kokkola		
28-FC Kuusankoski	Kuusankoski		
29-Korsholm	Mustasaari		

FRANCE

FEDERATION FRANCAISE DE FOOTBALL
60 Bis Avenue de d'iena, 75783 paris, FR
TEL 33-1/44 31 73 00 FAX/47 20 82 96
WEB www.fff.fr

REFERENCE
Official name
  French Republic

Date of formation	1685/1920
Capital	Paris
Population	59.1 Millions
Total area	212,930 sq mi, 551,500 sq km
Time zone	GMT +1 Hour
Density	270 per sq mi, 108 per sq km
Languages	French, provencal, breton, Catalan, Basque
Literacy rate	99%
Currency	Euro
Economy	Services 73%, Industry 20%, Agriculture 7%
Religions	Catholic 90%
Ethnic Mix	French 95%, Others 5%

GEOGRAPHY
Elevation
lowest point: Rhone River delta -2 m
highest point: Mont Blanc 4,807 m
Geography Note
largest west european nation
Natural Resources
coal, iron ore, bauxite, zinc, potash, timber, fish
Climate
generally cool winters and mild summers, but mild winters and hot summers along the Mediterranean; occasional strong, cold, dry, north-to-northwesterly wind known as mistral
French Food
fromage fonduebourguignone/ baguette/eclair au chocolat

WORLD CUP	
1930	First round
1934	1/8 finals
1938	1/4 finals
1950	Did not qualify
1954	First round
1958	1/2 finals
1962	Did not qualify
1966	First round
1970	Did not qualify
1974	Did not qualify
1978	First round
1982	1/2 finals
1986	1/2 finals
1990	Did not qualify
1994	Did not qualified
1998	World Champion
2002	First round

COUNTRY LEAGUE CHAMPIONS	
2004	Lyon
2003	Lyon
2002	Lyon
2001	Nantes
2000	Monaco
1999	Bordeaux
1998	Lens
1997	Monaco
1996	Auxerre
WOMEN'S LEAGUE CHAMPIONS	
2004	Montpellier HSC
2003	Juvisy FCF
2002	Toulouse OAC
2001	Toulouse OAC
2000	Toulouse OAC

NATIONAL TEAM COLORS

WORLD PICTURES OF SOCCER

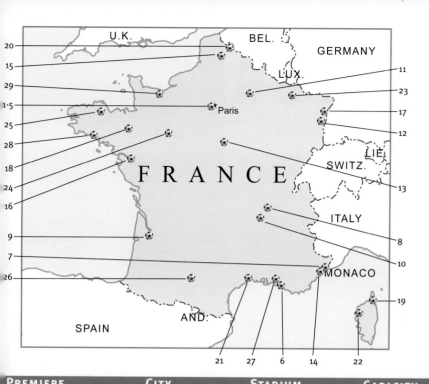

Premiere League Clubs	City	Stadium	Capacity
1-Paris Saint Germains FC	Paris	Parc des Princes	48 712
2-Paris Saint Germains FC-B	Paris	Municipal Georges Lefevre	1 500
3-Paris FC 2000	Paris	Stade Porte de Montreuil	3 000
4-AS Red Star	Paris	Stade de Marville	10 000
5-Racing Club de Paris	Paris	Stade Yves du Manoir	7 000
6-Olympique de Marseille	Marseille	Stade Velodrome	60 031
7-AS Monaco	Monaco	Stade Louis II	18 521
8-Olympique Lyon	Lyon	Stade Gerland	41 184
9-Girondins FC	Bordeaux	Stade Chaban-Delmas	34 327
10-AS Saint Etienne	Saint-Etienne	Stade Geoffroy-Guichard	35 616
11-Stade de Reims	Reims	Stade Auguste Delaune	9 592
12-FC Sochaux-Montbelliard	sochaux	Stade Auguste Bonal	20 025
13-AJ Auxerre	Auxerre	Stade Abbe Deschamps	23 493
14-OGC Nice	Nice	Municipal du ray	17 412
15-RC Lens	Lens	Stade Felix Bollaert	41 810
16-FC Nantes	Nantes	Stade de la Beaujoire	38 486
17-RC Strasbourg	Strasbourg	Stade de la Meinau	29 230
18-Stade Rennais FC	Rennes	Route de Lorient	31 716
19-SC Bastia	Bastia	Stade Armand Cesari	10 080
20-Lille OSC	Lille	Stade Grimonprez-Jooris	21 180
21-Montpellier HSC	Montpellier	Stade de la Mosson	31 250
22-AC Ajaccio	Ajaccio	Stade Francois Coty	10 660
23-FC Metz	Metz	Stade Symphorien	26 671
24-Le Mans	LeMans	Stade Omnisports	12 526
25-En Avant Guingamp	Guingamp	Municipal du Roudourou	18 016
26-Toulouse FC	Toulouse	Municipal	36 369
27-FC Istres	Istres	Bernard Bardin	11 000
28-FC Lorient	Lorient	Stade Le Moustoir	16 669
29-Stade de Caen	Caen	Stade Michel D'Ornano	21 500

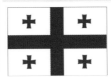

GEORGIA

GEORGIAN FOOTBALL FEDERATION
5, Shota Lamanidze Street, 380 012 Tbilisi
TEL 995 -32/960 710   FAX /001 128
WEB www.gff.ge

REFERENCE
Official name
Republic of Georgia

Date of formation 1991
Capital Tbilisi
Population 5.5 Million
Total area 26,911 sq MI (69,700 sq KM)
Time zone GMT+4
Density 188 per sq MI (73 per sq KM)
Languages Georgian, Russian
Literacy rate 95%
Currency Lari
Economy Services 44%
Religions Christian Orthodox 75%
Ethnic Mix Georgian 70%, Armenian

GEOGRAPHY
Elevation
lowest point: Black Sea 0 m
highest point: Mt'a Mqinvartsveri 5,047 m
Geography Note
strategically located east of the Black Sea;
Georgia controls much of the Caucasus
Mountains and the routes through them
Natural Resources
forests, hydropower, manganese
deposits, iron ore, copper, minor coal and
oil deposits; coastal climate and soils
allow for important tea and citrus growth.
Climate
warm and pleasant; Mediterranean-like on
Black Sea coast
Georgian Food
corn pie/fried eggplants with walnuts

WORLD CUP		COUNTRY LEAGUE CHAMPIONS	
1930	Did not qualify		
1934	Did not qualify		
1938	Did not qualify	2004	WIT Georgia Tbilisi
1950	Did not qualify	2003	Dinamo Tbilisi
1954	Did not qualify	2002	Torpedo Kutaisi
1958	Did not qualify	2001	Torpedo Kutaisi
1962	Did not qualify	2000	Torpedo Kutaisi
1966	Did not qualify	1999	Dinamo Tbilisi
1970	Did not qualify	1998	Dinamo Tbilisi
1974	Did not qualify	1997	Dinamo Tbilisi
1978	Did not qualify	1996	Dinamo Tbilisi
1982	Did not qualify	**WOMEN'S LEAGUE CHAMPIONS**	
1986	Did not qualify	2004	Not Known
1990	Did not qualify	2003	Not Known
1994	Did not qualify	2002	Not Known
1998	Did not qualify	2001	Not Known
2002	Did not qualify	2000	Not Known

NATIONAL TEAM COLORS

WORLD PICTURES OF SOCCER

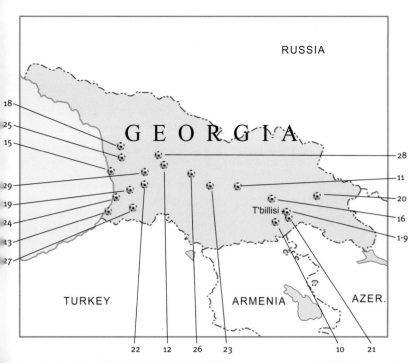

PREMIERE LEAGUE CLUBS	CITY	STADIUM	CAPACITY
1-Dinamo Tbilisi	Tbilisi	Boris Paichadze	74 380
2-Dinamo Tbilisi2	Tbilisi	Boris Paichadze	74 380
3-WIT Georgia Tbilisi	Tbilisi	Sinatle	2 500
4-FC Tbilisi	Tbilisi	Boris Paichadze	74 380
5-Lokomotivi Tbilisi	Tbilisi	Mikheil Meshki	35 000
6-Lokomotivi Tbilisi2	Tbilisi	Mikheil Meshki	35 000
7-TSU Tbilisi	Tbilisi	Central Mtskheta	3 000
8-U-17 National Team	Tbilisi		
9-FK Arsenali	Tbilisi	ASC	2 000
10-FC Sioni	Bolnisi	Tamaz Stepania	3 000
11-FC Dila	Gori	Municipal	8 230
12-Torpedo Kutaisi	Kutsaisi	Givi Kaladze	28 800
13-FC Dinamo Batumi	Batumi	Central	18 000
14-Kolkheti 1913	Poti	Phazisi	6 000
15-Kolkheti Poti FC	Poti	Central	12 000
16-FK Mtskheta	Mtskheta		
17-Spartak-Lazika	Zugdidi	Municipal	7 500
18-FC Odishi	Zugdidi		
19-Mertskhali Ozurgeti	Ozugerti		
20-Alazani Gurjaani	Gurjaani		
21-Gorda Rustavi	Rustavi	Poladi	10 720
22-FC Guria Lanchkhuti	Lanchkhuti	Evgrapi Shevardnaze	22 000
23-Iveria Khashuria	Khasuria		
24-FK Kobuleti	Kobuleti		
25-Kokheti Khobi	Khobi		
26-Metalurgi Zestaponi	Zestaponi		
27-Milani Tsnori	Tsnori		
28-FC Samgurali	Tskhaltubo	26 Maisi	12 000
29-FK Samtredia	Samtredia		

GERMANY

DEUTSCHER FUSSBALL-BUND
postfach 71 02 65
60492 Frankfurt AM Main
TEL 49-69/678 80 FAX /678 8266
WEB www.dbf.de

REFERENCE
Official name
  Federal Republic of Germany
Date of
formation   1871/1990
Capital   Berlin
Population   80.6 Million
Total area   137,800 sq MI (356,910 sq KM)
Time zone   GMT+1
Density   596per sq MI (230 per sq KM)
Languages   German, Turkish
Literacy rate 99%
Currency   Euro
Economy   Services 53%
Religions   Protestant 45%
Ethnic Mix   German 96%, Turkish

GEOGRAPHY
Elevation
lowest point: Freepsum Lake -2 m
highest point: Zugspitze 2,963 m
Geography Note
strategic location on North European Plain
and along the entrance to the Baltic Sea
Natural Resources
iron ore, coal, potash, timber, lignite,
uranium, copper, natural gas, salt, nickel,
arable land
Climate
temperate and marine; cool, cloudy, wet
winters and summers; occasional warm
foehn wind
German Food
spaetzle/black forest cake/sourcrote

WORLD CUP

1930	Did not qualify
1934	Finish Third
1938	First round exit
1950	Did not qualify
1954	World cup champ
1958	Finish Fourth
1962	1/4 final exit
1966	Finish second
1970	Finish third
1974	World cup champ
1978	Scd round exit
1982	Finish second
1986	Finish second
1990	World cup champ
1994	1/4 final exit
1998	1/4 final exit
2002	Finish second

COUNTRY LEAGUE CHAMPIONS

2004	SV Werder Bremen
2003	FC Bayern Munich
2002	Borussia Dortmund
2001	FC Bayern Munich
2000	FC Bayern Munich
1999	FC Bayern Munich
1998	FC Kaiserslautern
1997	FC Bayern Munich
1996	Borussia Dortmund

WOMEN'S LEAGUE CHAMPIONS

2004	FFC Turbine Postdam
2003	FFC Frankfurt
2002	FFC Frankfurt
2001	FFC Frankfurt
2000	FCR Duisbourg

NATIONAL TEAM COLORS

WORLD PICTURES OF SOCCER

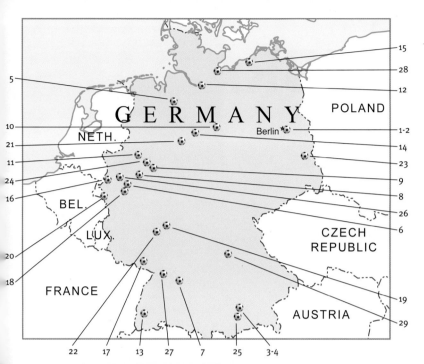

PREMIERE LEAGUE CLUBS	CITY	STADIUM	CAPACITY
1-Hertha BSC Berlin	Berlin	Olympiastadion	76 065
2-FC Union Berlin	Berlin	Stadion Alte Fosterei	18 051
3-Bayern Munchen FC	Munchen	Olympiastadion	69 060
4-FSV 1860 Munchen	Munchen	Olympiastadion	69 060
5-SV Werder Bremen	Bremen	Weserstadion	42 466
6-Bayer 04 Leverkusen	Leverkusen	Bay Arena	22 500
7-VFB Stuttgart	Stuttgart	Gotlieb-Daimler Stadion	54 267
8-VFL Bochum	Bochum	Ruhrstadion	32 645
9-Borussia Dortmund	Dortmund	Westfalenstadion	82 678
10-VFL Wolfsburg	Wolfsburg	Volkswagen Arena	30 122
11-FC Schalke 04	Gelsenkirchen	Arena auf Schalke	61 027
12-Hamburger SV	Hamburger	AOL Arena	55 000
13-SC Freiburg	Freiburg	Dreisamstadion	24 918
14-Hannover 96	Hannover	AWD Arena	48 933
15-FC Hansa Rostock	Rostock	Ostseestadion	30 000
16-Borussia	Monchengladbach	Bokelberg Stadion	34 500
17-1.FCKaiserslautern	Kaiserslautern	Fritz-Walter Stadion	41 582
18-1.FC Koln	Koln	Rhein Energy Stadion	50 997
19-Eintrach Frankfurt	Frankfurt	Waldstadion	61 146
20-Alemannia Aachen	Aachen	Tivoli Stadion	24 816
21-Arminia Bielefeld	Bielefeld	Alm Stadion	26 512
22-FSV Mainz 05	Mainz	Stadion am Brushweg	18 600
23-Energie Cottbus	Cottbus	Stadion der Freundschaft	21 000
24-MSV Duisburg	Duisburg	Wedaustadion	30 128
25-SPVGG Unterhaching	Unterhaching	Sportpark	15 053
26-SVWacker	Burghausen	Stadion Liebigstrabe	8 000
27-Karlsruher SC	Karlsruher	Wildparkstadion	33 800
28-VFB Lubeck	Lubeck	Lohmuhle	18 000
29-1.FC Nurnberg	Nurnberg	Frankenstadion	44 968

GIBRALTAR

Gibraltar Football Assoc.
WEB www.gibraltarfa.com

Reference
Official name
The Crown Colony of Gibraltar

Date of formation 1713
Capital Gibraltar
Population 27,086
Total area 2.5sq acres(6.5 sq Km)
Time zone Pacific
Density Not Known
Languages English, Spanish
Literacy rate 99%
Currency British Pound
Economy Military, Tourism
Religions Catholic
Ethnic Mix English, Spanish

Geography
Elevation
lowest point: Mediterranean Sea o m
highest point: Rock of Gibraltar 426 m
Geography Note
strategic location on Strait of Gibraltar that links the North Atlantic Ocean and Mediterranean Sea
Natural Resources
NEGL
Climate
mediterranean with mild winters and warm summers
Gibraltar Food
calentita/panissa

WORLD CUP		COUNTRY LEAGUE CHAMPIONS	
1930	Did not qualify		
1934	Did not qualify		
1938	Did not qualify	2004	Newcastle FC
1950	Did not qualify	2003	Newcastle FC
1954	Did not qualify	2002	Gibraltar United FC
1958	Did not qualify	2001	Lincoln FC
1962	Did not qualify	2000	Glacis United FC
1966	Did not qualify	1999	Manchester United
1970	Did not qualify	1998	ST. Theresas FC
1974	Did not qualify	1997	Glacis United
1978	Did not qualify	1996	St Joseph's FC
1982	Did not qualify	**WOMEN'S LEAGUE CHAMPIONS**	
1986	Did not qualify	2003	Bishop Fitgerald MC
1990	Did not qualify	2002	Lincoln ABG
1994	Did not qualify	2001	Gibraltar United
1998	Did not qualify	2000	Gibraltar United
2002	Did not qualify	1999	Unknown

NATIONAL TEAM COLORS

WORLD PICTURES OF SOCCER

SPAIN

GIBRALTAR

1-14

Premiere League Clubs	City	Stadium	Capacity
1-Newcastle FC	Gibraltar	Victoria Stadium	1 500
2-Gibraltar United	Gibraltar	Victoria stadium	1 500
3-Glacis United	Gibraltar	Victoria stadium	1 500
4-Manchester united	Gibraltar	Victoria stadium	1 500
5-St Joseph's FC	Gibraltar	Victoria stadium	1 500
6-Lions FC	Gibraltar	Victoria stadium	1 500
7-Newcastle Reserve	Gibraltar	Victoria stadium	1 500
8-St Theresa's FC	Gibraltar	Victoria stadium	1 500
9-Glacis United Reserve	Gibraltar	Victoria stadium	1 500
10-Manchester United Reserve	Gibraltar	Victoria stadium	1 500
11-St Joseph's FC Reserve	Gibraltar	Victoria stadium	1 500
12-UTD Monteverde Reserve	Gibraltar	Victoria stadium	1 500
13-Moroccan Star	Gibraltar	Victoria stadium	1 500
14-College Cosmos FC	Gibraltar	Victoria stadium	1 500

GREECE

HELLENIC FOOTBALL FED.
137 Singrou Av. Nea Smirni,17121 Athens
TEL 30-10/930 6000   FAX /935 9666
WEB www.epo.gr

REFERENCE
Official name
Hellenic Republic
Date of formation 1830/1947
Capital Athens
Population 10.5 Million
Total area 50,961 sq MI (131 sq KM)
Time zone GMT+1
Density 210 perm sq MI (81 per sq KM)
Languages Greek, English
Literacy rate 97%
Currency Euro
Economy Services 56%
Religions Greek Orthodox 98%
Ethnic Mix Greek 98%

GEOGRAPHY
Elevation
lowest point: Mediterranean Sea 0 m
highest point: Mount Olympus 2,917 m
Geography Note
strategic location dominating the Aegean
Sea and southern approach to Turkish
Straits; a peninsular country, possessing an
archipelago of about 2,000 islands
Natural Resources
bauxite, lignite, magnesite, petroleum,
marble, hydropower potential
Climate
temperate; mild, wet winters; hot dry
summers
Greek Food
dolmas/mousska

WORLD CUP		COUNTRY LEAGUE CHAMPIONS	
1930	Did not qualify		
1934	Did not qualify		
1938	Did not qualify	2004	Panathinaikos
1950	Did not qualify	2003	Olympiakos
1954	Did not qualify	2002	Olympiakos
1958	Did not qualify	2001	Olympiakos
1962	Did not qualify	2000	Olympiakos
1966	Did not qualify	1999	Olympiakos
1970	Did not qualify	1998	Olympiakos
1974	Did not qualify	1997	Olympiakos
1978	Did not qualify	1996	Panathinaikos
1982	Did not qualify	**WOMEN'S LEAGUE CHAMPIONS**	
1986	Did not qualify	2004	A.E Aigina
1990	Did not qualify	2003	A.E Aigina
1994	First round exit	2002	PAOK Thessaloniki
1998	Did not qualify	2001	AO Kavala
2002	Did not qualify	2000	M.E.A.O Fyliriakos Flor

NATIONAL TEAM COLORS

WORLD PICTURES OF SOCCER

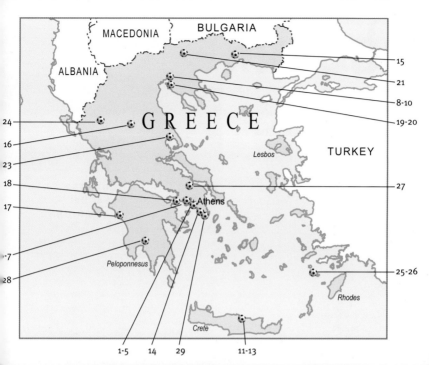

PREMIERE LEAGUE CLUBS	CITY	STADIUM	CAPACITY
1-AEK Athens	Athens	Nikos Doumas	23 000
2-Olympiakos CFP	Athens	Rizpouli Stadium	14 200
3-Apollon FC	Athens	Rizpouli Stadium	14 200
4-Panathinaikos FC	Athens	Apostolos Nikolaidis	16 620
5-Egaleo FC Athens	Athens	Apostolos Nikolaidis	16 620
6-Olympiakos CFP	Piraes	Karaiskaki Stadium	33 500
7-Ethnikos FC	Piraes	Karaiskaki Stadium	33 500
8-Paok FC	Thessaloniki	Toumba Stadium	28 701
9-Iraklis FC	Thessaloniki	Kaftanzoglio Stadium	28 028
10-Aris FC	Thessaloniki	Harilaou Stadium	18 308
11-FC OFI Kriti	Heraklion	Pankritiko Stadium	33 240
12-Ergotelis FC	Heraklion	Pankritiko Stadium	33 240
13-IFI Crete	Heraklion	OFI Stadium	9 000
14-Panionios FC	Nea Smyrni	Nea Smyrni Stadium	11 700
15-Skoda Xanthi FC	Xanthi	Xanthi Stadium	9 500
16-A.O Trikala	Trikala	Trikala Stadium	18 000
17-Paniliakos FC	Pyrgos	Pyrgos Stadium	6 750
18-Proodeftiki FC	Korydhallos	Korydallos Stadium	4 361
19-Apollon Kalamarias FC	Kalamaria	Kalamaria Stadium	7 000
20-Panaeghialos FC	Kalamaria	Kalamaria Stadium	7 000
21-Panserraikos FC	Serrai	Serres Stadium	10 000
22-Niki Volou	Volos	Niki Volou Stadium	4 500
23-Olympiakos Volos FC	Volos	Panthessalian Stadium	20 000
24-PAS Giannina	Ioannina	Zossimades Stadium	7 600
25-Ionikos FC	Nikia	Neapoli Stadium	5 123
26-Halkidona FC	Nikia	Neapoli Stadium	5 123
27-Akratitos FC	Ano Liossia	Akratitos Stadium	4 944
28-Kalamata FC	Kalamata	Messiniakos Stadium	5 613
29-Kalithea FC	Kalithea	Kalithea Stadium	4 250

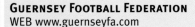

GUERNSEY

REFERENCE
Official name
Guernsey

Claimed	1066
Capital	St Peter Port
Population	56,681
Total area	25 sq Mi(65 sq Km)
Time zone	GMT +/- 0
Density	Not Known
Languages	English,
Literacy rate	99%
Currency	Guernsey Pound
Economy	Financial Services, Tourism, Manufacturing, Horticulture
Religions	64% Anglican, 8% Presbyterian, 14% Catholic, Methodist
Ethnic Mix	English 95%, Others 5%

GEOGRAPHY
Elevation
lowest point: Atlantic Ocean 0 m
highest point: Unnamed location on Sark 114 m
Geography Note
large, deepwater harbor at Saint Peter Port
Natural Resources
cropland
Climate
temperate with mild winters and cool
summers; about 50% of days are overcast
Guernsey Island Food
mock clotted cream/butter cookies

WORLD CUP		COUNTRY LEAGUE CHAMPIONS	
1930	Did not qualify		
1934	Did not qualify		
1938	Did not qualify	2005	Sylvans SC
1950	Did not qualify	2004	St. Martin's AC
1954	Did not qualify	2003	Vale Recreation FC
1958	Did not qualify	2002	Sylvans SC
1962	Did not qualify	2001	Sylvans SC
1966	Did not qualify	2000	Sylvans SC
1970	Did not qualify	1999	Sylvans SC
1974	Did not qualify	1998	Sylvans SC
1978	Did not qualify	1997	Sylvans SC
1982	Did not qualify	**WOMEN'S LEAGUE CHAMPIONS**	
1986	Did not qualify	2004	Not Known
1990	Did not qualify	2003	Not Known
1994	Did not qualify	2002	Not Known
1998	Did not qualify	2001	Not Known
2002	Did not qualify	2000	Not Known

NATIONAL TEAM COLORS

WORLD PICTURES OF SOCCER

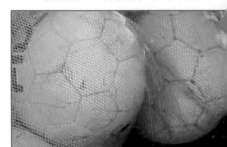

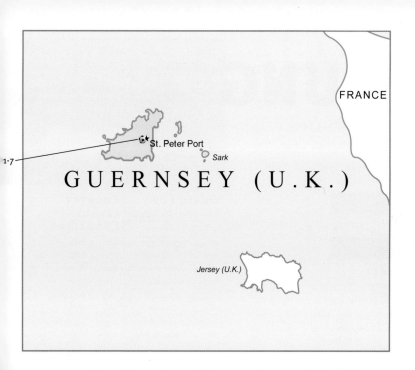

FRANCE

St. Peter Port

Sark

GUERNSEY (U.K.)

1-7

Jersey (U.K.)

Premiere League Clubs	City	Stadium	Capacity
1-Northerners	St. Peter Port		
2-Police	St. Peter Port		
3-Sylvans	St. Peter Port		
4-Vale Recreation	St. Peter Port		
5-Belgraves Wanderers	St. Peter Port		
6-Rovers AC	St. Peter Port		
7-Rangers	St. Peter Port		

HUNGARY

HUNGARIAN FOOTBALL FED.
Robert Karoly Krt. 61 65,Robert Haz
1134 Budapest
TEL 36-1/412 3340 FAX /452 0360
WEB www.mlsz.hu

REFERENCE
Official name
Republic of Hungary

Date of formation	1918
Capital	Budapest
Population	10 Millions
Total area	35,652 sq Mi (92,340 sq Km)
Time zone	GMT +1
Density	280 per sq Mi (109 per sq Km)
Languages	Hungarian (Magyar), German, Slovak
Literacy rate	99%
Currency	Forint
Economy	Services 48%
Religions	Catholic 64%
Ethnic Mix	Hungarian 69%, Gypsy 4%

GEOGRAPHY
Elevation
lowest point: Tisza River 78 m
highest point: Kekes 1,014 m
Geography Note
the north-south flowing Duna (Danube) and
Tisza Rivers divide the country into three
large regions.
Natural Resources
bauxite, coal, natural gas, fertile soils,
arable land
Climate
temperate; cold, cloudy, humid winters;
warm summers
Hungary Food
chicken paprika/paprikas krumpli

WORLD CUP

1930	Did not qualify
1934	1/4 final exit
1938	Finish second
1950	Did not qualify
1954	Finish second
1958	First roud exit
1962	1/4 final exit
1966	1/4 final exit
1970	Did not qualify
1974	Did not qualify
1978	First round exit
1982	Finish Fourth
1986	Finish Third
1990	Did not qualify
1994	Did not qualify
1998	Did not qualify
2002	Did not qualify

COUNTRY LEAGUE CHAMPIONS

2004	Ferencvaros
2003	MTK
2002	Zalaegerszegi TE
2001	Ferencvaros
2000	Dunaferr FC
1999	MTK
1998	Ujpesti TE
1997	MTK
1996	Ferencvaros
WOMEN'S LEAGUE CHAMPIONS	
2004	Iris FC
2003	Not Known
2002	Not Known
2001	Not Known
2000	Not Known

NATIONAL TEAM COLORS

WORLD PICTURES OF SOCCER

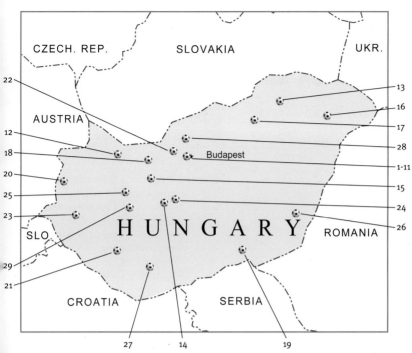

Premiere League Clubs	City	Stadium	Capacity
1-Ferencvarosi TC	Budapest	Stadion Ulloi Ut	18 100
2-Ujpest FC	Budapest	Stadion Szusza Ferenc	13 501
3-Vasas FC	Budapest	StadionLlovsky Rudolf	18 000
4-Budapest Honved FC	Budapest	Stadion Jozsef Bozsik	13 500
5-MTK Hungaria FC	Budapest	Stadion Hidegkuti Nandor	12 700
6-Csepel FC	Budapest	Stadion Beke Teri	10 000
7-Soroksari TE	Budapest	Stadion Haraszti Ut	10 000
8-Rakospalotai	Budapest	Stadion Budai II.Laszlo	10 000
9-BVSC-Zuglo	Budapest	Stadion Szonyi Ut	9 000
10-Kerulet FC	Budapest	StadionHevizi Ut	7 000
11-BKV Elore	Budapest	Stadion Sport Utcai	6 000
12-Gyory ETO FC	Gyor	Stadion ETO	27 000
13-DVTK Miskolc	Miskolc	DVTK Stadion	22 000
14-Kecskemeti TE	Kecskemet	Stadion Kecskemeti	20 000
15-Videoton FC	Szekesfehevar	Stadion Sostoi Ut	19 000
16-Nyirseg Spartacus FC	Nyiregyhaza	Stadion Sostoi Ut	16 500
17-Egeri SE	Eger	Stadion Nagy Jozsef Utcai	16 000
18-FC Tatabanya	Tatabanya	Stadion Varosi	15 500
19-FC Szeged	Szeged	Stadion Felso Tiszaparti	15 000
20-Haladas FC Lombard	Szombathely	Stadion Rohonci Ut	14 000
21-Kaposvari Rakoczi FC	Kaposvar	Stadion Voroshadsereg Ut	14 000
22-Dorogi FC	Dorog	Stadion Kollar Lajos Sport	13 000
23-Zalaegerszegi TE	Zalaegerszegi	Stadion ZTE	12 500
24-Dunaujvarosi FC	Dunaujvaros	Stadion Eszperanto Ut	12 000
25-Veszpremi LC	Veszprem	Stadion Varosi	12 000
26-Bekescsabai Elore FC	Bekescsaba	Stadion Korhaz Utcai	11 500
27-Komloi Banyasz	Komlo	Stadion Pecsi Ut	10 900
28-Dunakanyar Vac FC	Vac	Stadion Varosi	10 500
29-Balaton FC	Siofok	Stadion Revesz Geza Ut	10 500

 # ICELAND

KNATTSPYRNUSAMBAND ISLANDS
Laugardal,104 Reykjavik
TEL 354 /510 2900   FAX /568 9793
WEB www.ksi.is

REFERENCE
Official name
Republic of Iceland
Date of formation 1944
Capital Reykjavik
Population 281,000
Total area 35,652 sq Mi (92,340 sq Km)
Time zone GMT 0
Density 7 per sq Mi (2.7 per sq Km)
Languages Icelandic
Literacy rate 99%
Currency Krona
Economy Services 61%
Religions Evangelical Lutheran 93%
Ethnic Mix Icelandic 94%

GEOGRAPHY
Elevation
lowest point: Atlantic Ocean 0 m
highest point: Hvannadalshnukur 2,119 m
Geography Note
strategic location between Greenland and Europe; westernmost European country; Reykjavik is the northernmost national capital in the world; more land covered by glaciers than in all of continental Europe
Natural Resources
fish, hydropower, geothermal power, diatomite
Climate
temperate; moderated by North Atlantic Current; mild, windy winters; damp, cool summers
Iceland Food
tilapia grilled/bacalao tartar/laufabrand

WORLD CUP		COUNTRY LEAGUE CHAMPIONS	
1930	Did not qualify		
1934	Did not qualify		
1938	Did not qualify	2004	FH Hafnarfjor'ur
1950	Did not qualify	2003	KR Reykjavik
1954	Did not qualify	2002	KR Reykjavik
1958	Did not qualify	2001	IA Akranes
1962	Did not qualify	2000	KR Reykjavik
1966	Did not qualify	1999	KR Reykjavik
1970	Did not qualify	1998	IBV Vestmannaeyjar
1974	Did not qualify	1997	IBV Vestmannaeyjar
1978	Did not qualify	1996	IA Akranes
1982	Did not qualify	**WOMEN'S LEAGUE CHAMPIONS**	
1986	Did not qualify	2004	Valur
1990	Did not qualify	2003	KR
1994	Did not qualify	2002	KR
1998	Did not qualify	2001	Brei'Ablik
2002	Did not qualify	2000	Brei'Ablik

NATIONAL TEAM COLORS

WORLD PICTURES OF SOCCER

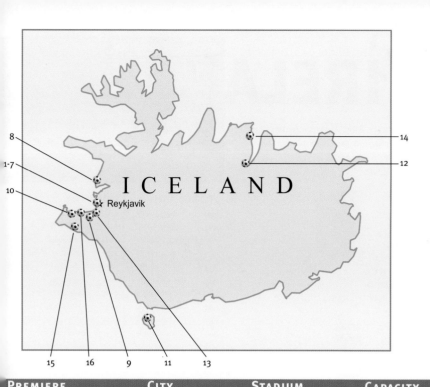

I C E L A N D

★ Reykjavik

PREMIERE LEAGUE CLUBS	CITY	STADIUM	CAPACITY
1-Fram Reykjavik	Reykjavik	Laugardalsvollur	7 176
2-Fylkir	Reykjavik	Fylkisvollur	4 000
3-KR Reykjavik	Reykjavik	KR-Vollur	3 000
4-Valur	Reykjavik	Hlidarendi	3 000
5-Throttur Reykjavik	Reykjavik	Valbjarnarvollur	2 500
6-IR Reykjavik	Reykjavik	IR-Vollur	1 000
7-Vikingur	Reykjavik	Vikin	1 000
8-IA Akranes	Akranes	Akranesvollur	4 850
9-FH Hafnarfjordhur	Hafnarfjordhur	Kaplakrikavollur	4 800
10-IBK Keflavik	Keflavik	Keflavikurvollur	4 000
11-IBV	Vestmannaeyjar	Hasteinsvollur	3 540
12-KA Akureyri	Akureyri	Akureyrarvollur	3 500
13-UBK Breidablik	Kopavogur	Kopavogsvollur	3 500
14-IF Leiftur	Olafsfjordhur	Olafsfiardarvollur	3 000
15-UMF Grindavik	Grindavik	Grindavikurvollur	2 500
16-Starnan	Gardabae	Stjornuvollur	1 000

IRELAND

THE FOOTBALL ASSOCIATION OF IRELAND
80, Merion Square, South, Dublin 2
TEL 353-1/676 6864 FAX /661 0931
WEB www.fai.ie

REFERENCE
Official name
Republic of Ireland

Date of formation 1922
Capital Dublin
Population 3.7 Million
Total area 26,598 sq Mi (68,890 sq Km)
Time zone GMT 0
Density 139 per sq Mi (52 per sq Km)
Languages English,Irish Gaelic
Literacy rate 99%
Currency Euro
Economy Industry 54%
Religions Catholic 88%
Ethnic Mix Irish 95%

GEOGRAPHY
Elevation
lowest point: Atlantic Ocean 0 m
highest point: Carrauntoohil 1,041 m
Geography Note
strategic location on major air and sea routes between North America and northern Europe; over 40% of the population resides within 97 km of Dublin
Natural Resources
zinc, lead, natural gas, barite, copper, gypsum, limestone, dolomite, peat, silver.
Climate
temperate maritime; modified by North Atlantic Current; mild winters, cool summers; consistently humid; overcast about half the time.
Irish Food
soda bread/potato Irish soup

WORLD CUP		COUNTRY LEAGUE CHAMPIONS	
1930	Did not qualify		
1934	Did not qualify		
1938	Did not qualify	2004	Shelbourne
1950	Did not qualify	2003	Bohemians & Shelb.
1954	Did not qualify	2002	Bohemians
1958	Did not qualify	2001	Shelbourne
1962	Did not qualify	2000	Bohemians
1966	Did not qualify	1999	St Patrick Athletic
1970	Did not qualify	1998	St Patrick Athletic
1974	Did not qualify	1997	Derry City
1978	Did not qualify	1996	St Patrick Athletic
1982	Did not qualify	**WOMEN'S LEAGUE CHAMPIONS**	
1986	Did not qualify	2004	UC Dublin
1990	1/4 final exit	2003	UC Dublin
1994	Scd round exit	2002	Shamrock Rovers
1998	Did not qualify	2001	Shamrock Rovers
2002	Scd round exit	2000	Shamrock Rovers

NATIONAL TEAM COLORS

WORLD PICTURES OF SOCCER

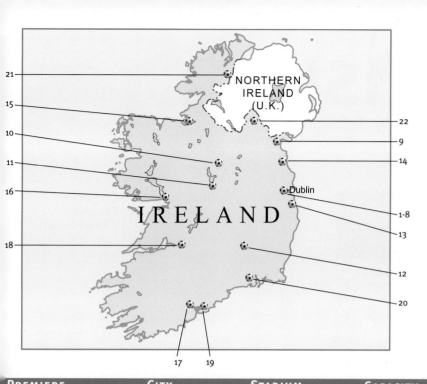

PREMIERE LEAGUE CLUBS	CITY	STADIUM	CAPACITY
1-Bohemians FC	Dublin	Dalymount Park	12 200
2-Dublin City FC	Dublin	Morton Stadium	12 000
3-Shelbourne FC	Dublin	Tolka Park	9 681
4-St.Patrick's Athletic	Dublin	Richmond Park	7 500
5-Shamrock Rovers	Dublin	Tallaght Stadium	6 000
6-University College of Dublin	Dublin	Belfield Park	5 250
7-St.Francis FC	Dublin	John Hyland Park	3 500
8-Home Farm Fingal	Dublin	Whitehall	3 000
9-Dundalk FC	Dundalk	Oriel Park	12 200
10-Longford Town	Longford	Strokestown Road	10 000
11-Athlone Town	Athlone	St.Mel's Park	7 200
12-Kilkenny City	Kilkenny	Buckley Park	6 850
13-Bray Wanderers	Bray	Carlisle Grounds	6 500
14-Drogheda United	Drogheda	United Park	5 400
15-Sligo Rovers	Sligo	Showgrounds	9 000
16-Galway United	Galway	Terryland Park	7 784
17-Cork City	Cork	Turner's Cross	11 500
18-Limerick FC	Limerick	Hogan Park	10 000
19-Cobh Ramblers	Cobh	St.Coleman's Park	10 000
20-Waterford United	Waterford	Regional Sports center	8 200
21-Finn Harps	Ballybofey	Finn Park	7 900
22-Monaghan United	Monaghan	Gortakeegan	6 600

ISLE OF MAN

ISLE OF MAN FOOTBALL ASOOC.
PO Box 53, The Bowl, Douglas, Im99164
TEL: 016 852853 FAX: 016 85852
WEB: www.isleofmanfa.com

REFERENCE
Official name
    Crown Dependency
Date of formation   1765
Capital   Douglas
Population   71,714
Total area   221 sq Mi (572 sq Km)
Time zone   GMT 0
Density   Not Known
Languages   English and Manx Gaelic
Literacy rate   99%
Currency   Pound
Economy   Fishing and Tourism
Religions   Catholic
Ethnic Mix   Briton, Manx

GEOGRAPHY
Elevation
lowest point: Irish Sea 0 m
highest point: Snaefell 621 m
Geography Note
one small islet, the Calf of Man, lies to the southwest, and is a bird sanctuary
Natural Resources
fish
Climate
temperate; cool summers and mild winters; overcast about one-third of the time
Isle of Man Food
braised beef with mushrooms/baked flounder

WORLD CUP

1930	Did not qualify
1934	Did not qualify
1938	Did not qualify
1950	Did not qualify
1954	Did not qualify
1958	Did not qualify
1962	Did not qualify
1966	Did not qualify
1970	Did not qualify
1974	Did not qualify
1978	Did not qualify
1982	Did not qualify
1986	Did not qualify
1990	Did not qualify
1994	Did not qualify
1998	Did not qualify
2002	Did not qualify

COUNTRY LEAGUE CHAMPIONS

2004	St George's FC
2003	St Mary's AFC
2002	Peel AFC
2001	Peel AFC
2000	Peel AFC
1999	Castletown FC
1998	St Mary's AFC
1997	Douglas HSOB
1996	St Mary's AFC

WOMEN'S LEAGUE CHAMPIONS

2004	Not Known
2003	Malew
2002	Rushen United
2001	Not Known
2000	Not Known

NATIONAL TEAM COLORS

WORLD PICTURES OF SOCCER

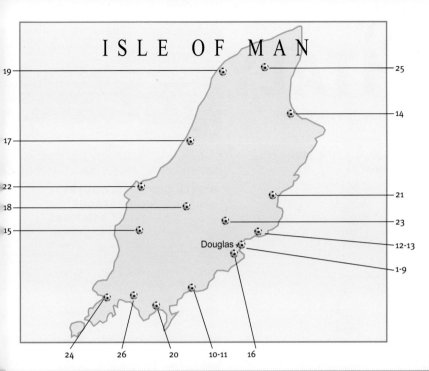

ISLE OF MAN

PREMIERE LEAGUE CLUBS	CITY	STADIUM	CAPACITY
1-St George's FC	Douglas	Glencrutcherry Rd Ground	100-500
2-St Mary's AFC	Douglas	The Bowl Football Ground	100-500
3-Gymnasium FC	Douglas	Tromodore Park Ground	100-500
4-Corinthians FC	Douglas	Nobles Road Ground	100-500
5-Braddan FC	Douglas	Victoria Road Ground	100-500
6-Douglas Royal FC	Douglas	Nobles Park Ground	100-500
7-Pulrose FC	Douglas	Groves Road Ground	100-500
8-Police FC	Douglas	Groves Road Ground	100-500
9-Douglas & District FC	Douglas	Groves Road Ground	100-500
10-Ronaldsway FC	Ballasalla	Ronaldsway Air.Sport Grd	100-500
11-Mallew FC	Ballasalla	Clagh Vane Ground	100-500
12-Douglas HS Old Boys	Onchan	BlackBerry Lane Ground	100-500
13-Onchan FC	Onchan	Onchan Stadium	2 000
14-RYCOB	Ramsey	Lezayre Road Ground	100-500
15-Foxdale FC	Foxdale	Billy Goat Park Ground	100-500
16-Union Mills FC	Kirk Braddon	Ballamona SportGround	100-500
17-Michael FC	Kirk Michael	Balleira Road Ground	100-500
18-St John's United FC	St John	Mullen-y-Cloie Ground	100-500
19-Jurby FC	Jurby	Jurby Football Ground	100-500
20-Metropolitan FC	Castletown	Malen Road	100-500
21-Laxey FC	Laxey	Glenroad Football Ground	100-500
22-Peel AFC	Peel	Douglas Road Ground	100-500
23-Marown Crosby	Crosby	Memorial Football Ground	100-500
24-Rushen United AFC	Porterin	Croit Lowey Ground	100-500
25-Ayre United FC	Andreas	Sportfield Football Ground	100-500
26-Colby FC	Colby	GlenRoad Football Ground	100-500

ITALY

FED.ITALIANA GIUOCO CALCIO
Via Gregorio Allegri, 14,
CP 2450 00198 Roma
TEL 39-06/84 911 FAX /84 912 526
WEB www.figc.it

REFERENCE
Official name
   Italian Republic
Date of
formation   1871
Capital   Rome
Population   57.3 Million
Total area   113,536 sq Mi (294,060 sq Km)
Time zone   GMT +1
Density   505 per sq Mi (188 per sq Km)
Languages   Italian, German, French
Literacy rate 99%
Currency   Euro
Economy   Services 71%
Religions   Catholic
Ethnic Mix   Italian 94%, Sardinian 2%

GEOGRAPHY
Elevation
lowest point: Mediterranean Sea o m
highest point: Mont Blanc (Monte Bianco)
               de Courmayeur 4,748 m
               (a secondary peak of Mont
               Blanc)
Geography Note
strategic location dominating central
Mediterranean as well as southern sea and air
approaches to Western Europe
Natural Resources
mercury, potash, marble, sulfur, natural gas
and crude oil reserves, fish, coal, arable land
Climate
predominantly Mediterranean; Alpine in far
north; hot, dry in south
Italian Food
pennetini in white sauce/bolognese sauce

WORLD CUP		COUNTRY LEAGUE CHAMPIONS	
1930	Did not qualify		
1934	World cup champ		
1938	World cup champ	2004	Miilan AC
1950	First round exit	2003	Juventus FC
1954	First round exit	2002	Juventus FC
1958	Did not qualify	2001	AS Roma
1962	First round exit	2000	SS Lazio
1966	First round exit	1999	Milan AC
1970	Finish second	1998	Juventus FC
1974	First round exit	1997	Juventus FC
1978	Finish Fourth	1996	Milan AC
1982	World cup champ	**WOMEN'S LEAGUE CHAMPIONS**	
1986	Scd round exit	2004	Foroni Verona
1990	Finish Third	2003	Foroni Verona
1994	Finish Second	2002	Ruco Line Verona
1998	1/4 final exit	2001	Torres Fos
2002	Scd round exit	2000	Torres Fos

NATIONAL TEAM COLORS

WORLD PICTURES OF SOCCER

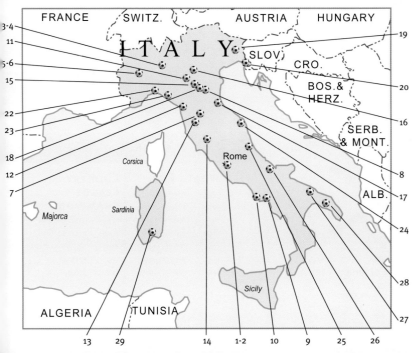

PREMIERE LEAGUE CLUBS	CITY	STADIUM	CAPACITY
1-AS Roma	Roma	Olimpico	82 307
2-SS Lazio Roma	Roma	Olimpico	82 307
3-AC Milan	Milano	Giuseppe Meazza	85 700
4-FC Internazionale	Milano	Giuseppe Meazza	85 700
5-Juventus FC	Torino	Delle Alpi	71 012
6-Torino Calcio	Torino	Delle Alpi	71 012
7-Fiorentina	Firenze	Artemio Franchi	47 232
8-Bologna FC 1909	Bologna	Renato Dallara	39 561
9-Salernitana Sport	Salerno	Arechi	37 894
10-SS Napoli Calcio	Napoli	San Paolo	78 210
11-AC Parma	Parma	Ennio Tardini	28 783
12-Pisa Sporting Club	Pisa	Arena Garibaldi	23 850
13-Empoli FC	Empoli	Carlo Castellani	19 847
14-Siena AC	Siena	Artemio Franchi	13 500
15-Reggiana Calcio	Reggio Emilia	Giglio	29 546
16-Piacenza FC	Piacenza	Leonardo Garilli	21 800
17-AC Cesena	Cesena	Dino Manuzzi	23 860
18-Modena FC	Modena	Alberto Braglia	20 507
19-Udinese Calcio	Udine	Friuli	41 652
20-US Triestina Calcio	Trieste	Nereo Rocco	31 350
21-Genoa 1893	Genova	Luigi Ferraris	41 917
22-UC Sampdoria	Genova	Luigi Ferraris	41 917
23-Spezia Calcio	La Spezia	Alberto Picco	12 000
24-Ancona Calcio	Ancona	Del Conero	26 000
25-Ascoli Calcio 1898	Ascoli Piceno	Cino Lillo del Duca	28 430
26-AC Campobasso	Campobasso	Selvapiana	18 000
27-AS Bari	Barri	San Nicola	58 270
28-US Lecce	Lecce	Via Del Mare	40 800
29-Cagliari Calcio	Cagliari	Sant Elia	39 905

 # JERSEY

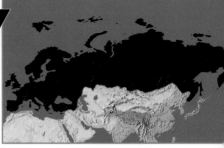

JERSEY FOOTBALL FEDERATION
Saint Helier
WEB www.jerseyfa.com

REFERENCE
Official name
Bailwick of Jersey (Crown Dependency of the U.K)

Claimed	1066
Capital	St Helier
Population	85,721
Total area	45 sq Mi (116 sq Km)
Time zone	GMT +/- 0
Languages	English
Literacy rate	99%
Currency	Jersey Pound
Economy	Financial Services, Agriculture, Tourism
Religions	Protestant 52%Catholic9%

GEOGRAPHY
Elevation
lowest point: Atlantic Ocean 0 m
highest point: Unnamed location 143 m
Geography Note
largest and southernmost of Channel Islands; about 30% of population concentrated in Saint Helier
Natural Resources
arable land
Climate
temperate; mild winters and cool summers
Jersey Food
moist chocolate cakes

WORLD CUP

1930	Did not qualify
1934	Did not qualify
1938	Did not qualify
1950	Did not qualify
1954	Did not qualify
1958	Did not qualify
1962	Did not qualify
1966	Did not qualify
1970	Did not qualify
1974	Did not qualify
1978	Did not qualify
1982	Did not qualify
1986	Did not qualify
1990	Did not qualify
1994	Did not qualify
1998	Did not qualify
2002	Did not qualify

COUNTRY LEAGUE CHAMPIONS

2005	Jersey Scottish
2004	Jersey Scottish
2003	Trinity FC
2002	St Peter
2001	St Peter
2000	St Paul
1999	Jersey Scottish
1998	Jersey Scottish
1997	Jersey Scottish
WOMEN'S LEAGUE CHAMPIONS	
2005	First Tower FC
2004	St Peter Ladies
2003	St Peter Ladies
2002	Wanderers Ladies
2001	Not Known

NATIONAL TEAM COLORS

WORLD PICTURES OF SOCCER

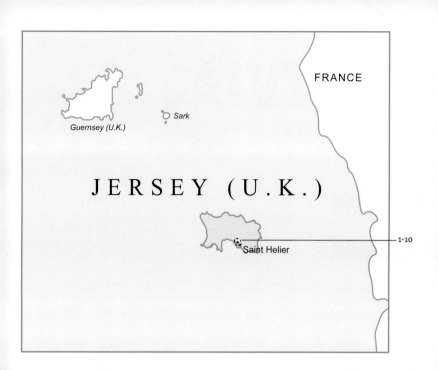

PREMIERE LEAGUE CLUBS	CITY	STADIUM	CAPACITY
1-Jersey Scottish	St. Helier		
2-Trinity FC	St. Helier		
3-Jersey Wanderers	St. Helier		
4-Portuguese Club	St. Helier		
5-St Paul's FC	St. Helier		
6-Rozel Rovers	St. Helier		
7-Magpies	St. Helier		
8-First Tower	St. Helier		
9-St.Peter FC	St. Helier		
10-Sporting Academics	St. Helier		
11-St.Martin FC			
12-S. John FC			
13-St.Lawrence			
14-St.Ouen			
15-First Tower United			
16-Beeches			
17-Sporting Club Francais			
18-Grouville FC			
19-St.Brelade FC			
20-St.Clement FC			
21-Jersey Nomads			

LATVIA

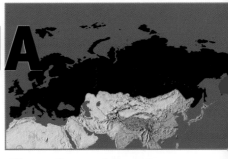

LATVIAN FOOTBALL ASSOC.
Augsiela 1, 1009 Riga
TEL 371/229 2988 FAX /731 5604
WEB www.lff.lv

REFERENCE
Official name
Republic of Latvia

Date of formation	1991
Capital	Riga
Population	2.4 Million
Total area	24,938 sq Mi (64,589 sq Km)
Time zone	GMT +3
Density	96 per sq Mi (37 per sq Km)
Languages	Latvian, Russian
Literacy rate	99%
Currency	Lat
Economy	Services 43%
Religions	Lutheran 55%, Catholic 24%
Ethnic Mix	Latvian 52%

GEOGRAPHY
Elevation
lowest point: Baltic Sea 0 m
highest point: Gaizinkalns 312 m
Geography Note
most of the country is composed of fertile,
low-lying plains, with some hills in the east.
Natural Resources
peat, limestone, dolomite, hydropower,
wood, arable land, minimal amber
Climate
maritime; wet, moderate winters
Latvian Food
piparkukas

WORLD CUP		COUNTRY LEAGUE CHAMPIONS	
1930	Did not qualify		
1934	Did not qualify		
1938	Did not qualify	2004	Skonto Riga
1950	Did not qualify	2003	Skonto Riga
1954	Did not qualify	2002	Skonto Riga
1958	Did not qualify	2001	Skonto Riga
1962	Did not qualify	2000	Skonto Riga
1966	Did not qualify	1999	Skonto Riga
1970	Did not qualify	1998	Skonto Riga
1974	Did not qualify	1997	Skonto Riga
1978	Did not qualify	1996	Skonto Riga
1982	Did not qualify	**WOMEN'S LEAGUE CHAMPIONS**	
1986	Did not qualify	2004	Ceriba 46 VSK
1990	Did not qualify	2003	Not Known
1994	Did not qualify	2002	Not Known
1998	Did not qualify	2001	Not Known
2002	Did not qualify	2000	Not Known

NATIONAL TEAM COLORS

WORLD PICTURES OF SOCCER

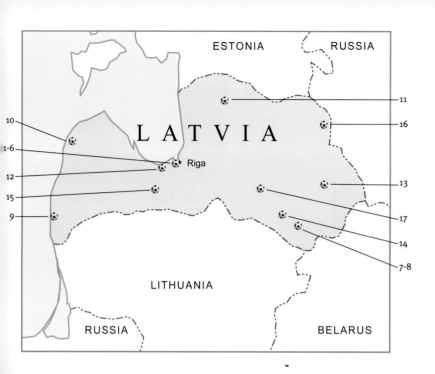

PREMIERE LEAGUE CLUBS	CITY	STADIUM	CAPACITY
1-Skonto Riga	Riga	Stadionas Skonto	8 207
2-FK Riga	Riga	Latvijas Universitates	5 000
3-Auda Riga	Riga	Stadionas Audas	2 000
4-RKB-Arma Riga	Riga	Stadionas Jurnieks	2 200
5-MultibankaRiga	Riga		
6-JFC Skonto Riga	Riga		
7-Ditton Daugavpils	Daugavpils		
8-FC Dinaburg Daugavpils	Daugavpils	Stadionas Celtnieks	4 070
9-FHK Liepajas Metalurgs	Liepaja	Stadionas Daugava	5 083
10-FK Ventspils	Ventspils	Stadionas Daugava	3 085
11-Gauja Valmiera	Valmiera	Stadionas Jana Dalina	2 000
12-FK Jurmala	Jurmala		
13-Dizvanagi Rezekne	Rezekne		
14-Zibens/Zemessardze	Ilukste		
15-RAF Jelgava	Jelgava		
16-Balvu Vilki/ATU Balvi	Balvi		
17-Jekabpils SC	Jekabpils		

LIECHTENSTEIN

LICHTENSTEINER FUSSBALL-VERBAND
Attenbach 11, Postfach 165, 9490 Vaduz
TEL 423/237 4747 FAX /237 4748
WEB www.sportnet.li/lfv

REFERENCE
Official name
Principality of Liechtenstein
Date of
formation   1719
Capital   Vaduz
Population   32,207
Total area   62 sq Mi (160 sq Km)
Time zone   GMT+1
Density   519 sq Mi (200 per sq Km)
Languages   German
Literacy rate   99%
Currency   Swiss Franc
Economy   Services 50%
Religions   Catholic 81%
Ethnic Mix   Liechtensteiner 62%

GEOGRAPHY
Elevation
lowest point: Ruggeller Riet 430 m
highest point: Grauspitz 2,599 m
Geography Note
along with Uzbekistan, one of only two
doubly landlocked countries in the world;
variety of microclimatic variations based on
elevation
Natural Resources
hydroelectric potential, arable land
Climate
continental; cold, cloudy winters with
frequent snow or rain; cool to moderately
warm, cloudy, humid summers
Liechtenstein Food
liechtestein knopfli/leber knodelsuppe

WORLD CUP		COUNTRY LEAGUE CHAMPIONS	
1930	Did not qualify		
1934	Did not qualify		
1938	Did not qualify	2004	FC Vaduz
1950	Did not qualify	2003	FC Vaduz
1954	Did not qualify	2002	FC Vaduz
1958	Did not qualify	2001	FC Vaduz
1962	Did not qualify	2000	FC Vaduz
1966	Did not qualify	1999	FC Vaduz
1970	Did not qualify	1998	FC Vaduz
1974	Did not qualify	1997	FC Balzers
1978	Did not qualify	1996	FC Vaduz
1982	Did not qualify	**WOMEN'S LEAGUE CHAMPIONS**	
1986	Did not qualify	2004	Not Known
1990	Did not qualify	2003	Not Known
1994	Did not qualify	2002	Not Known
1998	Did not qualify	2001	Not Known
2002	Did not qualify	2000	Not Known

NATIONAL TEAM COLORS

WORLD PICTURES OF SOCCER

SWITZERLAND   AUSTRIA

7

6

L I C H T E N S T E I N

4

1 — Vaduz

3

5 2

PREMIERE LEAGUE CLUBS	CITY	STADIUM	CAPACITY
1-FC Vaduz	Vaduz	Rheinpark Stadion	8 000
2-FC Balzers	Balzers	Sportplatz	1 000
3-FC Triesenberg	Triesenberg	Leitawis	1 000
4-FC Schaan	Schaan	Rheinwiese	1 000
5-FC Triesen	Triesen	Blumenau	1 500
6-USV Eschen-Mauren	Eschen	Eschen Sportpark	6 000
7-FC Ruggell	Ruggell	Gemeindesportplatz	1 000

LITHUANIA

LITHUANIAN FOOTBALL FED.
Selmyniskiu Str.15, 2005 Vilnius
TEL 370-2/723 654   FAX /723 651
WEB www.futbolas.it

REFERENCE
Official name
Republic of Lithuania
Date of formation 1991
Capital Vilnius
Population 3.7 million
Total area 25,174 sq Mi (65,200 sq Km)
Time zone GMT +3
Density 147 per sq Mi(55 per sq Km)
Languages Lithuanian, Russian
Literacy rate 99%
Currency Litas
Economy Industry 42%
Religions Catholic 83%
Ethnic Mix Lithuanian 80%

GEOGRAPHY
Elevation
lowest point: Baltic Sea 0 m
highest point: Juozapines/Kalnas 292 m
Geography Note
fertile central plains are separated by hilly
uplands that are ancient glacial deposits
Natural Resources
peat, arable land
Climate
transitional, between maritime and continental; wet, moderate winters and summers
Lithuanian Food
ausytes su grybais/didzkukuliai

WORLD CUP		COUNTRY LEAGUE CHAMPIONS	
1930	Did not qualify		
1934	Did not qualify		
1938	Did not qualify	2004	FBK Kaunas
1950	Did not qualify	2003	FBK Kaunas
1954	Did not qualify	2002	FBK Kaunas
1958	Did not qualify	2001	FBK Kaunas
1962	Did not qualify	2000	FBK kaunas
1966	Did not qualify	1999	Zalgiris Kaunas
1970	Did not qualify	1998	Kareda Siauliai
1974	Did not qualify	1997	Kereda Siauliai
1978	Did not qualify	1996	Inkaras Kaunas
1982	Did not qualify	**WOMEN'S LEAGUE CHAMPIONS**	
1986	Did not qualify	2004	Gintra Univ. Siauliai
1990	Did not qualify	2003	Gintra Univ. Siauliai
1994	Did not qualify	2002	Textilite Ukmerge
1998	Did not qualify	2001	Sventupe Ukmerge
2002	Did not qualify	2000	Gintra Siauliai

NATIONAL TEAM COLORS

WORLD PICTURES OF SOCCER

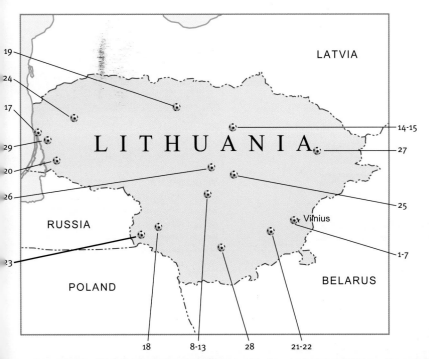

PREMIERE LEAGUE CLUBS	CITY	STADIUM	CAPACITY
1-Zalgiris Vilnius	Vilnius	Zalgiris	15 030
2-Sviesa Vilnius	Vilnius		
3-Panerys Vilnius	Vilnius	Panerys Stadium	3 000
4-Polonija Vilnius	Vilnius		
5-Gelezinis Vilkas Vilnius	Vilnius		
6-Zalgiris II Vilnius	Vilnius		
7-Lokomotyvas Vilnius	Vilnius	Lokomotyvas	2 000
8-FBK Kaunas	Kaunas	Darius Girenas	8 476
9-Kvintencija Kaunas	Kaunas		
10-Ranga Politechnika	Kaunas	KTU Stadium	4 000
11-LKAA Atletas Kaunas	Kaunas		
12-FK Inkaras Kaunas	Kaunas	Inkaras	4 000
13-Kareda Kaunas	Kaunas		
14-FK Ekranas Panevezys	Panevezys	Aukstaitija	10 000
15-Ekranas II Panevezys	Panevezys	Aukstaitija	10 000
16-Atlantas Klaipeda	Klaipeda	Zalgiris	5 000
17-Rodovitas Klaipeda	Klaipeda		
18-Suduva Marijampole	Marijampole		
19-Sakalas Siauliai	Siauliai	Savivaldbye	2 430
20-FK Silute	Silute		
21-Vetra Rudiskes	Rudiskes		
22-Vetra-II Rudiskes	Rudiskes		
23-Kauno Jegeriai	Jugeriai	Kariouomenes	1 000
24-Babrungas Plunge	Plunge		
25-Lietava Jonava	Jonava		
26-Nevezyz Kedainiai	Kedainiai	Kedainiai	3 000
27-Utenis Utena	Utena		
28-Dainava Alytus	Alytus	Alytus Stadium	2 000
29-Banga Gargzdai	Gargzdai	Gargzdai	2 000

LUXEMBOURG

Fed. Luxembourgeoise de Football
50, Rue de Strasbourg, 2560 Luxembourg
TEL 352/488 665   FAX /400 201
WEB www.football.lu

Reference
Official name
Grand Duchy of Luxembourg

Date of formation	1867
Capital	Luxembourg
Population	431,000
Total area	998 sq Mi (2585 sq Km)
Time zone	GMT +1
Density	432 per sq Mi (166 per sq Km)
Languages	Letzeburgish, French, German
Literacy rate	99%
Currency	Euro
Economy	Services 77%
Religions	Catholic 97%
Ethnic Mix	Lexemburger 73%

Geography
Elevation
lowest point: Moselle River 133 m
highest point: Buurgplaatz 559 m
Geography Note
landlocked; the only Grand Duchy in the world, it is the smallest of the European Union member states
Natural Resources
iron ore (no longer exploited), arable land
Climate
modified continental with mild winters, cool summers
Luxembourg Food
keiskuch/gromperekichelcher

World Cup

1930	Did not qualify
1934	Did not qualify
1938	Did not qualify
1950	Did not qualify
1954	Did not qualify
1958	Did not qualify
1962	Did not qualify
1966	Did not qualify
1970	Did not qualify
1974	Did not qualify
1978	Did not qualify
1982	Did not qualify
1986	Did not qualify
1990	Did not qualify
1994	Did not qualify
1998	Did not qualify
2002	Did not qualify

Country League Champions

2004	Jeunesse D'esch
2003	CS Grevenmacher
2002	F91 Dudelange
2001	F91 Dudelange
2000	F91 Dudelange
1999	Jeunesse D'Esh
1998	Jeunesse D'Esh
1997	Jeunesse D'Esh
1996	Jeunesse D'Esh

Women's League Champions

2004	Progress Niedercorn
2003	Progress Niedercorn
2002	Progress Niedercorn
2001	Progress Niedercorn
2000	Progress Niedercorn

National Team Colors

World Pictures of Soccer

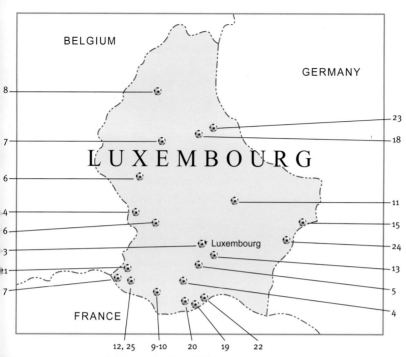

Premiere League Clubs	City	Stadium	Capacity
1-Ca Spora Luxembourg	Luxembourg	Josy Barthel	8 250
2-US Luxembourg	Luxembourg	Achille Hammerel	5 814
3-Alliance 01' Luxembourg	Luxembourg		
4-US Mondercange	Mondercange	Communal	2 050
5-Alliance 01'	Bonnevoie	Camille Polfer	3 500
6-F91 Rodange	Rodange	Jos Philippart	3 400
7-Sporting Mertzig	Mertzig	An De Burwiesen	2 800
8-Wiltz 71	Wiltz	Getzt	2 000
9-AS La Jeunesse D'Esh	Esh s. Alzette	De La Frontiere	5 400
10-CS Fola Esh	Esh s. Alzette		
11-FC Minerva	Lintgen		
12-FC Deifferdeng 03	Differdingen	Stade du Thillenberg	7 150
13-FC Hamm	Hamm		
14-CS Hobscheid	Hobscheid	Koericherberg	2 400
15-CS Grevenmacher	Grevenmacher	Op Flohr	4 000
16-FC AvenirBeggen	Henri Dunant	4 830	
17-Progress Niederkorn	Niederkorn		
18-FC Etzella	Ettelbruck	Deich	2 650
19-US Rumelange	Rumelange	Municipal	2 950
20-Schifflange 95	Schifflange	Am Emmeschbierchen	3 500
21-CS Petange	Petange	Municipal	3 300
22-F91 Dudelange	Dudelange	Jos Nosbaum	4 650
23-Young Boys Diekirch	Diekirch		
24-FC Wormeldange	Wormeldange		
25-FC Differdange 91'	Differdange		

MACEDONIA

FOOTBALL ASSOCIATION OF MACEDONIA

8-ma Udarna brigada 31-a, 2000 Skopje
TEL 389-2/128 065 FAX /165 448
WEB www.fsm.org.mk

REFERENCE

Official name
   FYR of Macedonia

Date of formation	1991
Capital	Skopje
Population	2 million
Total area	9929 sq Mi (925,715 sq Km)
Time zone	GMT +1
Density	201 per sq Mi (79 per sq Km)
Languages	Macedonian, Serbian, Croatian
Literacy rate	95%
Currency	Denar
Economy	Services & Agriculture 60%
Religions	Christian 74%
Ethnic Mix	Macedonian 67%

GEOGRAPHY

Elevation
lowest point: Vardar River 50 m
highest point: Golem Korab (Maja e Korabit) 2,753 m

Geography Note
landlocked; major transportation corridor from Western and Central Europe to Aegean Sea and Southern Europe to Western Europe

Natural Resources
chromium, lead, zinc, manganese, tungsten, nickel, low-grade iron ore, asbestos, sulfur, timber, arable land

Climate
warm, dry summers and autumns and relatively cold winters with heavy snowfall

Macedonian Food
kokoshka soupa/maced salad

WORLD CUP

1930	Did not qualify
1934	Did not qualify
1938	Did not qualify
1950	Did not qualify
1954	Did not qualify
1958	Did not qualify
1962	Did not qualify
1966	Did not qualify
1970	Did not qualify
1974	Did not qualify
1978	Did not qualify
1982	Did not qualify
1986	Did not qualify
1990	Did not qualify
1994	Did not qualify
1998	Did not qualify
2002	Did not qualify

COUNTRY LEAGUE CHAMPIONS

2004	Pobeda Prilep
2003	Vardar Skopje
2002	Vardar Skopje
2001	Sloga Jugomagnat
2000	Sloga Jugomagnat
1999	Sloga jugomagnat
1998	Sileks Kratovo
1997	Sileks Kratovo
1996	Silleks Kratovo

WOMEN'S LEAGUE CHAMPIONS	
2004	Not Known
2003	Not Known
2002	Not Known
2001	Not Known
2000	Not Known

NATIONAL TEAM COLORS

WORLD PICTURES OF SOCCER

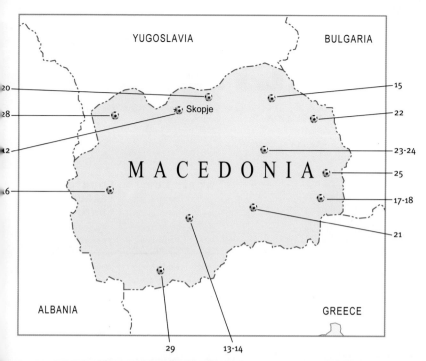

Premiere League Clubs	City	Stadium	Capacity
1-Sloga Jugomagnat	Skopje		
2-Vardar	Skopje	City Stadium Skopje	30 000
3-Rabotnicki Kometal	Skopje	City Stadium Skopje	30 000
4-Cementarnica 55	Skopje	Cementarnica	2 000
5-Madzari Solidarnost	Skopje		
6-Makedonija G.Petrov	Skopje	Gorce Petrov	3 000
7-Alumina	Skopje	Llinden	4 000
8-Shkendija Fortuna	Skopje		
9-Skopje	Skopje	Zelezarnica	4 000
10-Metalurg	Skopje	Zelezernica	4 000
11-Sloga Skopje	Skopje	Cair Stadium	5 000
12-Balkan	Skopje	Cair Stadium	5 000
13-Pobeda	Prilep		
14-Oktomvri	Prilep		
15-Sileks	Kratovo	Sileks	3 000
16-Napredok	Kicevo	City Stadium Kicevo	5 000
17-Belasica Geras Cunev	Strumica	Mladost	9 000
18-Strumica	Strumica	Mladost	9 000
19-Baskimi	Kumanovo		
20-Kumanovo	Kumanovo		
21-Tikves	Kavadarci	City Stadium Kavadarci	5 000
22-Brtegalnica	Delcevo		
23-Bregalnitsa	Shtip	City Stadium Shtip	15 000
24-Astibo	Shtip	City Stadium Shtip	15 000
25-Turnovo	Turnovo		
26-Shkendija 79'	Tetovo		
27-Teteks	Tetovo	City Stadium Tetovo	20 500
28-Ljuboten	Tetovo	City Stadium Tetovo	20 500
29-Pelister	Bitola	Tumbe Kafe Stadium	20 000

MALTA

MALTA FOOTBALL ASSOCIATION
280, St Paul Street, Valletta
TEL 356/2123 2581   FAX /2124 5136
WEB www.mfa.com

REFERENCE
Official name
Republic of Malta

Date of formation	1964
Capital	Valletta
Population	389,000
Total area	124 sq Mi (320 sq Km)
Time zone	GMT +1
Density	3137 sq Mi (1192 per sq Km)
Languages	Maltese, English
Literacy rate	86%
Currency	Lira
Economy	Government 37%, Services 30%
Religions	Catholic 98%
Ethnic Mix	Maltese 94%

GEOGRAPHY
Elevation
lowest point: Mediterranean Sea o m
highest point: Ta'Dmejrek 253 m
(near Dingli)
Geography Note
the country comprises an archipelago, with only the three largest islands (Malta, Ghawdex or Gozo, and Kemmuna or Comino) being inhabited.
Natural Resources
limestone, salt, arable land
Climate
mediterranean with mild, rainy winters and hot, dry summers
Maltese Food
stufat tat-tunnagg/pulpettun

WORLD CUP

1930	Did not qualify
1934	Did not qualify
1938	Did not qualify
1950	Did not qualify
1954	Did not qualify
1958	Did not qualify
1962	Did not qualify
1966	Did not qualify
1970	Did not qualify
1974	Did not qualify
1978	Did not qualify
1982	Did not qualify
1986	Did not qualify
1990	Did not qualify
1994	Did not qualify
1998	Did not qualify
2002	Did not qualify

COUNTRY LEAGUE CHAMPIONS

2004	Sliema Wanderers
2003	Sliema Wanderers
2002	Hibernians
2001	Valletta
2000	Birkirkara
1999	Valletta
1998	Valletta
1997	Valletta
1996	Sliema Wanderers
WOMEN'S LEAGUE CHAMPIONS	
2004	Hibernians
2003	Hibernians
2002	Hibernians
2001	Hibernians
2000	Hibernians

NATIONAL TEAM COLORS

WORLD PICTURES OF SOCCER

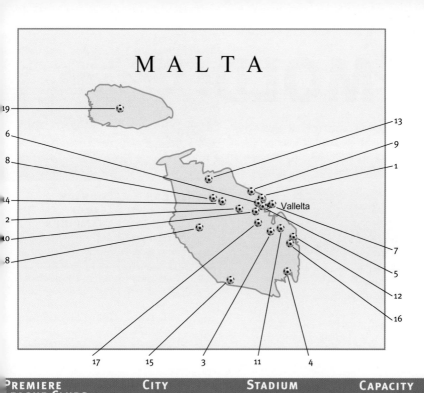

MALTA

Vallelta

MOLDOVA

FOOTBALL ASSOCIATION OF MOLDOVA
Tricolorului St 39, 2012 Chisinau
TEL 373-2/247 878 FAX /247 890
WEB www.fmf.md

REFERENCE
Official name
Republic of Moldova

Date of formation	1991
Capital	Chisinau
Population	4.4 Million
Total area	13,012 sq Mi (33,700 sq KM)
Time zone	GMT +3
Density	338 per sq Mi (133 per sq Km)
Languages	Moldovan, Russian
Literacy rate	99%
Currency	Leu
Economy	Services 46%
Religions	Eastern Orthodox 98%
Ethnic Mix	Moldovan 65%, Ukrainian 14%

GEOGRAPHY
Elevation
lowest point: Dniester River 2 m
highest point: Dealul Balanesti 430 m
Geography Note
landlocked; well endowed with various sedimentary rocks and minerals including sand, gravel, gypsum, and limestone
Natural Resources
lignite, phosphorites, gypsum, arable land, limestone
Climate
moderate winters, warm summers
Moldovan Food
chicken stew/potato pancakes

WORLD CUP

1930	Did not qualify
1934	Did not qualify
1938	Did not qualify
1950	Did not qualify
1954	Did not qualify
1958	Did not qualify
1962	Did not qualify
1966	Did not qualify
1970	Did not qualify
1974	Did not qualify
1978	Did not qualify
1982	Did not qualify
1986	Did not qualify
1990	Did not qualify
1994	Did not qualify
1998	Did not qualify
2002	Did not qualify

COUNTRY LEAGUE CHAMPIONS

2004	Sheriff Tiraspol
2003	Sheriff Tiraspol
2002	Sheriff Tiraspol
2001	Sheriff Tiraspol
2000	Zimbru Chisinau
1999	Zimbru Chisinau
1998	Zimbru Chisinau
1997	Const. Chisinau
1996	Zimbru Chisinau

WOMEN'S LEAGUE CHAMPIONS

2004	Not Known
2003	Not Known
2002	Not Known
2001	Not Known
2000	Not Known

NATIONAL TEAM COLORS

WORLD PICTURES OF SOCCER

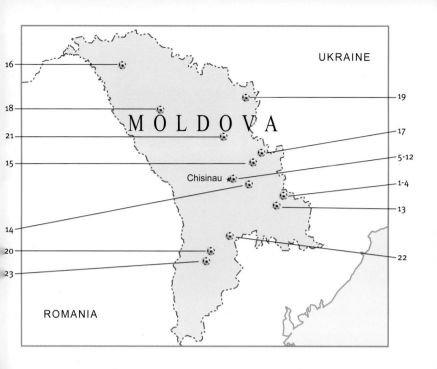

PREMIERE LEAGUE CLUBS	CITY	STADIUM	CAPACITY
1-Sheriff Tiraspol	Tiraspol	Bolshaya Sportivna	14 300
2-FC Tiraspol	Tiraspol	Bolshaya Sportivnaya	14 300
3-Tiligul Tiraspol	Tiraspol	Stadionul Orasenesc	3 525
4-Sheriff II	Tiraspol	Bolshaya Sportivnaya	14 300
5-Zimbru Chisinau	Chisinau	Republika Stadionul	8 084
6-Dacia Chisinau	Chisinau	Republika Stadionul	8 084
7-Unisport-Auto Chisinau	Chisinau	Stadionul Dinamo	2 692
8-FC Agro Chisinau	Chisinau	Stadionul Moldova	8 550
9-CS Steaua	Chisinau		
10-Politechnica	Chisinau		
11-FCA Viktoria	Chisinau		
12-Zimbru II	Chisinau	Republika Stadionul	8 084
13-Dinamo	Bender	Stadionul Selkovic	1 000
14-Roso	Floren		
15-FK Grigoriopol	Grigoriopol		
16-Nistru II	Yedintsi		
17-Energetik	Dubassari	Stadionul Municipal	3 000
18-Olympia Balti	Balti	Stadionul Municipal	5 000
19-IskraRybnitsa			
20-USC Garauzia	Comrat		
21-FK Orhei	Orhei		
22-Lokomotiv	Besarabeasca		
23-Majak	Kirsova		

NETHERLANDS

KONINKLIJKE NEDERLANDSE VOETBALBOND
Wounddenbergseweg 56-58, Postbus 515, 3700 AM Zeist
TEL 31-343/499 201 WEB www.knvb.nl

REFERENCE
Official name
Kingdom of Netherlands

Date of formation	1815
Capital	Amsterdam,The Hague
Population	15.8 Millions
Total area	13,096 sq Mi (33,920 sq Km)
Time zone	GMT+1
Density	1206 per sq Mi (423 per sq Km)
Languages	Arabic, Turkish, English
Literacy rate	99%
Currency	Euro
Economy	Services 79%
Religions	Catholic 36%, Orostetant 27%
Ethnic Mix	Dutch 96%, Others

GEOGRAPHY
Elevation
lowest point: Zuidplaspolder -7 m
highest point: Vaalserberg 322 m
Geography Note
located at mouths of three major European rivers (Rhine, Maas or Meuse, and Schelde)
Natural Resources
natural gas, petroleum, arable land
Climate
temperate; marine; cool summers and mild winters
Netherlands Food
banketstaaf/dutch apple pie

WORLD CUP

1930	Did not qualify
1934	First round exit
1938	First round exit
1950	Did not qualify
1954	Did not qualify
1958	Did not qualify
1962	Did not qualify
1966	Did not qualify
1970	Did not qualify
1974	Finish second
1978	Finish second
1982	Did not qualify
1986	Did not qualify
1990	Scd round exit
1994	Quarter final exit
1998	Semi final exit
2002	Did not qualify

COUNTRY LEAGUE CHAMPIONS

2004	Ajax
2003	P.S.V
2002	Ajax
2001	P.S.V
2000	P.S.V
1999	Feyernoord
1998	Ajax
1997	P.S.V
1996	Ajax

WOMEN'S LEAGUE CHAMPIONS	
2004	Ter Leede
2003	Ter Leede
2002	Saestum
2001	Ter Leede
2000	Saestum

NATIONAL TEAM COLORS

WORLD PICTURES OF SOCCER

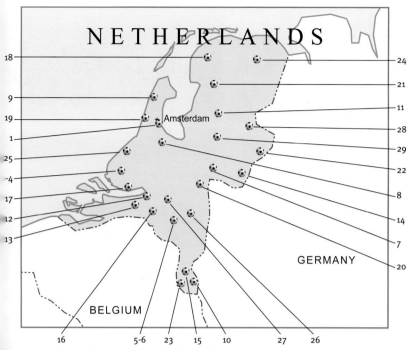

PREMIERE LEAGUE CLUBS	CITY	STADIUM	CAPACITY
1-Ajax Amsterdam	Amsterdam	Amsterdam Arena	51 324
2-Feyenoord	Roterdam	Stadion Feijenoord	51 180
3-Sparta Rotterdam	Rotterdam	Sparta Stadion	11 500
4-SC Excelsior	Rotterdam	S.R Verz Stadion	4 500
5-PSV Eindhoven	Eindhoven	Philips Stadion	36 500
6-FC Eidhoven	Eindhoven	Jan Louwers Stadion	4 600
7-Vitesse	Arnhem	Gelredome	29 600
8-FC Utrecht	Utrecht	Nieuw Galgenwaard	21 072
9-AZ Alkmaar	Alkmaar	Alkmaarderhout	8 390
10-Roda JC	Kerkrade	Parkstad Limburg	19 200
11-FC Zwolle	Zwolle	Oosterenk	6 800
12-RKC Waalwijk	Waalwijk	Mandemakers Stadion	6 200
13-NAC Breda	Breda	MyCom Stadion	17 064
14-De Graafschap	Doetinchem	De Vijverberg	10 900
15-Fortuna Sittard	Sittard	Wagner&Partners Stadion	13 000
16-Willem II	Tilburg	Stadion Willem II	14 700
17-Dordrecht 90'	Dordrecht	GN Bouw Stadion	4 500
18-Cambuur Leeuwarden	Leeuwarden	Caambur Stadion	10 000
19-HFC Harlem	Haarlem	Haarlem Stadion	3 500
20-NEC Nijmegen	Nijmegen	De Goffert	12 500
21-SC Heerenveen	Heerenveen	Abe Lenstra Stadion	14 200
22-FC Twente	Enshede	Arke Stadion	13 500
23-MVV Maastricht	Maastricht	De Geusselt	10 000
24-FC Groningen	Groningen	Oosterpark	13 000
25-ADO Den Haag	Den Haag	Zuiderpark	11 000
26-Helmond Sport	Helmond	De Braak Stadion	4 000
27-FC Den Bosch	Hertogenbosch	Ecco Stadion	9 000
28-Heracles Almelo	Almelo	Polman Stadion	6 650
29-Go Ahead Eagles	Deventer	Adelaashorst	4 800

NORTHERN IRELAND

IRISH FOOTBALL ASSOC. LTD.
20 Windsor Ave., Belfast BT9 6EE
TEL 44-28/9066 9458 FAX /9066 7620
WEB www.irishfa.com

REFERENCE
Official name
Northern Ireland

Date of formation	1707/1921
Capital	Belfast
Population	1.6 Million
Total area	5,452 sq Mi (14,121 sq Km)
Time zone	GMT
Density	117 per sq Km
Languages	English
Literacy rate	99%
Currency	British Pound
Economy	Services 80%
Religions	Presbytarian, Church of Ireland
Ethnic Mix	British Mix

GEOGRAPHY
Elevation
lowest point: Fenland -4 m
highest point: Ben Nevis 1,343 m

Geography Note
Belfast was transformed by the Industrial Revolution, and the stack of grand public buildings give it a vigorous, 19th-century feel.

Natural Resources
zinc, lead, natural gas, barite, copper, gypsum, limestone, dolomite, peat, silver

Climate
temperate; moderated by prevailing southwest winds over the North Atlantic Current; more than one-half of the days are overcast.

North Ireland Food
clotted cream/cheese cake/dumplings

WORLD CUP

1930	Did not qualify
1934	Did not qualify
1938	Did not qualify
1950	Did not qualify
1954	Did not qualify
1958	Quarter final exit
1962	Did not qualify
1966	Did not qualify
1970	Did not qualify
1974	Did not qualify
1978	Did not qualify
1982	Scd round exit
1986	First round exit
1990	Did not qualify
1994	Did not qualify
1998	Did not qualify
2002	Did not qualify

COUNTRY LEAGUE CHAMPIONS

2004	Linfield FC
2003	Glentoran FC
2002	Portadown FC
2001	Linfield FC
2000	Linfield FC
1999	Glentoran FC
1998	Cliftonville FC
1997	Crusaders FC
1996	Portadown FC

WOMEN'S LEAGUE CHAMPIONS

2004	Gentoran FC Ladies
2003	Newtownabbey Strikers
2002	Newtownabbey Strikers
2001	Lisburn D.Predators
2000	Not Known

NATIONAL TEAM COLORS

WORLD PICTURES OF SOCCER

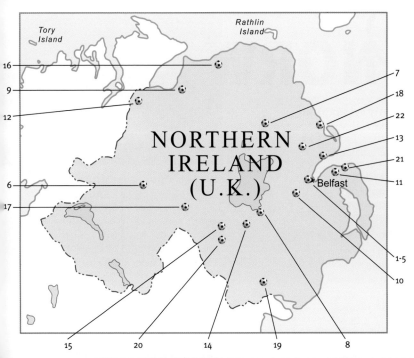

PREMIERE LEAGUE CLUBS	CITY	STADIUM	CAPACITY
1-Linfield	Belfast	Windsor Park	20 332
2-Glentoran	Belfast	Windsor Park	20 332
3-Crusaders	Belfast	Seaview	6 500
4-Cliftonville	Belfast	Solitude	6 000
5-Brantwood FC	Belfast	Skegoneil Avenue	5 000
6-Omagh Town	Omagh	St Julians Road	4 500
7-Ballymena United	Ballymena	The Showgrounds	8 000
8-Glenavon	Lurgan	Mourneview	5 000
9-Limavady	Limavady	The Showgrounds	1 500
10-Distillery	Lisburn	New Grosvenor	8 000
11-Ards	Newtownards	Taylor's Avenue	6 000
12-Institute	Londonderry	YMCA Grounds	2 000
13-Carrick Rangers	Carrickfergus	Taylor's Avenue	6 000
14-Portadown	Portadown	Shamrock Park	8 000
15-Loughgall United	Loughgall	Lakeview Park	3 000
16-Coleraine	Coleraine	The Showgrounds	6 500
17-Dungannon Swifts	Dungannon	Stangmore Park	3 000
18-Larne FC	Larne	Inver Park	6 000
19-Newry Town	Newry	The Showgrounds	6 500
20-Armagh City	Armagh	Holm Park	3 000
21-Bangor	Bangor	Clandeboye Park	4 000
22-Ballyclare Comrades	Ballyclare	Dixon Park	4 000

NORWAY

NORGE FOTBALLFORBUND
Serviceboks 1, Ullvaal Stadion, 0840 Oslo
TEL 47-21/029 300 FAX 47-21/029 301
WEB www.fotball.no

REFERENCE
Official name
  Kingdon of Norway
Date of formation   1905
Capital   Oslo
Population   4.5 Million
Total area   118,487 sq Mi (306,830 sq Km)
Time zone   GMT +1
Density   38 per sq Mi (14 per sq Km)
Languages   Norwegian, Lappish
Literacy rate   99%
Currency   Krone
Economy   Services 61%
Religions   Evangelical Lutheran 89%
Ethnic Mix   Norwegian 95%

GEOGRAPHY
Elevation
lowest point: Norwegian Sea 0 m
highest point: Galdhopiggen 2,469 m
Geography Note
about two-thirds mountains; some 50,000
islands off its much indented coastline;
strategic location adjacent to sea lanes and
air routes in North Atlantic; one of most
rugged and longest coastlines in world
Natural Resources
petroleum, copper, natural gas, pyrites,
nickel, iron ore, zinc, lead, fish, timber,
hydropower
Climate
temperate along coast, modified by North
Atlantic Current; colder interior and colder
summers; rainy year-round on west coast
Norway Food
whole glazed trout/almond paste

WORLD CUP		COUNTRY LEAGUE CHAMPIONS	
1930	Did not qualify		
1934	Did not qualify		
1938	First round exit	2004	Rosenborg BK
1950	Did not qualify	2003	Rosenborg BK
1954	Did not qualify	2002	Rosenborg BK
1958	Did not qualify	2001	Rosenborg BK
1962	Did not qualify	2000	Rosenborg BK
1966	Did not qualify	1999	Rosenborg BK
1970	Did not qualify	1998	Rosenborg BK
1974	Did not qualify	1997	Rosenborg BK
1978	Did not qualify	1996	Rosenborg BK
1982	Did not qualify	**WOMEN'S LEAGUE CHAMPIONS**	
1986	Did not qualify	2004	ROA
1990	Did not qualify	2003	Trondheim/Orn
1994	First round exit	2002	Kolbotn
1998	Scd round exit	2003	Trondheim/Orn
2002	Did not qualify	2000	Trondheim/Orn

NATIONAL TEAM COLORS

WORLD PICTURES OF SOCCER

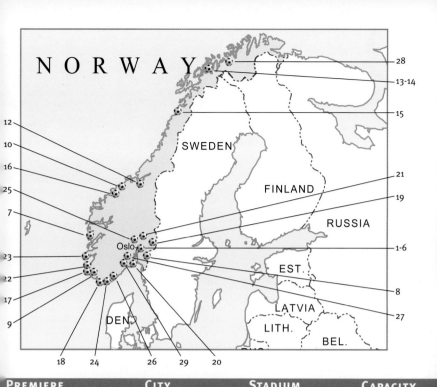

PREMIERE LEAGUE CLUBS	CITY	STADIUM	CAPACITY
1-SFK Lyn	Oslo	Ullevaal	25 572
2-Valerenga IF	Oslo	Ullevaal	25 572
3-Stabaek IF	Oslo	Nadderud	6 500
4-Kjelsas	Oslo	Grefsenstadion	3 000
5-Skeid	Oslo	Voldslokka	4 000
6-Oslo Ost	Oslo		
7-SK Brann	Bergen	Brann	19 269
8-Lillestrom SK	Lillestrom	Arasen	15 000
9-Sogndal IL	Sogndal	Fosshaugene	7 000
10-Molde FK	Molde	Molde Stadion	11 167
11-Rosenborg BK	Trondheim	Lerkendal	21 166
12-Byasen	Trondheim	Rosenborgbanen	3 000
13-Tromso IL	Tromso	Alfheim	11 000
14-Tromsdalen	Tromso	Tromsdalen Kunstgress	3 500
15-Bodo/Glimt	Bodo	Aspmyra	10 400
16-Alesund FK	Alesund		
17-Bryne IL	Bryne	Bryne	10 000
18-Harmarkameratene FK	Harmark		
19-Kongsvinger IL	Kongsvinger	Gjemselund	6 500
20-Sandefjord	Sandelfjord		
21-Raufoss	Raufoss	Hydrohallen	4 000
22-Viking FK	Stavanger	Stavanger Stadion	17 000
23-Haugesund FK	Haugesund	Haugesund	10 000
24-Mandalskameratene	Mandal		
25-Honefoss BK	Honefoss		
26-Start	Kristiansand	Kristiansand	17 000
27-Stromsgodset	Drammen	Marielyst	12 000
8-Hoddoy	Indre Hodoy		
29-Moss	Moss	Mellos	11 410

POLAND

Polsi Zwiazek Pilki Noznej
Miodowa 1, 00-080 Warsaw
TEL 48-22/827 1211 FAX /827 0704
WEB www.pzpn.pl

Reference
Official name
Republic of Poland
Date of formation 1945
Capital Warsaw
Population 38.8 Million
Total area 117,552 sq Mi (304 sq Km)
Time zone GMT+1
Density 330 per sq Mi (123 per sq Km)
Languages Polish, German, Others
Literacy rate 99%
Currency Zloty
Economy Services 40%
Religions Catholic 93%
Ethnic Mix Polish 98%

Geography
Elevation
lowest point: Raczki Elblaskie -2 m
highest point: Rysy 2,499 m
Geography Note
historically, an area of conflict because of flat terrain and the lack of natural barriers on the North European Plain
Natural Resources
coal, sulfur, copper, natural gas, silver, lead, salt, arable land
Climate
temperate with cold, cloudy, moderately severe winters with frequent precipitation; mild summers with frequent showers and thundershowers
Polish Food
bakka bread/pierogi

World Cup		Country League Champions	
1930	Did not qualify		
1934	Did not qualify		
1938	First round exitl	2004	Wisla Krakow
1950	Did not qualify	2003	Wisla Krakow
1954	Did not qualify	2002	Legia Warszawa
1958	Did not qualify	2001	Wisla Krakow
1962	Did not qualify	2000	Polonia Warszawa
1966	Did not qualify	1999	Wisla Krakow
1970	Did not qualify	1998	LKS Ptak Lodz
1974	Finish Third	1997	Widzew Lodz
1978	Scd round exit	1996	Wizdew Lods
1982	Finish Third	**Women's League Champions**	
1986	Scd round exit	2004	Not Known
1990	Did not qualify	2003	Not Known
1994	Did not qualify	2002	Not Known
1998	Did not qualify	2001	Not Known
2002	First round exit	2000	AZS Wroclaw

National Team Colors

World Pictures of Soccer

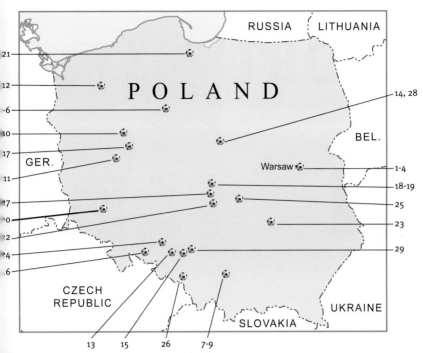

PREMIERE LEAGUE CLUBS	CITY	STADIUM	CAPACITY
1-Legia-Daewoo Warsaw	Warsaw	Stadion Wojska Polskiego	15 278
2-Gwardia Warsaw	Warsaw	Stadion Guardia	9 000
3-Hutnik Warsaw	Warsaw	Stadion Hutnik	7 000
4-Polonia Warsaw	Warsaw	Stadion Polonia	6 200
5-Zawisza Bydgoszcz	Bydgoszcz	Stadion Zawiszy	20 000
6-Polonia Bydgoszcz	Bydgoszcz	Stadion Polonia	20 000
7-Wisla Krakow	Krakow	Stadion Wisly	9 264
8-Hutnik Krakow	Krakow	Stadion Hutnik	12 200
9-Cracovia Krakow	Krakow	Stadion Cracovia	12 000
10-Amica Wronki	Wronki	Stadion Amiki	5 000
11-Groclin-Dysko.	Grodzisk Wielko P.	Stadion Groclin	7 000
12-Gornik Leczna	Leczna	Stadion Gornik	3 500
13-Gornik Zabrze	Zabrze	Stadion Gornika	23 000
14-Wisla Plock	Plock	Stadion Orlen	12 500
15-GKS Katowice	Katowice	Stadion GKS	9 690
16-Odra Wodislaw	Wodzislaw Slaski	Stadion Odry	10 000
17-Lech Poznan	Poznan	Stadion Lecha	15 000
18-Widzew Lodz	Lodz	Stadion Widzewa	12 500
19-LKS Lodz	Lodz	Stadion LKS	28 000
20-Gornik Polkowice	Polkowice	Stadion Gornik	7 000
21-Lukullus/Swit NowyDwor	Nowy Dwor	Stadion Swit	4 000
22-RKS Radomsko	Radomsko	Stadion Radomsko	8 000
23-KSZO Ostrowiec	Ostrowiec Swiet	Stadion Sport KSZO	10 000
24-Odra Opole	Opole	Stadion Odry	11 000
25-Ceramika Opoczno	Opoczno	Stadion Ceramika	4 000
26-Wlokniarz Kietrz	Kietrz	Stadion Wlokniarz	3 000
27-GKS Belchatow	Belchatow	Stadion GKS	7 000
28-Wisla Plock	Plock	Stadion Orlen	12 500
29-Bks Stal	Bielsko-Biala	Stadion Jagiellonia	3 000

PORTUGAL

FEDERACAO PORTUGUESA DE FUTEBOL
Praca de Alegria, N.25, cp21.100,
1250-004 Lisboa codex
TEL 351-21/325 2700
WEB www.fpf.pt

REFERENCE
Official name
Republic of Portugal

Date of formation	1640
Capital	Lisbon
Population	9.9 Million
Total area	35,501 per sq Mi (91,950 per sq Km)
Time zone	GMT +1
Density	279 per sq Mi (107 per sq Km)
Languages	Portuguese
Literacy rate	99%
Currency	Euro
Economy	Services 61%
Religions	Catholic 97%
Ethnic Mix	Portuguese 99%

GEOGRAPHY
Elevation
lowest point: Atlantic Ocean 0 m
highest point: Ponta do Pico (Pico or Pico
Alto) on Ilha do Pico in the Azores 2,351 m
Geography Note
Azores and Madeira Islands occupy strategic
locations along western sea approaches to
Strait of Gibraltar
Natural Resources
fish, forests (cork), tungsten, iron ore, urani-
um ore, marble, arable land, hydropower
Climate
maritime temperate; cool and rainy in north,
warmer and drier in south
Portuguese Food
Portuguese sweet bread/tomato rice

WORLD CUP

1930	Did not qualify
1934	Did not qualify
1938	Did not qualify
1950	Did not qualify
1954	Did not qualify
1958	Did not qualify
1962	Did not qualify
1966	Finish Third
1970	Did not qualify
1974	Did not qualify
1978	Did not qualify
1982	Did not qualify
1986	First round exit
1990	Did not qualify
1994	Did not qualify
1998	Did not qualify
2002	First round exit

COUNTRY LEAGUE CHAMPIONS

2004	FC Porto
2003	FC Porto
2002	Sporting CP
2001	Boavista FC
2000	Sporting CP
1999	FC Porto
1998	FC Porto
1997	FC Porto
1996	FC Porto

WOMEN'S LEAGUE CHAMPIONS

2004	S.U.1 Dezembro
2003	S.U.1 Dezembro
2002	S.U.1 Dezembro
2001	Gatoes FC
2000	S.U.1 Dezembro

NATIONAL TEAM COLORS

WORLD PICTURES OF SOCCER

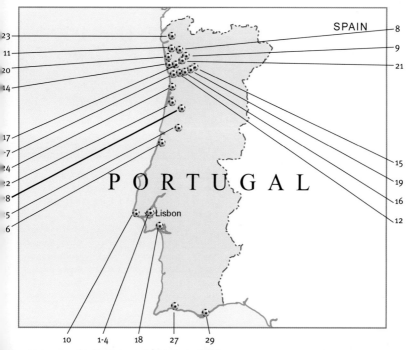

SPAIN

PORTUGAL

Lisbon

PREMIERE LEAGUE CLUBS	CITY	STADIUM	CAPACITY
1-Sporting Lisboa Benfica	Lisboa	Estadio da Luz	65 647
2-Sporting Portugal	Lisboa	Jose Alvalade	50 300
3-Atletico Portugal	Lisboa	Estadio da Tapadinha	15 000
4-Belenenses	Lisboa	Estadio Do Restelo	32 500
5-FC Porto	Porto	Estadio do Dragao	50 106
6-Boavista FC	Porto	Estadio do Bessa XXI	30 000
7-SC Salgueiros	Porto	Novo Estadio	12 151
8-Sporting de Braga	Braga	Municipal de Braga	30 154
9-Vitoria Sport Club	Guimaraes	Dom Afonso Henriques	29 643
10-GD Estoril Praia	Estoril	Antonio Coimbra da Mota	15 000
11-Varzim SC	Povoa Varzim	Estadio do Varzim	11 000
12-FC Penafiel	Penafiel	Municipal 25 de Abril	15 000
13-SC Salgueiros	Matosinhos	Estadio do Mar	30 000
14-Leixoes SC	Matosinhos	Estadio do Mar	30 000
15-Felgeiras	Felgeiras	Dr.Machado de Matos	15 000
16-FC Marco	M.Canavezes	Avelino Ferreira Torres	10 000
17-Maia	Maia	Munic. Vieira de Carvalho	12 000
18-Vitoria Setubal	Setubal	Estadio do Bonfim	25 000
19-FC Pacos de Fereira	Pacos Ferreira	Estadio do Mata Real	10 000
20-Rio Ave	Vila do Conde	Dos Arcos	12 815
21-FC Tirsense	Santo Tirso	Abel Alves de Figueiredo	15 000
22-SC Beira-Mar	Aveiro	Municipal de Aveiro	30 678
23-Feirense	Feira	Marcolino de Castro	14 000
24-Ovarense	Ovar	Marques da Silva	8 000
25-Academica de Coimbra	Coimbra	Cidade de Coimbra	30 154
26-Uniao Leiria	Leiria	Dr.Magalhaes Pessoa	29 771
27-Portimonense	Portimao	Estadio do Portimonense	16 500
28-SC Farense	S.joao da Venda	Estadio Algarve	30 305
29-Olhanense	Olhao	Estadio Jose Arcanjo	15 000

ROMANIA

FEDE. ROUMAMAINE DE FOOTBALL
Str. Poligrafiei 3, CP 83, OP 33, Sector 1
71556 Bucarest
TEL 40-1/224 1993
WEB www.frf.ro

REFERENCE
Official name
  Romania
Date of formation 1947
Capital Bucharest
Population 22.3 Million
Total area 88,934 sq Mi (230,340 sq Km)
Time zone GMT+2
Density 251 per sq Mi (94 per sq Km)
Languages Romanian, Hungarian
Literacy rate 97%
Currency Leu
Economy Industry 38 %
Religions Romanian Orthodox 87%, Catholic 5%
Ethnic Mix Romanian 89%,Magyar 9%

GEOGRAPHY
Elevation
lowest point: Black Sea 0 m
highest point: Moldoveanu 2,544 m
Geography Note
controls most easily traversable land route
between the Balkans, Moldova, and Ukraine
Natural Resources
petroleum (reserves declining), timber, natural gas, coal, iron ore, salt, arable land,
hydropower
Climate
temperate; cold, cloudy winters with
frequent snow and fog; sunny summers with
frequent showers and thunderstorms
Romanian Food
romanian chicken breasts/sausage rolls

WORLD CUP

1930	First round exit
1934	First round exit
1938	First round exit
1950	Did not qualify
1954	Did not qualify
1958	Did not qualify
1962	Did not qualify
1966	Did not qualify
1970	First round exit
1974	Did not qualify
1978	Did not qualify
1982	Did not qualify
1986	Did not qualify
1990	Scd round exit
1994	Quarter final exit
1998	Scd round exit
2002	Did not qualify

COUNTRY LEAGUE CHAMPIONS

2004	Dinamo Bucaresti
2003	Rapid Bucaresti
2002	Dinamo Bucaresti
2001	Steaua Bucaresti
2000	Dinamo Bucaresti
1999	Rapid Bucaresti
1998	Steaua Bucaresti
1997	Steaua Bucaresti
1996	Steaua Bucaresti

WOMEN'S LEAGUE CHAMPIONS

2004	Not Known
2003	Clujeana Cluj
2002	Regal Bucaresti
2001	Regal Bucaresti
2000	Conpet Ploiesti

NATIONAL TEAM COLORS

WORLD PICTURES OF SOCCER

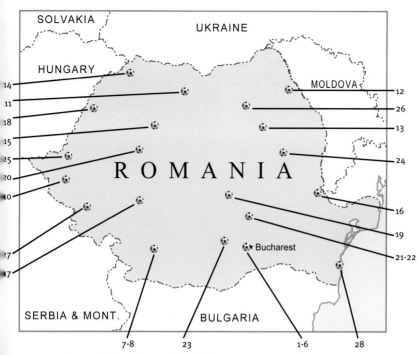

PREMIERE LEAGUE CLUBS	CITY	STADIUM	CAPACITY
1-Steaua Bucaresti	Bucaresti	Stadionul Steaua	27 063
2-Rapid Bucaresti	Bucaresti	Giulesti	19 100
3-Dinamo Bucaresti	Bucaresti	Stefan CelMare	15 300
4-Sportul Studentesc	Bucaresti	Aurica Radulescu	15 000
5-National FC	Bucaresti	Cotroceni	14 542
6-AS Rocar Bucaresti	Bucaresti	Rocar	8 000
7-Universitate Craiova	Craiova	Ion Oblemenco	28 000
8-Extensiv Craiova	Craiova	Romanescu Parc	10 000
9-Poli AEK Timisoara	Timisoara	Dan Paltinisanu	40 000
10-UM Timisoara	Timisoara	UMT	15 000
11-Gloria Bistrita	Bistrita	Gloria	15 000
12-FC Onesti	Onesti	FC Onesti	10 000
13-Ceahlaul P.N.	Pietra Neamt	Ceahlaul	12 500
14-Olimpia Satu Mare	Satu Mare	Olimpia	18 000
15-Universitatea Cluj	Cluj-Napoca	Ion Moinea	28 000
16-Otelul Galati	Galati	Otelul	13 000
17-Jiul Petrosani	Petrosani	Jiul	25 000
18-FC Oradea	Oradea	Municipal	22 500
19-FC Brasov	Brasov	Tineretului	15 000
20-Apulum Alba Lulia	Alba Lulia	Cetate	18 000
21-FC Petrolul Ploiesti	Ploiesti	Ilie Oana	20 000
22-SC Astra Ploiesti	Ploiesti	Astra	5 400
23-Chindia Tirgoviste	Tirgoviste	Municipal	12 000
24-FCM Bacau	Bacau	Dumitru Sechelariu	17 500
25-UT Arad	Arad	UTA	12 000
26-Foresta Falticeni	Falticeni	Areni	12 000
27-CSM Resita	Resita	Valea Domanului	12 000
28-Farul Constanta	Constanta	Gheorge Hagi	15 500

RUSSIA

FOOTBALL UNION OF RUSSIA
8 Luzhnetskaya Naberezhnaja,
119 992 moscow
TEL 7-095/201 1637 FAX /220 2037
WEB www.rfs.ru

REFERENCE
Official name
Russian Federation

Date of formation	1991
Capital	Moscow
Population	146 Million
Total area	6,562,100 sq Mi (16,995,800 sq Km)
Time zone	GMT+3-12
Density	22 per sq Mi (8 per sq Km)
Languages	Russian, Others
Literacy rate	99%
Currency	Rouble
Economy	Industry 27%, Agriculture 15%, Other47%
Religions	Russian Orthodox 75%
Ethnic Mix	Russian 82%

GEOGRAPHY
Elevation
lowest point: Caspian Sea -28 m
highest point: Gora El'brus 5,633 m
Geography Note
largest country in the world in terms of area but unfavorably located in relation to major sea lanes of the world; Mount Elbrus is Europe's tallest peak.
Natural Resources
wide natural resource base including major deposits of oil, natural gas, coal,minerals, timber
Climate
ranges from steppes in the south through humid continental in much of European Russia; subarctic in Siberia to tundra climate in the polar north; winters cool along Black Sea coast.
Russian Food
caviar/borschch soup/pancakes stuffed with meat

WORLD CUP

1930	Did not qualify
1934	Did not qualify
1938	Did not qualify
1950	Did not qualify
1954	Did not qualify
1958	1/4 final exit
1962	1/4 final exit
1966	Finish Fourth
1970	1/4 final exit
1974	Did not qualify
1978	Did not qualify
1982	Scd round exit
1986	Scd round exit
1990	First roud exit
1994	First round exit
1998	Did not qualify
2002	First round exit

COUNTRY LEAGUE CHAMPIONS

2004	Lokomotiv Moscow
2003	CSKA Moscow
2002	Lokomotiv Moskva
2001	Spartak Moskva
2000	Spartak Moskva
1999	Spartak Moskva
1998	Spartak Moskva
1997	Spartak Moskva
1996	Spartak Moskva

WOMEN'S LEAGUE CHAMPIONS

2004	Lada Togliatti
2003	Energyia Voronezh
2002	Energyia Voronezh
2001	CSK VVS Samara
2000	Ryazan TNK

NATIONAL TEAM COLORS

WORLD PICTURES OF SOCCER

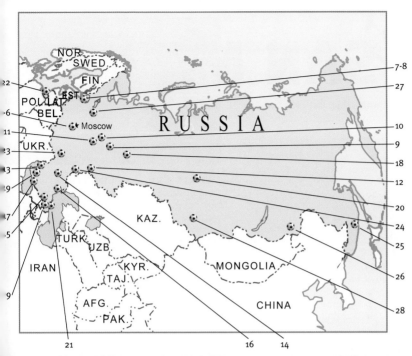

PREMIERE LEAGUE CLUBS	CITY	STADIUM	CAPACITY
1-FK Torpedo Moscow	Moscow	Luzhniki	80 480
2-FK Dinamo Moscow	Moscow	Dinamo	38 880
3-FK Lokomotiv Moscow	Moscow	Lokomotiv	30 000
4-FK Spartak Moscow	Moscow	Eduard Streltsov	13 200
5-FK Torpedo Metalurg	Moscow	Eduard Streltsov	13 200
6-CSKA Moscow	Moscow	CSKA Peshtchanoye	10 500
7-FK Dinamo SPB	Saint Petersburg	S.M Kirov	72 000
8-FK Zenith	Saint Petersburg	Petrovskiy	21 838
9-FK Rubin Kazan	Kazan	Tsentralnyi	32 000
10-Shinnik Yaroslav	Yaroslav	Shinnik	22 984
11-FK Saturn Ren TV	Ramenskoye	Saturn	16 500
12-Kryliya Sovetov Samara	Samara	Metallurg	35 330
13-SKA Rostov	Rostov Nadonu	SKA SKVO	33 000
14-SK Rotor Volgograd	Volgograd	Tsentralnyi	32 000
15-FK Alaniya Vladikavkaz	Vladikavkas	Republikan Spartak	32 674
16-FK Uralan Elista	Elista	Uralan	10 340
17-Chernomorets	Novorossiysk	Tsentralnyi	12 910
18-FK Amkar Perm	Perm	Zvezda	20 000
19-FK Kuban Krasnodar	Krasnodar	Kuban	28 000
20-FK Tom Tomsk	Tomsk	Trud	15 500
21-FK Anzhi	Makhatchkala	Anzhi	16 000
22-FK Baltika Kaliningrad	Kaliningrad	Baltika	14 500
23-Metallurg Lipestk	Lipetsk	Metallurg	14 330
24-FK Sokol Saratov	Saratov	Lokomotiv	14 800
25-SKA Energiya	Khabarovsk	SKA DVO	20 000
26-FK Lokomotiv Chita	Chita	Lokomotiv	12 500
27-FK Khimki	Khimki	Novator	5 260
28-FK Metallurg Kuzbass	Novokuznetsk	Metallurg	10 000
29-Spartak Naltchik	Naltchik	Spartak	18 000

SAN MARINO

FED. SAMMARINESE GIUOCO CALCIO
Viale Campo dei Giudei,14 47890 REP.
San Marino
TEL 378-054/999 0515
WEB www.fsgc.sm

REFERENCE
Official name
   Republic of San Marino

Date of formation	301
Capital	San Marino
Population	26,937
Total area	24 sq Mi (61 sq Km)
Time zone	GMT +1
Density	1122 per sq Mi(417 per sq Km)
Languages	Italian
Literacy rate	99%
Currency	Euro
Economy	Services 58%
Religions	Catholic 93%
Ethnic Mix	Sammarinese 80%, Italian 19%

GEOGRAPHY
Elevation
lowest point: Torrente Ausa 55 m
highest point: Monte Titano 755 m
Geography Note
landlocked; smallest independent state in
Europe after the Holy See and Monaco;
dominated by the Apennines
Natural Resources
building stone
Climate
mediterranean; mild to cool winters; warm,
sunny summers
San Marino Food
spicy steak

WORLD CUP

1930	Did not qualify
1934	Did not qualify
1938	Did not qualify
1950	Did not qualify
1954	Did not qualify
1958	Did not qualify
1962	Did not qualify
1966	Did not qualify
1970	Did not qualify
1974	Did not qualify
1978	Did not qualify
1982	Did not qualify
1986	Did not qualify
1990	Did not qualify
1994	Did not qualify
1998	Did not qualify
2002	Did not qualify

COUNTRY LEAGUE CHAMPIONS

2004	SS Pennarossa
2003	SP Domagnano
2002	SP Domagnano
2001	SP Cosmos
2000	SS Folgore Falciano
1999	SS Calcio Faetano
1998	SS Folgore Falciano
1997	SS Folgore Falciano
1996	SP Libertas

WOMEN'S LEAGUE CHAMPIONS

2004	Not Known
2003	Not Known
2002	Not Known
2001	Not Known
2000	Not Known

NATIONAL TEAM COLORS

WORLD PICTURES OF SOCCER

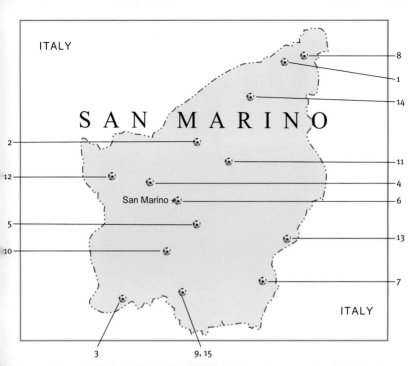

PREMIERE LEAGUE CLUBS	CITY	STADIUM	CAPACITY
1-Juvenes Dogana	Dogana	Dogana	1 000
2-SP Cailungo	Cailungo	Municipal Borgo Maggiore	3 500
3-Pennarossa	Chiesanuova	Chiesa Nuova	1 000
4-SP Libertas	Borgo Maggiore	Municipal Borgo Magiore	3 500
5-SS San Giovanni	San Giovanni	Municipal Borgo Magiore	3 500
6-SP Tre Penne	San Marino	Fonte Del Ovo	1 100
7-SP La Fiorita	Monte Giardino	Municipal Monte Giardino	2 200
8-SS Folgore Falciano	Falciano	Dogana	1 800
9-Tre Fiori	Fiorentina	Fiorentino	1 000
10-SS Murata	Murata	Municipal Monte Giordano	2 200
11-SP Domagnano	Domagnano	Olimpico	1 990
12-VirtusAcquaviva	Acquaviva	Acquaviva	1 000
13-SC Faetano	Faetano	Faetano	1 500
14-Cosmos Serravalle	Serravalle	Serravalle	4 667
15-Montevito	Fiorentino	Fiorentino	1 000

SCOTLAND

THE SCOTTISH FOOTBALL ASSOC.
Hampden Park, Glasgow G42 9AY
TEL 44-141/616 6000 FAX /616 6001
WEB www.scottishfa.co.uk

REFERENCE
Official name
Scotland
Date of formation 1707/1801
Capital Edinburg
Population 5.2 Million
Total area 30,414 sq mi(78,772 per sq Km)
Time zone GMT
Density 168 per sq Mi
Languages English, Scots Gaelic
Literacy rate 99%
Currency British Pound
Economy Services 72%
Religions Church of Scotland, Roman Catholic
Ethnic Mix Scottish 95%

GEOGRAPHY
Elevation
lowest point: Fenland -4 m
highest point: Ben Nevis 1,343 m
Geography Note
lies near vital North Atlantic sea lanes; only 35 km from France and now linked by tunnel under the English Channel; because of heavily indented coastline, no location is more than 125 km from tidal waters
Natural Resources
banking and finance, steel, transport equipment, oil and gas, whisky, tourism
Climate
temperate; moderated by prevailing southwest winds over the North Atlantic Current
Scotish Food
scottisch oat cake/almond shortbread biscuits

WORLD CUP		COUNTRY LEAGUE CHAMPIONS	
1930	Did not qualify		
1934	Did not qualify		
1938	Did not qualify	2004	Celtic
1950	Did not qualify	2003	Rangers
1954	First round exit	2002	Celtic
1958	First round exit	2001	Celtic
1962	Did not qualify	2000	Rangers
1966	Did not qualify	1999	Rangers
1970	Did not qualify	1998	Celtic
1974	First round exit	1997	Rangers
1978	First round exit	1996	Rangers
1982	First round exit	**WOMEN'S LEAGUE CHAMPIONS**	
1986	First round exit	2004	Hibernian
1990	First round exit	2003	Queens Park
1994	Did not qualify	2002	Kilmarnock FC
1998	First round exit	2001	Not Known
2002	Did not qualify	2000	Not Known

NATIONAL TEAM COLORS

WORLD PICTURES OF SOCCER

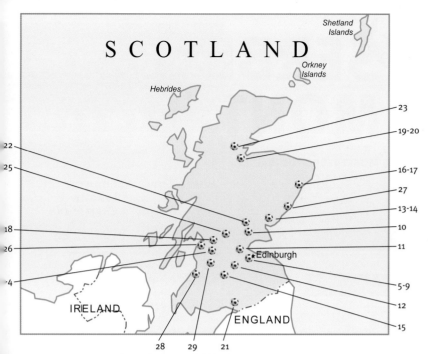

Premiere League Clubs	City	Stadium	Capacity
1-Celtic FC	Glasgow	Celtic Park	60 506
2-Rangers FC	Glasgow	Ibrox Stadium	50 420
3-Queens Park	Glasgow	Hampden Park	50 670
4-Partick Thistle FC	Glasgow	Firhill Stadium	13 079
5-Heart of Midlothian	Edinburg	Tynecastle Stadium	18 300
6-Edinburg City	Edinburg	Meadowpark Stadium	16 000
7-Hibernians FC	Edinburg	Easter Road Stadium	17 500
8-Edinburg Athletic	Edinburg	CS Sport Ground	1 500
9-CS Strollers	Edinburg	CS Sport Ground	1 500
10-Dunfermline Athletic	Dunfermline	East End Park	12 510
11-Livingston FC	Livingston	Almondvale Park	10 016
12-Motherwell	Motherwell	Fir Park	13 742
13-Dundee United	Dundee	Tannadice Park	14 200
14-Dundee FC	Dundee	Dens Park	14 000
15-Kilmarnock	Kilmarnock	Rugby Park	18 220
16-Aberdeen	Aberdeen	Pittodrie Stadium	22 200
17-Cove Rangers	Aberdeen	Allan Park	2 300
18-FC Clyde	Cumbernauld	Broadwood Stadium	8 029
19-Inverness CT	Inverness	Caledonian Stadium	6 500
20-Clachnacuddin	Inverness	Grant Street Park	3 000
21-Queen of the South	Dumfries	Palmerston Park	6 412
22-St Johnstone	Perth	McDiarmid Park	10 618
23-Ross County	Dingwall	Victoria Park	5 800
24-Falkirk	Falkirk	Brockville Park	7 576
25-East Stirlingshire	Falkirk	First Park	1 880
26-Saint Mirren	Paisley	St.Mirren Park	10 800
27-Brechin City	Brechin	Glebe Park	3 960
28-Ayr United	Ayr	Somerset Park	10 243
29-Hamilton Academicals	Hamilton	New Douglas Park	5 300

SERBIA & MONTENEGRO

SERBIA & MONTENEGRO FOOTBALL ASSOC.

HP.O Box 263, Belgrade, 1100
TEL 381-11/323 4253
WEB www.uefa.com

REFERENCE

Official name
Serbia & Montenegro

Date of formation February 4th,2003
Capital Belgrade
Population 10,829,175
Total area 102,350 sq km
Time zone GMT +1
Density 274 per sq Mi, 122 per sq Km
Languages Serbian 95%, Albanian 5%
Literacy rate 98%
Currency Dinar, Euro
Economy Machine building, Metallurgy
Religions Orthodox 65%, Muslim 19%,
Ethnic Mix Serb 62.6%, Albanian 16.5%

GEOGRAPHY

Elevation
lowest point: Adriatic Sea 0 m
highest point: Daravica 2,656 m

Geography Note
controls one of the major land routes from
Western Europe to Turkey and the Near East;
strategic location along the Adriatic coast

Natural Resources
oil, gas, coal, iron ore, bauxite, copper, lead,
zinc, antimony, chromite, nickel, gold, silver,
magnesium, pyrite, limestone, marble, salt,
hydropower, arable land

Climate
hot, dry summers and autumns and relatively
cold winters with heavy snowfall inland

Serbia & Montenegro Food
spicy pork, vesalica, mukalika

WORLD CUP

1930	Did not qualify
1934	Did not qualify
1938	Did not qualify
1950	Did not qualify
1954	First round exit
1958	First round exit
1962	Did not qualify
1966	Did not qualify
1970	Did not qualify
1974	Did not qualify
1978	Did not qualify
1982	Did not qualify
1986	Did not qualify
1990	Did not qualify
1994	Did not qualify
1998	Did not qualify
2002	Did not qualify

COUNTRY LEAGUE CHAMPIONS

2004	Crvena Zvezda Beograd
2003	Not Known
2002	Celtic
2001	Celtic
2000	Rangers
1999	Rangers
1998	Celtic
1997	Rangers
1996	Rangers

WOMEN'S LEAGUE CHAMPIONS

2004	Hibernian
2003	Queens Park
2002	Kilmarnock FC
2001	Not Known
2000	Not Known

NATIONAL TEAM COLORS

WORLD PICTURES OF SOCCER

PREMIERE LEAGUE CLUBS	CITY	STADIUM	CAPACITY
1-FK Partizan Beograd	Belgrade	Partizan	30 887
2-FK Crvena Zvezda Beograd	Belgrade	Crvena Zvezda	51 328
3-FK Zeleznik Beograd	Belgrade	Zeleznik	8 350
4-FK Beograd	Belgrade	Omladinski	13 912
5-FK Rad Beograd	Belgrade	Rad	6 000
6-FK Cukaricki Stakom	Belgrade	Cukaricki	5 000
7-FK Milicionar Beograd	Belgrade	Milicionar	5 000
8-Hajduk Beograd	Belgrade	Hajduk	4 000
9-FK Obolic Beograd	Belgrade	Obilic	3 000
10-FK Sartid Smederevo	Smederevo	Kraj Stare Zelezare	16 656
11-FK Hajduk Rodic	Kula	Hajduk	11 000
12-FK Zeta Golubovci	Golubac	Golubacima	5 000
13-FK Buducnost	Podgorica	FK Buducnost	17 000
14-FK Zemun	Zemun	Gradski	10 000
15-FK Sujetska	Niksic	Gradski	10 800
16-FK Vojvodina	Novi Sad	Gradski	15 745
17-FK Novi Sad	Novi Sad	Gradski	15 745
18-Borac Cacak	Cacak	Gradski	6 000
19-FK Radiniki	Obrenovac	Radnickog	5 000
20-Spartak Subotica	Subotica	Gradski	28 000
21-FK Nepradak	Krusevac	Mladost	22 100
22-FK Mladost Apatin	Apatin	Mladosti	7 000
23-FK Mladost Lucani	Lucani	Mladost	6 000
24-FK Becej	Becej	Gradski	5 000
25-FK Prostinac	Pristina	Gradski	25 000
26-FK Jedinstvo	Parain	Gradski	8 000
27-FK Radnicki Nis	Nis	Cair	8 900
28-FK Radnicki	Kragujevac	Cika Daca	22 058
29-FK ProleterZrenjanin	Gradski		18 700

SLOVAKIA

Slovak Football Assoc.
Junacka 6,832 80 Bratislava
TEL 421-2/4924 9151 FAX /4924 9595
WEB www.futbalsfz.sk

REFERENCE
Official name
Slovak Republic
**Date of
formation** 1993
Capital Bratislava
Population 5.4 Million
Total area 18,933 sq Mi (49,036 sq Km)
Time zone GMT+1
Density 285 per sq Mi (110 per sq Km)
Languages Slovak, Hungarian, Romany
Literacy rate 99%
Currency Koruna
Economy Services 44%, Industry 44%
Religions Catholic 60%
Ethnic Mix Slovak 85%, Magyar 6%

GEOGRAPHY
Elevation
lowest point: Bodrok River 94 m
highest point: Gerlachovsky Stit 2,655 m
Geography Note
landlocked; most of the country is rugged
and mountainous; the Tatra Mountains in
the north are interspersed with many scenic
lakes and valleys
Natural Resources
brown coal and lignite; small amounts of
iron ore, copper and manganese ore; salt;
arable land
Climate
temperate; cool summers; cold, cloudy,
humid winters
Slovakian Food
slovak gulash

WORLD CUP		COUNTRY LEAGUE CHAMPIONS	
1930	Did not qualify		
1934	Did not qualify		
1938	Did not qualify	2004	MSK Zilina
1950	Did not qualify	2003	MSK Zilina
1954	Did not qualify	2002	MSK Zilina
1958	Did not qualify	2001	Inter Bratislava
1962	Did not qualify	2000	Inter Bratislava
1966	Did not qualify	1999	SK Slovan Bratislava
1970	Did not qualify	1998	FC Kosice
1974	Did not qualify	1997	FC Kosice
1978	Did not qualify	1996	SK Slovan Bratislava
1982	Did not qualify	**WOMEN'S LEAGUE CHAMPIONS**	
1986	Did not qualify	2004	SK Slovan Bratislava
1990	Did not qualify	2003	SK ZSNP Nad Hronom
1994	Did not qualify	2002	SK ZSNP Nad Hronom
1998	Did not qualify	2001	SK Slovan Bratislava
2002	Did not qualify	2000	SK Slovan Bratislava

NATIONAL TEAM COLORS

WORLD PICTURES OF SOCCER

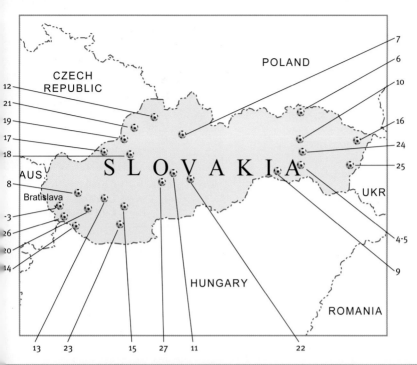

PREMIERE LEAGUE CLUBS	CITY	STADIUM	CAPACITY
1-SK Slovan Bratislava	Bratislava	Tehelne Pole	30 087
2-ASK Inter Bratislava	Bratislava	Pasienky	13 295
3-FC Artmedia Bratislava	Bratislava	Petrzalka	8 000
4-1.FC Kosice	Kosice	Vsesportovy Areal	30 312
5-Lokomotiva Kosice	Kosice	Lokomotiva	10 787
6-BSC Bardejov	Bardejov	Bardejov	12 000
7-MSK Ruzomberok	Ruzomberok	MSK Ruzomberok	5 030
8-FC Spartak Trnava	Trnava	Anton Malatinsky	18 448
9-FC Rimavska Sobota	Sobota	Rimavska Sobota	8 000
10-FC Tatran Presov	Presov	Tatran	14 000
11-Dukla Banska Byst	Banka Bystrica	Stiavnicky	11 500
12-MSK Zilina	Zilina	Pod Dubnon	6 233
13-FC Nitra	Nitra	Nitra	10 020
14-Dac Dunajska Streda	Streda	DAC	16 490
15-FK VTJ Koba Senec	Senec	Koba Senec	5 000
16-HF Chemlon Humenne	Humenne	Chemlon	18 000
17-FK Laugaricio Trencin	Trencin	Mestsky	15 712
18-HC Slovan Prievidza	Prievidza	Banik	6 500
19-FKZTS Dubnica	Dubnica NadVahom	Metsky	9 200
20-FC Sala	Sala		
21-SK Matador	Puchov		
22-Podbrezova	Podbrezova		
23-Druzstevnik Bac	Bac		
24-Steel Trans Licartovce	Licartvoce		
25-Bukocel	Vranov Nad Toplou		
26-FC Armedia Petrzalka	Petrzalka		
27-Kysucky Lieskoviec	Lieskoviec		

SLOVENIA

NOGOMETNA ZVEZA SLOVENIJE
Cerinova 4,pp 3986,1001 Ljubljana
TEL 386-1/530 0400 FAX /530 0410
WEB www.nzs.si

REFERENCE
Official name
  Republic of Slovenia
Date of formation   1991
Capital   Ljubljana
Population   2 million
Total area   7820 sq Mi (20,250 sq Km)
Time zone   GMT+1
Density   256 per sq Mi (97 per sq Km)
Languages   Slovene, Serbo-Croatian
Literacy rate 96%
Currency   Tolar
Economy   Services 52%
Religions   Catholic 96%
Ethnic Mix   Slovene 88%, Croat 3%, Serb 2%

GEOGRAPHY
Elevation
lowest point: Adriatic Sea 0 m
highest point: Triglav 2,864 m
Geography Note
despite its small size, this eastern Alpine
country controls some of Europe's major
transit routes
Natural Resources
lignite coal, lead, zinc, mercury, uranium, silver, hydropower, forests
Climate
mediterranean climate on the coast,
continental climate with mild to hot
summers and cold winters in the plateaus
and valleys to the east
Slovenian Food
srnci chrbat

WORLD CUP		COUNTRY LEAGUE CHAMPIONS	
1930	Did not qualify		
1934	Did not qualify		
1938	Did not qualify	2004	ND Gorica
1950	Did not qualify	2003	Maribor Branik
1954	Did not qualify	2002	Maribor Branik
1958	Did not qualify	2001	Maribor Branik
1962	Did not qualify	2000	Maribor Branik
1966	Did not qualify	1999	Maribor Branik
1970	Did not qualify	1998	Maribor Branik
1974	Did not qualify	1997	Maribor Branik
1978	Did not qualify	1996	HIT Nova Gorica
1982	Did not qualify	**WOMEN'S LEAGUE CHAMPIONS**	
1986	Did not qualify	2004	ZNK KRKA
1990	Did not qualify	2003	Not Known
1994	Did not qualify	2002	Not Known
1998	Did not qualify	2001	Not Known
2002	First round exit	2000	Not Known

NATIONAL TEAM COLORS

WORLD PICTURES OF SOCCER

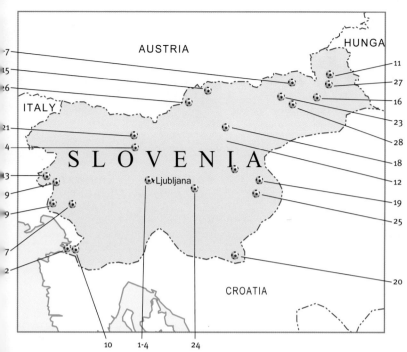

PREMIERE LEAGUE CLUBS	CITY	STADIUM	CAPACITY
1-NK KD Olimpija	Ljubljana	Bezigrad	8 211
2-NK Ljubljana	Ljubljana	ZSD Ljubljana	5 000
3-Set Vevce	Ljubljana Polje	Kodeljevo	3 000
4-Svoboda Ljubljana	Ljubljana		
5-NK Maribor	Maribor	Ljudski Vrt	10 210
6-Zeleznicar	Maribor	Sportni Park Tabor	5 000
7-Maribor PIV	Maribor		
8-ND Gorica	Nova Gorica	Sportni Park	5 000
9-HIT Nova Gorica	Nova Gorica	Sportni Park	5 000
10-NK Koper	Koper	SRC Bonifika	3 557
11-NK Mura	Murska Sobota	Fazanerija	5 400
12-CN Celje Publikum	Celje	Sportni Park	5 000
13-NK Esotech Smartno	Smartno	Smartno Obpaki	1 500
14-NK Domzale	Domzale	Sportni Park	2 500
15-NK Dravograd	Dravograd	Sportni Center	2 500
16-NK Drava Asfalti Ptuj	Ptuj	Mestni Stadion	1 950
17-NK Primorje	Ajdovscina	Nk Primorje Stadion	3 000
18-Rudar Velenje	Velenje	Ob Jezeru	3 800
19-NK Zagorge	Zagorge	Zagorge	2 000
20-NK Bela Krajina	Crnomelj	NK Bela Krajina Stadion	1 500
21-Supernova Triglav	Kranj	Mestni Stadion	4 600
22-MNK Izola Argeta	Izola	Mestni Stadion	4 000
23-Pohorje	Ruse	Ruse Stadion	3 000
24-Livar	Ivanca Gorica	Sportni Park	1 500
25-NK Krsko Posavje	Krsko	Matije Gubca	6 200
26-NK Korotan	Prevalje	Na Prevaljah	4 200
27-Beltinci	Beltinci	Sportni Park	4 000
28-NK Aluminij	Kidricevo	NK Aluminij Stadion	3 000
29-NK Goriska Brda	Rence	Vipotze	2 000

SPAIN

REAL FEDERATION ESPANOLA DE FUTBOL
Calle Alberto Bosh 13, AP 347, 28014
Madrid
TEL 34-91/420 1362 WEB www.futvol.com

REFERENCE
Official name
   Kingdom of Spain
Date of formation   1492
Capital   Madrid
Population   36 Million
Total area   192,834 sq Mi (499,440 sq Km)
Time zone   GMT+1
Density   205 sq Mi(77 sq Km)
Languages   Castilian Spanish 72%,
   Catalan, Galician, Basque
Literacy rate   97%
Currency   Euro
Economy   Services 68%
Religions   Catholic 96%
Ethnic Mix   Castilian Spanish 72%,
   Catalan 17%, Galician 6%,
   Basque 5%

GEOGRAPHY
Elevation
lowest point: Atlantic Ocean 0 m
highest point: Pico de Teide (Tenerife) on
Canary Islands 3,718 m
Geography Note
strategic location along approaches to Strait
of Gibraltar
Natural Resources
coal, lignite, iron ore, uranium, mercury,
pyrites, fluorspar, gypsum, zinc, lead, tungsten, copper, kaolin, potash, hydropower,
arable land
Climate
temperate; clear, hot summers in interior,
more moderate and cloudy along coast; cold
winters along coast.
Spanish Food
paella/camarones a la plancha

WORLD CUP

1930	Did not qualify
1934	1/4 final exit
1938	Did not qualify
1950	Finish Fourth
1954	Did not qualify
1958	Did not qualify
1962	First round exit
1966	First round exit
1970	Did not qualify
1974	Did not qualify
1978	First round exit
1982	Scd round exit
1986	1/4 final exit
1990	Scd round exit
1994	1/4 final exit
1998	First round exit
2002	1/4 final exit

COUNTRY LEAGUE CHAMPIONS

2004	Valencia CF
2003	Real Madris FC
2002	Valencia CF
2001	Real madrid CF
2000	RC Dep. Coruna
1999	FC Barcelona
1998	FC Barcelona
1997	Real Madrid CF
1996	Atletico Madrid

WOMEN'S LEAGUE CHAMPIONS

2004	Not Known
2003	Not Known
2002	Not Known
2001	Not Known
2000	Not Known

NATIONAL TEAM COLORS

WORLD PICTURES OF SOCCER

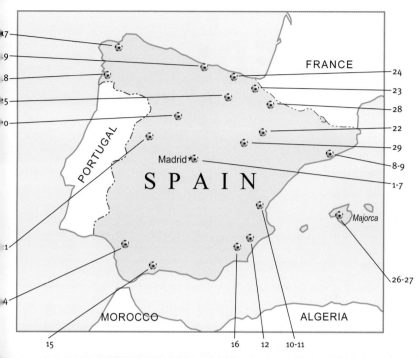

Premiere League Clubs	City	Stadium	Capacity
1-Real Madrid	Madrid	Santiago bernabeu	74 634
2-Atletico Madrid	Madrid	Vicente Calderon	57 500
3-Rayo Vallecano	Madrid	Teresa Rivero	15 500
-Moscardo	Madrid	Roman Valero	10 000
5-Santa Ana	Madrid	Polideportivo	8 500
-Real Madrid "B"	Madrid	Ciudad Deportiva	6 000
7-CD Carabanchel	Madrid	Campo da la Mina	5 000
-FC Barcelona	Barcelona	Camp Nou	98 000
-RCD Espanyol	Barcelona	Olimpico de Montjuic	56 000
10-Valencia	Valencia	Mestalla	53 000
11-Levante UD	Valencia	Ciudad de Valencia	27 792
12-Elche CF	Elche	Martinez Valero	38 740
13-Real Betis	Sevilla	Ruiz de Lopera	72 000
14-FC Sevilla	Sevilla	Ramon sanchez Pizjuan	55 000
15-Malaga CF	Malaga	La Rosaleda	33 000
16-Real Murcia CF	Murcia	La Condomina	15 805
17-RC Deportivo La Coruna	La Coruna	Riazor	35 800
18-Celta Vigo	Vigo	Balaidos	31 800
19-Racing Santander	Santander	El Sardinero	22 400
20-Real Valladolid	Valladolid	Nuevo Jose Zorilla	26 512
21-UD Salamanca	Salamanca	El Helmantico	17 341
22-Real Zaragoza	Zaragoza	La Romareda	34 700
23-Real Sociedad	San Sebastian	Anoeta	37 000
24-Athletic Bilbao	Bilbao	San Mames	40 300
25-Deportivo Alaves	Vitoria	Mendizorroza	19 500
26-Real Mallorca	Palma Mallorca	Son Moix	26 500
27-CA Baleares	Palma Mallorca	Balear	23 000
28-CA Osasuna	Pamplona	El Sadar	19 553
29-Villarreal CF	Villarreal	El Madrigal	22 157

SWEDEN

SVENSKA FOTBOLLFORBUNDET
Box1216, 17 123 Solna
TEL 46-8/735 0900 FAX /735 0901
WEB www.svenskfotboll.se

REFERENCE
Official name
Kingdom of Sweden
Date of formation 1905
Capital Stockholm
Population 8.9 Million
Total area 158,926 sq Mi (411,620 sq Km)
Time zone GMT+1
Density 56 per sq Mi (19 per sq Km)
Languages Swedish, Finnish, Lappish
Literacy rate 99%
Currency Krona
Economy Services 69%
Religions Evangelical Lutheran 89%
Ethnic Mix Swedish 91%, Finnish & Sami 3%

GEOGRAPHY
Elevation
lowest point: Baltic Sea 0 m
highest point: Kebnekaise 2,111 m
Geography Note
strategic location along Danish Straits linking Baltic and North Seas
Natural Resources
zinc, iron ore, lead, copper, silver, timber,
uranium, hydropower
Climate
temperate in south with cold, cloudy winters
and cool, partly cloudy summers; subarctic
in north
Swedish Food
swedish meatballs/salted herring

WORLD CUP	
1930	Did not qualify
1934	1/4 final exit
1938	Finish Fourth
1950	Finish Third
1954	Did not qualify
1958	Finish second
1962	Did not qualify
1966	Did not qualify
1970	First round exit
1974	Scd round exit
1978	First round exit
1982	Did not qualify
1986	Did not qualify
1990	First round exit
1994	Finish Third
1998	Did not qualify
2002	Scd round exit

COUNTRY LEAGUE CHAMPIONS	
2004	Malmo FF
2003	Djurgardens IF
2002	Djurgardens IF
2001	Hammarby IF
2000	Halmstads BK
1999	Helsinborgs IF
1998	AIK
1997	Halmstads BK
1996	IFK Goteborg
WOMEN'S LEAGUE CHAMPIONS	
2004	Kappa Ladies
2003	Kappa Ladies
2002	Umea IK
2001	Umea IK
2000	Umea IK

NATIONAL TEAM COLORS

WORLD PICTURES OF SOCCER

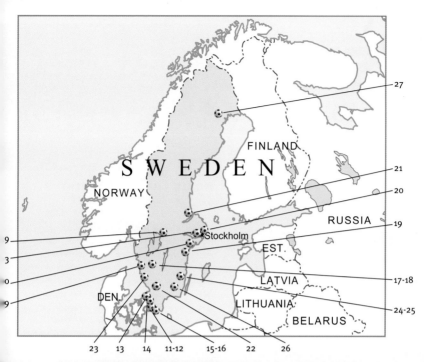

Premiere League Clubs	City	Stadium	Capacity
1-Djurgardens IF	Stockholm	Stockholm Stadion	14 500
2-FC Café Opera	Stockholm	Stockholm Stadion	14 500
3-Hammarby IF	Stockholm	Soderstadion	11 300
4-IFK Goteborg	Goteborg	Gamla Ullevi	15 845
5-Orgryte IS	Goteborg	Gamla Ullevi	15 845
-Goteborg AIS	Goteborg	Gamla Ullevi	15 845
7-BK Hacken	Goteborg	Rambergsvallen	8 480
8-Vastra Frolunda IF	Goteborg	Ruddalen	5 500
-Gunnilse IS	Goteborg	Hjallbovallen	3 000
10-AIK	Solna	Rasunda	37 000
11-Malmo FF	Malmo	Malmo Stadion	26 500
12-IFK Malmo	Malmo	Malmo IP	7 600
13-Helsinborgs IF	Helsingborgs	Olympia	16 673
14-Landroskona Bois	Landroskona	Landroskona IP	11 500
15-Trelleborgs FF	Trelleborg	Vangavallen	7 000
16-IFK Trelleborg	Trelleborg	Vangallen	7 000
17-IF Elfsborg	Boras	Ryavallen	18 900
18-Norrby IF	Boras	Ryavallen	18 900
19-Assyriska Foreningen	Sodertalje	Barsta IP	4 050
20-IF Brommapojkarna	Vallingby	Grimsta IP	4 500
21-Gefle IF	Gavle	Stromvallen	6 200
22-Halmstads BK	Halmstad	Orjans Vall	15 500
23-Falkenbergs FF	Falkenberg	Falkenbergs IP	4 000
24-Kalmar FF	Kalmar	Fredriksskans	8 500
25-Kalmar AIK	Kalmar	Fredriksskans	8 500
26-Osters IF	Vaxjo	Varendsvallen	15 062
27-Bodens BK	Boden	Bjorknasvallen	10 000
-BK Forward	Orebro	Trangens IP	4 700
-Orebro SK FK	Orebro	Eyravallen	13 000

SWITZERLAND

SCHEIZERISCHER FUSSBALL-VERBAND
Postfach, 3000 Bern 15
TEL 41-31/950 8111 FAX /950 8181
WEB www.football.ch

REFERENCE
Official name
Swiss Confederation

Date of formation	1815
Capital	Berne
Population	7.4 million
Total area	15,355 sq Mi(39,770 sq Km)
Time zone	GMT+1
Density	482 per sq Mi(176 per sq Km)
Languages	German, French, Italian
Literacy rate	99%
Currency	Franc
Economy	Services 64%
Religions	Catholic 48%, Protestant 44%
Ethnic Mix	German 65%, French 18%, Italian 10%

GEOGRAPHY
Elevation
lowest point: Lake Maggiore 195 m
highest point: Dufourspitze 4,634 m
Geography Note
landlocked; crossroads of northern and southern Europe; along with southeastern France, northern Italy, and southwestern Austria, has the highest elevations in the Alps
Natural Resources
hydropower potential, timber, salt
Climate
temperate, but varies with altitude; cold, cloudy, rainy/snowy winters; cool to warm, cloudy, humid summers with occasional showers
Switzerland Food
chard-wrapped asparagus dumplings/caramel-walnut torte

WORLD CUP

1930	Did not qualify
1934	1/4 final exit
1938	1/4 final exit
1950	First round exit
1954	1/4 finalexit
1958	Did not qualify
1962	First round exit
1966	First round exit
1970	Did not qualify
1974	Did not qualify
1978	Did not qualify
1982	Did not qualify
1986	Did not qualify
1990	Did not qualify
1994	Scd round exit
1998	Did not qualify
2002	Did not qualify

COUNTRY LEAGUE CHAMPIONS

2004	FC Basel
2003	Grasshopper Club
2002	FC Basel
2001	Grasshopper Club
2000	FC Sankt Gallen
1999	Servette FC
1998	Grasshopper Club
1997	FC Sion
1996	Grasshopper Club

WOMEN'S LEAGUE CHAMPIONS

2004	FC Surcee
2003	FC Surcee
2002	FC Sursee
2001	DFC Bern
2000	DFC Bern

NATIONAL TEAM COLORS

WORLD PICTURES OF SOCCER

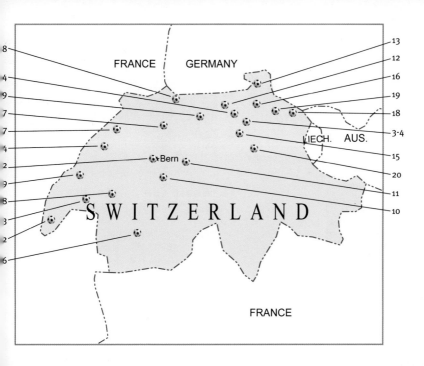

PREMIERE LEAGUE CLUBS	CITY	STADIUM	CAPACITY
-FC Bern	Bern	Neufeld	12 000
-BSC Young Boys	Bern	Neufeld	12 000
3-Zurich Grasshopper Club	Zurich	Hardturm	17 664
-FC Zurich	Zurich	Letzigrund	19 400
-FC Basel	Basel	St.Jakob Park	31 539
-BSC Old Boys	Basel	Schutzenmatte	11 700
-FC Nordstern	Basel	Rankhof	8 000
-FC Concordia	Basel	Rankhof	8 000
-FC Aarau	Aarau	Brugglifeld	13 500
ɔ-FC Thun	Thun	Lachen	7 250
1-FC Zollbruck	Zollbruck	Tannschachen	1 500
2-FC Baden	Baden	ESP Stadion	6 100
3-FC Schaffhausen	Schaffhausen	Breite	6 000
4-FC Wettingen 93	Wettingen	Altenburg	10 000
5-FC Wohlen	Wohlen	Paul-Walser Stiftung	3 300
-FC Winterthur	Winterthur	Schutzenwiese	14 987
7-FC Solothurn	Solothurn	Stadion Solothurn	6 747
8-FC St.Gallen	St.Gallen	Espenmoos	11 300
ɔ-FC Wil	Wil	Berghotz	5 800
ɔ-FC Glarus	Glarus	Bucholz	2 000
1-Servette de Geneve FC	Geneva	Stade de la Praille	31 124
2-Urania Geneve Sports	Geneva	Frontenex	4 000
3-Lausanne Sports	Lausanne	Pontaise	15 738
4-Xamax Neuchatel	Neuchatel	La Maladiere	13 300
5-FC Sion	Sion	Tourbillon	13 000
5-FC Bramois	Sion	Les Glareys	2 000
7-FC La Chaux	La Chaux-de-Fonds	Charriere	12 700
8-FC Bulle	Bulle	Bouleyres	5 150
-Yverdons Sports FC	Yverdon	Municipal	6 600

TURKEY

TURKIYE FUTBOL FEDERASYONU
Konaklar Mah.Ihlamurlu sok.9,4
Levent, 80620 Istanbul
TEL 90-212/282 7020 FAX /282 7015
WEB www.tff.org

REFERENCE
Official name
Republic of Turkey

Date of formation	1923
Capital	Ankara
Population	66.6 Million
Total area	297,154 sq Mi (769,630 sq Km)
Time zone	GMT+1
Density	224 per sq Mi (84 per sq Km)
Languages	Turkish, Kurdish, Arabic, Circas
Literacy rate	82%
Currency	Turkish Lira
Economy	Agriculture 50%, Services 35%
Religions	Muslim 99%
Ethnic Mix	Turkish 70%, Kurdish 20%, Arab 2%

GEOGRAPHY
Elevation
lowest point: Mediterranean Sea 0 m
highest point: Mount Ararat 5,166 m
Geography Note
strategic location controlling the Turkish
Straits (Bosporus, Sea of Marmara,
Dardanelles) that link Black and Aegean
Seas; Mount Ararat, the legendary landing
place of Noah's Ark, is in the far eastern
portion of the country
Natural Resources
antimony, coal, chromium, mercury,
copper, borate, sulfur, iron ore, arable land,
hydropower
Climate
temperate; hot, dry summers with mild, wet
winters; harsher in the interiors
Turkish Food
vartabit bread/Turkish shish kebab

WORLD CUP

1930	Did not qualify
1934	Did not qualify
1938	Did not qualify
1950	Did not qualify
1954	First round exit
1958	Did not qualify
1962	Did not qualify
1966	Did not qualify
1970	Did not qualify
1974	Did not qualify
1978	Did not qualify
1982	Did not qualify
1986	Did not qualify
1990	Did not qualify
1994	Did not qualify
1998	Did not qualify
2002	Finish Third

COUNTRY LEAGUE CHAMPIONS

2004	Fenerbahce
2003	Besiktas
2002	Galatasaray
2001	Fenerbahce
2000	Galatasaray
1999	Galatasaray
1998	Galatasaray
1997	Galatasaray
1996	Fenerbahce

WOMEN'S LEAGUE CHAMPIONS

2004	Not Known
2003	Gazi Universitesi
2002	Samsungucu
2001	Kuzeyspor Istanbul
2000	Delta Mobilya Istanbul

NATIONAL TEAM COLORS

WORLD PICTURES OF SOCCER

Premiere League Clubs	City	Stadium	Capacity
1-Galatasaray SK	Istanbul	Ataturk Olimpiyat	81 653
2-Fenerbahce SK	Istanbul	Fenerba. Sukru Saracolgu	54 000
3-Besiktas JK	Istanbul	Besiktas Inonu	20 863
4-Istanbulspor SFTAS	Istanbul	Gungoren Belediye	10 500
5-Buyuksehir BelediyesporSK	Istanbul	Bayrampasa Cetin Emec	12 000
6-Genclerbirligi SK	Ankara	Ankara 19 Mayis	21 250
7-MKE Ankaragucu SK	Ankara	Ankara 19 Mayis	21 250
8-BBS Ankaraspor	Ankara	Cebeci Inonu	15 000
9-Turk Telekom GSK Ankara	Ankara	Cebeci Inonu	15 000
10-Goztepe SHTAS	Izmir	Altay Alsancak	15 849
11-Altay GK Izmir	Izmir	Altay Alsancak	15 849
12-Izmirspor GSKD	Izmir	Altay Alsancak	15 849
13-Karsiyaka SK Izmir	Izmir	Altay Alsancak	15 849
14-Trabzonspor K	Trabzon	Huseyin Avni Aker	21 700
15-Jayserispor	Kayseri	Kayseri Ataturk	21 300
16-Hacilar Erciyesspor	Kayseri	Kayseri Ataturk	21 300
17-Diyarbakirspor	Diyarbakir	Diyarbakir Ataturk	16 000
18-Gaziantepspor K	Gaziantep	Kamil Ocak	19 000
19-Bursaspor K	Bursa	Bursa Ataturk	19 700
20-Adanaspor SFAS	Adana	5 Ocak	19 000
21-Adana Demirspor	Adana	5 Ocak	19 000
22-Caykur Rizespor K	Rize	Rize Ataturk	10 800
23-Konyaspor K	Konya	Konya Ataturk	19 440
24-Samsunspor	Samsun	Samsun 19 Mayis	13 500
25-Denizlispor	Denizli	Denizli Ataturk	15 000
26-Malatyaspor K	Malatya	Malatya Inonu	15 000
27-Akcaabat Sebatspor K	Akcaabat	Fatih	6 200
28-Elazigspor K	Elazig	Elazig Ataturk	14 467
29-Dardanelspor SFAS	Canakkale	18 Mart	12 500

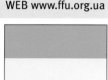

UKRAINE

FOOTBALL FED. OF UKRAINE
laboratorna St1, PB 293, 03150 kyiv
TEL 380-44/252 8498 FAX /252 8513
WEB www.ffu.org.ua

REFERENCE
Official name
   Ukraine

Date of formation	1991
Capital	Kiev
Population	50.5 Million
Total area	233,089 sq Mi (603,700 sq Km)
Time zone	GMT+3
Density	217 per sq Mi (82 per sq Km)
Languages	Ukrainian, Russian, Tartar
Literacy rate	80%
Currency	Hyrvna
Economy	Services 57%
Religions	Ukrainian Orthodox 95%, Jewish 1%
Ethnic Mix	Ukrainian 73%, Russian 22%, Jewish 1%

GEOGRAPHY
Elevation
lowest point: Black Sea 0 m
highest point: Hora Hoverla 2,061 m
Geography Note
Srategic position at the crossroads between
Europe and Asia; Second-largest country in
Europe
Natural Resources
iron ore, coal, manganese, natural gas, oil,
salt, sulfur, graphite, titanium,
magnesium, kaolin, nickel, mercury,
timber, arable land
Climate
temperate continental; Mediterranean only
on the southern Crimean coast; winters vary
from cool along the Black Sea to cold farther
inland; summers are warm across the
greater part of the country, hot in the south
Ukrainian Food
pashtet of liver/Ukrainian coffee torte

WORLD CUP

1930	Did not qualify
1934	Did not qualify
1938	Did not qualify
1950	Did not qualify
1954	Did not qualify
1958	Did not qualify
1962	Did not qualify
1966	Did not qualify
1970	Did not qualify
1974	Did not qualify
1978	Did not qualify
1982	Did not qualify
1986	Did not qualify
1990	Did not qualify
1994	Did not qualify
1998	Did not qualify
2002	Did not qualify

COUNTRY LEAGUE CHAMPIONS

2004	Dynamo Kyiv
2003	Dynamo Kyiv
2002	Shakhtar Donetsk
2001	Dynamo Kyiv
2000	Dynamo Kyiv
1999	Dynamo Kyiv
1998	Dynamo Kyiv
1997	Dynamo Kyiv
1996	Dynamo Kyiv
WOMEN'S LEAGUE CHAMPIONS	
2004	Not Known
2003	Not Known
2002	Not Known
2001	Lehenda-Cheksyl
2000	Not Known

NATIONAL TEAM COLORS

WORLD PICTURES OF SOCCER

15			29
16			26
23	Kiev		27
14			20
4	**UKRAINE**		24-25
18			17
			5-7
			28

11-12   19   22   9-10   21   8

Premiere League Clubs	City	Stadium	Capacity
1-FK Dinamo Kyyv	Kiev	Olimpiyskiy	83 300
2-FK CSKA Kyyv	Kiev	Stadion CSK ZSU	12 000
3-Obolon Kyyv	Kiev	Stadion CSK ZSU	12 000
4-Arsenal Kyyv	Kiev	Olimpiyskiy	83 300
5-FK Shakhtar Donetsk	Donetsk	Stadion Shakhtyor	31 718
6-FC Metalurh	Donetsk	Stadion Lokomotyv	24 510
7-FK Metalurh Donetsk	Donetsk	Stadion Metallurh	10 000
8-FK Dnipro	Dnipropetrovsk	Stadion Meteor	26 345
9-FK Tavvriya Simferopol	Simferopol	Stadion Lokomotyv	20 013
10-Dynamo Simferopol	Simferopol	Stadion Fiolent	6 500
11-FK Chornomorets 1959	Odesa	Tsentralnyi Chornomorets	30 767
12-Chernomorets II	Odesa	Stadion SCA	15 000
13-FKS Karpaty	Lviv	Stadion Karpaty	23 040
14-FK Karpaty Lviv	Lviv	Stadion Ukrajina	28 051
15-FK Volyn Lutsk	Lutsk	Stadion Avanhard	10 500
16-FK Nyva Ternopil	Ternopil	Stadion Tsentralnyi	18 500
17-FK Vorskla-Naftohaz	Poltava	Stadion Vorskla	24 810
18-Zakarpattya Uzhorod	Uzhorod	Stadion Avanhard	10 500
19-Zirka Kirovohrad	Kirovohrad	Stadion Zirka	20 000
20-Metalist Kharkiv	Kharkiv	Stadion Metalist	28 000
21-FK Metalurh	Zaporizhzhya	Stadion Metalurh	24 000
22-FK Kryvbas	Kryvyi Rih	Stadion Metalurh	29 782
23-Temp	Shepetovka	Stadion Temp	8 000
24-Zorja Luhansk	Luhansk	Stadion Avongard	34 000
25-Shakhtar Luhansk	Luhansk	Stadion Shakhtar	3 000
26-Spartak Sumy	Sumy	Stadion Yubileiny	29 300
27-Naftovyk Akhtyrka	Akhtyrka	Stadion Naftovnyk	9 700
28-FK Illichivets	Mariupol	Stadion Illichivets	13 000
29-Borysfen Borispil	Borispol	Stadion Kolos	7 500

WALES

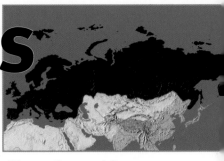

THE FOOTBALL ASSOCIATION OF WALES LTD
Plymouth Chambers, 3 Westgate
St.Cardiff CF10 1DP
TEL 44-29/2037 2325
WEB www.faw.org.uk

REFERENCE
Official name
Wales
Date of formation 1536/1707
Capital Cardiff
Population 2.9 Million
Total area 8,019 sq Mi(20,768 sq Km)
Time zone GMT 0
Density 364 per sq Mi, 141 per sq Km
Languages English, Scotts Gaelic
Literacy rate 99%
Currency British Pound
Economy Services 81%
Religions Church of Scotland, Roman Catholic
Ethnic Mix British

GEOGRAPHY
Elevation
lowest point: Fenland -4 m
highest point: Ben Nevis 1,343 m
Geography Note
lies near vital North Atlantic sea lanes; only
35 km from France and now linked by tunnel
under the English Channel; because of
heavily indented coastline, no location is
more than 125 km from tidal water
Natural Resources
agriculture and forestry, manufacturing,
tourism
Climate
temperate; moderated by prevailing southwest winds over the North Atlantic Current;
more than one-half of the days are overcast
Welsh Food
butterscotch/puddings/anglesey cake

WORLD CUP		COUNTRY LEAGUE CHAMPIONS	
1930	Did not qualify		
1934	Did not qualify		
1938	Did not qualify	2004	Rhyl
1950	Did not qualify	2003	Barry Town
1954	Did not qualify	2002	Barry Town
1958	1/4 final exit	2001	Barry Town
1962	Did not qualify	2000	Llansantfraid
1966	Did not qualify	1999	Barry Town
1970	Did not qualify	1998	Barry Town
1974	Did not qualify	1997	Barry Town
1978	Did not qualify	1996	Barry Town
1982	Did not qualify	**WOMEN'S LEAGUE CHAMPIONS**	
1986	Did not qualify	2004	Not Known
1990	Did not qualify	2003	Not Known
1994	Did not qualify	2002	Not Known
1998	Did not qualify	2001	Not Known
2002	Did not qualify	2000	Not Known

NATIONAL TEAM COLORS

WORLD PICTURES OF SOCCER

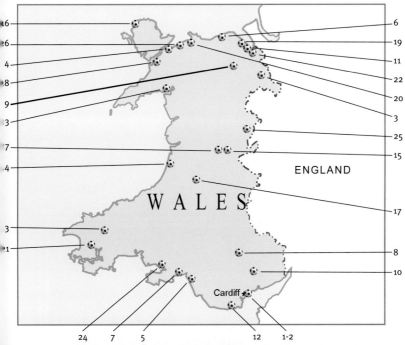

	16	
	26	
	4	
	8	
	9	
	3	
	7	
	4	
	3	
	1	
	3	

6
19
11
22
20
3
25
15

ENGLAND

WALES

17

8
10

Cardiff

24   7   5   12   1-2

Premiere League Clubs	City	Stadium	Capacity
1-Cardiff City AFC	Cardiff	Ninian Park	22 000
2-Inter Cable Tel FC	Cardiff	Leckwith Stadium	6 000
3-Wrexham Town	Wrexham	The Racecourse Ground	15 891
4-Bangor City	Bangor	Farrar Road	15 766
5-Afan Lido	Port Talbot	Afan Lido Sport Ground	5 000
6-FC Rhyl	Rhyl	Belle Vue	6 000
7-Swansea FC	Swansea	Vetch Field	9 975
8-Ebbw Vale RFC	Ebbw	Eugene Cross Park	8 000
9-Cefn Druids	Cefn	Plaskynaston Lane	2 500
10-Cwmbran Town	Cwmbran	Cwmbran	7 877
11-Flint Town United	Flint	Ca'er Castell	9 000
12-Barry Town	Barry	Jenner Park	6 000
13-Carmarthen Town	Carmarthen	Richmond Park	3 000
14-Aberystwyth Town	Aberystwyth	Park Avenue	5 500
15-FC Newton	Newton	Latham Park	5 000
16-Cemaes Bay	Cemaes Bay	School Lane	4 500
17-Rhayader Town FC	Rhayader	Y Weirglodd	2 000
18-Caernarfon Town	Caernarfon	The Oval	3 000
19-Holywell Town	Holywell	Halkyn Road	4 000
20-Conwy United	Conwy	Morfa Conwy Stadium	4 000
21-Haverfordwest CT	Haverfordwest	Bridge Meadow Stadium	2 000
22-Connah's Nomads	Connah's Quai	Halfway Ground	3 000
23-Porthmadog	Porthmadog	Y Traeth	4 000
24-FC Llaneli	Llaneli	Stebonhealth Park	3 700
25-Welshpool Town	Welshpool	Maesydre	3 000
26-TNS Llansantffraid	Llansantffraid	Recreation Field	2 000
27-FC Caersws	Caersws	Recreation Ground	3 500

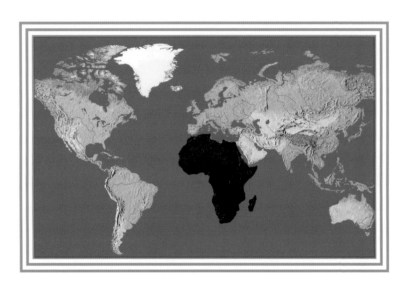

AFRICA

ALGERIA

FED. ALGERIENNE DE FOOTBALL
Chemin Ahmed Ouaked, BP39Dely-Ibrahim Alger
TEL/FAX 213 21/372929
WEB www.faf.org.dz

REFERENCE
Official name
Democratic & Popular Republic of Algeria

Date of formation	1962
Capital	Algiers
Population	31.5 million
Total area	919,590 sq Mi, 2,381,740 sq Km
Time zone	GMT 0
Density	34 per sq Mi, 13 per sq Km
Languages	Arabic,Berber, French
Literacy rate	60%
Currency	Dinar
Economy	Services 75%
Religions	Sunni Muslim 99%
Ethnic Mix	Arab 75%,Berber 24%

GEOGRAPHY
Elevation
lowest point: Chott Melrhir -40 m
highest point: Tahat 3,003 m
Geography Note
second-largest country in Africa (after Sudan)
Natural Resources
petroleum, natural gas, iron ore, phosphates, uranium, lead, zinc
Climate
arid to semiarid; mild, wet winters with hot, dry summers ; sirocco is a hot, dust/sand-laden wind especially in common summer
Algerian Food
couscous

WORLD CUP

1930	Did not qualify
1934	Did not qualify
1938	Did not qualify
1950	Did not qualify
1954	Did not qualify
1958	Did not qualify
1962	Did not qualify
1966	Did not qualify
1970	Did not qualify
1974	Did not qualify
1978	Did not qualify
1982	First round exit
1986	First roud exit
1990	Did not qualify
1994	Did not qualify
1998	Did not qualify
2002	Did not qualify

COUNTRY LEAGUE CHAMPIONS

2004	JS Kabylie
2003	USM Alger
2002	USM Alger
2001	CR Belouizdad
2000	CR Belouizdad
1999	MC Alger
1998	USM El Harrach
1997	CS Constantine
1996	USM Alger

Women's League Champions

2005	ASE Alger Centre
2004	ASE Alger Centre
2003	Not Known
2002	Not Known
2001	Not Known

NATIONAL TEAM COLORS

WORLD PICTURES OF SOCCER

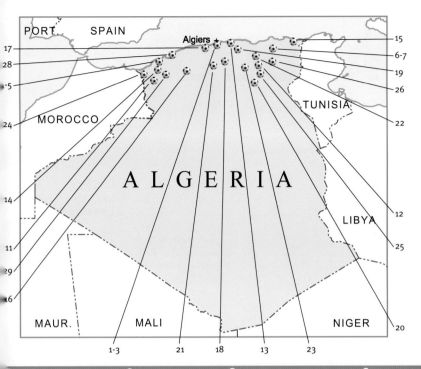

PORT   SPAIN

Algiers ★

17
28
4-5
24   MOROCCO

ALGERIA

14

11
29
16

MAUR.   MALI   NIGER

1-3   21   18   13   23

15
6-7
19
26

TUNISIA

22

12

LIBYA

25

20

PREMIERE LEAGUE CLUBS	CITY	STADIUM	CAPACITY
1-MC Algiers	Algiers	5 Juillet 1962	80 200
2-USM Algier	Algier	Omar Hamadi	15 000
3-CR Belouizdad	Algiers	20 Aout 1945	20 000
4-MC Oran	Oran	Ahmed Zabana	55 000
5-ASM Oran	Oran	Habib Bouakeul	20 000
6-CS Constantine	Constantine	Chahid Hamlaoui	25 000
7-MO Constantine	Constantine	Chahid Hamlaoui	25 000
8-WA Tlemcen	Tlemcen	Akit Lofti	10 000
9-ASPC Tlemcen	Tlemcen	Birouana	30 000
10-WA Tlemcen	Tlemcen	Akit Lofti	10 000
11-ASPC Tlemcen	Tlemcen	Birouana	30 000
12-HB Chelgoum-Laid	Chelgoum El Aid	11 Decembre 1961	
13-JS Kabylie	Tizi-Ouzou	1er Novembre	35 000
14-USM Bel Abbes	Sidi Bel Abbes	24 Fevrier 1956	50 000
15-USM Annaba	Annaba	19 Mai 1956	65 000
16-JSM Tiaret	Tiaret	Ahmed Kait	
17-USM Blida	Blida	Frere Brakni	35 000
18-RC Kouba	Kouba	Omar Benhaddad	20 000
19-JS Bordj Menaiel	Bordj Menaiel	Salah Takdjerad	15 000
20-US Biskra	Biskra	El Alia	
21-USM El Harrach	El Harrach	1er Novembre Mohamadia	8 000
22-ES Setif	Setif	8 Mai 1945	30 000
23-MC El Eulma	El Eulma	Messaoud Zeggar	
24-CR Temouchent	Ain Temouchent	Freha	
25-AS Ain M'Lila	Ain M'Lila	Freres Demene-Debbih	
26-CA BatnaBatna	Seffouhi		
27-ES Mostaganem	Mostaganem	Mohamed Bensaad	
28-WA mostaganem	Mostaganem	Mohamed Bensaad	
29-GC Mascara	Mascara	Meftah Aouard	5 000

ANGOLA

FED. ANGOLAISE DE FOOTBALL
Comp.da Cidadela Desportiva
BP 3449,Luanda
TEL 244-2/264948 FAX 244-2/260 566
WEB www.fafutebol.com

REFERENCE
Official name
Republic of Angola
Date of formation 1975
Capital Luanda
Population 12.9 million
Total area 481 sq Mi, 1,246,700 sq Km
Time zone GMT +1
Density 27 per sq Mi, 9 per sq Km
Languages Portuguese
Literacy rate 43%
Currency Kwanza
Economy agriculture 69%, services 21%
Religions Catholic50%, Protestant 20%,
Ethnic Mix Sovimbundu 37%, Kimbundu
25%, Bakongo 13%

GEOGRAPHY
Elevation
lowest point: Atlantic Ocean o m
highest point: Morro de Moco 2,620 m
Geography Note
Cabinda is separated from rest of country by
the Democratic Republic of the Congo
Natural Resources
petroleum, diamonds, iron ore, phosphates,
copper, feldspar, gold, bauxite, uranium
Climate
semiarid in south and along coast to
Luanda; north has cool, dry season (May to
October) and hot, rainy season (November
to April)
Angola Food
arroz de quilitas

WORLD CUP		COUNTRY LEAGUE CHAMPIONS	
1930	Did not qualify		
1934	Did not qualify		
1938	Did not qualify	2004	A. Sport Aviacao
1950	Did not qualify	2003	A. Sport Aviacao
1954	Did not qualify	2002	A. Sport Aviacao
1958	Did not qualify	2001	Petro Atletico
1962	Did not qualify	2000	Petro Atletico
1966	Did not qualify	1999	Primeiro de Agosto
1970	Did not qualify	1998	Primeiro de Agosto
1974	Did not qualify	1997	Petro Atletico
1978	Did not qualify	1996	Primeiro de Agosto
1982	Did not qualify	**Women's League Champion**	
1986	Did not qualify	2004	Progresso do Sambizan
1990	Did not qualify	2003	Progresso do Sambizan
1994	Did not qualify	2002	Progresso do Sambizan
1998	Did not qualify	2001	Desp.da Expresso
2002	Did not qualify	2000	Desp.da Expresso

NATIONAL TEAM COLORS

WORLD PICTURES OF SOCCER

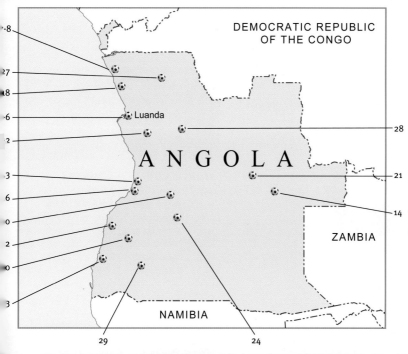

PREMIERE LEAGUE CLUBS	CITY	STADIUM	CAPACITY
Atletico Sport Aviacao	Luanda	Joaquim Dinis	10 000
Petro Atletico	Luanda	Est.Nacional da Cidadela	60 000
CD Primeiro de Agosto	Luanda	Est.Nacional da Cidadela	60 000
Inter Clube Angola	Luanda	Est.Nacional da Cidadela	60 000
CD Primeiro de Agosto	Luanda	Dos Coqueiros	12 000
Sport Luanda e Benfica	Luanda	Dos Coqueiros	12 000
Sporte Clube Cabinda	Cabinda	Estadio do Tafe	
Academica Soyo	Cabinda	Estadio do Tafe	
Petro Atletico Huambo	Huambo	Estadio da Ferroviario	
1er de Maio	Huambo	Estadio de Calcilhas	
Sonangol Namibe	Namibe	Estadio Joaquim Morais	
Independente Tombwa	Namibe	Estadio Joaquim Morais	
Academica Lobito	Lobito	Estadio do Electro Clube	
Progresso Sambuanga	Sambuanga	Campo de Sao Paulo	
Estrela Clube 1 de Maio	Benguela		
Sporting Benguela	Benguela		
Acad.Petroleo do Kwanda	Soyo		
Academica Soyo	Soyo		
Sport Lubango e Benfica	Lubango	Nossa senhora do Monte	
Ferroviaro da Huila	Lubango	Nossa Senhora do Monte	
FC Onze Bravos do Moxico	Luena	Campo de Sao Paulo	
Sagrada Esperanca	Dundo	Estad.Quintalao do Dundo	
Independente	Tombwa		
11 de Novembro	Kuando Kubango		
Cambonde Novo	Uije		
FC Constructores	Uije		
FC Uije	Uije		
Ritondo SC	Malanje	Comandante Valodia	
Desportivo Militar Huila	Huila		

BENIN

BENIN FOOTBALL ASSOCIATION
BP 965, Cotonou
TEL 229/330 537   FAX 229/330537
WEB

REFERENCE
Official name
  Republic of Benin

Date of formation	1960
Capital	Porto Novo
Population	6.1 million
Total area	42,710 sq Mi, 110,620 sq Km
Time zone	GMT +1
Density	143 per sq Mi, 56 per sq Km
Languages	French, Fon, Bariba, Adja, Houeda, Fulani
Literacy rate	36%
Currency	CFA Franc
Economy	middle
Religions	traditional beliefs 70%, Muslim 15%, Christian 15%
Ethnic Mix	Fon 47%, Adja 12%, Bariba 10%,

GEOGRAPHY
Elevation
lowest point: Atlantic Ocean o m
highest point: Mont Sokbaro 658 m
Geography Note
sandbanks create difficult access to a coast
with no natural harbors, river mouths, or
islands
Natural Resources
small offshore oil deposits, limestone,
marble, timber
Climate
tropical; hot, humid in south; semiarid in
north
Benin Food
Fritters
ginger beer (drink)

WORLD CUP

1930	Did not qualify
1934	Did not qualify
1938	Did not qualify
1950	Did not qualify
1954	Did not qualify
1958	Did not qualify
1962	Did not qualify
1966	Did not qualify
1970	Did not qualify
1974	Did not qualify
1978	Did not qualify
1982	Did not qualify
1986	Did not qualify
1990	Did not qualify
1994	Did not qualify
1998	Did not qualify
2002	Did not qualify

COUNTRY LEAGUE CHAMPIONS

2004	Abandoned
2003	Dragons de L'Oueme
2002	Dragons de L'Oueme
2001	AS Colombes
2000	Requins de l'atlantique
1999	Dragons de L'Oueme
1998	Dragons de L'Oueme
1997	Mogas 90
1996	Mogas 90
Women's League Champion	
2004	Not Known
2003	Not Known
2002	Fleche Noire SC
2001	Not Known
2000	Not Known

NATIONAL TEAM COLORS

WORLD PICTURES OF SOCCER

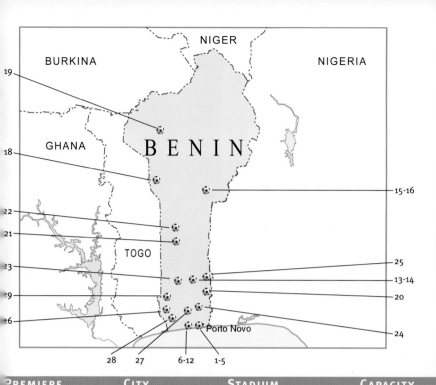

Premiere League Clubs	City	Stadium	Capacity
-Dragons de L'Oueme	Porto Novo	Stade Municipale	20 000
-Mogas 90	Porto Novo	Stade municipale	20 000
-Postel Sport	Porto Novo	Stade Charles de Gaule	15 000
-Etoile Sportive	Porto novo	Stade Cotonou II	6 000
-AS Porto Novo	Porto Novo	Stade Cotonou II	6 000
-Requins de L'Atlantique	Cotonou	Stade de L'Amitie	35 000
-Toffa	Cotonou	Stade de L'Amitie	35 000
-AS Cotonou	Cotonou	Stade Rene Pleven	12 000
-Ajijas	Cotonou	Quartier Akpakpa	12 000
-Soleil FC	Cotonou	Stade Rene Pleven	12 000
-Lions de L'Atakory	Cotonou	Quartier Akpakpa	12 000
-Energie Sport	Cotonou	Quartier Akpakpa	12 000
-Varietes de Bohicon	Bohicon		
-Tonnerre de Bohicon	Bohicon		
-Buffles de Borgou	Parakou	Stade Bourgou	8 000
-Cavaliers FC	Parakou	Stade Bourgou	8 000
-Sitex de Lokossa	Lokossa		
-Pantheres FC	Djougou	Stade Djougou	10 000
-Lions de L'Atacora FC	Natitingou	Stade Atakora	3 500
-JS de Pobe	Pobe		
-Savalou FC			
Agoua SA			
-Varietes FC	Abomey		
-Espoir FC	Zounke		
-Vautours D'Ilacondji	Ilacondji		
-Entente de L'Atlantique	Lokossa		
-JA Misserete	Misserete		
-AS Pythagore D'Akvakpa	Akvakpa	Stade D'Akvakpa	12 000
-JS Komondor	Gbanave		

BOTSWANA

BOTSWANA FOOTBALL ASSOC.
PO BOX 1396,Gaborone
TEL 267/300 279   FAX267/300 280
WEB

REFERENCE
Official name
Republic of Botswana

Date of formation	1966
Capital	Gaborone
Population	1.6 million
Total area	218,814 sq Mi, 566,730 sq Km
Time zone	GMT +2
Density	7 per sq Mi, 2 per sq Km
Languages	English, Tswana, Shona, San, Khoikhoi, Ndebele
Literacy rate	69%
Currency	Pula
Economy	services 51%, mining & agriculture 49%
Religions	traditional beliefs 50%, Christian 30%
Ethnic Mix	Tswana 98%

GEOGRAPHY
Elevation
lowest point: Junction of the Limpopo and Shashe Rivers 513 m
highest point: Tsodilo Hills 1,489 m
Geography Note
landlocked; population concentrated in eastern part of the country
Natural Resources
diamonds, copper, nickel, salt, soda ash, potash, coal, iron ore, silver
Climate
semiarid; warm winters and hot summers
Botswana Food
vegetable stew/Kalahari truffes morama/sorghum porridge

WORLD CUP

1930	Did not qualify
1934	Did not qualify
1938	Did not qualify
1950	Did not qualify
1954	Did not qualify
1958	Did not qualify
1962	Did not qualify
1966	Did not qualify
1970	Did not qualify
1974	Did not qualify
1978	Did not qualify
1982	Did not qualify
1986	Did not qualify
1990	Did not qualify
1994	Did not qualify
1998	Did not qualify
2002	Did not qualify

COUNTRY LEAGUE CHAMPIONS

2004	Botswana DF XI
2003	Mogoditshane Fight
2002	Botswana DF XI
2001	Mogoditshane Fight
2000	Mogoditshane Fight
1999	Mogoditshane Fight
1998	Notwane PG
1997	Botswana DF XI
1996	Notwane PG
Women's League Champion	
2004	Not Known
2003	Not Known
2002	Not Known
2001	Not Known
2000	Not Known

NATIONAL TEAM COLORS

WORLD PICTURES OF SOCCER

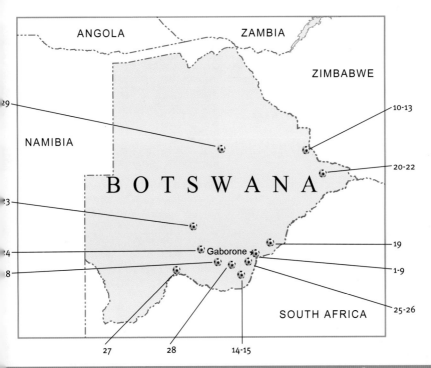

Premiere League Clubs	City	Stadium	Capacity
-Notwane FC	Gaborone	National stadium	22 500
-Mogaditshane Fighters	Gaborone	National stadium	22 500
-Botswana Defence Force XI	Gaborone	National stadium	22 500
-Police XI	Gaborone	National stadium	22 500
-Prisons XI	Gaborone	National stadium	22 500
-Township Rollers	Gaborone	National stadium	22 500
-Black Peril	Gaborone	National stadium	22 500
-Gaborone United	Gaborone	National stadium	22 500
-Wonder Sporting Club	Gaborone	National stadium	22 500
ɔ-TASC	Francistown		
ᴀ-TAFIC	Francistown		
2-Rhinos	Francistown		
ʒ-Great North Tigers	Francistown		
₄-Botswana Meat Commission	Lobatse		
₅-Extension Gunners	Lobatse		
₅-Comets	Jwaneng		
₇-Blue Diamonds	Jwaneng		
ʒ-Cosmos Blizzards	Jwaneng		
ɔ-Centre Chiefs	Mochudi		
ɔ-FC Satmos	Selebi Phikwe		
₁-Nico United	Selebi Phikwe		
₂-Continental Aces	Selebi Phikwe		
ʒ-Lehututu United	Lehututu		
₄-Gabane Santos	Gabane		
₅-Red Sparks	Tlokweng		
₅-Naughty Boys	Tlokweng		
₇-Young Fighters	Wezda		
ʒ-Southern Pirates	Kanye		
ɔ-Orapa Bucs	Orapa		

BURKINA FASO

FED. BURKINABE DE FOOTBALL
01 BP 57,Ouagadougou OI
TEL 226/318 815   FAX 226/318 843
WEB www.cafonline.com

REFERENCE
Official name
Burkina Faso

Date of formation	1960
Capital	Ouagadougou
Population	11.9 million
Total area	105,714 sq Mi, 273,800 sq Km
Time zone	GMT 0
Density	113 per sq Mi, 40 per sq Km
Languages	French, Mossi, Fulani, Tuareg, Dyula, Songhai
Literacy rate	19%
Currency	CFA Franc
Economy	agriculture 87%
Religions	traditional beliefs 55%,
Ethnic Mix	Muslim 35%,Catholic 9%, Mossi 50%, Others 50%

GEOGRAPHY
Elevation
lowest point: Mouhoun (Black Volta) River 200 m
highest point: Tena Kourou 749 m
Geography Note
landlocked savanna cut by the three principal
rivers of the Black, Red, and White Voltas
Natural Resources
manganese, limestone, marble; small deposits
of gold, antimony, copper, nickel, bauxite, lead,
phosphates, zinc, silver
Climate
tropical; warm, dry winters; hot, wet summers
Burkina Food
mango chutney/spiced lamb balls

WORLD CUP		COUNTRY LEAGUE CHAMPIONS	
1930	Did not qualify		
1934	Did not qualify		
1938	Did not qualify	2004	ASFA/Yennega
1950	Did not qualify	2003	ASFA/Yennega
1954	Did not qualify	2002	ASFA/Yennega
1958	Did not qualify	2001	Etoile Filante
1962	Did not qualify	2000	USFA Ouagadougou
1966	Did not qualify	1999	ASFA/Yennega
1970	Did not qualify	1998	USFA Ouagadougou
1974	Did not qualify	1997	Racing Bo Dioulaso
1978	Did not qualify	1996	Racing Bo Dioulaso
1982	Did not qualify	**Women's League Champion**	
1986	Did not qualify	2004	ASF Gazelles
1990	Did not qualify	2003	Princess Ouagadougou
1994	Did not qualify	2002	Not Known
1998	Did not qualify	2001	Not Known
2002	Did not qualify	2000	Not Known

NATIONAL TEAM COLORS

WORLD PICTURES OF SOCCER

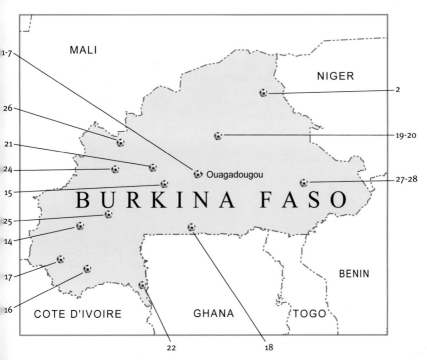

PREMIERE LEAGUE CLUBS	CITY	STADIUM	CAPACITY
1-Etoile Filante	Ouagadougou	Stade du 4 Aout	40 000
2-USFA	Ouagadougou	Stade du 4 Aout	40 000
3-ASFA Yennenga	Ouagadougou	Stade du 4 Aout	40 000
4-Rail Club Kadiogo	Ouagadougou	Stade Municipal	15 000
5-Santos FC	Ouagadougou	Stade Municipal	15 000
6-Union Sportive Ouaga	Ouagadougou	Stade Municipal	15 000
7-Etoile sportive Ouaga	Ouagadougou	Stade Manory	8 000
8-Racing Club BoBo	BoBo-Dioulasso	Stade Municipal	30 000
9-AS Fonctionnaires	Bobo-Dioulasso	Stade Municipal	30 000
10-USFRAN	BoBo-Dioulasso	Stade Wobi	10 000
11-Kiko FC	Bobo-Dioulasso	Stade Wobi	10 000
12-Les Scorpions FC	Bobo-Dioulasso	Stade Wobi	10 000
13-RC Bobo	Bobo-Dioulasso	Stade Wobi	10 000
14-AS Maya	Bobo-Dioulasso	Stade Municipal	30 000
15-ASEC Koudougou	Koudougou	Stade Balibie	
16-Rail Club de Kadio	Kadio		
17-USCO	Banfora		
18-Olympic Nahouri de Po	Po		
19-Equipe Provinciale de Nayala	Kaya		
20-Sanmatenga FC de Kaya	Kaya		
21-Lance FC de Reo	Reo		
22-US Batie	Batie		
23-Olympique Systeme	Dedougou		
24-Bankuy Sport	Dedougou		
25-Hounde FC	Hounde		
26-Sourou Sport	Tougan		
27-Nalambou FC	Fada N'Gourma		
28-Tidiany FC	Fada N'Gouma		
29-Dori FC	Dori		

BURUNDI

Fed. de Football du Burundi
1Bldg. Nyogozi, Boulevard de L'uprona
BP3426,Bujumbra
TEL 257/212 891   FAX257/242 892

Reference
Official name
Republic of Burundi
Date of formation 1962
Capital Bujumbura
Population 6.7 million
Total area 9903 sq Mi, 25,650 sq Km
Time zone GMT +2
Density 677 per sq Mi, 206 per sq Km
Languages Kirundi, French, Swahili,
Literacy rate 35%
Currency Franc
Economy agriculture 92%
Religions Catholic 60%,
traditional belief 39%
Ethnic Mix Hutu 85%, Tutsi 14%, Twa 1%

Geography
Elevation
lowest point: Lake Tanganyika 772 m
highest point: Mount Heha 2,670 m
Geography Note
landlocked; straddles crest of the Nile-
Congo watershed; the Kagera, which drains
into Lake Victoria, is the most remote headstream of the White Nile
Natural Resources
nickel, uranium, rareearth, cobalt,
copper, platinum, oxides, peat,
hydropower, arable land
Climate
average annual temperature varies with altitude from 23 to 17 degrees centigrade ; average annual rainfall is about 150 cm
Burundi Food
spinach potatoes

World Cup		Country League Champions	
1930	Did not qualify		
1934	Did not qualify		
1938	Did not qualify	2004	Atletico Olympique
1950	Did not qualify	2003	League Suspended
1954	Did not qualify	2002	Muzinga
1958	Did not qualify	2001	Prince Louis FC
1962	Did not qualify	2000	Vital'O
1966	Did not qualify	1999	Vital'O
1970	Did not qualify	1998	Vital'O
1974	Did not qualify	1997	Maniema
1978	Did not qualify	1996	Vital'O
1982	Did not qualify	**Women's League Champions**	
1986	Did not qualify	2004	Not Known
1990	Did not qualify	2003	Not Known
1994	Did not qualify	2002	Not Known
1998	Did not qualify	2001	Not Known
2002	Did not qualify	2000	Not Known

National Team Colors

World Pictures of Soccer

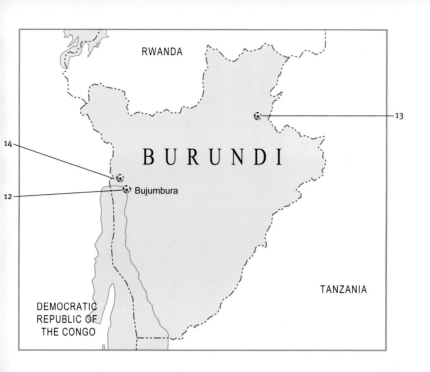

PREMIERE LEAGUE CLUBS	CITY	STADIUM	CAPACITY
1-Vital'O	Bujumbura	Prince Louis Rwagasore	22 000
2-Prince Louis FC	Bujumbura	Prince Louis Rwagasore	22 000
3-Fantastique	Bujumbura	Prince Louis Rwagasore	22 000
4-Burundi Sport Dynamic	Bujumbura	Prince Louis Rwagasore	22 000
5-Interstar	Bujumbura	Prince Louis Rwagasore	22 000
6-Atletico	Bujumbura	Prince Louis Rwagasore	22 000
7-Muzinga FC	Bujumbura	Prince Louis Rwagasore	22 000
8-Inter FC	Bujumbura	Prince Louis Rwagasore	22 000
9-Brother's Men	Bujumbura	Prince Louis Rwagasore	22 000
10-Elite FC	Bujumbura	Prince Louis Rwagasore	22 000
11-Universitaire Rumuri	Bujumbura	Prince Louis Rwagasore	22 000
12-Burundi direct	Bujumbura	Prince Louis Rwagasore	22 000
13-Muyinga FC	Muyinga		
14-Delta star	Gatumba		

CAMEROON

FED.CAMEROUNAISE DE FOOTBALL
BP 1116,Yaounde
TEL 237/221 0012 FAX 237/221 6662
WEB www.cameroon.fifa.com

REFERENCE
Official name
Republic of Cameroon

Date of formation 1961

Capital Yaounde

Population 15.1 million

Total area 179,691 sq Mi, 465,400 sq Km

Time zone GMT +1

Density 84 per sq Mi, 32 per sq Km

Languages English, French, Fang, Bulu, Yaunde, Duala, Mbum

Literacy rate 80%

Currency CFA Franc

Economy Services 98%, Industry 19%

Religions Catholic 35%, Traditional Belief 25%

Ethnic Mix Highlanders 31%, Equatorial Bantu 19%

GEOGRAPHY
Elevation
lowest point: Atlantic Ocean 0 m
highest point: Fako (on Cameroon
Mountain) 4,095 m

Geography Note
sometimes referred to as the hinge of Africa;
throughout the country there are areas of
thermal springs and indications of current or
prior volcanic activity; Mount Cameroon, the
highest mountain in Sub-Saharan west African

Natural Resources
petroleum, bauxite, iron ore, timber,
hydropower

Climate
varies with terrain, from tropical along coast to
semiarid and hot in north

Cameroon Food

WORLD CUP

1930	Did not qualify
1934	Did not qualify
1938	Did not qualify
1950	Did not qualify
1954	Did not qualify
1958	Did not qualify
1962	Did not qualify
1966	Did not qualify
1970	Did not qualify
1974	Did not qualify
1978	Did not qualify
1982	First round exit
1986	Did not qualify
1990	1/4 final exit
1994	First round exit
1998	First round exit
2002	First round exit

COUNTRY LEAGUE CHAMPIONS

2004	Cotonsport Garoua
2003	Cotonsport Garoua
2002	Canon Yaounde
2001	Cotonsport Garoua
2000	Fovu Baham
1999	Sable Batie
1998	Cotonsport Garoua
1997	Cotonsport Garoua
1996	Unisport Bafang
1995	RC bafoussam
1994	Aiglr Royale
1993	RC bafoussam

Women's League Champion

2004	Canon Yaounde
2003	Ngondi Nkam

NATIONAL TEAM COLORS

WORLD PICTURES OF SOCCER

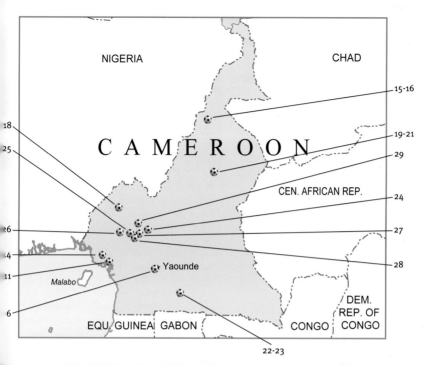

PREMIERE LEAGUE CLUBS	CITY	STADIUM	CAPACITY
-Canon Sportif	Yaounde	Omnispt.Ahmadou Ahidjo	60 000
-Tonnere Kalara Club	Yaounde	Omnispt.Ahmadou Ahidjo	60 000
-Olympic Mvolye	Yaounde	Omnispt.Ahmadou Ahidjo	60 000
-Prevoyance	Yaounde	Omnispt.Ahmadou Ahidjo	60 000
-Cintra	Yaounde	Omnispt.Ahmadou Ahidjo	60 000
-AS de la Mairie 1er	Yaounde	Omnispt.Ahmadou Ahidjo	60 000
-Union Sportive	Douala	Stade de la Reunification	35 000
-Caiman	Douala	Stade de la Reunification	35 000
-Dynamo Douala	Douala	Stade de la Reunification	35 000
ɔ-Port FC	Douala	Stade de la Reunification	35 000
-Kadji Sport Academy	Douala	Stade de la Reunification	35 000
ɔ-Mount Cameroon FC	Buea	Stade de Moliko	10 000
ɐ-Botafogo	Buea	Stade de Moliko	10 000
ɐ-Prison's	Buea	Stade de Moliko	10 000
ɐ-Cotonsport	Garoua	Omnispt. Poumpoum Rey	20 000
ɔ-Opep Cercle Sportif	Garoua	Omnispt. Poumpoum Rey	20 000
-PWD Bamenda	Bamenda	Municipal	10 000
ɪ-Free Boys	Bamenda	Municipal	10 000
ɔ-Girondins	Ngaoundere	Ndoumbe Oumar	10 000
ɔ-Olympic	Ngaoundere	Ndoumbe Oumar	10 000
-Universite	Ngaoundere	Ndoumbe Oumar	10 000
ɐ-Colombe	Sangmelima	Municipal	10 000
ɑ-Akon FC	Sangmelima	Municipal	10 000
ɐ-Panthere	Bangangte	Municipal	20 000
-Sable	Batie	Municipal de Batie	10 000
-Fovu Baham	Baham	Municipal de Baham	10 000
-Stade Bandjoun	Bandjoun	Fotso Victor	10 000
-Unisport Bafang	Bafang	Municipal	10 000
-Racing Bafoussam	Bafoussam	Municipalde Bamendzi	10 000

CAPE VERDE

FED.CAPVERDIENNE DEFOOTBALL
Oraia Cabo Verde,PO Box 234,234 Praia
TEL 238/611 362 FAX 238/611 362 WEB
www.cafonline.com

REFERENCE
Official name
   Republic of Cape Verde

Date of formation	1975
Capital	Praia
Population	428,000
Total area	1556 sq Mi, 4030 sq Km
Time zone	GMT -1
Density	275 per sq Mi, 100 sq Km
Languages	Portuguese, Creole
Literacy rate	70%
Currency	Escudo
Economy	agriculture 66%, services 20%
Religions	Catholic 97%
Ethnic Mix	Creole 60%, African 30%

GEOGRAPHY
Elevation
lowest point:
Atlantic Ocean 0 m
highest point:
Mt. Fogo 2,829 m (a volcano on Fogo Island)
Geography Note
strategic location 500 km from west coast of
Africa near major north-south sea routes;
important communications station; important sea and air refueling site
Natural Resources
salt, basalt rock, limestone, kaolin, fish
Climate
temperate; warm, dry summer; precipitation
meager and very erratic
Cape Verde Food
cachupa di cabo verde

WORLD CUP		COUNTRY LEAGUE CHAMPIONS	
1930	Did not qualify		
1934	Did not qualify		
1938	Did not qualify	2004	Sal Rei FC
1950	Did not qualify	2003	Academico do Sal
1954	Did not qualify	2002	SC da Praia Santiago
1958	Did not qualify	2001	Onze Unidos
1962	Did not qualify	2000	Derby FC
1966	Did not qualify	1999	GD Amarante
1970	Did not qualify	1998	CS Mindelense
1974	Did not qualify	1997	SC da Praia Santiago
1978	Did not qualify	1996	CD Travadores
1982	Did not qualify	**Women's League Champion**	
1986	Did not qualify	2004	Not Known
1990	Did not qualify	2003	Not Known
1994	Did not qualify	2002	Not Known
1998	Did not qualify	2001	Not Known
2002	Did not qualify	2000	Not Known

NATIONAL TEAM COLORS

WORLD PICTURES OF SOCCER

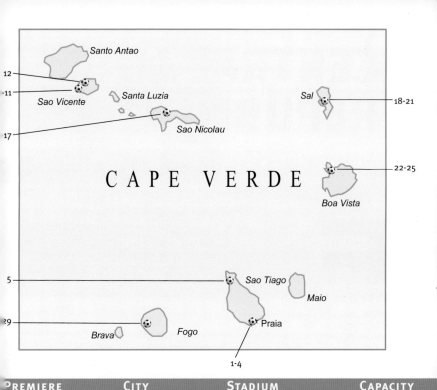

Premiere League Clubs	City	Stadium	Capacity
1-Sporting Praia	Praia/Sao tiago	Estadio da Varza	8 000
2-FC Boavista	Praia/Sao tiago	Estadio da Varza	8 000
3-CD Travadores	Praia/Sao tiago	Estadio da Varza	8 000
4-Academica de Praia	Praia/Sao tiago	Estadio da Varza	8 000
5-Barcelona	Tarrafal/Sao tiago	Estadio da Varza	8 000
6-GD Amarante	Mindelo/Sao Vicente	Estadio Mun.Aderito Sena	5 000
7-Academica	Mindelo/Sao Vicente	Estadio Mun.Aderito Sena	5 000
8-CS mindelense	Mindelo/Sao Vicente	Estadio Mun.Aderito Sena	5 000
9-AA do Mindelo	Mindelo/Sao Vicente	Estadio Mun.Aderito Sena	5 000
10-GS Castilho	Mindelo/Sao Vicente	Estadio Mun.Aderito Sena	5 000
11-Derby FC	Mindelo/Sao Vicente	Estadio Mun.Aderito Sena	5 000
12-Batuque FC	Madeiral/Sao Vicente		
13-FC Ultramarina	Tarrafal/Sao Nicolau	Joao de Deus Lopes Silva	5 000
14-SC Atletico	Sao Nicolau	Joao de Deus Lopes Silva	5 000
15-FC Belo Horizonte	Sao Nicolau		
16-FC Praia Branca	Sao Nicolau		
17-FCTalho	Sao Nicolau		
18-Academica	Espargos/Sal	Estadio Marcelo Leitao	5 000
19-Academico do Sal	Sal		
20-Santa Maria	Sal		
21-Palmeira	Sal		
22-Academica	Sal Rei/Boa vista		
23-Sanjoanse	Boa Vista		
24-Desportivo	Boa Vista		
25-Africa show	Boa Vista		
26-Botafogo	Sao Felipe/Fogo		
27-Vulcanicos	Sao Felipe/Fogo		
28-ABC de Patim	Sao Felipe/Fogo		
29-Desp. Cova Figueira	Sao Felipe/Fogo		

CENTRAL AFRICAN REPUBLIC

FED.CENTRAFRICAINE DE FOOTBALL
PO Box 344,Bangui
TEL 236/619 545 FAX 236/615660
WEB www.cafonline.com

REFERENCE
Official name
Central African Republic

Date of formation	1960
Capital	Bangui
Population	3.3 million
Total area	240,532 sq Mi, 622,980 sq Km
Time zone	GMT +1
Density	15 per sq Mi, 5 per sq Km
Languages	French, Sango, Banda
Literacy rate	58%
Currency	CFA Franc
Economy	agriculture 85%
Religions	traditional belief 60%,Christian 35%, Muslim 5%
Ethnic Mix	Baya 34%,Banda 27%, Mandjia 21%, Sara 10%,

GEOGRAPHY
Elevation
lowest point: Oubangui River 335 m
highest point: Mont Ngaoui 1,420 m
Geography Note
landlocked; almost the precise center of Africa
Natural Resources
diamonds, uranium, timber, gold, oil, hydropower
Climate
tropical; hot, dry winters; mild to hot, wet summers
Centrral African Republic Food
liboka/bidia/mbika/spinach stew

WORLD CUP		COUNTRY LEAGUE CHAMPIONS	
1930	Did not qualify		
1934	Did not qualify		
1938	Did not qualify	2004	Olympic Real bangui
1950	Did not qualify	2003	AS Tempete
1954	Did not qualify	2002	Discontinued
1958	Did not qualify	2001	Olympic Real bangui
1962	Did not qualify	2000	Olympic Real bangui
1966	Did not qualify	1999	Not Known
1970	Did not qualify	1998	Discontinued
1974	Did not qualify	1997	AS Tempete
1978	Did not qualify	1996	AS Tempete
1982	Did not qualify	**Women's League Champion**	
1986	Did not qualify	2004	Not Known
1990	Did not qualify	2003	Not Known
1994	Did not qualify	2002	Not Known
1998	Did not qualify	2001	Zarasclo Bangui
2002	Did not qualify	2000	Zarasclo Bangui

NATIONAL TEAM COLORS

WORLD PICTURES OF SOCCER

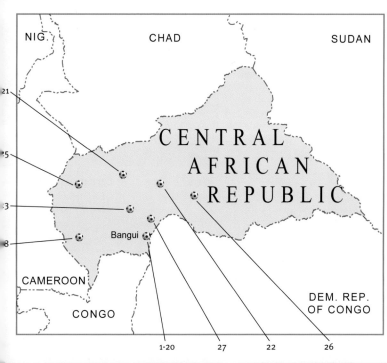

PREMIERE LEAGUE CLUBS	CITY	STADIUM	CAPACITY
Olympic Real Castel	Bangui	Barthelemy Boganda	12 000
-AS Tempete Mocaf	Bangui	Barthelemy Boganda	12 000
-SCAF	Bangui	Barthelemy Boganda	12 000
-ASOPT	Bangui	Barthelemy Boganda	12 000
-Les Anges de Fatima	Bangui	Barthelemy Boganda	12 000
-CS Plateau	Bangui	Barthelemy Boganda	12 000
-USCA Bangui	Bangui	Barthelemy Boganda	12 000
-M'Poko Sports	Bangui	Bangui M'Poko Field	10 000
US Centreafricaine	Bangui	Bangui M'Poko Field	10 000
-Abeilles centreafricaine	Bangui	Bangui M'Poko Field	10 000
-DFC-8	Bangui	Bangui M'Poko Field	10 000
-AC Real Bangui	Bangui	Bangui M'Poko Field	10 000
-ASFA	Bangui	Bangui M'Poko Field	10 000
-FCDN	Bangui	Bangui M'Poko Field	10 000
-Kemo FC	Bangui	Bangui M'Poko Field	10 000
-Lobaye	Bangui	Bangui M'Poko Field	10 000
-AS Petroca	Bangui	Bangui M'Poko Field	10 000
-Esperance du 5eme	Bangui	Bangui M'Poko Field	10 000
-US Catin	Bangui	Bangui M'Poko Field	10 000
-FACA	Bangui	Bangui M'Poko Field	10 000
-M'Bakara	Bossangoa		
-Ouaka	Sibut	Municipal Sibut	
-Ouham-Pende	Bossembele		
-Sangha-Mbaere	Bouar		
-Mambere Kadei	Bouar		
-Basse-Kotto	Bambari	Municipal Bambari	
-FC Tigres	Begoua		
-Berberati FC	Berberati	Municipal Berberati	

CHAD

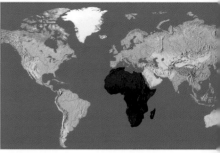

FED. CHADIENNE DE FOOTBALL
BP 886, N'Djamena
TEL 235/518 740   FAX 235/518 648
WEB www.cafonline.com

REFERENCE
Official name
  Republic Of Chad
**Date of
formation**   1960
Capital   Ndjamena
Population   7.7 million
Total area   496,177 sq Mi, 1,259,200 sq Km
Time zone   GMT +1
Density   16 per sq Mi, 6 per sq Km
Languages   French, Sara, Maba
Literacy rate   47%
Currency   CFA Franc
Economy   agriculture 85%, services &
                    Industry 15%
Religions   Muslim 50%, traditional beliefs
                    43%, Christian 7%
Ethnic Mix   Nomads Tuareg & Toubou 38%,
                    Sara 30%, Arab 15%

GEOGRAPHY
Elevation
lowest point:
Djourab Depression 160 m
highest point:
Emi Koussi 3,415 m
Geography Note
landlocked; Lake Chad is the most significant water body in the Sahel
Natural Resources
petroleum (unexploited but exploration
under way), uranium, natron, kaolin, fish
(Lake Chad)
Climate
tropical in south, desert in north
Chad Food
squash with peanuts/sweet potatoes salad

WORLD CUP

1930	Did not qualify
1934	Did not qualify
1938	Did not qualify
1950	Did not qualify
1954	Did not qualify
1958	Did not qualify
1962	Did not qualify
1966	Did not qualify
1970	Did not qualify
1974	Did not qualify
1978	Did not qualify
1982	Did not qualify
1986	Did not qualify
1990	Did not qualify
1994	Did not qualify
1998	Did not qualify
2002	Did not qualify

COUNTRY LEAGUE CHAMPIONS

2004	No Competition
2003	Renaissance FC
2002	No Competititon
2001	FC Tourbillon
2000	FC Tourbillon
1999	Renaissance FC
1998	AS Coton Chad
1997	FC Tourbillon
1996	AS Coton Chad
Women's League Champion	
2004	Not Known
2003	Not Known
2002	Not Known
2001	Not Known
2000	Not Known

NATIONAL TEAM COLORS

WORLD PICTURES OF SOCCER

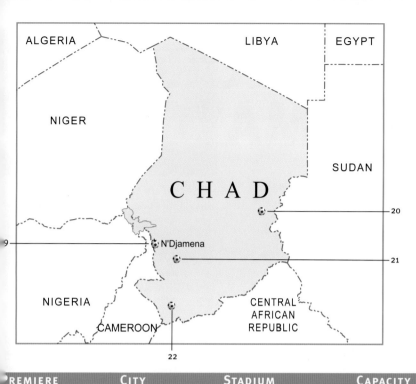

PREMIERE LEAGUE CLUBS	CITY	STADIUM	CAPACITY
FC Tourbillon	N'Djamena	Stade National N'Djamena	20 000
Renaissance FC	N'Djamena	Stade National N'Djamena	20 000
AS Coton Chad	N'Djamena	Stade National N'Djamena	20 000
Postel 2000	N'Djamena	Stade National N'Djamena	20 000
Tout Puissant Elect Sport	N'Djamena	Stade National N'Djamena	20 000
Gazelle	N'Djamena	Stade National N'Djamena	20 000
AS GSP	N'Djamena	Stade National N'Djamena	20 000
AS Kaleta	N'Djamena	Stade National N'Djamena	20 000
BFC	N'Djamena	Stade National N'Djamena	20 000
-Satellite	N'Djamena	Stade National N'Djamena	20 000
ASV N'Djamena	N'Djamena	Stade National N'Djamena	20 000
-Brande	N'Djamena	Stade National N'Djamena	20 000
-AS Douth	N'Djamena	Stade National N'Djamena	20 000
-AS Sahel	N'Djamena	Stade National N'Djamena	20 000
-USM	N'Djamena	Stade National N'Djamena	20 000
Africa Sport	N'Djamena	Stade National N'Djamena	20 000
AS Police N'Djamena	N'Djamena	Stade National N'Djamena	20 000
-AS Mairie	N'Djamena	Stade National N'Djamena	20 000
Elect sport N'Djamena	N'Djamena	Stade National N'Djamena	20 000
Renaissance	Abeche		
Massinya	Massenya		
-AS Moundou	Moundou		

COMOROS & MAYOTTE

FED. COMOROS DE FOOTBALL
PB #1006, Moroni, Comoros Island
TEL   FAX
WEB www.cafonline.com

REFERENCE
Official name
Federal Islamic Republic
of the Comoros

Date of
formation   1975
Capital   Moroni
Population   694,000
Total area   861 sq Mi, 2230 sq Km
Time zone   GMT +3
Density   806 per sq Mi, 259 per sq Km
Languages   Arabic, French, Comoran
Literacy rate   57%
Currency   Franc
Economy   Agriculture 80
Religions   Sunni Muslim 98%
Ethnic Mix   Comorian 97%, Makua 2%,

GEOGRAPHY
Elevation
lowest point: Indian Ocean 0 m
highest point: Le Kartala 2,360 m
Geography Note
important location at northern end of
Mozambique Channel
Natural Resources
vanilla and cloves
Climate
tropical marine; rainy season (November to
May)
Comoros Food
chicken with coconut, carrot and mashed
potatoes

WORLD CUP

1930	Did not qualify
1934	Did not qualify
1938	Did not qualify
1950	Did not qualify
1954	Did not qualify
1958	Did not qualify
1962	Did not qualify
1966	Did not qualify
1970	Did not qualify
1974	Did not qualify
1978	Did not qualify
1982	Did not qualify
1986	Did not qualify
1990	Did not qualify
1994	Did not qualify
1998	Did not qualify
2002	Did not qualify

COUNTRY LEAGUE CHAMPIONS

2004	Etoile D'or
2003	Volcan FC
2002	Etoile du Sud
2001	Rapid Club
2000	Apache de Mitsam.
1999	Not Known
1998	US Zlimadjou
1997	Not Known
1996	Not Known

Women's League Champio

2004	Not Known
2003	Not Known
2002	Not Known
2001	Not Known
2000	Not Known

NATIONAL TEAM COLORS

WORLD PICTURES OF SOCCER

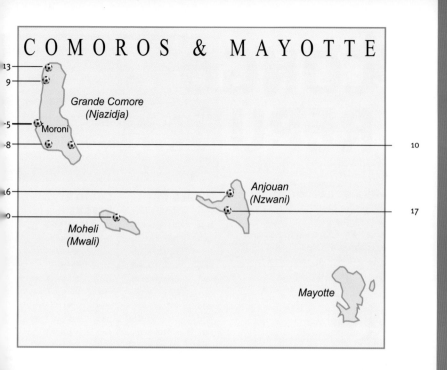

COMOROS & MAYOTTE

Grande Comore
(Njazidja)

Moroni

Anjouan
(Nzwani)

Moheli
(Mwali)

Mayotte

PREMIERE LEAGUE CLUBS	CITY	STADIUM	CAPACITY
Rapid	Moroni/Grand Comore	Stade de Baumer	
Bresil	Moroni/Grand Comore	Stade de Baumer	
Volcan Club	Moroni/Grand Comore	Stade de Baumer	
Nouvelle Vague	Moroni/Grand Com.	Stade de Baumer	
Etoile du Sud	Moroni/Grand Comore	Stade de Baumer	
Papillon Bleu	Misoud./Grand Comore	Stade Ajao	
Elan	Mitsoudje/Grand Comore	Stade Ajao	
JACM	Mitsoudje/Grand Comore	Stade Ajao	
US Zilimadjou	Grand Comore	Stade Ajao	
Avenir Comoros	Foumbouni/Gr.Co	Stade Ajao	
Coin Nord	Mitsamiouli/Grand Com.		
Apache	Mitsamiouli/Grand Comore		
Excellent	Mitsamiouli/Grand Comore		
Citadelle	Mutsamudu/Anjouan		
Groupe Choc	Mutsamudu/Anjouan		
Gambessa	Mutsamudu/Anjouan		
Le Gombessa FC	Pomoni/Anjouan		
Fomboni Club	Fomboni/Moheli	Stade de Fombonilors	
Etoile du sud	Fomboni/Moheli	Stade de Fombonilors	
Belle Lumiere Mdjoezi	Fomboni/M.	Stade de Fombonilors	

CONGO REPUBLIC

FED.CONGOLAISE DE FOOTBALL
180, Rue Eugenne Etienne, Centre Ville
BP 4041, Brazzaville
TEL 242/812 524 FAX 242/812 524
WEB www.cafonline.com

REFERENCE
Official name
The Republic of Congo

Dare of formation	1960
Capital	Brazzaville
Population	2.9 million
Total area	131,853 sq Mi, 341 sq Km
Time zone	GMT +1
Density	22 per sq Mi, 8 per sq Km
Languages	French,Kongo
Literacy rate	74%
Currency	CFA Franc
Economy	Agriculture 75%,Industry & Services 25%
Religions	Traditional 50%,Catholic 25%,Protestant 23%, Muslim 2%
Ethnic Mix	Bakongo 48%,Sangha 20%,Teke 17%,Mboshi 12%

GEOGRAPHY
Elevation
lowest point: Atlantic Ocean 0 m
highest point: Pic Marguerite on Mont
Ngaliema (Mount Stanley) 5,110 m
Geography Note
about 70% of the population lives in
Brazzaville & Pointe-Noire
Natural Resources
oil, timber, potash, lead, zinc, uranium, copper, phosphates, natural gas, hydropower
Climate
tropical; rainy season (March to June); dry
season (June to October); constantly high
temperatures and humidity; particularly
enervating climate astride the Equator
Congo Republic Food
chicken cumin sauce/capitaine in palm oil

WORLD CUP

1930	Did not qualify
1934	Did not qualify
1938	Did not qualify
1950	Did not qualify
1954	Did not qualify
1958	Did not qualify
1962	Did not qualify
1966	Did not qualify
1970	Did not qualify
1974	Did not qualify
1978	Did not qualify
1982	Did not qualify
1986	Did notqualify
1990	Did not qualify
1994	Did not qualify
1998	Did not qualify
2002	Did not qualify

COUNTRY LEAGUE CHAMPIONS

2004	Diables Noirs
2003	Saint Michel Ouenze
2002	AS Police
2001	Etoile du Congo
2000	Etoile du Congo
1999	Vita Club Mokanda
1998	Vita Club Mokanda
1997	Munisport
1996	Munisport

Women's League Champion

2004	FCF La Source
2003	FCF La Source
2002	FCF La Source
2001	FCF La Source
2000	FCF La Source

NATIONAL TEAM COLORS

WORLD PICTURES OF SOCCER

PREMIERE LEAGUE CLUBS	CITY	STADIUM	CAPACITY
Etoile du Congo	Brazaville	Stade de la Revolution	50 000
Union Sport Mbingui	Brazaville	Stade de la Revolution	50 000
Saint Michel de Ouenze	Brazaville	Stade de la Revolution	50 000
As Police	Brazaville	CS Alphonso Massamba	30 000
CARA	Brazaville	Stade Marchand	30 000
Diables Noirs	Brazaville	Stade Marchand	30 000
Jeunesse Sportive	Brazaville	Stade Marchand	30 000
Patronage Saint-Anne	Brazaville	Stade Marchand	30 000
Kotoko MFOA	Brazaville	Stade Marchand	30 000
Vita Club Mokanda	Point-Noire	Stade MunicipalP-N	30 000
AS Cheminots	Pointe-Noire	Stade MunicipalP-N	30 000
Pigeon Vert	Pointe-Noire	Stade MunicipalP-N	30 000
JS Bougaivillee	Pointe-Noire	Stade MunicipalP-N	30 000
La Mancha	Pointe-Noire	Stade MunicipalP-N	30 000
Munisport	Pointe-Noire	Stade MunicipalP-N	30 000
Nico-Nicoye	Pointe Noire	Stade MunicipalP-N	30 000
Electsport	Nkayi		
Olympique	Nkayi		
Inter Club	Ouesso		
Socobois de Dolisie	Niari		
AC Leopards de Dolisie	Niari		
Abeilles FC	Lekena		
CARA Lekena	Djambala		

COTE D'IVOIRE

Fed. Ivoirienne de Football
01 BP 1408, Abidjan 01
TEL 225/2124 0027 FAX 225/2135 7659
WEB www.cafonline.com

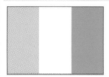

Reference
Official name
 Republic of cote D'Ivoire

Date of formation	1960
Capital	Yamoussoukro
Population	14.8 million
Total area	122,780 sq Mi, 318,000 sq Km
Time zone	GMT 0
Density	121 per sq Mi, 49 per sq Km
Languages	French, Akran
Literacy rate	40%
Currency	CFA Franc
Economy	agriculture 70%, services 25%, Industry 5%
Religions	traditional beliefs 63%,Muslim 25%, Christian 12%
Ethnic Mix	Baoule 23%, Bete 18%, Senufo 15%

Geography
Elevation
lowest point: Gulf of Guinea 0 m
highest point: Mont Nimba 1,752 m

Geography Note
most of the inhabitants live along the sandy coastal region; apart from the capital area, the forested interior is sparsely populated

Natural Resources
petroleum, natural gas, diamonds, manganese, iron ore, cobalt, bauxite, copper, hydropower

Climate
tropical along coast, semiarid in far north; three seasons - warm and dry (November to March), hot and dry (March to May), hot and wet (June to October)

Ivory Coast Food
kedjenou/aloko

WORLD CUP		COUNTRY LEAGUE CHAMPIONS	
1930	Did not qualify		
1934	Did not qualify		
1938	Did not qualify	2004	ASEC
1950	Did not qualify	2003	ASEC
1954	Did not qualify	2002	ASEC
1958	Did not qualify	2001	ASEC
1962	Did not qualify	2000	ASEC
1966	Did not qualify	1999	Africa Sports
1970	Did not qualify	1998	ASEC
1974	Did not qualify	1997	ASEC
1978	Did not qualify	1996	Africa Sports
1982	Did not qualify	**Women's League Champio**	
1986	Did not qualify	2004	Juventus Yopoungo
1990	Did not qualify	2003	Juventus Yopoungo
1994	Did not qualify	2002	Juventus Yopoungo
1998	Did not qualify	2001	Juventus Yopoungo
2002	Quarter Final exit	2000	Juventus Yopoungo

National Team Colors

World Pictures of Soccer

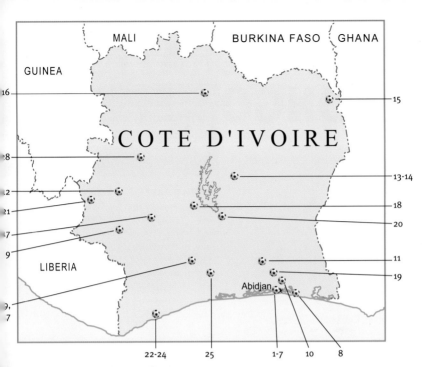

PREMIERE LEAGUE CLUBS	CITY	STADIUM	CAPACITY
-ASEC	Abidjan	Stade Houphout Boigny	30 000
-Africa Sport	Abidjan	Stade Houphout Boigny	30 000
-Stade	Abidjan	Stade Houphout Boigny	30 000
-Stella	Abidjan	Stade Robert Champroux	15 000
-Jeunesse Club	Abidjan	Stade Robert Champroux	15 000
-Satellite FC	Abidjan	Stade Robert Champroux	15 000
-Cosmos FC	Abidjan	Stade Robert Champroux	15 000
-Onze Frere	Bassam		
-SC Gagnoa	Gagnoa		
ɔ-Stella Club D'Adjame	Adjame		
1-FC Toumodi	Toumodi		
2-FC Man	Man		
3-Alliance	Bouake	Stade de Bouake	20 000
4-ASC Bouake	Bouake	Stade de Bouake	20 000
5-Sabe Sport	Bouna	Stade Grand Lahou	10 000
6-CO Korhogo	Korhogo	Sztade de Bonoua	10 000
7-Reveil Club Daloa	Daloa		
3-CO Bouafle	Bouafle		
ɔ-Rio Sport D'Anyama	Anyama		
ɔ-US Yamoussoukro	Yamoussoukro		
1-Ban FC de Danane	Danane		
2-Sewe de San Pedro	San Pedro	Municipal San Pedro	10 000
3-COSAP de San Pedro	San Pedro	Municipal San Pedro	10 000
4-Sirocco de San Pedro	San Pedro	Municipal San Pedro	10 000
5-Makan FC	Divo		
6-SC de Gagnoa	Gagnoa		
7-Mogan FC	Gagnoa		
3-Siguilolo de Seguela	Seguela		
ɔ-Nicla Sport de Guiglo	Guilo		

137

DEMOCRATIC CONGO REPUBLIC

FED.CONGOLAISE DE FOOTBALL
Av. de L'enseignemt 210, c/kasa vubu, Kinshasa
TEL 243/993 9635 FAX
WEB www.cafonline.com

WORLD CUP		COUNTRY LEAGUE CHAMPIONS	
1930	Did not qualify		
1934	Did not qualify		
1938	Did not qualify	2004	DC Motemba Pembe
1950	Did not qualify	2003	AS Vita Club
1954	Did not qualify	2002	FC Lupopo
1958	Did not qualify	2001	TP Mazembe
1962	Did not qualify	2000	TP Mazembe
1966	Did not qualify	1999	DC Motemba Pemba
1970	Did not qualify	1998	DC Motemba Pemba
1974	Did not qualify	1997	AS Vita
1978	Did not qualify	1996	DC Motemba Pemba
1982	Did not qualify	**Women's League Champion**	
1986	Did notqualify	2004	Not Known
1990	Did not qualify	2003	Grand Hotel FC
1994	Did not qualify	2002	Not Known
1998	Did not qualify	2001	Not Known
2002	Did not qualify	2000	Not Known

REFERENCE
Official name
Democratic Republic of Congo

Date of formation	1960
Capital	Kinshasa
Population	51.7 Million
Total area	875,520 sq Mi, 2,267,600 sq Km
Time zone	GMT +1/2
Density	59 per sq Mi, 21 per sq Km
Languages	French, Kiswahili, Tshiluba, Kikongo, Lingala
Literacy rate	76%
Currency	Congolese Franc
Economy	Agriculture72%, Services 15%, Industry 13%
Religions	Traditional 50%, Christian 50%
Ethnic Mix	Mix Bantu & Hamitic 45%

GEOGRAPHY
Elevation
lowest point:
Atlantic Ocean 0 m
highest point:
Mount Berongou 903 m
Geography Note
Straddles Equator; has very narrow strip of land that controls the lower Congo River and is only outlet to South Atlantic Ocean; dense tropical rain forest in central river basin
Natural Resources
cobalt, copper, cadmium, petroleum, industrial and gem diamonds, gold, silver, zinc, manganese, tin, germanium, uranium, radium, bauxite, iron ore, coal, hydropower, timber
Climate
tropical; hot and humid in equatorial river basin; cooler and drier in southern highlands; cooler and wetter in eastern highlands
Congo Republic Food
liboka/mbika

NATIONAL TEAM COLORS

WORLD PICTURES OF SOCCER

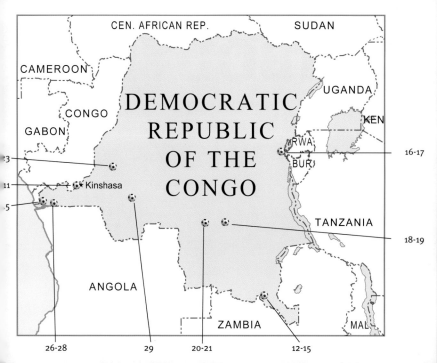

PREMIERE LEAGUE CLUBS	CITY	STADIUM	CAPACITY
AS Vita Club	Kinshasa	Stade Des martyrs	80 000
DC Motema Pembe	Kinshasa	Stade Des martyrs	80 000
AS Bilima	Kinshasa	Stade Des martyrs	80 000
AS Dragons	Kinshasa	Stade Des martyrs	80 000
Kintambo	Kinshasa	Stade Municipal	20 000
Kin City FC	Kinshasa	Stade Municipal	20 000
CS Style du Congo	Kinshasa	Stade Municipal	20 000
Utexafrica	Kinshasa	Stade Municipal	20 000
FC Spartak Ajeb	Kinshasa	Stade Municipal	20 000
AS Sodigraf	Kinshasa	Stade Municipal	20 000
Kinshasa City FC	Kinshasa	Stade Municipal	20 000
FC Lupopo	Lubumbashi	Municipal Lubumbashi	37 000
TP Mazembe	Lubumbashi	Municipal Lubumbashi	37 000
FC Saint Eloi Lupopo	Lubumbashi	Municipal Lubumbashi	37 000
Lubumbashi Sport	Lubumbashi	Municipal Lubumbashi	37 000
OC Bukavu Dawa	Bukavu	Stade de Kadutu	25 000
OC Muungano	Bukavu	Stade de Kadutu	25 000
SM Sanga Balende	Mbuji-Mayi	Stade Tshikasi	20 000
Mbongo Sport	Mbuji-Mayi	Stade Tshikasi	20 000
US Tshinkunku	Kananga		
AS Saint Luc	Kananga		
CS Matiti Mabe	Bandandu		
FC Kivunka	Bandundu		
AS Vuvu	Boma		
Entente de Boma	Boma		
Entente Urbaine de Matadi	Matadi		
FC Tonnerre	Matadi		
IC Onatra	Matadi		
AS Vutuka	Kikwit		

DJIBOUTI

FED. DJIBOUTIENNE DE FOOTBALL
BP 2964, Djibouti
TEL 253/341 964 FAX 253/341 063
WEB www.cafonline.com

REFERENCE
Official name
Republic of Djibouti
Date of formation 1977
Capital Djibouti
Population 638,000
Total area 8949 sq Mi, 23,180 sq Km
Time zone GMT +3
Density 71 per sq Mi, 20 per sq Km
Languages Arabic, French, Somali, Afar
Literacy rate 45%
Currency Franc
Economy services 45%, agriculture 14%
Religions Sunni Muslim 94%, Christian 6%
Ethnic Mix Issa 60%, Afar 35%

GEOGRAPHY
Elevation
lowest point: Lac Assal -155 m
highest point: Moussa Ali 2,028 m
Geography Note
strategic location near world's busiest shipping lanes and close to Arabian oilfields; terminus of rail traffic into Ethiopia; mostly wasteland; Lac Assal (Lake Assal) is the lowest point in Africa
Natural Resources
geothermal areas
Climate
desert; torrid, dry
Djibouti Food
mushroom pickles/fish Lemon grille

WORLD CUP

1930	Did not qualify
1934	Did not qualify
1938	Did not qualify
1950	Did not qualify
1954	Did not qualify
1958	Did not qualify
1962	Did not qualify
1966	Did not qualify
1970	Did not qualify
1974	Did not qualify
1978	Did not qualify
1982	Did not qualify
1986	Did not qualify
1990	Did not qualify
1994	Did not qualify
1998	Did not qualify
2002	Did not qualify

COUNTRY LEAGUE CHAMPIONS

2002	AS Boreh
2001	FNP Djibouti
2000	CDA Djibouti
1999	FNS djibouti
1998	Not known
1997	Not Known
1996	FNP Djibouti
1995	FNP Djibouti
1994	FNS Djibouti

Women's League Champion

2003	Bis Mer Rouge
2002	Bis Mer Rouge
2001	Bis Mer Rouge
2000	Bis Mer Rouge

NATIONAL TEAM COLORS

WORLD PICTURES OF SOCCER

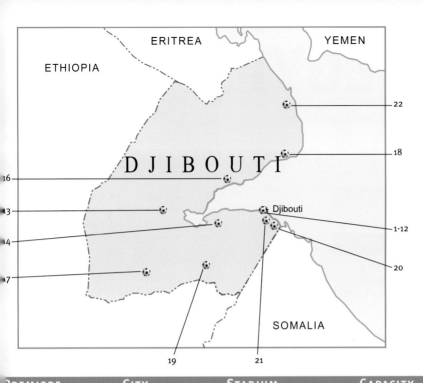

PREMIERE LEAGUE CLUBS	CITY	STADIUM	CAPACITY
-Force National de Police	Djibouti	Hadj Hassan Gouled Apti	10 000
-Aeroport	Djibouti	Hadj Hassan Gouled Apti	10 000
-AS Marill	Djibouti	Hadj Hassan Gouled Apti	10 000
-ASC Djibouti-Ethiopie	Djibouti	Stade de Ville Djibouti	10 000
-Gendarmerie Nationale	Djibouti	Stade de Ville Djibouti	10 000
-Chemin de Fer	Djibouti	Stade de Ville Djibouti	10 000
-Jeunesse Espoir	Djibouti	Stade de Ville Djibouti	10 000
-AS Port	Djibouti	Stade de Ville Djibouti	10 000
-Shell Djibouti	Djibouti	Stade de Ville Djibouti	10 000
o-ONT Balbala	Djibouti		
ı-Fratacci	Djibouti		
2-AC Balbala	Djibouti		
3-Sabieh	Assajog		
4-Osman Darar	Arta		
5-Djib-Telecom	Tadjoura		
5-Tadjoura FC	Tadjoura		
7-Dikhil FC	Dikhil		
3-Obock FC	Obock		
ɔ-AS Ali sabieh	Ali Sabieh		
o-AS Loyada	Loyada		
ı-Jeunesse Damerdjog	Damerdjog		
2-Port	Khor Angar		

# EGYPT

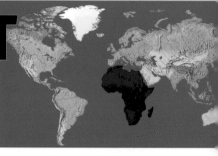

EGYPTIAN FOOTBALL ASSOC.
5, Gabalaya street, Gezira
El Borg Post Office, Cairo
TEL 20-2/735 1793 FAX 20-2/736 7817
WEB www.efa.com.eg

REFERENCE
Official name
  Arab republic of Egypt

Date of formation	1936
Capital	Cairo
Population	68.5 million
Total area	384 sq Mi, 995,450 sq Km
Time zone	GMT +2
Density	178 per sq Mi, 67 per sq Km
Languages	Arabic, French, English
Literacy rate	51%
Currency	Egyptian Pound
Economy	Services 55%, Agriculture 34%
Religions	Sunni Muslim94%, Coptic Christian3%
Ethnic Mix	Eastern Hamitic 90%,Nubian 5%

GEOGRAPHY
Elevation
lowest point: Qattara Depression -133 m
highest point: Mount Catherine 2,629 m

Geography Note
controls Sinai Peninsula, only land bridge
between Africa and remainder of Eastern
Hemisphere; controls Suez Canal, shortest
sea link between Indian Ocean and
Mediterranean Sea.

Natural Resources
petroleum, natural gas, iron ore, phosphates, manganese, limestone, gypsum,
talc, asbestos, lead, zinc

Climate
desert; hot,dry summers with moderate
winters

Egyptian Food
Egyptian kefta/yemiser selatta/dukkau

WORLD CUP

1930	Did not qualify
1934	First round exit
1938	Did not qualify
1950	Did not qualify
1954	Did not qualify
1958	Did not qualify
1962	Did not qualify
1966	Did not qualify
1970	Did not qualify
1974	Did not qualify
1978	Did not qualify
1982	Did not qualify
1986	Did not qualify
1990	First round exit
1994	Did not qualify
1998	Did not qualify
2002	Did not qualify

COUNTRY LEAGUE CHAMPIONS

2005	Al-Ahly
2004	Zamalek
2003	Zamalek
2002	Ismaily
2001	Zamalek
2000	Al Ahly
1999	Al Ahly
1998	Al Ahly
1997	Al Ahly

Women's League Champion

2004	Semoutha
2003	Goldi
2002	Maaden LFC
2001	Maaden LFC
2000	Maaden LFC

NATIONAL TEAM COLORS

WORLD PICTURES OF SOCCER

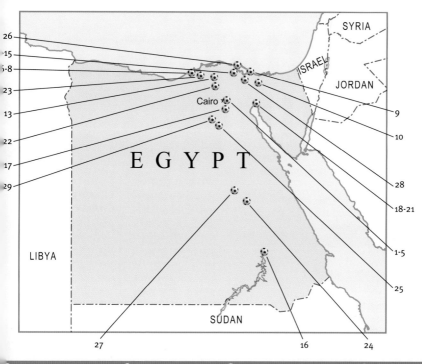

PREMIERE LEAGUE CLUBS	CITY	STADIUM	CAPACITY
-Zamalek	Cairo	Zamalek-Hassan Helmi	40 000
-Al-Ahly	Cairo	Mokhtar el Tetch	20 000
-ENPPI	Cairo	Cairo Stadium	50 000
Mazarea Dina	Cairo	Cairo Stadium	50 000
-Mokawloon-El Arab	Cairo	Arab Contractor Stadium	60 000
-Ittihad	Alexandria	Alexandria Stadium	22 500
-Sawahel	Alexandria	Alexandria Stadium	22 500
Koroum	Alexandria	Alexandria Stadium	22 500
-Al-Masry	Port Said	Port Said Stadium	30 000
-Ismaily	Ismailiya	Ismailiya Stadium	30 000
-Baladiyyat	Al-Mahalla	El Mahalla Stadium	20 000
-Ghazl	Al-Mahalla	El Mahalla Stadium	20 000
-Al Mahalla Fillery	Al Mahalla	El Mahalla Stadium	20 000
-Mansura	Al-Mansura	Al Mansura Stadium	20 000
-Baladia	Al-Mansura	Al Mansura Stadium	20 000
-Aswan	Aswan	Aswan Stadium	20 000
-Al-Tersa	Tersa	Mit Okba Stadium	25 000
-Gahzl Al Suez	Suez		
-Suez Fillery	Suez		
-Suez FC	Suez		
-Qanat	Suez	Suez Canal Stadium	30 000
-Tanta	Tanta		
-Damanhur	Damanhur		
-Aluminum	Naja Hammadi		
-Bani Suwayf	Bani Suwayf		
-Dumyat	Dumyat		
-Sohag	Sohag-Suhaj		
-Sharquiya	Zaqaziq	Sharkya Stadium	20 000
-Al Fayyum	Al Fayyum		

EQUATORIAL GUINEA

FED. ECUATOGUINEA DEFUTBOL

Patricio lumumba, 1071 Malabo
Stadium
TEL 240-9/2257 FAX 240-92257
WEB www.cafonline.com

REFERENCE
Official name
Republic Equatorial Guinea

Date of formation	1968
Capital	Malabo
Population	453,000
Total area	10,830 sq Mi, 28,050 sq Km
Time zone	GMT +1
Density	42 per sq Mi, 16 per sq Km
Languages	Spanish,Fang
Literacy rate	51%
Currency	CFA Franc
Economy	agriculture 64%, services 24%
Religions	Catholic 89%
Ethnic Mix	Fang 85%, Bubi 4%

GEOGRAPHY
Elevation
lowest point: Atlantic Ocean o m
highest point: Pico Basile 3,008 m
Geography Note
insular and continental regions rather widely
separated Eritrea
Natural Resources
oil, petroleum, timber, small unexploited
deposits of gold, manganese, uranium
Climate
tropical; always hot, humid
Equatorial Food
salsa of peanuts with chicken

WORLD CUP

1930	Did not qualify
1934	Did not qualify
1938	Did not qualify
1950	Did not qualify
1954	Did not qualify
1958	Did not qualify
1962	Did not qualify
1966	Did not qualify
1970	Did not qualify
1974	Did not qualify
1978	Did not qualify
1982	Did not qualify
1986	Did not qualify
1990	Did not qualify
1994	Did not qualify
1998	Did not qualify
2002	Did not qualify

COUNTRY LEAGUE CHAMPIONS

2004	Renacimiento FC
2003	Atletico
2002	CD Ela Nguema
2001	FC Akonangui
2000	CD Ela Nguema
1999	FC Akonangui
1998	CD Ela Nguema
1997	Dep. Mongomo
1996	Cafe Bank Sportif

Women's League Champion

2004	Aguilas Verdes
2003	Isla de Bioko
2002	Not Known
2001	Ewaiso Ipola
2000	Not Known

NATIONAL TEAM COLORS

WORLD PICTURES OF SOCCER

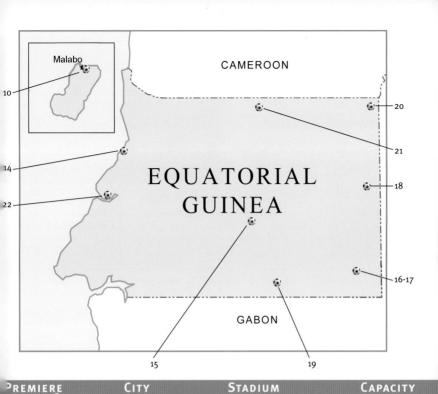

PREMIERE LEAGUE CLUBS	CITY	STADIUM	CAPACITY
-Atletico	Malabo/Bioco Island	Estadio La Paz	10 000
-Café Bank Sportif	Malabo/Bioco I.	Estadio La Paz	10 000
-Renacimiento FC	Malabo/Bioco I.	Estadio La Paz	10 000
-Sony de Ela Nguema	Malabo/Bioco I.	Estadio La Paz	10 000
-GD Lage	Malabo	Estadio La Paz	10 000
-Real Basile	Malabo/Bioco Island	Estadio La Paz	10 000
-Deportivo Unidad	Malabo/Bioco Island	Estadio La Paz	10 000
-ICEF	Malabo/Bioco Island	Estadio La Paz	10 000
-Panther FC	Malabo/Bioco Island	Estadio La Paz	10 000
ɔ-Rayos Lasser	Malabo/Bioco Island	Estadio La Paz	10 000
₁-Akonangui FC	Bata	Estadio La Libertad Bata	10 000
₂-Dragons FC	Bata	Estadio La Libertad Bata	10 000
₃-Union Vesper	Bata	Estadio La Libertad Bata	10 000
₄-Juveniles Reyes	Bata	Estadio La Libertad Bata	10 000
₅-Deportivo Evinayong	Evinayong		
₆-Estrella Nsok	Nsok	Real Nato de AkurenamAkurenam	
₇-Nsok-NsomoNsok			
₈-Deportivo Mongomo	Mongomo		
ɔ-Real Nato de Akurenam	Akurenam		
ɔ-Pedro Claver de Ebebiyin	Ebebiyin	Estadio Manuel Enguru	5 000
₁-Racing Micomeseng	Micomeseng		
₂-Real Boncoro de Cogo	Cogo		

ERITREA

ERITREAN NATIONAL FOOTBALL FEDERATION
Sematat Avenue 29-31, PB 3665 Asmara
TEL 291-1/120335   FAX 291-1/126 821
WEB www.cafonline.com

REFERENCE
Official name
State of Eritrea
Date of formation 1993
Capital Asmara
Population 3.9 million
Total area 45,405 sq Mi, 117,600 sq Km
Time zone GMT +3
Density 86 per sq Mi, 32 per sq Km
Languages Tigrinya, Arabic, Tigre, Afar, Bilen, Kunama, Nara
Literacy rate 25%
Currency Ethiopian Birr
Economy agriculture 80%, industry & services 20%
Religions Christian 45%, Muslim 45%
Ethnic Mix Tigray 50%, Kunama 40%, Afar 4%, Saho 3%

GEOGRAPHY
Elevation
lowest point: near Kulul within the Denakil depression -75 m
highest point: Soira 3,018 m
Geography Note
strategic geopolitical position along world's busiest shipping lanes; Eritrea retained the entire coastline of Ethiopia along the Red Sea upon de jure independence from Ethiopia on 24 May 1993
Natural Resources
gold, potash, zinc, copper, salt, possibly oil and natural gas, fish
Climate
hot, dry desert strip along Red Sea coast; cooler and wetter in the central highlands
Eritrean Food
alicha/Ingera/tsebhi zegni

WORLD CUP		COUNTRY LEAGUE CHAMPIONS	
1930	Did not qualify		
1934	Did not qualify		
1938	Did not qualify	2004	Adulis Club
1950	Did not qualify	2003	Ansaba SC
1954	Did not qualify	2002	Red Sea FC
1958	Did not qualify	2001	Hintsa Asmara
1962	Did not qualify	2000	Red Sea FC
1966	Did not qualify	1999	Red Sea FC
1970	Did not qualify	1998	Red Sea FC
1974	Did not qualify	1997	Mdlaw Megbi
1978	Did not qualify	1996	Not Known
1982	Did not qualify	**Women's League Champion**	
1986	Did not qualify	2004	Adulis Club
1990	Did not qualify	2003	Ansaba SC
1994	Did not qualify	2002	Red Sea FC
1998	Did not qualify	2001	Hintsa Asmara
2002	Did not qualify	2000	Red Sea FC

NATIONAL TEAM COLORS

WORLD PICTURES OF SOCCER

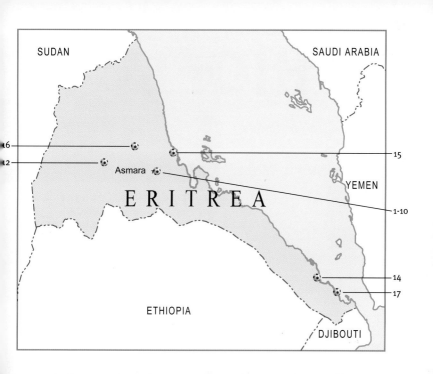

PREMIERE LEAGUE CLUBS	CITY	STADIUM	CAPACITY
Red Sea FC	Asmara	Chic Chero	10 000
Hintsa	Asmara	Chic Chero	10 000
Medalawi Megbi	Asmara	Chic Chero	10 000
Al-Tahrir	Asmara	Chic Chero	10 000
Food Victory	Asmara	Chic Chero	10 000
Adulis	Asmara	Chic Chero	10 000
Brewery	Asmara	Chic Chero	10 000
Dahlak	Asmara	Chic Chero	10 000
Awet	Asmara	Chic Chero	10 000
Berhan	Asmara	Chic Chero	10 000
Arkobkobai	Arkordat		
AdalArkordat			
Anseba Sport Club	Keren		
Beylul	Beylul		
Chemical	Masawa		
CH-Star	Keren		
Tesfa Sport	Assab		

ETHIOPIA

ETHIOPIAN FOOTBALL FEDERATION
Addis Ababa Std., PB 1080, Addis Abeba
TEL 251-1/514 453 FAX 251-1/515 899
WEB www.cafonline.com

REFERENCE

Official name
Federal Democratic republic of Ethiopia

Date of formation 1993
Capital Addis Ababa
Population 62.6 million
Total area 428,571 sq Mi, 1,110,000 sq Km
Time zone GMT +3
Density 179 per sq Mi, 53 per sq Km
Languages Amharic, English, Arabic
Literacy rate 35%
Currency Birr
Economy agriculture 80%, services 12%,
Religions Orthodox 40%, Muslim 40%, traditional beliefs 15%
Ethnic Mix Oromo 40%, Amhara 25%, Sidamo 9%

GEOGRAPHY

Elevation
lowest point: Denakil Depression -125 m
highest point: Ras Dejen 4,620 m

Geography Note
landlocked - entire coastline along the Red Sea was lost with the de jure independence of Eritrea on 24 May 1993; the Blue Nile, the chief headstream of the Nile

Natural Resources
small reserves of gold, platinum, copper, potash, natural gas, hydropower

Climate
tropical monsoon with wide topographic-induced variation

Ethiopian Food
amhari mesir wat/Injera/dorowat/chicken wotworld cup

WORLD CUP

1930	Did not qualify
1934	Did not qualify
1938	Did not qualify
1950	Did not qualify
1954	Did not qualify
1958	Did not qualify
1962	Did not qualify
1966	Did not qualify
1970	Did not qualify
1974	Did not qualify
1978	Did not qualify
1982	Did not qualify
1986	Did not qualify
1990	Did not qualify
1994	Did not qualify
1998	Did not qualify
2002	Did not qualify

COUNTRY LEAGUE CHAMPIONS

2004	Awassa Kenema
2003	St.George
2002	St.George
2001	Mebrat Hail
2000	St.George
1999	St.George
1998	Mebrat Hail
1997	Ethio Bunna
1996	St.George

Women's League Champior

2004	Not Known
2003	Not Known
2002	Not Known
2001	Not Known
2000	Not Known

NATIONAL TEAM COLORS

WORLD PICTURES OF SOCCER

PREMIERE LEAGUE CLUBS	CITY	STADIUM	CAPACITY
-St.George SA	Addis Abeba	Addis Abeba Stadium	35 000
-Eelpa	Addis Abeba	Addis Abeba Stadium	35 000
-Insurance	Addis Abeba	Addis Abeba Stadium	35 000
-Ethiopian Coffee	Addis Abeba	Addis Abeba Stadium	35 000
-Nyala	Addis Abeba	Addis Abeba Stadium	35 000
-Banks SC	Addis Abeba	Addis Abeba Stadium	35 000
-EEPCO Electric FC	Addis Abeba	Addis Abeba Stadium	35 000
-Mebrat Hail	Addis Abeba	Addis Abeba Stadium	35 000
-Ethio-Bunna	Addis Abeba	Addis Abeba Stadium	35 000
-Mechal	Addis Abeba	Addis Abeba Stadium	35 000
-Ermejachen	Addis Abeba	Addis Abeba Stadium	35 000
-Berhanena Selam FC	Addis Abeba	Addis Abeba Stadium	35 000
-Medhin	Addis Abeba	Addis Abeba Stadium	35 000
-Ethiopian Bunna	Addis Abeba	Addis Abeba Stadium	35 000
-Bunna Gebeya	Addis Abeba	Addis Abeba Stadium	35 000
-Muger Cement	Oromo		
-Wonji Sugar	Oromo		
-Adama City	Oromo		
-Trans Ethiopia	Tigray		
-Guna Trading FC	Mekele	Mekele Stadium	5 000
-Arba Minch Textile	Arba-Minch		
-Awassa City	Awasa		
-Awassa Flour Mill	Awassa	Municipal Awassa	5 000
-Awassa Kenema	Awassa		
-Wolaita Tussa	Awassa		
-Harar Beer Botling FC	Harar		
-Ogaden Anbassa	Harar		
-Harar City	Harar		
-Coton FC	Dire Dawa		

149

GABON

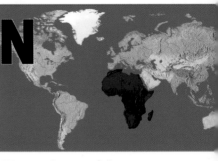

FED. GABONNAISE DE FOOTBALL
BP 181, Libreville
TEL 241/730 460   FAX 241/677 962
WEB www.cafonline.com

REFERENCE
Official name
The Gabonese Republic
Date of formation 1960
Capital Libreville
Population 1.2 million
Total area 99,486 Mi, 257,670 sq Km
Time zone GMT +1
Density 12 per sq Mi, 5 per sq Km
Languages French, Fang
Literacy rate 63%
Currency CFA Franc
Economy agriculture 65%, industry & commerce 30%
Religions Catholic 55%, traditional beliefs 40%
Ethnic Mix Fang 35%, Eshira 25%, Bantu 29%, French 2%

GEOGRAPHY
Elevation
lowest point: Atlantic Ocean 0 m
highest point: Mont Iboundji 1,575 m
Geography Note
a small population and oil and mineral reserves have helped Gabon become one of Africa's wealthier countries; in general, these circumstances have allowed the country to maintain and conserve its pristine rain forest and rich biodiversity
Natural Resources
petroleum, manganese, uranium, gold, timber, iron ore, hydropower
Climate
tropical; always hot, humid
Gabonese Food
baked banana

WORLD CUP

1930	Did not qualify
1934	Did not qualify
1938	Did not qualify
1950	Did not qualify
1954	Did not qualify
1958	Did not qualify
1962	Did not qualify
1966	Did not qualify
1970	Did not qualify
1974	Did not qualify
1978	Did not qualify
1982	Did not qualify
1986	Did not qualify
1990	Did not qualify
1994	Did not qualify
1998	Did not qualify
2002	Did not qualify

COUNTRY LEAGUE CHAMPIONS

2004	Mangasport
2003	US Bitam
2002	US Mbila Nzambi
2001	FC 105 Libreville
2000	Mangasport
1999	FC 105 Libreville
1998	Petrosport
1997	FC 105 Libreville
1996	Mbilinga FC

Women's League Champion

2004	Not Known
2003	Not Known
2002	Not Known
2001	Not Known
2000	Not Known

NATIONAL TEAM COLORS

WORLD PICTURES OF SOCCER

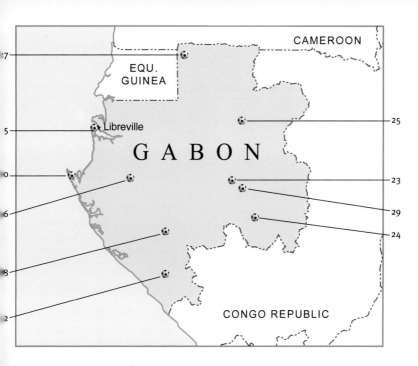

PREMIERE LEAGUE CLUBS	CITY	STADIUM	CAPACITY
FC 105	Libreville	Stade Omar Bongo	40 000
Cercle Mberi	Libreville	Stade Omar Bongo	40 000
Jeunesse Sportive	Libreville	Stade Omar Bongo	40 000
Stade D'Akebe	Libreville	Augustin Monedan	20 000
USM Libreville	Libreville	Stade Omar Bongo	40 000
TP Akwembe	Libreville	Augustin Monedan	20 000
Aigle Royal	Libreville	Stade Omar Bongo	40 000
Mangasport	Libreville	Stade Omar Bongo	40 000
US Mbila Nzambi	Libreville	Augustin Monedan	20 000
JAC	Libreville	Stade Omar Bongo	40 000
AS Scolaire	Libreville	Augustin Monedan	20 000
Ndzimba FC	Libreville	Stade Omar Bongo	40 000
Anges ABC	Libreville	Stade Omar Bongo	40 000
Delta Sport FC	Libreville	Augustin Monedan	20 000
Mbelinga FC	Libreville	Augustin Monedan	20 000
Petro Sport	Port Gentil	Pierre Claver Divounguy	10 000
AS Sogara	Port Gentil	Pierre Claver Divounguy	10 000
Mbilinga FC	Port Gentil	Pierre Claver Divounguy	10 000
Aigles Verts	Port Gentil	Pierre Claver Divounguy	10 000
Marathon	Sport Gentil	Augustin Monedan	20 000
Munadji 76	Tchibanga	Stade Dialogue	10 000
Algle Lunga	Tchibanga	Stade Dialogue	10 000
Wongo Sport	Lastoursville	Stade Mbeba	10 000
Manga Sport	Moanda	Stade Henry Sylvoz	5 000
Aigles de Belinga	Makokou	Stade Alexandre Sambat	10 000
AO Evizo	Lambarane	Stade de Lambarane	5 000
US Bitam	Bitam	Stade Municipal Bitam	10 000
Stade Mbombey	Mouila		
Union Sportive	Koulamoutou		

GAMBIA

GAMBIA FOOTBALL ASSOC.
c/o Independence Stadium
Bakau, PB 523, Banjul
TEL 220/496 980 FAX 241/677 962
WEB www.cafonline.com

REFERENCE
Official name
Republic of Gambia

Date of formation	1965
Capital	Banjul
Population	1.3 million
Total area	3861 sq Mi, 10,000 sq Km
Time zone	GMT 0
Density	337 per sq Mi, 118 per sq Km
Languages	English
Literacy rate	37%
Currency	Dalasi
Economy	agriculture 75%, industry, services & commerce 19%
Religions	Sunni Muslim 90%, Christian 9%
Ethnic Mix	Mandingo 42%, Fulani 18%, Wolof 16%, Jola 10%, Serahuli 9%

GEOGRAPHY
Elevation
lowest point: Atlantic Ocean 0 m
highest point: unnamed location 53 m
Geography Note
almost an enclave of Senegal; smallest country on the continent of Africa
Natural Resources
fish
Climate
tropical; hot, rainy season (June to November); cooler, dry season (November to May)
Gambian Food
jollof rice

WORLD CUP

1930	Did not qualify
1934	Did not qualify
1938	Did not qualify
1950	Did not qualify
1954	Did not qualify
1958	Did not qualify
1962	Did not qualify
1966	Did not qualify
1970	Did not qualify
1974	Did not qualify
1978	Did not qualify
1982	Did not qualify
1986	Did not qualify
1990	Did not qualify
1994	Did not qualify
1998	Did not qualify
2002	Did not qualify

COUNTRY LEAGUE CHAMPIONS

2004	Wallidan
2003	Armed Forces
2002	Wallidan
2001	Wallidan
2000	Real Banjul
1999	Ports Authority
1998	Real Banjul
1997	Real banjul
1996	Hawks

Women's League Champion

2004	Company 10 FC
2003	Not Known
2002	City Girls Banjul FC
2001	Company 10 FC
2000	Company 10 FC

NATIONAL TEAM COLORS

WORLD PICTURES OF SOCCER

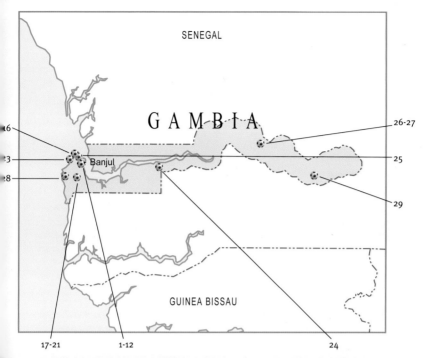

SENEGAL			
GAMBIA			26-27
16			
3	Banjul		25
8			
			29
	GUINEA BISSAU		
17-21	1-12	24	

PREMIERE LEAGUE CLUBS	CITY	STADIUM	CAPACITY
Banjul Hawks FC	Banjul	Independence Stadium	10 000
Wallidan FC	Banjul	Independence Stadium	10 000
Gambia Port Authority	Banjul	Independence Stadium	10 000
Armed Forces	Banjul	Independence Stadium	10 000
Real de Banjul FC	Banjul	Independence Stadium	10 000
Gambia Port Authority	Banjul	Independence Stadium	10 000
Starlight Gunners FC	Banjul	Brikama	15 000
Banjul Hawks	Banjul	Brikama	15 000
Flamenins FC`	Banjul	Brikama	15 000
Half Die United FC	Banjul	Brikama	15 000
Eliminite	Banjul	Brikama	15 000
Young Africans	Banjul	Brikama	15 000
Steve Biko FC	Bakau	Independence Stadium	10 000
Bakau United FC	Bakau	Independence Stadium	10 000
Sait Matty FC	Bakau	Independence Stadium	10 000
Latdior FC	Bakau	Independence Stadium	10 000
Sky Power	Brikama	Municipal Bikrama	7 000
Saraba FC	Brikama	Municipal Bikrama	7 000
Justice FC	Brikama	Municipal Bikrama	7 000
Tallinding United FC	Bikrama	Municipal Bikrama	7 000
Flamemins	Bikrama	Municipal Bikrama	7 000
Serrekunda United FC	Serrekunda	Municipal Serrekunda	5 000
Blackpool	Serrekunda	Municipal Serrekunda	5 000
Kiang West FC	Kiang W.-Batelling		
Rising Star FC	Latrakunda		
NPE Sukuta	Sukuta		
Sukuta Tigers	Sukuta		
Tanji FC	Tanji	Tanji Municipal Stadium	3 000
Basse FC	Basse Santa Su		

163

 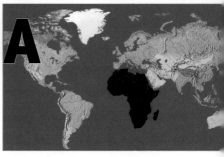

GHANA

GHANA FOOTBALL ASSOC.
General Secretariat, National Sport Consul
PB 1272, Accra
TEL 233-21/671 FAX 233-21/668 590
WEB www.cafonline.com

REFERENCE
Official name
Republic of Ghana

Date of formation	1957
Capital	Accra
Population	20.2 million
Total area	88,810 sq Mi, 230,020 sq Km
Time zone	GMT 0
Density	227 per sq Mi, 79 per sq Km
Languages	English, Akan, Mossi, Ewe, Ga' Twi, Fanti, Gurma
Literacy rate	64%
Currency	Cedi
Economy	agriculture 58%, services 31%
Religions	Christian 43%, traditional beliefs 38%, Muslim 11%
Ethnic Mix	Sashanti & Fanti 52%, Moshi 16%, Ewe 12%

WORLD CUP

1930	Did not qualify
1934	Did not qualify
1938	Did not qualify
1950	Did not qualify
1954	Did not qualify
1958	Did not qualify
1962	Did not qualify
1966	Did not qualify
1970	Did not qualify
1974	Did not qualify
1978	Did not qualify
1982	Did not qualify
1986	Did not qualify
1990	Did not qualify
1994	Did not qualify
1998	Did not qualify
2002	Did not qualify

COUNTRY LEAGUE CHAMPIONS

2004	Not Known
2003	Asante Kotoko
2002	Hearts of Oak
2001	Hearts of Oak
2000	Hearts of Oak
1999	Hearts of Oak
1998	Hearts of Oak
1997	Hearts of Oak
1996	Goldfields

Women's League Champion

2004	Ashiaman Ladies
2003	Post Ladies
2002	Post Ladies
2001	Ghatel Ladies
2000	Ghatel Ladies

NATIONAL TEAM COLORS

GEOGRAPHY
Elevation
lowest point: Atlantic Ocean 0 m
highest point: Mount Afadjato 880 m
Geography Note
Lake Volta is the world's largest artificial lake
Natural Resources
gold, timber, industrial diamonds, bauxite, manganese, fish, rubber, hydropower
Climate
tropical; warm and comparatively dry along southeast coast; hot and humid in southwest; hot and dry in north
Ghanean Food
jollof rice/kentumere/akotonshi

WORLD PICTURES OF SOCCER

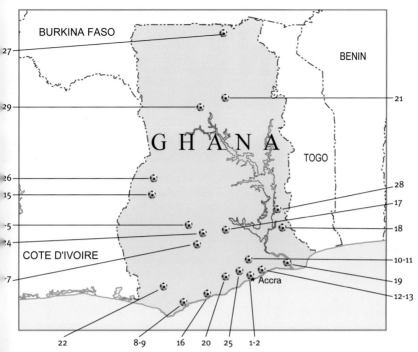

Premiere League Clubs	City	Stadium	Capacity
-Hearts of Oak	Accra	Accra Sports Stadium	35 000
-Great Olympics	Accra	Kaneshie Sport Complex	20 000
-Asante Kotoko	Kumasi	Kumasi Sport Stadium	45 000
-King Faisal Babies	Kumasi	Kumasi Sport Stadium	45 000
-Queen's Park Rangers	Kumasi	Prempeh College Park	2 000
-Goldfields SC	Obuasi	Len Clay Stadium	25 000
-Adansiman	Obuasi	Len Clay Stadium	25 000
-Hasaacas	Sekondi	Gyandu Park	15 000
-Eleven Wise	Sekondi	Gyandu Park	15 000
-Power FC	Koforidua	Koforidua Sports Stadium	5 000
-Maxbees Suhum	Koforidua	Koforidua Sports Stadium	5 000
-GHAPOHA Readers	Tema	Tema Sports Stadium	10 000
-Afienga United	Tema	Tema Sports Stadium	10 000
-Brong Ahafo United	Sunyani	Coronation Park	10 000
-Bofoakwa Tano	Sunyani	Coronation Park	10 000
-Ebusua Darf	Cape Coast	Cape Coast Stadium	15 000
-Okwawu United	Nkawkaw	Nkawkaw Stadium	5 000
-Vodarep	Ho	Ho Sports Stadium	5 000
-Dawa Youngstars	Dawa	Dawa Sports Stadium	10 000
-All Blacks	Swedru	Swedru Sports Stadium	5 000
-Real Tamale	Tamale	Kaladan Park	5 000
-Mine stars	Prestea	Scot Stadium	5 000
-Liberty Professionals	Danso	Dansoman Park	2 000
-Stay Cool	Danso	Dansoman Park	2 000
-Kwaebbirem United	Asuom	Asuom Park	5 000
-Arsenals	Berekum	Berekum Sports Stadium	5 000
-Bolgatanga FC	Bolgatanga	Bolgatanga Stadium	5 000
-Heart of Lions	Kpandu		
-Shooting Stars	Nyankpala		

GUINEA

FED. DE FUTEBOL DA GUINEA- BISSAU
Rua 4 #10-c, CP 375, 1035 Bissau CODEX
TEL 245/201 918 FAX 245/211 414
WEB www.cafonline.com

REFERENCE
Official name
   Republic of Guinea-Bissau

Date of	
formation	1974
Capital	Bissau
Population	1.2 million
Total area	10,570 sq Mi, 28,120 sq Km
Time zone	GMT 0
Density	114 per sq Mi, 34 per sq Km
Languages	Portuguese
Literacy rate	54%
Currency	Paso
Economy	agriculture 90%
Religions	indigenous beliefs 52%, Muslim 40%, Christian 8%
Ethnic Mix	Balanta 25%,Fula 20%, Madinka & Mandyako 23%

GEOGRAPHY
Elevation
lowest point: Atlantic Ocean 0 m
highest point: Mont Nimba 1,752 m
Geography Note
Niger and its important tributary the Milo
have their sources in the Guinean highlands
Natural Resources
bauxite, iron ore, diamonds, gold, uranium,
hydropower, fish
Climate
generally hot and humid; monsoonal-type
rainy season (June to November) with south-
westerly winds; dry season (December to
May) with northeasterly harmattan winds
Guinean Food
maffi hakko/gombo sauce/bissap juice

WORLD CUP

1930	Did not qualify
1934	Did not qualify
1938	Did not qualify
1950	Did not qualify
1954	Did not qualify
1958	Did not qualify
1962	Did not qualify
1966	Did not qualify
1970	Did not qualify
1974	Did not qualify
1978	Did not qualify
1982	Did not qualify
1986	Did not qualify
1990	Did not qualify
1994	Did not qualify
1998	Did not qualify
2002	Did not qualify

COUNTRY LEAGUE CHAMPIONS

2004	SC de Bissau
2003	UD Internacional
2002	SC de Bissau
2001	Season Cancelled
2000	SC de Bissau
1999	Season Cancelled
1998	SC de Bissau
1997	SC de Bissau
1996	ADR Mansaba

Women's League Champion

2004	Not Known
2003	Not Known
2002	Not Known
2001	Not Known
2000	Not Known

NATIONAL TEAM COLORS

WORLD PICTURES OF SOCCER

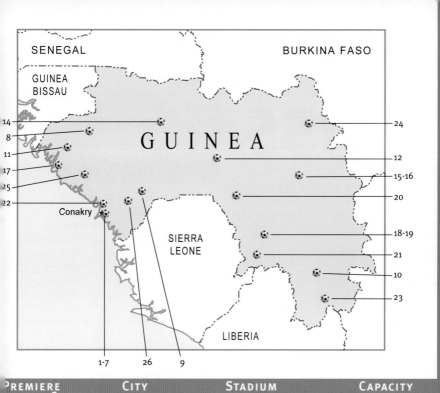

PREMIERE LEAGUE CLUBS	CITY	STADIUM	CAPACITY
-AS de Kaloum Stars	Conakry	Stade du 28 Septembre	40 000
-Hafia FC	Conakry	Stade du 28 Septembre	40 000
-Satellite FC	Conakry	Stade du 28 Septembre	40 000
-Horoya AC	Conakry	Stade du 28 Septembre	40 000
-Baraka SSG	Conakry	Stade du 28 Septembre	40 000
-Etoile de Guinee	Conakry	Stade du 28 Septembre	40 000
ASF Armee Guinea	Conakry	Stade du 28 Septembre	40 000
-AS des Mineurs	Sangaredi		
-Gangan FC	Kindia		
-Simandou FC	Beyla		
-CO Kakande	Boke		
-Sifo	Dabola		
-Fello Star	Labe	El Hadj Saifoulage Diallo	10 000
-Baredi de Labe	Labe	El Hadj Saifoulage Diallo	10 000
-Universite Club de Kankan	Kankan		
-Milo FC	Kankan		
-CI Kamsar	Kamsar	Stade Municipal Kamsar	5 000
-FC Niandan	Kissidougou		
-Kissidougou FC	Kissidougou		
-Sankaran	Faranah		
-Mankona	Gueckedou		
-Soumba Dubreka	Dubreka		
-Nzerekore FC	Nzerekore	Municipal Nzerekore	10 000
-SAG de Siguiri	Siguiri		
-Atletico de Koliyah	Koliyah		
-Friguiagbe FC	Friguiagbe		

GUINEA BISSAU

FED. GUINEENE DE FOOTBALL
PB 3645, Conakry
TEL 224/455 878 FAX 224/455 879
WEB www.cafonline.com

REFERENCE
Official name
Republic of Guinea

Date of formation	1958
Capital	Conakry
Population	7.4 million
Total area	94,926 sq Mi, 245,860 sq Km
Time zone	GMT 0
Density	78 per sq Mi, 30 per sq Km
Languages	French, Fulani, Malinke, Soussou, Kissi
Literacy rate	35%
Currency	Franc
Economy	agriculture 80%, industry & commerce 11%
Religions	Muslim 65%, traditional beliefs 33%, Fila 30%, Malinke 30%,
Ethnic Mix	Soussou 15%, Kissi 10%

GEOGRAPHY
Elevation
lowest point: Atlantic Ocean 0 m
highest point: Mont Nimba 1,752 m
Geography Note
Niger and its important tributary the Milo
have their sources in the Guinean highlands
Natural Resources
bauxite, iron ore, diamonds, gold, uranium,
hydropower, fish
Climate
generally hot and humid; monsoonal-type
rainy season (June to November) with south-
westerly winds; dry season (December to
May) with northeasterly harmattan winds
Guinea Bissau Food
maffi hakko/gombo sauce/bissap juice

WORLD CUP

1930	Did not qualify
1934	Did not qualify
1938	Did not qualify
1950	Did not qualify
1954	Did not qualify
1958	Did not qualify
1962	Did not qualify
1966	Did not qualify
1970	Did not qualify
1974	Did not qualify
1978	Did not qualify
1982	Did not qualify
1986	Did not qualify
1990	Did not qualify
1994	Did not qualify
1998	Did not qualify
2002	Did not qualify

COUNTRY LEAGUE CHAMPIONS

2004	Season Cancelled
2003	ASFAG Conakry
2002	Satellite FC
2001	Horoya AC
2000	Horoya AC
1999	Season Cancelled
1998	AS Kaloum Stars
1997	Season Cancelled
1996	AS Kaloum Stars

Women's League Champion

2004	Not Known
2003	Not Known
2002	Not Known
2001	Not Known
2000	Not Known

NATIONAL TEAM COLORS

WORLD PICTURES OF SOCCER

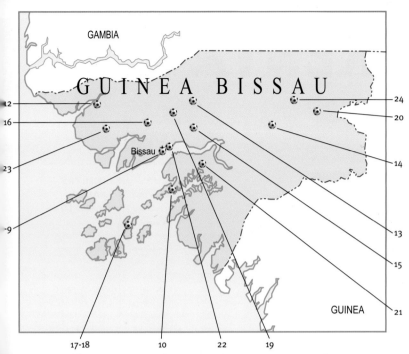

PREMIERE LEAGUE CLUBS	CITY	STADIUM	CAPACITY
-Sporting Clube Bissau	Bissau	Estadio 24 de Septembro	20 000
-Mavegro FC	Bissau	Estadio 24 de Septembro	20 000
-Sport Bissau e Benfica	Bissau	Estadio 24 de Septembro	20 000
-Sport Portos de Bissau	Bissau	Estadio 24 de Septembro	20 000
-UDI de Bissau	Bissau	Estadio Lino Correia	12 000
-Ajuda Sport Bissau	Bissau	Estadio Lino Correia	12 000
-Bissau FC	Bissau	Estadio Lino Correia	12 000
-FC Cuntum	Bissau	Estadio Lino Correia	12 000
-En Bissau	Bissau	Estadio Lino Correia	12 000
0-Estrela Negra de Bolama	Bolama		
1-Cacheu FC	Cacheu		
2-Vitoria FC	Cacheu		
3-AD Recreativa Mansaba	Mansaba		
4-Sporting Clube Batafa	Batafa		
5-CFOS Balantas	Mansoa		
6-Bula FCBula			
7-FC Tubaroes Bijagos	Bubaque		
8-Bubaque FC	Bubaque		
9-Atletico Bissora	Bissora		
0-Desportivo de Gabu	Gabu		
1-Fulacunda FC	Fulacunda		
2-Flamengo Pefine FC	Pefine		
3-FC Canchungo	Canchungo		
4-Contuboel	Contuboel		

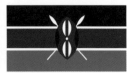

KENYA

KENYA FOOTBALL FEDERATION
Nyayo National Stadium
PB 40234, Nairobi
TEL 254-2/608 422 FAX 254-2/608 422
WEB www.cafonline.com

REFERENCE
Official name
Republic of Kenya
Date of formation 1963
Capital Nairobi
Population 30.1 million
Total area 218,907 sq Mi, 566,970 sq Km
Time zone GMT +3
Density 138 per sq Mi, 49 per sq Km
Languages Swahili, English, Kikuyu, Luo, Kamba
Literacy rate 77%
Currency Shilling
Economy agriculture 80%, services 12%, Industry 8%
Religions Christian 60%, traditional beliefs 25%
Ethnic Mix Kikuyu 21%, Luhya 14%, Luo 13%, Kamba 11%

GEOGRAPHY
Elevation
lowest point: Indian Ocean 0 m
highest point: Mount Kenya 5,199 m
Geography Note
Kenyan Highlands comprise one of the most successful agricultural production regions in Africa; glaciers are found on Mount Kenya, Africa's second highest peak
Natural Resources
gold, limestone, soda ash, salt barites, rubies, fluorspar, garnets, wildlife, hydropower
Climate
varies from tropical along coast to arid in interior
Kenyan Food
chapatis/ugli/samosa/sukuma wiki

WORLD CUP		COUNTRY LEAGUE CHAMPIONS	
1930	Did not qualify		
1934	Did not qualify		
1938	Did not qualify	2004	Ulinzi Stars
1950	Did not qualify	2003	Ulinzi Stars
1954	Did not qualify	2002	Oserian
1958	Did not qualify	2001	Oserian
1962	Did not qualify	2000	Tusker FC
1966	Did not qualify	1999	Tusker FC
1970	Did not qualify	1998	AFC Leopards
1974	Did not qualify	1997	Utalii FC
1978	Did not qualify	1996	Kenya Breweries
1982	Did not qualify	**Women's League Champion**	
1986	Did not qualify	2004	Not Known
1990	Did not qualify	2003	Makolanders
1994	Did not qualify	2002	Makolanders
1998	Did not qualify	2001	Telkom White FC
2002	Did not qualify	2000	Not Known

NATIONAL TEAM COLORS

WORLD PICTURES OF SOCCER

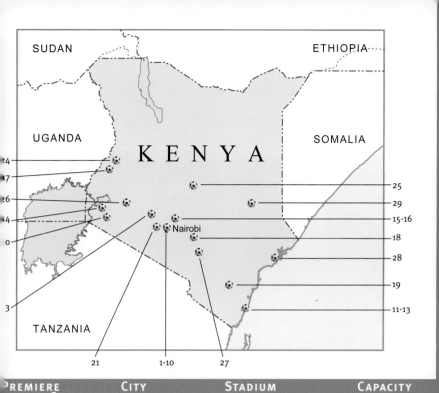

PREMIERE LEAGUE CLUBS	CITY	STADIUM	CAPACITY
AFC Leopards	Nairobi	Kasarani Stadium	60 000
Red Berets	Nairobi	Kasarani Stadium	60 000
Re-Union	Nairobi	Kasarani Stadium	60 000
Polica	Nairobi	Kasarani Stadium	60 000
Tusker FC	Nairobi	Kasarani Stadium	60 000
Kawangware	Nairobi	Kasarani Stadium	60 000
KCB FC	Nairobi	Kasarani Stadium	60 000
Gor Mahia	Nairobi	Kasarani Stadium	60 000
Mathare United	Nairobi	Kasarani Stadium	60 000
Kenya Pipeline	Nairobi	Kasarani Stadium	60 000
Coast Stars	Mombasa	Mombasa Coast	20 000
Cook n Lite FC	Mombasa	Mombasa Coast	20 000
Mombasa Liverpool	Mombasa	Mombasa Coast	20 000
Sony Sugar FC	Awundo's Village		
Ulinzi Stars	Thika	Thikan Stadium	10 000
Medisca Thika United	Thika	Thikan Stadium	10 000
Pan Paper	Webuye		
Kenap	Athi River		
Chemelil Sugar	Nyando		
Shabana	Kisii		
Utalii	Ruaka		
Sher Agencies	Naivasha	Municipal	10 000
Oserian Fastac	Naivasha	Municipal	10 000
Nzoia Sugar	Bungoma		
Meru Bombers	Meru		
Brooke Bond	Kericho		
Makindu United	Makindu		
FC Lamu	Lamu		
Garissa FC	Garissa		

LESOTHO

LESOTHO FOOTBALL ASSOC.
1PB 1879, Maseru-100
TEL 266/311 879   FAX 266/310 586
WEB www.cafonline.com

REFERENCE
Official name
Kingdom of Lesotho
Date of formation 1966
Capital Masuru
Population 2.2 million
Total area 11,718 sq Mi, 30,350 sq Km
Time zone GMT +2
Density 188 per sq Mi, 70 per sq Km
Languages English, Sesotho, Zulu
Literacy rate 71%
Currency Loti
Economy agriculture 75%, services & industry 25%
Religions Christian 90%, traditional beliefs 10%
Ethnic Mix Sotho 97%, European & Asian 3%

GEOGRAPHY
Elevation
lowest point: Junction of the Orange and Makhaleng Rivers 1,400 m
highest point: Thabana Ntlenyana 3,482 m
Geography Note
landlocked, completely surrounded by South Africa; mountainous, more than 80% of the country is 1,800 meters above sea level
Natural Resources
water, agricultural and grazing land, some diamonds and other minerals
Climate
temperate; cool to cold, dry winters; hot, wet summers
Lesotho Food
trout meuniere/banana souffle

WORLD CUP		COUNTRY LEAGUE CHAMPIONS	
1930	Did not qualify		
1934	Did not qualify		
1938	Dd not qualify	2004	RLDF
1950	Did not qualify	2003	Matlama FC
1954	Did not qualify	2002	Lesotho Prisons
1958	Did not qualify	2001	RLDF
1962	Did not qualify	2000	Lesotho Prisons
1966	Did not qualify	1999	RLDF
1970	Did not qualify	1998	RLDF
1974	Did not qualify	1997	RLDF
1978	Did not qualify	1996	Roma Rovers
1982	Did not qualify	**Women's League Champior**	
1986	Did not qualify	2004	Not Known
1990	Did not qualify	2003	Not Known
1994	Did not qualify	2002	Not Known
1998	Did not qualify	2001	Not Known
2002	Did not qualify	2000	Not Known

NATIONAL TEAM COLORS

WORLD PICTURES OF SOCCER

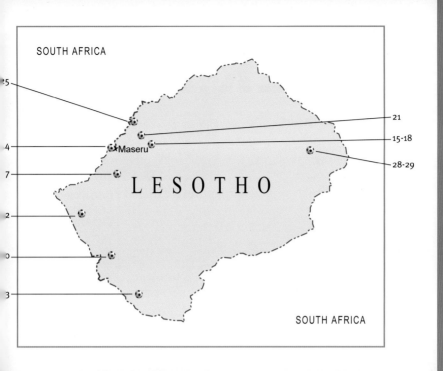

PREMIERE LEAGUE CLUBS	CITY	STADIUM	CAPACITY
Matlama FC	Maseru	Maseru national Stadium	20 000
RLDF	Maseru	Maseru national Stadium	20 000
Arsenal	Maseru	Maseru national Stadium	20 000
Lesotho PS	Maseru	Maseru national Stadium	20 000
Police FC	Maseru	Maseru national Stadium	20 000
Maseru FC	Maseru	Maseru national Stadium	20 000
Swallows FC	Maseru	Maseru national Stadium	20 000
Lijabatho FC	Maseru	Maseru national Stadium	20 000
LDS	Maseru	Maseru national Stadium	20 000
-LMP	Maseru	Maseru national Stadium	20 000
Lerotholi	Maseru	Maseru national Stadium	20 000
Maseru Brothers	Maseru	Maseru national Stadium	20 000
Maseru United	Maseru	Maseru national Stadium	20 000
Ambassadors	Maseru	Maseru national Stadium	20 000
Qalo FC	Koali		
Qoaling Flowers	Koali		
Highlanders	Koali		
Young Zebras	Koali		
Majantja	Mohales Hoek	Mohales Hoek Municipal	5 000
LMPS FC	Mohales Hoek	Mohales Hoek Municipal	5 000
Lioli FC	Teyateyaneng		
Bantu	Matefeng		
Liphakoe	Quthing		
Roaring Lions FC	Maputsoe	Municipal Maputsoe	5 000
Maputsoe Aces	Maputsoe	Municipal Maputsoe	5 000
NUL Rovers	Roma		
Manonyane	Roma		
Polytechnic FC	Makhotlong		
Balafe Makhotlong	Makhotlong		

LIBERIA

LIBERIA FOOTBALL ASSOC.
Broad & Center Streets
PB 10-1066 1000 Monrovia 10
TEL 231/226 385 FAX 231/226 843
WEB www.liberiansoccer.com

REFERENCE
Official name
Republic of Liberia

Date of formation	1847
Capital	Monrovia
Population	3.2 million
Total area	37,189 sq Mi, 96,320 sq Km
Time zone	GMT 0
Density	86 per sq Mi, 26 per sq Km
Languages	English, Kpelle, Bassa Vai, Grebo, Kru,Gola
Literacy rate	40%
Currency	Liberian
Economy	agriculture 70%, services 25%,Industry 5%
Religions	Christian 68%, traditional beliefs 18%, Muslim 14%
Ethnic Mix	indigenous tribes 95%, Americo-Liberians 5%

GEOGRAPHY
Elevation
lowest point: Atlantic Ocean 0 m
highest point: Mount Wuteve 1,380 m
Geography Note
facing the Atlantic Ocean, the coastline is characterized by lagoons, mangrove swamps, and river-deposited sandbars; the inland grassy plateau supports limited
Natural Resources
water, agricultural and grazing land, some diamonds and other minerals
Climate
temperate; cool to cold, dry winters; hot, wet summers
Liberian Food
Monrovian collards/jollof rice

WORLD CUP

1930	Did not qualify
1934	Did not qualify
1938	Did not qualify
1950	Did not qualify
1954	Did not qualify
1958	Did not qualify
1962	Did not qualify
1966	Did not qualify
1970	Did not qualify
1974	Did not qualify
1978	Did not qualify
1982	Did not qualify
1986	Did not qualify
1990	Did not qualify
1994	Did not qualify
1998	Did not qualify
2002	Did not qualify

COUNTRY LEAGUE CHAMPIONS

2004	Miighty Barolle
2003	LRPC Oilers
2002	LPRC Oilers
2001	Mighty Barolle
2000	Mighty Barolle
1999	LPRC Oilers
1998	Invincible Eleven
1997	Invincible Eleven
1996	Junior Professional

Women's League Champion

2004	Tito United
2003	Earth Angels FC
2002	Earth Angels FC
2001	Earth Angels FC
2000	Not Known

NATIONAL TEAM COLORS

WORLD PICTURES OF SOCCER

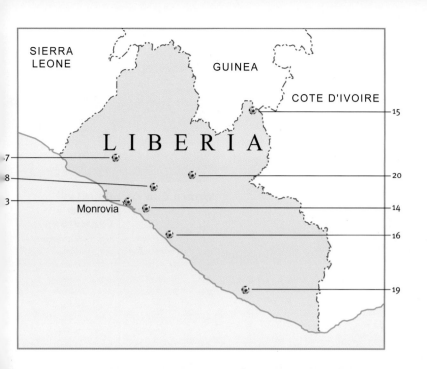

SIERRA LEONE			
GUINEA			
COTE D'IVOIRE			

PREMIERE LEAGUE CLUBS	CITY	STADIUM	CAPACITY
LPRC Oilers	Monrovia	Antoinette Tubman	20 000
Mighty Barolle	Monrovia	Antoinette Tubman	20 000
Invincible Eleven	Monrovia	National Complex	35 000
Junior Professional	Monrovia	National Complex	35 000
NPA Anchors	Monrovia	National Complex	35 000
Saint Joseph Warriors	Monrovia	National Complex	35 000
Sparrow	Monrovia	ATS Stadium	10 000
Baccus Marine	Monrovia	ATS Stadium	10 000
Black Stars	Monrovia	ATS Stadium	10 000
-Saint Joseph Warriors	Monrovia	ATS Stadium	10 000
-Fulani FC	Monrovia	ATS Stadium	10 000
-Cedar United	Monrovia	ATS Stadium	10 000
-Monrovia Club Brewery	Monrovia	ATS Stadium	10 000
-Mighty Blue Angels	Unification Town		
-Lamco Enforcers	Yakepa		
Saint Anthony FC	Buchanan		
Alliance FC	Tubmanburg		
Olympic FC	Kakata		
Bassa Defenders	Bassa		
-Bame FC	Bame		

# LIBYA

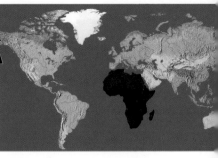

LIBYAN ARAB FOOTBALL FED.

Asayadi Street, Near Janat Al-Reef
PB 5137, Tripoli
TEL 218-21/334 3600 FAX /444 6610
WEB www.cafonline.com

REFERENCE

Official name
The great socialist People's Libyan
Arab Jamahiriya

Date of formation	1951
Capital	Tripoli
Population	5.6 million
Total area	679,358 sq Mi, 1,759,540 sq Km
Time zone	GMT +2
Density	8 per sq Mi, 3 per sq Km
Languages	Arabic , Tuareg
Literacy rate	75%
Currency	Dinar
Economy	services 51%, industry 32%, agriculture 17%
Religions	Sunni Muslim 97%
Ethnic Mix	Arab & Berber 95%

GEOGRAPHY

Elevation
lowest point: Sabkhat Ghuzayyil -47 m
highest point: Bikku Bitti 2,267 m
Geography Note
more than 90% of the country is desert or
semidesert
Natural Resources
petroleum, natural gas, gypsum
Climate
mediterranean along coast; dry, extreme
desert interior
Lybian Food
Shorba/Ruzz Jaari/Cuscus Bil-Khodra

WORLD CUP

1930	Did not qualify
1934	Did not qualify
1938	Did not qualify
1950	Did not qualify
1954	Did not qualify
1958	Did not qualify
1962	Did not qualify
1966	Did not qualify
1970	Did not qualify
1974	Did not qualify
1978	Did not qualify
1982	Did not qualify
1986	Did not qualify
1990	Did not qualify
1994	Did not qualify
1998	Did not qualify
2002	Did not qualify

COUNTRY LEAGUE CHAMPIONS

2004	Al-Olympique
2003	Al-Ittihad
2002	Al-Ittihad
2001	Al-Medina
2000	Al-Ahly
1999	Al-Mahalah
1998	Al-Mahalah
1997	Al-Tahaddy
1996	Al-Shaat
Women's League Champion	
2004	Not Known
2003	Not Known
2002	Not Known
2001	Not Known
2000	Not Known

NATIONAL TEAM COLORS

WORLD PICTURES OF SOCCER

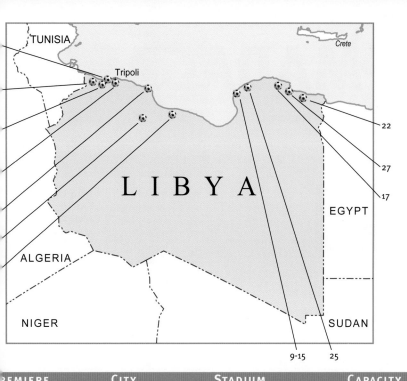

PREMIERE LEAGUE CLUBS	CITY	STADIUM	CAPACITY
Al-Ittihad	Tripoli	June 11th Stadium	80 000
Al-Ahly	Tripoli	June 11th Stadium	80 000
Al-Madina	Tripoli	June 11th Stadium	80 000
Al-Mahalah	Tripoli	June 11th Stadium	80 000
Al-Tirsana	Tripoli	June 11th Stadium	80 000
Al-Shaat	Tripoli	June 11th Stadium	80 000
Al-Dahra	Tripoli	June 11th Stadium	80 000
Al-Wahda	Tripoli	June 11th Stadium	80 000
Al-Nasr	Benghazi	March 28th Stadium	60 000
Al-Hilal	Benghazi	March 28th Stadium	60 000
Al-Ahly	Benghazi	March 28th Stadium	60 000
Al-Tahaddy	Benghazi	March 28th Stadium	60 000
Benghazi Al-Jadida	Benghazi	March 28th Stadium	60 000
Al-Jadida	Benghazi	March 28th Stadium	60 000
Al-Wifaq	Benghazi	March 28th Stadium	60 000
Rafik	Surman		
Al-Akhdar	Darnah		
Al-Swihli	Misurata		
Al-Shawehly	Misurata		
Al-Olympic	Az-Zawiyah		
Al-Wifak	Sabrata		
Al Soukour	Tobruk		
Al-Dhahra	Tarhunah		
Al-Thara	Tarhunah		
Al-Marooj	Al-Marj		
Surt Gulf FC	Surt		
Khalij Bamba	Bamba		

MADAGASCAR

FED. MALAGASY DE FOOTBALL
Pres. vie, 9b lot ibf,rue rabearivelo
pb 4409, antasahavola, Antananarivo 101
TEL 261-20/226 8374 FAX /226 8373
WEB www.cafonline.com

REFERENCE

Official name
Republic of Madagascar

Date of formation 1960
Capital Antananarivo
Population 15.9 million
Total area 224,532 sq Mi, 581,540 sq Km
Time zone GMT +3
Density 71 per sq Mi, 25 per sq Km
Languages Malagasy, French
Literacy rate 83%
Currency Franc
Economy agriculture 81%, services 13%, industry 6%
Religions traditional beliefs 52%, Christian 41%
Ethnic Mix Merina 26%, Betsimisaraka 15%, Betsileo 12%

GEOGRAPHY

Elevation
lowest point: Indian Ocean 0 m
highest point: Maromokotro 2,876 m
Geography Note
world's fourth-largest island; strategic location along Mozambique Channel
Natural Resources
graphite, chromite, coal, bauxite, salt, quartz, tar sands, semiprecious stones, mica, fish, hydropower
Climate
tropical along coast, temperate inland, arid in south
Madagascar Food
lasary voatabia/akoko sy voanio

WORLD CUP

1930	Did not qualify
1934	Did not qualify
1938	Did not qualify
1950	Did not qualify
1954	Did not qualify
1958	Did not qualify
1962	Did not qualify
1966	Did not qualify
1970	Did not qualify
1974	Did not qualify
1978	Did not qualify
1982	Did not qualify
1986	Did not qualify
1990	Did not qualify
1994	Did not qualify
1998	Did not qualify
2002	Did not qualify

COUNTRY LEAGUE CHAMPIONS

2004	USJF/Ravinala
2003	Ecoredipharm
2002	AS Adema
2001	SO de L'Emyrne
2000	AS Fortior
1999	AS Fortior
1998	DSA Antanarivo
1997	DSA Antanarivo
1996	FC BVF Antanarivo

Women's League Champio

2004	Not Known
2003	Not Known
2002	Not Known
2001	ASKA Anosizato
2000	Toamasina

NATIONAL TEAM COLORS

WORLD PICTURES OF SOCCER

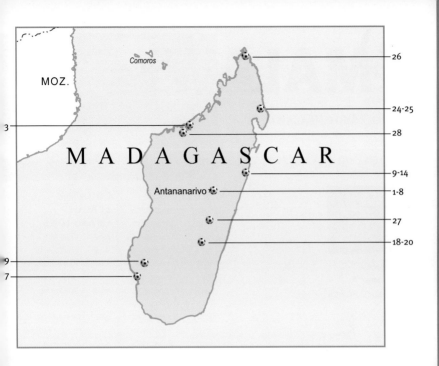

PREMIERE LEAGUE CLUBS	CITY	STADIUM	CAPACITY
AS Adema	Antanarivo	Mahama Sina Stadium	22 000
Stade Olymp. Lermyne	Antanarivo	Mahama Sina Stadium	22 000
DSA Antanarivo	Antanarivo	Mahama Sina Stadium	22 000
FC BVF Antanarivo	Antanarivo	Diego-Suarez Antsiranana	10 000
Dinamo Fima	Antanarivo	Diego-Suarez Antsiranana	10 000
COSFAP	Antanarivo	Diego-Suarez Antsiranana	10 000
BTM	Antanarivo	Diego-Suarez Antsiranana	10 000
USCA Foot	Antanarivo	Stade Mahamasina	10 000
Ecoredipharm	Toamasina		
Lions de Transfoot	Toamasina		
AS Fortior	Toamasina	Stade Mun.Toamasina	5 000
US Transfoot	Toamasina	Stade Mun.Toamasina	5 000
US Port	Toamasina		
ECO Redipharm	Toamasina		
FC Fobar	Toliara		
AS Somasud	Toliara		
Requins de Mahavatse	Toliara		
ASF Fianarantsoa	Fianarantsoa		
AS Jirama	Fianarantsoa		
Akon Ambatomena	Fianarantsoa		
AS Sotema	Mahajanga	Alex Rabemananjara	5 000
Fortior Club Cote Ouest	Mahajanga	Alex Rabemananjara	5 000
FCO	Mahajanga	Alex Rabemananjara	5 000
Antalaha	Antalaha		
Lazan	Antalaha		
So. Peche et Froid	Antsiranana		
EE AFOMA	Ambositra		
Namakia FC	Namakia		
Aigles FC	Sakaraha		

MALAWI

FOOTBALL ASSOC. MALAWI
Mpira House, Old Chileka Road
PB 865, 265 Blantyre
TEL 265/623 197 FAX 265/623 204
WEB www.cafonline.com

REFERENCE
Official name
Republic of Malawi

Date of formation	1964
Capital	Lilongwe
Population	10.9 million
Total area	36,324 sq Mi, 94,080 sq Km
Time zone	GMT +2
Density	300 per sq Mi, 83 per sq Km
Languages	English, Chewa
Literacy rate	56%
Currency	Kwacha
Economy	agriculture 79%, services 16%, industry 5%
Religions	Protestant 55%, Catholic 20%, Muslim 20%
Ethnic Mix	Bantu 99%

GEOGRAPHY
Elevation
lowest point: junction of the Shire River and international boundary
with Mozambique 37 m
highest point: Sapitwa (Mount Mlanje) 3,002 m
Geography Note
landlocked; Lake Nyasa,580 km long, is the country's most prominent physical feature
Natural Resources
limestone, arable land, hydropower, unexploited deposits of uranium, coal, and bauxite
Climate
sub-tropical; rainy season (November to May); dry season (May to November)
Malawi Food
nsima/mbatata/zitumbuwa

WORLD CUP

1930	Did not qualify
1934	Did not qualify
1938	Did not qualify
1950	Did not qualify
1954	Did not qualify
1958	Did not qualify
1962	Did not qualify
1966	Did not qualify
1970	Did not qualify
1974	Did not qualify
1978	Did not qualify
1982	Did not qualify
1986	Did not qualify
1990	Did not qualify
1994	Did not qualify
1998	Did not qualify
2002	Did not qualify

COUNTRY LEAGUE CHAMPIONS

2004	Bakili Bullets
2003	Bakili Bullets
2002	Total Big bullets
2001	Total Big bullets
2000	Bata Bullets
1999	Bata Bullets
1998	Telecom Wanderers
1997	Telecom Wanderers
1996	Telecom Wanderers
Women's League Champion	
2004	DD Sunshine Queens
2003	Not Known
2002	Not Known
2001	Not Known
2000	Not Known

NATIONAL TEAM COLORS

WORLD PICTURES OF SOCCER

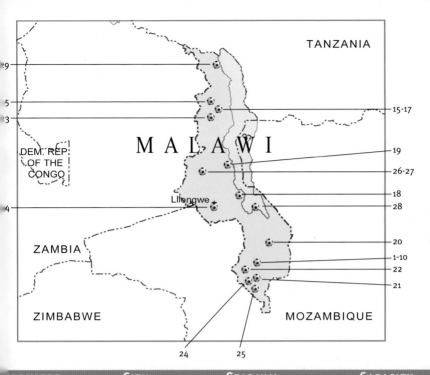

PREMIERE LEAGUE CLUBS	CITY	STADIUM	CAPACITY
Bakili Bullets	Blantyre	Kamuzu Stadium	50 000
MTL Strikers	Blantyre	Kamuzu Stadium	50 000
ADMARC Tigers	Blantyre	Kamuzu Stadium	50 000
Telecom Wanderers	Blantyre	Kamuzu Stadium	50 000
Michiru Castles	Blantyre	Kamuzu Stadium	50 000
Bata Bullets	Blantyre	Kamuzu Stadium	50 000
University FC	Blantyre	Kamuzu Stadium	50 000
Total Big Bullets	Blantyre	Chichiri Stadium	20 000
Super ESCOM	Blantyre	Chichiri Stadium	20 000
Limbe Leaf Wanderers	Blantyre	Chichiri Stadium	20 000
Silver Strikers	Lilongwe	CIVO Lilongwe Stadium	10 000
Blue Eagles	Lilongwe	CIVO Lilongwe Stadium	10 000
CIVO United	Lilongwe	CIVO Lilongwe Stadium	10 000
MDC United	Lilongwe	CIVO Lilongwe Stadium	10 000
Moyale Barracks	Mzuzu		
MZADD Rangers	Mzuzu		
Mzuzu University	Mzuzu		
MAFCO	Salima		
DWASCO	Nkhota Kota		
Red Lions	Zomba		
Illovo FC	Nachalo		
Sucoma	Chikwawa		
Raiply United	Chikangawa		
Goma United	Goma		
Rumphi Medicals	Rumphi		
Kasungu FC	Kasungu		
Kasungu Tobacco	Kasungu		
Army Marines	Monkey Bay		
Karonga United	Karonga		

MALI

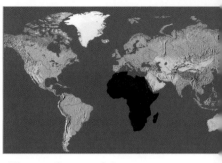

FED. MALIENNE DE FOOTBALL
Stade Mamadou Konate
PB 1020, Bamako
TEL 223/224 254   FAX 223/224 254
WEB www.cafonline.com

REFERENCE
Official name
   Republic of Mali
Date of formation 1960
Capital Bamako
Population 11.2 million
Total area 471,115 sq Mi, 1,220,190 sq Km
Time zone GMT 0
Density 24 per sq Mi, 8 per sq Km
Languages French, Bambara, Fulani, Senufo, Soninke
Literacy rate 30%
Currency CFA Franc
Economy agriculture 75%, services 13%, industry 2%
Religions Muslim 80%, traditional beliefs 18%
Ethnic Mix Bambara 32%, Fula 14%, Senufu 12%, Soninka 9%

GEOGRAPHY
Elevation
lowest point: Senegal River 23 m
highest point: Hombori Tondo 1,155 m
Geography Note
landlocked; divided into three natural zones: the southern, cultivated Sudanese; the central, semiarid Sahelian; and the northern, arid Saharan
Natural Resources
gold, phosphates, kaolin, salt, limestone, uranium, hydropower
Climate
subtropical to arid; hot and dry February to June; rainy, humid, and mild June to November; cool and dry November to February
Malian Food
Poulet Yassa/Foutou

WORLD CUP		COUNTRY LEAGUE CHAMPIONS	
1930	Did not qualify		
1934	Did not qualify		
1938	Did not qualify	2004	Djoliba AC
1950	Did not qualify	2003	Stade Malien
1954	Did not qualify	2002	Stade Malien
1958	Did not qualify	2001	Stade Malien
1962	Did not qualify	2000	Stade Malien
1966	Did not qualify	1999	Djoliba AC
1970	Did not qualify	1998	Djoliba AC
1974	Did not qualify	1997	Djoliba AC
1978	Did not qualify	1996	Djoliba AC
1982	Did not qualify	Women's League Champion	
1986	Did not qualify	2004	AS Mande
1990	Did not qualify	2003	Super Lionnes
1994	Did not qualify	2002	Super Lionnes
1998	Did not qualify	2001	Super Lionnes
2002	Did not qualify	2000	Super Lionnes

NATIONAL TEAM COLORS

WORLD PICTURES OF SOCCER

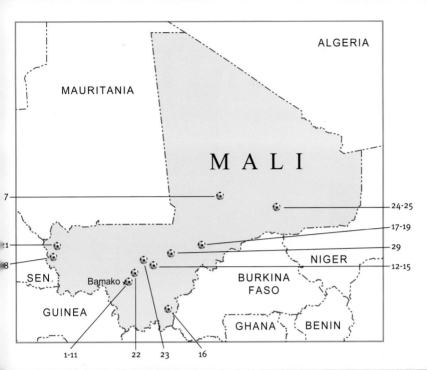

PREMIERE LEAGUE CLUBS	CITY	STADIUM	CAPACITY
-AS Real Bamako	Bamako	Stade Modibo Keita	25 000
-Djoliba AC	Bamako	Complex Heremakono	15 000
-Stade Malien	Bamako	Stade National 26 Mars	50 000
-Cercle Olympique	Bamako	Stade National 26 Mars	50 000
-JS Centre Setif Keita	Bamako	Stade National 26 Mars	50 000
-Commune II	Bamako	Stade National 26 Mars	50 000
-Etoile sportive Darsalam	Bamako	Stade National 26 Mars	50 000
-USFAS	Bamako	Stade National 26 Mars	50 000
-AS Mande	Bamako	Stade National 26 Mars	50 000
-AS Bamako	Bamako	Stade National 26 Mars	50 000
-AS Police	Bamako	Stade National 26 Mars	50 000
-AS Biton	Segou	Stade Amari Daou	15 000
-Renaissance de Segou	Segou	Stade Amari Daou	15 000
-AS comatex	Segou	Stade Amari Daou	15 000
-Avenir FC	Segou	Stade Amari Daou	15 000
-AS Tata National	Sikasso	Stade Omnisport	20 000
-Debo	Mopti	Taikiri	5 000
-Depot Club Mopti	Mopti	Taikiri	5 000
-Douga Club de Mopti	Mopti	Taikiri	5 000
-AS Sigui	Kayes	Abdoul Nakoro Cissoko	5 000
-AS Legal Segou	Kayes	Abdoul Nakoro Cissoko	5 000
-AS Nianan	Koulikoro	Stade Municipal Koulikoro	10 000
-AS Moribabougou	Moribabougou		
-Sonni Gao	Gao		
-Africa Sport	Gao		
-Al Farouk Tombouctou	Tombouctou		
-CM Tombouctou	Tombouctou		
-AS Fale	Macina		
-AS Sofa	Molodo		

MAURITANIA

FED. DE FOOTBALL DE LA REP.
Islamique de Mauritanie
BP 566, Nouakchott
TEL 222/529 1032 FAX 222/529 1031
WEB www.cafonline.com

REFERENCE
Official name
Islamic Republic Of Mauritania

Date of formation	1960
Capital	Nouackchott
Population	2.7 million
Total area	395,953 sq Mi, 1,025,520 sq Km
Time zone	GMT 0
Density	7 per sq Mi, 2 per sq Km
Languages	French, Hassaniyah Arabic, Wolof
Literacy rate	37%
Currency	Ouguiya
Economy	agriculture 70%,services 22%, Industry 8%
Religions	Sunni Muslim 100%
Ethnic Mix	Maure 81%, Wolof 7%, Tukulor 5%, Soninka 3%

GEOGRAPHY
Elevation
lowest point: Sebkha de Ndrhamcha -3 m
highest point: Kediet Ijill 910 m
Geography Note
most of the population concentrated in the cities of Nouakchott and Nouadhibou and along the Senegal River in the southern part of the country
Natural Resources
iron ore, gypsum, copper, phosphate, diamonds, gold, oil; fish
Climate
desert; constantly hot, dry, dusty
Mauritanian Food
harira

WORLD CUP

1930	Did not qualify
1934	Did not qualify
1938	Did not qualify
1950	Did not qualify
1954	Did not qualify
1958	Did not qualify
1962	Did not qualify
1966	Did not qualify
1970	Did not qualify
1974	Did not qualify
1978	Did not qualify
1982	Did not qualify
1986	Did not qualify
1990	Did not qualify
1994	Did not qualify
1998	Did not qualify
2002	Did not qualify

COUNTRY LEAGUE CHAMPIONS

2004	ACS Ksar
2003	NASR Sebhka
2002	FC Nouadhibou
2001	FC Nouadhibou
2000	Mauritel
1999	SPDA Rosso
1998	Garde nationale
1997	Not Known
1996	Not Known

Women's League Champion

2004	Not Known
2003	Not Known
2002	Not Known
2001	Not Known
2000	Not Known

NATIONAL TEAM COLORS

WORLD PICTURES OF SOCCER

Premiere League Clubs	City	Stadium	Capacity
-AS Guarde Nationale	Nouakchott	Stade National Nouakchott	40 000
-ASC Mauritel Mobile	Nouakchott	Stade National Nouakchott	40 000
-El Ahmedi FC	Nouakchott	Stade National Nouakchott	40 000
-ASC Ksar	Nouakchott	Stade National Nouakchott	40 000
-ASC Armee	Nouakchott		
-ASC Gendrim	Nouakchott		
-AS Amical Douane	Nouakchott		
-ASC Police	Nouakchott		
ASC Air mauritanie	Nouakchott		
-ASC Sonalec	Nouakchott		
-ASAC Concorde	Nouakchott		
-FC Nouadhibou	Nouadhibou		
-SNIM de Nouadhibou	Nouadhibou		
-Neimerwatt Nouadhibou	Nouadhibou		
-Jedida Nouadhibou	Nouadhibou		
-SMCP	Nadhibou		
NASR	Sebkha		
-ASC Entente Sebkha	Sebkha		
-Terrouzi FC	Rosso		
-Talhaya	Rosso		
-ASC Trarza	Rosso		
-Toro FC de Trarza	Rosso		
-ASC Kedia de Zouerate	Zouerate		
-Progres Zouerate	Zouerate		
-Delta FC	Tidjarat		
-AS Noujoum	Tidjarat		
-Gorgol FC	Kaedi		
-Adrar FC	Atar		
-Tidjikja	Tidjikja		

MAURITIUS

MAURITIUS FOOTBALL ASSOC.
Chancery House, 2nd Floor # 303-305
14 Lislet Geoffroy Street, Port Louis
TEL 230/211 5909 FAX 230/210 8125
WEB www.cafonline.com

REFERENCE
Official name
Mauritius

Date of formation 1968
Capital Port Louis
Population 1.2 million
Total area 718 sq Mi, 1860 sq Km
Time zone GMT +4
Density 1671 per sq Mi, 635 per sq Km
Languages English, French Creole, Hindi, Bhojpuri, Chinese
Literacy rate 83%
Currency Rupee
Economy services 73%, agriculture 27%, industry 22%
Religions Hindu 52%, Catholic 26%, Muslim 17%
Ethnic Mix Indo-Mauritian 68%, Creole 27%

GEOGRAPHY
Elevation
lowest point: Indian Ocean 0 m
highest point: Mont Piton 828 m
Geography Note
the main island, from which the country derives its name, is of volcanic origin and is almost entirely surrounded by coral reefs
Natural Resources
arable land, fish
Climate
tropical, modified by southeast trade winds; warm, dry winter (May to November); hot, wet, humid summer (November to May)
Mauritius Food
fricasse le chou/mulku/hakien

WORLD CUP	
1930	Did not qualify
1934	Did not qualify
1938	Did not qualify
1950	Did not qualify
1954	Did not qualify
1958	Did not qualify
1962	Did not qualify
1966	Did not qualify
1970	Did not qualify
1974	Did not qualify
1978	Did not qualify
1982	Did not qualify
1986	Did not qualify
1990	Did not qualify
1994	Did not qualify
1998	Did not qualify
2002	Did not qualify

COUNTRY LEAGUE CHAMPIONS	
2004	AS Port Louis 2000
2003	AS Port Louis 2000
2002	AS Port Louis 2000
2001	Olympique de Moka
2000	No Competition
1999	Fire Brigade SC
1998	Scouts Club
1997	Sunrise Flacq United
1996	Sunrise Flacq United
Women's League Champion	
2004	AS Quatre-Bornes
2003	Grand Port United
2002	AS Port Louis
2001	Not Known
2000	Not Known

NATIONAL TEAM COLORS

WORLD PICTURES OF SOCCER

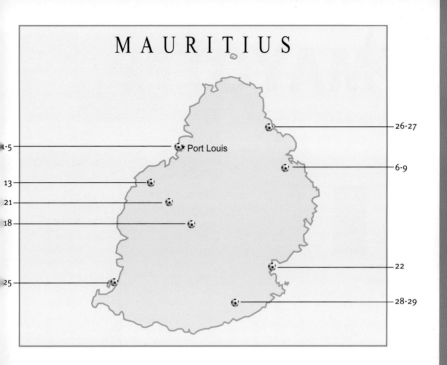

MAURITIUS

★ Port Louis

4-5 ·
13 ·
21 ·
18 ·
25 ·

26-27
6-9
22
28-29

PREMIERE LEAGUE CLUBS	CITY	STADIUM	CAPACITY
1-AS Port-Louis 2000	Port Louis	Stade Anjalay	
2-Scout s Club	Port louis	Stade Anjalay	
3-Police Club	Port Louis	Stade Anjalay	
4-New Sainte-Marie	Port-Louis	Stade Anjalay	
5-La Cur Sylvester	Port Louis	Stade Anjalay	
6-Faucon Flacq SC	Flacq	Stade Auguste Vollaire	
7-Sunrise Flacq United	Flacq	Stade Auguste Vollaire	
8-Tamil Cadets United	Flacq	Stade Auguste Vollaire	
9-Boulet Rouge SC	Flacq	Stade Auguste Vollaire	
10-Fire Brigade	Beau Bassin/Rose Hill	Stade Sir Gaetan Duval	
11-US BBRH	Beau Bassin/Rose Hill	Stade Sir Gaetan Duval	
12-Roche Brunes FC	Beau Bassin/RH	Stade Sir Gaetan Duval	
13-West bromwich Albion	Beau Bassin	Stade Sir Gaetan Duval	
14-Curepipe Starlight SC	Curepipe	Stade George V	
15-Jeanne D'Arc Malherbes	Curepipe	Stade George V	
16-Cercle de Joachim	Curepipe	Stade George V	
17-Forest Side SC	Curepipe	Stade George V	
18-Henrietta SC	Curepipe	Stade George V	
19-Sodnac	Quatres-Bornes	Stade Guy Rozemont	
20-AS Quatres-Bornes	Quatres-Bornes	Stade Guy Rozemont	
21-Jokers FC	Quatre-Bornes	Stade Guy Rozemont	
22-Grand Port United	Mahebourg	Stade Harry Latour	
23-Olympique de Moka	Moka	Stade Quartier-Militaire	
24-Young Men's SC	Moka	Stade Quartier-Militaire	
25-Cercle de Moka	Moka	Stade Quartier-Militaire	
26-Blue Birds FC	Riviere du Rempart	Stade Anjalay	
27-AS Rd.R	Riviere du Rempart	Stade Anjalay	
28-Savanne SC	Savanne	Stade Harry Latour	
29-Savanne Galets	Savanne	Stade Harry Latour	

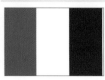# MAYOTTE

MAYOTTE FOOTBALL
Federation
Not Known
TEL: FAX:
WEB www.cafonline.com

REFERENCE
Official name
Mayotte (French Territory)

Date of
Claimed	1843
Capital	Mamoudzou
Population	131,320
Total area	144 sq Mi, 374 sq Km
Time zone	GMT +3
Density	398 per sq Km
Languages	French, English, Hindi
Literacy rate	85%
Currency	French franc
Economy	Tourism 80%
Religions	Catholic 80%,Others
Ethnic Mix	Black african 90%

GEOGRAPHY
Elevation
lowest point: Indian Ocean 0 m
highest point:Benara 660 m
Geography Note
part of Comoro Archipelago; 18 islands
Natural Resources
NEGL
Climate
tropical; marine; hot, humid, rainy season
during northeastern monsoon (November to
May); dry season is cooler (May to
November)
Mayotte Food
cassava/plantain/couscous

WORLD CUP		COUNTRY LEAGUE CHAMPIONS	
1930	Did not qualify		
1934	Did not qualify		
1938	Did not qualify	2004	AS Sada
1950	Did not qualify	2003	FC Kani-Bane
1954	Did not qualify	2002	FC Kani-Bane
1958	Did not qualify	2001	VCO Vahibe
1962	Did not qualify	2000	Rosador
1966	Did not qualify	1999	FC Jumeau
1970	Did not qualify	1998	AS Sada
1974	Did not qualify	1997	Not Known
1978	Did not qualify	1996	Not Known
1982	Did not qualify	Women's League Champion	
1986	Did not qualify	2004	Not Known
1990	Did not qualify	2003	Not Known
1994	Did not qualify	2002	Not Known
1998	Did not qualify	2001	Atlas Margaritas
2002	Did not qualify	2000	Not Known

NATIONAL TEAM COLORS

WORLD PICTURES OF SOCCER

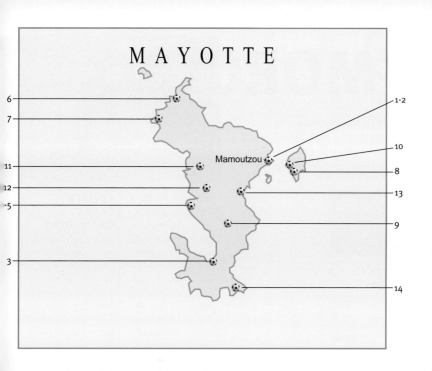

MAYOTTE

PREMIERE LEAGUE CLUBS	CITY	STADIUM	CAPACITY
-ASC Kaweni	Mamoudzou	Stade de Kavani	5 000
-Mairie Mamoudzou	Mamoudzou	Stade de Kavani	5 000
-FC Jumeaux	M'zioizie		
-AS Sada	Sada		
-UC Sada	Sada		
-Abeilles	Mtzamboro		
-Racine du Nord	Acoua		
-Pamandzi Sport Club	Pamandzi Be		
-Tchanga	M'Samouni		
-Mairie Dzaoudzi	Dzaoudzi		
-FCO Chingoni	Chingoni		
-Etincelles	Sohoa		
-Ouragan	Dembeni		
-Etoile du sud	Balembo		

MOROCCO

FED. ROYALE MAROCAINE DE FOOTBALL
51 bis av. ibn sina, BP 51 10.000 Rabat-A
TEL 212-3/767 2706 FAX /767 1070
WEB www.fedefoot.ma

REFERENCE
Official name
Kingdom of Morocco
Date of formation 1956
Capital Rabat
Population 28.4 million
Total area 172,316 sq Mi, 446,300 sq Km
Time zone GMT +1
Density 165 per sq Mi, 66 per sq Km
Languages Arabic, Berber, French
Literacy rate 42%
Currency Dirham
Economy agriculture 46%, services 30%, industry 24%
Religions Muslim 99%
Ethnic Mix Arab 70%, Berber 29%

GEOGRAPHY
Elevation
lowest point: Sebkha Tah -55 m
highest point: Jbel Toubkal 4,165 m
Geography Note
strategic location along Strait of Gibraltar
Natural Resources
phosphates, iron ore, manganese, lead, zinc, fish, salt
Climate
mediterranean, becoming more extreme in the interior
Moroccan Food
couscous/batinjaan zalud/kebab koutbane

WORLD CUP

1930	Did not qualify
1934	Did not qualify
1938	Did not qualify
1950	Did not qualify
1954	Did not qualify
1958	Did not qualify
1962	Did not qualify
1966	Did not qualify
1970	First round exit
1974	Did not qualify
1978	Did not qualify
1982	Did not qualify
1986	scd round exit
1990	Did not qualify
1994	First round exit
1998	First round exit
2002	Did not qualify

COUNTRY LEAGUE CHAMPIONS

2004	Raja Casablanca
2003	Hassania US
2002	Hassania US
2001	Raja Casablanca
2000	Raja Casablanca
1999	Raja Casablanca
1998	Raja Casablanca
1997	Raja Casablanca
1996	Raja Casablanca
Women's League Champion	
2005	Raja D'Agadir
2004	Not Known
2003	Not Known
2002	Not Known
2001	Not Known

NATIONAL TEAM COLORS

WORLD PICTURES OF SOCCER

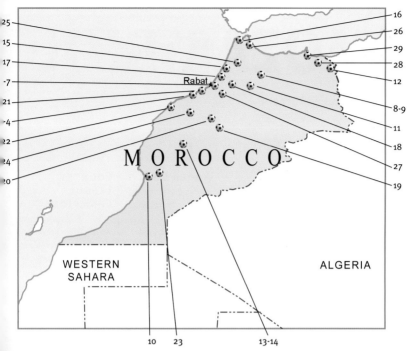

PREMIERE LEAGUE CLUBS	CITY	STADIUM	CAPACITY
-Raja Casablanca	Casablanca	Mohammed V	67 000
-WAC Casablanca	Casablanca	Mohammed V	67 000
-Racing Athletic Club	Casablanca	stade Pere Jego	10 000
-Tihad Sportif	Casablanca	Sidi Mohammed	5 000
-FAR Rabat	Rabat	Moulay Abdellah	60 000
-Stade Marocain	Rabat	El Barid	20 000
-FUS Rabat	Rabat	Stade du Fus	8 000
-MAS Fes	Fes	Complex Sportif	45 000
-WAF Fes	Fes	Hassan II	15 000
-Hassania US	Agadir	Al Inbiaate	15 000
-COD Meknes	Meknes	Stade D'Honneur	20 000
-MC Oujda	Oujda	Stade D'Honneur	35 000
-KAC Marrakech	Marrakech	El Harti	25 000
-Nejm Marrakech	Marrakech	El Harti	25 000
-KAC Kenitra	Kenitra	Municipal	15 000
-Ittihad Riadi	Tangier	Stade de Marchan	14 000
-SA Sale	Sale	Marche Verte	4 000
-Ittihad Zemmouri	Al-Khmissat	Stade du 20 Aout	6 000
-Raja Beni Melal	Beni Melal	D'Honneur	12 000
-Olympique	Khouribga	Municipal	5 000
-SCC Mohammedia	Mohammedia	El Bachir	5 000
-DH El Jadida	El Jadida	El Abdi	15 000
-JS El Massira	El Massira	Cheick Laaghdef	40 000
-RS Settat	Settat	Municipal	20 000
-UFC Sidi Kacem	Sidi Kacem		
-Maghreb Tetouan	Tetouan		
-Renaissance Tiflet	Tiflet		
-Renaissance Berkane	Berkane		
-Hilal Nador	Nador		

MOZAMBIQUE

FED. MOCAMBICINA DE FUTEBOL
Av. Samora Machel,11-2 Andar,1467
Map.
TEL 258-1/300 366 FAX /300 367
WEB www.cafonline.com

REFERENCE
Official name
Republic of Mozambique
Date of formation 1975
Capital Maputo
Population 19.7 million
Total area 302,737 sq Mi, 784,090 sq Km
Time zone GMT +2
Density 65 per sq Mi, 24 per sq Km
Languages Portuguese
Literacy rate 40%
Currency Metical
Economy agriculture 85%, services 8%, industry 7%
Religions traditional beliefs 60%, Christian 30%, Muslim 10%
Ethnic Mix Makua-Lomwe 47%,Thonga 23%,Malawi 12%

GEOGRAPHY
Elevation
lowest point: Indian Ocean 0 m
highest point: Monte Binga 2,436 m
Geography Note
the Zambezi flows through the north-central and most fertile part of the country
Natural Resources
coal, titanium, natural gas, hydropower, tantalum, graphite
Climate
tropical to subtropical
Mozambiques Food
sopa de feijao verde matata/frango a cafrial

WORLD CUP		COUNTRY LEAGUE CHAMPIONS	
1930	Did not qualify		
1934	Did not qualify		
1938	Did not qualify	2004	Ferroviario Maputo
1950	Did not qualify	2003	Maxaquene
1954	Did not qualify	2002	Ferroviario Maputo
1958	Did not qualify	2001	Costa do Sol
1962	Did not qualify	2000	Costa do Sol
1966	Did not qualify	1999	Ferroviario Maputo
1970	Did not qualify	1998	Not Known
1974	Did not qualify	1997	Ferroviario Maputo
1978	Did not qualify	1996	Ferroviario Maputo
1982	Did not qualify	**Women's League Champion**	
1986	Did not qualify	2004	Not Known
1990	Did not qualify	2003	Not Known
1994	Did not qualify	2002	Not Known
1998	Did not qualify	2001	Not Known
2002	Did not qualify	2000	Not Known

NATIONAL TEAM COLORS

WORLD PICTURES OF SOCCER

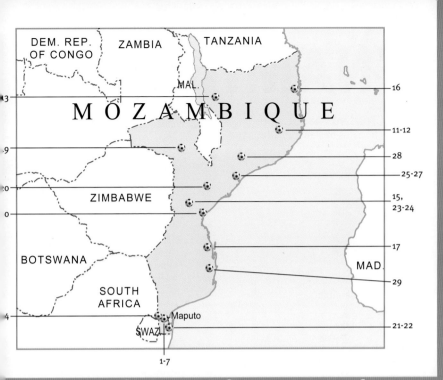

PREMIERE LEAGUE CLUBS	CITY	STADIUM	CAPACITY
-CD Da Maxaquene	Maputo	Do Maxaquene	15 000
-CD Costa do Sol	Maputo	Do Costa do Sol	10 000
-Grupo Desportivo Maputo	Maputo	Do Desportivo	10 000
Clube Ferroviario de Maputo	Maputo	Da Chava	60 000
-Academica de Maputo	Maputo		
-CDMatchedje	Maputo	Do Costa do Sol	10 000
-GD Mahafil	Maputo	Do Mahafil	4 000
Clube Ferroviario da Beira	Beira	Do Ferroviario	10 000
GDCT do Pungue	Beira		
ɔ-Textil Puenge	Beira	Chiveve	10 000
₅-Clube Ferroviario	Nampula		
₂-ECMEP	Nampula		
₃-FC de Lichinga	Lichinga		
₅-Desportivo da Matola	Matola		
-Textafrica do Chimoio	Chimoio		
₅-Clube Ferroviario de Pemba	Pemba		
-Wane Pone	Inhassaro-Maxixe	Do Conselho Municipal	10 000
₃-Chingale	Tete		
₃-Desportivos	Tete		
ɔ-Textil	Pungue		
-Catembe FC	Catembe		
₂-Amor FC da Catembe	Catembe		
₄-Desportivo Chimoio	Chimoio		
-Aves de Chimoio	Chimoio		
₅-Ferroviario Quelimane	Quelimane		
₃-Catedral de Quelimane	Quelimane		
-Quelimane FC	Quelimane		
-CBC de Mocuba	Mocuba		
ɔ-Sporting Bagu	Massinga		

NAMIBIA

NAMIBIA FOOTBALL ASSOC.
Coun. of churches of Namibia, Abraham Mashego st., CNN Bld. Katutura, PB 1345, 9000 Windhoek TEL 264-61/26691
WEB www.cafonline.com

REFERENCE
Official name
Republic of Namibia

Date of formation	1994
Capital	Windhoek
Population	1.7 million
Total area	317,872 sq Mi, 823,290 sq Km
Time zone	GMT +2
Density	5 per sq Mi, 2 per sq Km
Languages	English, Afrikaans, Ovambo, Kavango, German
Literacy rate	40%
Currency	Rand
Economy	agriculture 60%, industry & commerce 19%
Religions	Christian 90%, traditional beliefs 10%
Ethnic Mix	Ovambo 50%, Kavango 9%, Damara 8%

GEOGRAPHY
Elevation
lowest point: Atlantic Ocean 0 m
highest point: Konigstein 2,606 m
Geography Note
first country in the world to incorporate the protection of the environment into its constitution; some 14% of the land is protected, including virtually the entire Namib Desert coastal strip
Natural Resources
diamonds, copper, uranium, gold, lead, tin, lithium, cadmium, zinc, salt, vanadium, natural gas, hydropower, fish
note: deposits of oil, coal, and iron ore
Climate
desert; hot, dry; rainfall sparse and erratic
Namibian Food
black eyed peas/oshifima

WORLD CUP

1930	Did not qualify
1934	Did not qualify
1938	Did not qualify
1950	Did not qualify
1954	Did not qualify
1958	Did not qualify
1962	Did not qualify
1966	Did not qualify
1970	Did not qualify
1974	Did not qualify
1978	Did not qualify
1982	Did not qualify
1986	Did not qualify
1990	Did not qualify
1994	Did not qualify
1998	Did not qualify
2002	Did not qualify

COUNTRY LEAGUE CHAMPIONS

2004	Blue Waters
2003	Chief Santos
2002	Liverpool
2001	Liverpool
2000	Tunacor Blue Waters
1999	Black Africans
1998	Black Africans
1997	Not Known
1996	Tunacor Blue Waters

Women's League Champion

2004	Civics FC
2003	Not Known
2002	Not Known
2001	Unam Bokkies
2000	Not Known

NATIONAL TEAM COLORS

WORLD PICTURES OF SOCCER

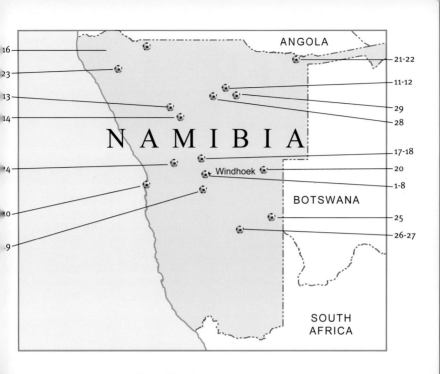

PREMIERE LEAGUE CLUBS	CITY	STADIUM	CAPACITY
-Civics FC	Windhoek	Independence Stadium	25 000
-Orlando Pirates	Windhoek	Independence Stadium	25 000
-Ramblers	Windhoek	Independence Stadium	25 000
-African Stars	Windhoek	Khomasdal Stadium	10 000
-Black Africa	Windhoek	Khomasdal Stadium	10 000
-United Africa Tigers	Windhoek	Khomasdal Stadium	10 000
-Young Ones	Windhoek	Khomasdal Stadium	10 000
-Sundowns	Windhoek	Khomasdal Stadium	10 000
-Blue Waters	Walvis Bay	Kuisebmond Stadium	10 000
-Eleven Arrows	Walvis Bay	Kuisebmond Stadium	10 000
-Chief Santos	Tsumeb		
-Benfica	Tsumeb		
-Golden Bees FC	Outjo		
-Life Fighters	Otjiwarongo	Otjiwarongo Municipal	5 000
-Oshakati City FC	Oshakati	Independence Stadium	5 000
-Young Chiefs	Oshakati	Independence Stadium	5 000
-Liverpool FC	Okahandja		
-Young Chiefs	Okahandja		
-Friends	Rehoboth		
-Mae Dae Chiefs	Gobabis		
-Gica Top	Rundu		
-Bingo FC	Rundu		
-Blue Birds	Opuwo		
-Blue Birds FC	Erongo		
-Aranos FC	Aranos		
-Bee Bob Brothers	Mariental	Mariental Sport Stadium	5 000
-Flying Eagles	Mariental	Mariental Sport Stadium	5 000
-Touch & Go	Otavi		
-Chelsea	Grootfontein	Omulunga Stadium	5 000

NIGER

FED. NIGERIENNE DE FOOTBALL
Std. du 29 Juillet, BP 10299, Rue de la
Topoa, Niamey
TEL 227/725 127
WEB www.cafonline.com

REFERENCE
Official name
  Republic of Niger
**Date of
formation** 1960
Capital Niamey
Population 10.7 million
Total area 489,072 sq Mi, 1,266,700 sq Km
Time zone GMT +1
Density 22 per sq Mi, 8 per sq Km
Languages French, Hausa, Djerma, Fulani,
  Tuareg, Teda
Literacy rate 13%
Currency CFA Franc
Economy agriculture87%, services 10%,
  industry 3%
Religions Muslim 84%,
  traditional belief 14%
Ethnic Mix Hausa 54%, Djerma 21%,
  Fulani 10%, Tuareg 9%

GEOGRAPHY
Elevation
lowest point: Niger River 200 m
highest point: Mont Bagzane 2,022 m
Geography Note
landlocked; one of the hottest countries in
the world: northern four-fifths is desert,
southern one-fifth is savanna, suitable for
livestock and limited agriculture
Natural Resources
uranium, coal, iron ore, tin, phosphates,
gold, petroleum
Climate
desert; mostly hot, dry, dusty; tropical in
extreme south
Niger Food
mango salad/jollof rice/groundmeat stew

WORLD CUP

1930	Did not qualify
1934	Did not qualify
1938	Did not qualify
1950	Did not qualify
1954	Did not qualify
1958	Did not qualify
1962	Did not qualify
1966	Did not qualify
1970	Did not qualify
1974	Did not qualify
1978	Did not qualify
1982	Did not qualify
1986	Did not qualify
1990	Did not qualify
1994	Did not qualify
1998	Did not qualify
2002	Did not qualify

COUNTRY LEAGUE CHAMPIONS

2004	Sahel SC
2003	Sahel SC
2002	AS Niamey
2001	JS Tenere
2000	JS Tenere
1999	Olympique FC
1998	Olympique FC
1997	Olympique FC
1996	Sahel SC

Women's League Champions

2004	Not Known
2003	Not Known
2002	Not Known
2001	Not Known
2000	Not Known

NATIONAL TEAM COLORS

WORLD PICTURES OF SOCCER

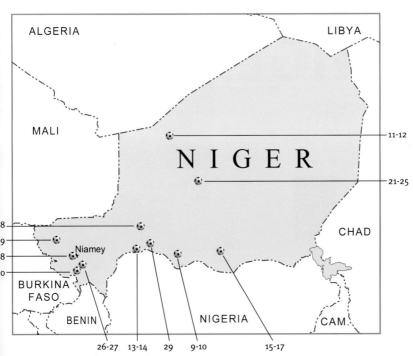

PREMIERE LEAGUE CLUBS	CITY	STADIUM	CAPACITY
-Sahel SC	Niamey	General Seyni Kountche	30 000
-Zumunta AC	Niamey	General Seyni Kountche	30 000
-Olympic FC	Niamey	General Seyni Kountche	30 000
-JS du Tenere	Niamey	General Seyni Kountche	30 000
-AS FINIS	Niamey	Niamey Municipal	10 000
-ASFAN	Niamey	Niamey Municipal	10 000
-Liberte FC	Niamey	Niamey Municipal	10 000
-AS Police	Niamey	Niamey Municipal	10 000
-Dan Baskore	Maradi	Maradi municipal	10 000
-Jangorzo FC	Maradi	Maradi municipal	10 000
-Akokana	Arlit	Arlit Municipal	7 000
-Urana	Arlit	Arlit Municipal	7 000
-AS CBK	Birnin Konni	Birnin Koni Municipal	5 000
-Gourama FC	Birnin Konni	Birnin Koni Municipal	5 000
-Espoir FC	Zinder	Zinder Municipal	10 000
-Alkali Nassara Club	Zinder	Zinder Municipal	10 000
-AS Tanimoune	Zinder	Zinder Municipal	10 000
-US Gendarmerie Nationale	Tillbery	Tillabery Municipal	5 000
-AS Douanes	Tillebery	Tillabery Municipal	5 000
-National Dendi	Gaya	Gaya municipal	5 000
-Aigles FC	Agadez	Agadez Municipal	5 000
-Akokana D'Arlit	Agadez	Agadez Municipal	5 000
-Lantarki FC	Agadez	Agadez Municipal	5 000
-Urana	Agadez	Agadez Municipal	5 000
-Generateur FC	Agadez	Agadez Municipal	5 000
-Entente FC	Dosso	Dosso Municipal	5 000
-Tagour Provincial Club	Dosso	Dosso Municipal	5 000
-Dan Garmou	Tahoua	Tahoua Municipal	10 000
-ASIC	Malbaza		

NIGERIA

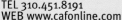

NIGERIA FOOTBALL ASSOC.
Plot 2033, Olusegun Obasanjo Way,
Zone 7
Wuse Abuja,PB 5101 Garki,Abuja
TEL 310.451.8191
WEB www.cafonline.com

REFERENCE

Official name
Federal Republic of Nigeria

Date of formation	1960
Capital	Abuja
Population	111.5 million
Total area	351,648 Sq Mi, 910,770 sq Km
Time zone	GMT +1
Density	317 per sq Mi, 123 per sq Km
Languages	English, Hausa, Yoruba
Literacy rate	56%
Currency	Naira
Economy	services 51%, agriculture 45%, industry 4%
Religions	Muslim 50%, Christian 40%, traditional beliefs 10%
Ethnic Mix	Hausa 21%, Yoruba 21%, Ibo 18%, Fulani 11%

GEOGRAPHY

Elevation
lowest point: Atlantic Ocean 0 m
highest point: Chappal Waddi 2,419 m

Geography Note
the Niger enters the country in the north-west and flows southward through tropical rain forests and swamps to its delta in the Gulf of Guinea

Natural Resources
natural gas, petroleum, tin, columbite, iron ore, coal, limestone, lead, zinc, arable land

Climate
varies; equatorial in south, tropical in center, arid in north

Nigerian Food
ikokore/ojojo/kulikuli/ewedu/amala

WORLD CUP

1930	Did not qualify
1934	Did not qualify
1938	Did not qualify
1950	Did not qualify
1954	Did not qualify
1958	Did not qualify
1962	Did not qualify
1966	Did not qualify
1970	Did not qualify
1974	Did not qualify
1978	Did not qualify
1982	Did not qualify
1986	Did not qualify
1990	Did not qualify
1994	Scd round exit
1998	Scd round exit
2002	First round exit

COUNTRY LEAGUE CHAMPIONS

2004	Dolphin FC
2003	Enyimba Aba
2002	Enyimba Aba
2001	Enyimba Aba
2000	Julius Berger
1999	Lobi Stars FC
1998	3 SC Shooting Stars
1997	Eagle Cement
1996	Udoji United FC

Women's League Champion

2004	Bayelsa Queens
2003	Delta Queens FC
2002	Pellican Stars FC
2001	Pellican Stars FC
2000	Pellican Stars FC

NATIONAL TEAM COLORS

WORLD PICTURES OF SOCCER

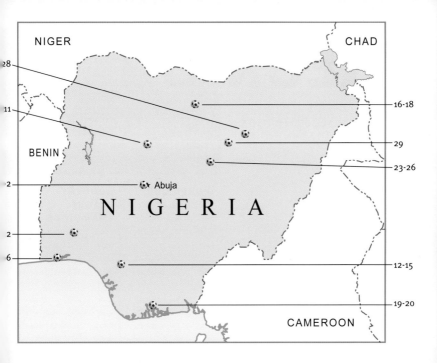

PREMIERE LEAGUE CLUBS	CITY	STADIUM	CAPACITY
-FCDA	Abuja	Old Paradise Ground	5 000
-NEPA Abuja FC	Abuja	Abuja Stadium	60 000
-Stationery Stores	Lagos	Taslim Balogoun	20 000
-Flaming Flamingos	Lagos	Taslim Balogoun	20 000
Union Bank FC	Lagos	Surelere	45 000
FC Julius Berger	Lagos	Onikan	5 000
UNTL	Kaduna	Ahmadou Bello	30 000
Avante United	Kaduna	Ahmadou Bello	30 000
Gray's International	Kaduna	Ahmadou Bello	30 000
-NUB	Kaduna	Ahmadou Bello	30 000
-Ranchers Bees	Kaduna	Ranchers Bees Stadium	10 000
-Insurance FC	Benin City	Samuel Ogbemudia	20 000
-Edo United	Benin City	Samuel Ogbemudia	20 000
-Igbino FC	Benin City	Samuel Ogbemudia	20 000
-Okomu	Benin City	Samuel Ogbemudia	20 000
-Rangers International	Kano	Sani Abacha	25 000
-Wreca Kano	Kano	Sani Abacha	25 000
-Dantata	Kano	Sani Abacha	25 000
-Dolphin FC	Port Hartcourt	Liberation Stadium	25 000
-Sharks FC	Port Hartcourt	Sharks Stadium	10 000
-Shooting Stars	Ibadan	Liberty Stadium	35 000
-Adepojou	Ibadan	Lekan Salami	18 000
-Plateau United	Jos	Rwang Pam	15 000
-Juth FC	Jos	Rwang Pam	15 000
-Mighty Jets	Jos	Rwang Pam	15 000
-JC Raiders	Jos	Rwang Pam	15 000
-Gombe United	Gombe	Abubakar Umar Memorial	10 000
-Black Stars FC	Gombe	Abubakar Umar Memorial	10 000
-Wikki Tourists	Bauchi	Abubakar Tafawa Balewa	25 000

REUNION

REUNION FOOTBALL FEDERATION
(No Address Found)
TEL: FAX:
WEB www.cafonline.com

REFERENCE
Official name
   Reunion (French Overseas Dept)

Claimed	1638
Capital	Saint Denis
Population	632,000
Total area	970 sq Mi, 2500 sq Km
Time zone	GMT +4
Density	not known
Languages	French, English, Hindi
Literacy rate	79%
Currency	French Franc
Economy	services 49%, agriculture 30%, industry 21%
Religions	Roman Catholic 86%, Hindu, Muslim, Buddhist (1995)
Ethnic Mix	French, African, Malagasy, Chinese, Pakistani, Indian

GEOGRAPHY
Elevation
lowest point: Indian Ocean 0 m
highest point: Piton des Neiges 3,069 m
Geography Note
this mountainous, volcanic island has an active volcano, Piton de la Fournaise; there is a tropical cyclone center at Saint-Denis, which is the monitoring station for the whole Indian Ocean
Natural Resources
fish, arable land, hydropower
Climate
tropical, but temperature moderates with elevation; cool and dry from May to November, hot and rainy from November to April
Reunion Food
espadon massale/le cari bichiques/le civet zourite

WORLD CUP

1930	Did not qualify
1934	Did not qualify
1938	Did not qualify
1950	Did not qualify
1954	Did not qualify
1958	Did not qualify
1962	Did not qualify
1966	Did not qualify
1970	Did not qualify
1974	Did not qualify
1978	Did not qualify
1982	Did not qualify
1986	Did not qualify
1990	Did not qualify
1994	Did not qualify
1998	Did not qualify
2002	Did not qualify

COUNTRY LEAGUE CHAMPIONS

2004	USS Tamponnaise
2003	USS Tamponnaise
2002	SS Saint Louisienne
2001	SS Saint Louisienne
2000	AS Marsouins
1999	USS Tamponnaise
1998	SS Saint Louisienne
1997	SS Saint Louisienne
1996	CS Saint Denis
Women's League Champion	
2004	FF Ouest FC
2003	FF Ouest FC
2002	Port Foot Feminin
2001	FF Ouest FC
2000	Not Known

NATIONAL TEAM COLORS

WORLD PICTURES OF SOCCER

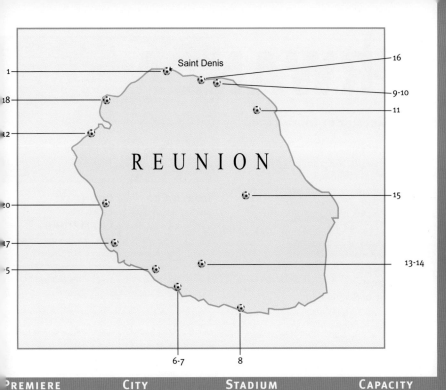

Saint Denis

REUNION

1	16
18	9-10
12	11
20	15
17	13-14
5	6-7
	8

PREMIERE LEAGUE CLUBS	CITY	STADIUM	CAPACITY
1-Saint-Denis FC	Saint-Denis	Stade de L'Est	7 500
2-SS Riviere Sports	Saint-Louis	Stade de L'Est	7 500
3-SS Saint-Louisienne	Saint-Louis	Stade de L'Est	7 500
4-RC Saint-Louis	Saint-Louis	Stade de L'Est	7 500
5-OL Saint-Louis	Saint-Louis	Stade de L'Est	7 500
6-JS Saint-Pierroise	Saint-Pierre		
7-SS Capricorne	Saint Pierre		
8-SS Excelsior	Saint-Joseph		
9-SS Dynamo	Sainte-Marie		
10-CS Sainte-Marie	Sainte-Marie		
11-US Saint-Andre Leopards	Saint-Andre		
12-FC Ouest Saint-Paul	Saint-Paul		
13-US Stade Tamponnaise	Le Tampon		
14-FC Pont-D'Yves	Le Tampon		
15-CS Plaine	Plaine des Palmistes		
16-US Chaudron	Chaudron		
17-FC Les Avirons	Les Avirons		
18-Jeanne D'Arc	Le Port		
19-AS Marsouins	Saint-Leu		
20-AS Pitons	Saint-Leu		

RWANDA

FED. RWANDAIDE DE FOOTBALL AMATEUR
1BP 2000, Kigali
TEL 250/71 596 FAX 250/71 597
WEB www.cafonline.com

REFERENCE
Official name
Republic of Rwanda

Date of formation	1962
Capital	Kigali
Population	7.7 million
Total area	9633 sq Mi, 24,950 sq Km
Time zone	GMT +2
Density	799 per sq Mi, 309 per sq Km
Languages	Kinyarwanda, French, Kiswahili
Literacy rate	41%
Currency	Franc
Economy	agriculture 93%, services 3%,Industry 2%
Religions	traditional beliefs 50%, Catholic 45%
Ethnic Mix	Hutu 90%, Tusi 6%, Twa 2%

GEOGRAPHY
Elevation
lowest point: Rusizi River 950 m
highest point: Volcan Karisimbi 4,519 m
Geography Note
landlocked; most of the country is savanna grassland with the population predominantly rural
Natural Resources
gold, cassiterite (tin ore), wolframite (tungsten ore), methane, hydropower, arable land
Climate
temperate; two rainy seasons (February to April, November to January); mild in mountains with frost and snow possible
Rwadan Food
amandazi/pinto beans with potatoes

WORLD CUP		COUNTRY LEAGUE CHAMPIONS	
1930	Did not qualify		
1934	Did not qualify		
1938	Did not qualify	2004	Rayon Sport Butare
1950	Did not qualify	2003	APR FC Kigali
1954	Did not qualify	2002	Rayon Sport Butare
1958	Did not qualify	2001	APR FC Kigali
1962	Did not qualify	2000	APR FC Kigali
1966	Did not qualify	1999	APR FC Kigali
1970	Did not qualify	1998	Rayon Sport Butare
1974	Did not qualify	1997	Rayon Sport Butare
1978	Did not qualify	1996	APR FC Kigali
1982	Did not qualify	Women's League Champion	
1986	Did not qualify	2004	Not Known
1990	Did not qualify	2003	Not Known
1994	Did not qualify	2002	Not Known
1998	Did not qualify	2001	Not Known
2002	Did not qualify	2000	Not Known

NATIONAL TEAM COLORS

WORLD PICTURES OF SOCCER

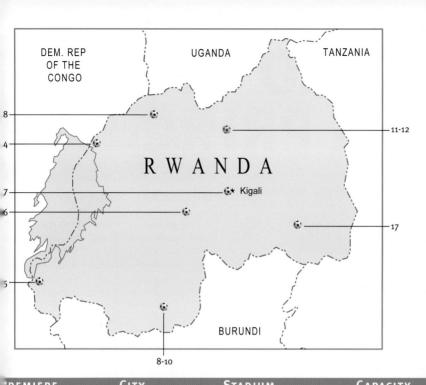

PREMIERE LEAGUE CLUBS	CITY	STADIUM	CAPACITY
APR FC	Kigali	Amahoro Stadium	10 000
Citadins	Kigali	Amahoro Stadium	10 000
Leopards FC	Kigali	Amahoro Stadium	10 000
Kiyovu Sport	Kigali	Amahoro Stadium	10 000
Rayon Sport	Kigali	Amahoro Stadium	10 000
Rwanda FC	Kigali	Amahoro Stadium	10 000
Pantheres Noires	Kigali	Amahoro Stadium	10 000
Nyanza FC	Butare		
Mukura Victory Sport	Butare		
Intare Ruhengeri FC	Butare		
Zebres de Byumba FC	Byumba		
Byumba FC	Byumba		
Etincelles	Gisenyi		
Marines FC	Gisenyi		
Espoir FC	Cyangugu		
Flash FC	Gitarama		
Police FC	Kibungo		
Muhungwa	Ruhengeri		

SAO TOME & PRINCIPE

FED. SANTOMENSE DE FUTEBOL
Rua da Mocambique, Sao Tome
TEL 239-12/24 231 FAX /21 333
WEB www.fsf.st

REFERENCE
Official name
Democratic Republic of Sao Tome & Principe

Date of formation	1975		
Capital	Sao Tome		
Population	159,883		
Total area	370 sq Mi, 960 sq Km		
Time zone	GMT 0		
Density	432 per sq Mi, 161 per sq Km		
Languages	Portuguese, Portuguese Creole		
Literacy rate	67%		
Currency	Dobra		
Economy	fishing & agriculture		
Religions	Catholic 84%		
Ethnic Mix	Black 90%, Portuguese & Creole 10%		

GEOGRAPHY
Elevation
lowest point: Atlantic Ocean 0 m
highest point: Pico de Sao Tome 2,024 m
Geography Note
the smallest country in Africa; the two main islands form part of a chain of extinct volcanoes and both are fairly mountainous
Natural Resources
fish, hydropower
Climate
tropical; hot, humid; one rainy season (October to May)
Sao Tome & Principe Food
sopa de santo

WORLD CUP		COUNTRY LEAGUE CHAMPIONS	
1930	Did not qualify		
1934	Did not qualify		
1938	Did not qualify	2004	Not Known
1950	Did not qualify	2003	Inter Bom-Bom
1954	Did not qualify	2002	No competition
1958	Did not qualify	2001	Bairros Unidos FC
1962	Did not qualify	2000	Inter Bom Bom
1966	Did not qualify	1999	Sporting Praia Cruz
1970	Did not qualify	1998	GSOS Operarios
1974	Did not qualify	1997	No competition
1978	Did not qualify	1996	Caixao Grande
1982	Did not qualify	**Women's League Champio**	
1986	Did not qualify	2004	Not Known
1990	Did not qualify	2003	Vitoria Riboque FC
1994	Did not qualify	2002	Not Known
1998	Did not qualify	2001	Not Known
2002	Did not qualify	2000	Not Known

NATIONAL TEAM COLORS

WORLD PICTURES OF SOCCER

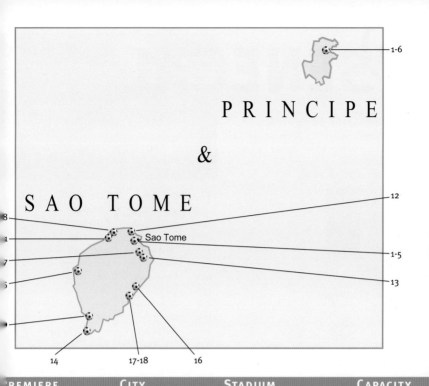

PRINCIPE

&

SAO TOME

Sao Tome

PREMIERE LEAGUE CLUBS	CITY	STADIUM	CAPACITY
Sporting Clube Sao Tome	Sao Tome	Estadio Nacional 12 julho	6 500
Alianca Nacional	Sao Tome	Estadio Nacional 12 julho	6 500
UDESCAI	Sao tome	Estadio Nacional 12 julho	6 500
Andorinhas	Sao Tome	Nacional Sao Tome	3 000
3es de Septembro	Sao Tome	Nacional Sao Tome	3 000
Caixao Grande FC	Caixao Grande		
Bairros Unidos FC	Caixao Grande		
Inter FC	Bombom		
Vitoria FC	Tou		
Sporting Praia	Praia Das Conchas		
DesportivoFolha Fede	Praia Das Conchas		
Desportivo Guadalupe	Guadalupe		
Santana FC	Santana		
Benfica Porto Alegre	Porto Alegre		
Deportivo St. Caterina	St.Caterina		
Varzim FC	Ribeira Afonso		
Maritimo	Santa Cruz		
GD Cruz Vermelha	Santa Cruz		
Principe Island			
Deportivo Porto Real	San Antonio	Est. da Regiao Autonoma	3 000
Desportivo Sundy	San Antonio	Est. da Regiao Autonoma	3 000
GDOS Operarios	San Antonio	Est. da Regiao Autonoma	3 000
DAPB	San Antonio	Est. da Regiao Autonoma	3 000
er de Maio	San Antonio	Est. da Regiao Autonoma	3 000
Desportivo S. Antonio	San Antonio	Est. da Regiao Autonoma	3 000

SENEGAL

FED. SENEGALAISE DE FOOTBALL
Stade Leopold Sedar Senghor. Route de
L'aeroport LS Senghor BP 13021 Dakar
TEL 221/827 2935
WEB www.cafonline.com

REFERENCE
Official name
Republic of Senegal
Date of formation 1960
Capital Dakar
Population 9.5 million
Total area 74,336 sq Mi, 192,530 sq Km
Time zone GMT 0
Density 128 per sq Mi, 51 per sq Km
Languages French,Wollof,Fulani,Serer,
Diola,Malinke,Soninke
Literacy rate 32%
Currency CFA Franc
Economy agriculture 81%,services 13%,
industry 6%
Religions Sunni Muslim 90%,
traditional Beliefs 5%
Ethnic Mix Wolof 44%, Serer 15%, Fula 12%,
Diola 5%

GEOGRAPHY
Elevation
lowest point: Atlantic Ocean 0 m
highest point: unnamed feature near
Nepen Diakha 581 m
Geography Note
westernmost country on the African continent; The Gambia is almost an enclave of
Senegal
Natural Resources
fish,phosphates,iron ore
Climate
tropical; hot, humid; rainy season (May to
November) has strong southeast winds; dry
season (December to April) dominated by
hot, dry, harmattan wind
Senegalese Food
yassaau poulet/mamadou's banana glace

WORLD CUP		COUNTRY LEAGUE CHAMPIONS	
1930	Did not qualify		
1934	Did not qualify		
1938	Did not qualify	2004	ASC Diaraf
1950	Did not qualify	2003	ASC Jeanne D'Arc
1954	Did not qualify	2002	ASC Jeanne D'Arc
1958	Did not qualify	2001	ASC Jeanne D'Arc
1962	Did not qualify	2000	ASC Diaraf
1966	Did not qualify	1999	ASC Jeanne D'Arc
1970	Did not qualify	1998	ASEC Ndiambour
1974	Did not qualify	1997	AS Douanes
1978	Did not qualify	1996	Sonacos
1982	Did not qualify	**Women's League Champio**	
1986	Did not qualify	2004	Sirenes du Grand Yoff
1990	Did not qualify	2003	Aigles Madina
1994	Did not qualify	2002	Sirenes de Dakar
1998	Did not qualify	2001	Sirenes de Dakar
2002	1/4 Final exit	2000	Not Known

NATIONAL TEAM COLORS

WORLD PICTURES OF SOCCER

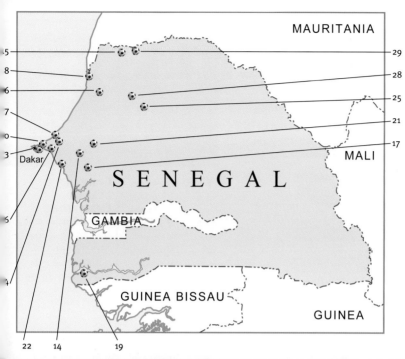

PREMIERE LEAGUE CLUBS	CITY	STADIUM	CAPACITY
ASC Diaraf	Dakar	Stade Leopold Senghor	60 000
AS Douanes	Dakar	Stade Leopold Senghor	60 000
Guediawaye FC	Dakar	Stade Leopold Senghor	60 000
Port Autonome	Dakar	Stade Leopold Senghor	60 000
ASFA	Dakar		
ASC HLM	Dakar		
ASC Police	Dakar		
Jeanne D'Arc	Dakar		
DUC	Dakar		
Renaissance	Dakar		
ADS de Dakar	Dakar		
ASC Niayes-Pikine	Dakar		
Inter de Dakar	Dakar		
SONACOS	Djourbel		
CSS	Richard-Toll		
ASEC Ndiambour	Louga		
ASC Saloum	Kaolack		
Linguere	Saint-Louis		
Casa Sport	Ziguinchor		
US Ouakam	Ouakam		
ASC Khombole	Khombole		
Stade Mbour	Mbour		
Us Rail	Thies	Stade Lat Dior	10 000
ASC Thies	Thies	Stade Lat Dior	10 000
US de Goree	Gore Tiango		
Yakaar FC	Rufisque		
ETICS	Mboro		
ASC Foyer	Dara		
Dagana FC	Dagana		

SEYCHELLES

Seychelles Football Fed.
PB 843, People's Stadium, Victoria, Mahe
TEL 248/324 632   FAX 248/225 468
WEB www.seychelles.nets/sff

REFERENCE
Official name
Republic of Seychelles
Date of formation   1976
Capital   Victoria
Population   79,326
Total area   104 sq Mi, 270 sq Km
Time zone   GMT +4
Density   763 per sq Mi, 201 per sq Km
Languages   Creole, French, English
Literacy rate   88%
Currency   Rupee
Economy   services 80%, agriculture 10%, industry 10%
Religions   Catholic 90%, Anglica 8%
Ethnic Mix   Creole 89%, Indian 55, Chinese 2%

GEOGRAPHY
Elevation
lowest point: Indian Ocean 0 m
highest point: Morne Seychellois 905 m
Geography Note
40 granitic and about 50 coralline islands
Natural Resources
fish, copra, cinnamon trees
Climate
tropical marine; humid; cooler season during southeast monsoon (late May to September); warmer season during northwest monsoon (March to May)
Seychelles Food
karikoko ton/soup de tectec

WORLD CUP

1930	Did not qualify
1934	Did not qualify
1938	Did not qualify
1950	Did not qualify
1954	Did not qualify
1958	Did not qualify
1962	Did not qualify
1966	Did not qualify
1970	Did not qualify
1974	Did not qualify
1978	Did not qualify
1982	Did not qualify
1986	Did not qualify
1990	Did not qualify
1994	Did not qualify
1998	Did not qualify
2002	Did not qualify

COUNTRY LEAGUE CHAMPIONS

2004	La Passe FC
2003	St Michel United
2002	La Passe FC
2001	Red Star
2000	St.Michel United
1999	St.Michel United
1998	Red Star
1997	St.Michel United
1996	St.Michel United

Women's League Champion

2004	Olympia Coast
2003	Dolphins FC
2002	Olympia Coast
2001	Olympia Coast
2000	Rovers FC

NATIONAL TEAM COLORS

WORLD PICTURES OF SOCCER

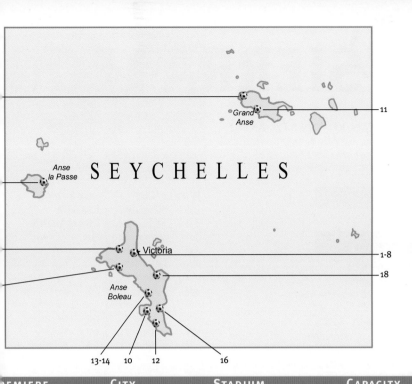

*Anse
la Passe*

S E Y C H E L L E S

*Grand
Anse* — 11

Victoria — 1-8

— 18

*Anse
Boleau*

13-14   10   12   16

PREMIERE LEAGUE CLUBS	CITY	STADIUM	CAPACITY
.Louis FC	Victoria	Stade Linite	10 000
scot United FC	Victoria	Stade Linite	10 000
unshine SC	Victoria	Stade Linite	10 000
t.Michel United FC	Victoria	Stade Linite	10 000
ed Star FC	Victoria	Stade Linite	10 000
nse-aux-Pins FC	Victoria	Stade Linite	10 000
nse Reunion	Victoria	Stade Linite	10 000
aiman FC	Victoria	Stade Linite	10 000
orthern Dynamo	Belombre	People's Stadium	7 000
Plaisance FC	Baie Lazare	People's Stadium	7 000
ight Stars FC	Grand Anse	People's Stadium	7 000
South Olympic	Takamaka	People's Stadium	7 000
Western Tigers	Anse Boileau	People's Stadium	7 000
Anse Boileau	Anse Boileau	People's Stadium	7 000
Foresters	Mont Fleuri	People's Stadium	7 000
ARSU	Anse Royale	People's Stadium	7 000
Saint Pierre	Praslin Island	People's Stadium	7 000
Cascade	Cascade	People's Stadium	7 000
La Passe FC	La Passe	People's Stadium	7 000
Port Glaud	Port Glaud	People's Stadium	7 000

SIERRA LEON

SIERRA LEONE FOOTBALL ASSO.
21 Battery Street, Kington, Freetown
TEL 232-22/241 872 FAX /227 771
WEB www.cafonline

REFERENCE
Official name
Republic of Sierra Leone
Date of formation 1961
Capital Freetown
Population 4.9 million
Total area 27,652 sq Mi, 71,620 sq Km
Time zone GMT 0
Density 177 per sq Mi, 74 per sq Km
Languages English, Krio
Literacy rate 30%
Currency Leone
Economy agriculture 70%, services 17%, industry 13%
Religions traditional beliefs 30%, Muslim 30%, Christian 30%
Ethnic Mix Mende 35%, Temne 32%, Limba 8%, Kuranko 4%

GEOGRAPHY
Elevation
lowest point: Atlantic Ocean 0 m
highest point: Loma Mansa (Bintimani) 1,948 m
Geography Note
rainfall along the coast can reach 495 cm (195 inches) a year, making it one of the wettest places along coastal, western Africa
Natural Resources
diamonds, titanium ore, iron ore, gold, chromite
Climate
tropical; hot, humid; summer rainy season (May to December); winter dry season (December to April)
Sierra Leone Food
prawn/palava/egusi soup/binch akara

WORLD CUP

1930	Did not qualify
1934	Did not qualify
1938	Did not qualify
1950	Did not qualify
1954	Did not qualify
1958	Did not qualify
1962	Did not qualify
1966	Did not qualify
1970	Did not qualify
1974	Did not qualify
1978	Did not qualify
1982	Did not qualify
1986	Did not qualify
1990	Did not qualify
1994	Did not qualify
1998	Did not qualify
2002	Did not qualify

COUNTRY LEAGUE CHAMPIONS

2004	Not Known
2003	Not Known
2002	Mighty Blackpool
2001	Mighty Blackpool
2000	East End Lions
1999	Mighty Blackpool
1998	Not Known
1997	Not Known
1996	Mighty Blackpool

Women's League Champio

2004	Not Known
2003	Not Known
2002	Not Known
2001	East End Lioness
2000	East End Lioness

NATIONAL TEAM COLORS

WORLD PICTURES OF SOCCER

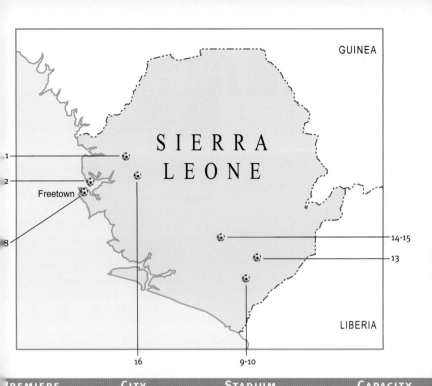

PREMIERE LEAGUE CLUBS	CITY	STADIUM	CAPACITY
Mighty Blackpool	Freetown	Brookfields Stadium	36 000
East End Lions	Freetown	Brookfields Stadium	36 000
Old Edwardians	Freetown	Brookfields Stadium	36 000
Real Republicans	Freetown	Brookfields Stadium	36 000
Sierra Fisheries	Freetown	Brookfields Stadium	36 000
Freetown United	Freetown	Brookfields Stadium	36 000
Port Authority	Freetown	Brookfields Stadium	36 000
Congo Constructors	Freetown	Brookfields Stadium	36 000
Diamond Stars	Konko		
Konko FC	Konko		
Bai Bureh Warriors	Port Loko		
Wusum Stars	Bombali		
Kamboi Eagles	Kenema		
Bo Rangers	Bo		
Kakua Rangers	Bo		
Lunsar FC	Lunsar		

SOMALIA

SOMALI FOOTBALL FEDERATION
P.O Box #222, Mogadishu, BN 03040
TEL 20-2/736 2497 FAX /738 0976
WEB www.cafonline.co

REFERENCE
Official name
Somali Democratic Republic

Date of formation	1960
Capital	Mogadishu
Population	10.1 million
Total area	242,215 sq Mi, 627,340 sq Km
Time zone	GMT +3
Density	42 per sq Mi, 11 per sq Km
Languages	Somali, Arabic
Literacy rate	24%
Currency	Shilling
Economy	agriculture 76%, services 16%, industry 8%
Religions	Sunni Muslim 98%, Christian 2%
Ethnic Mix	Somali 85%

GEOGRAPHY
Elevation
lowest point: Indian Ocean 0 m
highest point: Shimbiris 2,416 m
Geography Note
strategic location on Horn of Africa along southern approaches to Bab el Mandeb and route through Red Sea and Suez Canal
Natural Resources
uranium and largely unexploited reserves of iron ore, tin, gypsum, bauxite, copper, salt, natural gas, likely oil reserves
Climate
principally desert; December to February - northeast monsoon.May to October- southwest monsoon, torrid in the north and hot in the south.
Somalian Food
crabmeat stew/sorghum & peanuts

WORLD CUP		COUNTRY LEAGUE CHAMPIONS	
1930	Did not qualify		
1934	Did not qualify		
1938	Did not qualify	2004	Elman FC
1950	Did not qualify	2003	Elman FC
1954	Did not qualify	2002	Elman FC
1958	Did not qualify	2001	Elman FC
1962	Did not qualify	2000	Elman FC
1966	Did not qualify	1999	Not Known
1970	Did not qualify	1998	Port Authority
1974	Did not qualify	1997	Not Known
1978	Did not qualify	1996	Not Known
1982	Did not qualify	**Women's League Champion**	
1986	Did not qualify	2004	Not Known
1990	Did not qualify	2003	Not Known
1994	Did not qualify	2002	Not Known
1998	Did not qualify	2001	Not Known
2002	Did not qualify	2000	Not Known

NATIONAL TEAM COLORS

WORLD PICTURES OF SOCCER

PREMIERE LEAGUE CLUBS	CITY	STADIUM	CAPACITY
Elman FC	Mogadishu	Mogadishu Stadium	35 000
Morris Supplies	Mogadishu	Mogadishu Stadium	35 000
Mogadishu Municipality	Mogadishu	Mogadishu Stadium	35 000
Marine Club	Mogadishu	Mogadishu Stadium	35 000
Wagad	Mogadishu	Mogadishu Stadium	35 000
Horsed FC	Mogadishu	Mogadishu Stadium	35 000
Lavori Publici	Mogadishu	Mogadishu Stadium	35 000
Waxcol	Mogadishu	Mogadishu Stadium	35 000
NPA	Mogadishu	Mogadishu Stadium	35 000
Petroleum FC	Mogadishu	Mogadishu Stadium	35 000
Hoga	Mogadishu	Mogadishu Stadium	35 000
Somali Police	Mogadishu	Mogadishu Stadium	35 000
Port Authority	Mogadishu	Mogadishu Stadium	35 000
Marka Municipality FC	Marka		

SOUTH AFRICA

SOUTH AFRICAN FOOTBALL FEDERATION
First National bank Std. PB 910, 2000 J-burg
TEL 27-11/494 3522 FAX /494 3013
WEB www.safa.net

REFERENCE

Official name
Republic of South Africa

Date of formation	1994
Capital	Pretoria
Population	40.4 million
Total area	471,443 sq Mi, 1,221,040 sq Km
Time zone	GMT +2
Density	86 per sq Mi, 36 per sq Km
Languages	Afrikaans, English, (11 Africans Languages)
Literacy rate	81%
Currency	Rand
Economy	services 62%, industry 24%, agriculture 14%
Religions	Black Independent 17%, Dutch Reformed 11%
Ethnic Mix	Zulu 23%, Others 77%

GEOGRAPHY

Elevation
lowest point: Atlantic Ocean 0 m
highest point: Njesuthi 3,408 m
Geography Note
South Africa completely surrounds Lesotho and almost completely surrounds Swaziland
Natural Resources
gold, chromium, antimony, coal, iron ore, manganese, nickel, phosphates, tin, uranium, gem diamonds, platinum, copper, vanadium, salt, natural gas
Climate
mostly semiarid; subtropical along east coast; sunny days, cool nights
South African Food
biltong/skilpad/charkalaka/braai/potjiekos

WORLD CUP

1930	Did not qualify
1934	Did not qualify
1938	Did not qualify
1950	Did not qualify
1954	Did not qualify
1958	Did not qualify
1962	Did not qualify
1966	Did not qualify
1970	Did not qualify
1974	Did not qualify
1978	Did not qualify
1982	Did not qualify
1986	Did not qualify
1990	Did not qualify
1994	Did not qualify
1998	First round exit
2002	First round exit

COUNTRY LEAGUE CHAMPIONS

2004	Kaizer Chiefs
2003	Orlando Pirates
2002	Santos Cape Town
2001	Orlando Pirates
2000	Mamelodi Sundowns
1999	Mamelodi Sundowns
1998	Mamelodi Sundowns
1997	Manning Rangers
1996	Kaizer Chiefs

Women's League Champion

2004	Soweto Ladies
2003	Soweto ladies
2002	Soweto Ladies
2001	Not Known
2000	Not Known

NATIONAL TEAM COLORS

WORLD PICTURES OF SOCCER

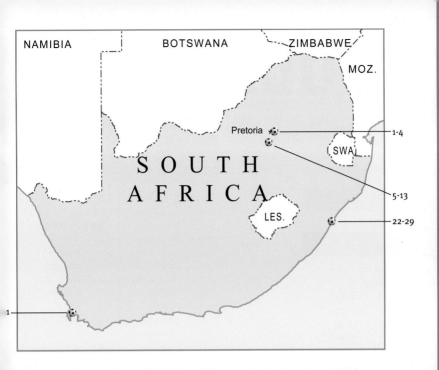

PREMIERE LEAGUE CLUBS	CITY	STADIUM	CAPACITY
Sundowns	Pretoria	Securior Loftus	52 000
Tycoon Silver Stars	Pretoria	Pilditch	20 000
Pretoria Spartak	Pretoria	Pilditch	20 000
Supersport United	Pretoria	Pilditch	20 000
Orlando Pirates	Johannesburg	FNB Stadium	90 000
Kaizer Chief	Johannesburg	Ellis Park	59 600
Moroka Swallows	Johannesburg	Rand Stadium	30 000
Dobsonville All Nations	Johannesbur.	Rand Stadium	30 000
Katlehong City	Johannesburg	Potgietersrus	20 000
Real Rovers	Johannesburg	Potgietersrus	20 000
Jomo Cosmos	Johannesburg	Vosloorus Stadium	25 000
Wits University	Johannesburg	Investek Milpark	12 000
Alexandra United	Johannesburg	Alexandra Complex	5 000
Ajax Cape Town	Cape Town	Newlands Stadium	51 000
FC Fortune	Cape Town	Newlands Stadium	51 000
Hellenic	Cape Town	Athlone Stadium	25 000
Mother City	Cape Town	Athlone Stadium	25 000
Santos	Cape Town	Greenpoint Stadium	18 000
Rainbow Stars	Cape Town	Greenpoint Stadium	18 000
Avendale Athletico	Cape Town	Silvermine Stadium	10 000
Zulu Royals	Cape Town	Silvermine Stadium	10 000
Durban United	Durban	ABSA Stadium	55 000
Amazulu FC	Durban	ABSA Stadium	55 000
Bush Bucks	Durban	ABSA Stadium	55 000
African Wanderers	Durban	ABSA Stadium	55 000
Manning Rangers	Durban	Chatsworth Stadium	35 000
Lamontville Golden Arrows	Durban	King Goodwill Zwelithini	25 000
Tembisa Classic	Durban	Makhulong Stadium	15 000
Phoenix City	Durban	Princess Magogo	10 000

SUDAN

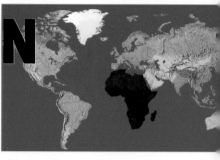

SUDAN FOOTBALL ASSOC.
PB 437, Khartoum
TEL 249-11/773 495 FAX /776 633
WEB www.cafonline.com

REFERENCE
Official name
Republic of Sudan

Date of formation	1956
Capital	Khartoum
Population	29.5 million
Total area	917,373 sq Mi, 2,376,000 sq mi)
Time zone	GMT +2
Density	32 per sq Mi, 14 per sq Km
Languages	Arabic
Literacy rate	45%
Currency	Pound
Economy	agriculture 65%, services 31%, industry 4%
Religions	Sunni Muslim 70%, Traditional Beliefs 20%, Christian 9%
Ethnic Mix	Arab 40%, Tribal 30%, Dinka & Beja 7%

GEOGRAPHY
Elevation
lowest point: Red Sea 0 m
highest point: Kinyeti 3,187 m
Geography Note
largest country in Africa; dominated by the Nile and its tributaries
Natural Resources
petroleum; small reserves of iron ore, copper, chromium ore, zinc, tungsten, mica, silver, gold, hydropower
Climate
tropical in south; arid desert in north; rainy season (April to October)
Sudanese Food
peanuts macaroons/shorba/maschi/shata

WORLD CUP		COUNTRY LEAGUE CHAMPIONS	
1930	Did not qualify		
1934	Did not qualify		
1938	Did not qualify	2004	Al Hilal
1950	Did not qualify	2003	Al Hilal
1954	Did not qualify	2002	Al Merreikh
1958	Did not qualify	2001	Al Merreikh
1962	Did not qualify	2000	Al Merreikh
1966	Did not qualify	1999	Al Hilal
1970	Did not qualify	1998	Al Hilal
1974	Did not qualify	1997	Al Merreikh
1978	Did not qualify	1996	Al Hilal
1982	Did not qualify	Women's League Champion	
1986	Did not qualify	2004	Not Known
1990	Did not qualify	2003	Not Known
1994	Did not qualify	2002	Not Known
1998	Did not qualify	2001	Not Known
2002	Did not qualify	2000	Not Known

NATIONAL TEAM COLORS

WORLD PICTURES OF SOCCER

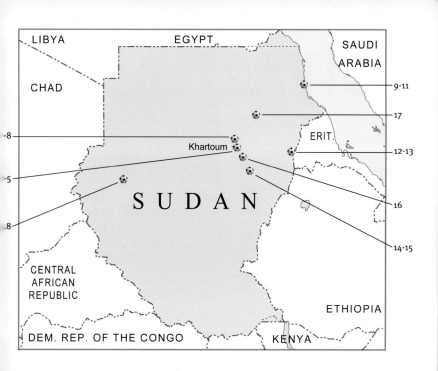

PREMIERE LEAGUE CLUBS	CITY	STADIUM	CAPACITY
-Khartoum-3	Khartoum	Stade Al-Merreikh	45 000
-Al-Ahli	Khartoum	Stade Al-Merreikh	45 000
-Burri	Khartoum	Stade Al-Hilal	40 000
-Shambat	Khartoum Bahri	Stade Al-Hilal	40 000
-Al-Nil	Khartoum	Stade Al-Hilal	40 000
-Hilal	Omdurman		
-Al-Merreikh	Omdurman		
-Mawrada	Omdurman		
-Al-Hilal El-Sahel	Port Sudan		
-Hay Al-Arab	Port Sudan		
-Al-Merreikh	Port Sudan		
-Al-Mirghani	Kassala		
-Taka	Kassala		
-Ittihad	Wad Medani		
-Al-Ahli	Wad Medani		
-Al-Hilal	Hasahisa		
-Amal	Atbara		
-Al-Merreikh	Abyah		

SWAZILAND

NATIONAL FOOTBALL ASSOCIATION OF SWAZILAND
PB 641, H100 Mbabane
TEL 268/404 6852 FAX 268/404 6206
WEB www.nfas.org.sz

REFERENCE
Official name
Kingdom of Swaziland

Date of formation	1968
Capital	Mbabane
Population	1,008,000
Total area	6641 sq Mi, 17,200 sq Km
Time zone	GMT +2
Density	152 per sq Mi, 57 per sq Km
Languages	Siswati, English, Zulu
Literacy rate	75%
Currency	Lilangeni
Economy	agriculture 60%, industry & services 40%
Religions	Christian 60%, traditional beliefs
Ethnic Mix	Swazi 97%

GEOGRAPHY
Elevation
lowest point: Great Usutu River 21 m
highest point: Emlembe 1,862 m
Geography Note
landlocked; almost completely surrounded by South Africa
Natural Resources
asbestos, coal, clay, cassiterite, hydropower, forests, small gold and
diamond deposits, quarry stone, and talc
Climate
varies from tropical to near temperate
Swaziland Food
swaziland slaai/mango chutney

WORLD CUP

1930	Did not qualify
1934	Did not qualify
1938	Did not qualify
1950	Did not qualify
1954	Did not qualify
1958	Did not qualify
1962	Did not qualify
1966	Did not qualify
1970	Did not qualify
1974	Did not qualify
1978	Did not qualify
1982	Did not qualify
1986	Did not qualify
1990	Did not qualify
1994	Did not qualify
1998	Did not qualify
2002	Did not qualify

COUNTRY LEAGUE CHAMPIONS

2004	Not Known
2003	Manzini Wanderers
2002	Manzini Wanderers
2001	Mbabane Highlanders
2000	Mbabane Highlanders
1999	Manzini Wanderers
1998	No Competition
1997	Mbabane Highlanders
1996	XI Men in Flight FC

Women's League Champion

2004	Kappa Ladies
2003	Kappa Ladies
2002	Not Known
2001	Not Known
2000	Not Known

NATIONAL TEAM COLORS

WORLD PICTURES OF SOCCER

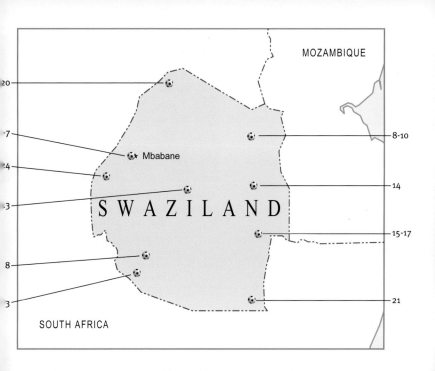

Premiere League Clubs	City	Stadium	Capacity
-Mbabane Highlanders	Mbabane	Somholo National Stadium	30 000
-Denver Sundowns	Mbabane	Somholo National Stadium	30 000
-Mbabane Swallows	Mbabane	Somholo National Stadium	30 000
-C&M Eagles	Mbabane	Somholo National Stadium	30 000
-Midas Mbabane City	Mbabane	Somholo National Stadium	30 000
-Umbelebele	Mbabane		
-Mhlume United	Mbabane		
-Royal Leopards	Simunye		
Simunye FC	Simunye		
-Young Buffaloes	Simunye		
-Manzini Wanderers	Manzini		
-Moneni Pirates	Manzini		
-City Stars Manzini	Manzini		
-XI Men in Flight	Siteki		
-Green Mamba FC	Big Bend		
-Pastor Limited FC	Big Bend		
-Delta StarsBig Bend	Big Bend		
-Hlathikhulu Tycoons	Hlathikhulu		
-Buch Bucks	Piggs Peak		
-Black Swallows	Piggs Peak		
-Lavumisa FC	Lavumisa		
-Nhlangano Police	Nhlangano		
-Nhlangano Black Terrors	Nhlangano		
-Mhlambanyatsi Rovers	Mhlambanyatsi		

TANZANIA

FOOTBALL ASSOCIATION OF TANZANIA
1PB 1574, Dar es Salaam
TEL 255-22/211 8668   FAX /213 0376
WEB www.cafonline.com

REFERENCE
Official name
United Republic of Tanzania

Date of formation	1964
Capital	Dar es Salaam
Population	33.5 million
Total area	342,100 sq Mi, 886,040 sq Km
Time zone	GMT +3
Density	98 per sq Mi, 37 per sq Km
Languages	English, Swahili
Literacy rate	67%
Currency	Shilling
Economy	agriculture 85%, services 10%, industry 5%
Religions	Muslim 33%, Christian 33%, traditioanal beliefs 30%
Ethnic Mix	Native African 99%, European & Asia 1%

GEOGRAPHY
Elevation
lowest point: Indian Ocean 0 m
highest point: Kilimanjaro 5,895 m
Geography Note
Kilimanjaro is highest point in Africa;
bordered by three of the largest lakes on the
continent: Lake Victoria (the world's second-
largest freshwater lake) in the north, Lake
Tanganyika (the world's second deepest) in
the west, and Lake Nyasa in the southwest
Natural Resources
hydropower, tin, phosphates, iron ore, coal,
diamonds, gemstones, gold, natural gas,
nickel
Climate
tropical along coast to temperate in
highlands
Tanzanian Food
Biriani/tanzanian meat stew ugali

WORLD CUP

1930	Did not qualify
1934	Did not qualify
1938	Did not qualify
1950	Did not qualify
1954	Did not qualify
1958	Did not qualify
1962	Did not qualify
1966	Did not qualify
1970	Did not qualify
1974	Did not qualify
1978	Did not qualify
1982	Did not qualify
1986	Did not qualify
1990	Did not qualify
1994	Did not qualify
1998	Did not qualify
2002	Did not qualify

COUNTRY LEAGUE CHAMPIONS

2004	Simba
2003	Not Known
2002	Simba
2001	Simba
2000	Young Africans
1999	Prisons
1998	Maji Maji
1997	Young Africans
1996	Young Africans

Women's League Champion

2005	Sayari FC
2004	Sayari FC
2003	Sayari FC
2002	Not Known
2001	Not Known

NATIONAL TEAM COLORS

WORLD PICTURES OF SOCCER

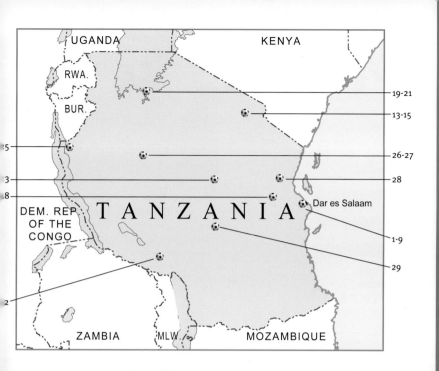

PREMIERE LEAGUE CLUBS	CITY	STADIUM	CAPACITY
Simba	Dar-es-Salaam	National Stadium	20 000
Young Africans	Dar-es-Salaam	National Stadium	20 000
Trans Camp FC	Dar-es-Salaam	National Stadium	20 000
Vijana	Dar-es-Salaam	National Stadium	20 000
Twiga Sports	Dar-es-Salaam	National Stadium	20 000
Msimbazi Rovers	Dar-es-Salaam	National Stadium	20 000
Pan-African	Dar-es-Salaam	National Stadium	20 000
Cosmopolitan	Dar-es-Salaam	National Stadium	20 000
Kumbukumbu	Dar-es-Salaam	National Stadium	20 000
Prisons	Mbeya		
44KJ Karume Rangers	Mbeya		
Tukuyu Stars	Mbeya		
Arusha FC	Arusha		
Pallsons	Arusha		
977KJ Meru Warriors	Arusha		
Moro United	Morogoro		
Reli Railways	Morogoro		
Uluguru	Morogoro		
Geita Mine	Mwanza		
Pamba Lira	Mwanza		
Toto African	Mwanza		
Police	Dodoma		
Ruvu Stars	Dodoma		
Reli	Kigoma		
M'banga	Kigoma		
Fire Rivers	Tabora		
Milambo	Tabora		
Rhino	Tambara		
Stilleto	Iringa		

 # TOGO

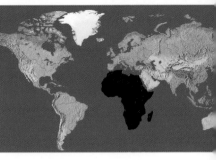

FED. TOGOLAISE DE FOOTBALL
CP 5, Lome
TEL 228/222 1412   FAX /222 1413
WEB www.ftf.gt

REFERENCE
Official name
Republic of Togo
Date of formation 1960
Capital Lome
Population 4.6 million
Total area 21,000 sq Mi, 54,390 sq Km
Time zone GMT 0
Density 219 per sq Mi, 84 per sq Km
Languages French, Ewe, Kabye, Gurma
Literacy rate 51%
Currency CFA Franc
Economy agriculture 68%,services 28%, industry 4%,
Religions traditional beliefs 50%, Christian 35%, Muslim 15%
Ethnic Mix Sewe 46%, European 1%, Other Regions Africans 53%

GEOGRAPHY
Elevation
lowest point: Atlantic Ocean 0 m
highest point: Mont Agou 986 m
Geography Note
the country's length allows it to stretch through six distinct geographic regions; climate varies from tropical to savanna
Natural Resources
phosphates, limestone, marble, arable land
Climate
tropical; hot, humid in south; semiarid in north
Togo Food
adohwe/botokoin/kouloukouli/beberebou emakoume

WORLD CUP		COUNTRY LEAGUE CHAMPIONS	
1930	Did not qualify		
1934	Did not qualify		
1938	Did not qualify	2004	Dynamic Togolais
1950	Did not qualify	2003	AS Douane Lome
1954	Did not qualify	2002	AS Douane Lome
1958	Did not qualify	2001	Dynamic Togolais
1962	Did not qualify	2000	Not Finished
1966	Did not qualify	1999	Semassi Sokode
1970	Did not qualify	1998	No Competition
1974	Did not qualify	1997	Dynamic Togolais
1978	Did not qualify	1996	ASKO Kara
1982	Did not qualify	**Women's League Champion**	
1986	Did not qualify	2004	Not Known
1990	Did not qualify	2003	Not Known
1994	Did not qualify	2002	Not Known
1998	Did not qualify	2001	Not Known
2002	Did not qualify	2000	Amies du Monde

NATIONAL TEAM COLORS

WORLD PICTURES OF SOCCER

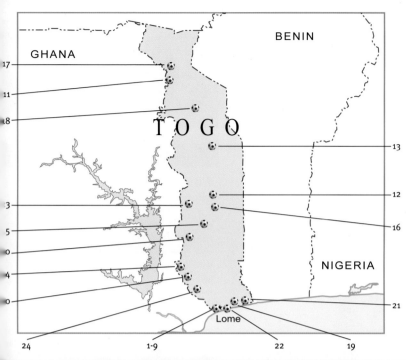

PREMIERE LEAGUE CLUBS	CITY	STADIUM	CAPACITY
Dynamic Togolais	Lome	General Eyadema	20 000
AS Togo-Port	Lome	General Eyadema	20 000
AS Douanes	Lome	General Eyadema	20 000
Etoile Filante	Lome	General Eyadema	20 000
OC Omnisports Agaza	Lome	General Eyadema	20 000
AC Merlan	Lome	General Eyadema	20 000
Togo Telecom FC	Lome	General Eyadema	20 000
FC La Semeuse	Lome	General Eyadema	20 000
Essor de Lome	Lome	General Eyadema	20 000
Maranatha FC	Fiokpo		
ASKO FC	Kara		
Kakadle FC	Defale		
AC Semassi FC	Sokode		
Gomido	Kpalime		
Ifodje D'Atakpame	Atakpame		
Abou Osse FC	Anie		
Doumbe FC	Sansanne Mango		
Sara Sport FC	Bafilo		
Gbohloe Su	Aneho		
Dzahini FC	Amou Oblo		
OTP	Kpeme		
Lumiere FC	Zongo		
Red Star	Bonkey		
US Kelegougan	Kelegougan		

 # TUNISIA

Fed. Tunisienne de Football
16, Rue de la Ligue Arabe
El Menzah VI, 2091 Tunis
TEL 216-71/233 303 FAX /767 929
WEB www.ftf.tn

Reference
Official name
Republic of Tunisia
Date of formation 1956
Capital Tunis
Population 9.6 million
Total area 59,984 sq Mi, 155,360 sq Km
Time zone GMT +1
Density 160 per sq Mi, 58 per sq Km
Languages Arabic, French
Literacy rate 65%
Currency Dinar
Economy agriculture 48%, services 42%, industry 10%
Religions Muslim 98%, Christian 1%
Ethnic Mix Arab & Berber 98%, European 1%

Geography
Elevation
lowest point: Shatt al Gharsah -17 m
highest point: Jebel ech Chambi 1,544 m
Geography Note
strategic location in central Mediterranean; Malta and Tunisia are discussing the commercial exploitation of the continental shelf between their countries, particularly for oil exploration
Natural Resources
petroleum, phosphates, iron ore, lead, zinc, salt
Climate
temperate in north with mild, rainy winters and hot, dry summers; desert in south
Tunisian Food
chackchouka/masfouf tunis/koukha/shakshuka

World Cup		Country League Champions	
1930	Did not qualify		
1934	Did not qualify		
1938	Did not qualify	2004	Esperance de Tunis
1950	Did not qualify	2003	Esperance de Tunis
1954	Did not qualify	2002	Esperance de Tunis
1958	Did not qualify	2001	Esperance de Tunis
1962	Did not qualify	2000	Esperance de Tunis
1966	Did not qualify	1999	Esperance de Tunis
1970	Did not qualify	1998	Esperance de Tunis
1974	Did not qualify	1997	ES Sahel
1978	First round exit	1996	Club Africain
1982	Did not qualify	**Women's League Champion**	
1986	Did not qualify	2005	ASF Sahel
1990	Did not qualify	2004	ES Djerba
1994	Did not qualify	2003	Not Known
1998	Did not qualify	2002	Not Known
2002	Did not qualify	2001	Not Known

National Team Colors

World Pictures of Soccer

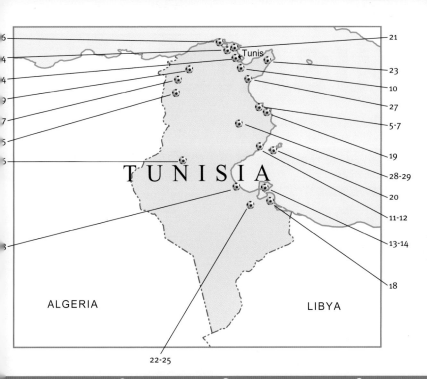

21		
Tunis	23	
	10	
	27	
	5-7	
	19	
	28-29	
T U N I S I A	20	
	11-12	
	13-14	
	18	
ALGERIA	LIBYA	
22-25		

PREMIERE LEAGUE CLUBS	CITY	STADIUM	CAPACITY
Esperance de Tunis	Tunis	Stade El Menzah	45 000
Club Africain	Tunis	Stade El Menzah	45 000
Stade Tunisien	Tunis	Stade Zouiten	18 000
Club Olympique Transports	Tunis	Stade Zouiten	18 000
Etoile du Sahel	Sousse	Stade Olympique	28 000
ES Hammam-Sousse	Sousse	Stade Olympique	28 000
Stade Soussien	Sousse	Stade Olympique	28 000
Avenir Sportive de Gabes	Gabes	Stade Municipal	10 000
Olympique de Beja	Beja	Stade Municipal	8 000
Club Sportif	Hammam-Lif	Stade Boui Kournine	8 000
Club Sfaxin	Sfax	Stade Taieb-Mhri	22 000
Sfax Railway Sport	Sfax	Stade Taieb-Mhri	22 000
Association Sportive Djerba	Djerba	Stade Houmet-Souk	6 000
ES Djerba	Djerba	Stade Houmet-Souk	6 000
Olympique du Kef	El-Kef	Stade 7 Novembre	7 000
CA Bizertin	Bizerte	Stade Municipal	20 000
Jundubah Sport	Jundubah		
ES Zarzis	Zarzis	Stade Jlidi	7 000
US Monastir	Monastir	Moustapha Benn Jenat	20 000
Ocean Club	Kerkennah	Stade Taieb-Mhri	15 000
Avenir Sportive La Marsa	La Marsa	Stade Chtioui	6 000
Olympique de medenine	Medenine	Stade Olympique	6 000
Etoile Sportive	Beni-Khalled	Stade Habib Tajouri	5 000
SA Menzel Bourghiba	Bourghiba		
CO Medenine	Medenine		
El-Gawafel	Gafsa		
AS Nabul	Nabul		
MS Kairouan	Kairouan		
S Kairouanaise	Kairouan	Stade Ali Zouaoui	15 000

215

UGANDA

FED. OF UGANDA FOOTBALL A.
PB 22518, Plot 743, Makerere Hill road
Wakulabye, Kampala
TEL 256-41/540 335 FAX /533 974
WEBwww.cafonline.com

REFERENCE
Official name
  Republic of Uganda
Date of formation 1962
Capital Kampala
Population 21.8 million
Total area 77,046 sq Mi, 199,550 sq Km
Time zone GMT +3
Density 283 per sq Mi, 91 per sq Km
Languages English, Uganda, Nkole, Chiga, Lango, Acholi, Teso
Literacy rate 61%
Currency Shilling
Economy agriculture 86%, services 10%, industry 4%
Religions Catholic 38%, Protestant 33%,traditional beliefs 29%
Ethnic Mix Bantu tribes 50%, Sudanese 5%, Others 45%

GEOGRAPHY
Elevation
lowest point: Lake Albert 621 m
highest point: Margherita Peak on Mount Stanley 5,110 m
Geography Note
landlocked; fertile, well-watered country with many lakes and rivers
Natural Resources
copper, cobalt, hydropower, limestone, salt, arable land
Climate
tropical; generally rainy with two dry seasons (December to February, June to August); semiarid in northeast
Ugandan Food
kampala kebobs

WORLD CUP		COUNTRY LEAGUE CHAMPIONS	
1930	Did not qualify		
1934	Did not qualify		
1938	Did not qualify	2004	Villa SC
1950	Did not qualify	2003	Villa SC
1954	Did not qualify	2002	Villa SC
1958	Did not qualify	2001	Villa SC
1962	Did not qualify	2000	Villa SC
1966	Did not qualify	1999	Villa SC
1970	Did not qualify	1998	Villa SC
1974	Did not qualify	1997	City council SC
1978	Did not qualify	1996	Express Red Eagles
1982	Did not qualify	**Women's League Champio**	
1986	Did not qualify	2004	Not Known
1990	Did not qualify	2003	Simba FC
1994	Did not qualify	2002	Not Known
1998	Did not qualify	2001	Not Known
2002	Did not qualify	2000	Not Known

NATIONAL TEAM COLORS

WORLD PICTURES OF SOCCER

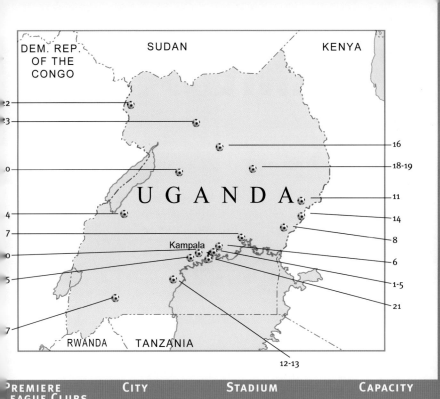

Premiere League Clubs	City	Stadium	Capacity
-SC Villa	Kampala	National Stadium	40 000
-Express Red Eagles	Kampala	National Stadium	40 000
-URA SC	Kampala	National Stadium	40 000
-Tower of Praise TV	Kampala	National Stadium	40 000
-Kampala City Council	Kampala	National Stadium	40 000
-SC Simba	Lugazi		
-Police	Jinja		
-Old Timers FC	Bugiri		
-Kinyara Sugar Works FC	Masindi		
-Masindi Packers	Masindi		
-Mbale Heroes	Mbale		
-Masaka Local Council	Masaka		
-Masaka Municipal	Masaka		
-Game Boys FC	Tororo		
-Buikwe Red Stars	Mukono		
-Akol FC	Lira		
-Mbarara United	Mbarara		
-Kumi Rangers	Kumi		
-Kumi TC	Kumi		
-Mpigi Works	Mpigi		
-Entebbe Rangers	Entebbe		
-Maecora	Arua		
-Black Rangers	Gulu		
-Mambugu FC	Mambugu		

ZAMBIA

FOOTBALL ASSOC. OF ZAMBIA
PB 34751, 9th Floor, Anchor House, Lusaka
TEL 260-1/221 145   FAX /224 561
WEB www.cafonline.com

REFERENCE
Official name
Republic of Zambia

Date of formation	1964
Capital	Lusaka
Population	9.2 million
Total area	285,992 sq Mi, 740,720 sq Km
Time zone	GMT +2
Density	32 per sq Mi, 13 per sq Km
Languages	English, Bemba, Tonga, Nyanja, Lozi, Lunda
Literacy rate	77%
Currency	Kwacha
Economy	agriculture 82%, services 10%, industry 8%
Religions	Christian 63%, indigenous beliefs 36$
Ethnic Mix	Bemba 34%, other African 65%, European 1%

GEOGRAPHY
Elevation
lowest point: Zambezi river 329 m
highest point: unnamed location in
Mafinga Hills 2,301 m
Geography Note
landlocked; the Zambezi forms a natural
riverine boundary with Zimbabwe
Natural Resources
copper, cobalt, zinc, lead, coal, emeralds,
gold, silver, uranium, hydropower
Climate
tropical; modified by altitude; rainy season
(October to April)
Zambian Food
amaranth with beans/cassava
pancakes/wild okra with beans

WORLD CUP

1930	Did not qualify
1934	Did not qualify
1938	Did not qualify
1950	Did not qualify
1954	Did not qualify
1958	Did not qualify
1962	Did not qualify
1966	Did not qualify
1970	Did not qualify
1974	Did not qualify
1978	Did not qualify
1982	Did not qualify
1986	Did not qualify
1990	Did not qualify
1994	Did not qualify
1998	Did not qualify
2002	Did not qualify

COUNTRY LEAGUE CHAMPIONS

2004	Red Arrows
2003	Zanaco
2002	Zanaco
2001	Nkana FC
2000	Power Dynamos
1999	Nkana FC
1998	Nchanga Rangers
1997	Power Dynamos
1996	Mufulira Wanderers

Women's League Champion

2004	Not Known
2003	Not Known
2002	Lass Connects FC
2001	Not Known
2000	Not Known

NATIONAL TEAM COLORS

WORLD PICTURES OF SOCCER

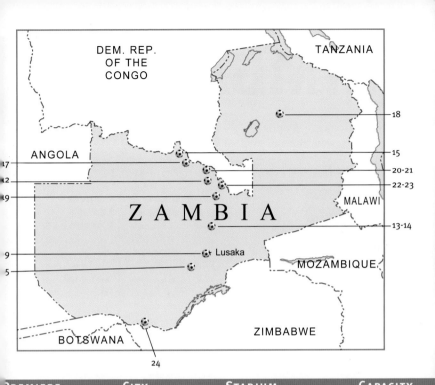

PREMIERE LEAGUE CLUBS	CITY	STADIUM	CAPACITY
-Green Buffaloes	Lusaka	Independence Stadium	30 000
-Zanaco	Lusaka	Independence Stadium	30 000
-Red Arrows	Lusaka	Independence Stadium	30 000
-Nkwazi	Lusaka	Independence Stadium	30 000
-National Assembly	Lusaka	Independence Stadium	30 000
-Lusaka Dynamos	Lusaka	Independence Stadium	30 000
-Lusaka Celtics	Lusaka	Independence Stadium	30 000
-City of Lusaka	Lusaka	Independence Stadium	30 000
-Lusaka Tigers	Lusaka	Independence Stadium	30 000
⊃-Power Dynamos	Kitwe		
⊣-Nkana FC	Kitwe		
₂-Kitwe United	Kitwe		
₃-Kabwe Warriors	Kabwe		
₄-Prisons Leopards	Kabwe		
₅-Konkola Blades	Chililabombwe		
₅-Nchanga Rangers	Chingola		
₇-Chingola Leopards	Chingola		
₈-Chambeshi Blackburn	Chambeshi		
₃-Roan United	Luanshya		
⊃-Mufulira Wanderers	Mufulira		
⊣-Mufulira blackpool	Mufulira		
₂-Forest Rangers	Ndola		
₃-Ndola United	Ndola		
₄-Livingstone Pirates	Livingstone		
₅-Nakambala Leopards	Nakambala		

ZIMBABWE

ZIMBABWE FOOTBALL ASSOC.
PB CY 114, Causeway, Harare
TEL 263-4/721 026 FAX /721 045
WEB www.sportcity.co.zw

REFERENCE
Official name
Republic of Zimbabwe

Date of formation   1980
Capital   Harare
Population   11.7 million
Total area   149,293 sq Mi, 386,670 sq Km
Time zone   GMT +2
Density   74 per sq Mi, 29 per sq Km
Languages   English, Shona, Ndebele
Literacy rate   85%
Currency   Zimbabwe $
Economy   agriculture 65%, services 29%, Industry 6%
Religions   Catholic, Syncretic 50%, Christian 25%, traditional beliefs 24%
Ethnic Mix   Shona 71%, Ndebele 16%, other African 16%, White 1%

GEOGRAPHY
Elevation
lowest point: junction of the Runde and Save rivers 162 m
highest point: Inyangani 2,592 m
Geography Note
the Zambezi forms a natural riverine boundary with Zambia;in full flood (February-April)the massive Victoria Falls on the river forms the world's largest curtain of falling water
Natural Resources
coal, chromium ore, asbestos, gold, nickel, copper, iron ore, vanadium, lithium, tin, platinum group metals
Climate
tropical; moderated by altitude;
Zimbabwe Food
sazda/doui/nanyama

WORLD CUP		COUNTRY LEAGUE CHAMPIONS	
1930	Did not qualify		
1934	Did not qualify		
1938	Did not qualify	2004	Caps United
1950	Did not qualify	2003	Amazulu
1954	Did not qualify	2002	Highlanders
1958	Did not qualify	2001	Highlanders
1962	Did not qualify	2000	Highlanders
1966	Did not qualify	1999	Highlanders
1970	Did not qualify	1998	No Competition
1974	Did not qualify	1997	Dynamos Harare
1978	Did not qualify	1996	CAPS United
1982	Did not qualify	Women's League Champion	
1986	Did not qualify	2004	Mufakose Queens
1990	Did not qualify	2003	Mufakose Queens
1994	Did not qualify	2002	Mufakose Queens
1998	Did not qualify	2001	Hollenbeck Queens
2002	Did not qualify	2000	Not Known

NATIONAL TEAM COLORS

WORLD PICTURES OF SOCCER

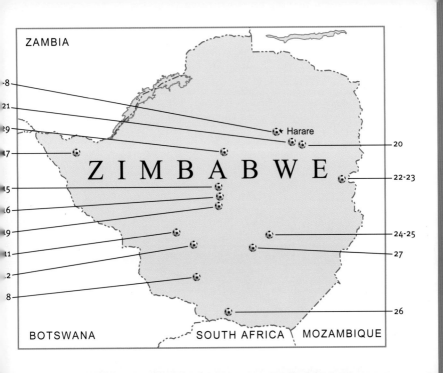

PREMIERE LEAGUE CLUBS	CITY	STADIUM	CAPACITY
-Dynamos	Harare	National Sport Stadium	60 000
-Circle United	Harare	National Sport Stadium	60 000
-CAPS United	Harare	National Sport Stadium	60 000
-Motor Action	Harare	Rufaro Stadium	35 000
-Sporting Lions	Harare	Rufaro Stadium	35 000
-Kambuzuma United	Harare	Rufaro Stadium	35 000
-Douglas Warriors	Harare	Rufaro Stadium	35 000
-Black Aces	Harare	Rufaro Stadium	35 000
-Amazulu	Bulawayo	Barbourfields	40 000
o-Highlanders	Bulawayo	Barbourfields	40 000
1-Njube Sundowns	Bulawayo	Barbourfields	40 000
2-Shabanie Mine	Shabanie		
3-Lancashire Steel	Kwekwe		
4-Kwekwe Cables	Kwekwe		
5-MM Burden	Kwekwe		
6-Ziscosteel	Redcliffe		
7-Hwange FC	Hwange		
8-Chapungu United	Gweru		
9-Gweru United	Gweru		
o-Blue Swallows	Marondera		
1-Buymore	Chitungwiza		
2-Black Rhinos	Mutare		
3-Red Seal Mutare	Mutare		
4-Gutu Leopards	Masvingo		
5-Masvingo United	Masvingo		
6-Border Stirkers	Beitbridge		
7-Mandava United	Zvishavane		
8-United Railstars	Gwanda		
9-Tongogara FC	Kadoma		

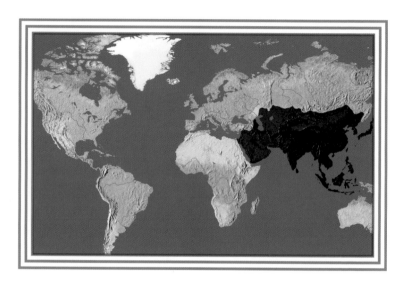

ASIA

AFGHANISTAN

AFGHANISTAN FOOTBALL FEDERATION
Mahmood Khan Wat, 5099Kabul
TEL:93-20/210 2417 FAX /210 2417
WEB www.footballasia.com

REFERENCE
Official name
　Islmic State of Afghanistan

Date of	
formation	1919
Capital	Kabul
Population	22.7 million
Total area	251,772 sq Mi, 652 sq Km
Time zone	GMT +4.5
Density	90 per sq Mi, 40 per sq Km
Languages	Persian, Pashtu
Literacy rate	32%
Currency	Afghani
Economy	agriculture 61%, services 21%, industry 14%
Religions	Sunni Muslim 84%,Shi'a Muslim 15%
Ethnic Mix	Spashto 52%, Tajik 21%, Hazara 19%, Uzbek 5%

GEOGRAPHY
Elevation
lowest point: Amu Darya 258 m
highest point: Nowshak 7,485 m
Geography Note
landlocked; the Hindu Kush mountains that
run northeast to southwest divide the
northern provinces from the rest of the
country; the highest peaks are in the
northern Vakhan (Wakhan Corridor)
Natural Resources
natural gas, petroleum, coal, copper,
chromite, talc, barites, sulfur, lead, zinc, iron
ore, salt, precious and semiprecious stones
Climate
arid to semiarid; cold winters and hot
summers
Afghanistan Food
abraysham kabaub/bonjan salat

WORLD CUP

1930	Did not qualify
1934	Did not qualify
1938	Did not qualify
1950	Did not qualify
1954	Did not qualify
1958	Did not qualify
1962	Did not qualify
1966	Did not qualify
1970	Did not qualify
1974	Did not qualify
1978	Did not qualify
1982	Did not qualify
1986	Did not qualify
1990	Did not qualify
1994	Did not qualify
1998	Did not qualify
2002	Did not qualify

COUNTRY LEAGUE CHAMPIONS

2004	Not Known
2003	Not Known
2002	Red Crescent Soc.
2001	Not Known
2000	Not Known
1999	Not Known
1998	Not Known
1997	Not Known
1996	Not Known

WOMEN'S LEAGUE CHAMPIONS

2004	Not Known
2003	Not Known
2002	Not Known
2001	Not Known
2000	Not Known

NATIONAL TEAM COLORS

WORLD PICTURES OF SOCCER

PREMIERE LEAGUE CLUBS	CITY	STADIUM	CAPACITY
Sabawun	Kabul	Kabul National stadium	25 000
Maiwand	Kabul	Kabul National stadium	25 000
Kabul Club	Kabul	Kabul National stadium	25 000
Milan Kabul	Kabul	Kabul National stadium	25 000
Kabul United	Kabul	Kabul National stadium	25 000
Pamir	Kabul	Kabul National stadium	25 000
Red Crescent Society	Kabul	Kabul National stadium	25 000

BAHRAIN

BAHRAIN FOOTBALL ASSOC.
PB 5464, Isa Town
TEL 973/689 569   FAX /781 188
WEB wwwfootballasia.com.

REFERENCE
Official name
State of Bahrain
Date of formation 1971
Capital Manama
Population 617,000
Total area 262 sq Mi, 680 sq Km
Time zone GMT +3
Density 2354 per sq Mi, 1,015 per sq Km
Languages Arabic, English,, Urdu, Farsi
Literacy rate 84%
Currency Manat
Economy industry & commerce 85%, agriculture 5%, services 7%
Religions Shi'a Muslim 99%, Bahrani 70%,
Ethnic Mix Iranian, Indian, Pakistani 24%, other Arab 4%, European 2%

GEOGRAPHY
Elevation
lowest point: Persian Gulf 0 m
highest point: Jabal ad Dukhan 122 m
Geography Note
close to primary Middle Eastern petroleum sources; strategic location in Persian Gulf, which much of Western world's petroleum must transit to reach open ocean
Natural Resources
oil, associated and nonassociated natural gas, fish, pearls
Climate
arid; mild, pleasant winters; very hot, humid summers
Bahrain Food
butter barbecued salmon/cheese sauce

WORLD CUP		COUNTRY LEAGUE CHAMPIONS	
1930	Did not qualify		
1934	Did not qualify		
1938	Did not qualify	2004	Muharraq
1950	Did not qualify	2003	Riffa
1954	Did not qualify	2002	Muharraq
1958	Did not qualify	2001	Muharraq
1962	Did not qualify	2000	West Riffa
1966	Did not qualify	1999	Muharraq
1970	Did not qualify	1998	West Riffa
1974	Did not qualify	1997	West Riffa
1978	Did not qualify	1996	Al Ahli
1982	Did not qualify	**WOMEN'S LEAGUE CHAMPIONS**	
1986	Did not qualify	2004	Muharraq
1990	Did not qualify	2003	Not Known
1994	Did not qualify	2002	Not Known
1998	Did not qualify	2001	Not Known
2002	Did not qualify	2000	Not Known

NATIONAL TEAM COLORS

WORLD PICTURES OF SOCCER

236

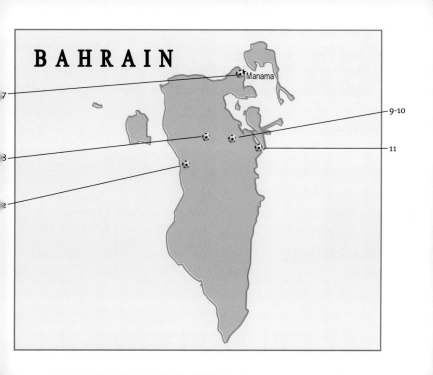

PREMIERE LEAGUE CLUBS	CITY	STADIUM	CAPACITY
Al-Ahli	Manama	Al-Ahli Stadium	10 000
Al-Najma	Manama	Bahrain National Stadium	30 000
Manama	Manama	Bahrain National Stadium	30 000
Muharraq	Muharraq	Al Muharraq Stadium	10 000
Bahrain	Muharraq	Al Muharraq Stadium	10 000
Al-Sahel	Muharraq	Al Muharraq Stadium	10 000
Al-Hala	Muharraq	Al Muharraq Stadium	10 000
Riffa	West Riffa		
East Riffa	East Riffa		
Busaiteen	East Riffa		
Sitrah	Sitrah		
Malikiya	Malikiya		

 # BANGLADESH

BANGLADESH FOOTBALL FEDERATION
Bangabandhu National Stadium,
1000 Dhaka   TEL 880 2/955 6072
WEB www.footballasia.com

REFERENCE
Official name
  People's Republic of Bangladesh
Date of formation 1971
Capital Dhaka
Population 129.2 Million
Total area 51,702 sq Mi, 133,910 sq Km
Time zone GMT +6
Density 2336 per sq Mi, 902 per sq Km
Languages Bangla, Urdu, Chakma, Marma
Literacy rate 37%
Currency Taka
Economy agriculture 57%, services 33%, industry 10%
Religions Muslim 87%, Hindu 12%
Ethnic Mix Bengali 98%

GEOGRAPHY
Elevation
lowest point: Indian Ocean 0 m
highest point: Keokradong 1,230 m
Geography Note
most of the country is situated on deltas of large rivers flowing from the Himalayas: the Ganges unites with the Jamuna (main channel of the Brahmaputra) and later joins the Meghna to eventually empty into the Bay of Bengal
Natural Resources
natural gas, arable land, timber, coal
Climate
tropical; mild winter (October to March); hot, humid summer (March to June); humid, warm rainy monsoon (June to October)
Bangladesh Food
meat Rrezalla/tikya kabab/makhani chicken

WORLD CUP

1930	Did not qualify
1934	Did not qualify
1938	Did not qualify
1950	Did not qualify
1954	Did not qualify
1958	Did not qualify
1962	Did not qualify
1966	Did not qualify
1970	Did not qualify
1974	Did not qualify
1978	Did not qualify
1982	Did not qualify
1986	Did not qualify
1990	Did not qualify
1994	Did not qualify
1998	Did not qualify
2002	Did not qualify

COUNTRY LEAGUE CHAMPIONS

2004	Brothers Union
2003	Muktijoddha SKC
2002	Mohammedan SC
2001	HAbahani Limited
2000	Muktijoddha SKC
1999	Mohammedan SC
1998	Muktijoddha SKC
1997	Not Known
1996	Mohammedan SC

WOMEN'S LEAGUE CHAMPIONS

2004	Dhaka FC
2003	Not Known
2002	Not Known
2001	Not Known
2000	Not Known

NATIONAL TEAM COLORS

WORLD PICTURES OF SOCCER

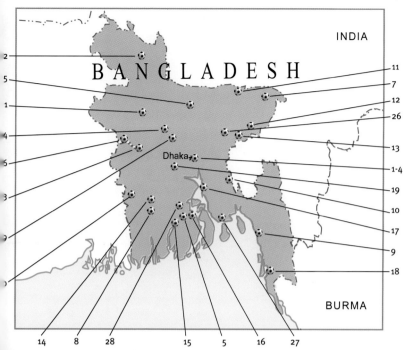

BANGLADESH

INDIA

BURMA

Dhaka

2
5
1
4
6
3
9

11
7
12
26
13
1-4
19
10
17
9
18

14 8 28 15 5 16 27

PREMIERE LEAGUE CLUBS	CITY	STADIUM	CAPACITY
Mohammedan SC	Dhaka	Kamlapur Stadium	20 000
Muktijoddha Sangsad	Dhaka	Kamlapur Stadium	20 000
Abahani Limited	Dhaka	Kamlapur Stadium	20 000
Arambagh Krira Sangha	Dhaka	Kamlapur Stadium	20 000
T&T Club	Barisal		
Abahani KC	Rajshahi		
Charutanga Jubu Sangha	Sylhet		
Abahani KC	Khulna		
Abahani KC	Chittatong	MA Aziz Stadium	20 000
Mohsin Club	Narayanganj		
Target SC	Sunamganj		
Raj Nagar Ekadah	Habiganj		
New Nation Club	Brahmanbaria		
AL Smitri Sangsad	Gopalganj*		
Udaykathi Jubo Samity	Pirojpur		
Kalinath Ekota Sangha	Bhola		
Natun Bazar	Chandpur		
Tarun Muslim	Cox's Bazaar		
Sabuj Sena	Faridpur		
SM Moyeen Sangsad	Jessore		
Memorial Club	Bogra		
New Million Sangha	Rangpur		
Brothers Union	Pabna		
Jamuna Traders	Sirajganj		
Al Helal Green SC	Mymensingh		
GRC SC	Narsingdi		
Friends Club	Noakhali		
Sabujbagh KC	Madaripur		
Greater Baby Stand Club	Tangail		

BHUTAN

BHUTAN FOOTBALL FEDERATION
PB 365, Thimphu
TEL 975 2/322 350 FAX /321 131
WEB www.footballasia.com

REFERENCE
Official name
Kingdom of Bhutan

Date of formation 1865
Capital Thimphu
Population 2.1 Million
Total area 18,147 sq Mi, 47,000sq Km
Time zone GMT +5.5
Density 116 per sq Mi, 42 per sq Km
Languages Dzongkha, Nepali
Literacy rate 41%
Currency Ngultrum
Economy agriculture 93%,services 5%, industry & commerce 2%
Religions Mahayana Buddhist 70%, Hindu 24%
Ethnic Mix Bhute 50%, Nepalese 35%

GEOGRAPHY
Elevation
lowest point: Drangme Chhu 97 m
highest point: Kula Kangri 7,553 m
Geography Note
landlocked; strategic location between China and India; controls several key Himalayan mountain passes
Natural Resources
timber, hydropower, gypsum, calcium carbide
Climate
varies; tropical in southern plains; cool winters and hot summers in central valleys; severe winters and cool summers in Himalayas
Bhutan Food
curry rice

WORLD CUP

1930	Did not qualify
1934	Did not qualify
1938	Did not qualify
1950	Did not qualify
1954	Did not qualify
1958	Did not qualify
1962	Did not qualify
1966	Did not qualify
1970	Did not qualify
1974	Did not qualify
1978	Did not qualify
1982	Did not qualify
1986	Did not qualify
1990	Did not qualify
1994	Did not qualify
1998	Did not qualify
2002	Did not qualify

COUNTRY LEAGUE CHAMPIONS

2004	Transport United
2003	Druk Pol
2002	Not Known
2001	Druk Star FC
2000	Phuentsholing FC
1999	Not Known
1998	Not Known
1997	Not Known
1996	Bhutan Telecom FC

WOMEN'S LEAGUE CHAMPIONS

2004	Not Known
2003	Not Known
2002	Not Known
2001	Not Known
2000	Not Known

NATIONAL TEAM COLORS

WORLD PICTURES OF SOCCER

PREMIERE LEAGUE CLUBS	CITY	STADIUM	CAPACITY
Thimpu FC	Thimpu	Changlimithang	15 000
Drukpol FC	Thimpu	Changlimithang	15 000
Royal Bhutan Police	Thimpu	Changlimithang	15 000
Royal Bhutan Army	Thimpu	Changlimithang	15 000
Finance	Thimpu	Changlimithang	15 000
Health School	Thimpu	Changlimithang	15 000
Social services	Thimpu	Changlimithang	15 000
Thimpu Ravens	Thimpu	Changlimithang	15 000
Bhutan Telecom Co.	Thimpu	Changlimithang	15 000
Drukstars	Thimpu	Changlimithang	15 000
Bumtang Tang FC	Bumthang	Bumtang Stadium	7 000
Phuentsholing	Phuentsholing	P.S.A Phuentsholing	6 000
Gomtu FC	Phuentsholing	P.S.A Phuentsholing	6 000
Chukha FC	Phuentsholing	P.S.A Phuentsholing	6 000
Samtse FC	Phuentsholing	P.S.A Phuentsholing	6 000
Paro FC	Paro	Paro Stadium	4 000

BRUNEI

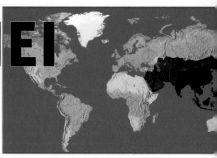

THE FOOTBALL ASSOCIATION OF BRUNEI DARUSSALAM

PB 2010, BS8674 Bandar Seri Begawan
TEL 673 2/382 761 FAX 382 760
WEB www.footballasia.com

REFERENCE

Official name
State of Brunei

Date of formation	1984
Capital	Bandar Seri Begawan
Population	328,000
Total area	2034 sq mi(5270 sq Km
Time zone	GMT +8
Density	161 per sq Mi (56 per sq Km
Languages	Malay, English, Chinese
Literacy rate	88%
Currency	Brunei $
Economy	services 87%, industry 9%, agriculture 4%
Religions	Muslim 66%, Buddhist 14%, Christian 10%
Ethnic Mix	Malay 67%, Chinese 16%, iIndigenous 6%

GEOGRAPHY

Elevation
lowest point: South China Sea 0 m
highest point: Bukit Pagon 1,850 m
Geography Note
close to vital sea lanes through South China
Sea linking Indian and Pacific Oceans; two
parts physically separated by Malaysia;
almost an enclave of Malaysia
Natural Resources
petroleum, natural gas, timber
Climate
tropical; hot, humid, rainy
Brunei Food
tofu & ginger/rujak brunei salad

WORLD CUP		COUNTRY LEAGUE CHAMPIONS	
1930	Did not qualify		
1934	Did not qualify		
1938	Did not qualify	2004	DPMM FC
1950	Did not qualify	2003	Wijaya United
1954	Did not qualify	2002	Wijaya United
1958	Did not qualify	2001	DPMM FC
1962	Did not qualify	2000	Kasuka FC
1966	Did not qualify	1999	Not Known
1970	Did not qualify	1998	Not Known
1974	Did not qualify	1997	Not Known
1978	Did not qualify	1996	Not Known
1982	Did not qualify	WOMEN'S LEAGUE CHAMPIONS	
1986	Did not qualify	2004	Not Known
1990	Did not qualify	2003	Not Known
1994	Did not qualify	2002	Not Known
1998	Did not qualify	2001	Not Known
2002	Did not qualify	2000	Not KNown

NATIONAL TEAM COLORS

WORLD PICTURES OF SOCCER

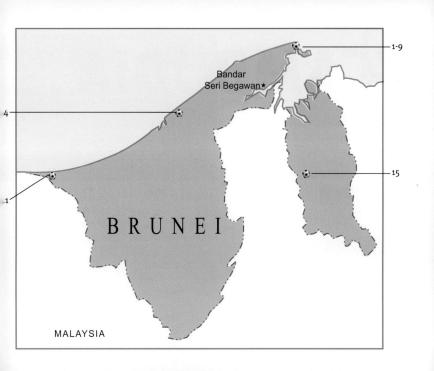

PREMIERE LEAGUE CLUBS	CITY	STADIUM	CAPACITY
Wijaya United FC	Brunei-Muara Dist.	SultanHassal Bolkiah	30 000
Kasuka FC	Brunei-Muara District	SultanHassal Bolkiah	30 000
Ah United FC	Brunei-Muara District	SultanHassal Bolkiah	30 000
Mulaut FC	Brunei-Muara District	SultanHassal Bolkiah	30 000
DPMM FC	Brunei-Muara District	SultanHassal Bolkiah	30 000
Kota Rangers FC	Brunei-Muara Dist.	SultanHassal Bolkiah	30 000
Jerudong FC	Brunei-Muara District	SultanHassal Bolkiah	30 000
Indera FC	Brunei-Muara District	SultanHassal Bolkiah	30 000
Kilanas FC	Brunei-Muara District	SultanHassal Bolkiah	30 000
-Mengellela	Belait District		
-BSRC	Belait District		
-Kamudi FC	Tutong District		
-Pesaka	Tutong District		
-Kiudang Mungkom	Tutong District		
-Ikatan Belia Mukim Bubok	Temburong D.		

CAMBODIA

CAMBODIA FOOTBALL FEDERATION
#47, St. Sangkat Boeung, Kengkang1,
Chamkamon Dist., Phnom Penh
TEL 855 23/364 889
WEB www. footballasia.com

REFERENCE
Official name
Kingdom of Cambodia
Date of formation 1953
Capital Phnom Penh
Population 11.2 Million
Total area 68,154 sq Mi, 176,520 sq Km
Time zone GMT +7
Density 164 per sq Mi, 65 per sq KM)
Languages Khmer,French
Literacy rate 35%
Currency Riel
Economy agriculture 80%, services & industry 20%
Religions Theravada Buddhism 95%
Ethnic Mix Khmer 94%, Chinese 4%, Vietnamese 1%

GEOGRAPHY
Elevation
lowest point: Gulf of Thailand 0 m
highest point: Phnum Aoral 1,810 m
Geography Note
a land of paddies and forests dominated by the Mekong River and Tonle Sap
Natural Resources
timber, gemstones, some iron ore, manganese, phosphates, hydropower potential
Climate
tropical; rainy, monsoon season (May to November); dry season (December to April); little seasonal temperature variation
Cambodian Food
aioan chua noeung phset kretni/trey chap kampot

WORLD CUP		COUNTRY LEAGUE CHAMPIONS	
1930	Did not qualify		
1934	Did not qualify		
1938	Did not qualify	2004	Hello United
1950	Did not qualify	2003	Not Known
1954	Did not qualify	2002	Samart United
1958	Did not qualify	2001	Not Known
1962	Did not qualify	2000	National Police
1966	Did not qualify	1999	Royal Dolphins
1970	Did not qualify	1998	Royal Dolphins
1974	Did not qualify	1997	Body Guards Club
1978	Did not qualify	1996	Body Guard Club
1982	Did not qualify	**WOMEN'S LEAGUE CHAMPIONS**	
1986	Did not qualify	2004	Not Known
1990	Did not qualify	2003	Not Known
1994	Did not qualify	2002	Not Known
1998	Did not qualify	2001	Not Known
2002	Did not qualify	2000	Not Known

NATIONAL TEAM COLORS

WORLD PICTURES OF SOCCER

PREMIERE LEAGUE CLUBS	CITY	STADIUM	CAPACITY
Nokorbal Krung	Phnom Penh	Stade National	50 000
Nokorbak Cheat	Phmon Penh	Stade National	50 000
Kang Yothipoikhemara	Phnom Penh	Stade National	50 000
Salsa Vekvoeun Yothes	Phnom Penh	Stade National	50 000
Kelia Rifh	Phnom Penh	Stade National	50 000
Kangtorp Choeung Tek	Phnom Penh	Old Stadium	15 000
Prey Veng	Phnom Penh	Old Stadium	15 000
Khemara	Phnom Penh	Old Stadium	15 000
Kampot	Phnom Penh	Old Stadium	15 000
Siem Reap	Phnomh Penh	Old Stadium	15 000

CHINA

FOOTBALL ASSOC. OF THE PEOPLE'S REPUBLIC OF CHINA

9 Tiyuguan Road, 100763, Beijing
TEL 86 10/6711 FAX /6714 2533
WEB www.fa.org.cn

REFERENCE

Official name
People's Republic of China

Date of formation 1912
Capital Beijing
Population 1,28 Billion
Total area 3,600,927 sq Mi, 9,326,410 sq Km
Time zone GMT +8
Density 355 per sq Mi, 130 per sq Km
Languages Mandarin
Literacy rate 81%
Currency Yuan
Economy agriculture 74%, industry 14%,
services 12%
Religions non religious 59%,
Buddhist6%, Muslim 2%
Ethnic Mix Han 93%, Zhaung 1%, Hui 1%

GEOGRAPHY

Elevation
lowest point: Turpan Pendi -154 m
highest point: Mount Everest 8,850 m
(1999 est.)

Geography Note
world's fourth-largest country (after Russia,
Canada, and US); Mount Everest on the
border with Nepal, is the world's tallest peak.

Natural Resources
coal, iron ore, petroleum, natural gas,
mercury, tin, tungsten, antimony,
manganese, molybdenum, vanadium,
magnetite, aluminum, lead, zinc, uranium,
hydropower

Climate
extremely diverse; tropical in south to subarctic in north

Chinese Food
sczchuan noodles/sweet sour shrimp

WORLD CUP		COUNTRY LEAGUE CHAMPIONS	
1930	Did not qualify		
1934	Did not qualify		
1938	Did not qualify	2004	Shenzhen Jianlibao
1950	Did not qualify	2003	Shanghai Shenua
1954	Did not qualify	2002	Dalian Shide
1958	Did not qualify	2001	Dalian Shide
1962	Did not qualify	2000	Dalian Shide
1966	Did not qualify	1999	Shandong Luneng
1970	Did not qualify	1998	Dalian Wanda
1974	Did not qualify	1997	Dalian Wanda
1978	Did not qualify	1996	Dalian Wanda
1982	Did not qualify	**WOMEN'S LEAGUE CHAMPIONS**	
1986	Did not qualify	2004	Shanghai SVA
1990	Did not qualify	2003	Beijing Chengjian
1994	Did not qualify	2002	Beijing Chengjian
1998	Did not qualify	2001	Shanghai STV
2002	First round exit	2000	Shanghai STV

NATIONAL TEAM COLORS

WORLD PICTURES OF SOCCER

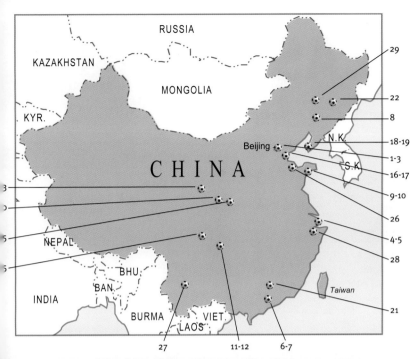

PREMIERE LEAGUE CLUBS	CITY	STADIUM	CAPACITY
Beijing Hyundai	Beijing	Worker's Stadium	72 000
Lioning Bird	Beijing	Olympic Sport Center	40 000
Liaoning Bodao	Beijing	Shijingshan Stadium	20 000
Shanghai Shenhua FC	Shanghai	Hongkou Stadium	35 000
Shanghai Zhongyuan Huili	Shanghai	Shanghai Stadium	80 000
Apollo Club	Guangzhou	Tianhe Stadium	60 000
Guangzhou Xiangxue	Guangzhou	Yuexiu Mountain	35 000
Shenyang Jinde	Shenyang	Wulihe Stadium	65 000
Qingdao Aoujuma	Qingdao	Qingdao Yizhong Center	60 000
-Qingdao Hademen	Qingdao	Hongchen Stadium	40 000
-Chongqing Lifan	Chongqing	Datianwan Stadium	32 000
-Xinganjue	Chongqing	Datianwan Stadium	32 000
-Sichuan Quanxing	Chengdu	Sichuan Stadium	40 000
-Sichuan Dahe	Chengdu	Chengdu Sports Center	40 000
-Chengdu Taihe	Chengdu	Chengdu Sports Center	40 000
-Tianjin Teda	Tianjin	Minyuan Stadium	20 000
-Tianjin Kangshifu	Tianjin	Minyuan Stadium	20 000
-Dalian Shide	Dalia	People's Stadium	50 000
-Dalian Sande Cars	Dalian	Jinzhou Stadium	
-Shaanxi Lijun Guoli	Baoji	City Stadium	27 000
-Guangdong Hongyuan	Shaoguan	Dongguan County	9 000
-Jilin Aodong	Jilin	People's Stadium	50 000
-Gansu Nogken	Lanzhou	Qilihe Stadium	40 000
-Shaanxi Lijun Guoli	Xi'an	Jiaodaruisun Stadium	51 000
-Ba Yi	Xi'an	Skydome Shhijiashunang	30 000
-Shandong Luneng Taishan	Jinan	Shandong Stadium	50 000
-Yunnan Hongta	Kunming	Kunming Tuodong	40 000
-Zhejiang Sanchua Luch.	Hangzhou	Huanglong Stadium	48 000
-Jilin Aodong Yanbian	Changchun	City Stadium	38 000

EAST TIMOR

EAST TIMOR FOOTBALL FEDERATION
P.O Box #122 Dili, East Timor
TEL   FAX
WEB www.footballasia.com

REFERENCE

Official name
DR East Timor

Date of formation May 20, 2002

Capital Dili

Population 1,040,880

Total area 15,077 sq km

Time zone Pacific

Density unknown

Languages Tetum, Portuguese and English

Literacy rate 60%

Currency US Dollar

Economy agriculture and mining

Religions Catholic, Muslim

Ethnic Mix Austronesian and Papuan

GEOGRAPHY

Elevation
lowest point: Savu Sea 0 m
highest point: Foho Tatamailau 2,963 m

Geography Note
The largest and easternmost of the Lesser Sunda Islands

Natural Resources
gold, petroleum, natural gas, manganese, marble

Climate
tropical; hot, humid, distinct rainy and dry seasons

East Timor Food
Not Known

WORLD CUP

1930	Did not Qualify
1934	Did not Qualify
1938	Did not Qualify
1950	Did not Qualify
1954	Did not Qualify
1958	Did not Qualify
1962	Did not Qualify
1966	Did not Qualify
1970	Did not Qualify
1974	Did not Qualify
1978	Did not Qualify
1982	Did not Qualify
1986	Did not Qualify
1990	Did not Qualify
1994	Did not Qualify
1998	Did not Qualify
2002	Did not Qualify

COUNTRY LEAGUE CHAMPIONS

2004	Not Known
2003	Not Known
2002	Not Known
2001	Not Known
2000	Not Known
1999	Not Known
1998	Not Known
1997	Not Known
1996	Not Known

Women's League Champ

2004	Not Known
2003	Not Known
2002	Not Known
2001	Not Known
2000	Not Known

NATIONAL TEAM COLORS

WORLD PICTURES OF SOCCER

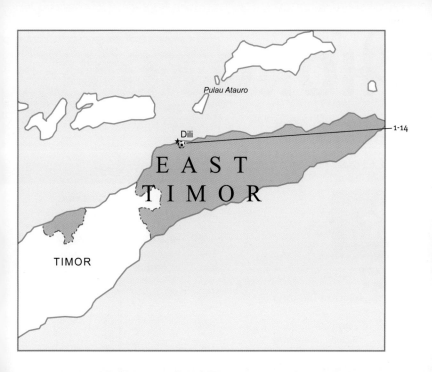

PREMIERE LEAGUE CLUBS	CITY	STADIUM	CAPACITY
-Akademik	Dili	Stadion NasionalDili	
-AC Mamura	Dili	Estadio Desportivo de Dili	
-FC Irmao Unidos	Dili		
-FC Café	Dili		
-FC Rusa Fuik	Dili		
-AD Esperanca	Dili		
-FC Audian	Dili		
-Palmonstown Lafaek	Dili		
-FC Porto Taibesi	Dili		
-Polisi Timor Leste	Dili		
-Sporting Lorosae	Dili		
-Dom Maululu	Dili		
-Ribeira Moloa	Dili		
-Cacusan Becora	Dili		

HONG KONG

Hong Kong Football Assoc.
55 Fat Kwong Street, Homantin, Kowloon, HK
TEL 852/2712 9122 FAX /2760 4303
WEB www.hkfa.com

Reference
Official name
Hong kong (Chinese Territory)

Date of formation   1997 (China)

Capital   Victoria (Hong Kong Island) (Beijing)

Population   6,847,125
Total area   416 sq Mi, 1,077 sq Km
Time zone   GMT+8
Density   16,459 per sq Mi
Languages   Chinese, English
Literacy rate   81%
Currency   Hong Kong $
Economy   services82%
Religions   Buddhist
Ethnic Mix   Chinese

Geography
Elevation
lowest point: South China Sea 0 m
highest point: Tai Mo Shan 958 m
Geography Note
more than 200 islands
Natural Resources
outstanding deepwater harbor, feldspar
Climate
tropical monsoon; cool and humid in winter, hot and rainy from spring through summer, warm and sunny in fall
Hong Kong Food
sesame chicken salad

World Cup		Country League Champions	
1930	Did not qualify		
1934	Did not qualify		
1938	Did not qualify	2004	Sun Hei
1950	Did not qualify	2003	Happy Valley
1954	Did not qualify	2002	Sun Hei
1958	Did not qualify	2001	Happy Valley
1962	Did not qualify	2000	South China
1966	Did not qualify	1999	Happy Valley
1970	Did not qualify	1998	Instant Dict
1974	Did not qualify	1997	South China
1978	Did not qualify	1996	Instant Dict
1982	Did not qualify	**Women's League Champions**	
1986	Did not qualify	2004	Not Known
1990	Did not qualify	2003	Not Known
1994	Did not qualify	2002	Not Known
1998	Did not qualify	2001	Not Known
2002	Did not qualify	2000	Not Known

National Team Colors

World Pictures of Soccer

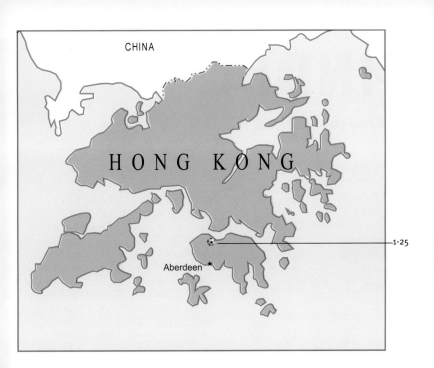

PREMIERE LEAGUE CLUBS	CITY	STADIUM	CAPACITY
South China Sea	Hong Kong	Hong Kong Stadium	40 000
-Happy Valley Athletic	Hong Kong	Hong Kong Stadium	40 000
Hong Kong FC	Hong Kong	Hong Kong Stadium	40 000
-Po Chai FC	Hong Kong	Mongkok Stadium	8 500
Sun Hei FC	Hong Kong	Mongkok Stadium	8 500
Instant-Dict FC	Hong Kong	Mongkok Stadium	8 500
Buller Rangers	Hong Kong	Tsing Yi Sports Ground	2 500
Kitchee SC	Hong Kong	Tuen TSK Sports Ground	2 500
Orient & Yee Hope Union	Hong Kong	Shatin Sports Ground	5 000
-Fukien	Hong Kong		
-Double Flowers FC	Hong Kong		
-Lucky Mile	Hong Kong		
-Fire services	Hong Kong		
-Kwok Keung	Hong Kong		
-Tung Po	Hong Kong		
-Eastern FC	Hong Kong		
-Mutual	Hong Kong		
-Citizens	Hong Kong		
-Art & Sales	Hong Kong		
-Ornaments	Hong Kong		
-Tung Sing	Hong Kong		
-Golden Sun	Hong Kong		
-Kowloon Fruit FC	Hong Kong		
-Hong Kong 08	Hong Kong		

INDIA

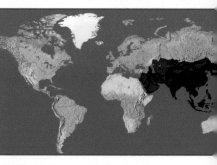

ALL INDIA FOOTBALL FEDERATION
Nehru Stadium (West Stand),
Fatorda, Margao-GOA 403 602
TEL 91 832/741 173 FAX /741 172
WEB www.footballasia.com

REFERENCE
Official name
Republic of India
Date of formation 1947
Capital New Delhi
Population 1,013 Billion
Total area 1,147,949 sq Mi, 2,973,190 sq Km
Time zone GMT +5.5
Density 882 per sq Mi, 304 per sq Km
Languages Hindi, English
Literacy rate 51%
Currency Rupee
Economy agriculture 63%, services2 6%, industry 11%
Religions Hindu 83%, Muslim11%, Christian 2%, Sikh 2%, Buddhist 1%
Ethnic Mix Indo-Aryan 72%, Dravidian 25%, Mongoloid 2%

GEOGRAPHY
Elevation
lowest point: Indian Ocean 0 m
highest point: Kanchenjunga 8,598 m
Geography Note
dominates South Asian subcontinent; near important Indian Ocean trade routes
Natural Resources
coal (fourth-largest reserves in the world), iron ore, manganese, mica,
bauxite, titanium ore, chromite, natural gas, diamonds, petroleum, limestone, arable land
Climate
varies from tropical monsoon in south to temperate in north
Indian Food
fish koliwada/brinjal prawn curry

WORLD CUP

1930	Did not qualify
1934	Did not qualify
1938	Did not qualify
1950	Did not qualify
1954	Did not qualify
1958	Did not qualify
1962	Did not qualify
1966	Did not qualify
1970	Did not qualify
1974	Did not qualify
1978	Did not qualify
1982	Did not qualify
1986	Did not qualify
1990	Did not qualify
1994	Did not qualify
1998	Did not qualify
2002	Did not qualify

COUNTRY LEAGUE CHAMPIONS

2004	East Bengal Club
2003	East Bengal Club
2002	Mohun Bagan AC
2001	East Bengal Club
2000	Mohun Bagan AC
1999	Salgaocar SC
1998	Mohun Bagan AC
1997	JCT Mills
1996	Not Known

WOMEN'S LEAGUE CHAMPIONS

2005	Manipur
2004	Manipur
2003	Manipur
2002	Manipur
2001	Manipur

NATIONAL TEAM COLORS

WORLD PICTURES OF SOCCER

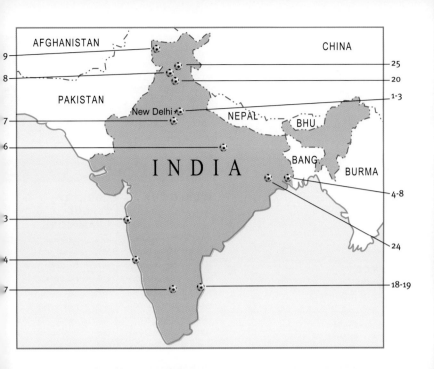

PREMIERE LEAGUE CLUBS	CITY	STADIUM	CAPACITY
Hindustan Club	New Delhi	Jawaharlal Nehru	75 000
New Delhi Heroes	New Delhi		
Indian Nationals FC	New Delhi		
Mohun Bagan AC	Calcutta	CFC Ground	22 000
East Bengal Club	Calcutta	East Bengal Ground	23 500
Tollygunge Agragami	Calcutta	Rabindra Sarobar Stadium	18 000
Mohammedan SC	Calcutta	Mohammedan Stadium	15 000
Calcutta Port Trust FC	Calcutta		
Salgaocar SC	Goa	Fatorda Stadium	35 000
Vasco SC	Goa	Fatorda Stadium	35 000
Churchill Brothers SC	Goa	Fatorda Stadium	35 000
Dempo SC	Goa	Fatorda Stadium	35 000
Sporting Club de Goa	Goa		
Fransa FC	Goa		
Hindustan Aeronautics	Bangalore	Sree Kanteerawa	40 000
Indian Telephone	Bangalore	Bangalore Stadium	15 000
Madras Engineering	Bangalore		
Integral Coach Factory	Chennai	Jawaharlal Nehru	40 000
Indian Bank	Chennai	Jawaharlal Nehru	40 000
JCT Mills	Phagwara		
Mahindra United	Mumbai		
Air India FC	Mumbai		
Central Railway FC	Mumbai		
Tata Football Academy	Jamshedpur		
Punjab State Elect.	Hoshiapur		
Uttar Pradesh Police	Uttar Pradesh		
Rewari FC	Rewari, Haryana		
Border Security Force	Jalandhar		
Jammu & Kashmir Bank	Srinagar		

INDONESIA

FOOTBALL ASSOCIATION OF INDONESIA
Gelora Bung Karno, Pintu X-XI, 10023 Jak.
TEL 62-21/570 4762 FAX /573 4386 WEB
www.sepak-bola.tv

REFERENCE
Official name
   Republic of Indonesia
Date of formation   1945
Capital   Jakarta
Population   699,447 sq Mi, 1,811,570 sq Km
Time zone   GMT +7/9
Density   303 per sq Mi, 113 per sq Km
Languages   Bahasa Indonesia, 250 + Dialects
Literacy rate   83%
Currency   Rupiah
Economy   agriculture 54%, services 38%, industry 8%
Religions   Sunni Muslim 87%, Christian 9%, Hindu 2%
Ethnic Mix   Javanese 45%,Sundanese 14%, Madurese 8%

GEOGRAPHY
Elevation
lowest point: Indian Ocean 0 m
highest point: Puncak Jaya 5,030 m
Geography Note
tarchipelago of 17,000 islands (6,000 inhabited); straddles Equator; strategic location astride or along major sea lanes from Indian Ocean to Pacific Ocean
Natural Resources
petroleum, tin, natural gas, nickel, timber, bauxite, copper, fertile soils, coal, gold, silver
Climate
tropical; hot, humid; more moderate in highlands
Indonesian Food
dayak style shrimp/indonesian satay

WORLD CUP

1930	Did not qualify
1934	Did not qualify
1938	Did not qualify
1950	Did not qualify
1954	Did not qualify
1958	Did not qualify
1962	Did not qualify
1966	Did not qualify
1970	Did not qualify
1974	Did not qualify
1978	Did not qualify
1982	Did not qualify
1986	Did not qualify
1990	Did not qualify
1994	Did not qualify
1998	Did not qualify
2002	Did not qualify

COUNTRY LEAGUE CHAMPIONS

2004	Persebaya
2003	Persik
2002	Petrokimia Putra
2001	Persija Jakarta
2000	PSM Ujungpandang
1999	PSIS Semarang
1998	Season Not Finished
1997	Persebaya Surabaya
1996	Matrans Bandung

WOMEN'S LEAGUE CHAMPIONS

2004	Not Known
2003	Not Known
2002	Not Known
2001	Not Known
2000	Not Known

NATIONAL TEAM COLORS

WORLD PICTURES OF SOCCER

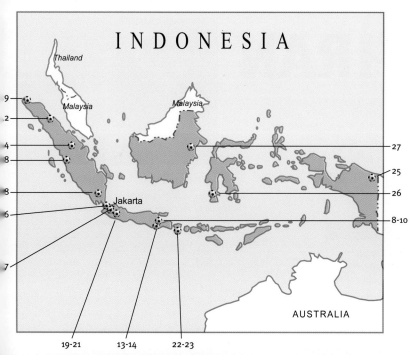

INDONESIA

Thailand

Malaysia

Malaysia

Jakarta

AUSTRALIA

9
2
4
8
8
6
7
27
25
26
8-10

19-21   13-14   22-23

PREMIERE LEAGUE CLUBS	CITY	STADIUM	CAPACITY
PSIS	Jakarta	Jatidiri	35 000
Pelita Solo	Jakarta	Sanggraha Pelita	20 000
Persija Jakarta FC	Jakarta	Sanggraha Pelita	20 000
Pelita Solo	Jakarta	Solo Manahan	20 000
Jakarta FC	Jakarta	Bea Cukai Rawamangun	15 000
Persija Jakarta	Jakarta	Menteng Stadium	10 000
Krama Yudha Tiga Berlian	Jakarta	Menteng Stadium	10 000
Persebaya	Surabaya	Gelora 10 November	40 000
Surabaya FC	Surabaya	Jombang	20 000
Tambak Sari	Surabaya	Tambak Sari Stadium	20 000
Medan Jaya FC	Medan	Teladan	25 000
PSMS Medan FC	Medan	Teladan	25 000
Arema Malang	Malang	Gajayana	15 000
Persema Malang	Malang	Gajayana	15 000
Persita Tangerang	Tangerang	Benteng Stadium	25 000
Persikota Tangerang	Tangerang	Benteng Stadium	25 000
PSP Padang	Padang	Haji Agus Salim	22 000
Semen Padang	Padang	Haji Agus Salim	22 000
Persib Bandung	Bandung	Siliwangi	25 000
Persikab Bandung	Bandung	Sangkuriang	12 000
Mastrans Bandung Raya	Bandung	Sangkuriang	12 000
Gelora Putra Delta	Denpasar	Ngurah Rai	20 000
Perseden	Denpasar		
PSPS Pekanbaru	Pekanbaru	Hang Tuah	10 000
Persipura Jayapura	Hollandia	Mandala	20 000
PSM Makassar	Makassar	Mattoangin	30 000
Putra Samarinda	Samarinda	Segiri	20 000
PSBL	Bandar Lampung	Pahoman	20 000
Persiraja	Banda AcehBanda Aceh	Harapan Bangsa	25 000

IRAN

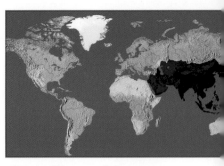

IR Iran Football Federation
Shahid Keshvari Sports Complex,
Mirdamad Av., Razan Jonoobi St. PB
15875-6967, 15875 Tehran
TEL 98 21/225 8151
www.iriff.org

Reference
Official name
Islamic Republic of Iran

Date of formation	1906
Capital	Tehran
Population	67.7 Million
Total area	631,659 sq Mi, 1,636,000 sq Km
Time zone	GMT + 3.5
Density	107 per sq Mi, 42 per sq Km
Languages	Farsi (Persian)
Literacy rate	70%
Currency	Rial
Economy	services 46%, agriculture 33%, industry 21%
Religions	Shi'a Muslim 95%, Sunni Muslim 4%
Ethnic Mix	Persian 50%, Azeri 20%, Lur & Bakhtiari 10%, Kurds 8%

Geography
Elevation
lowest point: Caspian Sea -28 m
highest point: Kuh-e Damavand 5,671 m
Geography Note
strategic location on the Persian Gulf and
Strait of Hormuz, which are vital maritime
pathways for crude oil transport
Natural Resources
petroleum, natural gas, coal, chromium, copper, iron ore, lead, manganese, zinc, sulfur
Climate
mostly arid or semiarid, subtropical along
Caspian coast
Iranian Food
khoresht-e badenjan/kabab e barg

World Cup		Country League Champions	
1930	Did not qualify		
1934	Did not qualify		
1938	Did not qualify	2004	Paas
1950	Did not qualify	2003	Sepahan
1954	Did not qualify	2002	Piroozi
1958	Did not qualify	2001	Esteghlal
1962	Did not qualify	2000	Piroozi
1966	Did not qualify	1999	Piroozi
1970	Did not qualify	1998	Esteghlal
1974	Did not qualify	1997	Piroozi
1978	First round exit	1996	Piroozi
1982	Did not qualify	**Women's League Champions**	
1986	Did not qualify	2004	Not Known
1990	Did not qualify	2003	Not Known
1994	Did not qualify	2002	Not Known
1998	First round exit	2001	Not Known
2002	Did not qualify	2000	Not Known

National Team Colors

World Pictures of Soccer

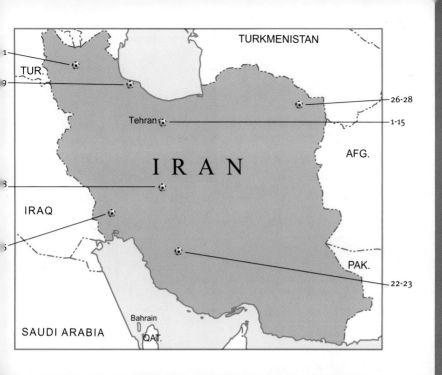

PREMIERE LEAGUE CLUBS	CITY	STADIUM	CAPACITY
Esteghlal Tehran	Tehran	Azadi Stadium	100 000
Piroozi	Tehran	Azadi Stadium	100 000
Bank Melli Tehran	Tehran	Azadi Stadium	100 000
Saypa	Tehran	Azadi Stadium	100 000
Paas	Tehran	Dastgerdi Stadium	15 000
Ararat	Tehran	Ararat Stadium	15 000
Tehran FC	Tehran	Shirodi Stadium	30 000
Paykan	Tehran	Iran Khodro Stadium	10 000
Tehran club	Tehran	Takhti Stadium	30 000
Saba Battery	Tehran		
Rah Ahan	Tehran		
Barq Tehran	Tehran		
HOMA	Tehran		
Ground Force	Tehran		
Oghab	Tehran		
Zob-Ahan	Esfehan	Naghsh e Jahan Stadium	75 000
Sepahan	Esfehan	Takhti Stadium	15 000
Polyacryl	Esfehan	Takhti Stadium	15 000
Traktor Sazi	Tabriz	Bagh Shomal Takhti	20 000
Shahrdari	Tabriz	Bagh Shomal Takhti	20 000
Mashin Sazi	Tabriz	Bagh Shomal Takhti	20 000
Bargh	Shiraz	Hafezieh Stadium	30 000
Fajr Sepasi	Shiraz	Hafezieh Stadium	30 000
Foolad	Ahvaz	Takhti Stadium	30 000
Estaghlal Ahvaz	Ahvaz	Takhti Stadium	30 000
Payam	Mashdad	Takhti Stadium	15 000
Abomoslem	Mashdad	Takhti Stadium	15 000
PartSazan Khorasan	Mashdad	Takhti Stadium	15 000
Esteghlal Rasht	Rasht	Dr.Azody Stadium	20 000

IRAQ

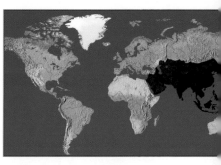

IRAQI FOOTBALL ASSOCIATION
Olympic Bldg. Palestine Street,
PB 484, Baghdad
TEL 964-1/772 9990 FAX /885 4321
WEB www.footballasia.com

REFERENCE
Official name
Republic of Iraq
Date of formation 1906
Capital Bagdad
Population 23.1 million
Total area 168,869 sq Mi, 437,370 sq Km
Time zone GMT +3
Density 137 per sq Mi, 55 per sq Km
Languages Arabic,Kurdish,Turkish,Farsi(Persian)
Literacy rate 57%
Currency Dinar
Economy services 48%, agriculture 30%, industry 22%
Religions Shi'a Ithna, Muslim 63%, Sunni Muslim 33%
Ethnic Mix Arab 79%, Kurdish 16%, Persian 3%, Turkoman 2%

GEOGRAPHY
Elevation
lowest point: Persian Gulf 0 m
highest point: Haji Ibrahim 3,600 m
Geography Note
strategic location on Shatt al Arab waterway
and at the head of the Persian Gulf
Natural Resources
petroleum, natural gas, phosphates,
sulfur
Climate
mostly desert; mild to cool winters with dry,
hot, cloudless summers; northern
mountainous regions along Iranian and
Turkish borders
Iraqi Food
lis-san el qua-thi

WORLD CUP		COUNTRY LEAGUE CHAMPIONS	
1930	Did not qualify		
1934	Did not qualify		
1938	Did not qualify	2004	No Competition
1950	Did not qualify	2003	Abandoned
1954	Did not qualify	2002	Al Talaba
1958	Did not qualify	2001	Al Zawra
1962	Did not qualify	2000	Al Zawra
1966	Did not qualify	1999	Al Zawra
1970	Did not qualify	1998	Al Shurta
1974	Did not qualify	1997	Al Quwa Al Jawia
1978	Did not qualify	1996	Al Zawra
1982	Did not qualify	WOMEN'S LEAGUE CHAMPIONS	
1986	First round exit	2004	Not Known
1990	Did not qualify	2003	Not Known
1994	Did not qualify	2002	Not Known
1998	Did not qualify	2001	Not Known
2002	Did not qualify	2000	Not Known

NATIONAL TEAM COLORS

WORLD PICTURES OF SOCCER

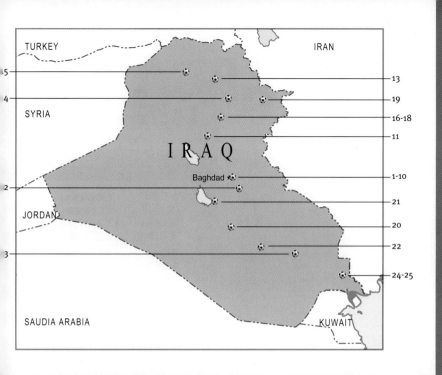

PREMIERE LEAGUE CLUBS	CITY	STADIUM	CAPACITY
Al-Quwa	Baghdad	Baghdad stadium	90 000
Al-Jawiya	Baghdad	Baghdad stadium	90 000
Al-Talaba	Baghdad	Baghdad stadium	90 000
Al Nafat	Baghdad	Baghdad stadium	90 000
Al-Jaish	Baghdad	Baghdad stadium	90 000
Al-Zawraa	Baghdad	Al Shaab	45 000
Al Sinaa	Baghdad	Al Shaab	45 000
Al-Estiglal	Baghdad	Al Shaab	45 000
Al-Karkh	Baghdad	Al Shaab	45 000
Al-Shurta	Baghdad	Al Shaab	45 000
Salah al Deen	Tikrit		
Diyala	Diyala		
Arbil	Arbil		
Kirkurk	Kirkurk		
Mosul	Mosul		
Dahuk	Dahuk		
Zakho	Dahuk		
Pire	sDahuk		
Sulimaniya	Sulimaniya		
Al-Najaf	Najaf		
Karbala	Karbala		
Samawa	Samawa		
Al-Nassriya	Nassriya		
Al-Minaa	Basra		
Basr	aBasra		

ISRAEL

THE ISRAEL FOOTBALL ASSOC.
Ramat-Gan Stadium, 299 Aba Hilel
Street 52134 Ramat Gan
TEL 972-3/617 1503   FAX/570 2044
WEB www.uefa.com

REFERENCE
Official name
  State of Israel
**Date of
formation** 1948
Capital Jerusalem
Population 6.2 Million
Total area 7849 sq Mi, 20,330 sq Km
Time zone GMT+2
Density 790 per sq Mi, 277 per sq Km
Languages Hebrew, Arabic, Yiddish
Literacy rate 98%
Currency New Chekel
Economy servces 95%
Religions Jewish 92%, Muslim 14%
Ethnic Mix Jewish 82%, Arab 18%

GEOGRAPHY
Elevation
lowest point: Dead Sea -408 m
highest point: Har Meron 1,208 m
Geography Note
there are 231 Israeli settlements and civilian
land use sites in the West Bank, 42 in the
Israeli-occupied Golan Heights, 25 in the
Gaza Strip,and 29 in East Jerusalem (2001
est.); Sea of Galilee is an important freshwater source.
Natural Resources
timber, potash, copper ore, natural gas,
phosphate rock, magnesium bromide, clays,
sand
Climate
temperate; hot and dry in southern and
eastern desert areas
Israel Food
humus/pita bread

WORLD CUP		COUNTRY LEAGUE CHAMPIONS	
1930	Did not qualify		
1934	Did not qualify		
1938	Did not qualify	2004	Maccabi Haifa
1950	Did not qualify	2003	Maccabi Tel Aviv
1954	Did not qualify	2002	Maccabi Tel Aviv
1958	Did not qualify	2001	Maccabi Tel Aviv
1962	Did not qualify	2000	Hapoel Tel Aviv
1966	Did not qualify	1999	Hapoel Haifa
1970	First round exit	1998	Beitar jerusalem
1974	Did not qualify	1997	Beitar Jerusalem
1978	Did not qualify	1996	Maccabi Tel Aviv
1982	Did not qualify	**WOMEN'S LEAGUE CHAMPIONS**	
1986	Did not qualify	2004	ASSA Tel Aviv
1990	Did not qualify	2003	Maccabi Holon
1994	Did not qualify	2002	Maccabi Haifa
1998	Did not qualify	2001	Maccabi Haifa
2002	Did not qualify	2000	Hapoel Tel Aviv

NATIONAL TEAM COLORS

WORLD PICTURES OF SOCCER

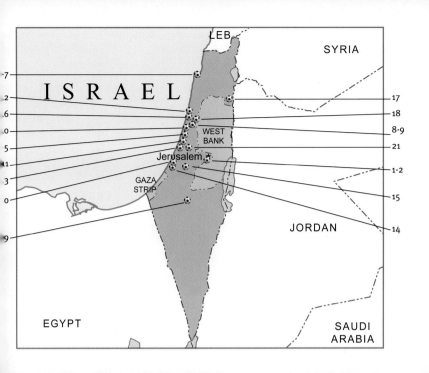

PREMIERE LEAGUE CLUBS	CITY	STADIUM	CAPACITY
Beitar Jerusalem	Jerusalem	Teddi	20 000
Hapoel Jerusalem	Jerusalem	Teddi	20 000
Maccabi Tel-Aviv	Tel-Aviv	Bloomfield Stadium	16 500
Hapoel Tel-Aviv	Tel-Aviv	Bloomfield Stadium	16 500
Bnei-Yehuda	Tel-Aviv	Sehunat Hatikva	7 000
Maccabi Haifa	Haifa	Kiryat Eli'Ezer	18 500
Hapoel Haifa	Haifa	Kiryat Eli'Ezer	18 500
Maccabi Petah-Tikva	Petah-Tikva	Hapoel Petah-Tikva	8 400
Hapoel Petah-Tikva	Petah-Tikva	Hapoel Petah-Tikva	8 400
Maccabi Herzliyya	Herzliyya	Herzliyya Stadium	9 000
Maccabi Jaffa	Jaffa	R.I Gaon Stadium	5 000
Maccabi Netanya	Netanya	Sar-Tov	6 500
Zafririm Holon	Holon	Zafririm Stadium	3 500
Hapoel Ashqelon	Ashqelon	Sela Stadium	10 000
Maccabi Kiryat-Gat	Kiryat-Gat	Kiryat-Gat City Stadium	3 500
Hakoah Ramat-Gan	Ramat-Gan	Winter Stadium	8 000
Hapoel Beit-She'an	Beit She'an	Beit She'an Stadium	5 000
Hapoel Kefar-Saba	Kefar-Saba	Kfar Saba Stadium	8 000
Hapoel Be'er-Sheva	Be'er-Sheva	Vasermil	13 000
Ironi Ashdod	Ashdod	Ashdod Stadium	8 000
Ironi RishonLetsion	Rishon-Letsion	Superland	

JAPAN

JAPAN FOOTBALL ASSOCIATION
3rd Floor, Shibuya Nomura Bldg. 1-10-8
Dogenzaka, Shibuya-Ku, 150-0043 Tokyo
TEL 81 3/3476 2011 FAX /3476 2291
WEB www.jfa.or.jp

REFERENCE

Official name
Japan
Date of formation 1945
Capital Tokyo
Population 126 Million
Total area 145,374 sq Mi, 376,520 sq Km
Time zone GMT +9
Density 871 sq Mi, 334 per sq Km
Languages Japanese, Korean
Literacy rate 99%
Currency Yen
Economy services 69%, industry 24%, agriculture 7%
Religions Shinto & Buddhist 76%, Buddhist 16%, Christian 8%
Ethnic Mix Japenese 99%

GEOGRAPHY
Elevation
lowest point: Hachiro-Gata -4 m
highest point: Fujiyama 3,776 m
Geography Note
strategic location in northeast Asia
Natural Resources
negligible mineral resources, fish
Climate
varies from tropical in south to cool temperate in north
Japenese Food
sushi/tempura/yarisoba/soba

WORLD CUP		COUNTRY LEAGUE CHAMPIONS	
1930	Did not qualify		
1934	Did not qualify		
1938	Did not qualify	2004	Yokohama F.Marinos
1950	Did not qualify	2003	Yokohama F.Marinos
1954	Did not qualify	2002	Jubilo Iwata
1958	Did not qualify	2001	Kashima Antlers
1962	Did not qualify	2000	Kashima Antlers
1966	Did not qualify	1999	Jubilo Iwata
1970	Did not qualify	1998	Kashima Antlers
1974	Did not qualify	1997	Jubilo Iwata
1978	Did not qualify	1996	Kashima Antlers
1982	Did not qualify	**WOMEN'S LEAGUE CHAMPIONS**	
1986	Did not qualify	2004	Tasaki Perule FC
1990	Did not qualify	2003	Tasaki Perule FC
1994	Did not qualify	2002	Iga FC Kunoichi
1998	First round exit	2001	Ni-Tele Beleza
2002	Scd round exit	2000	Tasaki Perule FC

NATIONAL TEAM COLORS

WORLD PICTURES OF SOCCER

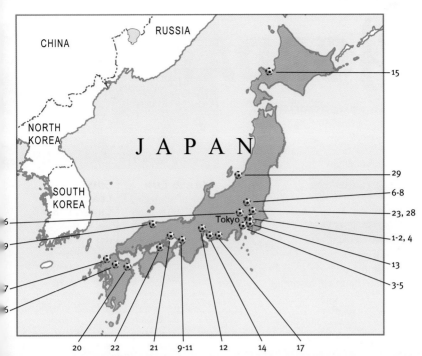

PREMIERE LEAGUE CLUBS	CITY	STADIUM	CAPACITY
-Tokyo FC	Tokyo	Ajinamoto Stadium	50 000
-Tokyo verdy 1969	Tokyo	Ajinamoto Stadium	50 000
Yokohama Marinos	Yokohama	Yokohama International	70 000
Sagawa Tokyo	Tokyo		
Yokohama FC	Yokohama	Mitsuzawa Stadium	15 000
Saitama FC	Saitama	Stadium 2002	63 000
Urawa Red Diamonds	Saitama	Komaba Stadium	21 500
Omiya Ardija	Saitama	Omiya Football Stadium	12 500
Cerezo Ozaka	Ozaka	Nagai stadium	50 000
-Gamba Osaka	Ozaka	Expo 70' Stadium	23 000
-Sagawa Osaka	Osaka		
-Nagoya Grampus	Nagoya	Mizuho Football Stadium	15 000
-Kawasaki Frontale	Kawasaki	Todoroki Stadium	25 000
-Nagoya Grampus	Toyota	Toyota Stadium	45 000
-Consadole Sapporo	Sapporo	Atsubetsu Stadium	20 000
-Ventforet Kofu	Kofu	Kose Sports Stadium	13 000
-Jubilo Iwata	Iwata	Jubilo Iwata Stadium	17 300
-SC Tottori	Tottori	Tottori"Bird" Stadium	25 000
-Ehime FC	Tottori	Tottori"Bird" Stadium	25 000
-Oita Trinita	Oita	Oita stadium"Big Eye"	43 200
-Vissel Kobe	Kobe	Kobe Universiade	45 000
-Takamatsu United FC	Takamatsu	Kagawa Stadium	30 100
-Kashima Antlers	Kashima	Kashima soccer Stadium	41 800
-Sanfrecce Hiroshima	Hiroshima	Hiroshima "Big Arch"	45 000
-Jef United Ichihara	Hiroshima	Ichihara Stadium	15 000
-Sagan Tosu	Tosu	Tosu Stadium	25 000
-Avispa Fukuoka	Fukuoka	Hakatanomori Stadium	23 000
-Kashiwa Reysol	Kashiwa	Hitachi Kashiwa Stadium	16 000
-Albirex Nigata	Nigata	Nigata Stadium	42 700

JORDAN

JORDAN FOOTBALL ASSOCIATION
PB 962024, Al Hussein Sports City,
11196 Amman
TEL 962 6/565 7662 FAX /565 7660
WEB www.jfa.com.jo

REFERENCE
Official name
Hashemite Kingdom of Jordan

Date of formation	1946
Capital	Amman
Population	6.7 Million
Total area	34,335 sq Mi, 88,930 sq Km
Time zone	GMT +2
Density	195 per sq Mi, 51 per sq Km
Languages	Arabic
Literacy rate	86%
Currency	Dinar
Economy	services 64%, industry 26%, agriculture 10%
Religions	Muslim 92%, Christian 7%
Ethnic Mix	Arab 98%, Armenian 1%, Circassian 1%

GEOGRAPHY
Elevation
lowest point: Dead Sea -408 m
highest point: Jabal Ram 1,734 m
Geography Note
strategic location at the head of the Gulf of Aqaba and as the Arab country that shares the longest border with Israel and the occupied West Bank
Natural Resources
phosphates, potash, shale oil
Climate
mostly arid desert; rainy season in west (November to April)
Jordanese Food
mansaf/shish kebab

WORLD CUP

1930	Did not qualify
1934	Did not qualify
1938	Did not qualify
1950	Did not qualify
1954	Did not qualify
1958	Did not qualify
1962	Did not qualify
1966	Did not qualify
1970	Did not qualify
1974	Did not qualify
1978	Did not qualify
1982	Did not qualify
1986	Did not qualify
1990	Did not qualify
1994	Did not qualify
1998	Did not qualify
2002	Did not qualify

COUNTRY LEAGUE CHAMPIONS

2004	Al Faisaly
2003	Al Faisaly
2002	Al Faisaly
2001	Al Faisaly
2000	Al Faisaly
1999	Al Faisaly
1998	No Competition
1997	Al Wahdat
1996	Al Wahdat
WOMEN'S LEAGUE CHAMPIONS	
2005	Shabab
2004	Not Known
2003	Not Known
2002	Not Known
2001	Not Known

NATIONAL TEAM COLORS

WORLD PICTURES OF SOCCER

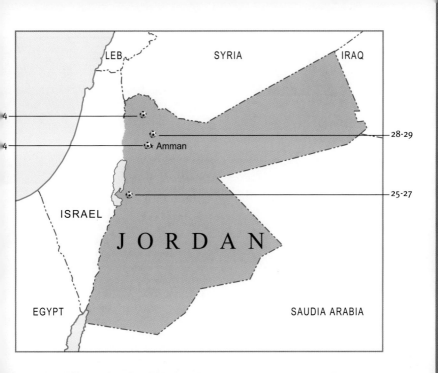

PREMIERE LEAGUE CLUBS	CITY	STADIUM	CAPACITY
Al-Wehdat	Amman		
-Al-Faysali	Amman		
Al-Baq'aa	Amman		
Yarmouk	Amman		
Shabab Al-Hussein	Amman		
Hashmy	Amman		
Hai Al-Ameer Hasan Club	Amman		
Al-Jazeera	Amman		
Al-Yarmouk	Amman		
-Al-Ahly	Amman		
-Hai Al-Ameer Hasan Club	Amman		
-Sahab	Amman		
-Al-Qadesiya	Amman		
-Ain Karem	Amman		
-Al-Hussein Club	Irbed		
-Al-Ramtha	Irbed		
-Kufer soom	Irbed		
-Al-Arabi	Irbed		
-Al-Turra	Irbed		
-Mghayyar	Irbed		
-Sareeh	Irbed		
-Al-Karmel	Irbed		
-Al-Jaleel	Irbed		
-Saham	Irbed		
-Mua'ab	Karak		
-That Ras	Karak		
-Ghour Al Safy	Karak		
Zarka	Zarka		
-As-Rusayfa	Zarka		

KAZAKHSTAN

THE FOOTBALL UNION OF KAZAKHSTAN

Satpayev Street, 29/3,480 072 Almaty
TEL 7 3272/929 244 FAX /921 885
WEB www.fsk.kz

REFERENCE

Official name
   Republic of Kazakhstan

Date of formation 1991
Capital Astana
Population 6.7 million
Total area 34,335 sq Mi, 88,930 sq Km
Time zone GMT +6
Density 15 per sq Mi, 6 per sq Km
Languages Kazakh, Russian
Literacy rate 98%
Currency Tenge
Economy services 43%, industry 31%, agriculture 26%
Religions Muslim 50%, Russian Orthodox 13%, Protestant 1%
Ethnic Mix Kazakh 53%, Russian 30%, Ukrainian 4%

GEOGRAPHY

Elevation
lowest point: Vpadina Kaundy -132 m
highest point: Khan Tangiri Shyngy (Pik Khan-Tengri) 6,995 m
Geography Note
landlocked; Russia leases approximately 6,000 sq km of territory enclosing the Baykonur Cosmodrome
Natural Resources
major deposits of petroleum, natural gas, coal, iron ore, manganese, chrome ore, nickel, cobalt, copper, molybdenum, lead, zinc, bauxite, gold, uranium
Climate
continental, cold winters and hot summers, arid and semiarid
Kazakhstan Food
beliashi

WORLD CUP		COUNTRY LEAGUE CHAMPIONS	
1930	Did not qualify		
1934	Did not qualify		
1938	Did not qualify	2004	Kairat Almaty
1950	Did not qualify	2003	Irtysh Pavlodar
1954	Did not qualify	2002	Irtysh Pavlodar
1958	Did not qualify	2001	Zhenis Astana
1962	Did not qualify	2000	Zhenis Astana
1966	Did not qualify	1999	Irtysh Pavlodar
1970	Did not qualify	1998	Yelimay Semipalatinsk
1974	Did not qualify	1997	Yelimay Semipalatinsk
1978	Did not qualify	1996	Taraz Jambul
1982	Did not qualify	**WOMEN'S LEAGUE CHAMPIONS**	
1986	Did not qualify	2004	Not Known
1990	Did not qualify	2003	Not Known
1994	Did not qualify	2002	Not Known
1998	Did not qualify	2001	Not Known
2002	Did not qualify	2000	Not Known

NATIONAL TEAM COLORS

WORLD PICTURES OF SOCCER

PREMIERE LEAGUE CLUBS	CITY	STADIUM	CAPACITY
Dostyk	Shymkent	Imeni Kashi Mukana	30 000
Karabastau	Shymkent	Imeni Kashi Mukana	30 000
Ordabasy	Shymkent		
Aqsu-Kent	Shymkent		
FK Kairat	Almaty	Tsentralny	25 000
CSKA Zhyger	Almaty	Kazgau	3 000
Yesil Bogatyr	Petropavl	Avangard	10 000
Batys Plus	Oral	Avangard	10 000
FK Taraz	Taraz	Khimik	23 000
JambylTaraz			
Shakhtyor Ispat-Karmet	Karagandy	Shakhtyor	33 000
Munayly	Atyrau		
FK Atyrau	Atyrau	Nephtyanik	10 000
Tobol	Kostanaj	Tsentralny	10 000
Yesil Bogatyr	Petropavl	Avangard	10 000
Ekibastuzets	Ekibastuz	Shakhtyor	9 000
Zhenis	Astana	K.Mukana Munajtpasov	13 500
Kaspiy	Aktau	Munaishi	3 500
Vostok-Altyn	Oskermen	Vostok	12 000
Zhetysu	Taldykorgan	Spartak	8 000
Aktobe Lento	Aktobe	Tsentralny	12 000
Yelimai Semey	Semej	Spartak	15 000
Yesil	Kokshetau	Khimik	8 000
Irtysh	Bastau	Tsentralny	15 000
Qaysar-Jas	Qyzylorda		
Irtish	Pavlodar		
Gornyak	Krasnyy Gornyak		
Yassi-Rahat	Turkestan		

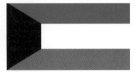

KUWAIT

KUWAIT FOOTBALL ASSOC.
PB 2029 Safat, 13021 Safat
TEL 965/255 585 FAX /255 5935
WEB www.alazraq.com

REFERENCE

Official name
State of Kuwait

Date of formation	1961
Capital	Kuwait City
Population	2 Million
Total area	6880 sq Mi, 17,820 sq Km
Time zone	GMT +3
Density	291 per sq Mi, 111 per sq Km
Languages	Arabic, English
Literacy rate	78%
Currency	Dinar
Economy	services 90%, industry 9%, agriculture 1%
Religions	Muslim 75%, Christian 10%, Hindu 15%
Ethnic Mix	Kuwaiti 45%,Arab 35%, South Asian 9%

GEOGRAPHY

Elevation
lowest point: Persian Gulf 0 m
highest point: Unnamed location 306 m
Geography Note
strategic location at head of Persian Gulf
Natural Resources
petroleum, fish, shrimp, natural gas
Climate
dry desert; intensely hot summers; short, cool winters
Kuwaiti Food
chicken mechbous

WORLD CUP

1930	Did not qualify
1934	Did not qualify
1938	Did not qualify
1950	Did not qualify
1954	Did not qualify
1958	Did not qualify
1962	Did not qualify
1966	Did not qualify
1970	Did not qualify
1974	Did not qualify
1978	Did not qualify
1982	First round exit
1986	Did not qualify
1990	Did not qualify
1994	Did not qualify
1998	Did not qualify
2002	Did not qualify

COUNTRY LEAGUE CHAMPIONS

2004	Al Qadisiya
2003	Al Qadisiya
2002	Al Arabi
2001	Al Kuwait
2000	Al Salmiya
1999	Al Qadisiya
1998	Al Salmiya
1997	Al Arabi
1996	Kazma

WOMEN'S LEAGUE CHAMPIONS

2004	Not Known
2003	Not Known
2002	Not Known
2001	Not Known
2000	Not Known

NATIONAL TEAM COLORS

WORLD PICTURES OF SOCCER

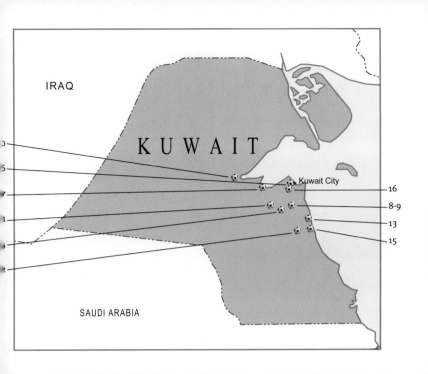

PREMIERE LEAGUE CLUBS	CITY	STADIUM	CAPACITY
Al-Kuwait SC	Kuwait City	Kazma SC Stadium	20 000
Al-Arabi	Kuwait City		
Alqadisiya Al-Kuwait	Kuwait City	Mohammed Al-Hamad	20 000
Salmiya	Kuwait City		
Al-Kuwait City	Kuwait City		
Kazma Al-Kuwait	Kuwait City	Al-Sadaqua Walsalam	20 000
Solaybeekhat	Solaybeekhat		
Al-Yarmouk	Khitan		
Khitan	Khitan		
Jahra	Jahra		
Al-Tadamon	Farwaniya		
Al-Shabab	Ahmadi		
Al-Sahel	Abu Hlaifa		
Al-Nasr	Jleeb Al-Shyookh		
Fehayheel	Fehayheel		
Al-Kuwait City	Kaifan		

KYRGYZSTAN

FOOTBALL FEDERATION OF KYRGYZSTAN REPUBLIC
PB 1484, Kurenkeeva Str. 195,720
040 Bishkek/TEL 996-31/267 0573
web www.football.gratis.kg

REFERENCE
Official name
Republic of Kyrgyzstan

Date of formation	1991
Capital	Bishkek
Population	4.7 million
Total area	76,640 sq Mi, 198,500 sq Km
Time zone	GMT +6
Density	61 per sq Mi, 23 per sq Km
Languages	Kyrgyz,Russian,Uzbek
Literacy rate	97%
Currency	Som
Economy	services 41%,agriculture 38%, industry 21%
Religions	Sunnu Muslim 70%, Russian Orthodox 30%
Ethnic Mix	Kyrgyz 57%,Russian 19%, Uzbek 13%

GEOGRAPHY
Elevation
lowest point: Kara-Daryya (Karadar'ya) 132 m
highest point: Jengish Chokusu
(Pik Pobedy) 7,439 m
Geography Note
landlocked; entirely mountainous, dominated
by the Tien Shan range; many tall peaks,
glaciers, and high-altitude lakes
Natural Resources
abundant hydropower; significant deposits of
gold and rare earth metals; locally exploitable
coal, oil, and natural gas; other deposits of
nepheline, mercury, bismuth, lead
Climate
dry continental to polar in high Tien Shan; subtropical in southwest (Fergana Valley); temperate in northern foothill zone
Kyrgyzstan Food
gutap/plov

WORLD CUP		COUNTRY LEAGUE CHAMPIONS	
1930	Did not qualify		
1934	Did not qualify		
1938	Did not qualify	2004	Dordoy-DinamoNaryn
1950	Did not qualify	2003	Jashtyk AK altyn
1954	Did not qualify	2002	SKA PVO Bishkek
1958	Did not qualify	2001	SKA PVO Bishkek
1962	Did not qualify	2000	SKA PVO Bishkek
1966	Did not qualify	1999	CAG Dinamo
1970	Did not qualify	1998	CAG Dinamo
1974	Did not qualify	1997	Dinamo Bishkek
1978	Did not qualify	1996	Metallurg Kadanjay
1982	Did not qualify	**WOMEN'S LEAGUE CHAMPIONS**	
1986	Did not qualify	2004	Not Known
1990	Did not qualify	2003	Not Known
1994	Did not qualify	2002	Not Known
1998	Did not qualify	2001	Not Known
2002	Did not qualify	2000	Not Known

NATIONAL TEAM COLORS

WORLD PICTURES OF SOCCER

PREMIERE LEAGUE CLUBS	CITY	STADIUM	CAPACITY
SKA PVO	Bishkek	National stadium	23 000
Dinamo-Polyot Bishkek	Bishkek	National stadium	23 000
RUOR Guardia Bishkek	Bishkek	National stadium	23 000
Olimpia-85 Bishkek	Bishkek	National stadium	23 000
Shoro Bishkek	Bishkek	Dynamo Stadium	10 000
Bishkek-87	Bishkek	Dynamo Stadium	10 000
Bishkek-88	Bishkek	Dynamo Stadium	10 000
Erkin Farm Bishkek	Bishkek	Dynamo Stadium	10 000
Dordoy Naryn	Naryn		
Kol Tor Karakol	Karakol		
Jayil Baatyr Kara-Balta	Kara-Balta		
Abdysh Ata Kant	Kant		
Orto Nur Sokuluk	Sokuluk		
Manas Ordo Talas	Talas		
Dinamo UVD Osh	Osh		
Issyk Ata	Ata		

LAOS

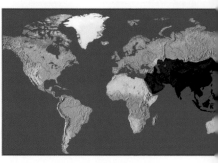

Lao Football Federation
National Stadium, PB 3777,856
Vientiane
TEL 856 21/213 460 FAX /213 460
WEB:www.footballasia.com

Reference
Official name
Laos People's Democratic Republic

Date of formation	1953
Capital	Vientiane
Population	5.4 million
Total area	89,112 sq Mi, 230,800 sq Km
Time zone	GMT +7
Density	61 per sq Mi, 23 per sq Km
Languages	La, Mio, Yao
Literacy rate	56%
Currency	Kip
Economy	agriculture 80%,services & industry 20%
Religions	Buddhist 85%, Anmist 15%
Ethnic Mix	Lao Loum 56%, Lao Theung 34%, Lao Soung 9%

Geography
Elevation
lowest point: Mekong River 70 m
highest point: Phou Bia 2,817 m
Geography Note
landlocked; most of the country is mountainous and thickly forested; the Mekong forms a large part of the western boundary with Thailand
Natural Resources
timber, hydropower, gypsum, tin, gold, gemstones
Climate
tropical monsoon; rainy season (May to November); dry season (December to April)
Laos Food
papaya salad/som tom/larp beef

World Cup		Country League Champions	
1930	Did not qualify		
1934	Did not qualify		
1938	Did not qualify	2004	Telecom & Trans FC
1950	Did not qualify	2003	Telecom & Trans FC
1954	Did not qualify	2002	Telecom & Trans FC
1958	Did not qualify	2001	Not Known
1962	Did not qualify	2000	Vientiane Municipal
1966	Did not qualify	1999	Not Known
1970	Did not qualify	1998	Khammouan Province
1974	Did not qualify	1997	Sayaboury FC
1978	Did not qualify	1996	Lao Army
1982	Did not qualify	**Women's League Champions**	
1986	Did not qualify	2004	Not Known
1990	Did not qualify	2003	Not Known
1994	Did not qualify	2002	Not Known
1998	Did not qualify	2001	Not Known
2002	Did not qualify	2000	Not Known

National Team Colors

World Pictures of Soccer

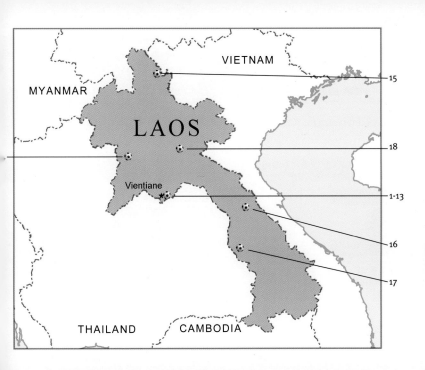

PREMIERE LEAGUE CLUBS	CITY	STADIUM	CAPACITY
Telecom & Transportation	Vientiane	National stadium	18 000
Vientiane Municipality	Vientiane		
Bank	Vientiane		
National University	Vientiane		
Army FC	Vientiane		
Security Ministry	Vientiane		
National Radio	Vientiane		
Education Ministry	Vientiane		
Lao Soft Drink	Vientiane		
Interior Ministry	Vientiane		
Vientiane Police FC	Vientiane		
Electricity of Laos	Vientiane		
Morning Market	Vientiane		
Houayxay	Houayxay		
Phongsali	Phongsali		
Khammouan Province	Khammouan		
Savannakhet	Savannakhet		
Xiangkhoang	Xiangkhoang		

LEBANON

LEBANESE FOOTBALL ASSOC.
Verdun St. Bristol, Radwan Center,
PB 4732,Beirut
TEL 961 1/745 745 FAX /349 529
WEB www.lebansefa.com

REFERENCE
Official name
Republic of Lebanon
Date of formation 1944
Capital Beirut
Population 3.3 Million
Total area 3949 sq Mi, 10,230 sq Km
Time zone GMT +2
Density 836 sq Mi, 343 per sq Km
Languages Arabic, French, Armenian, English
Literacy rate 92%
Currency Pound
Economy services 60%, industry 28%, agriculture 12%
Religions Muslim 70%, Christian 30%
Ethnic Mix Arab 94%, Armenian 4%
GEOGRAPHY
Elevation
lowest point: Mediterranean Sea 0 m
highest point: Qurnat as Sawda' 3,088 m
Geography Note
Nahr el Litani only major river in Near East not crossing an international boundary; rugged terrain historically helped isolate, protect, and develop numerous factional
Natural Resources
limestone, iron ore, salt, water-surplus state in a water-deficit region, arable land
Climate
mediterranean; mild to cool, wet winters with hot, dry summers; Lebanon mountains experiences heavy winter snows.
Lebanese Food
fatoush salad

WORLD CUP		COUNTRY LEAGUE CHAMPIONS	
1930	Did not qualify		
1934	Did not qualify		
1938	Did not qualify	2004	Al Nijmeh
1950	Did not qualify	2003	Olympic Beirut
1954	Did not qualify	2002	Al Nijma
1958	Did not qualify	2001	Al Ansar
1962	Did not qualify	2000	Al Nijma
1966	Did not qualify	1999	Al Ansar
1970	Did not qualify	1998	Al Ansar
1974	Did not qualify	1997	Al Ansar
1978	Did not qualify	1996	Al Ansar
1982	Did not qualify	**WOMEN'S LEAGUE CHAMPIONS**	
1986	Did not qualify	2004	Not Known
1990	Did not qualify	2003	Not Known
1994	Did not qualify	2002	Not Known
1998	Did not qualify	2001	Not Known
2002	Did not qualify	2000	Not Known

NATIONAL TEAM COLORS

WORLD PICTURES OF SOCCER

PREMIERE LEAGUE CLUBS	CITY	STADIUM	CAPACITY
Al-Nejmeh SC	Beirut	Camille Chamoun	57 600
Homenetmen	Beirut	Bourj Hammoud Stadium	10 000
Homenmen	Beirut	Bourj Hammoud Stadium	10 000
Al-Bourj	Beirut	Bourj Hammoud Stadium	10 000
Al-Ansar	Beirut	Beirut Municipality	18 000
Al-Ahed	Beirut	Beirut Municipality	18 000
Shabab Al-Sahel	Beirut	Beirut Municipality	18 000
Olympic Beirut	Beirut	Beirut Municipality	18 000
Safa FC	Beirut	Safa stadium	4 000
CS La Sagesse	Beirut	Fouad Shehab Stadium	5 000
Racing Club	Beirut	Fouad Shehab Stadium	5 000
Haraket Al-Shabab	Tripoli	International Olympic	22 400
Riyadha Wal-Adab	Tripoli	International Olympic	22 400
Shabibe Al-Mazraa	Tripoli	International Olympic	22 400
Al-Tadamon	Sour	Sour Stadium	6 500
Salam Zghorta	Zgharta	International Olympic	22 500
Ahly Saida	Saida	Saide International	22 600
Al-Tadamon Tyre	Tyre	Tyre Municipal	

MACAO

ASSOC. DE FUTBOL DE MACAU
Ave. da Amizade 405
Seng Vo Kok 13 andar "a" Macau
TEL 853/26 0148 FAX 853/78 5178
WEB www.macaofutbol.com

REFERENCE
Official name
  Macao

Date of formation	1557
Capital	Macao
Population	461,833
Total area	6 sq Mi
Time zone	Pacific
Density	3200 per sq Mi
Languages	Chinese, Portuguese, English
Literacy rate	99%
Currency	Pataca
Economy	Casino gambling 60% of revenues
Religions	Catholic 15% , Buddhist 50%
Ethnic Mix	Chinese 95%, Macanese, Portuguese 5%

GEOGRAPHY
Elevation
Lowest point: South China Sea 0 m
Highest point: Coloane Alto 172.4 m
Geography Note
essentially urban; one causeway and two
bridges connect the two islands of Coloane
and Taipa to the peninsula on mainland
Natural Resources
NEGL
Climate
subtropical; marine with cool winters, warm
summers
Macao Food
spiced shin of beef/serradura

WORLD CUP		COUNTRY LEAGUE CHAMPIONS	
1930	Did not qualify		
1934	Did not qualify		
1938	Did not qualify	2004	Monte Carlo FC
1950	Did not qualify	2003	Monte Carlo FC
1954	Did not qualify	2002	Monte Carlo FC
1958	Did not qualify	2001	GD Lam Pak
1962	Did not qualify	2000	Policia SP
1966	Did not qualify	1999	Not Known
1970	Did not qualify	1998	GD Lam Pak
1974	Did not qualify	1997	Not Known
1978	Did not qualify	1996	Not Known
1982	Did not qualify	**WOMEN'S LEAGUE CHAMPIONS**	
1986	Did not qualify	2004	Skiponjat
1990	Did not qualify	2003	Skiponjat
1994	Did not qualify	2002	Not Known
1998	Did not qualify	2001	Not Known
2002	Did not qualify	2000	Not Known

NATIONAL TEAM COLORS

WORLD PICTURES OF SOCCER

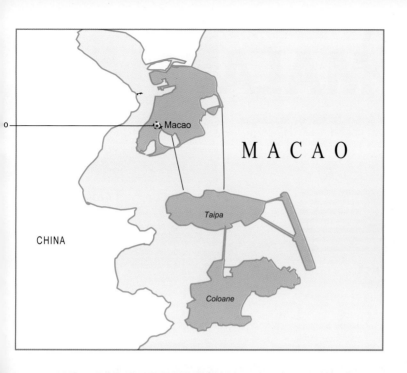

PREMIERE LEAGUE CLUBS	CITY	STADIUM	CAPACITY
Monte Carlo	Macao	Estadio Campo Desportivo	15 000
Heng Tai	Macao	Estadio Campo Desportivo	15 000
Policia de Seguranca Publica	Macao	Estadio Campo Desportivo	15 000
Servicos de Alfandega	Macao	Estadio Campo Desportivo	15 000
Lam Pak	Macao	Estadio Campo Desportivo	15 000
Va Luen	Macao	Estadio Campo Desportivo	15 000
Bombeiros	Macao	Estadio Campo Desportivo	15 000
Autoridade Monetaria	Macao	Estadio Campo Desportivo	15 000
Hong Lok	Macao	Estadio Campo Desportivo	15 000
Kei Lun	Macao	Canidromo	2 000
Hoi Fan	Macao	Canidromo	2 000
Tim Tec	Macao	Canidromo	2 000
Policia Maritima	Macao	Canidromo	2 000
Leng Ngan	Macao	Canidromo	2 000
Kuan Tai	Macao	Canidromo	2 000
San Cheong Seng	Macao	Canidromo	2 000
Va Luen	Macao	Canidromo	2 000
Jardim Amizade	Macao	Canidromo	2 000
Associacao Si Tong	Macao	Canidromo	2 000

MALAYSIA

FOOTBALL ASSOCIATION OF MALAYSIA
Wisma Fam, Tingkat 3, Jalan SS5A/9,
Kelana Jaya, 47301 Peteling Jaya,
Selangor
TEL 60 3/7876 37 66
WEB www.fam.org.my

REFERENCE

Official name
    Federation of Malaysia

Date of formation	1965
Capital	Kuala Lumpur
Population	22.2 Million
Total area	126,853 sq Mi, 328,550 sq Km
Time zone	GMT +8
Density	175 per sq Mi, 65 per sq Km
Languages	Malay, Chinese, Tamil
Literacy rate	83%
Currency	Ringgit
Economy	agriculture 42%, services 39%, industry 19%
Religions	Muslim 53% ,Buddhist 19%, Chinese Faith 12%, Christian 7%
Ethnic Mix	Malay 47%, Chinese 32%, Indian 8%

GEOGRAPHY

Elevation
lowest point: Indian Ocean 0 m
highest point: Gunung Kinabalu 4,100 m
Geography Note
strategic location along Strait of Malacca and
southern South China Sea
Natural Resources
tin, petroleum, timber, copper, iron ore, natural
gas, bauxite
Climate
tropical; annual southwest (April to October)
and northeast (October to February) monsoons
Malaysian Food
rojak/nonya chicken/rendang/nasi minyak

WORLD CUP

1930	Did not qualify
1934	Did not qualify
1938	Did not qualify
1950	Did not qualify
1954	Did not qualify
1958	Did not qualify
1962	Did not qualify
1966	Did not qualify
1970	Did not qualify
1974	Did not qualify
1978	Did not qualify
1982	Did not qualify
1986	Did not qualify
1990	Did not qualify
1994	Did not qualify
1998	Did not qualify
2002	Did not qualify

COUNTRY LEAGUE CHAMPIONS

2004	Pahang
2003	Perak
2002	Perak
2001	Penang
2000	Selangor
1999	Brunei
1998	Perak
1997	Selangor
1996	Selangor

WOMEN'S LEAGUE CHAMPIONS

2004	Not Known
2003	Not Known
2002	Not Known
2001	Not Known
2000	Not Known

NATIONAL TEAM COLORS

WORLD PICTURES OF SOCCER

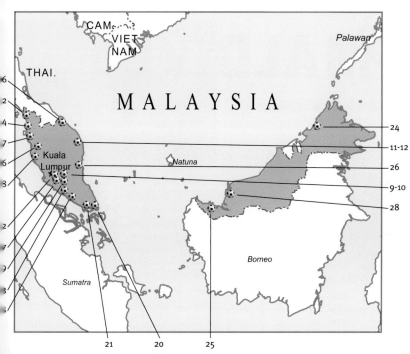

PREMIERE LEAGUE CLUBS	CITY	STADIUM	CAPACITY
Kuala Lumpur FA	Kuala Lumpur	KLFA Stadium	18 000
Kuala Lumpur Malay Mail	Kuala Lu.	KLFA Stadium	18 000
Kelantan FA	Kota Bahru	Sultan Mohammed IV	30 000
Kelantan JPS	Kota Bahru	Sultan Mohammed IV	30 000
Kelantan SKMK	Kota Bahru	Sultan Mohammed IV	30 000
Kelantan TNB	Kota Bahru	Sultan Mohammed IV	30 000
Malacca Telekom	Malacca	HangTuah Stadium	20 000
Malacca FA	Malacca	HangTuah Stadium	20 000
Selangor Public Bank	Selayang	Selayang Stadium	20 000
Police	Selayang	Selayang Stadium	20 000
Kelantan JPS	Kuala Terengganu	Sultan Is.Nasiruddin Shah	25 000
Terrengganu FA	Kuala Terengganu	Sultan Is.Nasiruddin Shah	25 000
Kedah FA	Alor Setar	Darulaman Stadium	32 387
Kedah JKR	Alor Setar	Darulaman Stadium	32 387
Perak TKN	Ipoh	DBI Stadium	40 000
Perak FA	Ipoh	DBI Stadium	40 000
Selangor FA	Shah Alam	Shah Alam Stadium	81 000
Armed Forces	Lumut	Naval base Stadium	12 000
Selangor MPPJ	Peteling Jaya	MPPJ Stadium	25 000
Johor FC	Pasir Gudang	Pasir Gudang Stadium	15 000
Johor FA	Johor Baru	Tan Sri hassan Yunus	30 000
Perlis FA	Kangar	Utama Stadium	30 000
Negeri Sembilan FA	Seremban	Tuanku Abdul Rahman	30 000
Sabah FA	Kota Kinabalu	Likas Stadium	35 000
Sarawak FA	Kuching	Sarawak Stadium	30 000
Pahang FA	Kuantan	Darulmakur Stadium	40 000
Penang FA	Penang	State Batu Kawan	40 000
Brunei	Sibu		

MALDIVES

FOOTBALL ASSOCIATION OF MALDIVES
National Stadium, Banafusaa Magu,
Galolhul 20-04
TEL 960/317 006
WEB www.famaldives.gov.mv

REFERENCE
Official name
  Republic of the Maldives
Date of
formation 1965
Capital Male
Population 286,000
Total area 116 sq Mi, 300sq Km
Time zone Gmt +5
Density 2466 per sq Mi, 1000 per sq Km
Languages Dhivehi, Sinhala, Tamil
Literacy rate 93%
Currency Rufiyaa
Economy tourism, fishing, manufacturing
Religions Muslim 100%
Ethnic Mix Mixed Arab, Sinhalese & Malay
           100%

GEOGRAPHY
Elevation
lowest point: Indian Ocean 0 m
highest point: Unnamed location on Wilingili
island in the Addu Atoll 2.4 m
Geography Note
1,190 coral islands grouped into 26 atolls
(200 inhabited islands, plus 80 islands with
tourist resorts).
Natural Resources
fishing industry
Climate
tropical; hot, humid; dry, northeast monsoon
(November to March); rainy, southwest
monsoon (June to August)
Maldives Food
fish and rice

WORLD CUP		COUNTRY LEAGUE CHAMPIONS	
1930	Did not qualify		
1934	Did not qualify		
1938	Did not qualify	2004	Not Known
1950	Did not qualify	2003	Victory SC
1954	Did not qualify	2002	Victory SC
1958	Did not qualify	2001	Victory SC
1962	Did not qualify	2000	Victory SC
1966	Did not qualify	1999	Club Valencia
1970	Did not qualify	1998	Club Valencia
1974	Did not qualify	1997	New Radiant
1978	Did not qualify	1996	Club Lagoons
1982	Did not qualify	**WOMEN'S LEAGUE CHAMPIONS**	
1986	Did not qualify	2004	Not Known
1990	Did not qualify	2003	Not Known
1994	Did not qualify	2002	Not Known
1998	Did not qualify	2001	Not Known
2002	Did not qualify	2000	Not Known

NATIONAL TEAM COLORS

WORLD PICTURES OF SOCCER

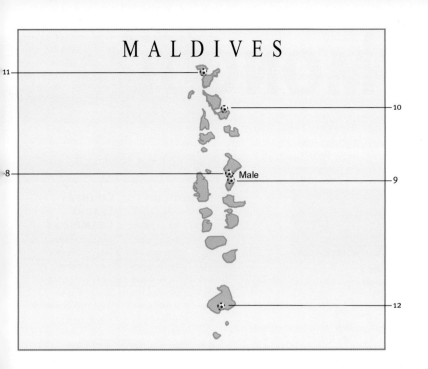

MALDIVES

	City	Stadium	Capacity
Premiere League Clubs			
-Victory	Male	Galolhu Stadium	11 800
-Valencia	Male	Galolhu Stadium	11 800
-IFC	Male	Galolhu Stadium	11 800
-Mecano	Male	Galolhu Stadium	11 800
BG Sport	Male	Galolhu Stadium	11 800
-New Radiant	Male	Galolhu Stadium	11 800
Eagles	Male	Galolhu Stadium	11 800
-STELCO	Male	Galolhu Stadium	11 800
Hurriyya	Huraa		
-Guaidhoo ZJ	Guraidhoo		
-Kelaa YF	Kelaa		
-Radshoo JU	Gan		

MONGOLIA

MONGOLIAN FOOTBALL FEDERATION
PB 259, 210646 Ulaan Baatar
TEL 976 1/131 2145 FAX /131 2145
WEB www.footballasia.com

REFERENCE

Official name
Mongolia

Date of formation 1924

Capital Ulan Bator

Population 2.7 Million

Total area 604 sq Mi, 1,565,000sq Km

Time zone GMT +8

Density 4 per sq Mi, 1.5 per sq Km

Languages Khalkha, Mongol, Turkic, Russian, Chinese

Literacy rate 85%

Currency Tughrik

Economy agriculture 85%, industry 8%, services 7%

Religions Tibetan Buddhist 96%, Muslim 4%

Ethnic Mix Mongol 90%, Kazakh 4%, Chinese 2%, Russian 2%

GEOGRAPHY

Elevation
lowest point: Hoh Nuur 518 m
highest point: Nayramadlin Orgil
(Huyten Orgil) 4,374 m

Geography Note
landlocked; strategic location between
China and Russia

Natural Resources
oil, coal, copper, molybdenum, tungsten,
phosphates, tin, nickel, zinc, wolfram,
fluorspar, gold, silver, iron, phosphate

Climate
desert; continental (large daily and seasonal
temperature ranges)

Mongolian Food
mongolian barbecue/sanbusak/shula

WORLD CUP		COUNTRY LEAGUE CHAMPIONS	
1930	Did not qualify		
1934	Did not qualify		
1938	Did not qualify	2004	Khangarid
1950	Did not qualify	2003	Khangarid
1954	Did not qualify	2002	Erchim
1958	Did not qualify	2001	Khangarid
1962	Did not qualify	2000	Erchim
1966	Did not qualify	1999	ITI Bank Bars FC
1970	Did not qualify	1998	Erchim FC
1974	Did not qualify	1997	Delger Ulan Bator
1978	Did not qualify	1996	Erchim FC
1982	Did not qualify	**WOMEN'S LEAGUE CHAMPIONS**	
1986	Did not qualify	2004	Not Known
1990	Did not qualify	2003	Not Known
1994	Did not qualify	2002	Not Known
1998	Did not qualify	2001	Not Known
2002	Did not qualify	2000	Not Known

NATIONAL TEAM COLORS

WORLD PICTURES OF SOCCER

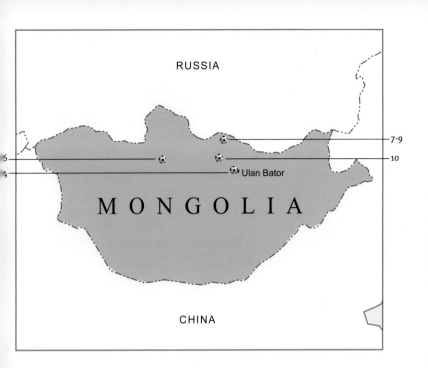

PREMIERE LEAGUE CLUBS	CITY	STADIUM	CAPACITY
Derger	Ulan Bator	Ulan Bator Nat. Stadium	30 000
ITR Bank	Ulan Bator	Ulan Bator Nat. Stadium	30 000
Khudulmur	Ulan Bator	Ulan Bator Nat. Stadium	30 000
Khuch	Ulan Bator		
Khangarid	Edernet		
Edrenet Ninj	Edernet		
Suhbaator	Suhbaator		
Selenge CCB	Suhbaator		
Suhbaator district Select	Suhbaator		
-Friendship Darhan	Darhan		

MYANMAR

MYANMAR FOOTBALL FEDERATION
Youth Training Center, Thuwunna,
Yangon
TEL 951/57 73 66   FAX /57 12 53
WEB www.footballasia.com

REFERENCE
Official name
   Union of Myanmar
Date of formation   1948
Capital   Yangon (Rangoon)
Population   45.6 million
Total area   253,876 sq Mi, 657,540 sq Km
Time zone   GMT + 6.5
Density   180 per sq Mi, 71 per sq Km
Languages   Burmese, Karen, Shan, Chin,
                     Kachin, Mon, Palaung, Wa
Literacy rate   83%
Currency   Kyat
Economy   agriculture 64%, services 27%,
                     industry 9%
Religions   Buddhist 87%, Christian 6%,
                     Muslim 4%
Ethnic Mix   Burman 68%, Shan 9%

GEOGRAPHY
Elevation
lowest point: Andaman Sea 0 m
highest point: Hkakabo Razi 5,881 m
Geography Note
strategic location near major Indian Ocean shipping
lanes
Natural Resources
petroleum, timber, tin, antimony, zinc, copper,
tungsten, lead, coal, some marble, limestone,
precious stones, natural gas, hydropower
Climate
tropical monsoon; cloudy, rainy, hot, humid
summers (southwest monsoon, June to
September); less cloudy, scant rainfall, mild
temperatures, lower humidity during
Myanmar Food
peiwahlay hincho/pebo chet/mounlar ou chinye

WORLD CUP		COUNTRY LEAGUE CHAMPIONS	
1930	Did not qualify		
1934	Did not qualify		
1938	Did not qualify	2004	Custom
1950	Did not qualify	2003	Shan State
1954	Did not qualify	2002	Mandalay
1958	Did not qualify	2001	Mandalay
1962	Did not qualify	2000	Finance & Revenues
1966	Did not qualify	1999	Finance & Revenues
1970	Did not qualify	1998	Yangon City Devlp.
1974	Did not qualify	1997	Finance & Revenues
1978	Did not qualify	1996	Finance & Revenues
1982	Did not qualify	**WOMEN'S LEAGUE CHAMPIONS**	
1986	Did not qualify	2004	Not Known
1990	Did not qualify	2003	Yangon state
1994	Did not qualify	2002	Not Known
1998	Did not qualify	2001	Not Known
2002	Did not qualify	2000	Not Known

NATIONAL TEAM COLORS

WORLD PICTURES OF SOCCER

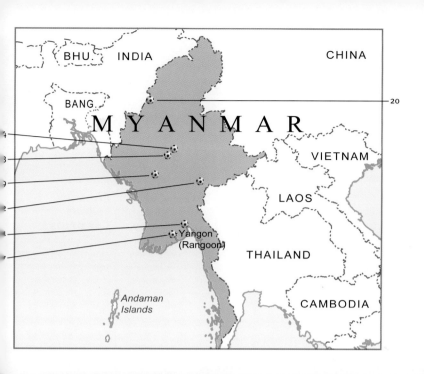

PREMIERE LEAGUE CLUBS	CITY	STADIUM	CAPACITY
Ministry Finance & Revenue	Yangon	Aung San Stadium	45'000
Ministry Home Affairs	Yangon		
Ministry of Energy	Yangon		
Ministry of Defence	Yangon		
Ministry of Forestry	Yangon		
Ministry of Constructions	Yangon		
Yangon City Development	Yangon		
Ministry of Commerce	Yangon		
Ministry of agriculture	Yangon		
Ministry of Railway	Yangon		
Mines Minestry	Yangon		
Royal FC	Yangon		
Tatmadaw	Yangon		
Yangon FC	Yangon		
Yangon University	Yangon		
Transport-A	Yangon		
Defence services	Yangon		
Magwe Division	Magwe		
Maung Maung	Magwe		
Central Ordnance	Indaing		
Bago Division	Bago		
Kayah State	Loi-Kaw		
Mandalay	Mandalay		
Sagaing	Sagaing		

NEPAL

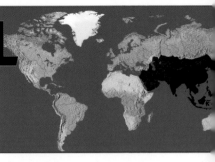

ALL NEPAL FOOTBALL ASSOC.
PB 12454, Wardd #4, Bishalnagar, Kathmandu
TEL 977 1/414 710 FAX /424 314
WEB www.footballasia.com

REFERENCE
Official name
Kingdom of Nepal

Date of formation	1769
Capital	Kathmandu
Population	23.9 Million
Total area	52,818 sq Mi, 136,800sq Km
Time zone	GMT +5.5
Density	452 per sq Mi, 173 per sq Km
Languages	Nepali, Maithilli
Literacy rate	27%
Currency	Rupee
Economy	agriculture 93%, services 6%, industry 1%
Religions	Hindu 90%, Buddhist 5%, Muslim 3%
Ethnic Mix	Nepalese 52%, Maithilli 11%, Tibeto-Burmese 10%, Bhojpuri 8%

GEOGRAPHY
Elevation
lowest point: Kanchan Kalan 70 m
highest point: Mount Everest 8,850 m
(1999 est.)
Geography Note
landlocked; strategic location between China and India; contains eight of world's 10 highest peaks, including Mount Everest - the world's tallest - on the border with China
Natural Resources
quartz, water, timber, hydropower, scenic beauty, small deposits of lignite, copper, cobalt, iron ore
Climate
varies from cool summers and severe winters in north to subtropical summers and mild winters in south
Nepalese Food
daal bhat/bhancha ghar/aloo tareko/shikarni

WORLD CUP		COUNTRY LEAGUE CHAMPIONS	
1930	Did not qualify		
1934	Did not qualify		
1938	Did not qualify	2004	Three Stars Club
1950	Did not qualify	2003	Manang Maryangdi
1954	Did not qualify	2002	No Competition
1958	Did not qualify	2001	No Competition
1962	Did not qualify	2000	Manang Marsyanghdi
1966	Did not qualify	1999	Mahendra Police
1970	Did not qualify	1998	Three Star Club
1974	Did not qualify	1997	Three Star Club
1978	Did not qualify	1996	New Road Team
1982	Did not qualify	**WOMEN'S LEAGUE CHAMPIONS**	
1986	Did not qualify	2004	Not Known
1990	Did not qualify	2003	Not Known
1994	Did not qualify	2002	Not Known
1998	Did not qualify	2001	Not Known
2002	Did not qualify	2000	Not Known

NATIONAL TEAM COLORS

WORLD PICTURES OF SOCCER

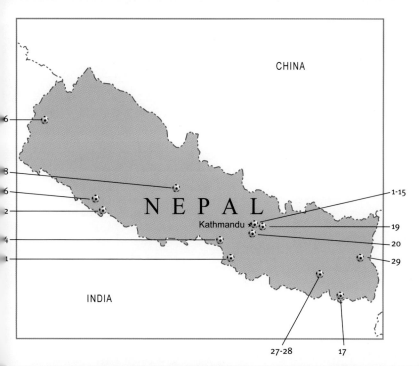

PREMIERE LEAGUE CLUBS	CITY	STADIUM	CAPACITY
Kathmandu Club	Kathmandu	Dasarath Rangasala	25 000
New Road Team	Kathmandu	Sano Gaucharan	2 000
Annapurna Club	Kathmandu		
Mahendra Police Club	Kathmandu		
Manang Marsyangdi FC	Kathmandu		
Friends Club	Kathmandu		
Sankata Boys SC	Kathmandu		
Jawalakhel Youth	Kathmandu		
Ranipokhari Corner team	Kathmandu		
Boys Sports Club	Kathmandu		
Boys Union Club	Kathmandu		
Brigade Boys Club	Kathmandu		
Mahavir Club	Kathmandu		
Tribhuvan Club	Kathmandu	Police Training Ground	2 000
Naxal Yuwa Mandal	Kathmandu		
Three Star Club	Patan		
Biratnagar FC	Biratnagar	Saheed Stadium	10 000
Sahara Club	Pokhara	Anapurna Stadium	5 000
Madhyapur YC	Bhakhtapur		
Lalitpur FC	Lalitpur	ANFA Sadobato	1 000
Birgunj Club	Birgunj	Narayani Stadium	15 000
Jaya Kisan SC	Banke District		
Amar YC	Chitwan District		
Shihar Club	Chitwan District		
Aikta Tiger Club	Dang District		
Dipendra Prahari Club	Dang District		
Mithila FC	Dhanukha District		
Madimandhup	Dhanusa District		
Helibod Team	Ilam District		

# NORTH KOREA

DPR KOREA FOOTBALL ASSOC.
kumsong-Dong 2, PB 56,
Pyongyang
TEL 850 2/18 111 FAX /381 4403
WEB www.footballasia.com

REFERENCE
Official name
Democratic People's Republic of Korea

Date of formation	1948
Capital	Pyongyang
Population	24 Million
Total area	46,490 sq Mi, 120,410 sq Km
Time zone	GMT +9
Density	516 per sq Mi, 185 per sq Km
Languages	Korean, Chinese
Literacy rate	95%
Currency	Won
Economy	services & industry64%, agriculture 36%
Religions	Traditional beliefs 16%, Ch'ondogyo 14%, Buddhist 2%, Nonreligious 68%
Ethnic Mix	Korean 100%

GEOGRAPHY
Elevation
lowest point: Sea of Japan o m
highest point: Paektu-san 2,744 m
Geography Note
strategic location bordering China, South
Korea, and Russia; mountainous interior is
isolated and sparsely populated
Natural Resources
coal, lead, tungsten, zinc, graphite,
magnesite, iron ore, copper, gold, pyrites,
salt, fluorspar, hydropower
Climate
temperate with rainfall concentrated in
summer
North Korean Food
kimchi/tokkuk

WORLD CUP

1930	Did not qualify
1934	Did not qualify
1938	Did not qualify
1950	Did not qualify
1954	Did not qualify
1958	Did not qualify
1962	Did not qualify
1966	Quarter final exit
1970	Did not qualify
1974	Did not qualify
1978	Did not qualify
1982	Did not qualify
1986	Did not qualify
1990	Did not qualify
1994	Did not qualify
1998	Did not qualify
2002	Did not qualify

COUNTRY LEAGUE CHAMPIONS

2004	Pyongyang CSG
2003	Not Known
2002	April 25 FC
2001	Not Known
2000	Locomotive
1999	Not Known
1998	Not Known
1997	Not Known
1996	Lokomotive FC

WOMEN'S LEAGUE CHAMPIONS

2004	Amnokang SG
2003	Not Known
2002	April 25 FC
2001	Not Known
2000	Not Known

NATIONAL TEAM COLORS

WORLD PICTURES OF SOCCER

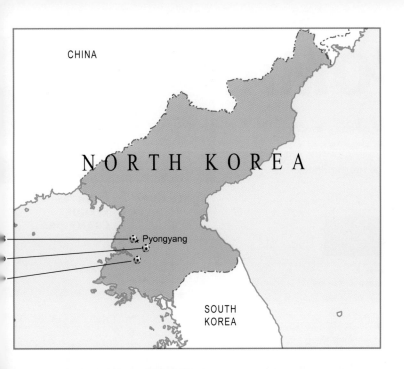

PREMIERE LEAGUE CLUBS	CITY	STADIUM	CAPACITY
Pyongyang City SG	Pyongyang	Yanggakdo Stadium	30 000
Pyongyang Club	Pyongyang	Yanggakdo Stadium	30 000
April 25 SG	Pyongyang	Yanggakdo Stadium	30 000
Locomotive	Pyongyang	Sosan Stadium	25 000
Rimyongsu SG	Pyongyang	Sosan Stadium	25 000
Amnokang SG	Pyongyang	Sosan Stadium	25 000
Wolmido SG	Pyongyang	Sosan Stadium	25 000
Sport University	Pyongyang	Sosan Stadium	25 000
North Hwangju	Hwangju		
Songnim	Songnim		

 # OMAN

OMAN FOOTBALL ASSOC.
PB 3462, 112 Ruwi
TEL 968/787 635 FAX /787 632
WEB www.footballasia.com

REFERENCE
Official name
Sultanate of Oman

Date of formation	1561
Capital	Muscat
Population	2.5 Million
Total area	82,031 sq Mi, 212,460 sq Km
Time zone	GMT +4
Density	30 per sq Mi, 12 per sq Km
Languages	Arabic, Baluchi
Literacy rate	35%
Currency	Rial
Economy	agriculture 50%, services 28%, industry 22%
Religions	Ibadi Muslim 75%, Hindu & other Muslim 25%
Ethnic Mix	Arab 88%, Baluch4%, Indian & Pakistani 3%, Persian 3%, African 2%

GEOGRAPHY
Elevation
lowest point: Arabian Sea 0 m
highest point: Jabal Shams 2,980 m
Geography Note
strategic location on Musandam Peninsula
adjacent to Strait of Hormuz, a vital transit
point for world crude oil
Natural Resources
petroleum, copper, asbestos, some
marble, limestone, chromium, gypsum, natural gas
Climate
dry desert; hot, humid along coast; hot, dry
interior; strong southwest summer monsoon
(May to September) in far south
Oman Food
lamb & dates stew/oatmeal date bars

WORLD CUP		COUNTRY LEAGUE CHAMPIONS	
1930	Did not qualify		
1934	Did not qualify		
1938	Did not qualify	2004	Al-Nasr
1950	Did not qualify	2003	Rowi
1954	Did not qualify	2002	Al Oruba
1958	Did not qualify	2001	Zofar
1962	Did not qualify	2000	Al Oruba
1966	Did not qualify	1999	Zofar
1970	Did not qualify	1998	Al Nasr
1974	Did not qualify	1997	Oman Club
1978	Did not qualify	1996	Sur
1982	Did not qualify	**WOMEN'S LEAGUE CHAMPIONS**	
1986	Did not qualify	2004	Not Known
1990	Did not qualify	2003	Not Known
1994	Did not qualify	2002	Not Known
1998	Did not qualify	2001	Not Known
2002	Did not qualify	2000	Not kNown

NATIONAL TEAM COLORS

WORLD PICTURES OF SOCCER

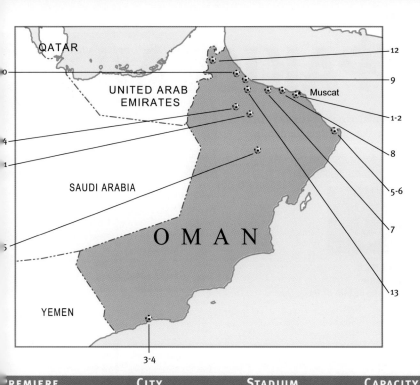

PREMIERE LEAGUE CLUBS	CITY	STADIUM	CAPACITY
Rowi	Muscat	Sultan Qaboos Stadium	40 000
Oman	Muscat	Sultan Qaboos Stadium	40 000
Al-Nasr	Salala	Salala Complex	8 000
Dhofar	Salala	Salala Complex	8 000
Al-Arooba	Sur		
Sur	Sur		
Suwaiq	Barka		
Seeb	Seeb		
Khaboora	Khaboora		
Saham	Saham		
Al-Tali'aa	Al-Tali'aa		
Al-Mahda	Al-Mahda		
Sedadib	Sedadib		
Ibri	Ibri		
Nizwa	Nizwa	Nizwa Complex	11 000

PAKISTAN

PAKISTAN FOOTBALL FEDERATION
183, Abu Bakar Blk, New Garden Tn,
Lahore
TEL 92 42/571 6855 FAX /571 6854
WEB www.footballasia.com

REFERENCE
Official name
Islamic Republic of Pakistan

Date of formation	1947
Capital	Islamabad
Population	156.5 Million
Total area	297,637 sq Mi, 770,880 sq Km
Time zone	GMT +5
Density	526 per sq Mi, 171 per sq Km
Languages	Urdu, Punjabi
Literacy rate	37%
Currency	Rupee
Economy	agriculture 50%, services 38%, industry 12%
Religions	Sunni Muslim 77%, Shi'A Muslim 20%, Hindu 2%, Christian 1%
Ethnic Mix	Punjabi 50%, Sindi 15%, Pashtu 15%, Mohajir 8%

GEOGRAPHY
Elevation
lowest point: Indian Ocean 0 m
highest point: K2 (Mt. Godwin-Austen) 8,611 m
Geography Note
controls Khyber Pass and Bolan Pass, traditional invasion routes between Central Asia and the Indian Subcontinent
Natural Resources
land, extensive natural gas reserves, limited petroleum, poor quality coal, iron ore, copper, salt, limestone
Climate
mostly hot, dry desert; temperate in northwest; arctic in north
Pakistanese Food
chicken jalfraizi/naan/karkhai gosht/ras malai

WORLD CUP

1930	Did not qualify
1934	Did not qualify
1938	Did not qualify
1950	Did not qualify
1954	Did not qualify
1958	Did not qualify
1962	Did not qualify
1966	Did not qualify
1970	Did not qualify
1974	Did not qualify
1978	Did not qualify
1982	Did not qualify
1986	Did not qualify
1990	Did not qualify
1994	Did not qualify
1998	Did not qualify
2002	Did not qualify

COUNTRY LEAGUE CHAMPIONS

2004	WAPDA
2003	WAPDA
2002	WAPDA
2001	WAPDA
2000	Allied Bank Limited
1999	Allied Bank Limited
1998	P.I.A
1997	Allied Bank Limited
1996	Not Known

WOMEN'S LEAGUE CHAMPIONS

2004	Not Known
2003	Not Known
2002	Not Known
2001	Not Known
2000	Not Known

NATIONAL TEAM COLORS

WORLD PICTURES OF SOCCER

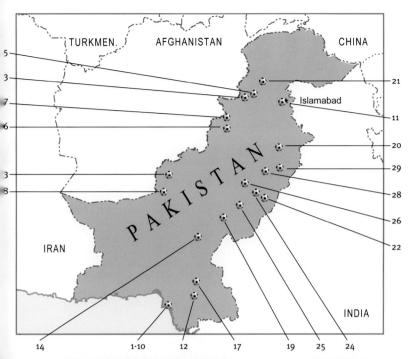

PREMIERE LEAGUE CLUBS	CITY	STADIUM	CAPACITY
PCJSS Karachi	Karachi	Karachi National Stadium	34 228
Karachi Port Trust	Karachi	Karachi National Stadium	34 228
Allied Bank Limited	Karachi	Karachi National Stadium	34 228
Habib Bank Limited	Karachi	Karachi National Stadium	34 228
Pakistan Army	Karachi	KMC Stadium	
Khan Research Lab	Karachi	KMC Stadium	
Pakistan Navy	Karachi	KMC Stadium	
Pakistan Telecommunication	Karachi	KMC Stadium	
Water & Power	Karachi	KMC Stadium	
Railway FC	Karachi	KMC Stadium	
Islamabad FC	Islamabad	Jinnah Sport Stadium	48 200
Hyderabad FC	Hyderabad#	Hyderabad Football Stad.	25 000
DFA Quetta Club	Quetta	Sadiq Shaheed Park	20 000
Sukur FC	Sukur	Sukkur Football Stad.	17 500
Nowshera FC	Nowshera	Nowshera Football stad.	6 000
Kohat sFC	Kohat	Kohat Football Stadium	6 000
Sindh FC	Nawabshah		
Tamaz FC	Tamaz Khan	Tehmas Khan Football St.	6 000
Sargodha FC	Sargodha	Municipal Stadium	7 000
C.T.M	Faisalabad		
Mardan FC	Mardan	Mardan Stadium	7 000
Punjab Police	Punjab Region		
Din Bahar	Peshawar	Tehmas Khan Stadium	
Sajid Club	Vihari		
Bahawalpur Club	Bahawalpur		
Multan Club	Multan		
Tatai Shaheed Club	Tatai	Tatai Shaheed Stadium	
Sahiwal Club	Sahiwal		
Okara Club	Okara		

PALESTINE

PALESTINE FOOTBALL FED.
Al-Yarmuk
Gaza
TEL 70-8/283-4339 FAX 970-8/282-5208
WEB www.palfa.com

REFERENCE
Official name
Palestine
Date of formation Disputed
Capital Bethlehem
Population 2,385,615
Total area 5,860 sq km
Time zone GMT +2
Density NA
Languages Arabic and English
Literacy rate NA
Currency Jordanian Dinar
Economy NA
Religions 75% Muslim
Ethnic Mix Palentinian Arab 83%, others 17%

GEOGRAPHY
Elevation
lowest point: Dead Sea - 408 m
highest point: Tall Asur 1,022 m
Geography Note
NA
Natural Resources
agriculture
Climate
temperate, warm to hot summers, cool to mild winters
Palestine Food
lamb, humus, pita bread,

WORLD CUP		COUNTRY LEAGUE CHAMPIONS	
1930	Did not Qualify		
1934	Did not Qualify		
1938	Did not Qualify	2004	Not Known
1950	Did not Qualify	2003	Not Known
1954	Did not Qualify	2002	Not Known
1958	Did not Qualify	2001	Not Known
1962	Did not Qualify	2000	Not Known
1966	Did not Qualify	1999	Not Known
1970	Did not Qualify	1998	Not Known
1974	Did not Qualify	1997	Not Known
1978	Did not Qualify	1996	Not Known
1982	Did not Qualify	**Women's League Champ**	
1986	Did not Qualify	2004	Not Known
1990	Did not Qualify	2003	Not Known
1994	Did not Qualify	2002	Not Known
1998	Did not Qualify	2001	Not Known
2002	Did not Qualify	2000	Not Known

NATIONAL TEAM COLORS

WORLD PICTURES OF SOCCER

PREMIERE LEAGUE CLUBS	CITY	STADIUM	CAPACITY
Wadi Al-Neiss	Bethlehem		
Islami Sahwan	Bethlehem		
Orthodox Club Bei Sahur	Bethlehem		
Shabab Al-Karas	Hebron		
Shabab Beit Amt	Hebron		
Tarek Bin Zeyad	Hebron		
Al-Quds	Al-Quds		
Sulwan	Al-Quds		
Al-Wuwathafeen	Al-Quds		
Hattein SC	Nablus		
Shabab Share	Nablus		
Shabab Balatah	Nablus		
Rafah SC	Rafah		
Khadamat Rafah	Rafah		
Azoun SC	Qalqiliyah		
Gaza SC	Gaza	Palestine Stadium	10 000
Jenin SC	Jenin		
Shabat Akabat Jabr	Jericho	Jericho Stadium	10 000
Al-Aqsa	Jericho		
Shabab Khan Younis	Khan Younis	Khan Younis Stadium	

PHILIPPINES

PHILIPPINE FOOTBALL FED.
Rm #405-406, Bldg B, Philsports Cplx,
Meralco Ave., Pasig City, Metro Manila
TEL 62 2/687 1594 FAX 687 1598
WEB www.

REFERENCE
Official name
  Repubic of the Philippines
Date of formation   1946
Capital   Manila
Population   76 Million
Total area   115,123 sq Mi, 298 sq Km
Time zone   GMT +8
Density   660 per sq Mi, 265 per sq Km
Languages   Pilipino, English
Literacy rate   94%
Currency   Peso
Economy   services 48%,agriculture 42%, industry 10%
Religions   Catholic 84%, Protestant 9%, Muslim 5%
Ethnic Mix   Malay 50%, Indonesian %, Polynesian 30%,

GEOGRAPHY
Elevation
lowest point: Philippine Sea 0 m
highest point: Mount Apo 2,954 m
Geography Note
favorably located in relation to many of
Southeast Asia's main water bodies: the
South China Sea, Philippine Sea, Sulu Sea,
Celebes Sea, and Luzon Strait
Natural Resources
timber, petroleum, nickel, cobalt, silver,
gold, salt, copper
Climate
tropical marine; northeast monsoon
(November to April); southwest monsoon
(May to October)
Philippines Food
fish, rice

WORLD CUP

1930	Did not qualify
1934	Did not qualify
1938	Did not qualify
1950	Did not qualify
1954	Did not qualify
1958	Did not qualify
1962	Did not qualify
1966	Did not qualify
1970	Did not qualify
1974	Did not qualify
1978	Did not qualify
1982	Did not qualify
1986	Did not qualify
1990	Did not qualify
1994	Did not qualify
1998	Did not qualify
2002	Did not qualify

COUNTRY LEAGUE CHAMPIONS

2005	NCR
2004	NCR
2003	Not known
2002	Not Known
2001	Not Known
2000	Not Known
1999	NCRB FC
1998	NCR South FC
1997	Air Force Hawks FC

WOMEN'S LEAGUE CHAMPIONS

2004	Davao
2003	UP Diliman
2002	Not known
2001	Not known
2000	Not known

NATIONAL TEAM COLORS

WORLD PICTURES OF SOCCER

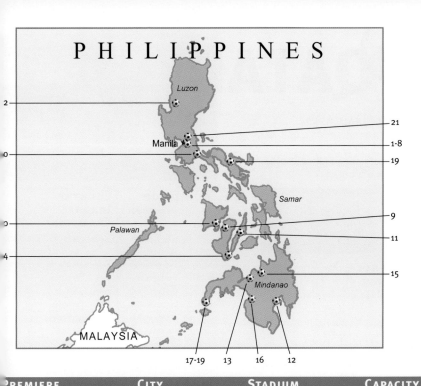

PHILIPPINES

Luzon

Manila

21

1-8

19

Samar

Palawan

9

11

15

Mindanao

MALAYSIA

17-19   13   16   12

PREMIERE LEAGUE CLUBS	CITY	STADIUM	CAPACITY
Manilla FC	Manilla	Ninoy Aquino Stadium	25 000
-Navy Dolphins FC	Manilla		
-Army Tamaraws	Manilla		
Alabang United	Manilla		
Espana United Tigers	Manilla		
Loyola Falcons FC	Manilla		
Mendiola United	Manilla		
Taft FC	Manilla		
Bacolod FC	Bacolod	Pana-Ad Stadium	15 000
-Iloilo FC	Iloilo	National Stadium	10 000
-Cebu FC	Cebu		
-Davao Club	Davao		
-Iligan FC	Iligan		
-Dumaguete FC	Dumaguete		
-Cagayan de Oro FC	Cagayan de Oro		
-Cotabato Club	Cotabato		
-Zamboanga City	Zamboanga		
-Zamboanga del Sur	Zamboanga		
-Naga City-Camarines Sur	Naga		
-Lucona Occidental	Lucona		
-Quezon FC	Quezon City		
-Baguio City FC	Baguio		

 QATAR

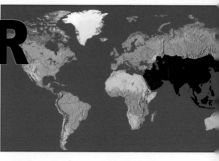

QATAR FOOTBALL ASSOC.
Olympic Committee Bldg, 2nd Floor,
Cornich, PB 5333, Doha
TEL 974/443 4455 FAX /441 1660
WEB www.qfa.org.qa

REFERENCE
Official name
    State of Qatar

Date of formation	1971
Capital	Doha
Population	699,000
Total area	4247 sq Mi, 11,000sq Km
Time zone	GMT +3
Density	165 per sq Mi, 66 per sq Km
Languages	Arabic, Farsi, Urdu, Hindi, English
Literacy rate	80%
Currency	Riyal
Economy	services 50%, industry (oil production mainly) 48%, agriculture 2%
Religions	Muslim 95%
Ethnic Mix	Arab 40%,Indian 18%, Pakistani 18%,Iranian 10%

GEOGRAPHY
Elevation
lowest point: Persian Gulf o m
highest point: Qurayn Abu al Bawl 103 m
Geography Note
strategic location in central Persian Gulf
near major petroleum deposits
Natural Resources
petroleum, natural gas, fish
Climate
arid; mild, pleasant winters; very hot, humid summers
Qatar Food
shish kebab

WORLD CUP		COUNTRY LEAGUE CHAMPIONS	
1930	Did not qualify		
1934	Did not qualify		
1938	Did not qualify	2004	Al-Sadd
1950	Did not qualify	2003	Qatar SC
1954	Did not qualify	2002	Al Ittihad
1958	Did not qualify	2001	Al Wakra
1962	Did not qualify	2000	Al Saad
1966	Did not qualify	1999	Al Wakra
1970	Did not qualify	1998	Al Ittihad
1974	Did not qualify	1997	Al Arabi
1978	Did not qualify	1996	Al Arabi
1982	Did not qualify	**WOMEN'S LEAGUE CHAMPIONS**	
1986	Did not qualify	2004	Not known
1990	Did not qualify	2003	Not known
1994	Did not qualify	2002	Not known
1998	Did not qualify	2001	Not known
2002	Did not qualify	2000	Not known

NATIONAL TEAM COLORS

WORLD PICTURES OF SOCCER

مدرب قطر يتطلع للاستعانة بلاعبين من فرنسا

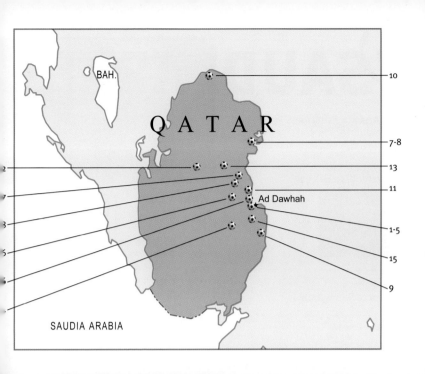

PREMIERE LEAGUE CLUBS	CITY	STADIUM	CAPACITY
Al-Sadd	Doha	Ad-Doha Stadium	25 000
Qatar SC	Doha	Ad-Doha Stadium	20 000
Al-Ittihad	Doha	Al-Gharaffah Stadium	25 000
Al-Arabi	Doha	Ad-Doha Stadium	20 000
Al-Ahli	Doha		
Al-Ryyan	Rayyan		
Khor	Khor	Al-Khor Stadium	20 000
Al-Taawun	Khor	Al-Khor Stadium	20 000
Al-Wakra	Wakra	Al-Wakra Stadium	20 000
Al-Shamal	Shamal	Shamal Stadium	
Al-Ittifaq	Markhiyah		
Al-Nasr	Ash Shahanyiah		
Al-Tadamun	Umm Salal	Umm Affai	25 000
Al-Shabab	Muaydhir Abu ad Dawm		
Al-Shoala	Abu Hamur		
Al-Qadisiya	Madinat Khalifa	Al-Qadisiyah Stadium	
Al-Hilal	Al Kharitiyat		
Al-Siliya	Al Gharatah		

 # SAUDI ARABIA

SAOUDI ARABIA FOOTBALL FED.
Al Mather Quarter Prince Faisal Bin
Fahad Street, Prince Faisal Bin Fahad
PB 5844, 11432 Riyadh
TEL 966 1/482 2240
WEB www.footballasia.com

REFERENCE
Official name
Kingdom of Saudi Arabia

Date of formation	1932
Capital	Riyadh
Population	21.6 million
Total area	816,480 sq Mi, 2,114,690 sq Km
Time zone	GMT +3
Density	26 per sq Mi, 11 per sq Km
Languages	Arabic
Literacy rate	62%
Currency	Riyal
Economy	agriculture 49%, services 37%, industry 14%
Religions	Sunni Muslim 85%, Shi'A Muslim 15%
Ethnic Mix	Arab 90%, Afro-Asian 10%

GEOGRAPHY
Elevation
lowest point: Persian Gulf 0 m
highest point: Jabal Sawda' 3,133 m
Geography Note
extensive coastlines on Persian Gulf and Red
Sea provide great leverage on shipping
(especially crude oil) through Persian Gulf
and Suez Canal
Natural Resources
petroleum, natural gas, iron ore, gold,
copper
Climate
harsh, dry desert with great temperature
extremes
Saudi Arabian Food
aish bel-lahm/saudi samboosak

WORLD CUP

1930	Did not qualify		
1934	Did not qualify		
1938	Did not qualify		
1950	Did not qualify		
1954	Did not qualify		
1958	Did not qualify		
1962	Did not qualify		
1966	Did not qualify		
1970	Did not qualify		
1974	Did not qualify		
1978	Did not qualify		
1982	Did not qualify		
1986	Did not qualify		
1990	Did not qualify		
1994	scd round exit		
1998	First round exit		
2002	First round exit		

COUNTRY LEAGUE CHAMPIONS

2004	Al-Shabab
2003	Al-Ittihad
2002	Al Hilal
2001	Al Ittihad
2000	Al Ittihad
1999	Al Ittihad
1998	Al Hilal
1997	Al Ittihad
1996	Al Hilal

WOMEN'S LEAGUE CHAMPIONS

2004	Not known
2003	Not known
2002	Not known
2001	Not known
2000	Not known

NATIONAL TEAM COLORS

WORLD PICTURES OF SOCCER

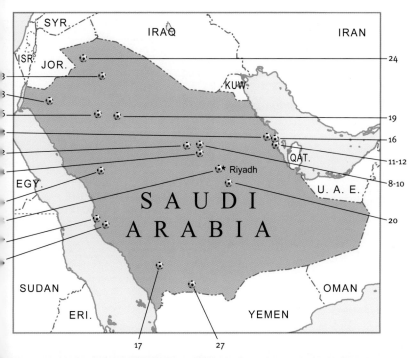

PREMIERE LEAGUE CLUBS	CITY	STADIUM	CAPACITY
Al-Shabab	Riyadh	King Fadh Stadium	70 000
Al-Nasr	Riyadh		
Al-Hilal	Ryadh		
Al-Riyadh SC	Riyadh		
Sudoos	Riyadh		
Al-Ittihad	Jeddah	Al Ittihad Stadium	20 000
Al-Ahly	Jeddah	Prince Sultan Bin Fahad	40 000
Al-Ra'ed	Beraida		
Al-Taawun	Bereida		
Jawaa	Bereida		
Al-Qadisiya	Al Khubar		
Thaqba	Al Khubar		
Ohod	Medina		
Al-Ansar	Medina		
Al-Wahda	Mecca		
Al-Ittifaq	Damman	Fin Fohad Bin Abdul Aziz	12 000
Abha	Abha		
Al-Khaleej	Saihat		
Al-Ta'ee	Ha'il		
Al-Sho'ala	Karjal		
Al-Nimjeh	Unayzah		
Al-Hazm	Ar Rass		
Al-Arooba	Al Jawf		
Hamada	Ghatti		
Hajr	Ihsa'a		
Al-Rowdha	Ihsa'a		
Najran	Najran		
Al-Watani	Tabook		

# SINGAPORE

FOOTBALL ASSOCIATION OF SINGAPORE
15 StadiumRd, Natl Std, South Ent.
397718 Singapore
TEL 65/293 1477
WEB www.fas.org.sg

REFERENCE
Official name
Republic of Singapore
Date of formation 1965
Capital Singapore
Population 3.6 Millions
Total area 236 sq Mi, 610 sq Km
Time zone GMT +8
Density 15,254 per sq Mi, 5,579 per sq Km
Languages Malay, Chinese, English
Literacy rate 91%
Currency Singapore $
Economy services 70%, industry 29%, agriculture 1%
Religions Buddhist 55%, Taoism 22%, Muslim 16%,
Ethnic Mix Chinese 78%, Malay 14%, Indian 6%

GEOGRAPHY
Elevation
lowest point: Singapore Strait 0 m
highest point: Bukit Timah 166 m
Geography Note
focal point for Southeast Asian sea routes
Natural Resources
fishing industry,Deepwater ports
Climate
tropical; hot, humid, rainy; two distinct monsoon seasons - Northeastern monsoon from December to March and Southwestern monsoon from June to September; inter-monsoon - frequent afternoon and early evening thunderstorms
Singapore Food
hainan chicken/laksa

WORLD CUP

1930	Did not qualify
1934	Did not qualify
1938	Did not qualify
1950	Did not qualify
1954	Did not qualify
1958	Did not qualify
1962	Did not qualify
1966	Did not qualify
1970	Did not qualify
1974	Did not qualify
1978	Did not qualify
1982	Did not qualify
1986	Did not qualify
1990	Did not qualify
1994	Did not qualify
1998	Did not qualify
2002	Did not qualify

COUNTRY LEAGUE CHAMPIONS

2004	Tampines Rovers
2003	Home United
2002	Singapore AF
2001	Geylang United
2000	Singapore IF
1999	Home United
1998	Singapore IF
1997	Singapore IF
1996	Geylang United

WOMEN'S LEAGUE CHAMPIONS

2004	Guangzhou Sunray Ca
2003	Tampines Rovers
2002	Tampines Rovers
2001	Not known
2000	Tampines Rovers

NATIONAL TEAM COLORS

WORLD PICTURES OF SOCCER

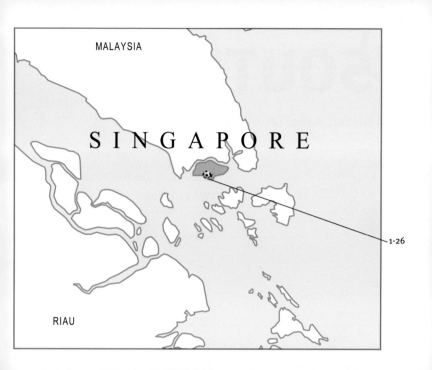

PREMIERE LEAGUE CLUBS	CITY	STADIUM	CAPACITY
Singapore SC	Singapore	Singapore stadium	12 000
Albirex Niigata	Singapore	Jalan Besar Stadium	
Home United	Singapore	Bishan Stadium	3 000
Tampines Rovers	Singapore	Tampines stadium	4 000
Woodlands Wellington	Singapore	Woodlands Stadium	4 500
Singapore Armed Forces	Singapore	Jurong Town Stadium	6 000
Balestier Khalsa	Singapore		
Young Lions	Singapore		
Geylang United	Singapore	Bedok Stadium	4 000
Sinchi	Singapore		
Tanjong Pagar United	Singapore	Queenstown Stadium	4 500
Sembawang Rangers	Singapore	Yishun Stadium	3 000
Sengkang Marine	Singapore		
Jurong FC	Singapore	Jurong East Stadiu	2 000
Gombak United	Singapore	Bukiy Gombak Stadium	2 000
Balestier Central	Singapore	Toa Payoh Stadium	3 500
Tanjong Pagar United	Singapore		
Clementi khalsa	Singapore		
Marine Castle United	Singapore	Hougang Stadium	3 000
Kaki Bukit	Singapore		
Changi United	Singapore		
Pioneer Arsenal	Singapore		
South Avenue	Singapore		
Redhill Rangers	Singapore		
And Mio Kio	Singapore		
Commonwealth Palace	Singapore		
Bukit Merah	Singapore		

SOUTH KOREA

KOREA FOOTBALL ASSOCIATION

1-131 Shinmunro, 2-Ka,Jongno-Gu,
110-062, Seoul
TEL 82 2/733 6764   FAX /735 2755
WEB www.kfa.or.kr

REFERENCE
Official name
Republic of South Korea

Date of formation	1948
Capital	Seoul
Population	46.8 million
Total area	38,119 sq Mi, 98,730 sq Km
Time zone	GMT +9
Density	1,228 per sq Mi, 476 per sq Km
Languages	Korean, Chinese
Literacy rate	99%
Currency	Won
Economy	services 55%, industry 27%, agriculture 18%
Religions	Mahayana Buddhist 47%, Protestant 38%, Catholic 11%, Confucian 3%
Ethnic Mix	Korean 100%

GEOGRAPHY
Elevation
lowest point: Sea of Japan 0 m
highest point: Halla-san 1,950 m
Geography Note
strategic location on Korea Strait
Natural Resources
coal, tungsten, graphite, molybdenum, lead, hydropower potential
Climate
temperate, with rainfall heavier in summer than winter
South Korean Food
korean barbecue/kimchi

WORLD CUP

1930	Did not qualify
1934	Did not qualify
1938	Did not qualify
1950	Did not qualify
1954	First round exit
1958	Did not qualify
1962	Did not qualify
1966	Did not qualify
1970	Did not qualify
1974	Did not qualify
1978	Did not qualify
1982	Did not qualify
1986	First round exit
1990	First round exit
1994	First round exit
1998	First round exit
2002	Finish Fourth

COUNTRY LEAGUE CHAMPIONS

2004	Suwon Bluewings
2003	Songnam Ilhwa chunm
2002	Songnam Ilhwa chunm
2001	Songnam Ilhwa chunm
2000	Anyang LG Cheetah
1999	Suwon S. Bluewings
1998	Suwon S. Bluewings
1997	Pusan Daewoo Horang
1996	Ulsan Hyundai Horang

WOMEN'S LEAGUE CHAMPIONS

2004	Not Known
2003	Sungmin Wonders
2002	Sungmin Wonders
2001	Not Known
2000	Sungmin Wonders

NATIONAL TEAM COLORS

WORLD PICTURES OF SOCCER

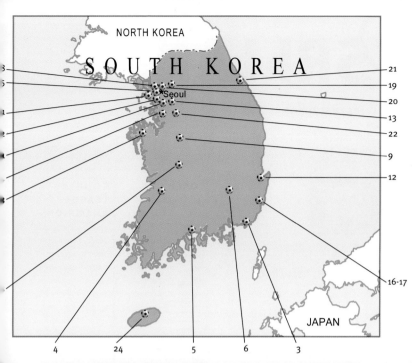

PREMIERE LEAGUE CLUBS	CITY	STADIUM	CAPACITY
Anyang LG Cheetahs	Anyang	Anyang Stadium	18 210
Bucheon SK	Bucheon	Bucheon Stadium	35 000
Busan Icons	Busan	Busan Asiad Stadium	53 860
Chonbuk Hyundai Motors	Jeonju	Jeonju World Cup Stadium	43 350
Chunnam Dragons	Gwangyang	Gwangyang Stadium	15 000
Deagu FC	Deagu	Deagu World Cup Stadium	65 750
Daejeon Citizen	Deajeon	Deajon WC Stadium	41 300
Deajeon Korea Hydro	Deajeon	Deajeon Hanbat Stadium	
Gwangju Sangmu Phoenix	Gwangju	Gwangju WC Stadium	44 120
Incheon United	Incheon	Munhak Stadium	50 250
Incheon Korea Railway	Incheon	Munhak Stadium	50 250
Pohang Steelers	Pohang	Steelyard Stadium	20 240
Ilhwa Chunma	Seongnam	Seongnam Stadium	21 240
Suwon Samsung Bluewings	Suwon	Suwon World cup Stadium	43 920
Suwon City	Suwon	Suwon Stadium	
Ulsan Hyunday Horangi	Ulsan	Ulsan Munsu Stadium	44 460
Ulsan Hyundai Mipo Dockyard	Ulsan	Ulsan Munsu Stadium	
Gimpo Halleluja	Gimpo	Gimpo Stadium	
Uijeongbu Hummel	Uijeongbu	Uijeongbu	
Goyang Koomin Bank	Goyang	Goyang Stadium	
Gangneung City	Gangneung	Gangneung Stadium	
Icheon Sangmu	Icheon	Icheon Stadium	
Seosan Citizen FC	Seosan	Seosan Stadium	
Jeju FC	Jeju	Jeju Stadium	30 000
Seoul FC	Seoul	Seoul Sang-Am Stadium	64 600

SRI LANKA

FOOTBALL FEDERATION OF SRI LANKA
100/9 Independence Ave., Colombo 7
TEL 94 1/696 179 FAX /682 471
WEB www.footballasia.com

REFERENCE

Official name
Democratic Socialist Republic of Sri Lanka

Date of formation	1948
Capital	Colombo
Population	18.8 Million
Total area	24,996 sq Mi, 64,740 sq Km
Time zone	GMT +5.5
Density	752 sq Mi, 291 per sq Km
Languages	Sinhala, Tamil, English
Literacy rate	90%
Currency	Rupee
Economy	services 45%, agriculture 43%, industry 12%
Religions	Buddhist 69%, Hindu 15%, Christian 8%, Muslim 8%
Ethnic Mix	Sinhalese 74%, Tamil 18%, Moor 7%

GEOGRAPHY

Elevation
lowest point: Indian Ocean 0 m
highest point: Pidurutalagala 2,524 m

Geography Note
strategic location near major Indian Ocean sea lanes

Natural Resources
limestone, graphite, mineral sands, gems, phosphates, clay, hydropower

Climate
tropical monsoon; northeast monsoon (December to March); southwest monsoon (June to October)

Sri Lanka Food
kudu badum/mulligatawny soup/mustard beef curry

WORLD CUP		COUNTRY LEAGUE CHAMPIONS	
1930	Did not qualify		
1934	Did not qualify		
1938	Did not qualify	2004	Blue Stars SC
1950	Did not qualify	2003	Negombo Youth SC
1954	Did not qualify	2002	Saunders SC
1958	Did not qualify	2001	Saunders SC
1962	Did not qualify	2000	Ratnams SC
1966	Did not qualify	1999	Saunders SC
1970	Did not qualify	1998	Ratnams SC
1974	Did not qualify	1997	Saunders SC
1978	Did not qualify	1996	Saunders SC
1982	Did not qualify	**WOMEN'S LEAGUE CHAMPIONS**	
1986	Did not qualify	2004	Army Ladies SC
1990	Did not qualify	2003	Police Ladies SC
1994	Did not qualify	2002	Not Known
1998	Did not qualify	2001	Not Known
2002	Did not qualify	2000	Not Known

NATIONAL TEAM COLORS

WORLD PICTURES OF SOCCER

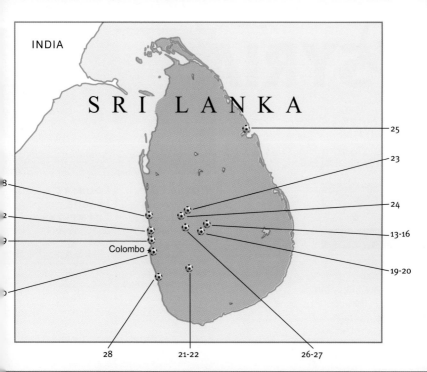

PREMIERE LEAGUE CLUBS	CITY	STADIUM	CAPACITY
Renown SC	Colombo	Sugathadasa Stadium	25 000
Ratnams SC	Colombo		
Saunders SC	Colombo	Premadadsa Stadium	40 000
Old Benedictans SC	Colombo		
Air Force SC	Colombo		
Pettah United SC	Colombo		
Maligawatte SC	Colombo		
Cooray SC	Colombo		
Java Lane SC	Colombo		
Navy SC	Colombo		
Jupiter SC	Negombo		
Negombo Youth SC	Negombo		
York SC	Kandy		
Municipal SC	Kandy		
Red Diamonds SC	Kandy		
Hyline SC	Kandy		
New Youngsters SC	Wennapuwa		
Marians SC	Wennappuwa		
Red Sun SC	Gampola		
Manchester United SC	Gampola		
New Stars SC	Ratnapura		
Sapphire SC	Ratnapura		
Pelican SC	Kurunegala		
Hyline SC	Dangolla		
Olympic SC	Trincomalee		
Maya SC	Kegalle		
Kegalle SC	Kegalle		
Super Beach SC	Kalutara		
Youngsters	Kandana		

SYRIA

SYRIAN FOOTBALL ASSOC.
Maysaloon St, PB 421, Damascus
TEL 963 11/333 5866 FAX/33315 11
WEB www.footballasia.com

REFERENCE
Official name
Syrian Arab Republic
Date of formation 1946
Capital Damascus
Population 16.1 Million
Total area 71,065 sq Mi, 184,060 sq Km
Time zone GMT +2
Density 227 per sq Mi, 93 per sq Km
Languages Arabic, French, Kurdish, Armenian, Circassian, Aramaic
Literacy rate 71%
Currency Pound
Economy services 63%, agriculture 22%, industry 15%
Religions Sunni Muslim 74%, other Muslim 16%, Christian 10%
Ethnic Mix Arab 89%, Kurdish 6%

GEOGRAPHY
Elevation
lowest point: unnamed location near Lake Tiberias -200 m
highest point: Mount Hermon 2,814 m
Geography Note
there are 42 Israeli settlements and civilian land use sites in the Israeli-occupied Golan Heights (August 2001 est.)
Natural Resources
petroleum, phosphates, chrome and manganese ores, asphalt, iron ore, rock salt, marble, gypsum, hydropower
Climate
mostly desert; hot, dry, sunny summers and mild, rainy winters along coast; cold weather with snow or sleet periodically in Damascus
Syrian Food
batlawa/hummus/shish kebab

WORLD CUP		COUNTRY LEAGUE CHAMPIONS	
1930	Did not qualify		
1934	Did not qualify		
1938	Did not qualify	2004	Wahda
1950	Did not qualify	2003	Jaish
1954	Did not qualify	2002	Jaish
1958	Did not qualify	2001	Jaish
1962	Did not qualify	2000	Jabala
1966	Did not qualify	1999	Jaish
1970	Did not qualify	1998	Jaish
1974	Did not qualify	1997	Teshrin
1978	Did not qualify	1996	Karama
1982	Did not qualify	**WOMEN'S LEAGUE CHAMPIONS**	
1986	Did not qualify	2004	Not known
1990	Did not qualify	2003	Not known
1994	Did not qualify	2002	Not known
1998	Did not qualify	2001	Not known
2002	Did not qualify	2000	Not known

NATIONAL TEAM COLORS

WORLD PICTURES OF SOCCER

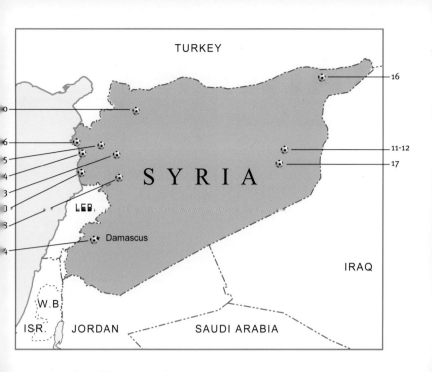

PREMIERE LEAGUE CLUBS	CITY	STADIUM	CAPACITY
Al-Majd	Damascus	Abbasiyn Stadium	45 000
Al-Jaish	Damascus		
Al-Wahda	Damascus		
Al-Shorta	Damascus		
Teshrin	Latakia	Al-Assad	35 000
Hottin	Latakia	Al-Assad	35 000
Al-Karama	Homs		
Al-Wathba	Homs		
Al-Ittihad	Aleppo	Al Hamadaniah	20 000
Al-Horriya	Aleppo	Al Hamadaniah	20 000
Al-Foutoua	Dayr az Zawr		
Al-Yaqaza	Dayr az Zawr		
Umayya	Idlib		
Jablah	Jablah		
Qardaha	Qardaha		
Al-Jihad	Qameshli		
Al-Mayadin	Mayadin		
Al-Arabi	Tartus		

TAIWAN

CHINESE TAIPEI NATIONAL FOOTBALL FEDERATION
#2F Yu Men St., 104 Taipei, Taiwan
TEL 886 2/2596 1185 FAX /2595 1594
WEB www.football.org.tw

REFERENCE
Official name
Republic of China (Taiwan)

Date of formation	1949
Capital	Taipei
Population	22.2 Million
Total area	12,456 sq Mi, 32,260 sq Km
Time zone	GMT +8
Density	1782 sq Mi, 615 per sq Km
Languages	Mandarin
Literacy rate	Average
Currency	Taiwan $
Economy	services 49%, industry 30%, agriculture 21 %
Religions	Buddhist, Confucian & Taoist 93%, Christian 5%
Ethnic Mix	indigenous Chinese 84%, Mainland Chinese 14%

GEOGRAPHY
Elevation
lowest point: South China Sea 0 m
highest point: Yu Shan 3,997 m
Geography Note
strategic location adjacent to both the
Taiwan Strait and the Luzon Strait
Natural Resources
small deposits of coal, natural gas, limestone, marble, and asbestos
Climate
tropical; marine; rainy season during southwest monsoon (June to August); cloudiness
is persistent and extensive all year
Taiwanese Food
apring rolls/miso soup/taiwanese sushi

WORLD CUP

1930	Did not qualify
1934	Did not qualify
1938	Did not qualify
1950	Did not qualify
1954	Did not qualify
1958	Did not qualify
1962	Did not qualify
1966	Did not qualify
1970	Did not qualify
1974	Did not qualify
1978	Did not qualify
1982	Did not qualify
1986	Did not qualify
1990	Did not qualify
1994	Did not qualify
1998	Did not qualify
2002	Did not qualify

COUNTRY LEAGUE CHAMPIONS

2004	Taipower FC
2003	Taipower FC
2002	Taipower FC
2001	Taipower FC
2000	Taipower FC
1999	Taipower FC
1998	Taipower FC
1997	Taipower FC
1996	Taipower FC

WOMEN'S LEAGUE CHAMPIONS

2004	Not known
2003	Not known
2002	Not known
2001	Wei Da
2000	Wei Da

NATIONAL TEAM COLORS

WORLD PICTURES OF SOCCER

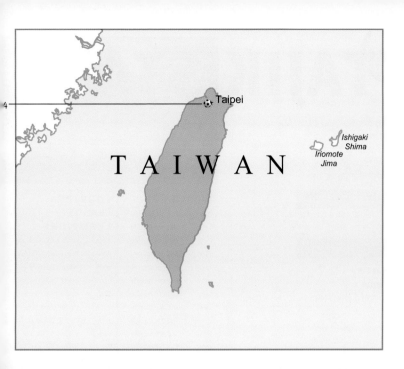

Taipei

Ishigaki
Shima

Iriomote
Jima

T A I W A N

PREMIERE LEAGUE CLUBS	CITY	STADIUM	CAPACITY
Taipower	Taipei	Chungshan Soccer	25 000
Ta Tung	Taipei		
Wei dan	Taipei		
Taiwan PEC	Taipei		
I-Lain Youth	Taipei		
Ming Chuan	Taipei		
City Bank	Taipei		
Flying Camel	Taipei		
Mingchuang	Taipei		
-Lukuang	Taipei		
-Taipei Bank	Taipei		
-Chun Li	Taipei		
-Taiwan AC	Taipei		
-Taipei FC	Taipei		

 # TAJIKISTAN

TAJIKISTAN NATIONAL FOOTBALL FEDERATION
44 Rudaki Ave., PB 26, 734 025 Dushanbe
TEL 992 372/212 363 FAX /212 447
WEB www.footballasia.com

REFERENCE
Official name
Republic of Tajikistan

Date of formation	1991
Capital	Dushanbe
Population	6.2 Million
Total area	55,251 sq Mi, 143,100 sq Km
Time zone	Gmt +6
Density	112 per sq Mi, 43 per sq Km
Languages	Tajik ,Uzbek, Russian
Literacy rate	98%
Currency	Tajik Rouble
Economy	agriculture 43%, services 35%, industry 22%
Religions	Sunni Muslim 80%, Shi'A Muslim 5%
Ethnic Mix	Tajik 62%, Uzbek 24%, Russian 8%, Tatar 1%, Kyrgyz 1%

GEOGRAPHY
Elevation
lowest point: Syr Darya (Sirdaryo) 300 m
highest point: Qullai Ismoili Somoni 7,495 m
Geography Note
landlocked; mountainous region dominated by the Trans-Alay Range in the north and the Pamirs in the southeast; highest point, Qullai Ismoili Somoni (formerly Communism Peak), was the tallest mountain in the former USSR
Natural Resources
hydropower, some petroleum,uranium,mercury, brown coal,lead,zinc,tungsten,silver, gold
Climate
midlatitude continental, hot summers, mild winters; semiarid to polar in Pamir Mountains
Tajikistan Food
pachlava/tajik non

WORLD CUP

1930	Did not qualify
1934	Did not qualify
1938	Did not qualify
1950	Did not qualify
1954	Did not qualify
1958	Did not qualify
1962	Did not qualify
1966	Did not qualify
1970	Did not qualify
1974	Did not qualify
1978	Did not qualify
1982	Did not qualify
1986	Did not qualify
1990	Did not qualify
1994	Did not qualify
1998	Did not qualify
2002	Did not qualify

COUNTRY LEAGUE CHAMPIONS

2005	Regar-Tadaz Turzun.
2004	Regar-Tadaz Turzun.
2003	Varzob Dushanbe
2002	Regar-Tadaz Turzun.
2001	Regar-Tadaz Turzun.
2000	Varzob Dushanbe
1999	Varzob Dushande
1998	Varzob Dushande
1997	Vakhsh Kurgan Tyube

WOMEN'S LEAGUE CHAMPIONS

2004	Not Known
2003	Not Known
2002	Not Known
2001	Not Known
2000	Not Known

NATIONAL TEAM COLORS

WORLD PICTURES OF SOCCER

PREMIERE LEAGUE CLUBS	CITY	STADIUM	CAPACITY
CSKA Dusanbe	Dusanbe	Dusanbe Central Stadium	20 000
BDA Dusanbe	Dusanbe		
SKA Pamir Dusanbe	Dusanbe	Pamir Stadium	10 000
Varzob Dusanbe	Dusanbe		
Sitora Dusanbe	Dusanbe		
Dinamo Dusanbe	Dusanbe		
Samar-Umed	Dusanbe		
Oriyon Dusanbe	Dusanbe		
POISK Dusanbe	Dusanbe		
Bofanda Dusanbe	Dusanbe		
Lokomotiv Dusanbe	Dusanbe		
Regar-Tadaz	Tursunzade		
Anicon Tursunzade	Tursunzade		
Safarbek Karim	Sheykhon		
Khuja Karim	Khujand		
Olimp-Ansol Kulob	Kulob		
Ravshan Kulob	Kulob		
Istravshan Ura-Tyube	Tyube		
Nuri Vakhsh Kurgan-Tyube	Tyube		
Saddam Surband Kurgan	Tyube		
Shodmon Ghissar	Ghissar		
Farruh Ghissar	Ghissar		
Aviator Chkalovsk	Chkalovsk		
FK Dangara	Dangara		
Istravshan Uroteppa	Uroteppa		
FK Khujand	Khujand		
Vash Qurghonteppa	Qurghonteppa		
SKA Nurek	Nurek		
Panjsher Kolhozabad	Kolhozabad		

THAILAND

THE FOOTBALL ASSOCIATION OF THAILAND
Natl. Stad. Gate #3, Roma 1 Rd, Patumwan,
10330 Bangkok
TEL 66 2/214 1058
WEB www.footballasia.com

REFERENCE
Official name
   Kingdom of Thailand

Date of formation	1882
Capital	Bangkok
Population	61.4 million
Total area	197,255 sq Mi, 510,890 sq Km
Time zone	GMT +7
Density	311 per sq Mi, 117 per sq Km
Languages	Thai, Chinese, Malay, Khmer Mon, Karen, Miao, English
Literacy rate	95%
Currency	Baht
Economy	agriculture 70%, services 24%, industry 6%
Religions	Buddhist 95%, Muslim 4%, Hindu Christian 1%
Ethnic Mix	Thai 80%, Chinese 12%, Malay 4%, Khmer 4%

GEOGRAPHY
Elevation
lowest point: Gulf of Thailand 0 m
highest point: Doi Inthanon 2,576 m
Geography Note
controls only land route from Asia to
Malaysia and Singapore
Natural Resources
tin, rubber, natural gas, tungsten,
tantalum, timber, lead, fish, gypsum,
lignite, fluorite, arable land
Climate
tropical; rainy, warm, cloudy southwest
monsoon (mid-May to September); dry, cool
northeast monsoon (November to mid-
March); southern isthmus always hot and
Thailand Food
laap neua/tam lao/chicken curry

WORLD CUP		COUNTRY LEAGUE CHAMPIONS	
1930	Did not qualify		
1934	Did not qualify		
1938	Did not qualify	2004	Krung Thai Bank
1950	Did not qualify	2003	Krung Thai Bank
1954	Did not qualify	2002	BEC Tero Sasana
1958	Did not qualify	2001	BEC Tero Sasana
1962	Did not qualify	2000	BEC Tero Sasana
1966	Did not qualify	1999	Royal Thai AF
1970	Did not qualify	1998	Sinthana
1974	Did not qualify	1997	Bangkok Bank FC
1978	Did not qualify	1996	Not Known
1982	Did not qualify	**WOMEN'S LEAGUE CHAMPIONS**	
1986	Did not qualify	2004	Not Known
1990	Did not qualify	2003	Not Known
1994	Did not qualify	2002	Not Known
1998	Did not qualify	2001	Not Known
2002	Did not qualify	2000	Not Known

NATIONAL TEAM COLORS

WORLD PICTURES OF SOCCER

PREMIERE LEAGUE CLUBS	CITY	STADIUM	CAPACITY
BEC Tero Sassana	Bangkok	Mahanakorn UNI	5 000
Bangkok Bank	Bangkok	Bangna Stadium	2 000
Port Authority	Bangkok	Tarua Stadium	3 000
Sinthana	Bangkok	Sinthana Stadium	1 000
Bangkok Commerce	Bangkok	Mee Suwan	3 000
Royal Thai Army	Bangkok	Thai Army Sports Stadium	20 000
Royal Thai Air Force	Bangkok	Thupatemee	20 000
T.O Thailand	Bangkok	Turakitbundit	4 000
Bangkok M.A	Bangkok	Thai Stadium	10 000
Krung Thai Bank	Bangkok	Suphachalasai	40 000
Bangkok Tobacco	Bangkok	Thai Stadium	10 000
BangkokChristian College	Bangkok	Thai Stadium	10 000
Bangkok Police FC	Bangkok	Thai Stadium	10 000
Ratana Bundit Bangkok	Bangkok	Turakitbundit	4 000
Chiang Mai FC	Chiang Mai	700th Anniversary Stadia	25 000
Sonkhla	Sonkhla	Tinsulanon	20 000
Phitsanulok	Phitsanulok		
Samut Songkhram	Samut Songkhra.		
Nakhon Sawan	Nakhon Sawan		
Chon Buri	Chon Buri		
Nakhon R.	Nakhon Ratchasima		
Sisaket	Sisaket		

TURKMENISTAN

FOOTBALL FEDERATION OF TURKMENISTAN
32 Belinskiy, Turkmembashi Spt. Cplx
Stadium Kopetdag, 744 001 Ashgabat
TEL 993 12/362 392
WEB www.footballasia.com

REFERENCE
Official name
Turkmenistan
Date of formation 1991
Capital Ashgabat
Population 4.5 Million
Total area 188,455 sq Mi, 488,100 sq Km
Time zone GMT +5
Density 24 per sq Mi, 9 per sq Km
Languages Turkmen,Uzbek
Literacy rate 98%
Currency Manat
Economy agriculture 44%,services 36%, industry 20%
Religions Sunni Muslim 87%, Eastern Orthodox 11%
Ethnic Mix Turkmen 73%, Russian 10%, Uzbek 9%, Kazakh 2%, Tatar 1%

GEOGRAPHY
Elevation
lowest point: Vpadina Akchanaya -81 m
highest point: Gora Ayribaba 3,139 m
Geography Note
landlocked; the western and central low-lying, desolate portions of the country make up the great Garagum (Kara-Kum) desert, which occupies over 80% of the country; eastern part is plateau
Natural Resources
petroleum, natural gas, coal, sulfur, salt
Climate
subtropical desert
Turkmenistan Food
chaihana/shurpa

WORLD CUP		COUNTRY LEAGUE CHAMPIONS	
1930	Did not qualify		
1934	Did not qualify		
1938	Did not qualify	2004	Nebitci Balkanabat
1950	Did not qualify	2003	Nisa Ashgabat
1954	Did not qualify	2002	Shagadam Turkmenbas
1958	Did not qualify	2001	Nisa Ashgabat
1962	Did not qualify	2000	Kpetdag Ashgabat
1966	Did not qualify	1999	Nisa Ashgabat
1970	Did not qualify	1998	Kopetdag Ashgabat
1974	Did not qualify	1997	Not Known
1978	Did not qualify	1996	Nisa Ashgabat
1982	Did not qualify	**WOMEN'S LEAGUE CHAMPIONS**	
1986	Did not qualify	2004	Not Known
1990	Did not qualify	2003	Not Known
1994	Did not qualify	2002	Not Known
1998	Did not qualify	2001	Not Known
2002	Did not qualify	2000	Not Known

NATIONAL TEAM COLORS

WORLD PICTURES OF SOCCER

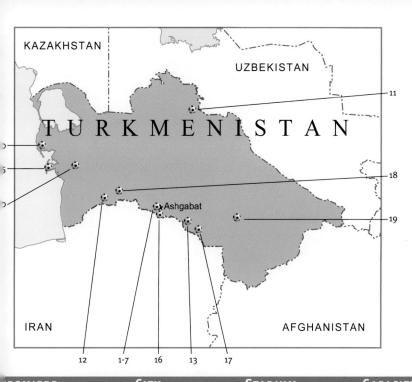

PREMIERE LEAGUE CLUBS	CITY	STADIUM	CAPACITY
Kopetdag	Ashgabat	Kopetdag Stadium	26 000
Nisa Ashgabat	Ashgabat	Dagdan stadium	1 500
Asudalyk	Ashgabat	Dagdan stadium	1 500
TTU Ashgabat	Ashgabat		
Galkan Ashgabat	Ashgabat		
Serhetchi Ashgabat	Ashgabat		
Melik Ashgaba	Ashgabat		
Garagum	Turkmenbashi	Turkmanabat	5 000
Jeykhun	Turkmenbashi		
Sagadam	Turkmenbashi		
Turan Dashovuz	Dashovuz	Dashovuz stadium	12 000
Gazci Gaz	Akak		
Ahal Ak	Dasayak		
Nisa Cheleken	Cheleken		
Nebitchi	Cheleken	Balkanabat Stadium	10 000
SMM Plus Karatamak	Karatamak		
Linkveyu Tedzhen	Tejen		
Geoktepe	Geoktepe		
FK Merv Mary	Mary		
Lokomotiv	Nebitdag		

UNITED ARAB EMIRATES

UAE Football Association
PB 916, Abu Dhabi
TEL 971-2/44 56 00   FAX /44 85 58
WEB www.uaefootball.ae

REFERENCE
Official name
United Arab Emirates

Date of	
formation	1971
Capital	Abu Dhabi
Population	2,344,402
Total area	32,278 sq Mi, 83,600 sq Km
Time zone	GMT +4
Density	74 per sq Mi, 29 per sq Km
Languages	Arabic, Farsi
Literacy rate	79%
Currency	Dirham
Economy	services 57%, industry 38%, agriculture 5%
Religions	Muslim (Mainly sunni) 96%, Christian, Hindu 4%
Ethnic Mix	Asian 50%, Emirian 19%, Other Arab 23%, Others 8%

GEOGRAPHY
Elevation
lowest point: Persian Gulf 0 m
highest point: Jabal Yibir 1,527 m
Geography Note
strategic location along southern
approaches to Strait of Hormuz, a vital
transit point for world crude oil
Natural Resources
petroleum, natural gas
Climate
desert; cooler in eastern mountains
UAE Food
khameer bread/sago ma Lheeb

WORLD CUP

1930	Did not qualify		
1934	Did not qualify		
1938	Did not qualify		
1950	Did not qualify		
1954	Did not qualify		
1958	Did not qualify		
1962	Did not qualify		
1966	Did not qualify		
1970	Did not qualify		
1974	Did not qualify		
1978	Did not qualify		
1982	Did not qualify		
1986	Did not qualify		
1990	Did not qualify		
1994	Did not qualify		
1998	Did not qualify		
2002	Did not qualify		

COUNTRY LEAGUE CHAMPIONS

2004	Al-Ain
2003	Al-Ain
2002	Al-Ain
2001	Al-Wahda
2000	Al-Ain
1999	Al-Wahda
1998	Al-Ain
1997	Al-Wasl
1996	Sharjah

WOMEN'S LEAGUE CHAMPIONS

2004	Not Known
2003	Not Known
2002	Not Known
2001	Not Known
2000	Not Known

NATIONAL TEAM COLORS

WORLD PICTURES OF SOCCER

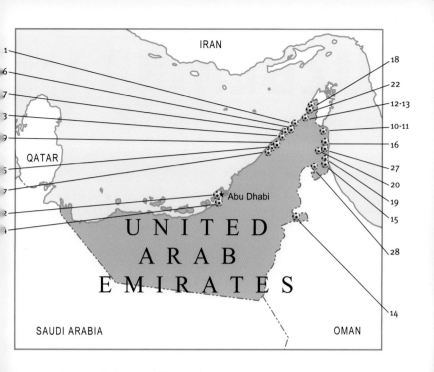

PREMIERE LEAGUE CLUBS	CITY	STADIUM	CAPACITY
Al-Wahda	Abu Dhabi	Mohammed Bin Zayed	15 000
Al-Jazeera	Abu Dhabi	Al Nuhayyan Stadium	12 000
Al-Shabab	Dubai	Al-Maktoum Stadium	12 000
Al-Nasr	Dubai	Al-Maktoum Stadium	12 000
Al-Wasl	Dubai	Al-Maktoum Stadium	12 000
Al-Ahly	Dubai	Al-Maktoum Stadium	12 000
Dubai FC	Dubai	Al-Maktoum Stadium	12 000
Al-Shaab	Sharjah	Sharjah Stadium	12 000
Sharjah SC	Sharjah	Sharjah Stadium	12 000
Dibba	Dibba		
Dibba Al-Hisn	Dibba		
Ras Al-Khaima	Ras-Al-Khaima		
Emirates	Ras Al-Khaima		
Al-Ayn	Al-Ayn	Tahnoon Mohammed	10 000
Al-Ittihad	Kalba		
Al-Khaleej	Khor Fakkan		
Al Hamriya	Al Hamriya		
Al-Taawun	Sha'am		
Al-Fujayrah	Al Fujayrah		
Masafi	Masafi		
Hamra Island	Hamra Island		
Ramms	Ramms		
Ajman	Ajman	Ajman Stadium	
Al-Arooba	Batin		
Shanqah	Ash Shanqah		
Al-Arabi	Um Al-Qiwain		
Sharm	Sharm		
Masfoot	Masfut	Masfoot Stadium	

UZBEKISTAN

FOOTBALL FED. REP. OF UZBEKISTAN
Massiv Almazar, Furkat Str. 15/1,700
003 Tashkent
TEL 998 71/144 1684
WEB www.footballasia.com

REFERENCE
Official name
Republic of Uzbekistan
Date of formation 1991
Capital Tashkent
Population 24.3 Million
Total area 127,741 sq Mi, 447,400 sq Km
Time zone GMT +6
Density 190 per sq Mi, 54 per sq Km
Languages Uzbek, Russian
Literacy rate 98%
Currency Sum
Economy agriculture 43%, services 35% industry 22%
Religions Sunni Muslim 88%, Eastern Orthodox 9%
Ethnic Mix Uzbek 71%, Russian 8%, Tajik 5%, Kazakh 4%

GEOGRAPHY
Elevation
lowest point: Sariqarnish Kuli -12 m
highest point: Adelunga Toghi 4,301 m
Geography Note
along with Liechtenstein, one of the only two doubly landlocked countries in the world
Natural Resources
natural gas, petroleum, coal, gold, uranium, silver, copper, lead and zinc, tungsten, molybdenum
Climate
mostly midlatitude desert, long, hot summers, mild winters; semiarid grassland in east
Uzbekistan Food
uzbek plov/manty/sabzi piez/non

WORLD CUP		COUNTRY LEAGUE CHAMPIONS	
1930	Did not qualify		
1934	Did not qualify		
1938	Did not qualify	2004	Pakhtakor Tashkent
1950	Did not qualify	2003	Pakhtakor Tashkent
1954	Did not qualify	2002	Pakhtakor Tashkent
1958	Did not qualify	2001	Neftchi Freghana
1962	Did not qualify	2000	Dustlik Tashkent
1966	Did not qualify	1999	Dustlik Tashkent
1970	Did not qualify	1998	Pakhtaktor Tashkent
1974	Did not qualify	1997	MHSK Tashkent
1978	Did not qualify	1996	Nawbahor Namangan
1982	Did not qualify	**WOMEN'S LEAGUE CHAMPIONS**	
1986	Did not qualify	2004	Not Known
1990	Did not qualify	2003	Not Known
1994	Did not qualify	2002	Not Known
1998	Did not qualify	2001	Not Known
2002	Did not qualify	2000	Not Known

NATIONAL TEAM COLORS

WORLD PICTURES OF SOCCER

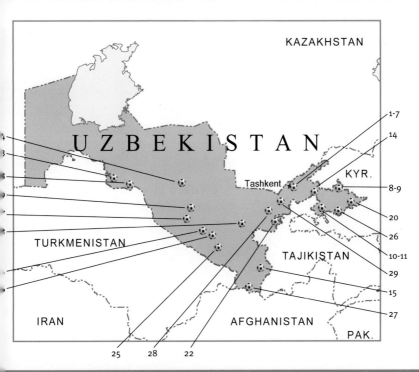

PREMIERE LEAGUE CLUBS	CITY	STADIUM	CAPACITY
Pakhtakor Tashkent	Tashkent	Pakhtakor Central	54 000
Lokomotiv Tashkent	Tashkent		
Traktor Tashkent	Tashkent		
Dostlik Tashkent	Tashkent		
NBU Osiyo	Tashkent		
FK Tashkent	Tashkent		
Shayxontaur XXI	Tashkent		
Navbahor Namangan	Namangan	Markaziy Stadium	25 000
Papsen Namagan	Namagan		
FK Qogon 1912	Qogon		
Temiryulchi Qogon	Qogon		
Khorazm Urgench	Urgench	Khorazm Urgench	25 000
Jaichun Urgench	Urgench		
FK Kasansay	Kasansay	Markaziy Stadium	30 000
Chaganiyon Denow	Denow		
Navabahor Konsonsoy-	Kasan		
FK Bukhoro	Bukhoro	Markaziy Stadium	40 000
FK Hazorasp	Hazorasp		
Gizdhouan FK	Gizdhouan		
FK Andijon	Andijon		
Mashal Mubarek	Mubarek		35 000
Metallurg Bekabad	Bekabad		
Samarquand-Dinamo	Samarquand		
Qizilqum Zarafshon	Zarafshon		
Nasaf Qarshi	Qarshi	Markaziy Stadium	20 000
Neftchi Fergana	Fergana		
Surkhon Termiz	Termiz		
Sogdiyona Jizzax	Jizzax		
FK Gulitson	Gulitson		

VIETNAM

VIETNAM FOOTBALL FEDERATION
141, Nguyen Thai Hoc Str., Dis Dongda, Hanoi
TEL 84 4/845 2480
WEB www.vff.org.vn

REFERENCE
Official name
Socialist Republic of Vietnam

Date of formation	1976
Capital	Hanoi
Population	79.8 Million
Total area	125,621 sq Mi, 325,360 sq Km
Time zone	GMT +7
Density	635 per sq Mi, 235 per sq Km
Languages	Vietnamese
Literacy rate	64%
Currency	Dong
Economy	agriculture 65%, industry & services 35%
Religions	Buddhist 55%, Catholic 7%, Non religious 38%
Ethnic Mix	Vietnamese 88%, Chinese 4%, Thai 2%

GEOGRAPHY
Elevation
lowest point: South China Sea 0 m
highest point: Ngoc Linh 3,143 m
Geography Note
extending 1,650 km north to south, the country is only 50 km across at its narrowest point
Natural Resources
phosphates, coal, manganese, bauxite, chromate, offshore oil and gas deposits, forests, hydropower
Climate
tropical in south; monsoonal in north with hot, rainy season (mid-May to mid-September) and warm, dry season (mid-October to mid-March).
Vietnamese
Pho (beef noodle), Banh cuon (rice steam rolls)

WORLD CUP

1930	Did not qualify
1934	Did not qualify
1938	Did not qualify
1950	Did not qualify
1954	Did not qualify
1958	Did not qualify
1962	Did not qualify
1966	Did not qualify
1970	Did not qualify
1974	Did not qualify
1978	Did not qualify
1982	Did not qualify
1986	Did not qualify
1990	Did not qualify
1994	Did not qualify
1998	Did not qualify
2002	Did not qualify

COUNTRY LEAGUE CHAMPIONS

2004	Hoang Anh Gia Lai
2003	Hoang Anh Gia Lai
2002	Cang Saigon
2001	Song Lam Nghe An
2000	Song Lam Nghe An
1999	No Competition
1998	The Cong
1997	Cang Saigon
1996	Dong Thap
WOMEN'S LEAGUE CHAMPIONS	
2004	Ho Chi Minh City
2003	Hanoi
2002	Ho Chi Minh City
2001	Not Known
2000	Not Known

NATIONAL TEAM COLORS

WORLD PICTURES OF SOCCER

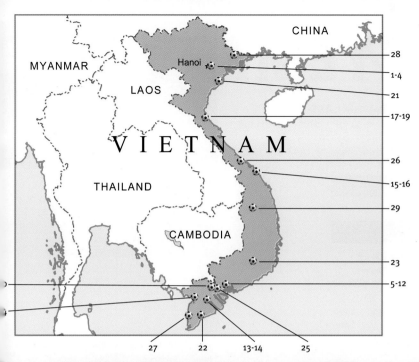

PREMIERE LEAGUE CLUBS	CITY	STADIUM	CAPACITY
The Cong	Hanoi	Hanoi Stadium	23 000
LG-ACB	Hanoi	Hanoi Stadium	23 000
Hang Kong Vietnam	Hanoi	Hanoi Stadium	23 000
Thanh Nien	Hanoi	Hanoi Stadium	23 000
Cang Saigon	Ho Chi Minh	Thong Nhat Stadium	25 000
Sinhancon	Ho Cho Minh	Thong Nhat Stadium	25 000
Ngan Hang Dong A	Ho Chi Minh	Thong Nhat Stadium	25 000
KS Khai Hoan	Ho Chi Minh	Thong Nhat Stadium	25 000
Bu'u Dien	Ho Cho Minh	Thong Nhat Stadium	25 000
Hai Quan	Ho Chi Minh	Thong Nhat Stadium	25 000
Quan Khu 7	Ho Chi Minh	Cu Chi Stadium	
Van Chinh	Ho Chi Minh	Cu Chi Stadium	
Can Tho	Can Tho	Can Tho Stadium	
Quan Khu 9	Can Tho	Can Tho Stadium	
Danang	Danang	Chi lang Stadium	
Quan Khu 5	Danang	Quan Khu 5 Stadium	
Quan Khu 4	Vinh	Quan Khu 4 Stadium	
Song Lam Nghe An	Vinh	Vinh Stadium	
Tra Vinh	Tra Vinh	Tra Vinh Stadium	
Dong Thap	Cao Lanh	Cao Lanh Stadium	23 000
Nam Dinh	Nam Dinh	Chua Cuoi Stadium	20 000
Bac Lieu	Bac Lieu	Bac Lieu Stadium	
Lam Dong	Dat Lat	Dat Lat Stadium	
Kien Giang	Rach Gia	Kien Giang Stadium	
Gach Dong Tam Long An	Tan An	Quy Nhon Stadium	
Thua Thien Hue	Hue	Tu Do Stadium	12 000
Ca mau	Ca mau	Ca Mau Stadium	
Quang Ninh	Ha long	Cua Ong Stadium	
Hoang Anh Gia Lai	Pleiku	Pleiku Stadium	10 000

 # YEMEN

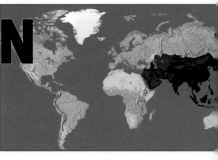

YEMEN FOOTBALL ASSOC.
Abu Baker Al Seddiq Street, Branching
Djibouti Street, Sanaa
TEL 967 1/442 240 FAX /442 261
WEB www.footballasia.com

REFERENCE
Official name
Republic of Yemen

Date of formation	1990
Capital	Sana'a
Population	18.1 million
Total area	217,362 sq Mi, 562,970 sq Km
Time zone	GMT +3
Density	83 per sq Mi, 32 per sq Km
Languages	Arabic
Literacy rate	41%
Currency	Rial
Economy	agriculture 63%, services 26%, industry 11%
Religions	Sunni Muslim 55%, Shi'a Muslim 42%, Christian, Hindu & Jewish 3%
Ethnic Mix	Arab 95%, Afro- Arab 3%, Somali, European 2%

GEOGRAPHY
Elevation
lowest point: Arabian Sea 0 m
highest point: Jabal an Nabi Shu'ayb 3,760 m
Geography Note
strategic location on Bab el Mandeb, the strait linking the Red Sea and the Gulf of Aden, one of world's most active shipping lanes
Natural Resources
petroleum, fish, rock salt, marble, small deposits of coal, gold, lead, nickel, and copper, fertile soil in west
Climate
mostly desert; hot and humid along west coast; temperate in western mountains extraordinarily hot, dry, harsh desert in east
Yemen Food
samak yemeni/baked guava

WORLD CUP		COUNTRY LEAGUE CHAMPIONS	
1930	Did not qualify		
1934	Did not qualify		
1938	Did not qualify	2004	Al-Shabab
1950	Did not qualify	2003	Al-Shabab
1954	Did not qualify	2002	Al-Wahda
1958	Did not qualify	2001	Al-Ahli
1962	Did not qualify	2000	Al-Ahli
1966	Did not qualify	1999	Al-Ahli
1970	Did not qualify	1998	Al-Wahda
1974	Did not qualify	1997	Al-Wahda
1978	Did not qualify	1996	No competition
1982	Did not qualify	**WOMEN'S LEAGUE CHAMPIONS**	
1986	Did not qualify	2004	Not known
1990	Did not qualify	2003	Not known
1994	Did not qualify	2002	Not known
1998	Did not qualify	2001	Not known
2002	Did not qualify	2000	Not known

NATIONAL TEAM COLORS

WORLD PICTURES OF SOCCER

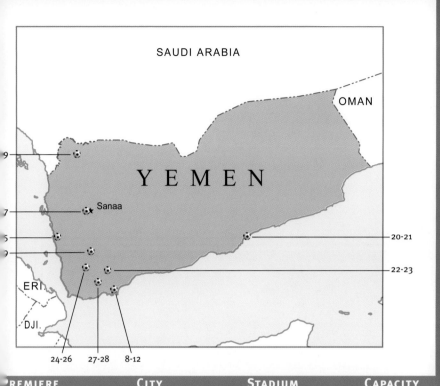

PREMIERE LEAGUE CLUBS	CITY	STADIUM	CAPACITY
Al-Wahda	Sanaa	Al-Murisi Stadium	20 000
Al-AhliSanaa	Sanaa		
May 22	Sanaa		
Yarmuk Al-Rawda	Sanaa	Althawra Sports City	30 000
Al-Sha'ab	Sanaa		
Qadisiya	Sanaa	Ali Muhesen	25 000
Al-Zohra	Sanaa		
Al-Tilal	Aden	Aden Stadium	22 000
Rawda	Aden		
-Nasir	Aden		
Shula	Aden		
Minaa	Aden		
Al-Hilal	Hudayda		
Al-Ahli	Hudayda		
Shabab Al-Jeel	Hudayda		
Al-Sha'ab	Ibb		
Shaab	Ibb		
Shabab Al-Khudus	Ibb		
Amal Ibb	Ibb		
Al-Sha'ab Hadramut	Mukalla	Baradem Mukalla	20 000
Mukalla	Mukalla		
Tadamun	Shabwa		
Raya	Shabwa		
Al-Saqr	Taaz		
Taliya	Taaz		
Rasheed	Taaz		
Hassan	Abya	Al-ShoHada'a Stadium	20 000
Shabab	Abya		
Ittihad	Saada		

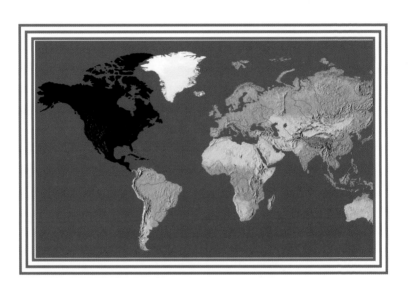

CONCACAF

ANGUILLA

ANGUILLA FOOTBALL ASSOC.
PB 608, The Valley
TEL 1 264/497 2595 FAX /497 2326
WEB www.concacaf.com

REFERENCE
Official name
Dependent Territory of Anguilla

Claimed	1650
Capital	The Valley
Population	10,300
Total area	37 sq Mi, 96 sq Km
Time zone	GMT -4
Density	126 per sq Km
Languages	English
Literacy rate	80%
Currency	East Caribbean $
Economy	Services 65%
Religions	Protestant, Christian
Ethnic Mix	Black African 85%

GEOGRAPHY
Elevation
lowest point: Caribbean Sea 0 m
highest point: Crocus Hill 65 m
Geography Note
the most northerly of the Leeward Islands in the Lesser Antilles
Natural Resources
Salt, fish, lobster
Climate
Tropical; moderated by northeast trade winds
Anguillan Food
spiny lobster bisque

WORLD CUP

1930	Did not qualify
1934	Did not qualify
1938	Did not qualify
1950	Did not qualify
1954	Did not qualify
1958	Did not qualify
1962	Did not qualify
1966	Did not qualify
1970	Did not qualify
1974	Did not qualify
1978	Did not qualify
1982	Did not qualify
1986	Did not qualify
1990	Did not qualify
1994	Did not qualify
1998	Did not qualify
2002	Did not qualify

COUNTRY LEAGUE CHAMPIONS

2004	Spartans Inter
2003	Spartans Inter
2002	Roaring Lions
2001	Roaring Lions
2000	Not held
1999	Attackers
1998	CC Spartans
1997	Not Known
1996	Not Known
1995	Not Known
Women's League Champio	
2004	Lil' Super Stars
2003	Shinning Stars
2002	Not Known
2001	Not Known

NATIONAL TEAM COLORS

WORLD PICTURES OF SOCCER

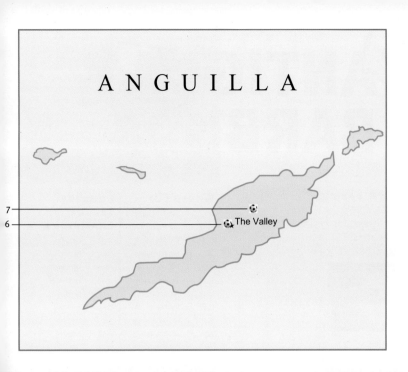

ANGUILLA

7
6 ⚽ The Valley

PREMIERE LEAGUE CLUBS	CITY	STADIUM	CAPACITY
-Spartans International	The valley		
-A.L.H.C.S Spartans	The Valley		
-Attackers FC	The Valley-North		
-Caribeans All-Stars	The Valley-South		
-Dolphins FC	The Valley-South		
-J.T Stars	The Valley-South		
-Roaring Lions FC	Stoney Ground		

ANTIGUA & BARBUDA

ANTIGUA & BARBUDA FOOTBALL ASSOCIATION
Newgate Street, PB 773, St John's
TEL 1 268/727 8869
WEB www.concacaf.com

REFERENCE
Official name
Antigua & Barbuda

Date of formation	1981
Capital	St. John's
Population	66,422
Total area	170 sq Mi, 440 sq Km
Time zone	GMT -4
Density	391 per sq Mi, 146 per sq Km
Languages	English, English Creole
Literacy rate	96%
Currency	E. Caribbean $
Economy	Services 67%
Religions	Anglican 44%, Protestant 42%
Ethnic Mix	African 95%

GEOGRAPHY
Elevation
lowest point: Caribbean Sea 0 m
highest point: Boggy Peak 402 m
Geography Note
Antigua has a deeply indented shoreline with many natural harbors and beaches; Barbuda has a very large western harbor
Natural Resources
pleasant climate fosters tourism
Climate
tropical marine; little seasonal temperature variation
Barbuda & Antigua Food
mango chow/banana bread

WORLD CUP

1930	Did not qualify
1934	Did not qualify
1938	Did not qualify
1950	Did not qualify
1954	Did not qualify
1958	Did not qualify
1962	Did not qualify
1966	Did not qualify
1970	Did not qualify
1974	Did not qualify
1978	Did not qualify
1982	Did not qualify
1986	Did not qualify
1990	Did not qualify
1994	Did not qualify
1998	Did not qualify
2002	Did not qualify

COUNTRY LEAGUE CHAMPIONS

2005	Bassa FC
2004	Bassa FC
2003	Parham FC
2002	Parham FC
2001	Empire
2000	Empire
1999	Empire
1998	Empire
1997	English Harbour
1996	English Harbour

Women's League Champi

2005	Otto Tigress
2004	Otto Tigress
2003	Otto Tigress
2002	Otto Tigress

NATIONAL TEAM COLORS

WORLD PICTURES OF SOCCER

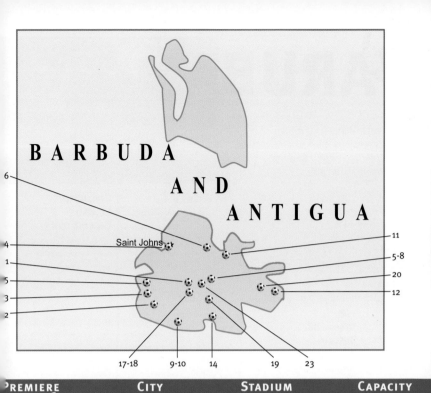

BARBUDA

AND

ANTIGUA

Saint Johns

PREMIERE LEAGUE CLUBS	CITY	STADIUM	CAPACITY
-Hoppers FC	Saint Johns		
-Villa Lions	Saint Johns		
-Lion Hill Spliff	Saint johns		
-Future Stars U-17 selection	St.Johns		
-Bassa FC	All Saints Village		
-Attackers FC	All Saints Village		
-West End Pressers	All Saints Village		
-Youth Vibes	All saints Village		
-Old Road FC	Old Road Village		
-Swamp FC	Old Road Village		
-Parham FC	Parham Town		
-Empire FC	Grays		
-SAP FC	Bolans Village		
-English Harbour FC	English Harbour		
-Jennings United	Jennings		
-Bullets FC	Pigotts		
-FreemansVille FC	Freemans		
-Cologne FC	Freemans		
-Glanvilles FC	Glanvilles		
-Liberta FC	Liberta		
-New Edition	Sea View Farm		
-Buckleys FC	Buckleys		
-John Hughes	John Hughes		

 # ARUBA

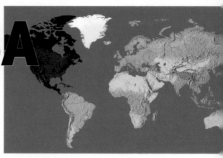

ARUBAANSE VOETBAL BOND
Ferguson Street Z/N, PB 376, Oranjestad
TEL 297/829 550   FAX /829 550
WEB www.avbaruba.aw

REFERENCE
Official name
    Aruba (Autonomous part of Holland)

Claimed	1643
Capital	Oranjestad
Population	88,000
Total area	75 sq Mi, 194 sq Km
Time zone	GMT-4
Density	355 per sq Km
Languages	Dutch, English
Literacy rate	95%
Currency	Arubin Florin
Economy	tourism, financial services
Religions	Protestant
Ethnic Mix	European 90%

GEOGRAPHY
Elevation
lowest point: Caribbean Sea 0 m
highest point: Mount Jamanota 188 m
Geography Note
a flat, riverless island renowned for its white
sand beaches; its tropical climate is
moderated by constant trade winds from the
Atlantic Ocean
Natural Resources
white sandy beaches
Climate
tropical marine; little seasonal temperature
variation
Aruban Food
papaya berde/webo yena/scabechi

WORLD CUP

1930	Did not qualify
1934	Did not qualify
1938	Did not qualify
1950	Did not qualify
1954	Did not qualify
1958	Did not qualify
1962	Did not qualify
1966	Did not qualify
1970	Did not qualify
1974	Did not qualify
1978	Did not qualify
1982	Did not qualify
1986	Did not qualify
1990	Did not qualify
1994	Did not qualify
1998	Did not qualify
2002	Did notqualify

COUNTRY LEAGUE CHAMPIONS

2004	Not Known
2003	Nacional
2002	RCA
2001	Dep. Nacional
2000	Dep. Nacional
1999	SV Estrella
1998	SV Estrella
1997	SV Riverplate
1996	SV Estrella

Women's League Champion

2004	Not Known
2003	Juventud Tanki
2002	Savaneta Stars
2001	SV Dakota
2000	Not Known

NATIONAL TEAM COLORS

WORLD PICTURES OF SOCCER

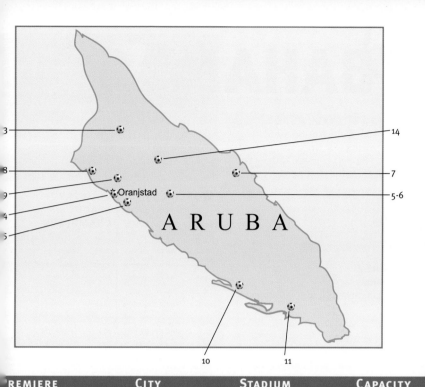

PREMIERE LEAGUE CLUBS	CITY	STADIUM	CAPACITY
Estrella Oranjstad	Oranjstad	Trinidad Stadium	10 000
RCA Solito	Oranjstad	Trinidad Stadium	10 000
SV Dakota	Oranjstad	Trinidad Stadium	10 000
SV Riverplate Modiki	Oranjstad	Trinidad Stadium	10 000
SV Estrella	Santa Cruz		
Brittania	Santa Cruz		
SV Independiente Caravel	Angochi		
Deportivo Nacional	Ponton		
Juventud	Tanki Leender		
Racing Club Savaneta	Savaneta		
Jong San Nicolas	San Nicolas		
Jong Aruba	Noord		
CD Caravel	Noord		
Caiquetio	Paradera		
CD Rooi Afo	Rooi Afo		

# BAHAMAS

Bahamas Football Assoc.

Plaza on the Way, West Bay St.
PB N-8434 Nassau, NP
TEL 1-242/829 550   FAX /820 550
www.bahamasfootballassoc.com

REFERENCE

Official name
The Commonwealth of the Bahamas

Date of formation	1973
Capital	Nassau
Population	307,000
Total area	3865 sq Mi, 10,010 sq Km
Time zone	GMT -5
Density	79 per sq Mi, 20 per sq Km
Languages	English, Engish Creole
Literacy rate	98%
Currency	Bahamian $
Economy	tourism 40%
Religions	Baptist 32%, Anglican 20%
Ethnic Mix	Black African 85%

GEOGRAPHY

Elevation
lowest point: Atlantic Ocean 0 m
highest point: Mount Alvernia, on Cat Island
63 m

Geography Note
strategic location adjacent to US and Cuba;
extensive island chain of which 30 are
inhabited

Natural Resources
salt, aragonite, timber, arable land

Climate
Tropical marine; moderated by warm waters
of Gulf Stream

Bahamian Food
carrot walnut salad
seafood chowder

WORLD CUP		COUNTRY LEAGUE CHAMPIONS	
1930	Did not qualify		
1934	Did not qualify		
1938	Did not qualify	2004	Final Not Played
1950	Did not qualify	2003	Bears FC
1954	Did not qualify	2002	Abacom United
1958	Did not qualify	2001	Cavalier FC
1962	Did not qualify	2000	Abacom United
1966	Did not qualify	1999	Cavalier FC
1970	Did not qualify	1998	Cavalier FC
1974	Did not qualify	1997	Cavalier FC
1978	Did not qualify	1996	Not Known
1982	Did not qualify	**Women's League Champion**	
1986	Did not qualify	2004	Predators
1990	Did not qualify	2003	Predators
1994	Did not qualify	2002	Predators
1998	Did not qualify	2001	Predators
2002	Did not qualify	2000	Predators

NATIONAL TEAM COLORS

WORLD PICTURES OF SOCCER

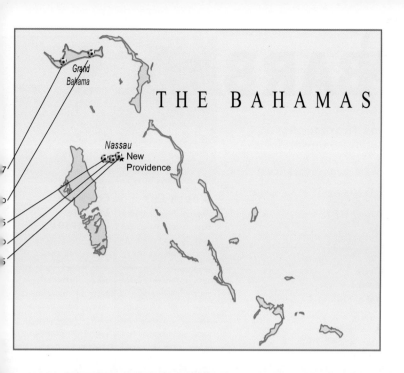

THE BAHAMAS

Grand Bahama

Nassau
New Providence

PREMIERE LEAGUE CLUBS	CITY	STADIUM	CAPACITY
Beck's Bear	New Providence		
Caledonia FC	New Providence		
Cavalier FC	New Providence		
Coca Cola FC	New Providence		
Racing Club Ath.	New Providence		
Strikers FC	New Providence		
Team Toyota	New Providence		
United FC	New Providence		
Rock & Roll FC	New Providence		
Dynamos	New Providence		
Florentina	New Providence		
Grizzlies FC	New Providence		
Juventus FC	New Providence		
Kickers FC	New Providence		
Rulado FC	New Providence		
Freeport FC	Grand Bahama		
Jamaicans Shrimp FC	Grand Baha.		
Sport Tigers	Grand Bahama		
Abacom United	Grand Bahama		
Brita Red Bulls	Grand Bahama		

BARBADOS

BARBADOS FOOTBALL ASSOC
PB 1362 Bridgetown-West Indies
TEL 1 246/228 1707 FAX /228 6484
WEB www.barbadossoccer.com

REFERENCE
Official name
　Barbados
Date of formation 1966
Capital Bridgetown
Population 270,000
Total area 169 sq Mi, 430 sq Km
Time zone GMT -4
Density 1598 per sq Mi, 602 per sq Km
Languages English, English Creole
Literacy rate 97%
Currency Barbados $
Economy services 76%
Religions Anglican 40%, Pentecostal 8%, Methodist 7%
Ethnic Mix Black African 90%

GEOGRAPHY
Elevation
lowest point: Atlantic Ocean 0 m
highest point: Mount Hillaby 336 m
Geography Note
Easternmost Caribbean island
Natural Resources
salt, aragonite, timber, arable land
Climate
Tropical marine; moderated by warm waters of Gulf Stream
Barbados Food
salt fish cakes

WORLD CUP

1930	Did not qualify
1934	Did not qualify
1938	Did not qualify
1950	Did not qualify
1954	Did not qualify
1958	Did not qualify
1962	Did not qualify
1966	Did not qualify
1970	Did not qualify
1974	Did not qualify
1978	Did not qualify
1982	Did not qualify
1986	Did not qualify
1990	Did not qualify
1994	Did not qualify
1998	Did not qualify
2002	Did not qualify

COUNTRY LEAGUE CHAMPIONS

2004	Notre Dame
2003	Paradise
2002	Notre Dame SC
2001	Paradise
2000	Notra Dame SC
1999	Notre Dame SC
1998	Notre Dame SC
1997	Notre Dame SC
1996	Paradise

Women's League Champio

2004	Not Known
2003	Not Known
2002	Not Known
2001	Not Known
2000	Not Known

NATIONAL TEAM COLORS

WORLD PICTURES OF SOCCER

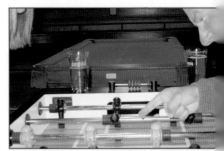

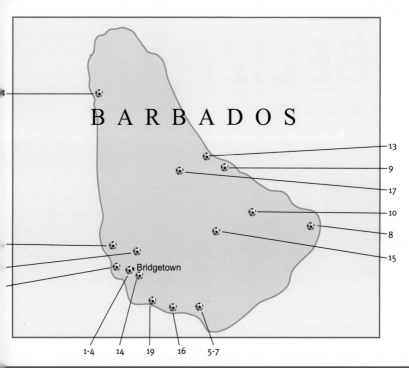

B A R B A D O S

Bridgetown

13
9
17
10
8
15

1-4   14   19   16   5-7

PREMIERE LEAGUE CLUBS	CITY	STADIUM	CAPACITY
Weymouth Wales FC	Bridgetown	National Stadium Bristol	5 000
Everton FC	Bridgetown	National Stadium Bristol	5 000
Spartan FC	Bridgetown	National Stadium Bristol	5 000
Barbados Defence Force	Bridgetown	National Stadium Bristol	5 000
Notre dame SC	Christchurch		
Paradise SC	Christchurch		
Pride of Gall Hill	Christchurch		
Ivy River	River		
Saint John's Sonnets	Saint johns		
Melverton FC	Melverton		
Hainesville United	Hainesville		
Pinelands FC	Pinelands		
Bathsehba	Bathsehba		
Brittons Hill United	Brittons Hill		
Ellerton United	Ellerton		
Silver Sands FC	Silver Hill		
Welchman Rovers	Welchman Hall Gully		
Speightstown	Speightstown		
Hasting United	Hastings		
Haggat Hall	Haggat Hall		

BELIZE

BELIZE NATIONAL ASSOC.
11 Simon Lamb Street, PB
1742, Belize city
TEL 501 2/36 563   FAX /36 564
WEB www.belizefootball.cjb.net

REFERENCE
Official name
  Belize
Date of formation   1981
Capital   Belmopan
Population   200,000
Total area   8803 sq Mi, 22,800 sq Km
Time zone   GMT -6
Density   23 per sq Mi, 10 per sq Km
Languages   English, English Creole, Spanish, Maya, Garifuna
Literacy rate   92%
Currency   Taka
Economy   services 60, agriculture 30%
Religions   Catholic 62%, Anglican 12%
Ethnic Mix   Mestizo 44%, Creole 30%, Mayan 11%, Garifuna 7%

GEOGRAPHY
Elevation
lowest point: Caribbean Sea 0 m
highest poin: Victoria Peak 1,160 m
Geography Note
Only country in Central America without a coastline on the North Pacific Ocean
Natural Resources
Arable land potential, timber, fish, hydropower
Climate
Tropical; very hot and humid; rainy season (May to November); dry season (February to May)
Belizean Food
Escabeche/Breadfruit Rolls

WORLD CUP		COUNTRY LEAGUE CHAMPIONS	
1930	Did not qualify		
1934	Did not qualify		
1938	Did not qualify	2004	Sagitun
1950	Did not qualify	2003	Kulture Yebra
1954	Did not qualify	2002	Kulture Yabra
1958	Did not qualify	2001	Kulture Yabra
1962	Did not qualify	2000	Sagitun
1966	Did not qualify	1999	Juventus
1970	Did not qualify	1998	Juventus
1974	Did not qualify	1997	Juventus
1978	Did not qualify	1996	Juventus
1982	Did not qualify	**Women's League Champic**	
1986	Did not qualify	2004	Millenium Girls
1990	Did not qualify	2003	Millenium Girls
1994	Did not qualify	2002	La Costena
1998	Did not qualify	2001	Northern Stars
2002	Did not qualify	2000	Not Known

NATIONAL TEAM COLORS

WORLD PICTURES OF SOCCER

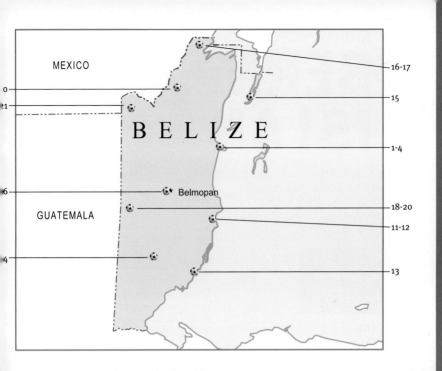

PREMIERE LEAGUE CLUBS	CITY	STADIUM	CAPACITY
-Kultura Yabra	Belize City	MCC Ground	2 500
-Acros Bombers	Belize city	MCC Ground	2 500
-Hattieville 2000 FC	Belize City	MCC Ground	2 500
-Metrostars FC	Belize City	MCC Ground	2 500
-Belmopan Bandits	Belmopan	Isidoro Beaton Stadium	1 000
-Capital United	Belmopan	Isidora Beaton Stadium	1 000
-Louisiana Area FC	Orange Walk	People's Stadium	3 000
-Lazio Jumex FC	Orange Walk	People's Stadium	3 000
Juventus Stars FC	Orange Walk	People's stadium	3 000
-Costena FC	Orange Walk	People's Stadium	3 000
-Griga Tropical United	Dangriga	Carl Ramos Ground	1 000
-New Erei FC	Dangriga		
-Sagitun FC	Mango Creek	M.Ashcroft Stadium	1 000
-Cosmos FC	Toledo		
-San Pedro Dolphins FC	San Pedro	Dolphins Stadium	1 000
-Corozal la Victoria FC	Corozal	Santiago Ricalde	1 000
-San Joaquin FC	Corozal	Santiago Ricalde	1 000
-Leslie's Verdes	Cayo San Ignacio	Norman Broaster	2 000
-Highlanders FC	Cayo San Ignacio	Norman Broaster	2 000
-Acros Real Verdes FC	Cayo San Ign.	Norman Broaster	
-Juventud Benquena	Benque Viejo	Juventud Estadio	2 000

BERMUDA ISLANDS

THE BERMUDA FOOTBALL ASSOC.
48 Cedar Ave., Hamilton HM 12
TEL 1 441/295 2199   FAX /295 0773
WEB www.concacaf.com

REFERENCE
Official name
Crown Colony of Bermuda

Claimed	1612
Population	60,144
Capital	Hamilton
Total area	20 sq Mi, 53 sq Km
Time zone	GMT -4
Density	1,249 per sq Km
Languages	English
Literacy rate	95%
Currency	Bermudian $
Economy	clerical 25%, services 29%, Laborers 21%
Religions	Anglican
Ethnic Mix	Black african 80%, European 20%

GEOGRAPHY
Elevation
lowest point: Atlantic Ocean 0 m
highest poin: Town Hill 76 m
Geography Note
Consists of about 138 coral islands and islets
with ample rainfall, but no rivers or freshwater
lakes; some land, reclaimed and otherwise,
was leased by US Government from 1941 to
1995
Natural Resources
subtropical; mild, humid; gales, strong winds
common in winter
Climate
Pleasant climate fostering tourism
Bermudan Food
Bermuda fish chowder
cassava pie/cod fish cake

WORLD CUP		COUNTRY LEAGUE CHAMPIONS	
1930	Did not qualify		
1934	Did not qualify		
1938	Did not qualify	2004	Dandy Town
1950	Did not qualify	2003	North Village Com.
1954	Did not qualify	2002	North Village Com.
1958	Did not qualify	2001	DandyTown Hornets
1962	Did not qualify	2000	PHC Zebras
1966	Did not qualify	1999	Vasco da Gama FC
1970	Did not qualify	1998	Vasco da Game FC
1974	Did not qualify	1997	Devonshire Colts
1978	Did not qualify	1996	Vasco da Gama FC
1982	Did not qualify	**Women's League Champio**	
1986	Did not qualify	2005	PCH Ladies
1990	Did not qualify	2004	PCH Ladies
1994	Did not qualify	2003	Rude Girls FC
1998	Did not qualify	2002	Rude Girls FC
2002	Did not qualify	2001	Rude Girls FC

NATIONAL TEAM COLORS

WORLD PICTURES OF SOCCER

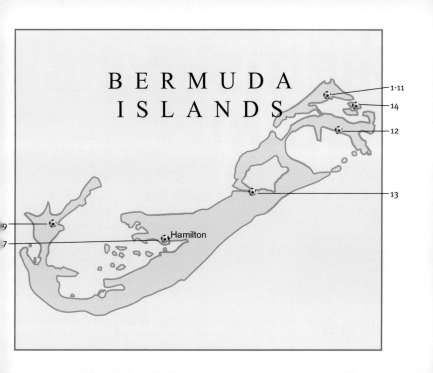

PREMIERE LEAGUE CLUBS	CITY	STADIUM	CAPACITY
North Village	Hamilton	PHC Stadium	1 000
Hamilton Parish	Hamilton	PHC Stadium	1 000
Boulevard Blazers	Hamilton	PHC Stadium	1 000
Southampton rangers	Hamilton	PCH Stadium1 000	
Vasco da Gama	Hamilton	St John's Field	1 000
Pembroke Hamilton Club	Hamilton	PHC Stadium	1 000
Pembroke Hamilton Zebras	Hamilton	PHC Stadium	1 000
Somerset Eagles	Somerset Village	White Hill Stadium	1 000
Somerset CC Trojans	Somerset Vill.	White Hill Stadium	1 000
-St George Colts	Saint George		
St George A.S	Saint George		
-St David's FC	Saint David's		
-Flatts FC	Flatts Village		
-Paget FC	Paget		

BRITISH VIRGIN ISLANDS

THE BRITISH VIRGIN ISLANDSSoccer FA
PO Box 4269 ,Tortola, BVI
TEL 284/494 5655 FAX /494 8968
WEB www.concacaf.com

REFERENCE
British Virgin Islands

Claimed	
Population	1672
Capital	Road Town
Total area	17,896
Time zone	59 sq Mi, 259 sq Km
Density	GMT --4
Languages	78 Sq Km
Literacy rate	English, English Creole
Currency	92%
Economy	U.S $
	Middle
Religions	Anglican, Protestant
Ethnic Mix	European, Black African

WORLD CUP		COUNTRY LEAGUE CHAMPIONS	
1930	Did not qualify		
1934	Did not qualify		
1938	Did not qualify	2004	Valencia FC
1950	Did not qualify	2003	Not Known
1954	Did not qualify	2002	HBA Panthers
1958	Did not qualify	2001	Future Stars United
1962	Did not qualify	2000	Hba Panthers
1966	Did not qualify	1999	Hba Panthers
1970	Did not qualify	1998	Veterans
1974	Did not qualify	1997	BDO B. Stingers
1978	Did not qualify	1996	Black Lions
1982	Did not qualify	**Women's League Champ**	
1986	Did not qualify	2004	Not Known
1990	Did not qualify	2003	HBA Panthers
1994	Did not qualify	2002	BVI School
1998	Did not qualify	2001	Not Known
2002	Did not qualify	2000	Not Known

NATIONAL TEAM COLORS

GEOGRAPHY
Elevation
lowest point:
Caribbean Sea o m
highest point:
Mount Sage 521 m
Geography Note
Strong ties to nearby US Virgin Islands and
Puerto Rico
Natural Resources
Climate
Subtropical; humid; temperatures moderat-
ed by trade winds
British Virgin Islands Food
island fish spice/jerk cooking

WORLD PICTURES OF SOCCER

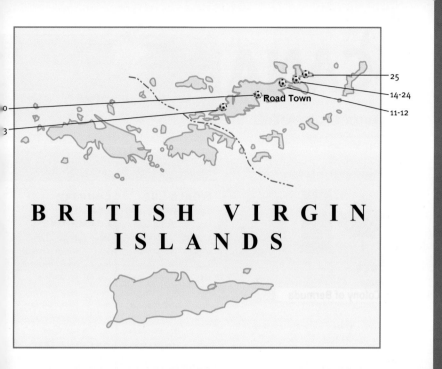

BRITISH VIRGIN ISLANDS

PREMIERE LEAGUE CLUBS	CITY	STADIUM	CAPACITY
Future Stars United	Roadtown		
Veterans	Roadtown		
Valencia United	Roadtown		
Combined Stars	Roadtown		
VP Bank Strikers	Roadtown		
HLSCC Stingrays	Roadtown		
Virgin Gorda United	The Valley		
HBA Panthers	East End		
East End Eagles	East End		
Jams Rock I			
Jams Rock II			
BDO BinderStingers	Roadtown		
Police	Roadtown		
Eagles FC	West End		
VG Kickers United			
LSL Strickers			
SA Bitter End	North Sound		
Willful Skillful			
Hazards			
Beverly Hills Strikers			
Spice United			
H&H Strikers			
Bitter End			
Codan Red Devils			
HallejujahStrikers			

# CANADA
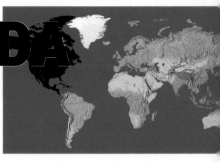

THE CANADIAN SOCCER ASSOC.
Place Soccer Canada, 237 Metcalfe St
Ottawa, ONT K2 1R2
TEL 1 613/237 7678
WEB www.soccercanada.com

REFERENCE
Official name
  Canada
Date of
formation   1867
Capital   Ottawa
Population   31.1 Million
Total area   3,560,216 sq Mi
        9,220,970 sq Km
Time zone   GMT-3.5/9
Density   9 per sq Mi, 3 per sq Km
Languages   English, French, Chinese,
        Inuktitut
Literacy rate   99%
Currency   Canadian $
Economy   Services 78%
Religions   Catholic 47%, Protestant 41%
Ethnic Mix   British Origin 44%, French
        Origin 25%, Indian/Inuit 4%

GEOGRAPHY
Elevation
lowest point: Atlantic Ocean 0 m
highest point: Mount Logan 5,959 m
Geography Note
second-largest country in world (after
Russia); strategic location between Russia
and US via north polar route
Natural Resources
Iron ore, nickel, zinc, copper, gold, lead,
molybdenum, potash, silver, fish, timber,
wildlife, coal, petroleum, natural gas,
hydropower
Climate
Varies from temperate in south to subarctic
and arctic in north
Canadian Food
orangepumpkin soup

WORLD CUP

1930	Did not qualify
1934	Did not qualify
1938	Did not qualify
1950	Did not qualify
1954	Did not qualify
1958	Did not qualify
1962	Did not qualify
1966	Did not qualify
1970	Did not qualify
1974	Did not qualify
1978	Did not qualify
1982	Did not qualify
1986	Did not qualify
1990	Did not qualify
1994	Did not qualify
1998	Did not qualify
2002	Did not qualify

COUNTRY LEAGUE CHAMPIONS

2004	Toronto Croatia
2003	Brampton Hitmen
2002	Ottawa Wizards
2001	St Catherine
2000	Toronto Croatia
1999	Toronto Olymp.
1998	St Catherine
1997	Not Played
1996	Not Played

Women's League Champ

2004	Edmonton Victoria
2003	Athens United
2002	Oakville Storm
2001	Burnaby Can.
2000	Edmonton Angels

NATIONAL TEAM COLORS

WORLD PICTURES OF SOCCER

PREMIERE LEAGUE CLUBS	CITY	STADIUM	CAPACITY
Ottawa Wizards	Ottawa-Ontario	OZ Optic Stadium	5 000
Toronto Lynx	Toronto-Ontario	Centennial Stadium	3 500
Toronto Croatia	Toronto-Ontario	Centennial Stadium	3 500
Metro Lions	Toronto-Ontario	Birchmount Stadium	6 000
Toronto Supra	Toronto-Ontario	Lamport Stadium	9 000
North York Astros	North York-Ontario	Esther Shiner Stadium	3 000
Chill FC	Thunder Bay-Ontario	Fort William Stadium	3 500
Western Ontario	London-Ontario	JW Little Stadium	7 500
London City SC	London-Ontario	JW Little Stadium	7 500
St.Catherines Wolves	St.Cat-Ontari	Club Roma	4 600
Vaughan Sun Devils	Mount.grove-O	Soccer Center	5 000
Brampton Hitmen	Brampton-Ont.	Victoria Park	5 000
Glen Shields Sun Devils	Thornhill-O	Dufferin Center Stadium	3 900
Hamilton Thunder	Hamilton-Ontario	Brian Timmis Stadium	5 000
Edmonton Aviators	Edmonton-Alber.	Commonwealth Stadium	60 217
Calgary Storm	Calgary-Alberta	Foothills Park	4 000
Alberta Golden Bears	Edmonton-Al.	Foote Field	3 000
Alberta Pandas	Edmonton-Alberta	Foote Field	3 000
Vancouver Whitecaps	Vancouver-BC	Swangard Stadium	7 100
UBC Thunderbirds	Vancouver-BC	Thunderbird Stadium	3 200
Victoria United	Victoria-BC	Royal Athletic Park	9 247
Victoria Vikes	Victoria-BC	Centennial Stadium	5 000
Abbotsford Rangers	Abbotsford-BC	Rotary Stadium	4 200
Okanagan Predators	Kelowna-BC	Apple Bowl	5 700
Memorial U.Seahawks	St. John's-NF	Memorial U. Field	2 000
Feildians FC	St.John's-NF	Feildian Grounds	1 000
Guards FC	St.John's-NF	Ayre Athletic Grounds	1 000
DalhousieTigers	Halifax-NovaScotia	F.B.W Memorial Field	2 000
Acadia Axemen	Wolfville-NovaS.	Raymond Field	3 000

CAYMAN ISLANDS

CAYMAN ISLANDS FOOTBALL

AssociationPB178GT,TrumanBoddenSpt.
cplx,Olympic way off walkers,Grand
Cayman TEL1345/9495775
WEBwww.caymanfootball.com

REFERENCE

Official name
Cayman Islands
(Crown Dependency Territory)

Date of formation	1670
Capital	Georgetown
Population	35,000
Total area	100 sq Mi, 259sq Km
Time zone	GMT -5
Density	151 Sq Km
Languages	English, English Creole
Literacy rate	95%
Currency	Caymanian $
Economy	Services 20%,Clerical
Religions	20%,Finance & Investment 10%
Ethnic Mix	Anglican,Catholic

GEOGRAPHY

Elevation
lowest point: Caribbean Sea 0 m
highest point: The Bluff 43 m
Geography Note
important location between Cuba and
Central America
Natural Resources
Fish, climate and beaches that foster
tourism
Climate
Tropical marine; warm, rainy summers (May
to October) and cool, relatively dry winters
(November to April)
Cayman Islands Food
lobsters fritters/smoked Cayman tuna

WORLD CUP

1930	Did not qualify
1934	Did not qualify
1938	Did not qualify
1950	Did not qualify
1954	Did not qualify
1958	Did not qualify
1962	Did not qualify
1966	Did not qualify
1970	Did not qualify
1974	Did not qualify
1978	Did not qualify
1982	Did not qualify
1986	Did not qualify
1990	Did not qualify
1994	Did not qualify
1998	Did not qualify
2002	Did not qualify

COUNTRY LEAGUE CHAMPIONS

2004	Latinos FC
2003	Scholars Inter
2002	Georgetown SC
2001	Scholars Inter
2000	Western Union FC
1999	Georgetown SC
1998	Scholars Inter
1997	Georgetown SC
1996	Not Known

Women's League Champ

2004	SC Inter
2003	GTSC
2002	Not Known
2001	SC Inter
2000	SC Inter

NATIONAL TEAM COLORS

WORLD PICTURES OF SOCCER

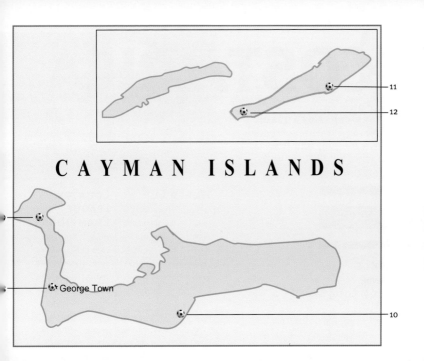

CAYMAN ISLANDS

REMIERE EAGUE CLUBS	CITY	STADIUM	CAPACITY
Western Union FC	Georgetown		
Naya FC	Georgetown		
Georgetown FC	Georgetown		
FC International	Georgetown		
Sunset FC	Georgetown		
Future FC	Georgetown		
Academy FC	Georgetown		
Links FC	Georgetown		
Scholars International FC	West Bay		
-Bodden Town FC	Bodden Town		
Cayman Brac	Cayman Brac Island		
-West End FC	West End		

COSTA RICA

FED.COSTARRICENSE DE FUTBOL
Costado Norte Estatua,Cortes en
la Sabana 670-1000 San Jose
TEL 506/222 154 FAX /2552674
www.fedefutbol.com

REFERENCE
Official name
Republic of Costa Rica
Date of formation 1821
Capital San Jose
Population 4 Million
Total area 19,714 sq Mi, 51,060 sq Km
Time zone GMT -6
Density 187 per sq Mi, 71 per sq Km
Languages Spanish, English Creole, Bribri, Cabecar
Literacy rate 94%
Currency Colon
Economy Services 57%, Agriculture 25%
Religions Catholic 76%
Ethnic Mix Mestizo & European 96%, Black 2%

GEOGRAPHY
Elevation
lowest point: Pacific Ocean 0 m
highest point: Cerro Chirripo 3,810 m
Geography Note
four volcanoes, two of them active, rise near
the capital of San Jose in the center of the
country; one of the volcanoes, Irazu, erupted
destructively in 1963-65
Natural Resources
Hydropower
Climate
tropical and subtropical; dry season
(December to April); rainy season (May to
November)
Costa Rican Food
hearts of palm salad/Costa Rican tilapia

WORLD CUP		COUNTRY LEAGUE CHAMPIONS	
1930	Did not qualify		
1934	Did not qualify		
1938	Did not qualify	2004	Saprissa
1950	Did not qualify	2003	Alajuelense
1954	Did not qualify	2002	Alajuelense
1958	Did not qualify	2001	Alajuelense
1962	Did not qualify	2000	Alajuelense
1966	Did not qualify	1999	Saprissa
1970	Did not qualify	1998	Saprissa
1974	Did not qualify	1997	Alajuelense
1978	Did not qualify	1996	Alajuelense
1982	Did not qualify	**Women's League Champ**	
1986	Did not qualify	2005	UCEN Alajuela
1990	Sd round exit	2004	UCEN Alajuela
1994	Did not qualify	2003	AD Desamporados
1998	Did not qualify	2002	AD Desamporados
2002	Sd round exit	2001	AD Desamporados

NATIONAL TEAM COLORS

WORLD PICTURES OF SOCCER

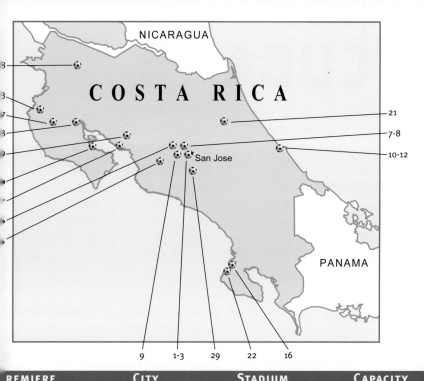

PREMIERE LEAGUE CLUBS	CITY	STADIUM	CAPACITY
Deportivo Saprissa	San Jose	Ricardo Saprissa Ayma	30 000
CS Libertad	San Jos		
Universidad Costa Rica	San Jose		
CD Alajuense	Alajuela	Alejandro Morera Soto	15 000
El Roble	Alajuela		
AD Carmelita	Alajuela	Edgardo Eli.PerezConejo	7 500
CS Herediano	Heredia	Eladio Rozabal Cordero	15 000
AD Santa Barbara	Heredia	C. Alvarado Villa Lobos	10 000
Ciudad Colon	Santa Ana		
AD Limonense	Limon	Estadio Juan Goban	10 000
Bananito	Limon		
Cahuita	Limon		
CS Catagines	Cartagena	Jose Rafael Fello Meza	10 000
ADM Perez Zeledon	Perez	Estadio Perez Zeledon	9 500
Generalena	Perez		
SL Municipal de Osa	Ciudad Cortez	Municipal Ciudad Cortez	10 000
Santacrucena	Santa Cruz		
Municipal Liberia	Guanacaste	Edg. Baltodano Briceno	9 700
AD Ramonenese	San Ramon		
Nandayurena	Nandayure		
Santos de Guapiles FC	Guapiles	Estadio Ebal Rodriguez	8 000
CS Uruguay	Coronado		
Muncpl.Punta Arenas	Punta Arenas		
Municipal Corredores	Punta Arenas		
Real Esparza	Punta Arenas		
Cobano	Punta Arenas		
Isla de Venado	Punta Arenas		
AD Belemita	Belen		
Goicochea	San Miguel		

CUBA

FED. CUBANA DE FUTBOL
Calle 13#601, Esq C Vedalo
La Habana, ZP4
TEL 537/40 35 81   FAX /40 909 37
WEB www.concacaf.com

REFERENCE
Official name
Republic of Cuba

Date of formation 1902
Capital Havana
Population 11.2 Million
Total area 42,803 sq Mi, 110,860 sq Km
Time zone GMT - 5
Density 262 per sq Mi, 100 per sq Km
Languages Spanish, English
Literacy rate 96%
Currency Cuban Peso
Economy services 48%, industry 29%, Agriculture 23%
Religions Catholic, Buddhist
Ethnic Mix White 66%, European African 22%

GEOGRAPHY
Elevation
lowest point: Caribbean Sea 0 m
highest point: Pico Turquino 2,005 m
Geography Note
largest country in Caribbean and western-most island of the Greater Antilles
Natural Resources
cobalt, nickel, iron ore, copper, manganese, salt, timber, silica, petroleum, arable land
Climate
tropical; moderated by trade winds; dry season (November to April); rainy season (May to October)
Cuban Food
Cuban lamb shanks/Cuban pesca limon

WORLD CUP		COUNTRY LEAGUE CHAMPIONS	
1930	Did not qualify		
1934	Did not qualify		
1938	Did not qualify	2004	FC Villa Clara
1950	Did not qualify	2003	FC Villa Clara
1954	Did not qualify	2002	Ciego De Avila
1958	Did not qualify	2001	Ciudad de la Habana
1962	Did not qualify	2000	FC Pinar del Rio
1966	Did not qualify	1999	Not Known
1970	Did not qualify	1998	Ciudad de la Haban
1974	Did not qualify	1997	FC Villa Clara
1978	Did not qualify	1996	FC Villa Clara
1982	Did not qualify	**Women's League Cham**	
1986	Did not qualify	2004	Ciudad de la Habana
1990	Did not qualify	2003	Ciudad de la Habana
1994	Did not qualify	2002	Not Known
1998	Did not qualify	2001	Ciudad de la Habana
2002	Did not qualify	2000	Not Known

NATIONAL TEAM COLORS

WORLD PICTURES OF SOCCER

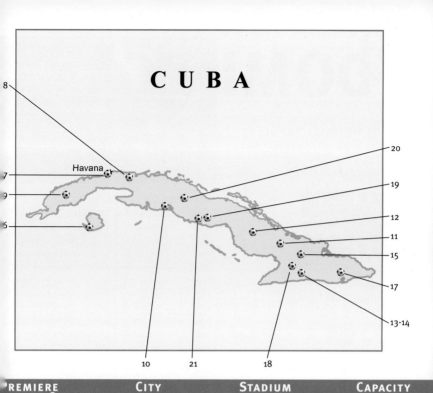

C U B A

Havana

PREMIERE LEAGUE CLUBS	CITY	STADIUM	CAPACITY
FC Real Liberia	La Habana		
Juventud Asturiana	La Habana		
Ciudad de La Habana	La Habana	Estadio Pedro Marrero	8 000
Hispano America	La Habana		
Industriales	La Habana	Estadio Campo Armada	4 000
La Habana FC	La Habana		
Provincia la Habana	La Habana	Terreno de Guanajay	1 000
Matanzas	Matanzas	Terreno de Colon	1 000
Pinar del Rio	Pinar del Rio	Estadio La Bombonera	5 000
-Cienfuegos	Cienfuegos		
-Las Tunas	Las Tunas	Esta.Ovidio Torres Manati	2 500
-Camaguey	Camaguey	Terreno de Florida	1 000
-Santiago de Cuba	Santiago de Cuba	Estadio Antonio Maceo	3 000
-Diablos Rojos	Santiago de Cuba	Estadio Rekortan	3 000
-Holguin	Holguin		
-Isla Juventud	Isla de la Juventud	Terreno de Rodeo	1 000
-Guantanamo	Guantanamo	Estadio Rogelio Palacio	2 500
-Granma	Bayamo	Conrade Benitez Jiguani	3 000
-Ciego de Avila	Ciego de Avila	CDV Deportivo de Moron	3 000
Villa Clara	Santa Clara	Estadio Santo Domingo	2 500
Sancti Spiritus	Sancti Spiritus	Rafael M. Demendives	2 000

DOMINICA

DOMINICA FOOTBALL ASSOC.
33 Great Marlborough Street, Roseau
TEL 1 767/448 7577 FAX /448 7587
WEB www.concacaf.com

REFERENCE
Official name
 Commonwealth of Dominica
Date of formation 1978
Capital Roseau
Population 73,000
Total area 290 sq Mi, 750 sq Km
Time zone GMT -4
Density 252 per sq Mi, 86 per sq Km
Languages English, French Creole,
 Carib,Ccoy
Literacy rate 94%
Currency E. Caribbean $
Economy services 55%, agriculture 25%
Religions Catholic 77%, Protestant 15%
Ethnic Mix black 91%, mixed 6%

GEOGRAPHY
Elevation
lowest point: Caribbean Sea 0 m
highest point: Morne Diablatins 1,447 m
Geography Note
known as "The Nature Island of the
Caribbean" due to its spectacular, lush, and
varied flora and fauna, which are protected
by an extensive natural park system
Natural Resources
timber, hydropower, arable land
Climate
tropical; moderated by northeast trade
winds; heavy rainfall
Dominican Food
banana & mango bread/cottage pie

WORLD CUP		COUNTRY LEAGUE CHAMPIONS	
1930	Did not qualify		
1934	Did not qualify		
1938	Did not qualify	2004	Harlem Bombers
1950	Did not qualify	2003	Harlem Bombers
1954	Did not qualify	2002	Saint Joseph
1958	Did not qualify	2001	Harlem Bombers
1962	Did not qualify	2000	Harlem Bombers
1966	Did not qualify	1999	Harlem Bombers
1970	Did not qualify	1998	ACS Zebians
1974	Did not qualify	1997	Harlem Bombers
1978	Did not qualify	1996	Black Rocks
1982	Did not qualify	**Women's League Champ**	
1986	Did not qualify	2004	Not Known
1990	Did not qualify	2003	Goodwill Runners FC
1994	Did not qualify	2002	Goodwill Runners FC
1998	Did not qualify	2001	Not Known
2002	Did not qualify	2000	Not Known

NATIONAL TEAM COLORS

WORLD WONDERS OF SOCCER

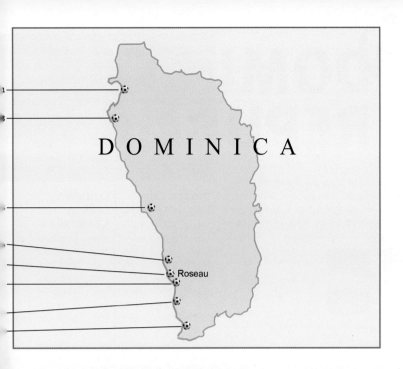

PREMIERE LEAGUE CLUBS	CITY	STADIUM	CAPACITY
Bluestars SC	Roseau		
Kensbro SC	Roseau		
South east Combined	Roseau		
Dame central SC	Roseau		
Zebians	Goodwill		
Saints SC	Goodwill		
Soufrieres FC	Soufrieres		
Saint Joseph	Saint Joseph		
Potters SC	Potters ville		
Pointe Milchel	Point Michel		
Bombers	Portsmouth		
Strikers	Dublanc		
Superwood United	Dublanc		

DOMINICAN REPUBLIC

FED.DOMINICANA DE FUTBOL

Estadio Olimpico, co Juan Pablo Duarte,
Apartado Postal 1953, Santo Domingo
TEL 1 809/542 6923 FAX /547 5363
WEB www.fedofutbol.com

REFERENCE

Official name
  Dominican Republic

Date of formation	1865
Capital	Santo Domingo
Population	8.5 million
Total area	18,679 sq Mi, 48,380 sq Km
Time zone	GMT -4
Density	455 per sq Mi, 166 per sq Km
Languages	Spanish,French Creole
Literacy rate	81%
Currency	Peso
Economy	Agriculture 46%
Religions	Catholic 92%
Ethnic Mix	Mixed 75%, White 15%

GEOGRAPHY

Elevation
lowest point: Lago Enriquillo -46 m
highest point: Pico Duarte 3,175 m

Geography Note
Shares island of Hispaniola with Haiti (eastern
two-thirds is the Dominican Republic, western
one-third is Haiti)

Natural Resources
nickel, bauxite, gold, silver

Climate
tropical maritime; little seasonal temperature
variation; seasonal variation in rainfall

Dominican Food
Chicken Roll with Pickles Vegetables/
Dominicana Flan

WORLD CUP

1930	Did not qualify
1934	Did not qualify
1938	Did not qualify
1950	Did not qualify
1954	Did not qualify
1958	Did not qualify
1962	Did not qualify
1966	Did not qualify
1970	Did not qualify
1974	Did not qualify
1978	Did not qualify
1982	Did not qualify
1986	Did not qualify
1990	Did not qualify
1994	Did not qualify
1998	Did not qualify
2002	Did not qualify

COUNTRY LEAGUE CHAMPIONS

2004	CD Pantoja
2003	Baninter Jarabacoa
2002	Baninter Jarabacoa
2001	CD Pantoja
2000	Not Known
1999	FC Don Bosco
1998	No Competition
1997	FC Santos
1996	Not known

Women's League Champ

2004	Not Known
2003	Not Known
2002	Not Known
2001	Not Known
2000	Not Known

NATIONAL TEAM COLORS

WORLD PICTURES OF SOCCER

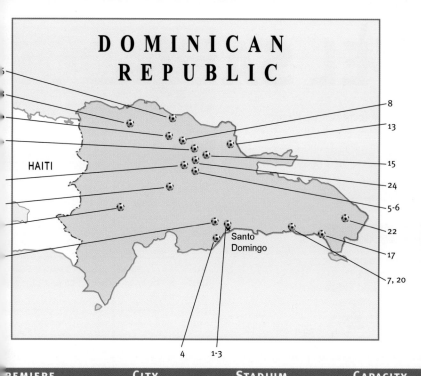

DOMINICAN REPUBLIC

HAITI

Santo Domingo

8
13
15
24
5-6
22
17
7, 20

4   1-3

PREMIERE LEAGUE CLUBS	CITY	STADIUM	CAPACITY
Bancredicard FC	Santo Domingo		
D Pantoja-Rowe FC	Santo Domingo		
Distrito Nacional U17	Santo Domingo		
San Cristobal FC	San Cristobal		
Jarabacoa	Jarabacoa		
Saninter	Jarabacoa		
ayaguana FC	San pedro de Marcoris		
Vivefut Moca FC	Moca, Prov. Espaillat		
porting FC de Santiago	Santiago		
La Canela	Santiago		
La Vega FC	La Vega		
Dosa	La Vega		
Canabrava	Monte Llano		
lusion Pibe	Salcedo		
Castillo	San Francisco de Marcoris		
Miramar FC	Puerto Plata		
La Romana	La Romana		
Mao FC	Mao		
Constanza FC	Constanza		
S.P Marcoris	San Pedro de Marcoris		
San Juan	San Juan de la Maguana		
Higuey FC	Highuey		
Deportivo Pantoja	Pantoja		
Villa Tapia	Villa Tapia		

EL SALVADOR

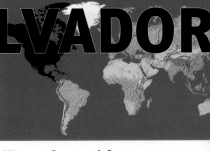

FED. SALVADORENA DE FUTBOL
Av. JM Delgado,Colonia Escalon, Frente
Centro Espanol, Apdo 1029 , San Salvador
TEL 503/263 7525   FAX /263 7583
WEB www.fesfut.org.sv

REFERENCE
Official name
Republic of El Salvador

Date of	
formation	1856
Capital	San Salvador
Population	6.3 Million
Total area	8000sq Mi, 20,720 sq Km
Time zone	GMT -6
Density	788 per sq Mi, 277per sq Km
Languages	Spanish,Nahua
Literacy rate	71%
Currency	Salvadoran Colon
Economy	Services 70%, Industry 22%
Religions	Catholic 80%, Evangelical 18%
Ethnic Mix	Mestizo 94%, Indian 5%

GEOGRAPHY
Elevation
lowest point: Pacific Ocean 0 m
highest point: Cerro El Pital 2,730 m
Geography Note
Smallest Central American country and only
one without a coastline on Caribbean Sea
Natural Resources
Hydropower, geothermal power, petroleum,
arable land
Climate
Tropical; rainy season (May to October); dry
season (November to April); tropical on
coast; temperate in uplands
El Salvadorian Food
Curtido Salad/Maria Luisa Cake

WORLD CUP

1930	Did not qualify
1934	Did not qualify
1938	Did not qualify
1950	Did not qualify
1954	Did not qualify
1958	Did not qualify
1962	Did not qualify
1966	Did not qualify
1970	Did not qualify
1974	Did not qualify
1978	Did not qualify
1982	Did not qualify
1986	Did not qualify
1990	Did not qualify
1994	Did not qualify
1998	Did not qualify
2002	Did not qualify

COUNTRY LEAGUE CHAMPIONS

2005	CD FAS(Aper)
2004	Alianza(Clau) C.D FAS(Ap
2003	San Salvador (Clau)CD F.
2002	C.D FAS (Clau) Alianza F(
2001	C.D Aguila (Clau) C.D Ag
(Aper)	
2000	L.A Firpo (Clau) C.D Agui
1999	L.A Firpo (Clau) Alianza
1998	L.A Firpo

Women's League Cham

2004	UCA
2003	I.D Usulutan
2002	Siervas de Dios
2001	Not Known
2000	Not Known

NATIONAL TEAM COLORS

WORLD PICTURES OF SOCCER

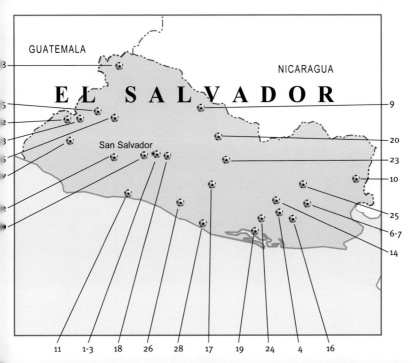

REMIERE EAGUE CLUBS	CITY	STADIUM	CAPACITY
Alianza FC	San Salvador		
San Salvador FC	San Salvador		
CD Atletico Marte	San Salvador	Estadio Cuscutlan	
Luis Angel Firpo	Usulatan	Estadio Sergio Torres	
CD FAS	Santa Ana	Estadio Oscar Quiterzo	
CD Aguila	San Miguel	Juan Francisco Barraza	
CD El Dragon	San Miguel	Juan Francisco barraza	
CD Isidro Metapan	Metapan		
CD Chalatenango	Chalatenango		
Municipal Limeno	Santa Rosa Lima	Jose Ramon Flores	
AD El Transito	La Libertad	Hacienda El Transito	
CD Espartano	San Julian		
CD Once Lobos	Chalchuapa		
CD Aspirante	Jucuapa		
Atletico Chaparrastique	Moncagua		
UDET	El Transito		
CD Platense	Zacatecoluca		
Coca Cola FC	Soyapango		
Mar y Plata	Puerto El Triunfo		
El Roble	Ilobasco		
CD Atiquizaya	Atiquizaya		
CD Huracan	Atiquizaya		
Independiente FC	San Vicente		
CO Topiltzin	Jiquilisco		
Jocoro FC	Jocoro		
San Luis FC	San Luis Talpa		
Sonsonate FC	Nahuizalco		
CD Espana Adese	San Sebastian		
CD El Vecandor	Santa Helena		

347

GREENLAND

GREENLAND FOOTBALL FEDERATION

PO Box 319, Nuuk Godthab, Greenland
TEL   FAX
WEB www.uefa.com

REFERENCE

Official name
Greenland

Date of formation 1953
Capital Nuuk Godthab
Population 59,827
Total area 839 sq MI 2,175,600 sq KM
Time zone GMT -1/4
Density 1 per sq Km
Languages Danish
Literacy rate 95%
Currency Danish Krone
Economy Fishing
Religions Protestant
Ethnic Mix Greenlanders, Danish

GEOGRAPHY

Elevation
lowest point: Atlantic Ocean 0 m
highest point: Gunnbjorn 3,700 m

Geography Note
Dominates North Atlantic Ocean between North America and Europe; sparse population confined to small settlements along coast, but close to one-quarter of the population lives in the capital, Nuuk; world's second largest ice cap

Natural Resources
zinc, lead, iron ore, coal, molybdenum, gold, platinum, uranium, fish, seals, whales, hydropower, possible oil and gas

Climate
arctic to subarctic; cool summers, cold winters

Greenland Food
fish steak with green peas

WORLD CUP		COUNTRY LEAGUE CHAMPIONS	
1930	Did not qualify		
1934	Did not qualify		
1938	Did not qualify	2004	Not Known
1950	Did not qualify	2003	Not Known
1954	Did not qualify	2002	Not Known
1958	Did not qualify	2001	Not Known
1962	Did not qualify	2000	Not Known
1966	Did not qualify	1999	B-67
1970	Did not qualify	1998	Kissaviarsuk 1933
1974	Did not qualify	1997	B-67
1978	Did not qualify	1996	B-67
1982	Did not qualify	**Women's League Champ**	
1986	Did not qualify	2004	Not Known
1990	Did not qualify	2003	Not Known
1994	Did not qualify	2002	Not Known
1998	Did not qualify	2001	Not Known
2002	Did not qualify	2000	Not Known

NATIONAL TEAM COLORS

WORLD PICTURES OF SOCCER

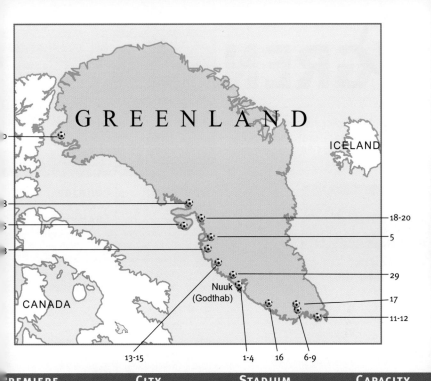

PREMIERE LEAGUE CLUBS	CITY	STADIUM	CAPACITY
B-67	Nuuk/Godthab		
Nuuk Idraetslag	Nuuk/Godthab		
IL Nuuk	Nuuk/Godthab		
Groenlands Sport	Nuuk/Godthab		
NBK-88	Niaqornaarsuk		
Kissaviarsuk 1933	Qaqortoq		
Qaa Qaqortoq	Qaqortoq		
Atrsaq Qaqortoq	Qaqortoq		
E-66 Qaqortoq	Qaqortoq		
-Tupilakken-41	Qaanak		
-Egaluk Nanortalik	Nanortalik		
-Siuterok Nanortalik	Nanortalik		
-Aqigssaq	Maniitsoq		
-Kagssagssuk	Maniitsoq		
-KT-85 Maniitsok	Maniitsoq		
-Pameq Arsuk	Arsuk		
-N-85	Narssaq		
-I-69 Illulisat	Illulisat		
-Nagdlunguaq	Illulisat		
-I-53	Illulisat		
-Siumut Amerdlok	Sisimiut		
-SAK	Sisimiut		
-S-68 Sisimiut	Sisimiut		
-Disko -76	Qeqertarsuaq		
-G-44	Qeqertarsuaq		
-Malamuk	Uummanaq		
-UB-68	Uummanaq		
-Ukaleg	Uummanaq		

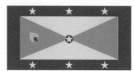 

GRENADA

Greneda Football Assoc.
PB 326, St Juilles Street, St.Georges
TEL 1 473/440 9903 FAX /440 9973
WEB www.concacaf.com

REFERENCE

Official name
Greneda

Date of formation 1974
Capital St. George
Population 99.500
Total area 131 sq Mi, 340 sq Km
Time zone GMT -4
Density 760 per sq Mi, 285 per sq Km
Languages EnglishEnglish Creole
Literacy rate 98%
Currency East Caribbean $
Economy Services 65%, Agriculture 20%
Religions Catholic 68%, Anglican 17%
Ethnic Mix Black African 82%,
Mulatto 13%, Indian 3%

GEOGRAPHY

Elevation
lowest point: Caribbean Sea 0 m
highest point: Mount Saint Catherine 840 m
Geography Note
the administration of the islands of the
Grenadines group is divided between Saint
Vincent and the Grenadines and Grenada
Natural Resources
timber, tropical fruit, deepwater harbors
Climate
tropical; tempered by northeast trade winds
Grenadian Food
Escoveitched Fish/Quick Fruit Cakes

WORLD CUP		COUNTRY LEAGUE CHAMPIONS	
1930	Did not qualify		
1934	Did not qualify		
1938	Did not qualify	2004	Not Known
1950	Did not qualify	2003	Hurricanes FC
1954	Did not qualify	2002	Not Known
1958	Did not qualify	2001	DML Grenada
1962	Did not qualify	2000	DML Grenada
1966	Did not qualify	1999	St.Andrews FLG
1970	Did not qualify	1998	Fontenoy United
1974	Did not qualify	1997	Seven Seas RC
1978	Did not qualify	1996	Not Known
1982	Did not qualify	1995	Not Known
1986	Did not qualify	1994	Not Known
1990	Did not qualify	1993	Not Known
1994	Did not qualify	**Women's League Champ**	
1998	Did not qualify	2004	Not Known
2002	Did not qualify	2003	Not Known

NATIONAL TEAM COLORS

WORLD PICTURES OF SOCCER

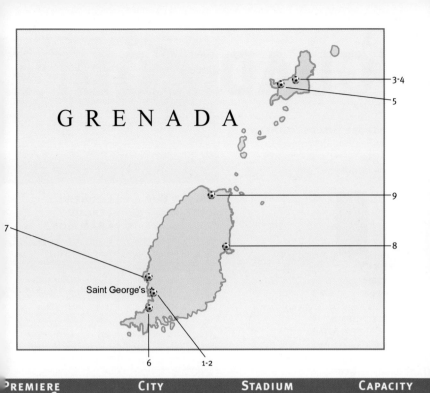

GRENADA

Saint George's

7
6   1-2
3-4
5
9
8

PREMIERE LEAGUE CLUBS	CITY	STADIUM	CAPACITY
-Queens Park Rangers	Saint George's		
-DML Mutual Life GBSS	Saint George's		
-Brunswuick United	Hillsborough		
-Clement Tigers	Hillsborough		
-Barba Super Stars	L'Esterre		
-BBH United	Belmont		
-Mt. Royal Strikers	Mt.Royal		
-St.Andrews FL	Grenville		
-Capital Bank Hurricane	Sauteurs		

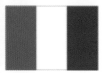

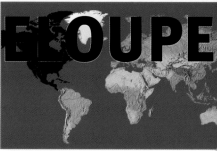

GUADELOUPE

FED.FOOTBALL GUADELOUPEEN
Rue de laville Dorly Berguin,97110,
Pointe a Pitre   TEL 590/212 888
WEB www.concacaf.com

REFERENCE
Official name
Guadeloupe
(French Overseas Department)
Claimed	1635
Capital	Basse Terre
Population	419,500
Total area	687 sq Mi, 1780 sq Km
Time zone	GMT -4
Density	246 per Sq Km
Languages	French, Creole, English
Literacy rate	99%
Currency	French Franc
Economy	Services 65%
Religions	Catholic 80%
Ethnic Mix	Black African 95%, Others

GEOGRAPHY
Elevation
lowest point: Caribbean Sea 0 m
highest point: Soufriere 1,484 m
Geography Note
A narrow channel, the Riviere Salee, divides
Guadeloupe proper into two islands: the
larger, western Basse-Terre and the smaller,
eastern Grande-Terre
Natural Resources
Cultivable land, beaches and climate that
foster tourism
Climate
Subtropical tempered by trade winds; mod-
erately high humidity
Guadeloupean Food
Pineapple Chicken Rundowns
Banana Flambe

WORLD CUP		COUNTRY LEAGUE CHAMPIONS	
1930	Did not qualify		
1934	Did not qualify		
1938	Did not qualify	2004	Racing Club
1950	Did not qualify	2003	Phare FC
1954	Did not qualify	2002	L'Etoile Filante
1958	Did not qualify	2001	L'Etoile Filante
1962	Did not qualify	2000	ASG Juventus
1966	Did not qualify	1999	Racing Club
1970	Did not qualify	1998	L'Etoile Filante
1974	Did not qualify	1997	L'Etoile Filante
1978	Did not qualify	1996	L'Etoile Filante
1982	Did not qualify	**Women's League Champi**	
1986	Did not qualify	2004	Solidarite 2000
1990	Did not qualify	2003	MJC FC
1994	Did not qualify	2002	Not Known
1998	Did not qualify	2001	Not Known
2002	Did not qualify	2000	Not Known

NATIONAL TEAM COLORS

WORLD PICTURES OF SOCCER

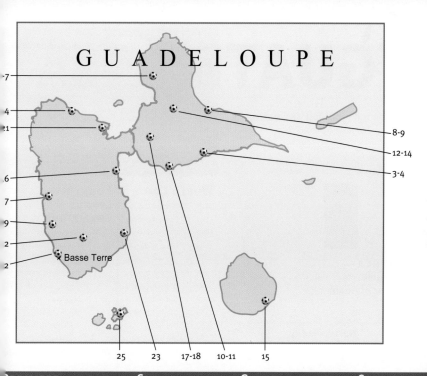

GUADELOUPE

PREMIERE LEAGUE CLUBS	CITY	STADIUM	CAPACITY
-Racing Club	Basse Terre		
-Cygne Noir	Basse Terre		
-Juventus	Sainte-Anne		
-Intrepide	Sainte-Anne		
-Rapid Club	Petit-Canal		
-Equinoxe	Petit-Canal		
-Phare	Petit Canal		
-AS Nenuphars	Moule		
-CS Moule	Moule		
-AS Dragon	Gosier		
-AS Gosier	Gosier		
-Etoile Filante	Morne-a-L'eau		
-Indomptable	Morne-a-L'eau		
-Olympic	Morne-a-L'eau		
-JS Capesterre	Cap Marie Galante		
-Arsenal Club	Petit Bourg		
-Siroco	Abymes		
-JS Abymes	Abymes		
-Red Star	Baie Mahault		
-US Baie Mahault	Baie Mahault		
-Solidarite Scolaire	Baie Mahault		
-Fumerolles	St.Claude		
-CS Capesterrien	Cap Belle Eau		
-Unite Sainte Rosienne	Sainte Rose		
-AJCS Terre-de-Haut	Terre-de-Haut		
-Resistance	Bouillante		
-CS Bouillante	Bouillante		
-JS Vieux Habitants	Vieux Habitants		
-Amical Club	Vieux Habitants		

GUATEMALA

Fed. Nacional de Football de Guatemala
7a Av.12-23 Zona9,Edificio Etisa,6
Nivel,Guatemala city 01009
TEL 502/3322424
www.futgt.com

REFERENCE

Official name
Republic of Guatemala

Date of formation 1838

Capital Guatemala City

Total area 41,864 sq Mi, 108,430 sq Km

Time zone GMT -6

Density 272 per sq Mi, 113 per sq Km

Languages Spanish,Quiche, Mam, kekchi,Cakchiquel, Mayan

Literacy rate 56%

Currency Quetzal

Economy Agriculture 50%,Services 38%

Religions Catholic 66%, Protestant 33%

Ethnic Mix Amerindian 60%,Mestizo 30%

GEOGRAPHY

Elevation
lowest point: Pacific Ocean o m
highest point: Volcan Tajumulco 4,211 m

Geography Note
no natural harbors on west coast

Natural Resources
petroleum, nickel, rare woods, fish, chicle, hydropower

Climate
tropical; hot, humid in lowlands; cooler in highlands

Guatemalan Food
Banana Bread/Atitlan Ceviche

WORLD CUP		COUNTRY LEAGUE CHAMPIONS	
1930	Did not qualify		
1934	Did not qualify		
1938	Did not qualify	2005	Municipal(A)
1950	Did not qualify	2004	Coban Imperial(C)
1954	Did not qualify		Municipal(A)
1958	did not qualify	2003	Communicaciones (C)
1962	Did not qualify		Communicaciones (A
1966	Did not qualify	2002	Municipal (C)
1970	Did not qualify		Municipal (A)
1974	Did not qualify	2001	Communicaciones (C
1978	Did not qualify		Municipal (A)
1982	Did not qualify	**Women's League Champ**	
1986	Did not qualify	2004	Communicaciones
1990	Did not qualify	2003	Communicaciones
1994	Did not qualify	2002	Communicaciones
1998	Did not qualify	2001	Communicaciones
2002	Did not qualify	2000	Communicaciones

NATIONAL TEAM COLORS

WORLD PICTURES OF SOCCER

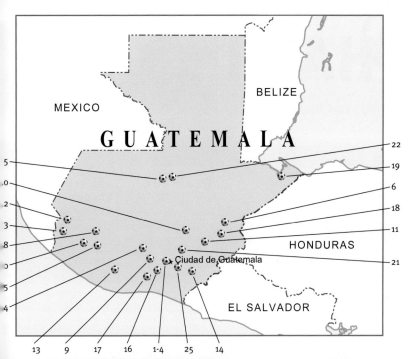

Premiere League Clubs	City	Stadium	Capacity
-Communicacione	Ciud.de Guatemala	Cementos Progresso	17 000
-Municipal	Ciudad de Guatemala	Estadio Mateo Flores	30 000
-Aurora FC	Ciudad de Guatemala	Estadio del Ejercito	12 500
-Univ.San Carlos	Ciud.de Guatemala	MF Carrera el Trebol	3 000
-Club Coban Imperial	Coban	Estadio Verapaz	13 000
-Club Deportivo Zacapa	Zacapa	David Ordonez Bardales	8 000
-CD Xelaju MC	Quetzaltenango	Mario Campeseco	7 000
-Rosario FC	Quetzaltenango	Mario Campesco	7 000
-Antigua GFC	Antigua	Pensativo	9 000
ɔ-Deportivo Teculutan	Teculutan	JH Pas Castilla	4 000
ᴀ-Deportivo Jalapa	Jalapa	Estadio Las Flores	4 000
2-Deportivo Marquense	San Marcos	Marquense Ensenada	9 000
3-SL Cotzumalguapa	Santa Lucia Ref	R.Munoz Galvez	15 000
4-Deportivo Achuapa	Jutiapa	El Condor	14 000
5-Dep.Suchitepequez	Mazatenango	C.Salazar Hijo	12 000
5-Deportivo Amatitlan	Amatitlan	Estadio Municipal	12 000
7-Deportivo Escuintla	Escuintla	Armanda Barillas	10 000
3-Deportivo Sacachispas	Chiquimula	Las Victorias	9 000
ɔ-Izabal JC	Puerto Barrios	Roy Fearon	8 000
ɔ-Juventud Retalteca	Retalhuleu	Monterroso Izaguire	8 000
ᴀ-Deportivo Copagsa	Santa Catarina	Estadio Copagsa	5 000
2-Deportivo Carcha	San Pedro Carcha	JR Ponce Way	4 000
3-Deportivo Coatepeque	Coatepeque		
4-Chimaltenango	Chimaltenango		
5-CD Petapa	Petapa		

HAITI

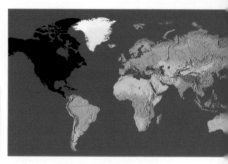

FED. HAITIENNE DE FOOTBALL
128 Av. Christophe,PB 2258,
Port au Prince
TEL 509/244 0115   FAX /244 0117
WEB www.concacaf.com

REFERENCE
Official name
   Repubublique of Haiti
Date of
formation   1804
Capital   Port-au-Prince
Total area   10,622 sq Mi, 27,555 sq Km
Time zone   GMT
Density   775 per sq Mi
Languages   French ,Creole, English
Literacy rate Average
Currency   Gourde
Economy   farming ,fishing
Religions   Catholic
Ethnic Mix   Black African 97%

GEOGRAPHY
Elevation
lowest point: Caribbean Sea 0 m
highest point: Cerro Las Minas 2,870 m
Geography Note
Has only a short Pacific coast but a long
Caribbean shoreline, including the virtually
uninhabited eastern Mosquito Coast
Natural Resources
Timber, gold, silver, copper, lead, zinc, iron
ore, antimony, coal, fish, hydropower
Climate
tropical & temperate
Haiti Food
lemon fish

WORLD CUP		COUNTRY LEAGUE CHAMPIONS	
1930	Did not qualify		
1934	Did not qualify		
1938	Did not qualify	2004	Not Known
1950	Did not qualify		Not Known
1954	Did not qualify	2003	Roulado (C)
1958	Did not qualify		Don Bosco (A)
1962	Did not qualify	2002	RC Haitien (C)
1966	Did not qualify		Roulado (A)
1970	Did not qualify	2001	FICA
1974	First round exit	2000	Racing Club Haitien
1978	Did not qualify	1999	Violette AC
1982	Did not qualify	1998	FICA
1986	Did not qualify	1999	Violette AC
1990	Did not qualify	**Women's League Champi**	
1994	Did not qualify	2004	Aigles Brillant
1998	Did not qualify	2003	Aigles Brillant
2002	Did not qualify	2002	Aigles Brillant

NATIONAL TEAM COLORS

WORLD PICTURES OF SOCCER

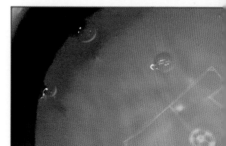

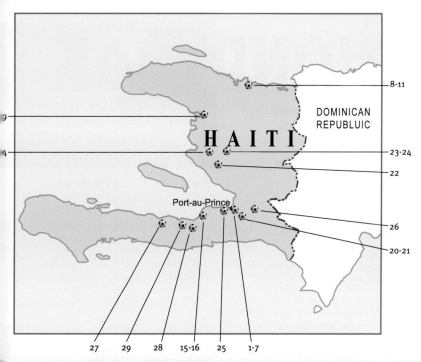

PREMIERE LEAGUE CLUBS	CITY	STADIUM	CAPACITY
Violette AC	Port-au-Prince	Stade Sylvio Cator	8 000
Carioca FC	Port-au-Prince	Stade Sylvio Cator	8 000
Amateur de Cite Soleil	Port-au-Prince	Stade Sylvio Cator	8 000
Racing Club Haitien	Port-au-Prince	Stade Sylvio Victor	8 000
Victory	Port-au-Prince	Stade Sylvio Victor	8 000
Etoile Haitienne	Port-au-Prince	Stade Sylvio Victor	8 000
Hatuey Bacardi Club	Port-au-Prince	Stade Sylvio Victor	8 000
FICA	Cap Haitien	Parc Saint Victor	1 000
AS Capoise	Cap Haitien	Parc saint Victor	1 000
JS Capoise	Cap Haitien	Parc Saint Victor	1 000
Zenith AC	Cap Haitien	Parc saint Victor	1 000
Tempete FC	Saint Marc	Parc Levelt	1 000
Baltimore SC	Saint Marc	Parc Levelt	1 000
Dynamite	Saint Marc	Parc Levelt	1 000
Cavaly AS	Leogane	Parc Gerard Christophe	1 000
Valencia FC	Leogane	Parc Gerard Christophe	1 000
Roulado	Gonaive		
Racing FC	Gonaive		
Éclair	Gonaive		
Don Bosco FC	Petionville		
All stars	Petionville		
Aigle Noir AC	Bel Air		
Triomphe	Liancourt		
Panthere Noire	Liancourt		
ASC de Carrefour	Carrefour		
Velox	Croix-des-Missions		
Rangers FC	Miragoane		
AS Grand Goave	Grand Goave		
AS Petit-Goave	Petit-Goave		

HONDURAS

FED. NACIONAL AUTONOMA
de Futbol de Honduras
Edif. Lomas del Mayar,Ave Rep.de CostaRica,
3er nivel,827 tegucigulpa,
DCTEL /504/235 4236 www.fenafuth.org

REFERENCE

Official name
   Republic of Honduras

Date of formation	1838
Capital	Tegucigalpa
Population	6.5 millions
Total area	43,200 sq Mi, 111,890 sq Km
Time zone	GMT -6
Density	150 per sq Mi, 53 per sq Km
Languages	Spanish, English Creole, Garifuna, Indian Languages 72%
Literacy rate	Lempira
Currency	agriculture 60%, services
Economy	24%, industry Catholic 97%
Religions	meztizo 90%,indian 5%,
Ethnic Mix	black African 5%

GEOGRAPHY

Elevation
lowest point: Caribbean Sea o m
highest point: Cerro Las Minas 2,870 m
Geography Note
Has only a short Pacific coast but a long
Caribbean shoreline, including the virtually
uninhabited eastern Mosquito Coast
Natural Resources
Timber, gold, silver, copper, lead, zinc, iron
ore, antimony, coal, fish, hydropower
Climate
Subtropical in lowlands, temperate in
mountains
Honduran Food
tortilla Pan Bread/Yucca Pie

WORLD CUP

1930	Did not qualify
1934	Did not qualify
1938	Did not qualify
1950	Did not qualify
1954	Did not qualify
1958	Did not qualify
1962	Did not qualify
1966	Did not qualify
1970	Did not qualify
1974	Did not qualify
1978	Did not qualify
1982	First round exit
1986	Did not qualify
1990	Did not qualify
1994	Did not qualify
1998	Did not qualify
2002	Did not qualify

COUNTRY LEAGUE CHAMPIONS

2005	Olimpia(A)
2004	Olimpia(C)
	Real Espana(A)
2003	Marathon(C)
	Olimpia (A)
2002	Marathon (C)
	Motagua (A)
2001	Platense (C)
	Olimpia (A)

Women's League Champ

2004	Not Known
2003	Banpais
2002	Fraternidad
2001	Fraternidad
2000	Fraternidad

NATIONAL TEAM COLORS

WORLD PICTURES OF SOCCER

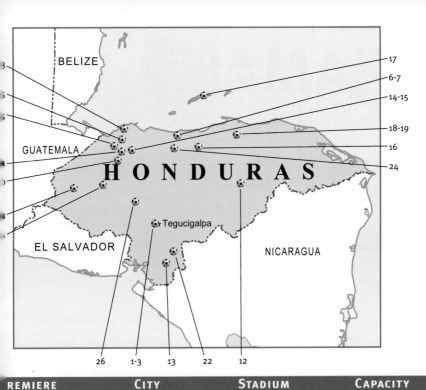

PREMIERE LEAGUE CLUBS	CITY	STADIUM	CAPACITY
Motagua	Tegucigalpa	Estad.Naci.Tiburcio Carias	25 000
Olimpia	Tegucigalpa	Estad.Naci.Tiburcio Carias	25 000
Universidad	Tegucigalpa	Estad.Naci.Tiburcio Carias	25 000
Marathon	San Pedro Sula	Estadio Francisco Morazan	30 000
Real Espana	San Pedro Sula	Estadio Francisco Morazan	30 000
Victoria	Ceiba	Estadio Nilmo Edwards	10 000
Vida	Ceiba	Estadio Nilmo Edwards	10 000
Platense	Puerto Cortez	Estadio Excelsior	7 000
Real Maya	Santa Barbara		
Real Patepluma	Santa Barbara		
Real Juventud	Santa Barbara		
Atletico Olanchuna	Catacamas		
Universidad Choluteca	Choluteca		
Salzburg	El Progresso		
Universal	El Progresso		
Social Sol	Olanchito		
Arsenal	Islas de la Bahia		
Union Arenense	Tocoa		
Real Sociedad	Tocoa		
Villanueva	Villanueva		
Parillas One	La Lima		
Aguan Valle	Sabana		
Dep. Santos	Santa Rosa de Copan		
America Marathon	San Juan Pueblo		
Real Choloma	Choloma		
Real Comayagua	Comayagua		

JAMAICA

JAMAICA FOOTBALL FED.LTD
20 St.Lucia,Crescent,Kingston 5
TEL 1 876/929 8036 FAX /929 0483
www.homeviewjamaica.com/jam-footballfed

REFERENCE
Official name
Jamaica
Date of formation 1962
Capital Kingston
Population 2.6 Million
Total area 4,181 sq Mi, 10,830 sq Km
Time zone GMT -5
Density 622 per sq Mi, 241 per sq Km
Languages English,English Creole,
Literacy rate Hindi, Spanish, Chinese
85%
Currency Jamaican $
Economy Services 63%, Agriculture 25%
Religions Christian 55%
Ethnic Mix Black African 75%,
Mulatto 13%,
Euro-Chinese 11%

GEOGRAPHY
Elevation
lowest point: Caribbean Sea 0 m
highest point: Blue Mountain Peak 2,256 m
Geography Note
strategic location between Cayman Trench
and Jamaica Channel, the main sea lanes for
the Panama Canal
Natural Resources
Bauxite, gypsum, limestone
Climate
Tropical; hot, humid; temperate interior
Jamaican Food
Beef & Okra(Jamaican Stir)
Plantan Fritters

WORLD CUP		COUNTRY LEAGUE CHAMPIONS	
1930	Did not qualify		
1934	Did not qualify		
1938	Did not qualify	2004	Tivoli Gardens
1950	Did not qualify	2003	Hazard United
1954	Did not qualify	2002	Arnett gardens FC
1958	Did not qualify	2001	Arnett Gardens FC
1962	Did not qualify	2000	Harbour View
1966	Did not qualify	1999	Tivoli Gardens
1970	Did not qualify	1998	Waterhouse
1974	Did not qualify	1997	Seba United
1978	Did not qualify	1996	Violet Kickers
1982	Did not qualify	**Women's League Cham**	
1986	Did not qualify	2004	Barbican
1990	Did not qualify	2003	Barbican
1994	Did not qualify	2002	Portmore Strikers
1998	First round exit	2001	Portmore Strikers
2002	Did not qualify	2000	Not Known

NATIONAL TEAM COLORS

WORLD PICTURES OF SOCCER

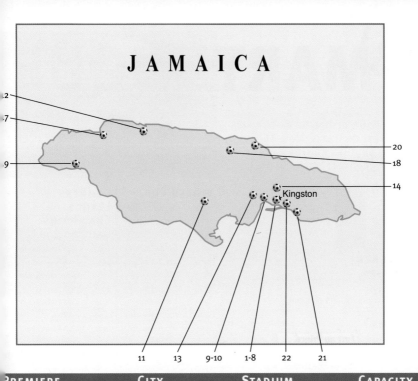

JAMAICA

Kingston

2
7
9
20
18
14
11   13   9-10   1-8   22   21

PREMIERE LEAGUE CLUBS	CITY	STADIUM	CAPACITY
-Arnett Gardens FC	Kingston	Tony Spaulding Complex	
Harbour View FC	Kingston		
-Tivoli Gardens	Kingston		
-Waterhouse	Kingston		
-Boy's Town	Kingston		
-Jamaica Defence Force	Kingston		
-Cavalier FC	Kingston		
-Santos	Kingston		
-Portmore United	Portmore		
o-Portmore Gardens	Portmore		
1-Hazard United	May Pen		
2-Village United	Falmouth		
3-Rivoli United	Spanish Town		
4-Constant Spring	Constant Spring		
5-Seba United	Montego Bay		
6-Wadadah	Montego Bay		
7-Violet Kickers	Montego Bay		
8-Invaders United	Breeze Hill		
9-Reno FC	Savannah del Mar		
o-Star Cosmos	Port Maria		
1-Bull Bay FC	Bull Bay		
2-August Town	August Town		

MARTINIQUE

MARTINIQUE LIGUE DE FOOTBALL
BP 307,Fort de france,Mart TEL
596/728-989 FAX 596/631 499
WEB www.concacaf.com

REFERENCE
Official name
Martinique
(French overseas Department)
Date of
formation   1635
Capital   Fort de France
Population   381,200
Total area   25 sq Mi, 1100 sq Km
Time zone   GMT -4
Density   388 per sq Km
Languages   French,French Creole
Literacy rate 93%
Currency   French Franc
Economy   Services 93%
Religions   Catholics 90%
Ethnic Mix   Black african,Mulatto,Europ.

GEOGRAPHY
Elevation
lowest point: Caribbean Sea o m
highest point: Montagne Pelee 1,397 m
Geography Note
the island is dominated by Mount Pelee,
which on 8 May 1902 erupted and completely destroyed the city of Saint Pierre, killing
30,000 inhabitants
Natural Resources
coastal scenery and beaches, cultivable land
Climate
tropical; moderated by trade winds; rainy
season (June to October); vulnerable to dev-
astating cyclones (hurricanes) every eight
years on average
Martinique Food
Baba au Rhum/Stuffed Crabs/Gratin au
Chayotte

WORLD CUP

1930	Did not qualify
1934	Did not qualify
1938	Did not qualify
1950	Did not qualify
1954	Did not qualify
1958	Did not qualify
1962	Did not qualify
1966	Did not qualify
1970	Did not qualify
1974	Did not qualify
1978	Did not qualify
1982	Did not qualify
1986	Did not qualify
1990	Did not qualify
1994	Did not qualify
1998	Did not qualify
2002	Did not qualify

COUNTRY LEAGUE CHAMPIONS

2004	Club Franciscain
2003	Club Franciscain
2002	Club Franciscain
2001	Club Franciscain
2000	Club Franciscain
1999	Club Franciscain
1998	Aiglons
1997	Club Franciscain
1996	Club Franciscain

Women's League Champ

2004	Not Known
2003	Not Known
2002	Not Known
2001	Not Known
2000	Not Known

NATIONAL TEAM COLORS

WORLD PICTURES OF SOCCER

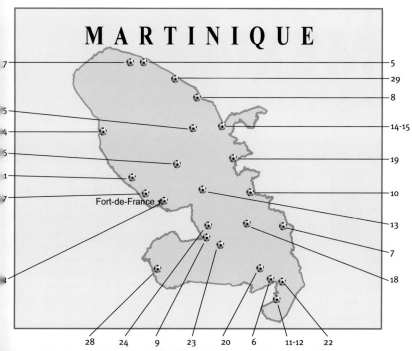

MARTINIQUE

PREMIERE LEAGUE CLUBS	CITY	STADIUM	CAPACITY
Club Colonial	Fort-de-France	Stade Dillon	5 000
Golden Star	Fort-de-France	Stade Dillon	5 500
Intrepide	Fort-de-France	Stade Dillon	5 000
Assaut	Saint-Pierre		
Etoile	Basse-Pointe		
Club Peleen	Morne Rouge		
CS Vauclinois	Vauclin		
Samaritaine	Sainte-Marie		
New Club	Petit-Bourg		
Club Franciscain	Le Francois		
Santanna Club	Sainte-Anne		
Renaissance	Sainte-Anne		
Aiglon	Lamentin		
Gauloise	Trinite		
AC Real Tartane	Trinite		
Excelsior	Schoelcher		
Emulation	Schoelcher		
Stade Spiritain	Saint-Esprit		
US Robert	Le Robert		
Racing Club	Riviere-Pilote		
CS Case Pilote	Case-Pilote		
US Marinoise	Marin		
Éclair	Riviere Salee		
New Star	Ducos		
Reveil Sportif	Gros Morne		
Racing Club	Saint-Joseph		
Rapid Club Lorrain	Lorrain		
RC Arlesien	Les Anses D'Arloet		

 # MEXICO

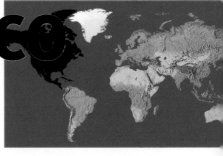

ed.Mexicana de
FutboAssociation
AC Colima #373,Colonia Roma,06700
Mexico DF   TEL 52-55/5241 0100
WEB www.femexfut.org.mx

REFERENCE
Official name
    United Mexican States

Date of formation	1936
Capital	Mexico City
Population	98.6 Million
Total area	736,945 sq Mi
	1,908,690 sq Km
Time zone	GMT -6/8
Density	134 per sq Mi, 50 per sq Km
Languages	Spanish, Mayan Dialects
Literacy rate	90%
Currency	Peso
Economy	Services 57%, Agriculture 23%
Religions	Catholic 95%, Protestant 2%
Ethnic Mix	Meztizo 55%, Indigenous Indian 20%

GEOGRAPHY
Elevation
lowest point: Laguna Salada -10 m
highest point: Volcan Pico de Orizaba 5,700 m
Geography Note
Strategic location on southern border of US;
corn (maize), one of the world's major grain
crops, is thought to have originated in Mexico
Natural Resources
Petroleum, silver, copper, gold, lead, zinc, nat-
ural gas, timber
Climate
Varies from tropical to desert
Mexican Food
Sopa de tortilla/Guacamole/Fajitas

WORLD CUP

1930	First round exit
1934	Did not qualify
1938	Did Not qualify
1950	First round exit
1954	First round exit
1958	First round exit
1962	First round exit
1966	First round exit
1970	1/4 final exit
1974	Did not qualify
1978	First round exit
1982	Did not qualify
1986	1/4 final exit
1990	Did not qualify
1994	Sd round exit
1998	Sd round exit
2002	Sd round exit

COUNTRY LEAGUE CHAMPIONS

2005	Pumas(Wint)
2004	Pumas(Sum)
	Pachuca(Wint)
2003	Monterrey(Sum)
	Toluca (Wint)
2002	America (Sum)
	Pachuca (Wint)
2001	Santos Laguna (Sum)
	Morelia (Wint)

Women's League Champ

2004	Not Known
2003	Not Known
2002	Not Known
2001	Atlas Margaritas
2000	Not Known

NATIONAL TEAM COLORS

WORLD PICTURES OF SOCCER

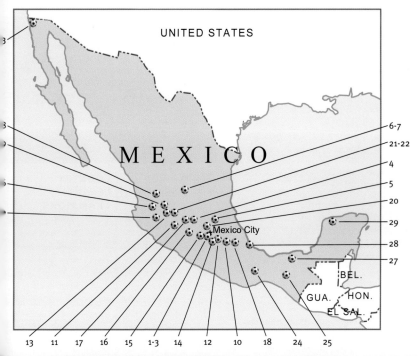

PREMIERE LEAGUE CLUBS	CITY	STADIUM	CAPACITY
America	Mexico City	Estadio Azteca	114 465
U.N.A.M Pumas	Mexico City	Olimpico Universitario	72 449
Cruz Azul	Mexico City	Estadio Azul	39 000
Queretaro	Queretaro	La Corregidorra	50 000
Pachuca	Pachuca	Miguel Hidalgo	25 000
Real San Luis	San Luis Potosi	Alfonso Lastras	24 000
Atl.San Luis Potosi	San luis Potosi	Estadio San Luis Potosi	10 000
Rayos de Necaxa	Aguascalientes	Estadio Victoria	20 000
Leon	Leon	Estadio Nou Camp	33 943
Puebla	Puebla	Estadio Morelos	38 384
Atlante	Nezahualcoyotl	Estadio NEZA 86	37 075
Irapuato	Irapuato	Sergio Leon Chavez	30 712
Colibries	Cuernavaca	Nido del Colibri	25 000
Club Toluca	Toluca	Nemesio Diez	26 000
Morelia Monarcas	Morelia	Estadio Morelos	38 000
Atletico Celaya	Celaya	Miguel Aleman	25 500
Zacatepec	Zacatepec	Coruco Diaz	18 000
La Piedad	La Piedad	Juan N.Lopez	15 000
C.A Hidalgo	Jasso	10 de Diciembre	17 000
Salmantino	Salamanca	El Molinito	4 000
Petroleros	Salamanca	Seccion XXIV	7 000
Trotamundos de Tijuana	Tijuana	Estadio de Tijuana	12 000
Veracruz	Veracruz	Luis Pirata Fuentes	43 154
Jaguares	Tuxtla Gutierrez	Victor manuel Reyna	25 000
Guadalajara Chivas	Guadalajara	Estadio Jalisco	66 000
Jaguares de Tabasco	Villahermosa	Olimpico	12 000
Orizaba FC	Orizaba	SOCUM	7 000
Atletico Yucatan	Merida	Carlos Iturralde	21 050

MONTSERRA

MONTSERRAT FOOTBALL ASSOC.
pb 505,Woodlands
TEL 1 664/491 8744 FAX /491 8801
WEB www.concacaf.com

REFERENCE
Official name
Montserrat
(British Dependency Territory)

Date of formation	1632
Capital	Plymouth (Uninhabitable)
Population	2850
Total area	40 sq Mi, 102 sq Km
Time zone	GMT -4
Density	128 per Sq Km
Languages	English,English creole
Literacy rate	95 %
Currency	EC $
Economy	tourism industry, agiculture
Religions	anglican, catholic
Ethnic Mix	Black african 85%,others

GEOGRAPHY
Elevation
lowest point: Caribbean Sea 0 m
highest point: Chances Peak 914 m
Geography Note
the island is entirely volcanic in origin and
contains seven active volcanoes
Natural Resources
fishing & tourism
Climate
Tropical; little daily or seasonal temperature
variation
Montserrat Food
cabbage au gratin
Montserrat Fish & Chips

WORLD CUP		COUNTRY LEAGUE CHAMPIONS	
1930	Did not qualify		
1934	Did not qualify		
1938	Did not qualify	2004	Ideal SC
1950	Did not qualify	2003	Royal Montserrat
1954	Did not qualify	2002	Royal Montserrat
1958	Did not qualify	2001	Royal Montserrat
1962	Did not qualify	2000	Royal Montserrat
1966	Did not qualify	1999	Not Known
1970	Did not qualify	1998	Not Known
1974	Did not qualify	1997	"Season interupted
1978	Did not qualify		Volcano soufriere"
1982	Did not qualify	1996	Royal Montserrat
1986	Did not qualify	**Women's League Champ**	
1990	Did not qualify	2004	Not Known
1994	Did not qualify	2003	Not Known
1998	Did not qualify	2002	Not Known
2002	Did not qualify	2001	Not Known

NATIONAL TEAM COLORS

WORLD PICTURES OF SOCCER

Soccer Culture

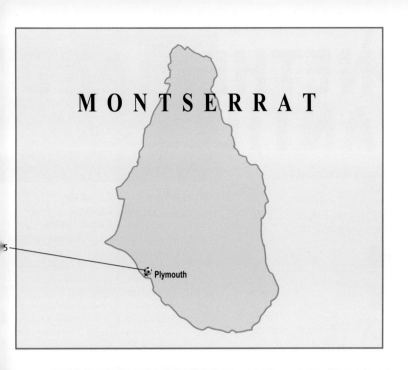

MONTSERRAT

5 —————— ⚽ Plymouth

PREMIERE LEAGUE CLUBS	CITY	STADIUM	CAPACITY
-Royal Montserrat Police	Plymouth	Blakes Football Complex	1 000
-Ideal Printers SC	Plymouth	Blakes Football Complex	1 000
-Montserrat Volcano Tremors	Plymouth	Blakes Football Complex	1 000
-Montserrat Secondary School	Plymouth	Blakes Football Complex	1 000
-Seventh Day Trendsetters	Plymouth	Blakes Football Complex	1 000

NETHERLAND ANTILLES

NETHERLANDS ANTILLIAANSE
Voetbal Unie
Bonamweg 49, Curacao, NA
TEL 599/9736 5040 FAX /9736 5047
WEB www.concacaf.com

REFERENCE
Official name
Netherlands Antilles

Date of formation 1816
Capital Willemstad
Population 207,175
Total area 308 sq Mi, 800 sq Km
Time zone GMT -4
Density Not Known
Languages Dutch,Creole
Literacy rate 90%
Currency Netherland Antilles Guilder
Economy Tourism , Offshore Finance
Religions Protestant, catholic
Ethnic Mix black 62%,european 40%

GEOGRAPHY
Elevation
lowest point: Caribbean Sea 0 m
highest point: Mount Scenery 862 m
Geography Note
the five islands of the Netherlands Antilles
are divided geographically into the Leeward
Islands (northern) group (Saba, Sint
Eustatius, and Sint Maarten) and the
Windward Islands (southern) group (Bonaire
and Curacao)
Natural Resources
Phosphates (Curacao only),
salt(Bonaire only)
Climate
Tropical
Netherlands Food
Dutch Indies Fruitcake/Shrimp Fritters/
Trotter Souse

WORLD CUP

1930	Did not qualify
1934	Did not qualify
1938	Did not qualify
1950	Did not qualify
1954	Did not qualify
1958	Did not qualify
1962	Did not qualify
1966	Did not qualify
1970	Did not qualify
1974	Did not qualify
1978	Did not qualify
1982	Did not qualify
1986	Did not qualify
1990	Did not qualify
1994	Did not qualify
1998	Did not qualify
2002	Did not qualify

COUNTRY LEAGUE CHAMPIONS

2004	Not Known
2003	SV Centro Barber
2002	SV Centro Barber
2001	Jong colombia
2000	Not Known
1999	Sithoc FC Mahuma
1998	Jong Colombia
1997	UD Banda Abou
1996	Not Known

Women's League Champi

2004	Not Known
2003	Not Known
2002	Not Known
2001	Not Known
2000	Not Known

NATIONAL TEAM COLORS

WORLD PICTURES OF SOCCER

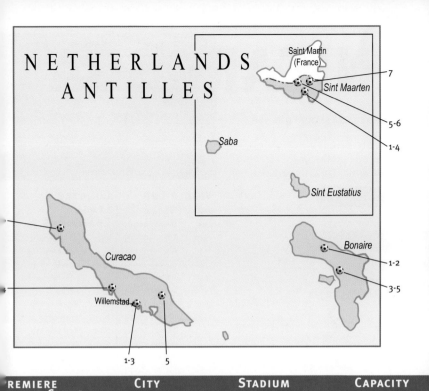

NETHERLANDS ANTILLES

Saint Martin (France)

Sint Maarten — 7

5-6

1-4

Saba

Sint Eustatius

Curacao

Bonaire — 1-2

Willemstad — 3-5

1-3 5

PREMIERE LEAGUE CLUBS	CITY	STADIUM	CAPACITY
SUBTWillemstad	Curacao		
CRKSV Jong Holland	Willemstad-C		
Inter Willemstad	Willemstad-C		
CRKSV Jong Colombia	Boka Sami-C		
RKSV Centro	Dominguito-Curacao		
Deportivo San Cruz	Santa Cruz-C		
BONAIRE ISLAND			
Real Rincon	Rincon		
Vespo	Rincon		
SV Uruguay	Rincon		
SV Vitesse	Kralendijk		
SV Juventus	Kralendijk		
SINT MARTEEN			
Victory Boys	Philipsburg		
United Warlords	Philipsburg		
Liberation Stars	Philipsburg		
Haitian United	Philipsburg		
Rebels	St. Peter		
Organized Youth	L.Prince Quarters		

NICARAGUA

FED. NICARAGUENSE DE FUTBOL
Hospital bautista 1,Cuadra Abajo,
1 Cuadra al sur y1/2 cuadra abajo,976 Managua
TEL 505/222 7035   FAX /222 7885
WEB www.concacaf.com

REFERENCE
Official name
   Republic of Nicaragua

Date of	
formation	1838
Capital	Managua
Population	5.1 Million
Total area	45,849 sq Mi, 118,750 sq Km
Time zone	GMT -6
Density	111 per sq Mi, 36 per sq Km
Languages	Spanish, English Creole, Miskito
Literacy rate	66%
Currency	Cordoba
Economy	agriculture 47%, services 37%
Religions	catholic 80%, protestant 17%
Ethnic Mix	mestizo 67%, white 14%, black 8%

GEOGRAPHY
Elevation
lowest point: Pacific Ocean 0 m
highest point: Mogoton 2,438 m
Geography Note
largest country in Central America; contains
the largest freshwater body in Central
America, Lago de Nicaragua
Natural Resources
gold, silver, copper, tungsten, lead, zinc, timber, fish
Climate
tropical in lowlands, cooler in highlands
Nicaraguan Food
oxtail Stew
fresco de pina y arroz (Drink)

WORLD CUP		COUNTRY LEAGUE CHAMPIONS	
1930	Did not qualify		
1934	Did not qualify		
1938	Did not qualify	2004	Diriangen (A)
1950	Did not qualify		Real Esteli (C)
1954	Did not qualify	2003	Real Esteli (A)
1958	Did not qualify		Real Esteli (C)
1962	Did not qualify	2002	Jalapa
1966	Did not qualify	2001	Walter Ferreti
1970	Did not qualify	2000	Diriangen
1974	Did not qualify	1999	Real Esteli
1978	Did not qualify	1998	Walter Ferreti
1982	Did not qualify	**Women's League Champ**	
1986	Did not qualify	2004	UNAN Managua
1990	Did not qualify	2003	Dirangen
1994	Did not qualify	2002	UAM
1998	Did not qualify	2001	Not Known
2002	Did not qualify	2000	Not Known

NATIONAL TEAM COLORS

WORLD PICTURES OF SOCCER

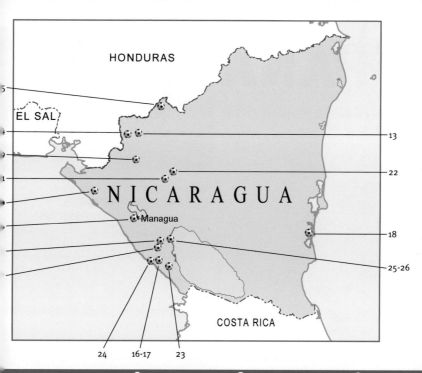

PREMIERE LEAGUE CLUBS	CITY	STADIUM	CAPACITY
Deportivo Walter Ferreti	Managua	Estadio T. Cranshaw	12 000
Acadamia de Policia	Managua		
Club Barrio de Cuba	Managua		
Parmalat FC	Managua	Estadio T. Cranshaw	12 000
UNAN Investa	Managua		
Deportivo Bautista	Managua		
Real Esteli FC	Esteli	Estadio Independencia	15 000
Junior Esteli	Esteli	Estadio Independencia	15 000
Atletico Esteli	Esteli	Estadio Independencia	15 000
Diriangen FC	Diriamba	Estadio Cacique	11 000
Masetepe	San marcos	Estadio Olimpico	5 000
San Marcos FC	San Marcos	Estadio Olimpico	5 000
Real Madriz FC	Madriz	Estadio Santiago	1 000
Deprtivo Somoto	Somoto	Estadio Santiago	1 000
Deportivo Jalapa	Jalapa	Estadio A.Ramos	1 000
Deportivo Masachapa	San Rafael/Sur		
Deportivo juniors	San Rafael/Sur		
Deportivo Bluefields	Bluefields		
Diriangen FC	Diriamba	Estadion Diriangen	5 000
FC Chinandega	Chinandega		
Club de Sebaco	Sebaco		
Matiguas	Matagalpa		
D. Bayardo lopez	San Antonio Arriba		
Delfines	Masachapa		
Intecna	Granada		
Deportivo Granada	Granad		

# PANAMA

FED. PANAMENA DE FUTBOL
Estadio Rommel Fernandez,Puerta 24,
Ave.Agustin A.AP 8-391 Zona 8,Panama
TEL 507/233 3896 FAX /233 0582
WEB www.marearoja.com/

REFERENCE
Official name
Republic of Panama
Date of formation 1903
Capital Panama City
Population 2.9 Million
Total area 29,340 sq Mi, 75,990 sq Km
Time zone GMT -5
Density 99 per sq Mi, 35 per sq Km
Languages Spanish, english Creole, indian languages
Literacy rate 90%
Currency Balboa
Economy services 60%
Religions catholic 86%, protestant 6%
Ethnic Mix meztizo 60%, white 14%, black 12%

GEOGRAPHY
Elevation
lowest point: Pacific Ocean o m
highest point: Volcan de Chiriqui 3,475 m
Geography Note
strategic location on eastern end of isthmus
forming land bridge connecting North and
South America; controls Panama Canal that
links North Atlantic Ocean via Caribbean Sea
with North Pacific Ocean
Natural Resources
copper, mahogany forests, shrimp,
hydropower
Climate
tropical maritime; hot, humid
Panamean Food
tamales Panamenos

WORLD CUP

1930	Did not qualify
1934	Did not qualify
1938	Did not qualify
1950	Did not qualify
1954	Did not qualify
1958	Did not qualify
1962	Did not qualify
1966	Did not qualify
1970	Did not qualify
1974	Did not qualify
1978	Did not qualify
1982	Did not qualify
1986	Did not qualify
1990	Did not qualify
1994	Did not qualify
1998	Did not qualify
2002	Did not qualify

COUNTRY LEAGUE CHAMPIONS

2004	Dep. Arabe Unido
2003	Tauro FC
2002	CD Plaza Amador
2001	Panama Viejo FC
2000	Tauro FC
1999	Deportivo Arabe
1998	Tauro FC
1997	Tauro FC
1996	San Francisco FC

Women's League Cham|

2004	CD Venus Santa Ana
2003	CD Santa Ana
2002	CD Santa Ana
2001	Embajadoras Veragua
2000	CD Santa Ana

NATIONAL TEAM COLORS

WORLD PICTURES OF SOCCER

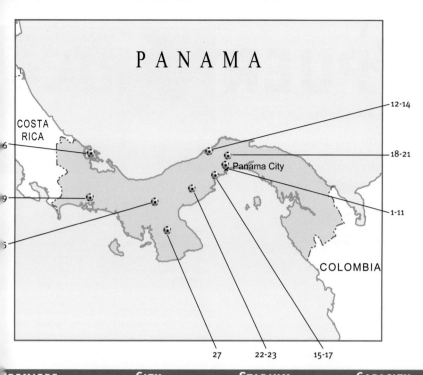

PANAMA

COSTA RICA

COLOMBIA

Panama City

6

9

5

12-14

18-21

1-11

27

22-23

15-17

PREMIERE LEAGUE CLUBS	CITY	STADIUM	CAPACITY
CD Plaza Amador	Panama City	Estadio Balboa	10 000
Tauro FC	Panama City	Estadio Giancarlo Gronchi	8 000
Panama Viejo	Panama City	Estadio Romel Fernandez	35 000
AFC Euro Kickers	Panama City	Estadio Romel Fernandez	35 000
El Chorillo FC	Panama City	Estadio JC Artes y Oficios	2 500
Alianza FC	Panama City	Estadio Romel Fernandez	35 000
Chorillo FC	Panama City		
Deportivo Italia	Panama City		
CD Espanol	Panama City		
Real Calidonia	Panama City		
Atletico Nacional FC	Panama City		
Deportivo Arabe Colon	Colon	Roberto Mariano Bula	7 500
Sporting Colon	Colon	Roberto Mariano Bula	7 500
Atletico Municipal	Colon	Roberto Mariano Bula	7 500
San Francisco FC	La Chorrera		
Atletico Guadalupe	La Chorrera		
CA Independiente	La Chorrera		
Sporting 89	San Miguelito		
Pan de Azucar	San Miguelito		
Cosmos FC	San Miguelito		
Ejecutivo Juniors	San Miguelito		
Sporting Cocle	Cocle		
Vista Hermosa	Cocle		
Atletico Veraguense	Veraguas		
La Primavera FC	Veraguas		
Zona Libre FC	Bocas del Toro		
Chitre FC	Herrera		
Chiriqui FC	Chiriqui	Estadio Kenny Cerracin	7 500
Solano FC	Chiriqui	Estadio Kenny Cerracin	7 500

PUERTO RICO

PUERTO RICO FOOTBALL FED,
PB 194355
Hato Rey,PR 00919-4355
TEL 1 787/764 2025   FAX /764 2025
WEB www.prfutbol.org

REFERENCE
Official name
Puerto Rico
(Commonwealth of the U.S.A)

Date of	
formation	1898
Capital	San Juan
Population	3,985,653
Total area	3,516 sq Mi, 9,104 sq Km
Time zone	GMT -4
Density	434 per sq km
Languages	Spanish,English
Literacy rate	89%
Currency	U.S $
Economy	Government 22%,manufactur-ing 17%,construction 6%
Religions	catholic 85%, crotestant 15% White (mostly Spanish origin)
Ethnic Mix	Hispanic 80.5%, black 8%

GEOGRAPHY
Elevation
lowest point: Caribbean Sea 0 m
highest point: Cerro de Punta 1,338 m
Geography Note
important location along the Mona Passage - a key shipping lane to the Panama Canal; San Juan is one of the biggest and best natural harbors in the Caribbean; many small rivers and high central mountains ensure land is well watered;south coast relatively dry
Natural Resources
some copper and nickel; potential for onshore and offshore oil
Climate
tropical marine, mild
Puerto Rican Food
pan de Maiz de carnaval
ensalada de bacalao

WORLD CUP		COUNTRY
1930	Did not qualify	**LEAGUE**
1934	Did not qualify	**CHAMPIONS**
1938	Did not qualify	2004 San Lorenzo
1950	Did not qualify	2003 Not Known
1954	Did not qualify	2002 Acad. De Quintana
1958	Did not qualify	2001 Acad. De Quintana
1962	Did not qualify	2000 Acad. De Quintana
1966	Did not qualify	1999 CF Nacional
1970	Did not qualify	1998 Acad. De Quintana
1974	Did not qualify	1997 Acad. De Quintana
1978	Did not qualify	1996 Acad. De Quintana
1982	Did not qualify	**Women's League Champ**
1986	Did not qualify	2004 Indias
1990	Did not qualify	2003 Indias
1994	Did not qualify	2002 Academia de Quintana
1998	Did not qualify	2001 Not Known
2002	Did not qualify	2000 Not Known

NATIONAL TEAM COLORS

WORLD PICTURES OF SOCCER

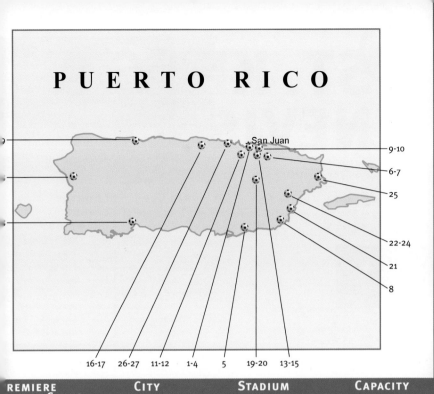

PUERTO RICO

San Juan

9-10
6-7
25
22-24
21
8

16-17　26-27　11-12　1-4　5　19-20　13-15

PREMIERE LEAGUE CLUBS	CITY	STADIUM	CAPACITY
CAF Quintana	San Juan		
Sporting Club San Juan	San Juan		
Islanders	San Juan		
Roosevelt	San Juan		
Brujos FC	Guayama		
Club Nacional de Carolina	Carolina		
Gigantes de Carolina	Carolina		
CF Maunabo Lions	Maunabo		
CF Roosevelt Pumas	Hato Rey		
Academia Quintana	Hato rey		
CF Byamon Lincoln	Bayamon		
Vaqueros	Bayamon		
Club Atleticos Rio Piedras	Rio Piedras		
Cardenales	Rio Piedras		
Club Fraigcomar	Rio Piedras		
CF Vega Alta	Vega Alta		
Maceteros	Vega Alta		
Atleticos de Anasco	Anasco		
Bairoa Huracanas	Caguas		
Criollos de Caguas	Caguas		
Boriken	Yabucoa		
Tornados FC	Hamacao		
Buhos	Hamacao		
Universidad	Hamacao		
Dorados	Ceiba		
Club Llaneros	Toa Baja		
Atleticos de Levittown	Toa Baja		
Club Guayacanes	Guayanilla		
Ganadores	Hatillo		

ST. KITTS & NEVIS

St. Kitts & Nevis Football
Association
PB 465, Warner Park, Basse Terre
TEL 1 869/4675 6809 FAX /465 1190
WEB www.sknfa.kn

Reference
Official name
St. Kitts & Nevis

**Date of
formation** 1983
Capital Basse Terre
Population 41.000
Total area 139 sq Mi, 360 sq Km
Time zone GMT -4
Density 412 per sq Mi, 159 per sq Km
Languages English, English creole
Literacy rate 90%
Currency East Caribbean $
Economy services 69%, industry & agri-
culture 31%
Religions anglican 33%, methodist
29%, Moravian 9%
Ethnic Mix black 95%, mixed 5%

Geography
Elevation
lowest point: Caribbean Sea 0 m
highest point: Mount Liamuiga 1,156 m
Geography Note
with coastlines in the shape of a baseball
bat and ball, the two volcanic islands are
separated by a three-km-wide channel
called The Narrows
Natural Resources
arable land
Climate
tropical tempered by constant sea breezes;
little seasonal temperature variation; rainy
season (May to November)
Saint Kitts & Nevis Food
jam cake/mango chutney

WORLD CUP		COUNTRY LEAGUE CHAMPIONS	
1930	Did not qualify		
1934	Did not qualify		
1938	Did not qualify	2004	Newtown United FC
1950	Did not qualify	2003	Village Superstars
1954	Did not qualify	2002	Canyon Rockets
1958	Did not qualify	2001	Garden Hotspurs FC
1962	Did not qualify	2000	Not Known
1966	Did not qualify	1999	St Paul's United
1970	Did not qualify	1998	Newton United FC
1974	Did not qualify	1997	Newton United FC
1978	Did not qualify	1996	Newton United FC
1982	Did not qualify	**Women's League Champ**	
1986	Did not qualify	2004	Not Known
1990	Did not qualify	2003	Not Known
1994	Did not qualify	2002	Not Known
1998	Did not qualify	2001	Not Known
2002	Did not qualify	2000	Not Known

NATIONAL TEAM COLORS

WORLD PICTURES OF SOCCER

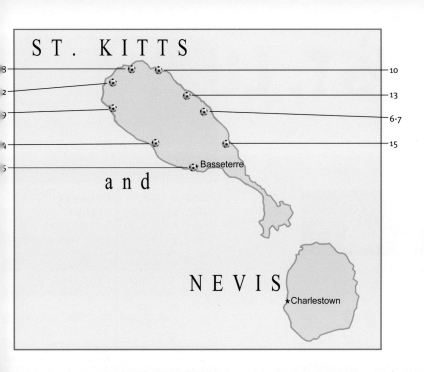

ST. KITTS and NEVIS

Basseterre

NEVIS

★Charlestown

PREMIERE LEAGUE CLUBS	CITY	STADIUM	CAPACITY
Village Superstars FC	Basseterre	Warner Park	10 000
Garden Hotspurs FC	Basseterre	Warner Park	10 000
Newton United FC	Basseterre	Warner Park	10 000
Basseterre HS FC	Basseterre	Warner Park	10 000
Blackburns FC	Basseterre	Warner Park	10 000
Cayon Rockets FC	Cayon		
Cayon Juniors FC	Cayon		
Saint Paul United	Saint Paul's		
Sandy Point FC	Sandy Point Town		
-Saddlers FC	Sadlers		
-Newton Juniors	Newton Ground		
-Newtown Ground FC	Newton Ground		
-Molineux FC	Molineux		
Old Roads FC	Old Road Town		
-Conaree FC	Upper Conaree		

ST. LUCIA

ST. LUCIA FOOTBALL ASSOC.
PB 255, Castries
TEL 1-785/453 0687 FAX /456 0510
WEB www.concacaf.com

REFERENCE
Official name
  Saint Lucia
Date of formation 1979
Capital Castries
Population 156,260
Total area 236 sq Mi, 610 sq Km
Time zone GMT -4
Density 662 per sq Mi, 248 per sq Km
Languages English , french Creole, Hindu Urdu
Literacy rate 82%
Currency East Caribbean $
Economy services 65%, agriculture 26%
Religions catholic 90%
Ethnic Mix black 90%, mulatto 6%, asian 3%

GEOGRAPHY
Elevation
lowest point: Caribbean Sea 0 m
highest point: Mount Gimie 950 m
Geography Note
the twin Pitons (Gros Piton and Petit Piton), striking cone-shaped peaks south of Soufriere, are one of the scenic natural highlights of the Caribbean
Natural Resources
forests, sandy beaches, minerals (pumice), mineral springs, geothermal potential
Climate
tropical, moderated by northeast trade winds; dry season from January to April, rainy season from May to August
Saint Lucian Food
canaoui/greenfig salad/petit piton

WORLD CUP		COUNTRY LEAGUE CHAMPIONS	
1930	Did not qualify		
1934	Did not qualify		
1938	Did not qualify	2004	Roots Alley Ballers
1950	Did not qualify	2003	Roots Alley Ballers
1954	Did not qualify	2002	VSADC
1958	Did not qualify	2001	VSADC
1962	Did not qualify	2000	Roots Alley Ballers
1966	Did not qualify	1999	Roots Alley Ballers
1970	Did not qualify	1998	Mabouya Valley Rov.
1974	Did not qualify	1997	Pioneers FC
1978	Did not qualify	1996	Not Known
1982	Did not qualify	**Women's League Champ**	
1986	Did not qualify	2005	Not Known
1990	Did not qualify	2004	Not Known
1994	Did not qualify	2003	Not Known
1998	Did not qualify	2002	Not Known
2002	Did not qualify	2001	Not Known

NATIONAL TEAM COLORS

WORLD PICTURES OF SOCCER

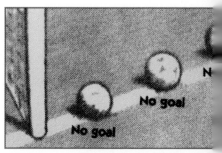

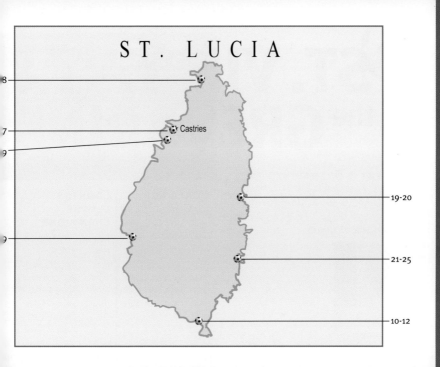

PREMIERE LEAGUE CLUBS	CITY	STADIUM	CAPACITY
VSADC	Castries	Vigie Field	
Lancers	Castries	Vigie Field	
Pioneers FC	Castries		
La Clery	Castries		
Black Mallet	Castries		
Spartans FC	Castries		
Shoppers FC	Castries		
Ghetto Stars	Soufriere		
Challengers SSC	Soufriere		
-Roots Alley Ballers	Vieux Fort	Friendship Park	
-Ghetto Lions	Vieux Fort	Friendship Park	
-BC Square United	Vieux Fort	Friendship Park	
-Cimpex Orion	Gros Islet		
-Northern United	Gros Islet		
-Orion FC	Gros Islet		
-Veterans FC	Gros Islet		
-Northern All Stars	Gros Islet		
-Borderline Rebels	Gros Islet		
-DCYO	Dennery		
-18 plus	Dennery		
-Pakis	Micoud		
-Boca Juniors	Micoud		
-Atlantic Ballers	Micoud		
-Leeds United	Micoud		
-Parks United	Micoud		
-Nyabinghi	Marchand		
-Skyzers	Marchand		
-Spurs United	Marchand		
-Pioneers	Marchand		

ST. VINCENT & the GRENADINES

ST. VINCENT & GRENADINES FOOTBALL FEDERATION

Sharp Street, PB 1278, Kingstown
TEL 1 784/456 2438   FAX /458 1177
WEB www.tnt.fifa.com

REFERENCE
Official name
St.Vincent & Grenadines

Date of formation	1979
Capital	Kingstown
Population	115,461
Total area	131 sq Mi, 340 sq Km
Time zone	GMT -4
Density	880 per sq Mi, 354 per sq Km
Languages	English, English Creole
Literacy rate	82%
Currency	East Caribbean $
Economy	agriculture 50%, services 30%
Religions	anglican 42%, methodist 20%
Ethnic Mix	black 66%, mulatto 19%, Asian 6%

GEOGRAPHY
Elevation
lowest point: Caribbean Sea 0 m
highest point: Soufriere 1,234 m
Geography Note
the administration of the islands of the
Grenadines group is divided between Saint
Vincent and the Grenadines and Grenada;
Saint Vincent and the Grenadines is comprised
of 32 islands and cays
Natural Resources
hydropower, cropland
Climate
tropical; little seasonal temperature variation;
rainy season (May to November)
Saint Vincent & Grenadines Food
pelau chicken/rava laddoo/cassava pone

WORLD CUP		COUNTRY LEAGUE CHAMPIONS	
1930	Did not qualify		
1934	Did not qualify		
1938	Did not qualify	2004	Samba FC
1950	Did not qualify	2003	BESCO
1954	Did not qualify	2002	San Juan Jablotech
1958	Did not qualify	2001	W.Connection FC
1962	Did not qualify	2000	W.Connection FC
1966	Did not qualify	1999	Defence Force
1970	Did not qualify	1998	Joe Public FC
1974	Did not qualify	1997	Defence Force
1978	Did not qualify	1996	Defence Force
1982	Did not qualify	**Women's League Champ**	
1986	Did not qualify	2004	Not Known
1990	Did not qualify	2003	Not Known
1994	Did not qualify	2002	Jane Public FC
1998	Did not qualify	2001	Stingrays FC
2002	Did not qualify	2000	United Petrotrin

NATIONAL TEAM COLORS

WORLD PICTURES OF SOCCER

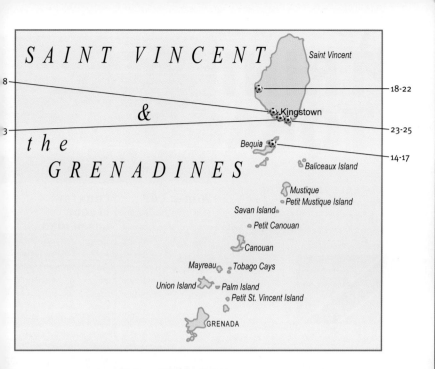

Premiere League Clubs	City	Stadium	Capacity
Frenches FC	Kingstown		
-Pepsi Sion Hill	Kingstown		
-Rose Place	Kingstown		
SVG Air Power Link	Kingstown		
Keartons U.	Kingstown		
Prospect U.	Kingstown		
Highpark Jugglers	Kingstown		
Richmond Hill	Kingstown		
De Freitas Hill Top	Arnos Vale		
-Cowdray Village	Arnos Vale		
-Brighton All Stars	Arnos Vale		
-Max Strikers	Arno Vale		
-English Pearls	Arno Vale		
-Lions FC	Bequia		
-High Times	Bequia		
-West Connection	Bequia		
-Fullness	Bequia		
-Keartons United	Barrouallie		
-North Stars	Barrouaille		
-Top Siders	Barouaille		
-St Vincent Motor system	Barouaille		
-Hill View	Barouaille		
-Prospect United FC	Calliaqua		
-Ascoli	Calliaqua		
-Play it Safe FC	Calliaqua		

TRINIDAD & TOBAGO

T & T FOOTBALL FEDERATION
24-26 dundonald Street,PB
400,Port of Spain
TEL 1 868/623 7312 FAX /623 8109
WEB www.tnt.fifa.com

REFERENCE
Official name
Republic of Trinida & Tobago

Date of	
formation	1962
Capital	Port of Spain
Population	1.3 Million
Total area	1981 sq Mi, 5130 sq Km
Time zone	GMT -4
Density	656 per Mi, 214 per sq Km
Languages	English, English creole
Literacy rate	98%
Currency	T&T $
Economy	Services 73%
Religions	catholic 32%, hindu 24%, anglican & protestant 28%
Ethnic Mix	Black african 90%,others 10%

WORLD CUP

1930	Did not qualify
1934	Did not qualify
1938	Did not qualify
1950	Did not qualify
1954	Did not qualify
1958	Did not qualify
1962	Did not qualify
1966	Did not qualify
1970	Did not qualify
1974	Did not qualify
1978	Did not qualify
1982	Did not qualify
1986	Did not qualify
1990	Did not qualify
1994	Did not qualify
1998	Did not qualify
2002	Did not qualify

COUNTRY LEAGUE CHAMPIONS

2004	Northeast Stars
2003	San Juan Jabloteh
2002	San Juan Jabloteh
2001	W.Connection FC
2000	W.Connection FC
1999	Defence Force
1998	Defence Force
1997	Defence Force
1996	Defence Force

Women's League Champ

2004	Joe Public Ladies FC
2003	Stingrays
2002	Jane Public FC
2001	Stingrays FC
2000	United Petrotrin FC

NATIONAL TEAM COLORS

GEOGRAPHY
Elevation
lowest point: Caribbean Sea 0 m
highest point: El Cerro del Aripo 940 m
Geography Note
Pitch Lake, on Trinidad's southwestern coast, is the world's largest natural reservoir of asphalt
Natural Resources
petroleum, natural gas, asphalt
Climate
tropical; rainy season (June to December)
Trinidad & Tobago Food
Pastelles/curry potatoes

WORLD PICTURES OF SOCCER

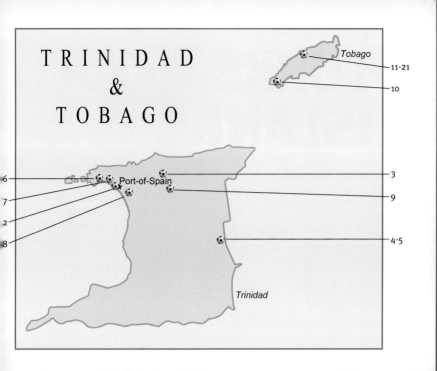

PREMIERE LEAGUE CLUBS	CITY	STADIUM	CAPACITY
-Maple Club	Port of Spain-TR Ils.	Hasely crawford Stadium	
-Malvern United	Port of Spain-TR Ils.	Hasely Crawford Stadium	
-Joe Public	Arouca-TR Ils.	Dr.Joao Havalenge Center	
-W Connection	Point Luisas-TR Ils.		
-Doc's Khelwalaas FC	Point Luisas-TR Ils.		
-Defence Force FC	Chaguaramas-TR Ils.		
-Police SC	Saint James-TR Ils.		
-San Juan Jabloteh	San Juan-TR Ils.		
-Arama Fire FC	Arima-TR Ils.		
-Phoenix Red	Canaan-Tobago Isl.		
-Tobago United	Tobago Island		
-Grafton Stokely Vale	Tobago Island		
-King David Enterprise	Tobago Island		
-Pepsi Hills United	Tobago Island		
-Georgia FC	Tobago Island		
-Earl Brooks	Tobago Island		
-KDE Goal City	Tobago Island		
-Golden Lane	Tobago Island		
-Main Street	Tobago Island		
-Charlotteville Unifiers	Tobago Island		
-Saint Clair's CS	Tobago Island		

TURKS & CAICOS ISLANDS

TURKS & CAYCOS ISLANDS
Football Association
PB 626, Tropicana Plaza, Leeward
HWY, Providenciales
TEL 1 649/941 5532 • www.football.tc

REFERENCE
Official name
Turks & Caicos (British Territory)

Claimed	1766
Capital	Cockburn Town
Population	13,800
Total area	166 sq Mi9430sq Km
Time zone	GMT -5
Density	44 per Sq Km
Languages	English, English creole
Literacy rate	92%
Currency	U.S $
Economy	tourism
Religions	anglican, protestant
Ethnic Mix	black african, mulatto, europ.

GEOGRAPHY
Elevation
lowest point: Caribbean Sea o m
highest point: Blue Hills 49 m
Geography Note
about 40 islands (eight inhabited)
Natural Resources
spiny lobster, conch
Climate
tropical; marine; moderated by trade winds;
sunny and relatively dry
Turks & Caicos Food
conch chowder/coconut rum
chessecake/conch fritters

WORLD CUP

1930	Did not qualify
1934	Did not qualify
1938	Did not qualify
1950	Did not qualify
1954	Did not qualify
1958	Did not qualify
1962	Did not qualify
1966	Did not qualify
1970	Did not qualify
1974	Did not qualify
1978	Did not qualify
1982	Did not qualify
1986	Did not qualify
1990	Did not qualify
1994	Did not qualify
1998	Did not qualify
2002	Did not qualify

COUNTRY LEAGUE CHAMPIONS

2004	KPMG United FC
2003	Carribean Allstars
2002	Beaches FC
2001	SWA Sharks FC
2000	Masters FC
1999	Tropic Allstars
1998	Not Known
1997	Not Known
1996	Not Known

Women's League Champ

2004	Horizon FC
2003	Blue Thunder FC
2002	Yellow Flames
2001	Grey Hurricanes
2000	Not Known

NATIONAL TEAM COLORS

WORLD PICTURES OF SOCCER

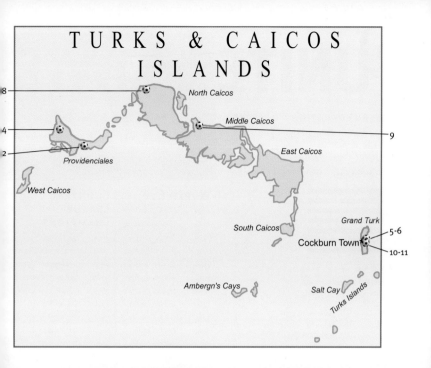

TURKS & CAICOS ISLANDS

PREMIERE LEAGUE CLUBS	CITY	STADIUM	CAPACITY
Caribbean Allstars FC	Providenciales	Providenciales Ground	1 500
Police FC	Providenciales	Providenciales Ground	1 500
ProvoPool Celtic FC	Providenciales	Providenciales Ground	1 500
Team TCIFA	Providenciales	Providenciales Ground	1 500
KPMG United FC	Grand Turk		
Grand Turk FC	Grand Turk		
RMC Master Hammer	North Caicos		
SWA Sharks FC	North Caicos		
Beaches Strikers FC	Conch Bar		
Barefoot FC	Cockburn Town		
Catholic Church	Cockburn Town		
Sans Complex	Five Cays		

UNITED STATES

US Soccer Federation
US Soccer House,1801-1811 S.Prairie
Ave.,Chicago,IL 60616
TEL 1 312/808 1300 FAX /808 1301
WEB www.ussoccer.com

Reference
Official name
United states of America

Date of formation	1776
Capital	Washington D.C.
Population	278.4 Million
Total area	3,539,224 sq Mi 9,166,600 sq Km
Time zone	GMT -5/11
Density	79 per sq Mi, 29 per sq Km
Languages	English,Spanish
Literacy rate	99%
Currency	U.S $
Economy	Services 80%, industry 18%
Religions	Protestant 61%, catholic 25%, jewish 2%
Ethnic Mix	White(Inc.Hispanic) 84%, Black 12%, Native Indian 1%

Geography
Elevation
lowest point: Death Valley -86 m
highest point: Mount McKinley 6,194 m
Geography Note
world's third-largest country by size (after
Russia and Canada) and by population
(after China and India); Mt. McKinley is
highest point in North America and Death
Valley the lowest point on the continent .
Natural Resources
coal, copper, lead, molybdenum, phosphates, uranium, bauxite, gold, iron, nickel,
potash, silver, tungsten, zinc, petroleum,
natural gas.
Climate
mostly temperate, tropical in Hawaii and
Florida, arctic in Alaska, semiarid in the
great plains , and arid in the southwest.
United States Food
cheeseburger & fries/Apple Pie

World Cup

1930	Finish Third
1934	First Round Exit
1938	Did not qualify
1950	First round exit
1954	Did not qualify
1958	Did not qualify
1962	Did not qualify
1966	Did not qualify
1970	Did not qualify
1974	Did not qualify
1978	Did not qualify
1982	Did not qualify
1986	Did not qualify
1990	First round exit
1994	Sd round exit
1998	First round exit
2002	1/4 final exit

Country League Champions

2004	D.C United
2003	San Jose Earthquakes
2002	Los Angeles Galaxy
2001	San Jose Earthquakes
2000	Kansas City Wizards
1999	D.C United
1998	Chicago Fire
1997	D.C United
1996	D.C United

Women's League Champ

2004	New Jersey Wildcats
2003	Washington Freedoms
2002	Carolina Courage
2001	Bay Area CyberRays
2000	San Diego W.F.C

National Team Colors

World Pictures of Soccer

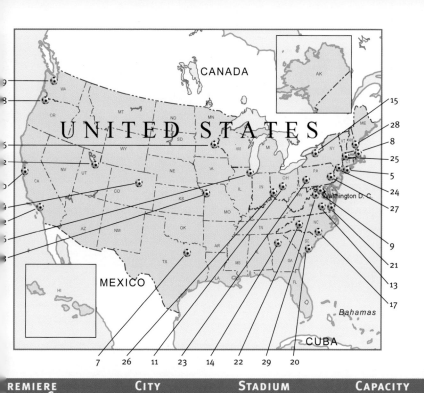

PREMIERE LEAGUE CLUBS	CITY	STADIUM	CAPACITY
laxy (MLS)	Los Angeles	Home Depot Center	27 000
USA (MLS)	Los Angeles	Home Depot Center	27 000
s City Wizards (MLS)	Kansas City	Arrowhead Stadium	79 451
do Rapids (MLS)	Denver	Rapids Stadium	20 000
ork Metrostars (MLS)	New York/New jersey	Giant Stadium	80 242
o Fires (MLS)	Chicago	Bridgeview Stadium	22 000
as (MLS)	Dallas	Pizza Hut Park	21 193
olution (MLS)	Foxboro	Foxboro Gillette Stadium	68 756
ted (MLS)	Washington D.C	RFK Memorial Stadium	56 000
ose Earthquakes (MLS)	San Jose	Spartan Stadium	25 525
bus Crew (MLS)	Columbus	Columbus Crew Stadium	22 555
alt Lake (MLS)	Salt Lake City	Rice-Eccles Stadium	46 500
ond Kickers (USL)	Richmond	Richmond Stadium	22 600
a Silverbacks (USL)	Atlanta	Dekalb Memorial	15 000
ster Rhinos (USL)	Rochester	Frontier Field	12 052
sota Thunder (USL)	Minneapolis	National Sport Center	12 000
gton Hammerhead (USL)	Wilmington	Legion Sports Cplx	5 500
nd Timbers (USL)	Portland	PGE Park	19 566
e Sounders (USL)	Seattle	Quest Field	67 000
eston Battery (USL)	Charleston	Black Baud Stadium	5 113
a Beach Mariners (USL)	Virginia Beach	VB Sportsplex	10 000
tte Eagles (USL)	Charlotte	Waddell H.S	4 000
urgh Riverhounds (USL)	Pittsburgh	Falconi Field	5 000
sland Roughriders (USL)	Uniondale	Mitchell Athletics Cplx	10 000
rn Mass Pioneers (USL)	Ludlow	Lusitano Stadium	3 000
nati Kings (USL)	Cincinnati	Corcoran Field	10 000
burg City Islanders (USL)	Harrisburg	Skyline Sports Cplx	10 000
ampshire Phantoms (USL)	Hudson	SNHU	5 000
ern Virginia Royals (USL)	Woodbridge	Forest Park Stadium	8 000

US VIRGIN ISLANDS

USVI Soccer Federation
54 castle Coakley,PB 2346,Kingshill
TEL 1 340/719 9676 FAX /719 9707
WEB www.usvisoccerfederation.com

Reference
Official name
  U.S Virgin Islands

Claimed	1917
Capital	Charlotte Amalie
Population	101,809
Total area	137 sq Mi, 355 sq Km
Time zone	GMT +7
Density	307 per sq Km
Languages	English,English Creole
Literacy rate	92%
Currency	U.S $
Economy	Tourism 90%
Religions	catholic,protestant
Ethnic Mix	Black African 90%,others

Geography
Elevation
lowest point: Caribbean Sea 0 m
highest point: Crown Mountain 474 m
Geography Note
important location along the Anegada
Passage - a key shipping lane for the
Panama Canal; Saint Thomas has one of the
best natural deepwater harbors in the
Caribbean
Natural Resources
Fishing
Climate
subtropical, tempered by easterly trade
winds, relatively low humidity
U.S. Virgin Islands Food
Jerk cooking/Crab Stuffed mushroom/
usvi spiced scallops

World Cup

1930	Did not qualify
1934	Did not qualify
1938	Did not qualify
1950	Did not qualify
1954	Did not qualify
1958	Did not qualify
1962	Did not qualify
1966	Did not qualify
1970	Did not qualify
1974	Did not qualify
1978	Did not qualify
1982	Did not qualify
1986	Did not qualify
1990	Did not qualify
1994	Did not qualify
1998	Did not qualify
2002	Did not qualify

Country League Champions

2005	Positive Vibes FC
2004	Not Known
2003	Waitikubuli United
2002	Haitian Stars SC
2001	UWS Upsetters DC
2000	UWS Upsetters DC
1999	MI Roc masters
1998	MI Roc Masters
1997	Saint John's United

Women's League Champ

2004	Not Known
2003	Not Known
2002	Not Known
2001	Not Known
2000	Not Known

National Team Colors

World Pictures of Soccer

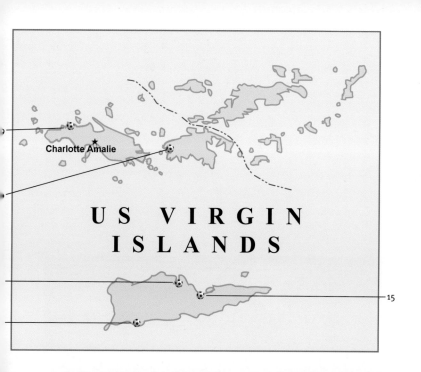

Charlotte Amalie

US VIRGIN ISLANDS

15

PREMIERE LEAGUE CLUBS	CITY	STADIUM	CAPACITY
Waitikubuli United SC	St.Thomas	Tortola Fields	
Haitian Stars SC	St.Thomas	Tortola Fields	
JWS Upsetters SC	St.Thomas	Tortola Fields	
Antilles Strikers SC	St.Thomas	Tortola fields	
M.I Roc Masters SC	St.Thomas	Tortola Fields	
Positive Vibes	St.Thomas	Tortola Fields	
St.Kitts United SC	St.Thomas	Tortola Fields	
Outlaws	St.Thomas	Tortola Fields	
JVI/School	St.Thomas	Tortola Fields	
Saint John United	Cruz Bay-St.John		
NT CROIX ISLAND			
Helenites	GroveplaceSt.Croix		
Rovers FC	St.Croix		
Chelsea United SC	St.Croix		
Skills SC	St.Croix		
Unique FC	ChristianstedSt.Croix		

SOUTH AMERICA

ARGENTINA

ASSOCIACION DEL FUTBOL ARGENTINO
Viamonte 1366(1053) Buenos Aires
TEL 54-11 4372 - 7900/4372
WEB www.afa.org.ar

REFERENCE
Official name
Argentine Republic
Date of formation 1816/1925
Capital Buenos Aires
Population 34 million
Total area 1,068,296 sq MI,
2,766,890 sq KM
Time zone GMT -3:00
Density 34 sq Mi, 13 sq Ki
Languages Spanish, English
Literacy rate 96%
Currency Argentine Peso
Economy 50% Services
Religions Catholic 90%
Ethnic Mix European 85%

Geography
Elevation
Lowest Point:
Salinas Chicas -40 m (located on Peninsula Valdes)
Highest Point: Cerro Aconcagua 6,960 m
Geography Note
second-largest country in South America (after Brazil); Cerro Aconcagua is South America's tallest mountain, while the Valdes Peninsula is the lowest point on the continent
Natural Resources
fertile plains of the Pampas, lead, zinc, tin, copper, iron ore, manganese, petroleum, uranium
Climate
mostly temperate; arid in southeast; subantarctic in southwest.
Argentinian Food
Matambre/Empanadas/Crillo de Pollo

WORLD CUP

1930	Final list
1934	First round exit
1938	Did not qualify
1950	Did not qualify
1954	Did not qualify
1958	First round exit
1962	First round exit
1966	1/4 finals
1970	Did not qualify
1974	Scd round exit
1978	World Champion
1982	Scd round exit
1986	World Champion
1990	Final list
1994	Scd round exit
1998	1/4 finals exit
2002	First round exit

COUNTRY LEAGUE CHAMPIONS

2004	Boca Juniors (A)
	River Plate (C)
2003	River Plate (A)
	Independiente(C)
2002	River plate (A)
	Racing Club (C)
2001	San Lorenzo (A)
	Boca Juniors (C)

Women's League Champions

2005	Boca Juniors (A)
2004	Boca juniors (A)
	River Plate (C)
2003	River Plate (A)
	River Plate (C)

NATIONAL TEAM COLORS

WORLD PICTURES OF SOCCER

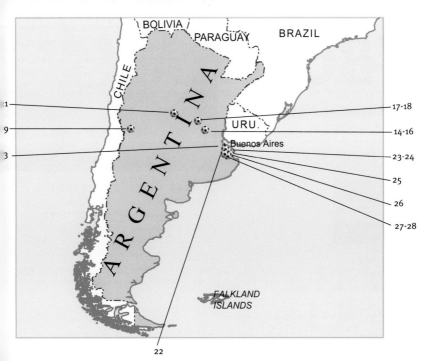

PREMIERE LEAGUE CLUBS	CITY	STADIUM	CAPACITY
River Plate	Buenos Aires	Antonio Vespucio Liberti	66 449
Boca Juniors	Buenos Aires	Alberto J.Armando	60 245
Ferrocarril Oeste	Buenos Aires	Arq.Ricardo Etcheverry	24 858
Chacarita Juniors	Buenos Aires	Chacarita Juniors	24 300
Velez Sarsfield	Buenos Aires	Jose Amalfitani	49 747
San Lorenzo	Buenos Aires	Pedro Bidegain	42 000
Nueva Chicago	Buenos Aires	Nueva Chicago	28 500
Huracan	Buenos Aires	Tomas Adolfo Duco	48 314
Argentinos Juniors	Buenos Aires	Estadio Argentinos Juniors	25 000
Defensor Belgrano	Buenos Aires	Defensor Belgrano	8 500
Platense	Buenos Aires	Ciudad de Vicente Lopez	31 000
Banfield	Buenos Aires	Florencio Sola	30 000
Almagro	Buenos Aires	Jose Ingenieros	12 000
Rosario Central	Rosario	Rosario Central	41 654
Newell's Old Boys	Rosario	Estadio 2 Abril	42 000
Tiro Federal	Rosario		
Colon Santa Fe	Santa Fe	Brigadier Lopez	32 000
Union Santa Fe	Santa Fe	15 de Abril	22 852
Talleres Cordoba	Cordoba	La Boutique	25 000
Instituto Cordoba	Cordoba	Juan Domingo Peron	26 535
Belgrano Cordoba	Cordoba	Gigante de Alberdi	28 000
Arsenal	Sarandi	Viaducto	10 000
Racing Club	Avallaneda	Presidente Peron	55 000
Independiente	Avallaneda	Estadio Independiente	57 901
Lanus	Lanus	Estadio Lanus	46 519
Quilmes AC	Quilmes	Centenario	33 000
Estudiantes	La Plata	Jorge Luis Hirschi	15 800
Gimnasia	La Plata	Juan Carlos Zerillo	33 500
San Martin	Mendoza	Gral.San Martin	9 000

 # BOLIVIA

FED. BOLIVIANA DE FUTBOL
Av. Libertador Bolivar#1148
Casilla de correo 484-Cochabamba-Bolivia
TEL 591-4 424-5889/ 424-5890
WEB:www.conmebol.com

REFERENCE
Official name
    The Repubic of Bolivia
Date of
formation   1825/1938
Capital   La Paz, Sucre
Population   8 million
Total area   424,162 sq Mi
    1,098,580 sq KM
Time zone   GMT -4:00
Density   18 sq Mi
Languages   Spanish, Quechua
Literacy rate 83%
Currency   Boliviano
Economy   50% Agriculture
Religions   Catholic 95%
Ethnic Mix   Indian and Mestizo

Geography
Elevation
lowest point: Rio Paraguay 90 m
highest point: Nevado Sajama 6,542 m
Geography Note
landlocked; shares control of Lago Titicaca,
world's highest navigable lake (elevation
3,805 m), with Peru
Natural Resources
tin, natural gas, petroleum, zinc, tungsten,
antimony, silver, iron, lead, gold, timber,
hydropower .
Climate
varies with altitude; humid and tropical to
cold and semiarid .
Bolivian Food
Picante de Gallina/Palta Rellenos

WORLD CUP

1930	First round exit
1934	Did not qualify
1938	Did not qualify
1950	First round exit
1954	Did not qualify
1958	Did not qualify
1962	Did not qualify
1966	Did not qualify
1970	Did not qualify
1974	Did not qualify
1978	Did not qualify
1982	Did not qualify
1986	Did not qualify
1990	Did not qualify
1994	First round exit
1998	Did not qualify
2002	Did not qualify

COUNTRY LEAGUE CHAMPIONS

2004	BOLIVAR (A)
2003	THE STRONGEST (A)
2002	Bolivar
2001	Oriente Petrolero
2000	J. Wilstermann
1999	Blooming
1998	Blooming
1997	Bolivar
1996	Bolivar
Women's League Champions	
2004	Enforma
2003	Atlantes
2002	Blooming
2001	Santa Cruz
2000	Santa Cruz

NATIONAL TEAM COLORS

WORLD PICTURES OF SOCCER

PREMIERE LEAGUE CLUBS	CITY	STADIUM	CAPACITY
The Strongest	La Paz	Hernando Siles	42 000
Club Bolivar	La Paz	Hernando Siles	42 000
Mariscal Braun	La Paz	Hernando Siles	42 000
La Paz FC	LaPaz		
Jorge Wilstermann	Cochabamba	FelixXCapriles	32 000
Aurora	Cochabamba	Felix Capriles	32 000
Atletico Independiente	Cochabamba		
Esparta	Cochabamba		
Oriente Petrolero	Santa Cruz	Ramon Tahuichi Aguilera	38 000
Blooming	Santa Cruz	Ramon Tahuichi Aguilera	38 000
Destroyers	Santa Cruz	Ramon Tahuichi Aguilera	38 000
Real Santa Cruz	Santa Cruz	Juan Carlos D. Saucedo	10 000
Real Potosi	Potosi	Mario Mercado v. Guzman	18 000
Nacional	Potosi		
Universitario Potosi	Potosi		
San Jose	Oruro	Jesus Bermudez	30 000
Ingenieros	Oruro		
Oruro Royal	Oruro		
Union Central	Tarija	IV Centenario	15 000
Royal Obrero	Tarija		
Universitario de Tarija	Tarija		
Independiente Petrolero	Sucre	Olimpico Patria	30 000
Stormers	Sucre		
Fancesa	Sucre		
Oriente Agropecuario	Pando		
Cobija FC	Pando		
Universitario de Beni	Beni		
1 de Mayo	Beni		
Guabira	Montero	Gilberto Parada	18 000

BRAZIL

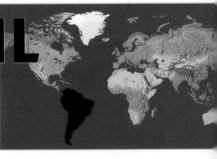

CONFEDERACAO BRASILEIRA DE FUTEBOL
Rua da Alfandega, 70, po box 1078
TEL 55-21/509 5937
WEB www.brasilfutebol.com

REFERENCE
Official name
Federative Republic of Brazil
Date of formation 1822/1929
Capital Brasilia
Population 164 million
Total area 3,286,472 sq Mi 8, 511,970 sq Km
Time zone GMT -3/5
Density 52 per sq Mi, 20 per sq Km
Languages Portuguese
Literacy rate 83%
Currency Real
Economy Services 55%
Religions Catholic
Ethnic Mix European, mix Euro-African

GEOGRAPHY
Elevation
lowest point: Salinas Chicas
-40 m (located on Peninsula Valdes)
highest point: Cerro Aconcagua 6,960 m
Geography Note
largest country in South America; Strait of Magellan, Beagle Channel, Drake Passage; Cerro Aconcagua is South America's tallest mountain, while the Valdes
Natural Resources
tin, natural gas, petroleum, zinc, tungsten, antimony, silver, iron, lead, gold, timber, hydropower
Climate
mostly tropical, but temperate in south
Brazilian Food
Sopa Leao Velloso/Empanadas de camarao/ Brazilian Feijoada

WORLD CUP

1930	First round exit
1934	First round exit
1938	Finish 3rd place
1950	Beaten Finalist
1954	1/4 final exit
1958	World Champion
1962	World Champion
1966	First round exit
1970	World Champion
1974	Finish fourth
1978	Finish third
1982	Scd round exit
1986	1/4 final exit
1990	Scd round exit
1994	World Champion
1998	Beaten Finalist
2002	World Champion

COUNTRY LEAGUE CHAMPIONS

2004	SANTOS
2003	CRUZEIRO EC
2002	Santos
2001	CA Paranaense
2000	Vasco Da Gama
1999	SC Corinthians
1998	SC Corinthians
1997	Vasco da Gama
1996	Gremio

Women's League Champions

2004	Gremio
2003	Botafogo
2002	Palmeiras
2001	Palmeiras

NATIONAL TEAM COLORS

WORLD PICTURES OF SOCCER

Map labels:
- COLOMBIA
- VEN.
- GUY.
- SUR.
- FR. GUI.
- ECU.
- PERU
- BRAZIL
- BOLIVIA
- Brasilia
- CHI.
- PARA.
- ARGENTINA
- URU.

Map numbers: 19, 16-18, 1-4, 11, 14, 9-10, 20-21, 22-23, 12, 5-8

PREMIERE LEAGUE CLUBS	CITY	STADIUM	CAPACITY
1-Botafogo FR	(Rio de Janeiro)	Jornalista Mario Filho	103 045
2-CR Flamengo	(Rio de Janeiro)	Jornalista Mario Filho	103 045
3-Fluminense FC	(Rio de Janeiro)	Jornalista Mario Filho	103 045
4-CR Vasco da Gama	(Rio de Janeiro)	Sao Januario	36 273
5-Sao Paulo FC	(Sao Paulo)	Cicero Pompeu de Toledo	80 000
6-SC Corinthians Paulista	(Sao Paulo)	Paulo Machado Carvalho	37 585
7-SE Palmeiras	(Sao Paulo)	Palestra Italia	32 000
8-A Portuguesa de Esportes	(SaoPaulo)	Osvaldo Teixeira Duarte	23 000
9-Guarani FC	(Campinas-SP)	Brinco de Ouro	30 988
10-AA Ponte Preta	(Campinas-SP)	Moises Lucarelli	18 806
11-Santos FC	(Santos-SP)	Urbano Caldeira	25 120
12-EC Sao Caetano	(Sao Caetano Sul-SP)	Anacleto Campanella	15 000
13-Marilia AC	(Marilia-SP)	Bento de Abreu	17 000
14-Mogo Mirim EC	(Mogo Mirim-SP)	W.Fernandes de Barros	32 000
15-Uniao Sao Joao EC	(Araras-SP)	Dr.Hermino Ometto	22 000
16-America FC	(Belo Horizonte-MG)	Raimundo Sampaio	18 000
17-CA Mineiro	(Belo Horizonte-MG)	Magalhaes Pinto	81 987
18-Cruzeiro EC	(Belo Horizonte-MG)	Magalhaes Pinto	81 987
19-Uberlandia EC	(Uberlandia-MG)	Joao Havalenge	72 000
20-Gremio FBPA(	Porto Alegre-RS)	Olimpico Monumental	51 081
21-SC Internacional	(Porto Alegre-RS)	Jose Pinheiro Borda	58 306
22-EC Juventude	(Caxias do Sul-RS)	Alfredo Jaconi	30 519
23-SER Caxias	(Caxia do Sul-RS)	Centenario	30 822
24-Goias EC	(Goiana-GO)	Serra Dourada	54 048
25-Vila Nova FC	(Goiana-GO)	Ones. Brasileiro Alverenga	8 000
26-Anapolis FC	(Anapolis-GO)	Jonas Duarte	20 000
27-Brasiliense FC	(Brasilia-DF)	Elmo Serejo Farias	25 000
28-SE Gama	(Brasilia-DF)	Walmir Campelo Bezarra	20 000
29-Brasilia EC	(Brasilia-DF)	Mane Garrincha	45 200

CHILE

FED. DE FUTBOL DE CHILE
Avda.Quilin #5635-Comuna
Penalolen Casilla Postal #3733
Correo cent.Santiago
TEL 56-2284-9000
WEB www.anfp.cl

REFERENCE
Official name
  Republic of Chile
Date of formation 1818/1929
Capital Santiago
Population 14 milltion
Total area 292,258 sq Mi
  756,950 sq Km
Time zone GMT -4:00
Density 47 sq Mi 20 sq Km
Languages Spanish
Literacy rate 95%
Currency Chilean Peso
Economy 63% Services
Religions Catholic 90%
Ethnic Mix European and Indigenous

GEOGRAPHY
Elevation
lowest point: Pacific Ocean o m
highest point: Nevado Ojos del Salado 6,880 m
Geography Note
a strategic location relative to sea lanes
between Atlantic and Pacific Oceans Strait of
Magellan, Beagle Channel, Drake Passage;
Atacama Desert is one of world's driest regions
Natural Resources
copper, timber, iron ore, nitrates, precious
metals, molybdenum, hydropower
Climate
temperate; desert in north; Mediterranean in
central region; cool and damp in south
Chilean Food
empanadas de horno, pebre

WORLD CUP

1930	First round exit
1934	Did not qualify
1938	Did not qualify
1950	First round exit
1954	Did not qualify
1958	Did not qualify
1962	Did not qualify
1966	Did not qualify
1970	Did not qualify
1974	Did not qualify
1978	Did not qualify
1982	Did not qualify
1986	Did not qualify
1990	Did not qualify
1994	First round exit
1998	Did not qualify
2002	Did not qualify

COUNTRY LEAGUE CHAMPIONS

2004	Cobreloa (C)
	Univ.de Chile (A)
2003	Cobreloa (C)
	Cobreloa (A)
2002	Colo Colo (C)
	Univ. Catolica (A)
2001	Santiago Wand.
2000	Univ. de Chile
1999	Univ. de Chile
1998	Colo Colo

Women's League Champions

2004	Santiago Morning
2003	Union Espanola
2002	Univ. de Chile
2001	Santiago Morning

NATIONAL TEAM COLORS

WORLD PICTURES OF SOCCER

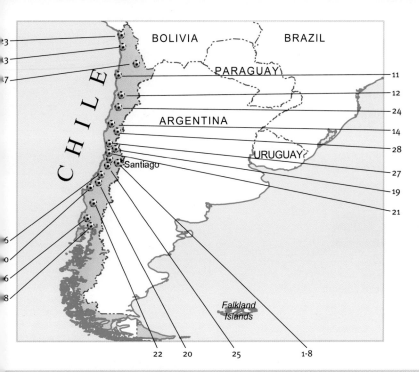

PREMIERE LEAGUE CLUBS	CITY	STADIUM	CAPACITY
1-Universidad de Chile	Santiago	Estadio Nacional	77 000
2-Colo Colo	Santiago	Monumental D. Arellano	62 500
3-Universidad Catolica	Santiago	San Carlos de Apoquindo	20 000
4-Union Espanola	Santiago	Santa Laura	25 000
5-Audax Italiano	Santiago	Municipal de la Florida	8 500
6-Palestino	Santiago	La Cisterna	12 000
7-Santiago morning	Santiago	Santiago Bueras	8 000
8-Magallanes	Santiago	Santiago Bueras	8 000
9-Deportes Concepcion	Concepcion	Municipal de Concepcion	35 000
10-Universidad Concepcion	Concepcion	Municipal de Concepcion	35 000
11-DaportesAntofagasta	Antofagasta	Estadio Regional	26 339
12-Cobresal	El Salvador	El Cobre	20 752
13-Deportes Iquique	Iquique	Tierra de Campeones	18 000
14-Coquimbo Unido	Coquimbo	Francisco S.Rumoroso	15 000
15-Huachipato	Talcahuano	Las Higueras	10 000
16-Deportes Talcahuano	Talcahuano	El Morro	13 000
17-Cobreloa	Calama	Municipal de Calama	20 180
18-Puerto Montt	Puerto Montt	Chinquihu	10 000
19-Union San Felipe	San Felipe	Municipal de San Felipe	13 162
20-Rangers	Talca	Fiscal de Talca	17 020
21-Santiago Wanderers	Valpairaiso	Playa Ancha	19 000
22-Deportes Temuco	Temuco	German Becker	20 930
23-Deportes Arica	Arica	Carlos Dittborn	17 786
24-Deportes Copiaco S.A	Copiaco	L.Vazenzuela Hermosilla	15 000
25-O'Higgins	Rancagua	El Teniente	25 000
26-Provincial Osorno	Osorno	Parque Schott	10 800
27-Union La Calera	La Calera	Nicolas Chahuan Nazar	18 000
28-Deportes Ovalle	Ovalle	Municipal de Ovalle	8 000

COLOMBIA

Fed.Colombiana de Futbol
Avenida 32#16-22 piso 4to, Apdo Aero
17606, Bogota,Colombia
TEL 57-1285 33 20
WEB www.colfutbol.org

Reference
Official name
  Republic of Colombia
Date of
formation   1819/1922
Capital   Bogota
Population   34 million
Total area   439,733 sq Mi
                   1,138,910 sq Km
Time zone   GMT -5:00
Density   78 sq Mi
Languages   Spanish, Indian
Literacy rate 91%
Currency   Columbian Peso
Economy   46% Services
Religions   Catholic 95%
Ethnic Mix   Mestizo 58%, White 20%

Geography
Elevation
lowest point: Pacific Ocean o m
highest point: Pico Cristobal Colon 5,775 m
Geography Note
only South American country with
coastlines on both North Pacific Ocean and
Caribbean Sea
Natural Resources
petroleum, natural gas, coal, iron ore,
nickel, gold, copper, emeralds, hydropower.
Climate
tropical along coast and eastern plains;
cooler in highlands .
Columbian Food
puchero bogateno/bolitas de piraruca

World Cup

1930	Did not qualify
1934	Did not qualify
1938	Did not qualify
1950	Did not qualify
1954	Did not qualify
1958	Did not qualify
1962	First round exit
1966	Did not qualify
1970	Did not qualify
1974	Did not qualify
1978	Did not qualify
1982	Did not qualify
1986	Did not qualify
1990	Scd round exit
1994	First round exit
1998	First round exit
2002	Did not qualify

Country League Champions

2004	Atletico Junior (C)
	Ind. Medellin (A)
2003	Deportes Tolima (C)
	Once Caldas (A)
2002	Ind. Medellin (C)
	America de Cali (A)
2001	America de Cali
2000	America de Cali
1999	Atletico Nacional
1998	Deportivo Cali

Women's League Champions

2004	Antioqua
2003	Bogota
2002	Bogota
2001	Tolima

National Team Colors

World Pictures of Soccer

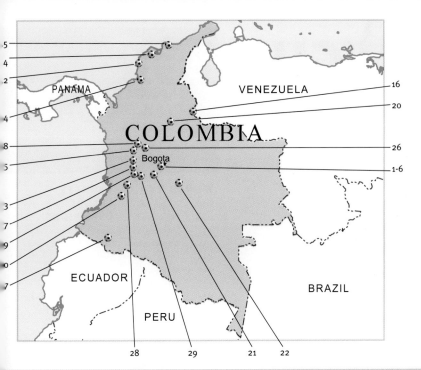

PREMIERE LEAGUE CLUBS	CITY	STADIUM	CAPACITY
-CD Millonarios	Bogota	El Campin	46 310
-Independiente Sant Fe	Bogota	El Campin	46 310
-Seguros La Equidad	Bogota	Olaya Herrera	
-Manpower Chico FC	Bogota	Olaya Herrera	
-Compensar	Bogota	Compensar	
-El Condor	Bogota	Metropolitano de Techo	
-Atletico de Medellin	Medellin	Atanasio Girardot	52 800
-Deportivo Independiente	Medellin	Atanasio Girardot	52 800
-America de Cali	Cali	Pascual Guerrero	45 000
-Deportivo de Cali	Cali	Pascual Guerrero	45 000
-Real Cartagena	Cartagena	Olimpico Pedro Heredia	14 000
-Expreso Rojo	Cartagena	Olimpico Pedro Heredia	14 000
-Atletico Junior CPD	Barranquilla	Metropolitano	75 000
-Johann FC	Barranquilla	Polideportivo Johann	3 000
-Union Magdalena	Santa Maria	Eduardo Santos	23 000
-Cucuta Deportivo	Cucuta	General Santander	35 000
-Deportivo Pasto	Pasto	Estadio Libertad	14 000
-Chia Fair Play FC	Chia	Municipal de Chia	
-Quindio Deportivo	Armenia	Centenario	35 000
-AtleticoBucaramanga	Bucaramanga	Alfonso Lopez	33 000
-Girardot FC	Girardot	Luis A.Duque Pena	15 000
-Centauros Villavicencio	Villavicencio	Manuel Calle Lombana	15 000
-Once Caldes	Manizales	Palogrande	33 000
-Real Sincelejo	Sincelejo	20 de Enero	8 000
-Envigado FC	Envigado	Polideportivo Sur	12 000
-Deportivo Rio Negro	Rionegro	Alberto Grisales	
-Deportes Pereira	Pereira	Hernan Ramirez Villegas	34 000
-Corporacion Cortulua	Tulua	12 de Octubre	12 000
-Deportes Tolima	Ibague	Manuel Murillo Toro	19 000

ECUADOR

Fed.Ecuatoriana de futbol
Via CostaKm 4.5- Av. del Bombero
Casilla 7447-Guayaquil,Ecuador
TEL (593-4)352-372
WEB www.ecuafutbolonline.org

REFERENCE
Official name
Republic of Ecuador
Official name Republic of Ecuador
Date of
formation   1830/1942
Capital   Quito
Population   11 million
Total area   109,483 sq Mi
283,560 sq Km
Time zone   GMT -5:00
Density   104/sq Mi, 44/sq Km
Languages   Spanish, Indigenous
Literacy rate   90%
Currency   Sucre
Economy   42% Services
Religions   Catholic 95%
Ethnic Mix   Indigenous, European

Geography
Elevation
lowest point: Pacific Ocean 0 m
highest point: Chimborazo 6,267 m
Geography Note
Cotopaxi in Andes is highest active volcano
in world
Natural Resources
Petroleum,Fish,Timber,Hydropower
Climate
coastal plain (costa), inter-Andean central
highlands (sierra), and flat to rolling eastern
jungle (oriente).
Ecuadorian Food
Locro/Pristinos/Chaulafan

WORLD CUP		COUNTRY LEAGUE CHAMPIONS	
1930	Did not qualify		
1934	Did not qualify		
1938	Did not qualify	2004	Deportivo Cuenca
1950	Did not qualify	2003	LD Universitaria
1954	Did not qualify	2002	Emelec
1958	Did not qualify	2001	Emelec
1962	Did not qualify	2000	Olmedo
1966	Did not qualify	1999	LD Universitaria
1970	Did not qualify	1998	LD Universitaria
1974	Did not qualify	1997	Barcelona
1978	Did not qualify	1996	El Nacional
1982	Did not qualify	1995	Barcelona
1986	Did not qualify	1994	Emelec
1990	Did not qualify	1993	Emelec
1994	Did not qualify	1992	El Nacional
1998	Did not qualify	**Women's League Champions**	
2002	First round exit	2000-2004	Not known

NATIONAL TEAM COLORS

WORLD PICTURES OF SOCCER

PREMIERE LEAGUE CLUBS	CITY	STADIUM	CAPACITY
LDU de Quito	Quito	La Casa Blanca	55 400
Deportivo Quito	Quito	Olimpico Atahualpa	45 000
El Nacional	Quito	Olimpico Atahualpa	45 000
Aucas	Quito	Chillogallo	25 000
CD America	Quito	La Armenia	1 000
Barcelona SC	Guayaquil	Isidro Romero Carbo	72 535
Emelec	Guayaquil	Capwell	18 614
Calvi	Guayaquil	Estadio Modelo	50 000
9 de Octubre	Guayaquil	Estadio Modelo	50 000
Deportivo Cuenca	Cuenca	Alejandro Serrano Aguilar	19 500
Esmeraldas Petrolero	Esmeraldas	Folke Anderson	14 000
Tecnico Universitario	Ambato	Bellavista de Ambato	22 000
Macara	Ambato	Bellavista de Ambato	22 000
Olmedo	Riobamba	Olimpico de Riobamba	12 000
Deportivo Saquisili	Saquisili	La Cocha Latacunga	17 000
Espoli	Ibarra	Estadio Olimpico	20 000
Manta FC	Manta	Jocay	12 000
Delfin	Manta	Jocay	12 000
Milagro Sporting	Milagro	Los Chirijos	18 000
Deportivo Quevedo	Quevedo	7 de Octubre	16 000
UD Juvenil	Quininde	Pascual Mina	4 000
Santa Rita	Vinces	El Sol	4 000
Audaz Octubrino	Machala	9 de Mayo	25 000
Real Madrid FC	Machachi	El Chan	4 000
LDU Porto Viejo	PortoViejo	Reales Tamanrindos	24 000
Universidad Catolica	Tulcan	Olimpico	8 000
Babahoyo	Babahoyo	Rafael Vera Yepez	11 000

FRENCH GUIANA

FRENCH GUIANA FOOTBALL FEDERATION
Not Known
TEL: FAX: WEB:

REFERENCE
Official name
French Guiana (Overseas Department of France)

Claimed	1817
Catital	Cayenne
Total area	35,135 sq Mi, 91,000 sq Km
Time zone	GMT - 3
Density	Not Known
Languages	French
Literacy rate	85%
Currency	French Franc
Economy	Services 61%, Industry21%, Agriculture 18%
Religions	Catholic
Ethnic Mix	European, Indigenous

Geography
Elevation
lowest point: Atlantic Ocean o m
highest point: Bellevue de l'Inini 851 m
Geography Note
mostly an unsettled wilderness; the only non-independent portion of the South American continent
Natural Resources
bauxite, timber, gold (widely scattered), cinnabar, kaolin, fish
Climate
Tropical; hot, humid; little seasonal temperature variation
French Guyana Food
Chicken Carame/Shrimps with hot sauce

WORLD CUP

1930	Did not qualify
1934	Did not qualify
1938	Did not qualify
1950	Did not qualify
1954	Did not qualify
1958	Did not qualify
1962	Did not qualify
1966	Did not qualify
1970	Did not qualify
1974	Did not qualify
1978	Did not qualify
1982	Did not qualify
1986	Did not qualify
1990	Did not qualify
1994	Did not qualify
1998	Did not qualify
2002	Did not qualify

COUNTRY LEAGUE CHAMPIONS

2003	US Matoury
2002	Aj Saint George
2001	AS C le Geldar
2000	Aj Saint George
1999	AJ Saint George
1998	AS Jahouvey
1997	US Sinnamary
1996	AS Club Colonial
1995	AS Jahouvey
1994	US Sinnamary
1993	SUS Sinnamary
1992	AS Club Colonial
1991	AS Club Colonial

Women's League Champions

2000-2004	not known

NATIONAL TEAM COLORS

WORLD PICTURES OF SOCCER

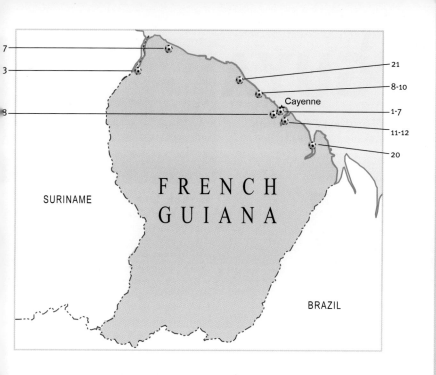

PREMIERE LEAGUE CLUBS	CITY	STADIUM	CAPACITY
AJSt.Georges	Cayenne	Stade de Baduel	7 000
ASPTT	Cayenne	Stade de Baduel	7 000
ASCGeldar	Cayenne	Stade de Baduel	7 000
ClubColonial	Cayenne	Stade de Baduel	7 000
ASCRemire	Cayenne	Stade de Baduel	7 000
ASLSportGuyanais	Cayenne	Stade Scolaire	1 000
ASSt.Elie	Cayenne	Stade Scolaire	1 000
SCKouroucien	Kourou	Stade Bois Chaudat	4 000
CosmaFoot	Kourou	Stade Bois Chaudat	4 000
ESDEKourou	Kourou	Stade Bois Chaudat	4 000
AJNalataAbriba	Matoury	Stade Municipal Matoury	1 000
USMatoury	Matoury	Stade Municipal Matoury	1 000
ASCAgouado	St.Laurent	Stade Long rene	1 500
USSinnamary	Sinnamary	Stade Municipal	2 500
AjAmesClaires	AmesClaire	Stade Roura	1 000
ASJMana	Mana	Stade municipal de Mana	1 500
USMananaise	Mana	Stade Municipal de Mana	1 500
USMacouria	Macouria	Stade Municipal	2 000
USLMontjoly	VieuxChemin	Stade Municipal	1 000
FCApprouague	Kaw	Stade Municipal de Kaw	1 000
EFIracoubo	Iracoubo	Stade Municipal Iracoubo	1 000

GUYANA

GUYANA FOOTBALL FEDERATION
159 Rupununi Street, Bel Air Park,
PB 10727, Georgetown
TEL 592-2/278 758   FAX /262 641
WEB:www.concacaf.com

REFERENCE
Official name
Cooperative Republic of Guyana

Date of formation	1966
Capital	Georgetown
Total area	76,003 sq Mi(196,850 sq Km)
Time zone	GMT -3
Density	11 per sq Mi(3 per sq Km)
Languages	English, Creole, Hindi, Urdu, Indian Languages
Literacy rate	98%
Currency	Guyana $
Economy	Industry 44%, Agriculture 34%
Religions	Christian 57%
Ethnic Mix	East Indian 52%, Black African 38%

Geography
Elevation
lowest point: Atlantic Ocean 0 m
highest point: Mount Roraima 2,835 m
Geography Note
the third-smallest country in South America after Suriname and Uruguay.
Natural Resources
bauxite, gold, diamonds, hardwood timber, shrimp, fish
Climate
Tropical; hot, humid, moderated by northeast trade winds; two rainy seasons (May to mid-August, mid-November to mid-January)
Guyana Food
Peperpot/Creole roti

WORLD CUP

1930	Did not qualify
1934	Did not qualify
1938	Did not qualify
1950	Did not qualify
1954	Did not qualify
1958	Did not qualify
1962	Did not qualify
1966	Did not qualify
1970	Did not qualify
1974	Did not qualify
1978	Did not qualify
1982	Did not qualify
1986	Did not qualify
1990	Did not qualify
1994	Did not qualify
1998	Did not qualify
2002	Did not qualify

COUNTRY LEAGUE CHAMPIONS

2004	Not Known
2003	Not Known
2002	Not Known
2001	Conquerors
2000	Not Held
1999	Not Hrld
1998	Santos FC
1997	Top XX
1996	Omai Gold Seekers
1995	Milerock
1994	Western Tigers FC

Women's League Champions

2000-2004	Not known

NATIONAL TEAM COLORS

WORLD PICTURES OF SOCCER

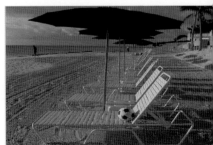

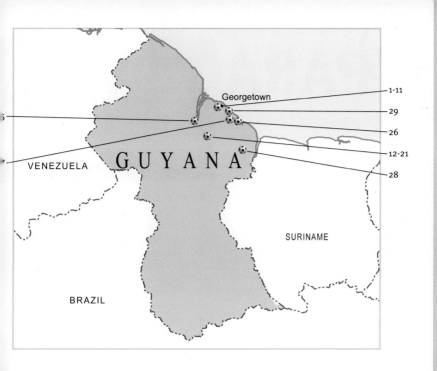

PREMIERE LEAGUE CLUBS	CITY	STADIUM	CAPACITY
Pele FC	Georgetown	Georgetown Stadium	2 000
Georgetown FC	Georgetown	Georgetown Stadium	2 000
Conquerors	Georgetown		
Camptown	Georgetown		
Western Tigers FC	Georgetown		
Police FC	Georgetown		
Kitty Vizion	Georgetown		
Beacon FC	Georgetown		
Thomas United	Georgetown		
Santos FC	Georgetown		
Fruta Conquerors	Georgetown		
Bakewell Topp XX	Linden		
Netrockers	Linden		
High Stars	Linden		
Milerock	Linden		
Botafogo	Linden		
Notre Dame	Linden		
MSC Lions	Linden		
Rose Bowl FC	Linden		
Eagle United	Linden		
Amelia's Ward	Linden		
Beacon	Bartica		
Wolves United	Bartica		
Rising Stars	Bartica		
East Coast's Golden Stars	Bartica		
Arsenal	New Amsterdam		
Rosignol United	Rosignol		
Kwakwani Strikers	Kwakwani		
Cougars	Berbice		

PARAGUAY

Assoc. Paraguaya de Futbol

Estadio Defensores del chaco, calle mayor
Martinez,1393 Asuncion
TEL (595-21)48-0122/24
WEB:www.apf.org.py

REFERENCE

Official name
Republic of Paraguay

Date of formation	1811/1938
Capital	Asuncion
Population	5 million
Total area	157,046 sq Mi , 406,750 sq Km
Time zone	GMT -4:00
Density	29 per sq Mi, 13 per sq Km
Languages	Spanish, Guarani
Literacy rate	92%
Currency	Guarani
Economy	50% Agriculture
Religions	Catholic 90%
Ethnic Mix	European

Geography

Elevation
lowest point: Junction of Rio Paraguay & Rio Parana 46 m
highest point: Cerro Pero (Cerro Tres Kandu) 842 m

Geography Note
landlocked; lies between Argentina, Bolivia, and Brazil; population concentrated in southern part of the country

Natural Resources
hydropower, timber, iron ore, manganese, limestone .

Climate
subtropical to temperate; substantial rainfall in the eastern portions, becoming semiarid in the far west

Paraguayan Food
So'o-yosopy

WORLD CUP

1930	1/4 Final
1934	Did not qualify
1938	1/2 Final
1950	Did not qualify
1954	Did not qualify
1958	1/4 Final
1962	Did not qualify
1966	1/2 Final
1970	Did not qualify
1974	Did not qualify
1978	1/4 Final
1982	Did not qualify
1986	1/2 Final
1990	Did not qualify
1998	Did not qualify
2002	Did not qualify

COUNTRY LEAGUE CHAMPIONS

2004	Cerro Porteno
2003	Libertad
2002	Libertad
2001	Cerro Porteno
2000	Olimpia
1999	Olimpia
1998	Olimpia
1997	Olimpia
1996	Cerro Porteño
1995	Olimpia
Women's League Champions	
2004	Univ. Autonoma
2003	Univ. Autonoma
2002	Real Sajonia
2001	Not Known

NATIONAL TEAM COLORS

WORLD PICTURES OF SOCCER

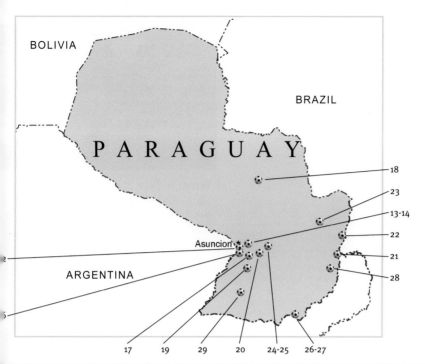

BOLIVIA

BRAZIL

P A R A G U A Y

Asuncion

ARGENTINA

18	
23	
13-14	
22	
21	
28	
17	19	29	20	24-25	26-27

PREMIERE LEAGUE CLUBS	CITY	STADIUM	CAPACITY
Club Cerro Porteno	Asuncion	General Pablo Rojas	25 000
Club Olimpia	Asuncion	Manuel Ferreira	20 000
Club Libertad	Asuncion	Alfredo Stroessner	16 000
Nacional	Asuncion		
Club Guarani	Asuncion	Rogelio Lorenzo Livieres	10 000
Club Sol de America	Asuncion	Luis Alfonso Giagni	10 000
Tacuary	Asuncion		
CS Colombia	Asuncion	Alfonso Colman	7 000
Cerro Cora	Asuncion	General Andres Rodriguez	6 000
Resistencia	Asuncion		
Rercoleta	Asuncion		
Presidente Hayes	Asuncion	Kiko Reyes	4 200
CS Luqueno	Luque	Feliciano Caceres	24 000
Teniente Herreros Bueno	Luque		
CS San Lorenzo	San Lorenzo	Ciudad Universitaria	10 000
Barrio Guarani	San Lorenzo		
12 de Octubre FC	Itagua	Carlos Pettengil	8 000
Tacuary FBC	Tacuary	Toribo Vargas	4 000
Olimpia de Ita	Ita		
8 de Diciembre	Caacupe		
Nacional	Hernanderia		
Tres Corrales	Ciudad del Este		
General Caballero	Juan Mallorquin		
San Lorenzo	Caaguazu		
8 of Diciembre	Caaguazu		
Nueva Estrella	Encarnacion		
Universal	Encarnacion		
Nanawa	Presidente Franco		
24 de Junio	San Juan-Misiones		

PERU

FED. PERUANA DE FUTBOL
Av. Aviacion 2085-San Luis-Lima 30, Peru
TEL (51-1) 225-8236
WEB www.fpf.com.pe

REFERENCE
Official name
Republic of Peru
Date of formation 1824/1942
Capital Lima
Population 23 million
Total area 496,223 sq Mi, 1,285,220 sq Km
Time zone GMT -5:00
Density 104 per sq Mi, 20 per sq Km
Languages Spanish, Quechua
Literacy rate 89%
Currency Nuevo Sol
Economy 53% Services
Religions Catholic 90%
Ethnic Mix Indigenous 45%, European37%

Geography
Elevation
lowest point: Pacific Ocean 0 m
highest point: Nevado Huascaran 6,768 m
Geography Note
shares control of Lago Titicaca, world's highest navigable lake, with Bolivia; remote Lake McIntyre is the ultimate source of the Amazon River
Natural Resources
Copper, Silver, Gold, Petrol, Timber, Fish, Iron, Coal, Phosphate, Potash, Hydropower, Natural gas
Climate
varies from tropical in east to dry desert in west; temperate to frigid in Andes
Peruvian Food
Pollo al Ajo Estillo Peruano/Lomo Saltado

WORLD CUP

1930	First round exit
1934	Did not qualify
1938	Did not qualify
1950	Did not qualify
1954	Did not qualify
1958	Did not qualify
1962	Did not qualify
1966	Did not qualify
1970	1/4 final exit
1974	Did not qualify
1978	Scd round exit
1982	First round exit
1986	Did not qualify
1990	Did not qualify
1994	Did not qualify
1998	Did not qualify
2002	Did not qualify

COUNTRY LEAGUE CHAMPIONS

2004	Allianza Lima
2003	Allianza Lima
2002	Sporting Crystal
2001	Alianza Lima
2000	Univ. de dep
1999	Univ. de dep
1998	Univ. de dep
1997	Alianza Lima
1996	Sporting Crystal
1995	Sporting Crystal
1994	Sporting Crystal

Women's League Champions

2004	JC Sport Girls
2003	Univ. deportes
2002	Not Known

NATIONAL TEAM COLORS

WORLD PICTURES OF SOCCER

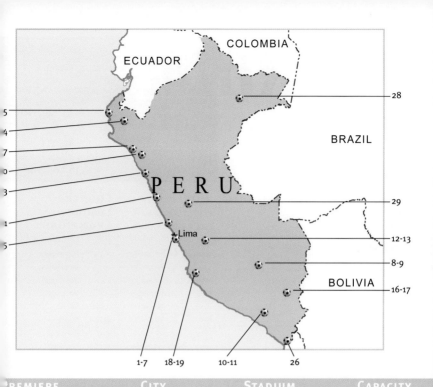

PREMIERE LEAGUE CLUBS	CITY	STADIUM	CAPACITY
Universitario	Lima	Teodoro Fernandez	80 000
Alianza Lima	Lima	Alejandro Villanueva	35 000
Universidad de San Marcos	Lima	Universidad San Marcos	60 000
Sporting Cristal	Lima	San martin de Porras	18 000
Deportivo Municipal	Lima	Teodoro Lolo Fernandez	15 000
Nicolas de Pierola	Lima		
Deportivo Aviacion	Lima	Municipal de Chorillos	15 000
Cienciano de Cuzco	Cuzco	Garcilazo de la Vega	30 000
Deportivo Garcilazo	Cuzco		
Melgar FBC	Arequipa	Monumental Arequipa	60 000
Sportivo Huracan	Arequipa		
Deportivo Wanka	Huancayo	Estadio Huancayo	20 000
Meteor Junin	Huancayo	Estadio Huancayo	20 000
Atletico Torino	Talara	Campeonisimo	8 000
IMI Talara	Talara	Campeonisimo	8 000
Alfonso Ugarte	Puno	Torres Bellon	20 000
Franciscano San Roman	Puno		
Octavio Espinoza	Ica	Jose Picasso Peratta	6 000
Abraham Valdelomar	Ica		
UTC Cajamarca	Cajamarca	Heroes de San Ramon	18 000
Jose Galves	Chimbote	Manuel Gomez Arellano	15 000
Deportivo Upao	Trujillo	Mansiche	18 000
Coopsol Trujillo	Trujillo		
Alianza Atletico	Sullana	Campeones del 36	10 000
Union Huaral	Huaral	Julio Lores Colan	10 000
Coronel Bolognesi	Tacna	Modelo	20 000
Juan Aurich	Chiclayo	Elias Aguirre	20 000
CNI de Iquitos	Iquitos	Max Austin	20 000
Leon de Huanaco	Huanaco	Heraclio Tapia	8 000

SURINAME

SURINAASME VOETBAL BOND
Letitia Vriesdelaan 7, PB 1223, Paramaribo
TEL 597/473 112 FAX /479 718
WEB:www.concacaf.com

REFERENCE
Official name
Republic of Suriname
Date of formation 1975
Catital Paramaribo
Population 417,000
Total area 62,343 sq Mi, 161,470 sq Km
Time zone GMT -3
Density 7 per sq Mi, 2 per sq Km
Languages Dutch, Pidgin, English, TakiTaki, Hindi, Javnese
Literacy rate 92%
Currency Guilder
Economy Industry 45%
Religions Hindu 27%, Protestant 25%,Catholic 23%
Ethnic Mix South Asian 34%, Creole 34%, Javanese 18%

Geography
Elevation
lowest point: Unnamed location in the coastal plain -2 m
highest point: Juliana Top 1,230 m
Geography Note
smallest independent country on South American continent; mostly tropical rain forest; great diversity of flora and fauna that, for the most part, is increasingly threatened by new development
Natural Resources
timber, hydropower, fish, kaolin, shrimp, bauxite, gold,nickel, copper, platinum, iron
Climate
tropical; moderated by trade winds
Suriname Food
Peanut soup, Rice Chicken

WORLD CUP

1930	Did not qualify
1934	Did not qualify
1938	Did not qualify
1950	Did not qualify
1954	Did not qualify
1958	Did not qualify
1962	Did not qualify
1966	Did not qualify
1970	Did not qualify
1974	Did not qualify
1978	Did not qualify
1982	Did not qualify
1986	Did not qualify
1990	Did not qualify
1994	Did not qualify
1998	Did not qualify
2002	Did not qualify

COUNTRY LEAGUE CHAMPIONS

2004	Walking About FC
2003	FCS Nacional
2002	Voorwaarts
2001	Not Played
2000	Transvaal
1999	SNL
1998	Transvaal
1997	Transvaal
1996	Transvaal
1995	Robinhood
1994	Transvaal
1993	Robinhood

Women's League Champions

2004	Merodia
2003	OEMA SOSO

NATIONAL TEAM COLORS

WORLD PICTURES OF SOCCER

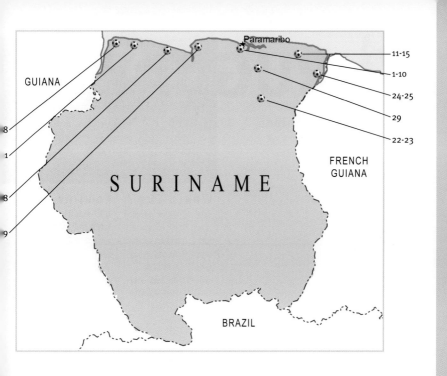

PREMIERE LEAGUE CLUBS	CITY	STADIUM	CAPACITY
Transvaal	ParaMaribo	Flora Stadion	7 000
Robinhood	Paramaribo	Andre Kamperveen	18 000
Leo Victor	Paramaribo	Andre Kamperveen	18 000
SNL	Paramaribo	Frank Essed Stadion	
HOB	Paramaribo	Frank Essed Stadion	
Royal 95'	Paramaribo	Vel de Hut	
OSV	Paramaribo		
Voorwaarts	Paramaribo	George Streepe Stadion	3 000
RCS Nacional	Paramaribo	N.G.G.B Stadion	3 100
Meo	Paramaribo		
Inter Moengotapoe	Moengo	Moengo Stadion	
Ricanaumofo	Moengo	Moengo Stadion	
SV Moengotapoe	Moengo	Juliana Stadion	
Robruns	Moengo		
Peto	Moengo		
Jai Hind Nickerie	Nieuw Nickerie	Nickerie Stadion	3 400
Atlantic FC	Neuw Nickerie	Nickerie Stadion	3 400
Zeedijk	Nieuw Nickerie	Nickerie Stadion	3 400
Boskamp FC	Boskamp		
Vitesse	Waganingen		
Bintang Merah	Waganingen		
SVG	Brokopondo		
BSV	Brokopondo		
Papatam	Albina		
Balate	Albina		
Arsenal	Coronie		
Flamingo	Coronie		
FC Corona	Coronie		
Indo	Commewijne		

 # URUGUAY

Assoc. Uruguaya de Futbol
Guayabo 1531,11200 Montevideo, UY
TEL (598-2) 400-7101 FAX/409 0550
WEB www.auf.org.uy

Reference
Official name
　Repubic of Uruguay
Date of formation 1825/1909
Capital Montevideo
Population 3 million
Total area 68,498 sq Mi, 177,410 sq Km
Time zone GMT -3:00
Density 45 per sq Mi, 19 per sq Km
Languages Spanish
Literacy rate 98%
Currency Uruguayan Peso
Economy 70% Services
Religions Catholic and Protestant
Ethnic Mix European and Indigenous 90%

Geography
Elevation
lowest point: Atlantic Ocean 0 m
highest point: Cerro Catedral 514 m
Geography Note
second-smallest South American country (after Suriname); most of the low-lying landscape (three-quarters of the country) is grassland, ideal for cattle and sheep raising
Natural Resources
arable land, hydropower, minor minerals, fisheries
Climate
warm temperate; freezing temperatures almost unknown
Uruguayan Food
Parilla

World Cup

1930	World Champion
1934	Did not qualify
1938	Did not qualify
1950	World Champion
1954	Finish 4th
1958	Did not qualify
1962	First round exit
1966	1/4 Final
1970	Finish 4th
1974	First round exit
1978	Did not qualify
1982	Did not qualify
1986	Scd round exit
1990	Scd round exit
1994	Did not qualify
1998	Did not qualify
2002	First round exit

Country League Champions

2004	Danubio
2003	Penarol
2002	Nacional
2001	Nacional
2000	Nacional
1999	Penarol
1998	Nacional
1997	Penarol
1996	Penarol
1995	Penarol
1994	Penarol
1993	Penarol
1993	Penarol

Women's League Champions

2000-2004	Rampla Jur

NATIONAL TEAM COLORS

WORLD PICTURES OF SOCCER

ARGENTINA

BRAZIL

28

7

U R U G U A Y

9

Montevideo ★ 1-25

PREMIERE LEAGUE CLUBS	CITY	STADIUM	CAPACITY
-Penarol	Montevideo	Estadio Centenario	73 609
-Club Nacional	Montevideo	Parque central	16 000
-CA Cerro	Montevideo	Luis Troccoli	25 000
-Montevideo Wanderers	Montevideo	Alfredo Victor Viera	12 500
-Danubio FC	Montevideo	Jardines del Hipodromo	16 000
-CS Cerrito	Montevideo	Estadia Charrua	12 000
-Colon FC	Montevideo	Parque Suero	2 000
-CA Progresso	Montevideo	Abraham Paladino	8 000
-IA Sud America	Montevideo	Carlos Angel Fossa	6 000
-Racing Club	Montevideo	Osvaldo Roberto	8 500
-CA Bella Vista	Montevideo	Jose Nasazzi	15 000
2-El Tanque Sisley	Montevideo	Victor della Valle	6 000
3-Uruguay Montevideo FC	Montevideo		3 000
-Allianza Montevideo FC	Montevideo	Parque Salus	4 000
-CSYD Huracan Buceo	Montevideo	Parque Huracan	8 000
-Liverpool FC	Montevideo	Estadio Belvedere	9 500
-Rampla Juniors FC	Montevideo	Estadio Olimpico	9 500
-CA Rentista	Montevideo	Complejo Rentistas	10 000
-CA Basanez	Montevideo	La Bombonera	6 000
-CA Fenix	Montevideo	Parque Carpurro	10 000
-CA River Plate	Montevideo	Federico Saroldi	12 000
-CSYD Villa Espanola	Montevideo	Obdulio Varela	8 000
-Defensor sporting Club	Montevideo	Luis Franzini	18 000
-Central Espanol FC	Montevideo	Parque Palermo	6 500
-Miramar misiones	Montevideo	Mendez Piana	4 000
-Paysandu FC	Paysandu	Estadio Artigas	25 000
-CA Paysandu Bella Vista	Paysandu	Estadio Artigas	25 000
-Tacuarembo FC	Tacuarembo	Raul Goyenola	12 000
-CA Plaza Colonia	Colonia d.Sacra.	Estadio Supicci	12 000

VENEZUELA

FED. VENEZOLANA DE FUTBOL
Av. Santos Erminy, Torre Mega II-Penthouse
BE/Sabana Grande y Solano-Caracas, Vz
TEL (58-212)762-0362/5691
WEB www.fvf.org.ve

REFERENCE
Official name
Republic of Venezuela
Date of formation 1830/1929
Capital Caracas
Population 21 million
Total area 352,143 sq Mi, 912,050 sq Km
Time zone GMT -4:00
Density 57 per sq Mi, 25 per sq Km
Languages Spanish and Indian
Literacy rate 91%
Currency Bolivar
Economy 63% Services
Religions Catholic 96%
Ethnic Mix Mestizo and White

Geography
Elevation
lowest point: Caribbean Sea 0 m
highest point: Pico Bolivar (La Columna) 5,007 m

Geography Note
on major sea and air routes linking North and
South America; Angel Falls in the Guiana
Highlands is the world's highest waterfall
Natural Resources
Petroleum, Natural gas, Iron, Ore, Gold,
Bauxite, Other Minerals, Hydropower, Diamonds
Climate
tropical; hot, humid; more moderate in
highlands
Venezuelan Food
Arepas Rellenascon guiso de Carne/
Arroz con bananas

WORLD CUP

1930	Did not qualify
1934	Did not qualify
1938	Did not qualify
1950	Did not qualify
1954	Did not qualify
1958	Did not qualify
1962	Did not qualify
1966	Did not qualify
1970	Did not qualify
1974	Did not qualify
1978	Did not qualify
1982	Did not qualify
1986	Did not qualify
1990	Did not qualify
1994	Did not qualify
1998	Did not qualify
2002	Did not qualify

COUNTRY LEAGUE CHAMPIONS

2004	Caracas FC
2003	Caracas FC
2002	Nacional Tachira
2001	Caracas FC
2000	Dep. Tachira
1999	Italchacao
1998	Atletico Zulia
1997	Caracas FC
1996	Minerven
1995	Caracas FC
1994	Caracas FC
1993	CS Maritimo
1992	Caracas FC

Women's League Champions

2000-2004	UCAB(Cara

NATIONAL TEAM COLORS

WORLD PICTURES OF SOCCER

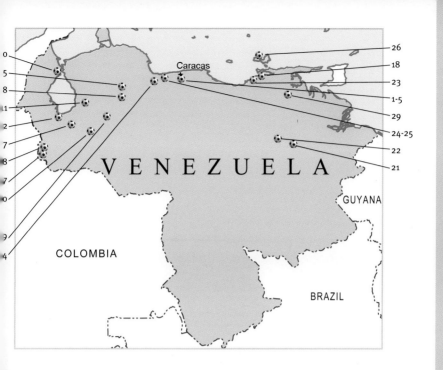

PREMIERE LEAGUE CLUBS	CITY	STADIUM	CAPACITY
Caracas FC	Caracas	Olimpico	25 000
Deportivo Italchacao	Caracas	Brigido Iriarte	15 000
UD Maritimo	Caracas		
UCV Caracas	Caracas		
Galicia FC	Caracas		
Deportivo Tachira	San Cristobal	Pueblo Nuevo	27 500
Nacional Tachira FC	San Cristobal	Pueblo Nuevo	27 500
San Cristobal FC	San Cristobal		
Union Atletico Maracaibo	Maracaibo	Jose Pachencho Romero	35 000
Atletico Zulia	Maracaibo		
Trujillanos FC	Valera	Luis Loreto Lira	14 000
Union Atletico El Vigia	El Vigia	12 de Febrero	12 765
Carabobo FC	Valencia	Misael Delgado	10 000
Hermandad Gallega	Valencia		
Union Lara FC	Barquisimeto	Farid Richa	12 480
Universidad de Los Andes	Merida	Guillermo Soto Rosa	14 000
Estudiantes FC Merida	Merida	Guillermo Soto Rosa	14 000
Nueva Cadiz FC	Cumana	F.Velazquez	15 000
Llaneros FC	Guanare	Rafael Calles Pinto	6 000
Atletico Zamora	Barinas	La Carolina	12 000
Mineros de Guyana	Puerto Ordaz	Cachamay	15 000
Industr. Caroni FC	Ciudad Bolivar		
Dep. Anzoategui SC	Puerto La Cruz		
Aragua FC	Maracay		
Academia Maracay	Maracay		
Atletico El Espinal	El Espinal		
UPEL Andina	Rubio		
Portuguesa FC	Acarigua		
UD Aragua Maturin	Aragua de Mat.		

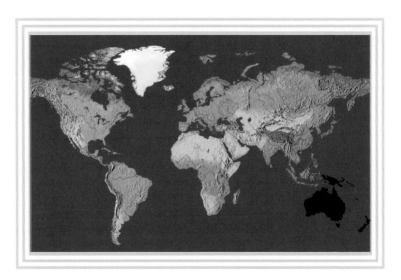

OCEANIA

AMERICAN SAMOA

AMERICAN SAMOA FOOTBALL FEDERATION

PB 282, AS 96799 Pago Pago
TEL 684/699 7380 FAX /699 7381
WEB www.oceaniafootball.com

REFERENCE

Official name
Unincorporated Territory

Date of formation	1900
Capital	Pago Pago
Population	60,000
Total area	75 sq Mi(195 sq Km)
Time zone	GMT-11
Density	828 per sq Mi
Languages	Samoan, English
Literacy rate	98%
Currency	U.S Dollars
Economy	Industry 37%
Religions	Baptist 42%, Catholic 34%
Ethnic Mix	Samoan(Polunesian) 89%, Tongan 4%, Caucasian 4%

GEOGRAPHY

Elevation
lowest point: Pacific Ocean 0 m
highest point: Lata 966 m
Geography Note
Pago Pago has one of the best natural deep-water harbors in the South Pacific Ocean, sheltered by shape from rough seas and protected by peripheral mountains from high winds
Natural Resources
pumice, pumicite
Climate
tropical marine, moderated by southeast trade winds; annual rainfall averages about 3 m; little seasonal temperature variation
American Samoa Food
suppo esi-dessert

WORLD CUP

1930	Did not qualify
1934	Did not qualify
1938	Did not qualify
1950	Did not qualify
1954	Did not qualify
1958	Did not qualify
1962	Did not qualify
1966	Did not qualify
1970	Did not qualify
1974	Did not qualify
1978	Did not qualify
1982	Did not qualify
1986	Did not qualify
1990	Did not qualify
1994	Did not qualify
1998	Did not qualify
2002	Did not qualify

COUNTRY LEAGUE CHAMPIONS

2004	Pago United
2003	Manumea
2002	Pansa Soccer Clib
2001	Pansa Soccer Club
2000	Pansa & Wild West
1999	Konika Machine FC
1998	Not Known
1997	Not Known
1996	Not Known

Women's League Champions

2004	Not Known
2003	Not Known
2002	Pago Girls
2001	Not Known
2000	Not Known

NATIONAL TEAM COLORS

WORLD PICTURES OF SOCCER

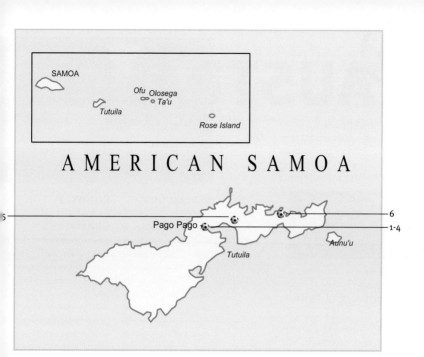

AMERICAN SAMOA

PREMIERE LEAGUE CLUBS	CITY	STADIUM	CAPACITY
Pansa SC	Pago Pago	Veteran Memorial	10 000
Pago Pago	Pago Pago		
Pago Eagles	Pago Pago		
Pago Boys	Pago Pago		
Aua Strikers	Aua		
Fagaitua Vikings	Fagaitua		

AUSTRALIA

SOCCER AUSTRALIA
Level 3,447 Kent Street, PB Q 1645 QVB
Post Office, NSW 1230 Sydney
TEL 61-2/8251 1000FAX /82511099
www.socceraustralia.com.au

REFERENCE
Official name
   Commonwealth of Australia

Date of formation	1901
Capital	Canberra
Population	18.9 Million
Total area	2,941,282 sq Mi (7,617,930 sq Km)
Time zone	GMT+10
Density	6.4 per sq Mi(2.4 per sq Km)
Languages	English,
Literacy rate	99%
Currency	Australian $
Economy	Services 78% Catholic26%,
Religions	Anglican 24%
	European 95%, Asian
Ethnic Mix	4%, Aboriginal 1%

GEOGRAPHY
Elevation
lowest point: Lake Eyre -15 m
highest point: Mount Kosciuszko 2,229 m
Geography Note
world's smallest continent but sixth-largest
country; population concentrated along the
eastern and southeastern coasts.
Natural Resources
bauxite, coal, iron ore, copper, tin, gold,
silver, uranium, nickel, tungsten, mineral
sands, lead, zinc, diamonds, natural gas,
petroleum
Climate
generally arid to semiarid; temperate in
south and east; tropical in north
Australian Food
meat Pie/anzac biscuits

WORLD CUP

1930	Did not qualify
1934	Did not qualify
1938	Did not qualify
1950	Did not qualify
1954	Did not qualify
1958	Did not qualify
1962	Did not qualify
1966	Did not qualify
1970	Did not qualify
1974	First round exit
1978	Did not qualify
1982	Did not qualify
1986	Did not qualify
1990	Did not qualify
1994	Did not qualify
1998	Did not qualify
2002	Did not qualify

COUNTRY LEAGUE CHAMPIONS

2004	Perth Glory
2003	Perth Glory
2002	Olympique Sharks
2001	Wollongong City
2000	Wollongong City
1999	South Melbourne
1998	South Melbourne
1997	Brisbane Strikers
1996	Melbourne Knights

Women's League Champions

2005	Queensland Stings
2004	NSW Sapphires
2003	Queensland Stings
2002	Queensland Stings
2001	Canberra Eclipse

NATIONAL TEAM COLORS

WORLD PICTURES OF SOCCER

AUSTRALIA

Canberra

9

8

1-3

6

10   4-5   12   7

PREMIERE LEAGUE CLUBS	CITY	STADIUM	CAPACITY
Sydney Olympic FC	Sydney	Oki Jubilee Stadium	18 000
Parramatta Power FC	Sydney	Parramatta Stadium	20 000
Sydney United SC	Sydney	Edensor Park	12 000
Melbourne Knights SC	Melbourne	Knights Stadium	15 000
South Melbourne	Melbourne	Bob jane Stadium	14 000
Wollongong Wolves SC	Wollongong	WIN Stadium	18 400
Marconi Stallions FC	Fairfield	Marconi Stadium	11 500
Newcastle United SC	Newcastle	Energy Australia Stadium	28 000
Brisbane Strikers SC	Brisbane	Perry Park	5 000
Adelaide Force SC	Adelaide	Hindmarsh Stadium	15 000
Perth Glory SC	Perth	Perth Oval	18 500
Hobart Olympic SC	Hobart	Nortn Warrane park	1 000

COOK ISLANDS

COOK ISLANDS FOOTBALL FEDERATION

Victoria road, Tupapa, Rarotonga, PB 29, Avarua, Rarotonga TEL /682/28 980
WEB www.oceaniafootball.com

REFERENCE

Official name
Cooks Islands

Claimed	1901
Capital	Avarua
Population	20,200
Total area	113 sq Mi(293 sq Km)
Time zone	GMT-10
Density	80 sq Mi
Languages	English,
Literacy rate	98%
Currency	New Zealand $
Economy	Agriculture, Services
Religions	Anglican, Presbyterian
Ethnic Mix	New Zealanders, Polynesians

GEOGRAPHY

Elevation
lowest point: Pacific Ocean 0 m
highest point: Te Manga 652 m
Geography Note
the northern Cook Islands are seven low-lying, sparsely populated, coral atolls; the southern Cook Islands consist of eight elevated, fertile, volcanic isles where most of the populace lives
Natural Resources
NEGL
Climate
tropical; moderated by trade winds
Cook Islands Food
ika mata/rukau/raro tarati

WORLD CUP

1930	Did not qualify
1934	Did not qualify
1938	Did not qualify
1950	Did not qualify
1954	Did not qualify
1958	Did not qualify
1962	Did not qualify
1966	Did not qualify
1970	Did not qualify
1974	Did not qualify
1978	Did not qualify
1982	Did not qualify
1986	Did not qualify
1990	Did not qualify
1994	Did not qualify
1998	Did not qualify
2002	Did not qualify

COUNTRY LEAGUE CHAMPIONS

2005	Sokattatck Nikao
2004	Tupapa FC
2003	Tupapa FC
2002	Tupapa FC
2001	Sokattack Nikao
2000	Avatiu FC
1999	Tupapa
1998	Not Known
1997	Avatiu FC

Women's League Champio

2004	Not Known
2003	Tupapa FC
2002	Nikao FC
2001	Tupapa FC
2000	Not Known

NATIONAL TEAM COLORS

WORLD PICTURES OF SOCCER

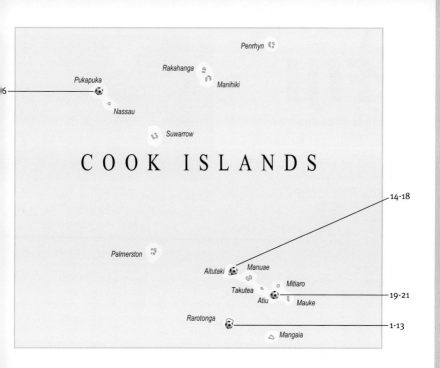

PREMIERE LEAGUE CLUBS	CITY	STADIUM	CAPACITY
Avarua FC	Rarotonga Island	Avarua National Stadium	3 000
Tupapa FC	Rarotonga Island		
Avatiu FC	Rarotonga Island		
Avatiu Goal	Rarotonga Island		
Nikao Sokattack	Rarotonga Island		
Takuvaine FC	Rarotonga Island		
United	Rarotonga		
Puaikara	Rarotonga Island		
Ataviu FC	Rarotonga Island		
-Arorangi FC	Rarotonga Island		
-Matavera FC	Rarotonga Island		
-Puaikura	Rarotonga Island		
-Titikaveka FC	Rarotonga Island		
-Aitutaki FC	Aitutaki Island		
-USA	Aitutaki Island		
-Vaipea	Aitutaki Island		
-Arenikau FC	Aitutaki Island		
-Tautu	Aitutaki Island		
-Teenui Raiders	Atui Island		
-Mighty Spo	Atui Island		
Southerners	Atui island		
-Walelangi	Pukapuka Island		
-Fake FC	Pukapuka Island		
-Lovely Boys FC	Pukapuka Island		
-Roto Village	Pukapuka Island		
-Yato Village	Pukapuka Island		

FIJI

FIJI FOOTBALL FEDERATION
PB 2514, Government Buildings, Suva
TEL 679/300 453 FAX /304 642
WEB www.fijifootball.com

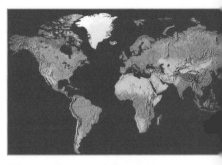

REFERENCE
Official name
Republic of Fiji

Date of formation	1970
Capital	Suva
Population	817,000
Total area	7054 sq Mi(18,270 sq Km)
Time zone	GMT+12
Density	116 per sq Mi(44 per sq Km)
Languages	English, Fijian, Hindi
Literacy rate	92%
Currency	Fiji $
Economy	Agriculture 67%
Religions	Hindu 38%, Methodist 37%
Ethnic Mix	Melanesian 48%, Indian 46%

GEOGRAPHY
Elevation
lowest point: Pacific Ocean 0 m
highest point: Tomanivi 1,324 m
Geography Note
includes 332 islands of which approximately 110 are inhabited
Natural Resources
timber, fish, gold, copper, offshore oil potential, hydropower
Climate
tropical marine; only slight seasonal temperature variation
Fiji Food
Fijian chicken

WORLD CUP

1930	Did not qualify
1934	Did not qualify
1938	Did not qualify
1950	Did not qualify
1954	Did not qualify
1958	Did not qualify
1962	Did not qualify
1966	Did not qualify
1970	Did not qualify
1974	Did not qualify
1978	Did not qualify
1982	Did not qualify
1986	Did not qualify
1990	Did not qualify
1994	Did not qualify
1998	Did not qualify
2002	Did not qualify

COUNTRY LEAGUE CHAMPIONS

2004	Ba
2003	Olympians
2002	BA
2001	Ba
2000	Nadi
1999	Ba
1998	Nadi
1997	Suva
1996	Suva

Women's League Champio

2004	Not Known
2003	Ba FC
2002	Ba FC
2001	Suva FC
2000	Nadi FC

NATIONAL TEAM COLORS

WORLD PICTURES OF SOCCER

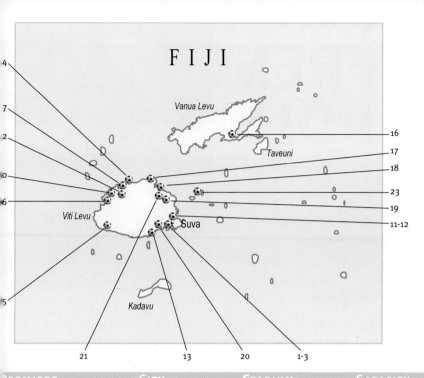

FIJI

Vanua Levu

Taveuni

Viti Levu

Suva

Kadavu

4
7
2
0
6
5
16
17
18
23
19
11-12
21
13
20
1-3

PREMIERE LEAGUE CLUBS	CITY	STADIUM	CAPACITY
Suva	Suva	Suva National stadium	5 000
Police	Suva		
Vatuga	Suva		
Nadi	Nadi	Prince Charles Park	1 000
Nawaicoba Blues	Nadi		
Forest eagles	Nadi		
Ba	Ba	Govind Park	4 000
Lautoka	Lautoka	Churchill Park	1 000
Press	Lautoka		
Foodtown Warriors	Lautoka		
Rewa	Nausori	Rato Cakobeau Park	1 000
Labasa	Nausori	Subrail Park	1 000
Navua	Navua	Thomson Park	1 000
Tavua	Tavua	Garvey park	1 000
Nadroga	Sigatoka	Lawaqa Park	1 000
Nasinu	Nasinu		
Rakiraki	Rakiraki		
Savusavu	Savusavu		
Taulevu/Naitasiri	Taulevu		
Lami	Lami		
Nawala	Nawala		
Vatukoula	Vatukoula		

FRENCH POLYNESIA

FEDERATION TAHITIENNE DE FOOTBALL
Rue Coppemoth Stade de Fautana,
BP50358, 98716 Pirae
TEL 689/540 954
WEB www.oceaniafootball.com

REFERENCE
Official name
Territory of French Polynesia

Claimed	1959
Capital	Papeete
Population	242,073
Total area	1,608 sq Mi(4265 sq Km)
Time zone	GMT-10
Density	75 per sq Mi
Languages	French, Polynesian
Literacy rate	95%
Currency	CFP
Economy	Tourism 68%,Industry 19%
Religions	Catholic, Protestant
Ethnic Mix	French, Polynesian, Melanesian

GEOGRAPHY
Elevation
lowest point: Pacific Ocean o m
highest point: Mont Orohena 2,241 m
Geography Note
includes five archipelagoes (4 volcanic, 1
coral); Makatea in French Polynesia is one of
the three great phosphate rock islands in
the Pacific Ocean
Natural Resources
timber, fish, cobalt, hydropower
Climate
tropical, but moderate
French Polynesia Food
coconut shrimps with vanilla

WORLD CUP

1930	Did not qualify
1934	Did not qualify
1938	Did not qualify
1950	Did not qualify
1954	Did not qualify
1958	Did not qualify
1962	Did not qualify
1966	Did not qualify
1970	Did not qualify
1974	Did not qualify
1978	Did not qualify
1982	Did not qualify
1986	Did not qualify
1990	Did not qualify
1994	Did not qualify
1998	Did not qualify
2002	Did not qualify

COUNTRY LEAGUE CHAMPIONS

2004	AS Manu-Ura Paea
2003	AS Pireas
2002	AS Venus
2001	AS Pireas
2000	AS Venus
1999	AS Venus
1998	AS Venus
1997	AS Venus
1996	AS Manu Ura

Women's League Champion

2004	Not Known
2003	Not Known
2002	AS Pirea
2001	AS Tefana
2000	Not Known

NATIONAL TEAM COLORS

WORLD PICTURES OF SOCCER

FRENCH POLYNESIA

Moorea

Papeete

Tahiti

9

11

8

6

3

1-7

10

Premiere League Clubs	City	Stadium	Capacity
Jeunes Tahitiens	Papeete	Stade Fautana	5 000
Excelsior	Papeete		
Central Sport	Papeete		
AS PTT	Papeete	Place To'ata	1 500
Fei Pi	Papeete		
Punaruu	Papeete		
AS Dragons	Papeete		
AS Pirae	Pirae	Stade Pater	15 000
AS Venu	Mahina		
AS Manu-Ura	Paea		
JS Arue	Arue		
Tefana	Faa'a		
Tamarii Faa'a	Faa'a		
AS Tiare Hinano	Moorea Island		
Mira	Moorea Island		
Tohiea	Moorea Island		

 # KIRIBATI

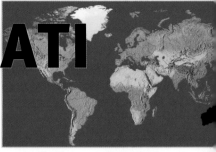

KIRIBATI FOOTBALL FEDERATION
Not Known
TEL: FAX:
WEB www.oceaniafootball.com

REFERENCE
Official name
  Republic of Kiribati

Date of formation	1979
Capital	Baikiri (Tarawa Atoll)
Total area	274 sq Mi (710 sq Km)
Time zone	GMT +12/11
Density	308 per sq Mi (119 per sq Km)
Languages	English, Kiribati
Literacy rate	90%
Currency	Ausralian $
Economy	Agriculture, Copra production, Fishing
Religions	Catholic 53%, Kiribati
Ethnic Mix	Protestant 39% Micronesian 98%

GEOGRAPHY
Elevation
lowest point: Pacific Ocean 0 m
highest point: Unnamed location on
              Banaba 81 m
Geography Note
21 of the 33 islands are inhabited; Banaba
(Ocean Island) in Kiribati is one of the three
great phosphate rock islands in the Pacific
Ocean - the others are Makatea in French
Polynesia, and Nauru
Natural Resources
phosphate (production discontinued in 79')
Climate
tropical; marine, hot and humid, moderated
by trade winds
Kiribati Food
te bua toro ni baukin

WORLD CUP

1930	Did not qualify
1934	Did not qualify
1938	Did not qualify
1950	Did not qualify
1954	Did not qualify
1958	Did not qualify
1962	Did not qualify
1966	Did not qualify
1970	Did not qualify
1974	Did not qualify
1978	Did not qualify
1982	Did not qualify
1986	Did not qualify
1990	Did not qualify
1994	Did not qualify
1998	Did not qualify
2002	Did not qualify

COUNTRY LEAGUE CHAMPIONS

2004	Flying Tigers Ambo
2003	Not Known
2002	Arorae
2001	Not Known
2000	Not Known
1999	BOK & Abaiang FC
1998	Not Known
1997	Not Known
1996	Not Known
199	Not Known

Women's League Champion

2004	Butaritari FC
2003	Not Known
2002	Abaiang FC
2001	Not Known

NATIONAL TEAM COLORS

WORLD PICTURES OF SOCCER

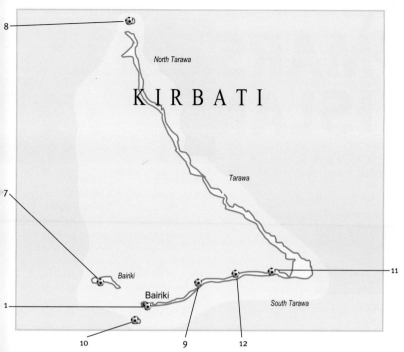

North Tarawa

KIRBATI

Tarawa

8

7

Bairiki

Bairiki

1

South Tarawa

11

10

9

12

Premiere League Clubs	City	Stadium	Capacity
-Tarawa Motors	Bairiki-South Tarawa	Bairiki National Stadium	
-ANZ Bank of Kiribati	Betio-South Tarawa		
-Kiribati ports Authority	Betio-South Tarawa		
-Marine Training Center	Betio-South Tarawa		
-Frigate	Betio-South Tarawa		
-Shipyard	Betio-South Tarawa		
-Betio Boys	Betio-South Tarawa		
-Koinawa	Koinawa-Abayang Island		
-Nei Wirara	Teoraereke		
-Tabiteuea	Tabiteuea		
-Bikenibeu Boys	Bikenibeu		
-Eita	Eita		

MARSHALL ISLANDS

MARSHALL ISLANDS FOOTBALL FEDERATION
Not Known
TEL: FAX:
WEB www.oceaniafootball.com

REFERENCE
Official name
Republic of the Marshall Islands

Date of formation	1964
Capital	Dalap -Uliga-Darrit
Population	68,126
Total area	70 sq Mi (181 sq Mi)
Time zone	GMT+12
Density	937 per sq Mi (361 per sq Km)
Languages	English, Maltese
Literacy rate	93%
Currency	U.S $
Economy	Agriculture, Fishing, Tourism
Religions	Protestant 90%, Catholic 8%
Ethnic Mix	Maltese 96%

GEOGRAPHY
Elevation
lowest point: Pacific Ocean o m
highest point: Unnamed location on
Likiep 10 m

Geography Note
two archipelagic island chains of 30 atolls
and 1,152 islands; Bikini and Enewetak are
former US nuclear test sites; Kwajalein, the
famous World War II battleground, is now
used as a US missile test range

Natural Resources
coconut products, marine products, deep
seabed minerals

Climate
wet season from May to November; hot and
humid; islands border typhoon belt

Marshall Islands Food
Barbecue limas

WORLD CUP

1930	Did not qualify
1934	Did not qualify
1938	Did not qualify
1950	Did not qualify
1954	Did not qualify
1958	Did not qualify
1962	Did not qualify
1966	Did not qualify
1970	Did not qualify
1974	Did not qualify
1978	Did not qualify
1982	Did not qualify
1986	Did not qualify
1990	Did not qualify
1994	Did not qualify
1998	Did not qualify
2002	Did not qualify

COUNTRY LEAGUE CHAMPIONS

2004	Not Known
2003	Not Known
2002	Not Known
2001	Not Known
2000	Kobeer FC
1999	Star Motion FC
1998	Star Motion FC
1997	Not Known
1996	Not Known
1995	Not Known

Women's League Champion

2004	Not Known
2003	Not Known
2002	Not Known
2001	Not Known

NATIONAL TEAM COLORS

WORLD PICTURES OF SOCCER

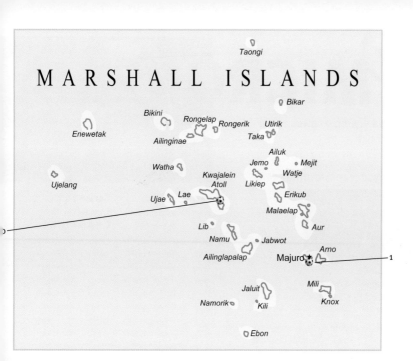

MARSHALL ISLANDS

Taongi

Bikar

Bikini
Rongelap
Rongerik
Utirik

Enewetak
Ailinginae
Taka

Ailuk

Jemo
Mejit

Watha
Watje

Kwajalein
Atoll
Likiep

Ujelang
Ujae
Lae
Erikub

Malaelap

Lib
Aur

Namu
Jabwot

Ailinglapalap
Arno

Majuro
1

Jaluit
Mili

Namorik
Kili
Knox

Ebon

PREMIERE LEAGUE CLUBS	CITY	STADIUM	CAPACITY
Majuro AllStars	Majuro	Dalap-Uliga Darit Stadium	
Kobbeer	Kwajalein		
Spartans	Kwajalein		
Spartans II	Kwajalein		
Locals	Kwajalein		
Queen of Peace	Kwajalein		
Spartans White	Kwajalein		
Calvary	Kwajalein		
Calvary II	Kwajalein		
-Spartans Reds	Kwajalein		

MICRONESIA

MICRONESIA FOOTBALL FEDERATION
Not Known
TEL: FAX:
WEB:www.oceaniafootball.com

REFERENCE
Official name
　Federated States of Micronesia
Date of formation 1986
Capital Palikir (Ponhpei Island)
Population 133,144
Total area 271 sq Mi (702 sq Km)
Time zone GMT+10
Density 491 per sq Mi (187 per sq Km)
Languages English, Trukese, Pohnpeian, Mortlockese
Literacy rate 90%
Currency U.S $
Economy Agriculture, Fishing, Services, textiles
Religions Catholic 50%
Ethnic Mix Micronesian 100%

GEOGRAPHY
Elevation
lowest point: Pacific Ocean 0 m
highest point: Dolohmwar (Totolom) 791 m
Geography Note
four major island groups totaling 607 islands
Natural Resources
forests, marine products, deep-seabed minerals
Climate
tropical; heavy year-round rainfall, especially in the eastern islands; located on southern edge of the typhoon belt with occasionally severe damage
Micronesia Food
Micronesian chicken

WORLD CUP

1930	Did not qualify
1934	Did not qualify
1938	Did not qualify
1950	Did not qualify
1954	Did not qualify
1958	Did not qualify
1962	Did not qualify
1966	Did not qualify
1970	Did not qualify
1974	Did not qualify
1978	Did not qualify
1982	Did not qualify
1986	Did not qualify
1990	Did not qualify
1994	Did not qualify
1998	Did not qualify
2002	Did not qualify

COUNTRY LEAGUE CHAMPIONS

2003	Not Known
2002	Not Known
2001	Not Known
2000	Not Known
1999	Not Known
1998	Not Known
1997	Not Known
1996	Not Known
1995	Not Known

Women's League Champio

2003	Not Known
2002	Not Known
2001	Not Known
2000	Not Known
1999	Not Known

NATIONAL TEAM COLORS

WORLD PICTURES OF SOCCER

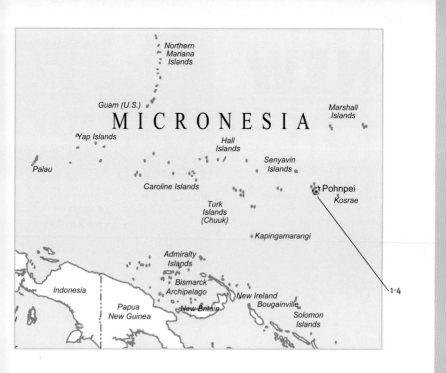

PREMIERE LEAGUE CLUBS	CITY	STADIUM	CAPACITY
Ponape Agricultural	Palikir		
Seventh Day Adventist	Palikir		
Local Warriors	Palikir		
Team International	Palikir		

NEW CALEDONIA

NEW CALEDONIA FOOTBALL FEDERATION
PO Box 117, Noumea 01346, NC
TEL: FAX:
WEB:www.oceaniafootball.com

REFERENCE
Official name
Nouvelle Caledonie

Claimed	1853
Capital	Noumea
Population	216,494
Total area	19,060 sq Km
Time zone	GMT+12
Density	24 per sq Mi
Languages	French, Polynesian, English
Literacy rate	92%
Currency	CFP
Economy	Tourism 80%
Religions	Roman Catholic 60%, Protestant 30%, Others 10%
Ethnic	Mix Melanesian 42.5% European 37.1 %

WORLD CUP

World Cup		Country League Champions	
1930	Did not qualify	2003	Not Known
1934	Did not qualify	2002	Not Known
1938	Did not qualify	2001	Not Known
1950	Did not qualify	2000	Not Known
1954	Did not qualify	1999	Not Known
1958	Did not qualify	1998	Not Known
1962	Did not qualify	1997	Not Known
1966	Did not qualify	1996	Not Known
1970	Did not qualify	1995	Not Known
1974	Did not qualify		
1978	Did not qualify	Women's League Champions	
1982	Did not qualify		
1986	Did not qualify	2003	Not Known
1990	Did not qualify	2002	Not Known
1994	Did not qualify	2001	Not Known
1998	Did not qualify	2000	Not Known
2002	Did not qualify	1999	Not Known

NATIONAL TEAM COLORS

GEOGRAPHY
Elevation
lowest point: Pacific Ocean o m
highest point: Mont Panie 1,628 m
Geography Note
one of the largest in the Pacific Ocean), the archipelago of Iles Loyaute, and numerous small, sparsely populated islands and atolls
Natural Resources
nickel, chrome, iron, cobalt, manganese, silver, gold, lead, copper
Climate
tropical; modified by southeast trade winds; hot, humid
New Caledonian Food
Lemon Fish

WORLD PICTURES OF SOCCER

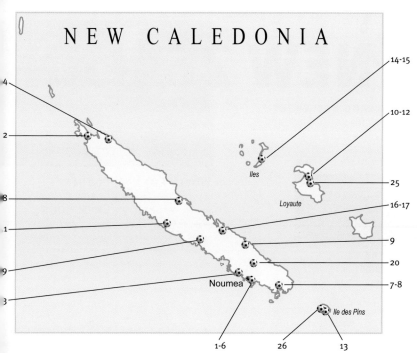

NEW CALEDONIA

Iles

Loyaute

25

14-15

10-12

16-17

9

20

7-8

Noumea

Ile des Pins

1-6   26   13

4

2

8

1

9

3

PREMIERE LEAGUE CLUBS	CITY	STADIUM	CAPACITY
-AS Magenta	Noumea	Numa-Daly Magenta	
-USC Noumea	Noumea		
-Olympique	Noumea		
-JS Vallee du Tir Noumea	Noumea	Stade Pentecost	
-JS Mare Noumea	Noumea	Stade Pentecost	
-JS Ouvea	Noumea	Stade Pentecost	
-AS Mont Dore	Mont Dore		
-AS Fregate	Mont Dore		
-ASLN Thio	Thio		
-JS Traput	Lifou Island		
-Nathalo	Lifou Island		
-We-Luecilla	Lifou Island		
-Iles des Pins	Pines Island		
-Uniforme Fayaoue	Ouvea Island		
-JS Ouvea	Ouvea Island		
-Entente de Galima	Gelima		
-USL Gelima	Gelima		
-ASLN Kouaoua	Kouaoua		
-ACB Poya	Poya		
-AS Auteuil	Auteuil		
-JS Baco	Baco		
-AS Poum	Poum		
-AS Paita	Paita		
-CA Saint Louis	Saint Louis		
-Wedoumel	Wedoumel		
-AS Kunie	Kunie		

NEW ZEALAND

New zealand Soccer Inc.
PB 11-357, Ellerslie, Auckland
TEL 64 9/525 6120
FAX /525 6123
WEB www.nzsoccer.com

Reference
Official name
The Dominion of New Zealand

Date of formation	1926
Capital	Wellington
Population	3.9 Million
Total area	103,733 sq Mi (268,670 sq Km)
Time zone	GMT+12
Density	35 per sq Mi (13 per sq Km)
Languages	English, Maori
Literacy rate	99%
Currency	New Zealand $
Economy	Services 70%
Religions	Anglican 24%, Presbyterian
Ethnic Mix	18%, European 82%, Maori 9%

Geography
Elevation
lowest point: Pacific Ocean o m
highest point: Mount Cook 3,764 m
Geography Note
about 80% of the population lives in cities;
Wellington is the southernmost national
capital in the world
Natural Resources
natural gas, iron ore, sand, coal, timber,
hydropower, gold, limestone
Climate
temperate with sharp regional contrasts
New Zealand Food
cashmere chutney/lamb barbecue

World Cup

1930	Did not qualify
1934	Did not qualify
1938	Did not qualify
1950	Did not qualify
1954	Did not qualify
1958	Did not qualify
1962	Did not qualify
1966	Did not qualify
1970	Did not qualify
1974	Did not qualify
1978	Did not qualify
1982	First round exit
1986	Did not qualify
1990	Did not qualify
1994	Did not qualify
1998	Did not qualify
2002	Did not qualify

Country League Champions

2005	Auckland City
2004	Central United
2003	Miramar Rangers
2002	Miramar Rangers
2001	Central United
2000	Napier City Rovers
1999	Central United
1998	Napier City Rovers
1997	Waitekere City

Women's League Champion

2003	Auckland-Manukau
2002	Auckland-Manukau
2001	Capital Soccer
2000	Auckland Soccer 2
1999	Not Known at this t

National Team Colors

World Pictures of Soccer

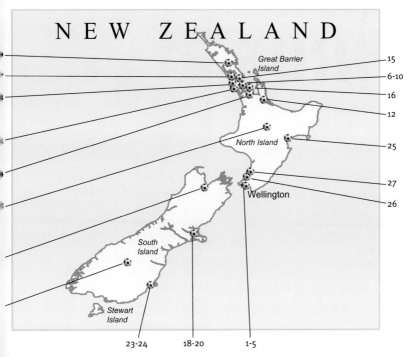

NEW ZEALAND

Great Barrier Island

North Island

South Island

Stewart Island

Wellington

15
6-10
16
12
25
27
26

23-24   18-20   1-5

PREMIERE LEAGUE CLUBS	CITY	STADIUM	CAPACITY
Miramar Rangers	Wellington		
Wellington marist	Wellington		
North Wellington	Wellington		
Wellington Olympic	Wellington		
Wellington United	Wellington		
Football Kingz FC	Auckland	Ericson Stadium	30 000
Central United	Auckland	Kiwitea Street	1 000
Eastern Suburbs	Auckland		
East Auckland	Auckland		
West Auckland	Auckland		
Mangere United	Mangere		
Tauranga City United	Tauranga City		
Onehunga Sports	Onehunga		
Papakura	Papakura	Melville United(Melville)	
Glenfield Rovers	Glenfield		
Ellerslie	Ellerslie		
Waitekere City	Waitekere City		
Christchurch Rangers	Christchurch		
Christchurch Technical	Christchurch		
Christchurch United	Christchurch		
Nelson Suburbs	Nelson		
Queenstown Rovers	Queenstown		
Dunedin Technical	Dunedin		
Caversham	Dunedin		
Napier City Rovers	Napier	Blue Water Park	
Waterside Karori	Karori		
Lower Hutt City	Lower Hutt City		
Taupo FC	Taupo		
Whangarei FC	Whangarei		

NIUE

Niu Football Federation
PO Box 106, Alofi, Niue 73920
TEL: FAX:
WEB:www.oceaniafootball.com

Reference
Official name
Niue (Associated territory of new Zealand)

Claimed	1901
Capital	Alofi
Population	2080
Total area	102 sq Mi(264 sq Km)
Time zone	GMT -11
Density	6 per sq Km
Languages	English, Melanesian
Literacy rate	95%
Currency	New Zealand $
Economy	Agriculture (coconut, Food Processing)

Religions
Ethnic Mix

Geography
Elevation
lowest point: Pacific Ocean 0 m
highest point: unnamed location near Mutalau settlement 68 m
Geography Note
one of world's largest coral islands
Natural Resources
fish, arable land
Climate
tropical; modified by southeast trade winds
Niue Food
niue coconut chicken/luae fish

World Cup

1930	Did not qualify
1934	Did not qualify
1938	Did not qualify
1950	Did not qualify
1954	Did not qualify
1958	Did not qualify
1962	Did not qualify
1966	Did not qualify
1970	Did not qualify
1974	Did not qualify
1978	Did not qualify
1982	Did not qualify
1986	Did not qualify
1990	Did not qualify
1994	Did not qualify
1998	Did not qualify
2002	Did not qualify

Country League Champions

2004	Not Known
2003	Not Known
2002	Not Known
2001	Alofi
2000	Talava
1999	Talava
1998	Lakepa
1997	Not Known
1996	Not Known

Women's League Champio

2004	Not Known
2003	Not Known
2002	Not Known
2001	Not Known

National Team Colors

World Pictures of Soccer

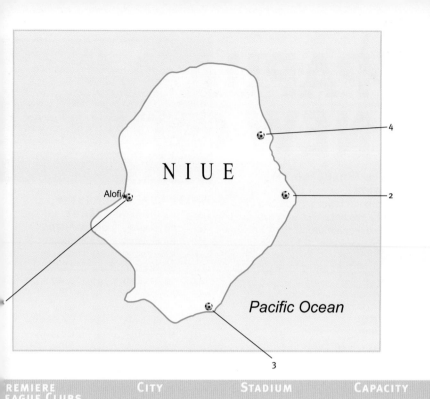

NIUE

Alofi

Pacific Ocean

4

2

3

PREMIERE LEAGUE CLUBS	CITY	STADIUM	CAPACITY
Alofi	Alofi		
Liku	Liku		
Hakupu	Hakupu		
Lakepa	Lakepa		

PAPUA NEW GUINEA

PAPUA NEW GUINEA FOOTBALL ASSOCIATION

PB 957, Room II Level 1, Haus Tisa LXE
411 Morobe Province TEL 675/479 1998
WEB www.oceaniafootball.com

REFERENCE

Official name
The Independent State of
Papua New guinea

Date of formation	1975
Capital	Port Moresby
Population	4.8 Million
Total area	174,849 sq Mi (452,860 sq Km)
Time zone	GMT +10
Density	27 per sq Mi (10 per sq Km)
Languages	Pidgin English, Motu, Papuan, 75% Native languages
Literacy rate	71%
Currency	Kina
Economy	Agriculture 64%
Religions	Christian 62%, Indg. Beliefs 34%
Ethnic Mix	Melanesian/Mixed 100%

GEOGRAPHY

Elevation
lowest point: Pacific Ocean 0 m
highest point: Mount Wilhelm 4,509 m

Geography Note
shares island of New Guinea with Indonesia;
one of world's largest swamps along southwest coast

Natural Resources
gold, copper, silver, natural gas, timber, oil,
fisheries

Climate
tropical; northwest monsoon (December to
March), southeast monsoon (May to
October); slight seasonal temperature
variation

Papua New Guinea Food
Tinned meat in dalo leaves/talautu

WORLD CUP

1930	Did not qualify
1934	Did not qualify
1938	Did not qualify
1950	Did not qualify
1954	Did not qualify
1958	Did not qualify
1962	Did not qualify
1966	Did not qualify
1970	Did not qualify
1974	Did not qualify
1978	Did not qualify
1982	Did not qualify
1986	Did not qualify
1990	Did not qualify
1994	Did not qualify
1998	Did not qualify
2002	Did not qualify

COUNTRY LEAGUE CHAMPIONS

2004	Sobou
2003	Sobou
2002	Sobou
2001	Sobou
2000	Unitech
1999	Guria
1998	ICF University
1997	ICF University
1996	ICF University

Women's League Champio

2004	Not Known
2003	Not Known
2002	Not Known
2001	Not Known
2000	Not Known

NATIONAL TEAM COLORS

WORLD PICTURES OF SOCCER

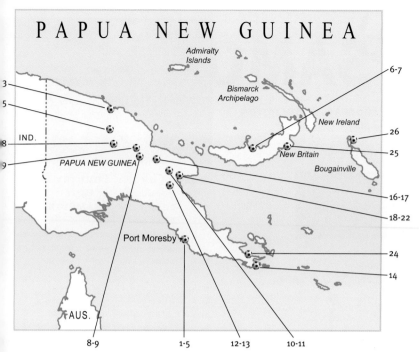

PAPUA NEW GUINEA

Admiralty Islands

Bismarck Archipelago

New Ireland

IND.

PAPUA NEW GUINEA

New Britain

Bougainville

Port Moresby

AUS.

3
5
8
9
6-7
26
25
16-17
18-22
24
14
8-9
1-5
12-13
10-11

Premiere League Clubs	City	Stadium	Capacity
-University ICF	Port Moresby	Hubbert Murray	10 000
-Defence	Port Moresby		
-Pangtel	Port Moresby		
-Rapatona	Port Moresby		
-Cosmos	Port Moresby		
-South Coast	Kimbe		
-Hoba	Kimbe		
-Guria	Goroka		
-Murat	Goroka		
-Tanang	Nadzab		
-Pulung	Nadzab		
-Huxley	Bulolo		
-Mt Rebels	Bulolo		
-Samarai South	Samarai		
-Momase	Chimbut		
-Yarus	Kaiapit		
-Banabin	Kaiapit		
-Sobou	Lae		
-Guria	Lae		
-Unitech	Lae		
-Blue Kumuls	Lae		
-Tolec Buresong	Lae		
-Central Hood	Kaup		
-Kutu West	Kutu		
-Dolphins	Buka		
-Hatolol	Kieta		
-Momads	Mt Hagen		
-Tarangau	Mt Hagen		
-Blue Kumuls	Kundiawa		

453

SAMOA

SAMOA FOOTBALL ASSOCIATION
PB 960, Apia
TEL 68A5/26 504   FAX 685/20 341
WEB:www.oceaniafootball.com

REFERENCE
Official name
Independent State of Samoa

Date of formation 1962
Capital Apia
Population 180,000
Total area 1093 sq Mi (2830 sq Km)
Time zone GMT +11
Density 165 per sq Mi (80 per sq Km)
Languages Samoan, English
Literacy rate 98%
Currency Tala
Economy Agriculture 65%
Religions Christian 99%
Ethnic Mix Polynesian 90%, Euronesian 9%

GEOGRAPHY
Elevation
lowest point: Pacific Ocean 0 m
highest point: Mauga Silisili 1,857 m
Geography Note
Occupies an almost central position within Polynesia
Natural Resources
hardwood forests, fish, hydropower
Climate
Tropical; rainy season (October to March), dry season (May to October)
Samoa Food
Suppo Esi

WORLD CUP

1930	Did not qualify
1934	Did not qualify
1938	Did not qualify
1950	Did not qualify
1954	Did not qualify
1958	Did not qualify
1962	Did not qualify
1966	Did not qualify
1970	Did not qualify
1974	Did not qualify
1978	Did not qualify
1982	Did not qualify
1986	Did not qualify
1990	Did not qualify
1994	Did not qualify
1998	Did not qualify
2002	Did not qualify

COUNTRY LEAGUE CHAMPIONS

2004	Strickland Bros.
2003	Strickland Bros.
2002	Strickland Bros.
2001	Gold Star
2000	Tiyavi FC
1999	Moataa
1998	Vaivase Tai
1997	Kiwi FC
1996	Not Known

Women's League Champions

2004	Kiwi FC
2003	Lepea FC
2002	Kiwi FC
2001	Kiwi FC
2000	Matautu Youth FC

NATIONAL TEAM COLORS

WORLD PICTURES OF SOCCER

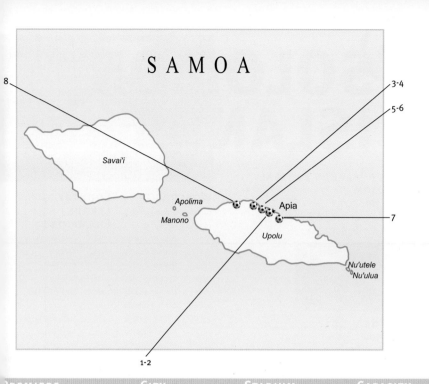

PREMIERE LEAGUE CLUBS	CITY	STADIUM	CAPACITY
Central United	Apia	J. Sepp Blatter Field	
Vikings	Apia	J. Sepp Blatter Field	
Gold Star FC	Sogi		
Sogi FC	Sogi		
Strickland Brothers	Lepea		
Lepea	Lepea		
Vaivase-Tai	Vaivase		
Moamoa	Moamoa		

SOLOMON ISLANDS

SOLOMON ISLANDS FOOTBALL FEDERATION
PB 854, Honiara
TEL 677/26 496 FAX 677/26 497
WEB www.siff.com.sb

REFERENCE
Official name
Solomon Islands

Date of formation	1978
Capital	Honiara
Population	444,000
Total area	10,806 sq Mi (27,990 sq Km)
Time zone	GMT +11
Density	41 per sq Mi(16 per sq Km)
Languages	English,Pidgin English,87 Native Languages
Literacy rate	62%
Currency	Solomon Islands $
Economy	Agriculture 85%
Religions	Anglican 34%, Catholic 19%
Ethnic Mix	Melanesian 94%, Polynesian 4%

GEOGRAPHY
Elevation
lowest point: Pacific Ocean o m
highest point: Mount Makarakomburu 2,447 m
Geography Note
strategic location on sea routes between the South Pacific Ocean, the Solomon Sea, and the Coral Sea
Natural Resources
fish, forests, gold, bauxite, phosphates, lead, zinc, nickel
Climate
tropical monsoon; few extremes of temperature and weather
Solomon Islands Food
kara snacks/fish lemon

WORLD CUP

1930	Did not qualify
1934	Did not qualify
1938	Did not qualify
1950	Did not qualify
1954	Did not qualify
1958	Did not qualify
1962	Did not qualify
1966	Did not qualify
1970	Did not qualify
1974	Did not qualify
1978	Did not qualify
1982	Did not qualify
1986	Did not qualify
1990	Did not qualify
1994	Did not qualify
1998	Did not qualify
2002	Did not qualify

COUNTRY LEAGUE CHAMPIONS

2004	Central Realas
2003	Koloale
2002	Koloale
2001	Koloale
2000	Laugu United
1999	Not Known
1998	Malaita Eagles FC
1997	Not Known
1996	Rangers

Women's League Champior

2004	Naha FC
2003	Naha FC
2002	Naha FC
2001	Not Known
2000	Not Known

NATIONAL TEAM COLORS

WORLD PICTURES OF SOCCER

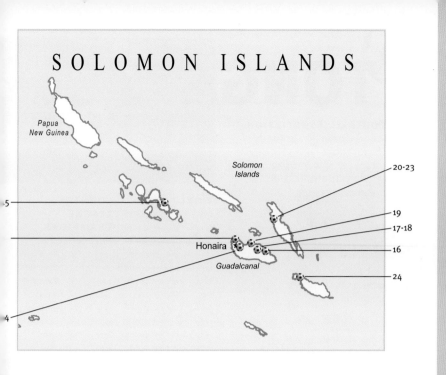

SOLOMON ISLANDS

Papua New Guinea

Solomon Islands

20-23

19

17-18

16

Honaira

Guadalcanal

24

5

4

PREMIERE LEAGUE CLUBS	CITY	STADIUM	CAPACITY
1-Koloale FC	Honiara	Lawson Tawa Stadium	10 000
2-Rangers	Honiara		
3-Naha	Honiara		
4-Marist	Honiara		
5-Mars	Honiara		
6-Laugu United FC	Honiara		
7-Walas	Honiara		
8-KOSSA	Honiara		
9-Sunbeam	Honiara		
10-Uncles	Honiara		
11-Las United	Honiara		
12-Eku	Honiara		
13-Vura	Honiara		
14-Honiara Police	Honiara		
15-Eastern Kingz	Temotu		
16-Senga	Lauru		
17-Kuara	Guadalcanal		
18-Banika	Guadalcanal		
19-East Kaio	Kaio		
20-Auki Kingz FC	Malaita		
21-Malaita Eagles	Malaita		
22-West Kwara'ae	Malaita		
23-West Are Are	Malaita		
24-Mareeba Bulls	Unawa		

# TONGA

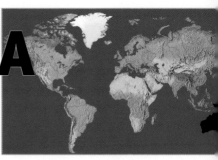

TONGA FOOTBALL ASSOCIATION
Tungi Arcade, Taufa'Ahau Road,
PB 852, Nuku'Alofa
TEL 676/24 442 FAX 676/23 340
WEB www.tongafootball.com

REFERENCE
Official name
  Kingdom of Tonga
**Date of
formation**   1970
Capital   Nuku'Alofa
Population   102,231
Total area   278 sq Mi (720 sq Km)
Time zone   GMT +12
Density   368 per sq Mi (145 per sq Km)
Languages   Tongan, English
Literacy rate 97%
Currency   Pa'Anga
Economy   Agriculture 70%
Religions   PFree Wesyan 64%,
                  Catholic 15%
Ethnic Mix   Polynesian 99%

GEOGRAPHY
Elevation
lowest point: Pacific Ocean o m
highest point: Unnamed location on Kao
                  Island 1,033 m
Geography Note
archipelago of 169 islands (36 inhabited)
Natural Resources
fish, fertile soil
Climate
tropical; modified by trade winds; warm
season (December to May), cool season
(May to December)
Tonga Food
veihalo(drink)
tonga chicken

WORLD CUP		COUNTRY LEAGUE CHAMPIONS	
1930	Did not qualify		
1934	Did not qualify		
1938	Did not qualify	2004	Not Known
1950	Did not qualify	2003	SC Lotoha'Apai
1954	Did not qualify	2002	SC Lotoha'Apai
1958	Did not qualify	2001	SC Lotoha'Apai
1962	Did not qualify	2000	SC Lotoha'Apai
1966	Did not qualify	1999	SC Lotoha'Apai
1970	Did not qualify	1998	SC Lotoha'Apai
1974	Did not qualify	1997	Not Known
1978	Did not qualify	1996	Not Known
1982	Did not qualify	**Women's League Champion**	
1986	Did not qualify	2004	Not Known
1990	Did not qualify	2003	Nuku'Alofa II
1994	Did not qualify	2002	Kumifonua
1998	Did not qualify	2001	Not Known
2002	Did not qualify	2000	Not Known

NATIONAL TEAM COLORS

WORLD PICTURES OF SOCCER

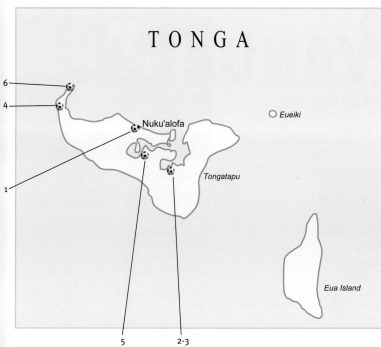

TONGA

Eueiki

Nuku'alofa

Tongatapu

Eua Island

Premiere League Clubs	City	Stadium	Capacity
-SC Lotoha'apai	Nuku'alofa	Mangweni Stadium	3 000
-Ngele'ia	Kolofou		
-Kolofou FC	Kolofou		
-Ahi'o Ulakai	Ahau		
-Veitango	Veitango		
-Ha'atafu XI	Ha'atafu		
-Makave	Makave Islands		
-Vava'u	Vava'u Islands		
-Niuaufo'ou	Niuaufo'ou Islands		

VANUATU

VANUATU FOOTBALL
Federation
PB 266, Port Villa
TEL 678/25 236   FAX 678/25 463
WEB www.oceaniafootball.com

REFERENCE
Official name
Republic of Vanuatu

Date of formation	1980
Capital	Port- Vila
Population	200,000
Total area	4706 sq mi (12,190 sq Km)
Time zone	GMT +11
Density	42 per sq Mi (12 per sq Km)
Languages	Bislama, English, French
Literacy rate	64%
Currency	Vatu
Economy	Agriculture 75%
Religions	Protestant 77%, Catholic 15%
Ethnic Mix	Melanesian 94%, Polynesian 3%

GEOGRAPHY
Elevation
lowest point: Pacific Ocean o m
highest point: Tabwemasana 1,877 m
Geography Note
a Y-shaped chain of four main islands and 80
smaller islands; several of the islands have
active volcanoes
Natural Resources
manganese, hardwood forests, fish
Climate
tropical; moderated by southeast trade
winds
Vanuatu Food
laplap

WORLD CUP

1930	Did not qualify
1934	Did not qualify
1938	Did not qualify
1950	Did not qualify
1954	Did not qualify
1958	Did not qualify
1962	Did not qualify
1966	Did not qualify
1970	Did not qualify
1974	Did not qualify
1978	Did not qualify
1982	Did not qualify
1986	Did not qualify
1990	Did not qualify
1994	Did not qualify
1998	Did not qualify
2002	Did not qualify

COUNTRY LEAGUE CHAMPIONS

2004	Not Known
2003	Tafea FC
2002	Tupuji Imere Mele
2001	Tafea FC
2000	Tafea FC
1999	Tafea FC
1998	Tafea FC
1997	Tafea FC
1996	Tafea FC

Women's League Champion

2004	Not Known
2003	Not Known
2002	Not Known
2001	Not Known
2000	Not Known

NATIONAL TEAM COLORS

WORLD PICTURES OF SOCCER

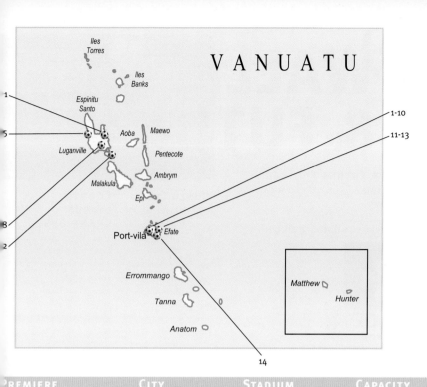

PREMIERE LEAGUE CLUBS	CITY	STADIUM	CAPACITY
Tafea FC	Port Vila/Efate Isl.	Port Vila Municipal Stad.	1 000
Sheperds University	Port Vila/Efate		
Amical	Port Vila/Efate Isl.		
Erakor GS	Port Vila/Efate Isl.		
Sia Raga	Port Vila/Efate Isl.		
Tupuji Imere	Port Vila/Efate Isl.	Korman Stadium	1 000
Seveners University	Port Vila/Efate		
Yatel FC	Port Vila/Efate Isl.		
Olympic	Port Vila/Efate Isl.		
Port Vila FC	Port Vila/Efate Isl.		
North Efate University	Efate Isl.		
Falefa	North Efate Isl.		
Ifira	South Efate Isl.		
Pango	Pango		
Pwele	Pwele		
Concord FC	Luganville/Santo Isl.		
Milo FC	Luganville/Santo Isl.		
Luganville FC	Luganville/Santo Isl.		
Korena	Santo Isl.		
Lorum	East Santo Isl.		
Black Spider	North Santo Isl.		
South seas FC	Malo		

WALLIS & FUTUNA

**WALLIS & FUTUNA FOOTBALL
Association**
Not Known
TEL: FAX:
WEB www.oceaniafootball.com

REFERENCE
Official name
  Territory of Wallis & Futuna

Claimed	1842
Capital	Mata Utu
Population	15,000
Total area	106 sq Mi(274 sq Km)
Time zone	GMT +12
Density	56 per sq Km
Languages	French, English, Polynesian
Literacy rate	91%
Currency	CPF
Economy	Agriculture, Fishing
Religions	Protestant, Catholic, Christian
Ethnic Mix	Polynesian, Melanesian

GEOGRAPHY
Elevation
lowest point: Pacific Ocean 0 m
highest point: Mont Singavi 765 m
Geography Note
both island groups have fringing reefs
Natural Resources
NEGL
Climate
tropical; hot, rainy season (November to
April); cool, dry season (May to October);
rains 2,500-3,000 mm per year (80% humidity); average temperature 26.6 degrees C
Wallis & Futuna Food
breadfruit/copra/poisson guave grillade

WORLD CUP

1930	Did not qualify
1934	Did not qualify
1938	Did not qualify
1950	Did not qualify
1954	Did not qualify
1958	Did not qualify
1962	Did not qualify
1966	Did not qualify
1970	Did not qualify
1974	Did not qualify
1978	Did not qualify
1982	Did not qualify
1986	Did not qualify
1990	Did not qualify
1994	Did not qualify
1998	Did not qualify
2002	Did not qualify

COUNTRY LEAGUE CHAMPIONS

2004	Not Known
2003	Not Known
2002	Not Known
2001	FANC
2000	Not Known
1999	Not Known
1998	AS Aka Aka
1997	AS Aka Aka
1996	AS Aka Aka

Women's League Champion

2004	Not Known
2003	Nuku'Alofa II
2002	Kumifonua
2001	Not Known
2000	Not Known

NATIONAL TEAM COLORS

WORLD PICTURES OF SOCCER

WALLIS

&

FUTUNA

Ile Wallis

Mata-Utu — 1, 3

Ile Uvea — 4

Iles de Home

Ile Futuna

2 — Ile Alofi

PREMIERE LEAGUE CLUBS	CITY	STADIUM	CAPACITY
Iles de Wallis	Wallis Island		
Iles de Futuna	Futuna Island		
Mata-Utu	Mata-Utu		
AS Aka-Aka	Aka-Aka		

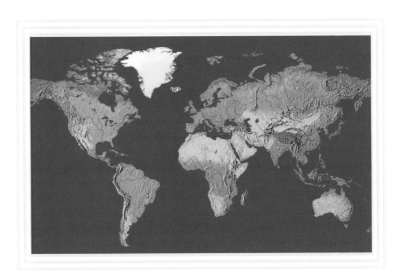

FAR & AWAY

AKROTIRI

CYPRUS
Area controlled by
Cyprus Government
(Greek Cypriot area)

COUNTRY FACTS

Official name: Akrotiri
Overseas territory of UK
Date of formation: June 6,1956
Capital: Episkopi
Location: peninsula on the southwest coast of Cyprus
Total area: 123 Sq KM
Population: about 5000
Languages: English
Literacy rate: 99%
Currency: British pound
Climate: Temperate, Mediterranean with hot, dry summers and cool winters
Note: includes a salt lake and wetlands

SOCCER FACTS

Football is alive and kicking in Akrotiri.

The Carter Cup kicks-off next season in Akrotiri, with all Minor Units and Major Units.

Akrotiri has one Stadium "Happy Valley Stadium" in Episkopi.

Akrotiri has a military Men's league/Women's league.

Men's Champion 2005: CSSU
Women's Champion 2005: Dhekelia

ANTARCTICA

COUNTRY FACTS

Official name: Antarctica
Total area: 14 million sq km, 280,000 sq km ice-free, 13.72 million sq km ice-covered (est.)
Note: fifth-largest continent, following Asia, Africa, North America, and South America
Elevation extremes:
lowest point:
Bentley Subglacial Trench -2,555 m
highest point:
Vinson Massif 4,897 m

Geography & Climate note: the coldest, windiest, highest (on average), and driest continent; during summer, more solar radiation reaches the surface at the South Pole than is received at the Equator in an equivalent period; mostly uninhabited.

SOCCER FACTS

Sir Ernest Shackleton's trans-antarctic expedition of 1914-1917 was one of the great feats of human endurance-one vividly captured in the powerful and dramatic pictures taken by Frank Hurley, the expedition's official photographer.

Frank Hurley is the first man to capture a picture of a game played in Antarctica.
On Feb 16,1916 at 4p.m The Crew of the "Endurance" had a Football game on the ice frozen Wendell Sea in Antarctica.

Multi-National

ARCTIC OCEAN

COUNTRY FACTS

Official name: Arctic Ocean
Total area: 14.056 million sq km
Elevation extremes:
lowest point:
Fram Basin -4,665 m
highest point:
sea level 0 m

Geography & Climate Note: polar climate characterized by persistent cold and relatively narrow annual temperature ranges; winters characterized by continuous darkness, cold and stable weather stations, and clear skies; summers characterized by continuous daylight, damp and foggy weather, and weak cyclones with rain or snow

The Arctic Ocean is the smallest of the world's five oceans.

SOCCER FACTS

Soccer on ice in the arctic (Near the North pole) On August 23th, the three most important research icebreakers worldwide met in the Arctic Ocean, about 500 km from the North Pole Crews from 17 nations had a scientific meeting and refueling session. By day's end they met for a soccer tournament on a 3 meter thick and 1 square kilometer, in area ice floe, where the sporting events took place. It was the docking place for the three icebreakers. The exact position was at 85°30'N and 15°00'E.

Multi-National

ASHMORE & CARTIER ISLANDS

COUNTRY FACTS

Official name: Ashmore & Cartier Island
Status External territory of Australia
Claimed: 1978
Administered from Canberra
Population: no permanent population
Total area: 2 sq Mi, 5.2 Sq KM
Time zone: GMT +8
Languages: English
Climate: Tropical
Natural resources: fish
Elevation extremes:
lowest point:
Indian Ocean 0 m
highest point:
unnamed location 3 m

SOCCER FACTS

No information available at this time.

To update information for this location please contact our world atlas web site.
www.soccerexplorers.com

BAKER & HOWLAND ISLANDS

North   Pacific   Ocean

COUNTRY FACTS

Official name: Baker & Howland
Islands unincorporated land of the
U.S.A.
Claimed: 1856
Capital: administered from
Washington D.C.
Population: no permanent
population
Total area: 0.5 sq Mi, 1.4 Sq Km
Time zone: GMT -10
Languages: English
Climate: hot, dry, windy
Natural resources: guano (deposits
worked until 1891), terrestrial and
aquatic wildlife.
Elevation extremes:
lowest point:
Pacific Ocean 0 m
highest point:
unnamed location 8 m

SOCCER FACTS

No information available
at this time.

To update information for
this location please
contact our world atlas
web site.
www.soccerexplorers.com

BASAS DA INDIA

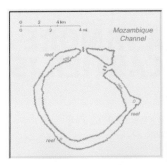

Mozambique
Channel

COUNTRY FACTS

Official name: Basas da India
Frence Dependency
Area: 0.2 Sq Km
Coastline: 35.2 Km
Climate: tropical
Population: uninhabited
Location: Southern Africa, islands in
the southern Mozambique Channel,
about one-half of the way from
Madagascar to Mozambique

This atoll is a volcanic rock
surrounded by reefs and is awash at
high tide. A French possession since
1897, it was placed under the
administration of a commissioner
residing in Reunion in 1968.

SOCCER FACTS

No information available
at this time.

To update information for
this location please
contact our world atlas
web site.
www.soccerexplorers.com

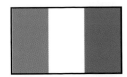

BOUVET ISLAND

COUNTRY FACTS

Official name: Bouvet Island
Dependency of Norway
Claimed: 1928
Capital: not applicable Administerd
from Oslo
Population: no permanent
population
Time zone: GMT +/_ 0
Total area: 22 sq Mi, 58 sq Km
Climate: Antarctic
Natural resources: none
Elevation extremes:
lowest point:
South Atlantic Ocean 0 m
highest point:
Olav Peak 935 m

SOCCER FACTS

No information available
at this time.

To update information for
this location please
contact our world atlas
web site.
www.soccerexplorers.com

BRITISH INDIAN OCEAN TERRITORY

COUNTRY FACTS

Official name: British Indian Ocean
Territory
Claimed: 1814
Capital: Diego Garcia
Population: 930
Total area: 23 sq Mi, 60 sq Km
Time zone: GMT -4
Climate: tropical marine; hot,
humid, moderated by trade winds
Natural resources: coconuts, fish,
sugarcane
Elevation Extremes:
lowest point:
Indian Ocean 0 m
highest point:
unnamed location on Diego Garcia
15 m

SOCCER FACTS

No information available
at this time.

To update information for
this location please
contact our world atlas
web site.
www.soccerexplorers.com

CANARY ISLANDS

COUNTRY FACTS

Official name: Canary Islands
Capital: Las Palmas de Gran Canaria
Population: 1,930,015
Total Area: 2,855 sq Mi,
7,500 sq Km
Time Zone: GMT +1
Climate: mild temperature, sub Saharan wind in the summer.
Religion: Roman Catholic
Note: The Canary Islands are an archipelago of seven islands of volcanic origin in the Atlantic Ocean, off the northwestern coast of Africa (Morocco and Western Sahara). The islands belong to Spain, and form an autonomous community of that country. The name comes from the Latin Insularia Canaria meaning Island of the Dogs.

SOCCER FACTS

King's Cup holders Deportivo Coruna were handed a trip to the Canary islands on Thursday to play third division minnows Corralejo in the first round of the competition Deportivo Tenerife, the Canary Islands' own fútbol (soccer) club Tenerife avoided the drop to second division for at least one more week with a win over Las Palmas in the Canary Island derby last weekend.

Canary Futebol.es

CEUTA

COUNTRY FACTS

Official name: Ceuta
Claimed: 1988
Capital: Ceuta
Population: 68,500
Total area: 19 sq Km
Time zone: GMT +1
Climate: hot
Natural resources: military, toursim
Elevation extremes:
lowest point:
Mediterranean o m
highest point:
unknown location

SOCCER FACTS

Club Name: AD Ceuta
Plays in the League Segunda División B - Grupo IV [Level: 3] of Spain.

One stadium : Estadio Alfonso Murube

Postal Address:
Agrupación Deportiva Ceuta
Camoens, 11
E-51001 CEUTA
Spain

Phone number:
+34 956 516799
Fax number:
+34 956 516799

CHRISTMAS ISLAND

COUNTRY FACTS

Official name: Chistmas Island
External territory of Australia
Claimed: 1958
Capital: Flying Fish Cove
Population: 1,275
Total area: 52 sq Mi, 135 sq Km
Time zone: GMT +7
Climate: tropical; heat and humidity moderated by trade winds
Natural resources: phosphate, beaches
Elevation extremes:
lowest point:
Indian Ocean 0 m
highest point:
Murray Hill 361 m

SOCCER FACTS

1994 Inter Island Cup
Played in Keeling (Cocos Island)
1- 7-1994 Cocos Islands
1-4 Christmas Islands
4- 7-1994 Cocos Islands
4-0 Christmas Islands
Cocos Islands win 5-4 on aggragate

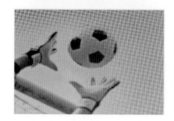

CLIPPERTON ISLAND

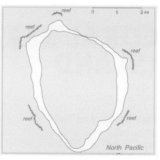

COUNTRY FACTS

Official name: Clipperton Island
Dependency of French Polynesia
Claimed: 1930
Capital: not applicable
Population: no permanent population
Total area: 2.7 sq Mi, 7 Sq Km
Time zone: GMT -8
Climate: tropical; humid, average temperature 20-32 degrees C, rains May-October
Natural resources: fish
Elevation extremes:
lowest point:
Pacific Ocean 0 m
highest point:
Rocher Clipperton 29 m

SOCCER FACTS

Clipperton WW2 Soccer Games
In November 1948 Qantas Empire Airways flew a survey flight from Perth, Via Coco and Mauratius Island to Johannesburg. During the war on Clipperton Individuals worked six days before being given a day of relaxation. A 3 match series of soccer was usually played between squadron and Malays who were employed by one of the owner of the island.

COCOS ISLAND

COUNTRY FACTS

Official name: Cocos Island or the Keelings Islands (External territory of Australia)
Claimed: 1955
Capital: not applicable
Population: 670
Total area: 5.% sq Mi, 14 sq Km
Time zone: GMT -10
Climate: tropical with high humidity, moderated by the southeast trade winds for about nine months of the year.
Natural resources: fish
Elevation extremes:
lowest point: Indian Ocean 0 m
highest point: unnamed location 5 m

SOCCER FACTS

No information available at this time.

To update information for this location please contact our world atlas web site.
www.soccerexplorers.com

CORAL SEA ISLAND

COUNTRY FACTS

Official name: Coral Sea Islands
Claimed: 1969
Capital: not applicable
Population: 8 Meteorologist
Total area: 1.2 Sq Mi, 3 Sq Km
Time zone: GMT +7
Climate: tropical
Natural resources: not known
Elevation extremes:
lowest point:
Pacific Ocean 0 m
highest point:
unnamed location on Cato Island 6 m

SOCCER FACTS

No information available at this time.

To update information for this location please contact our world atlas web site.
www.soccerexplorers.com

DHEKELIA

COUNTRY FACTS

Official name: Dhekelia
Overseas territorry of the UK
Claimed: Feb 6,1952
Capital: Episkopi Cantonment
Located in Akrotiri
Population: about 5000
Area: 130.8 sq Km
Language: English, Greek
Location: on the southeast coast of
Cyprus near Famagusta
Climate: temperate, Mediterranean
with hot, dry summers and cool
winters
Geography note: British extraterri-
torial rights also extended to several
small off-post sites scattered across
Cyprus.
Environment notes: netting and
trapping of small migrant songbirds
in the spring and autumn

SOCCER FACTS

Army Football
Association
Founded 1888

There is a ladies Major
Units League and Cup
competition, and exten-
sive opportunities for the
children, from toddler to
teenager.

Ladies Football Dhekelia
were crowned league
champions after their 5-3
victory against Akrotiri in
the final match of the
season.

EUROPA ISLAND

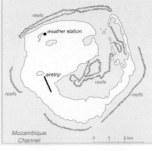

COUNTRY FACTS

Official Name: Europa Island
Claimed: 1897 (French territory)
Capital: not applicable
Area: 28 sq Km
Coastline: 22.2 Km
Climate: tropical
Population: uninhabited (researcher
and weather station scientist)
Location: Southern Africa, island in
the Mozambique Channel, about
half way between southern
Madagascar and southern
Mozambique.

SOCCER FACTS

No information available
at this time.

To update information for
this location please
contact our world atlas
web site.
www.soccerexplorers.com

FALKLAND ISLANDS

COUNTRY FACTS

Official name: Falkland Islands Dependent Territory of the United Kingdom
Claimed: 1832
Capital: Stanley
Population: 2562
Total area: 4,699 sq Mi, 12,173 sq Km
Time zone: GMT -4
Climate: cold marine; strong westerly winds, cloudy, humid; rain occurs on more than half of days in year; occasional snow all year, except in January and February, but does not accumulate
Natural resources: fish, wildlife
Elevation extremes:
lowest point:
Atlantic Ocean 0 m
highest point:
Mount Usborne 705 m

SOCCER FACTS

Falkland Islands Football League

Local football league, with outdoor season from November through March, and indoor season from April through October.

Football has long been played in the islands, but apart from internal competition which includes a long-running annual series against the Royal Navy Ice Patrol vessel HMS Endurance, the players have yet to experience overseas soccer.

FRENCH ANTARCTICA TERRITORY

COUNTRY FACTS

Official name: French Southern Antarctic Territories
Claimed: 1840 (French territories)
Capital: not applicable
Area: 7,829 Sq Km
Population: about 150 researchers depending on the season of the year.
Climate: Antarctic
Natural resources : fish, crayfish
Note: French Southern and Antarctic Lands include Ile Amsterdam, Ile Saint-Paul, Iles Crozet, and Iles Kerguelen in the southern Indian Ocean, along with the French-claimed sector of Antarctica, "Adelie Land".
The Antarctic portion consists of "Adelie Land," a thin slice of the Antarctic continent discovered and claimed by the French in 1840.

SOCCER FACTS

No information available at this time.

To update information for this location please contact our world atlas web site.
www.soccerexplorers.com

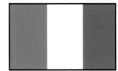

46

GLORIOSO ISLANDS

COUNTRY FACTS
Official name: Glorioso Islands
Territory of France
Claimed: 1892
Capital: not applicable
Total area: 2.1 sq Mi, 5 sq Km
Note: includes Ile Glorieuse, Ile du Lys, Verte Rocks, Wreck Rock, and South Rock
Time zone: GMT +3
Climate: tropical
Natural resources: guano, coconuts
Elevation extremes:
lowest point:
Indian Ocean 0 m
highest point:
unnamed location 12 m

SOCCER FACTS
No information available at this time.

To update information for this location please contact our world atlas web site.
www.soccerexplorers.com

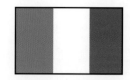

HEARD & McDONALD ISLANDS

COUNTRY FACTS
Official name: Territory of Heard & McDonald Islands
External territory of Australia
Claimed: 1947
Capital: not applicable
Population: none
Total area: 159 sq Mi, 412 sq Km
Time zone: GMT +5
Climate: Antarctic
Natural resources: fish
Elevation extreme:
lowest point:
Southern Ocean 0 m
highest point:
Big Ben 2,745 m

SOCCER FACTS
No information available at this time.

To update information for this location please contact our world atlas web site.
www.soccerexplorers.com

JAN MAYEN ISLAND

COUNTRY FACTS

Official name: Jan Mayen Island
(Dependency of Norway)
Claimed: 1929
Capital: not applicable
Population: none
Total area: 147 sq Mi, 381 sq Km
Time zone: GMT -1
Climate: Arctic maritime with
frequent storms and persistent fog
Natural resources: none
Elevation extremes:
lowest point:
Norwegian Sea 0 m
highest point:
Haakon VII Toppen/Beerenberg
2,277 m

SOCCER FACTS

No information available
at this time.

To update information for
this location please
contact our world atlas
web site.
www.soccerexplorers.com

JARVIS ISLAND

COUNTRY FACTS

Official name: Jarvis Island
Unincorporated territory of the U.S.A.
Claimed: 1856
Capital: not applicable
Population: none
Total area: 1.7 sq Mi, 2.8 sq Km
Time zone: GMT -10
Climate: tropical; scant rainfall,
constant wind, burning sun
Natural resources: guano (deposits
worked until late 1800s), terrestrial
and aquatic wildlife
Elevation extremes:
lowest point:
Pacific Ocean 0 m
highest point:
unnamed location 7 m

SOCCER FACTS

No information available
at this time.

To update information for
this location please
contact our world atlas
web site.
www.soccerexplorers.com

JOHNSTON ATOLL ISLAND

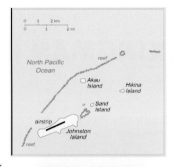

COUNTRY FACTS

Official name: Johnston Atoll
unincorporated territory of the
U.S.A.
Claimed: 1858
Capital: not applicable
Population: None
Total area: 1 sq Mi, 2.8 sq Km
Time zone: GMT -10
Climate: tropical, but generally dry;
consistent northeast trade winds
with little seasonal temperature
variation.
Natural resources: guano deposits
worked until depletion about 1890,
terrestrial and aquatic wildlife
Elevation extremes:
lowest point:
Pacific Ocean 0 m
highest point:
Summit Peak 5 m

SOCCER FACTS

No information available
at this time.

To update information for
this location please
contact our world atlas
web site.
www.soccerexplorers.com

JUAN DA NOVA ISLAND

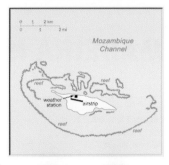

COUNTRY FACTS

Official name: Juan de Nova
French Territory
Claimed: 1897
Capital: not applicable
Area: 4.4 sq Km
Coastline: 24.1 Km
Population: small community of
Researchers and Meteorologist
Climate: tropical
Location: Southern Africa island, in
the Mozambique Channel, about
one-third of the way between
Madagascar and Mozambique
Presently a small amount of
researchers oversees a meteorologi-
cal station.

SOCCER FACTS

No information available
at this time.

To update information for
this location please
contact our world atlas
web site.
www.soccerexplorers.com

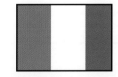

KINGMAN REEF

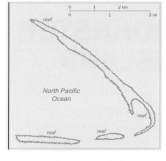

COUNTRY FACTS

Official name: Kingman Reef
Administered Territory of the U.S.A.
Claimed: 1856
Capital: not applicable
Population: none
Total area: 0.4 sq Mi, 1 sq Km
Time zone: GMT -10
Climate: tropical, but moderated by prevailing winds.
Natural resources:
terrestrial and aquatic wildlife
Elevation extremes:
lowest point:
Pacific Ocean 0 m
highest point:
unnamed location 1 m

SOCCER FACTS

No information available at this time.

To update information for this location please contact our world atlas web site.
www.soccerexplorers.com

MADEIRA ISLAND

COUNTRY FACTS

Official name: Madeira Island
Claimed: Portugal
Capital: not applicable
Population: 260,000
Total area: 459 sq Mi, 741 sq Km
Time zone: GMT 0
Climate: subtropical
Religion: Roman Catholic

Madeira Archipelago was discovered by the Portuguese in 1418, it consists of the islands of Madeira, Porto Santo and the uninhabited islands of the Selvagens and Desertas.

Madeira is 378 Mi (608 Km) from the Marocco and 620 Mi (1,000 km) from the European continent (1h30m flight from Lisbon).

SOCCER FACTS

Clube Sport Maritimo
Baira-Mar
Pontassolanse
Dsquim
Pnafiel

www.soccerexplorers.com

MARION ISLAND

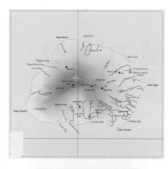

COUNTRY FACTS

Official name: Marion Island
South African
Claimed: 1772
Capital: not applicable
Population: 302
Total area: 290 sq Km
Time zone: GMT - 10
Climate: cold, temperate
Elevation extremes:
lowest point:
Atlantic Ocean 0 m
highest point:
President Peak 1,230 m

SOCCER FACTS

No information available
at this time.

To update information for
this location please
contact our world atlas
web site.
www.soccerexplorers.com

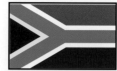

MIDWAY ISLANDS

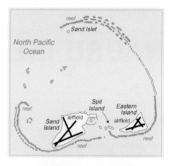

COUNTRY FACTS

Official name: Midway Islands
Administered Territory of the U.S.A.
Claimed: 1867
Capital: not applicable
Population: 453
Total area: 2 sq Mi, 5.2 sq Km
Time zone: GMT -10
Climate: Subtropical, but moderat-
ed by prevailing easterly winds
Elevation extremes:
lowest point:
Pacific Ocean 0 m
highest point:
unnamed location 13 m

SOCCER FACTS

No Information available
at this time.

To update information for
this location please
contact our world atlas
web site.
www.soccerexplorers.com

MONACO

COUNTRY FACTS

Official name: Principality of Monaco
Capital: Villes de Monaco
Population: 232,000
Total area: 1 sq Mi, 2 sq Km
Time zone: GMT +1
Climate: Mediterranean
Religion: Roman Catholic

SOCCER FACTS

Monaco plays in the French premiere League. They won that league in 1978, 1982, 1988, 1997 and 2000. They played the UEFA Cup Final in 2004 and lost Porto.

There are regional club level competitions within the city.

NAURU ISLANDS

COUNTRY FACTS

Official name: Republic of Nauru
Date of formation: 1968
Capital: no official
Population: 11,000
Total area: 8.1 sq Mi, 21 sq Km
Time zone: GMT +12
Density: 1358 per sq Mi, 505 per sq Km
Languages: Nauruan, English
Literacy rate: 99%
Currency: Australian $
Natural resources: phosphate mining, coconut production
Religions: Nauruan Church 60%, Christian 35%
Ethnic Mix: Nauruan 62%
Elevation Extremes:
lowest point:
Pacific Ocean 0 m
highest point:
Plateau rim 61 m

SOCCER FACTS

On October 2, 1994 a friendly match was played in Denigomodu against the Solomon Islands; a match recognized by the OFC. This was the first ever Internationally recognized game for Nauru. Nauru surprisingly won the match 2-1, and it became the greatest sporting event on the island. Especially since the Solomon Islands just won the Melanesian Cup that same year.

Nauru has a small stadium not completed called Menen Stadium.

NAVASSA ISLAND

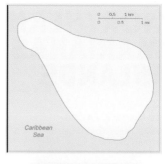

COUNTRY FACTS

Official name: Navassa Island
Unincorporated Territory of the U.S.A.
Claimed: 1856
Capital: not applicable
Population: none
Total area: 2 sq Mi, 5.2 sq Km
Time zone: GMT -5
Climate: marine, tropical
Natural resources: guano
Elevation extremes:
lowest point:
Caribbean Sea 0 m
highest point:
unnamed location on southwest
side 77 m

SOCCER FACTS

No information available
at this time.

To update information for
this location please
contact our world atlas
web site.
www.soccerexplorers.com

NORFOLK ISLANDS

COUNTRY FACTS

Official name: Norfolk Island
External Territory of Australia
Claimed: 1774
Capital: Kingston
Population: 2181
Total area: 13 sq Mi, 34 sq Km
Time zone: GMT + 11.5
Climate: subtropical, mild, little
seasonal temperature variation
Natural resources: fish
Elevation extremes:
lowest point:
Pacific Ocean 0 m
highest point:
Mount Bates 319 m

SOCCER FACTS

Apart from school soccer,
Norfolk Island does not
have a league at the
senior level.

They have a field for the
Pacific game that was
played in 1999.

NORTHERN MARIANAS ISLANDS

COUNTRY FACTS

Official name: Commonwealth Territory of the U.S.A
Claimed: 1947
Capital: Saipan
Population: 58,846
Total area: 177 sq Mi, 457 sq Km
Time zone: GMT + 10
Climate: tropical marine; moderated by northeast trade winds, little seasonal temperature variation; dry season December to June, rainy season July to October
Natural resources: arable land, fishing Industry
Elevation extremes:
lowest point:
Pacific Ocean o m
highest point:
Unnamed location on Agrihan 965 m

SOCCER FACTS

No name of club found when I was in Saipan in 1999. I could not recall if the teams were a full 11.

(7 on 7-rsssf source)
White Sharks
Blue Diamonds
Light Blue Panders
Red Rocks
F & B Dragons
Bangladesh Lions
Prince Roulette

There are no stadiums on the island. Most games are played on school fields. There are multi mini leagues for youth teams. No team on Rota Island.

PALAU

COUNTRY FACTS

Official name: Republic of Palau
Date of formation: 1994
Capital: Koror
Population: 18,766
Total area: 196 sq Mi, 508 sq Km
Time zone: GMT +9
Density: 96 per sq Mi, 39 per sq Km
Languages: Palauan, English
Literacy rate: 99%
Currency: U.S $
Economy: government, agriculture, fishing, tourism
Religions: Catholic 40%, indeginous Modekngei religion 34%,
Ethnic mix: Micronesian 100%
Elevation extremes:
lowest point:
Pacific Ocean o m
highest point:
Mount Ngerchelchuus 242 m

SOCCER FACTS

No information available at this time.

To update information for this location please contact our world atlas web site.
www.soccerexplorers.com

PALMYRA ATOLL

COUNTRY FACTS

Official name: Palmyra Atoll
unincorporated territory of the U.S.A.
Claimed: 1898
Capital: not applicable
Population: none
Total area: 5 sq Mi, 12 sq Km
Time zone: GMT -10
Climate: equatorial, hot, and very rainy
Natural resources: terrestrial and aquatic wildlife
Elevation extremes:
lowest point:
Pacific Ocean 0 m
highest point:
unnamed location 2 m

SOCCER FACTS

No information available at this time.

To update information for this location please contact our world atlas web site.
www.soccerexplorers.com

PARACELL ISLANDS

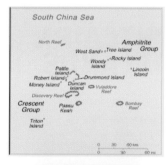

COUNTRY FACTS

Official name: Paracel Islands
Chinese external territorry
Claimed: 1974
Capital: not applicable
Population: no permanent
Population: Chinese Troops
Total area: not available
Time zone: GMT +8
Climate: tropical
Natural resources: none
Elevation extremes:
lowest point:
South China Sea 0 m
highest point: unnamed location on Rocky Island 14 m

SOCCER FACTS

No information available at this time.

To update information for this location please contact our world atlas web site.
www.soccerexplorers.com

PETER I ISLAND

COUNTRY FACTS

Official name: Peter I Island
Dependent Territory of Norway
Claimed: 1933
Capital: not applicable
Population: no permanent
population
Total area: 70 sq Mi (180 sq Km)
Time zone: GMT -6
Climate: very cold weather
Natural resources: none
Elevation extremes:
highest elevation:
Lars Kristensen's Topp 1695 m
lowest elevation:
sea level 0 m

SOCCER FACTS

No information available
at this time.

To update information for
this location please
contact our world atlas
web site.
www.soccerexplorers.com

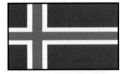

PITCAIRN ISLANDS

COUNTRY FACTS

Official name: Pitcairn Islands
Dependent territory of the U.K.
Claimed: 1887
Capital: Adamstown
Population: 55
Total area: 1.4 sq Mi, 3.5 sq Km
Time zone: GMT -8.5
Climate: tropical, hot, humid; modi-
fied by southeast trade winds; rainy
season (November to March)
Natural resources: miro trees (used
for handicrafts), fish; minerals -
manganese, iron, copper, gold, sil-
ver, and zinc have been discovered
offshore
Elevation extremes:
lowest point:
Pacific Ocean 0 m
highest point:
Pawala Valley Ridge 347 m

SOCCER FACTS

No information available
at this time.

To update information for
this location please
contact our world atlas
web site.
www.soccerexplorers.com

SAINT HELENA ISLAND

COUNTRY FACTS

Official name: Saint Helena Dependent Territory of the U.K
Claimed: 1673
Capital: Jamestown
Population: 6472
Total area: 47 sq Mi, 122 sq Km
Time zone: GMT +/- 0
Climate: tropical; marine, mild, tempered by trade winds
Natural resources: fish

SOCCER FACTS

Saint Helena premier league
1. Bellboys
2. Rovers
3. Harts
4. Prince Andrew United
5. Wideawakes
6. Alleyvaiders
7. Wanderers
8. Fugees

Saint Helena - List of Champions

1998	Rovers
1999	Bellboys
2000	Raiders
2001	Rovers
2002	Harts

SAINT PIERRE & MIQUELON

COUNTRY FACTS

Official name: St Pierre & Miquelon Territorial Collectivity of France
Claimed: 1604
Capital: Saint Pierre
Population: 6600
Total area: 93 sq Mi (242 sq Km)
Time zone: GMT -4
Climate: cold and wet, with much mist and fog; spring and autumn are windy
Natural resources: fish, deepwater ports
Elevation extremes:
lowest point:
Atlantic Ocean 0 m
highest point:
Morne de la Grande Montagne 240 m

SOCCER FACTS

There is a league that plays in the Summer from June until September.

The teams are:
1. ASIA (Champions in 2002, 03, 04)
2. ASM
3. ASSP

The Stadiums are:
1. Stade de L'Avenir
2. J. Girardin (500 seats)
3. L. Claireaux

The cup final is called: "Coupe de l'archipel" and it is played in October

SHETLAND ISLANDS

COUNTRY FACTS

Official name: Shetland
Claimed: 1472
Capital: not applicable
Population: 22,830
Total area: 551 sq Mi, 1,427 sq Km
Time zone: GMT: 0
Climate: humid, cold or mild
Note: The Shetlands are known for their ancient relics. Picturesque forts are scattered throughout the islands, and a village from the Bronze Age has been unearthed at Jarlshof on the Mainland.
The archipelago is 70 mi (110 km) long and consists of some 100 islands, of which fewer than one fourth are inhabited. Mainland, Yell, Unst, Fetlar, Whalsey, and Bressay are the largest islands. Lerwick, on Mainland, is the principal town of the Shetland Islands.

SOCCER FACTS

Eleven venues are to be used for the footbal tournament, which are spread across the length and breadth of our islands. From Balatsound on Shetland's most northerly island of Unst to Boddam in the south mainland and form Harbison Park in Walsay in the east to Strom Park in the rural west side.

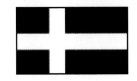

SOUTH GEORGIA & SANDWICH ISLANDS

COUNTRY FACTS

Official name: South Georgia & The Sandwich Islands
Dependent territory of the U.K.
Claimed: 1775
Capital: not applicable
Population: none
Total area: 1387 sq Mi, 3592 sq Km
Time zone: GMT - 4
Climate: mostly westerly winds throughout the year interspersed with periods of calm; nearly all precipitation falls as snow
Natural resources: fish
Elevation extremes:
lowest point:
Atlantic Ocean 0 m
highest point:
Mount Paget (South Georgia) 2,934 m

SOCCER FACTS

Yes, of course, there is a soccer field! It has to be the most remote (far and away) soccer field on earth.

Picture courtesy of a scientist working on the island.

www.sgisland.org

SPRATLY ISLANDS

COUNTRY FACTS

Official name: Spratly Island
Disputed territory between China, Taiwan, Vietnam, Malaysia and the Philippines
Claimed: not yet
Capital: not applicable
Population: not permanent
Population: troops of different nationalities are based on the islands
Total area: 1.9 sq Mi (5.4 sq Km)
Time zone: GMT +8
Climate: tropical
Natural resources: fish, guano, undetermined oil and natural gas potential
Elevation extremes:
lowest point:
South China Sea 0 m
highest point:
unnamed location on Southwest Cay 4 m

SOCCER FACTS

No information available at this time.

To update information for this location please contact our world atlas web site.
www.soccerexplorers.com

SVALBARD

COUNTRY FACTS

Official name: Svalbard
Dependency of Norway
Claimed: 1920
Capital: Longyearbyen
Population: 3231
Total area: 24,289 sq Mi, 62,906 sq Km
Time zone: GMT +1
Climate: Arctic; tempered by warm North Atlantic current; cool summers, cold winters; North Atlantic current flows along west and north coasts of Spitsbergen, keeping water open and navigable
Natural resources: coal, copper, iron ore, phosphate, zinc, wildlife, fish
Elevation extremes:
lowest point:
Arctic Ocean 0 m
highest point:
Newtontoppen 1,717 m

SOCCER FACTS

What sports are played in Svalbard? Almost all kinds of sports. Skiing, snowboarding, handball, volleyball, badminton, football (soccer).

Indoor Soccer is played in the Svalbard Sportshall.

www.svalbard.com

487

TOKELAU

COUNTRY FACTS

Official name: Tokelau
Dependent Territory of New Zealand
Claimed: 1926
Capital: not applicable
Population: 1577
Total area: 4 sq mi (10 sq Km)
Time zone: GMT - 11
Climate: tropical; moderated by
trade winds (April to November)
Natural resources: fish
Elevation extremes:
lowest point:
Pacific Ocean 0 m
highest point:
unnamed location 5 m

SOCCER FACTS

Tokelau has a small
stadium "Hemoana
Stadium".

We found only one team
"Ninguno FC".

TRISTAN DA CUHNA ISLANDS

COUNTRY FACTS

Official Name: Tristan da Cunha
Dependency Territory of the U.K.
Claimed: 1816
Capital: not applicable
Population: 300
Total area: 35 sq Mi, 78 sq Km
Time zone: GMT +4
Climate: cold tempeture, mild
summers
Natural Resources: none
Elevation Extremes:
lowest point:
sea level 0 m
highest elevation:
Tristan da Cunha Volcano 6,760 m

SOCCER FACTS

Royal Navy frigate HMS
Portland visited Tristan da
Cuhna on May 6 - 7 2001,
on her way to the
Falklands. Despite the
wet and windy weather,
most of the Ship's
Company were able to get
ashore at some stage
over the two days of the
visit to enjoy a traditional
Tristan welcome.
Recreational events
included a football match
at the only soccer field on
the Island which the visi-
tors were victorious
(despite having to play
uphill) against the
Islanders.
No Soccer League known
on Tristan da Cunha
Island.

TROMELIN ISLAND

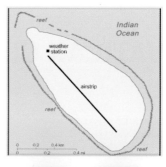

COUNTRY FACTS

Official name: Tromelin Island (France)
Date of formation: 1814
Population: not applicable
Capital: not applicable
Total area: 1 sq km
Time zone: GMT+/- 0
Languages: English
Climate: tropical
Resources: fish
Background: First explored by the French in 1776. At present, it serves as a sea turtle sanctuary. Serves as an important meteorological station.
Elevation extremes :
lowest point:
Indian Ocean 0 m
highest point:
unnamed location 7 m
Geography note: climatologically important location for forecasting cyclones.

SOCCER FACTS

No information available at this time.

To update information for this location please contact our world atlas web site.
www.soccerexplorers.com

TUVALU

COUNTRY FACTS

Official name: Tuvalu
Date of formation: 1978
Capital: Fongale on funafuti atoll
Total area: 10 sq Mi (26 sq Km)
Time zone: GMT +12
Density: 1084 per sq Mi,
407 per sq Km
Languages: Tuvaluan, Kiribati
Literacy rate: 95%
Currency: Australian $
Economy: Agriculture & fishing 70%
Religions: Church of Tuvalu
Ethnic Mix: Polynesian96%
Elevation extremes:
lowest point:
Pacific Ocean 0 m
highest point:
unnamed location 5 m

SOCCER FACTS

"Funafuti" is Tuvalu A League Champion for the 2005 season.

There are 8 teams in the league and each name represents an island or an Atoll.
Amatuku
Funafuti
Nanumanga
Nanumea
Niutao
Nui
Nukufetau
Vaitupu

There are also 2 other division(B & C)

VATICAN CITY

COUNTRY FACTS

Official name: Vatican City State
Date of formation: 1929
Capital: Vatican city
Population: 1000
Total area: 0.17 sq Mi, 0.44 sq Km
Time zone: GMT +1
Density: 5,882 per sq Mi, 2,272 per sq Km
Languages: Italian, Latin
Literacy rate: 99%
Currency: Vatican Lira
Economy: Services 100%
Religions: Roman Catholic
Ethnic Mix: Italian 90%, Swiss 10% (Swiss Guards)

SOCCER FACTS

The Vatican city League has 16 Teams.
1. Vatican Fire Brigades
2. Secret Archives FC
3. Radio Vaticana
4. St Peter Basilica
5. Team X
6. IW Religion
7. Sistine Sporting
8. Vatican Guards

Standards have now reached the point at which the league feels confident to field a national team.

The Vatican Football league has been around 27 years.

WAKE ISLAND

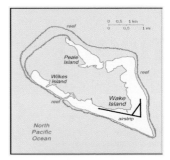

COUNTRY FACTS

Official Name: Wake island Unincorporated Territory of the U.S.A.
Claimed: 1898
Capital: not applicable
Population: 302
Total area: 2.5 sq Mi (6.5 sq km)
Time zone: GMT - 10
Climate: tropical
Natural resources: none
Elevation extremes:
lowest point:
Pacific Ocean 0 m
highest point:
unnamed location 6 m

SOCCER FACTS

No information available at this time.

To update information for this location please contact our world atlas web site.
www.soccerexplorers.com

WESTERN SAHARA

COUNTRY FACTS

Official Name: Western Sahara Territory disputed by Morocco & Polisario Front Independence Movement
Claimed: not yet
Capital: not applicable
main cities are;Tarfaya, La'youn, Ad Dakhla
Population: 239,333
Total area: 102,703 sq Mi, 266,000 sq Km
Time zone: GMT +/- 0
Climate: hot, dry desert; rain is rare; cold offshore air currents produce fog and heavy dew
Natural resources: phosphates, iron ore
Elevation extremes:
lowest point:
Sebjet Tah -55 m
highest point:
unnamed location 462 m

SOCCER FACTS

Laayoune, capital of Western Sahara has probably the only grass playing field in the Sahara. (Laayoune Stadium-30.000 Seats). Club-JSM Laayoune

ZANZIBAR

COUNTRY FACTS

Official name: Zanzibar (Tanzania)
Date of formation: 1963
Capital: Stone Town
Population: 621,000
Total area: 650 sq Mi, 17,494 sq Km
Time zone: GMT +3
Density: not known
Languages:
Literacy rate: 85%
Currency: Tanzanian Schilling
Note: Zanzibar is an archipelago made up of Zanzibar and Pemba Islands, and several islets. It is located in the Indian Ocean, about 25 miles from the Tanzanian coast, and 6° south of the equator.

SOCCER FACTS

Zanzibar Football Clubs:

1. Kaskazini Unguja (North Zanzibar)
2. Sharp Boys of Nungwi
3. Kusini Unguja (South Zanzibar)
4. Mjini Magharibi (Urban West)
5. KMKM
6. Miembeni
7. Mlandege
8. Shangani
9. Kaskazini Pemba (North Pemba)
10. Jamhuri ,Mwenge
11. Kusini Pemba (South Pemba)
12. Chipukizi
13. Maendeleo
14. Polisi

Soccer to New Heights

Wonderful stories of the human spirit rising to challenges
under adverse circumstances.

The eclectic world of soccer demonstrates an exceptional ability to adapt
and create global competition around the planet for humans with disabilities.
The game has been shaped to accommodate players with specific disabilities as well as making the sport more fun to participate in.

BLIND SOCCER is played in two different ways, One is five-a-side for blind or
visually impaired athletes (B1) and seven-a-side for athletes who are partially blind (B2).
The rules are the same as FIFA except the soccer ball has been designed
with bells inside, the throw-in can be made with one arm and there are no
offside rules.

The Argentina Blind National Soccer Team beat Spain with a score of 4-2 at
The 2003 Blind Soccer World Cup held in Rio de Janeiro from November 30
to December 8, 2003.
The Brazilian team won the previous World Championship of 1998 in
Campinas, Brazil and 2002 in Jerez, Spain.

Semifinal Argentina 5-0 Colombia
Semifinal Spain 4-1 Brazil

(Photos courtesy of IBSA)

7th	Korea 1-3	England
5th	Paraguay 1-0	Greece
3rd	Colombia 0-2	Brazil
Final	Argentina 4-2	Spain

IBSA:International Blind Sport Assoc.
IBSA has 108 Associates Countries
www.ibsa.es/eng/

AMPUTEE SOCCER is a recreational activity for people overcoming their disability with an opportunity to share time with others and compete in the game they love.

The Brazil Amputee National Soccer Team beat Russia with a score of 2-1 at the 2005 Amputee Soccer World Cup in the U.S.

Results from the 2005 Amputee Soccer World Cup

Semi Finals	Brazil	6 - 1	England
Semi Finals	Russia	3 - 0	Ukraine
Bronze Medal Match	England	1 - 0	Ukraine
Gold Medal Match	Brazil	2 - 1	Russia

Russia won the First Amputee Soccer World cup in 1998 with a score of Russia 3–0 against Uzbekistan.

(Pictures courtesy of ampsoccer.org)

DEAF SOCCER

Deaf olympic athletes have a hearing loss of at least 55 decibels in their better ear, as measured by a three-tone frequency average at 500, 1000 and 2000 Hertz, ISO 1964 Standard.

Great Britain Deaf National Soccer team beat Iran with a score of 2-1 at the 2005 Deafolympics in Melbourne Australia.

Sat 15/Jan	3rd - 4th Place	Ireland	0 - 2	Germany
Sat 16/Jan 2005	Final	Iran	1 - 2	UK

The United States Deaf Women national Team beat Russia with a score of 3- 0 at the 2005 Deafolympics in Melbourne Australia.

Sun 16/Jan	3rd - 4th Place	Denmark Women	1 – 2	UK Women
Sun 16/Jan 2005	Final	USA Women	3 – 0	Russia Women

Map Credits

All maps featured in the Europe, Africa, Asia, North America, South America and Oceania sections in addition to the Madeira map in Far and Away are copyright © 2005 by Kemari, Inc.

Thank you to cia.gov for maps featured in the Far and Away section. Specific credit to Shetland.com for the map on Shetland Islands; to Btinternet.com for the Tristan da Cunha and Marion Island maps; to Zanzibar.net for the Zanzibar map.

Photo Credits

All photography copyright © 2005 Marc Asmode with the exception of the following. Gene Gilsdorf for the photo for Clipperton Island; International Blind Sports Association for the photographs featuring blind soccer players; Thank You to Rick Hofmann,Steve wilber and ampsoccer.org for their images for Amputee world Cup pictures;David Nicholls for the South Georgia and Sandwich Island photograph; Royal Geographic Society on behalf of Frank Hurley for the Shackleton Antarctica photograph.

Bibliography

Much of the research done for this book would not have been possible without the following organizations:
rsssf.com
cia.gov
fifa.com
worldstadium.com

For corrections or to contribute new information, please contact us at newinfo@soccerexplorers.com.

Index

Malaysia	268
Maldives	270
Mali	172
Malta	70
Marion Island	469
Marshall Islands	432
Martinique	362
Mauritania	174
Mauritius	176
Mayotte	178
Mexico	364
Micronesia	434
Midway Islands	469
Moldova	72
Monaco	470
Mongolia	272
Montserrat	366
Morocco	180
Mozambique	182
Myanmar	274
Namibia	184
Nauru	470
Navassa Island	471
Nepal	276
Netherland Antilles	368
Netherlands	74
New Caledonia	436
New Zealand	438
Nicaragua	370
Niger	186
Nigeria	188
Niue	440
Norfolk Island	471
North Korea	278
Northern Ireland	76
Northern Marianas Islands	472
Norway	78
Oman	280
Pakistan	282
Palau	472
Palestine	284
Palmyra Atoll	473
Panama	372
Papua new Guinea	442
Paracell island	473
Paraguay	408
Peru	410
Peter I Island	474
Philippines	286
Pitcairn Island	474
Poland	80
Portugal	82
Puerto Rico	374
Qatar	288
Reunion	190
Romania	84
Russia	86
Rwanda	192
Samoa	444
San Marino	88
Sao Tome & Principe	194
Saudi Arabia	290
Scotland	90
Senegal	196
Serbia & Montenegro	92
Seychelles	198
Shetland	476
Sierra Leone	200
Singapore	292
Slovakia	94
Slovenia	96
Solomon Islands	446
Somalia	202
South Africa	204

South Africa	294
South Georgia & Sandwich Islands	476
Spain	98
Spratly Island	477
Sri Lanka	296
St.Helena Island	475
St.Kitts & Nevis	376
St.Lucia	378
St.Pierre & Miquelon	475
St.Vincent & Grenadines	380
Sudan	206
Suriname	412
Svalbard	477
Swaziland	208
Sweden	100
Switzerland	102
Syria	298
Taiwan	300
Tajikistan	302
Tanzania	210
Thailand	304
Togo	212
Tokelau	478
Tonga	448
Trinidad & Tobago	382
Tristan da Cunha	478
Tromelin Island	479
Tunisia	214
Turkey	104
Turkmenistan	306
Turks & Caicos	384
Tuvalu	479
U.S Virgin Islands	388
UAE	308
Uganda	216
Ukraine	106
United States	386
Uruguay	414
Uzbekistan	310
Vanuatu	450
Vatican City	480
Venezuela	416
Vietnam	312
Wake Island	480
Wales	108
Wallis & Futuna	452
Western Sahara	481
Yemen	314
Zambia	218
Zanzibar	481
Zimbabwe	220